Performance Modeling and Design of Computer Systems

Computer systems design is full of conundrums:

- Given a choice between a single machine with speed s, or n machines each with speed s/n, which should we choose?
- If both the arrival rate and service rate double, will the mean response time stay the same?
- Should systems really aim to balance load, or is this a convenient myth?
- If a scheduling policy favors one set of jobs, does it necessarily hurt some other jobs, or are these "conservation laws" being misinterpreted?
- Do greedy, shortest-delay, routing strategies make sense in a server farm, or is what is good for the individual disastrous for the system as a whole?
- How do high job size variability and heavy-tailed workloads affect the choice of a scheduling policy?
- How should one trade off energy and delay in designing a computer system?
- If 12 servers are needed to meet delay guarantees when the arrival rate is 9 jobs/sec, will we need 12,000 servers when the arrival rate is 9,000 jobs/sec?

Tackling the questions that systems designers care about, this book brings queueing theory decisively back to computer science. The book is written with computer scientists and engineers in mind and is full of examples from computer systems, as well as manufacturing and operations research. Fun and readable, the book is highly approachable, even for undergraduates, while still being thoroughly rigorous and also covering a much wider span of topics than many queueing books.

Readers benefit from a lively mix of motivation and intuition, with illustrations, examples, and more than 300 exercises – all while acquiring the skills needed to model, analyze, and design large-scale systems with good performance and low cost. The exercises are an important feature, teaching research-level counterintuitive lessons in the design of computer systems. The goal is to train readers not only to customize existing analyses but also to invent their own.

Mor Harchol-Balter is an Associate Professor in the Computer Science Department at Carnegie Mellon University. She is a leader in the ACM Sigmetrics Conference on Measurement and Modeling of Computer Systems, having served as technical program committee chair in 2007 and conference chair in 2013.

Performance Modeling and Design of Computer Systems

Queueing Theory in Action

Mor Harchol-Balter

Carnegie Mellon University, Pennsylvania

CAMBRIDGE
UNIVERSITY PRESS

32 Avenue of the Americas, New York NY 10013-2473, USA

Cambridge University Press is part of the University of Cambridge.

It furthers the University's mission by disseminating knowledge in the pursuit of education, learning, and research at the highest international levels of excellence.

www.cambridge.org
Information on this title: www.cambridge.org/9781107027503

First published 2013
Reprinted 2014

A catalog record for this publication is available from the British Library.

Library of Congress Cataloging in Publication data
Harchol-Balter, Mor, 1966–
Performance modeling and design of computer systems : queueing theory in action / Mor Harchol-Balter.
    pages cm
Includes bibliographical references and index.
ISBN 978-1-107-02750-3
1. Transaction systems (Computer systems) – Mathematical models. 2. Computer systems – Design and construction – Mathematics. 3. Queueing theory.
4. Queueing networks (Data transmission) I. Title.
QA76.545.H37 2013
519.8′2–dc23   2012019844

ISBN 978-1-107-02750-3 Hardback

To my loving husband Andrew, my awesome son Danny,
and my parents, Irit and Micha

I have always been interested in finding better designs for computer systems, designs that improve performance without the purchase of additional resources. When I look back at the problems that I have solved and I look ahead to the problems I hope to solve, I realize that the problem formulations keep getting simpler and simpler, and my footing less secure. Every wisdom that I once believed, I have now come to question: If a scheduling policy helps one set of jobs, does it necessarily hurt some other jobs, or are these "conservation laws" being misinterpreted? Do greedy routing strategies make sense in server farms, or is what is good for the individual actually disastrous for the system as a whole? When comparing a single fast machine with n slow machines, each of 1/nth the speed, the single fast machine is typically much more expensive – but does that mean that it is necessarily better? Should distributed systems really aim to balance load, or is this a convenient myth? Cycle stealing, where machines can help each other when they are idle, sounds like a great idea, but can we quantify the actual benefit? How much is the performance of scheduling policies affected by variability in the arrival rate and service rate and by fluctuations in the load, and what can we do to combat variability? Inherent in these questions is the impact of real user behaviors and real-world workloads with heavy-tailed, highly variable service demands, as well as correlated arrival processes. Also intertwined in my work are the tensions between theoretical analysis and the realities of implementation, each motivating the other. In my search to discover new research techniques that allow me to answer these and other questions, I find that I am converging toward the fundamental core that defines all these problems, and that makes the counterintuitive more believable.

Contents

IV From Markov Chains to Simple Queues

Preface

The ad hoc World of Computer System Design

The design of computer systems is often viewed very much as an art rather than a science. Decisions about which scheduling policy to use, how many servers to run, what speed to operate each server at, and the like are often based on *intuitions* rather than mathematically derived formulas. Specific policies built into kernels are often riddled with secret "voodoo constants,"[1] which have no explanation but seem to "work well" under some benchmarked workloads. Computer systems students are often told to *first* build the system and *then* make changes to the policies to improve system performance, rather than first creating a formal model and design of the system on paper to ensure the system meets performance goals.

Even when trying to evaluate the performance of an *existing* computer system, students are encouraged to *simulate* the system and spend many days running their simulation under different workloads waiting to see what happens. Given that the search space of possible workloads and input parameters is often huge, vast numbers of simulations are needed to properly cover the space. Despite this fact, mathematical models of the system are rarely created, and we rarely characterize workloads stochastically. There is no formal analysis of the parameter space under which the computer system is likely to perform well versus that under which it is likely to perform poorly. It is no wonder that computer systems students are left feeling that the whole process of system evaluation and design is very ad hoc. As an example, consider the trial-and-error approach to updating resource scheduling in the many versions of the Linux kernel.

Analytical Modeling for Computer Systems

But it does not have to be this way! These same systems designers could mathematically model the system, stochastically characterize the workloads and performance goals, and then analytically derive the performance of the system as a function of workload and input parameters. The fields of *analytical modeling* and *stochastic processes* have existed for close to a century, and they can be used to save systems designers huge numbers of hours in trial and error while improving performance. Analytical modeling can also be used in conjunction with simulation to help guide the simulation, reducing the number of cases that need to be explored.

---

[1] The term "voodoo constants" was coined by Prof. John Ousterhout during his lectures at the University of California, Berkeley.

Unfortunately, of the hundreds of books written on stochastic processes, almost none deal with computer systems. The examples in those books and the material covered are oriented toward operations research areas such as manufacturing systems, or *human* operators answering calls in a call center, or some assembly-line system with different priority jobs.

In many ways the analysis used in designing manufacturing systems is not all that different from computer systems. There are many parallels between a human operator and a computer server: There are faster human operators and slower ones (just as computer servers); the human servers sometimes get sick (just as computer servers sometimes break down); when not needed, human operators can be sent home to save money (just as computer servers can be turned off to save power); there is a startup overhead to bringing back a human operator (just as there is a warmup cost to turning on a computer server); and the list goes on.

However, there are also many differences between manufacturing systems and computer systems. To start, computer systems workloads have been shown to have extremely high variability in job sizes (service requirements), with squared coefficients of variation upward of 100. This is very different from the low-variability service times characteristic of job sizes in manufacturing workloads. This difference in variability can result in performance differences of orders of magnitude. Second, computer workloads are typically preemptible, and time-sharing (Processor-Sharing) of the CPU is extremely common. By contrast, most manufacturing workloads are non-preemptive (first-come-first-serve service order is the most common). Thus most books on stochastic processes and queueing omit chapters on Processor-Sharing or more advanced preemptive policies like Shortest-Remaining-Processing-Time, which are very much at the heart of computer systems. Processor-Sharing is particularly relevant when analyzing server farms, which, in the case of computer systems, are typically composed of Processor-Sharing servers, not First-Come-First-Served ones. It is also relevant in any computing application involving bandwidth being shared between users, which typically happens in a processor-sharing style, not first-come-first-serve order. Performance metrics may also be different for computer systems as compared with manufacturing systems (e.g., power usage, an important metric for computer systems, is not mentioned in stochastic processes books). Closed-loop architectures, in which new jobs are not created until existing jobs complete, and where the performance goal is to maximize throughput, are very common in computer systems, but are often left out of queueing books. Finally, the particular types of interactions that occur in disks, networking protocols, databases, memory controllers, and other computer systems are very different from what has been analyzed in traditional queueing books.

The Goal of This Book

Many times I have walked into a fellow computer scientist's office and was pleased to find a queueing book on his shelf. Unfortunately, when questioned, my colleague was quick to answer that he never uses the book because "The world doesn't look like an M/M/1 queue, and I can't understand anything past that chapter." The problem is that the queueing theory books are not "friendly" to computer scientists. The applications are not computer-oriented, and the assumptions used are often unrealistic for computer systems. Furthermore, these books are abstruse and often impenetrable by anyone who has not studied graduate-level mathematics. In some sense this is hard to avoid: If one wants to do more than provide readers with formulas to "plug into," then one has to *teach* them to derive their own formulas, and this requires learning a good deal of math. Fortunately, as one of my favorite authors, Sheldon Ross, has shown, it *is* possible to teach a lot of stochastic analysis in a fun and simple way that does not require first taking classes in measure theory and real analysis.

My motive in writing this book is to improve the design of computer systems by introducing computer scientists to the powerful world of queueing-theoretic modeling and analysis. Personally, I have found queueing-theoretic analysis to be extremely valuable in much of my research including: designing routing protocols for networks, designing better scheduling algorithms for web servers and database management systems, disk scheduling, memory-bank allocation, supercomputing resource scheduling, and power management and capacity provisioning in data centers. Content-wise, I have two goals for the book. First, I want to provide enough applications from computer systems to make the book relevant and interesting to computer scientists. Toward this end, almost half the chapters of the book are "application" chapters. Second, I want to make the book mathematically rich enough to give readers the ability to actually *develop new queueing analysis*, not just apply existing analysis. As computer systems and their workloads continue to evolve and become more complex, it is unrealistic to assume that they can be modeled with known queueing frameworks and analyses. As a designer of computer systems myself, I am constantly finding that I have to invent new queueing concepts to model aspects of computer systems.

How This Book Came to Be

In 1998, as a postdoc at MIT, I developed and taught a new computer science class, which I called "Performance Analysis and Design of Computer Systems." The class had the following description:

> In designing computer systems one is usually constrained by certain performance goals (e.g., low response time or high throughput or low energy). On the other hand, one often has many choices: One fast disk, or two slow ones? What speed CPU will suffice? Should we invest our money in more buffer space or a faster processor? How should jobs be scheduled by the processor? Does it pay to migrate active jobs? Which routing policy will work best? Should one balance load among servers? How can we best combat high-variability workloads? Often answers to these questions are counterintuitive. Ideally, one would like to have answers to these questions before investing the time and money to build a system. This class will introduce students to analytic stochastic modeling, which allows system designers to answer questions such as those above.

Since then, I have further developed the class via 10 more iterations taught within the School of Computer Science at Carnegie Mellon, where I taught versions of the class to both PhD students and advanced undergraduates in the areas of computer science, engineering, mathematics, and operations research. In 2002, the Operations Management department within the Tepper School of Business at Carnegie Mellon made the class a qualifier requirement for all operations management students.

As other faculty, including my own former PhD students, adopted my lecture notes in teaching their own classes, I was frequently asked to turn the notes into a book. This is "version 1" of that book.

Outline of the Book

This book is written in a question/answer style, which mimics the Socratic style that I use in teaching. I believe that a class "lecture" should ideally be a long sequence of bite-sized questions, which students can easily provide answers to and which lead students to the right intuitions. In reading this book, it is extremely important to try to answer each question *without* looking at the answer that follows the question. The questions are written to remind the reader to "think" rather than just "read," and to remind the teacher to ask questions rather than just state facts.

There are exercises at the end of each chapter. The exercises are an integral part of the book and should not be skipped. Many exercises are used to illustrate the application of the theory to problems in computer systems design, typically with the purpose of illuminating a key insight. All exercises are related to the material covered in the chapter, with early exercises being straightforward applications of the material and later exercises exploring extensions of the material involving greater difficulty.

The book is divided into seven parts, which mostly build on each other.

Part I introduces queueing theory and provides motivating examples from computer systems design that can be answered using basic queueing analysis. Basic queueing terminology is introduced including closed and open queueing models and performance metrics.

Part II is a probability refresher. To make this book self-contained, we have included in these chapters all the probability that will be needed throughout the rest of the book. This includes a summary of common discrete and continuous random variables, their moments, and conditional expectations and probabilities. Also included is some material on generating random variables for simulation. Finally we end with a discussion of sample paths, convergence of sequences of random variables, and time averages versus ensemble averages.

Part III is about operational laws, or "back of the envelope" analysis. These are very simple laws that hold for all well-behaved queueing systems. In particular, they do not require that any assumptions be made about the arrival process or workload (like Poisson arrivals or Exponential service times). These laws allow us to quickly reason at a high level (averages only) about system behavior and make design decisions regarding what modifications will have the biggest performance impact. Applications to high-level computer system design are provided throughout.

Part IV is about Markov chains and their application toward stochastic analysis of computer systems. Markov chains allow a much more detailed analysis of systems by representing the full space of possible states that the system can be in. Whereas the operational laws in Part III often allow us to answer questions about the overall mean number of jobs in a system, Markov chains allow us to derive the probability of exactly i jobs being queued at server j of a multi-server system. Part IV includes both discrete-time and continuous-time Markov chains. Applications include Google's PageRank algorithm, the Aloha (Ethernet) networking protocol, and an analysis of dropping probabilities in finite-buffer routers.

Part V develops the Markov chain theory introduced in Part IV to allow the analysis of more complex networks, including server farms. We analyze networks of queues with complex routing rules, where jobs can be associated with a "class" that determines their route through the network (these are known as BCMP networks). Part V also derives theorems on capacity provisioning of server farms, such as the "square-root staffing rule," which determines the minimum number of servers needed to provide certain delay guarantees.

The fact that Parts IV and V are based on Markov chains necessitates that certain "Markovian" (memoryless) assumptions are made in the analysis. In particular, it is assumed that the service requirements (sizes) of jobs follow an Exponential distribution and that the times between job arrivals are also Exponentially distributed. Many applications are reasonably well modeled via these Exponential assumptions, allowing us to use Markov analysis to get good insights into system performance. However, in some cases, it is important to capture the high-variability job size distributions or correlations present in the empirical workloads.

Part VI introduces techniques that allow us to replace these Exponential distributions with high-variability distributions. Phase-type distributions are introduced, which allow us to model virtually any general distribution by a *mixture of Exponentials*, leveraging our understanding of Exponential distributions and Markov chains from Parts IV and V. Matrix-analytic techniques are then developed to analyze systems with phase-type workloads in both the arrival process and service process. The M/G/1 queue is introduced, and notions such as the Inspection Paradox are discussed. Real-world workloads are described including heavy-tailed distributions. Transform techniques are also introduced that facilitate working with general distributions. Finally, even the service order at the queues is generalized from simple first-come-first-served service order to time-sharing (Processor-Sharing) service order, which is more common in computer systems. Applications abound: Resource allocation (task assignment) in server farms with high-variability job sizes is studied extensively, both for server farms with non-preemptive workloads and for web server farms with time-sharing servers. Power management policies for single servers and for data centers are also studied.

Part VII, the final part of the book, is devoted to scheduling. Smart scheduling is extremely important in computer systems, because it can dramatically improve system performance without requiring the purchase of any new hardware. Scheduling is at the heart of operating systems, bandwidth allocation in networks, disks, databases, memory hierarchies, and the like. Much of the research being done in the computer systems area today involves the design and adoption of new scheduling policies. Scheduling can be counterintuitive, however, and the analysis of even basic scheduling policies is far from simple. Scheduling policies are typically evaluated via simulation. In introducing the reader to analytical techniques for evaluating scheduling policies, our hope is that more such policies might be evaluated via analysis.

We expect readers to mostly work through the chapters in order, with the following exceptions: First, any chapter or section marked with a star (*) can be skipped without disturbing the flow. Second, the chapter on transforms, Chapter 25, is purposely moved to the end, so that most of the book does not depend on knowing transform analysis. However, because learning transform analysis takes some time, we recommend that any teacher who plans to cover transforms introduce the topic a little at a time, starting early in the course. To facilitate this, we have included a large number of exercises at the end of Chapter 25 that do not require material in later chapters and can be assigned earlier in the course to give students practice manipulating transforms.

Finally, we urge readers to please check the following websites for new errors/software:

 http://www.cs.cmu.edu/~harchol/PerformanceModeling/errata.html

 http://www.cs.cmu.edu/~harchol/PerformanceModeling/software.html

Please send any additional errors to harchol@cs.cmu.edu.

Acknowledgments

Writing a book, I quickly realized, is very different from writing a research paper, even a very long one. Book writing actually bears much more similarity to teaching a class. That is why I would like to start by thanking the three people who most influenced my teaching. Manuel Blum, my PhD advisor, taught me the art of creating a lecture out of a series of bite-sized questions. Dick Karp taught me that you can cover an almost infinite amount of material in just one lecture if you spend enough time in advance simplifying that material into its cleanest form. Sheldon Ross inspired me by the depth of his knowledge in stochastic processes (a knowledge so deep that he never once looked at his notes while teaching) and by the sheer clarity and elegance of both his lectures and his many beautifully written books.

I would also like to thank Carnegie Mellon University, and the School of Computer Science at Carnegie Mellon, which has at its core the theme of interdisciplinary research, particularly the mixing of theoretical and applied research. CMU has been the perfect environment for me to develop the analytical techniques in this book, all in the context of solving hard applied problems in computer systems design. CMU has also provided me with a never-ending stream of gifted students, who have inspired many of the exercises and discussions in this book. Much of this book came from the research of my own PhD students, including Sherwin Doroudi, Anshul Gandhi, Varun Gupta, Yoongu Kim, David McWherter, Takayuki Osogami, Bianca Schroeder, Adam Wierman, and Timothy Zhu. In addition, Mark Crovella, Mike Kozuch, and particularly Alan Scheller-Wolf, all longtime collaborators of mine, have inspired much of my thinking via their uncanny intuitions and insights.

A great many people have proofread parts of this book or tested out the book and provided me with useful feedback. These include Sem Borst, Doug Down, Erhun Ozkan, Katsunobu Sasanuma, Alan Scheller-Wolf, Thrasyvoulos Spyropoulos, Jarod Wang, and Zachary Young. I would also like to thank my editors, Diana Gillooly and Lauren Cowles from Cambridge University Press, who were very quick to answer my endless questions, and who greatly improved the presentation of this book. Finally, I am very grateful to Miso Kim, my illustrator, a PhD student at the Carnegie Mellon School of Design, who spent hundreds of hours designing all the fun figures in the book.

On a more personal note, I would like to thank my mother, Irit Harchol, for making my priorities her priorities, allowing me to maximize my achievements. I did not know what this meant until I had a child of my own. Lastly, I would like to thank my husband, Andrew Young. He won me over by reading all my online lecture notes and doing every homework problem – this was his way of asking me for a first date. His ability to understand it all without attending any lectures made me believe that my lecture notes might actually "work" as a book. His willingness to sit by my side every night for many months gave me the motivation to make it happen.

Introduction to Queueing

Part I serves as an introduction to analytical modeling.

We begin in Chapter 1 with a number of paradoxical examples that come up in the design of computer systems, showing off the power of analytical modeling in making design decisions.

Chapter 2 introduces the reader to basic queueing theory terminology and notation that is used throughout the rest of the book. Readers are introduced to both open and closed queueing networks and to standard performance metrics, such as response time, throughput, and the number of jobs in the system.

CHAPTER 1

Motivating Examples of the Power of Analytical Modeling

1.1 What Is Queueing Theory?

Queueing theory is the theory behind what happens when you have lots of jobs, scarce resources, and subsequently long queues and delays. It is literally the "theory of queues": what makes queues appear and how to make them go away.

Imagine a computer system, say a web server, where there is only one job. The job arrives, it uses certain resources (some CPU, some I/O), and then it departs. Given the job's resource requirements, it is very easy to predict exactly when the job will depart. There is no delay because there are no queues. If every job indeed got to run on its own computer, there would be no need for queueing theory. Unfortunately, that is rarely the case.

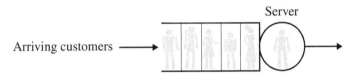

Figure 1.1. Illustration of a queue, in which customers wait to be served, and a server. The picture shows one customer being served at the server and five others waiting in the queue.

Queueing theory applies anywhere that queues come up (see Figure 1.1). We all have had the experience of waiting in line at the bank, wondering why there are not more tellers, or waiting in line at the supermarket, wondering why the express lane is for 8 items or less rather than 15 items or less, or whether it might be best to actually have *two* express lanes, one for 8 items or less and the other for 15 items or less. Queues are also at the heart of any computer system. Your CPU uses a time-sharing scheduler to serve a queue of jobs waiting for CPU time. A computer disk serves a queue of jobs waiting to read or write blocks. A router in a network serves a queue of packets waiting to be routed. The router queue is a finite capacity queue, in which packets are dropped when demand exceeds the buffer space. Memory banks serve queues of threads requesting memory blocks. Databases sometimes have lock queues, where transactions wait to acquire the lock on a record. Server farms consist of many servers, each with its own queue of jobs. The list of examples goes on and on.

The goals of a queueing theorist are twofold. The first is *predicting* the system performance. Typically this means predicting mean delay or delay variability or the probability that delay exceeds some Service Level Agreement (SLA). However, it can also mean predicting the number of jobs that will be queueing or the mean number of servers

3

being utilized (e.g., total power needs), or any other such metric. Although prediction is important, an even more important goal is finding a superior system *design* to improve performance. Commonly this takes the form of capacity planning, where one determines which additional resources to buy to meet delay goals (e.g., is it better to buy a faster disk or a faster CPU, or to add a second slow disk). Many times, however, without buying any additional resources at all, one can improve performance just by deploying a smarter scheduling policy or different routing policy to reduce delays. Given the importance of smart scheduling in computer systems, all of Part VII of this book is devoted to understanding scheduling policies.

Queueing theory is built on a much broader area of mathematics called stochastic modeling and analysis. Stochastic modeling represents the service demands of jobs and the interarrival times of jobs as random variables. For example, the CPU requirements of UNIX processes might be modeled using a Pareto distribution [84], whereas the arrival process of jobs at a busy web server might be well modeled by a Poisson process with Exponentially distributed interarrival times. Stochastic models can also be used to model dependencies between jobs, as well as anything else that can be represented as a random variable.

Although it is generally possible to come up with a stochastic model that adequately represents the jobs or customers in a system and its service dynamics, these stochastic models are not always analytically tractable with respect to solving for performance. As we discuss in Part IV, *Markovian assumptions*, such as assuming Exponentially distributed service demands or a Poisson arrival process, greatly simplify the analysis; hence much of the existing queueing literature relies on such Markovian assumptions. In many cases these are a reasonable approximation. For example, the arrival process of book orders on Amazon might be reasonably well approximated by a Poisson process, given that there are many independent users, each independently submitting requests at a low rate (although this all breaks down when a new Harry Potter book comes out). However, in some cases Markovian assumptions are very far from reality; for example, in the case in which service demands of jobs are highly variable or are correlated.

While many queueing texts downplay the Markovian assumptions being made, this book does just the opposite. Much of my own research is devoted to demonstrating the impact of workload assumptions on correctly predicting system performance. I have found many cases where making simplifying assumptions about the workload can lead to very inaccurate performance results and poor system designs. In my own research, I therefore put great emphasis on integrating measured workload distributions into the analysis. Rather than trying to hide the assumptions being made, this book *highlights* all assumptions about workloads. We will discuss specifically whether the workload models are accurate and how our model assumptions affect performance and design, as well as look for more accurate workload models. In my opinion, a major reason why computer scientists are so slow to adopt queueing theory is that the standard Markovian assumptions often do not fit. However, there are often ways to work around these assumptions, many of which are shown in this book, such as using phase-type distributions and matrix-analytic methods, introduced in Chapter 21.

1.2 Examples of the Power of Queueing Theory

The remainder of this chapter is devoted to showing some concrete examples of the power of queueing theory. Do *not* expect to understand everything in the examples. The examples are developed in much greater detail later in the book. Terms like "Poisson process" that you may not be familiar with are also explained later in the book. These examples are just here to highlight the types of lessons covered in this book.

As stated earlier, one use of queueing theory is as a *predictive tool*, allowing one to predict the performance of a given system. For example, one might be analyzing a network, with certain bandwidths, where different classes of packets arrive at certain rates and follow certain routes throughout the network simultaneously. Then queueing theory can be used to compute quantities such as the mean time that packets spend waiting at a particular router i, the distribution on the queue buildup at router i, or the mean overall time to get from router i to router j in the network.

We now turn to the usefulness of queueing theory as a *design tool* in choosing the best system design to minimize response time. The examples that follow illustrate that system design is often a *counterintuitive* process.

Design Example 1 – Doubling Arrival Rate

Consider a system consisting of a single CPU that serves a queue of jobs in First-Come-First-Served (FCFS) order, as illustrated in Figure 1.2. The jobs arrive according to some random process with some average arrival rate, say $\lambda = 3$ jobs per second. Each job has some CPU service requirement, drawn independently from some distribution of job service requirements (we can assume any distribution on the job service requirements for this example). Let's say that the average service rate is $\mu = 5$ jobs per second (i.e., each job on average requires $1/5$ of a second of service). Note that the system is not in overload ($3 < 5$). Let $\mathbf{E}[T]$ denote the mean response time of this system, where **response time** is the time from when a job arrives until it completes service, a.k.a. sojourn time.

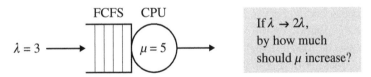

Figure 1.2. A system with a single CPU that serves jobs in FCFS order.

Question: Your boss tells you that starting tomorrow the arrival rate will double. You are told to buy a faster CPU to ensure that jobs experience the same mean response time, $\mathbf{E}[T]$. That is, customers should not notice the effect of the increased arrival rate. By how much should you increase the CPU speed? (a) Double the CPU speed; (b) More than double the CPU speed; (c) Less than double the CPU speed.

Answer: (c) Less than double.

Question: Why not (a)?

Answer: It turns out that doubling CPU speed together with doubling the arrival rate will generally result in cutting the mean response time in half! We prove this in Chapter 13. Therefore, the CPU speed does not need to double.

Question: Can you immediately see a rough argument for this result that does not involve any queueing theory formulas? What happens if we double the service rate and double the arrival rate?

Answer: Imagine that there are two types of time: Federation time and Klingon time. Klingon seconds are faster than Federation seconds. In fact, each Klingon second is equivalent to a half-second in Federation time. Now, suppose that in the Federation, there is a CPU serving jobs. Jobs arrive with rate λ jobs per second and are served at some rate μ jobs per second. The Klingons steal the system specs and reengineer the same system in the Klingon world. In the Klingon system, the arrival rate is λ jobs per Klingon second, and the service rate is μ jobs per Klingon second. Note that both systems have the same mean response time, $\mathbf{E}\left[T\right]$, except that the Klingon system response time is measured in Klingon seconds, while the Federation system response time is measured in Federation seconds. Consider now that Captain Kirk is observing both the Federation system and the Klingon reengineered system. From his perspective, the Klingon system has twice the arrival rate and twice the service rate; however, the mean response time in the Klingon system has been halved (because Klingon seconds are half-seconds in Federation time).

Question: Suppose the CPU employs time-sharing service order (known as Processor-Sharing, or PS for short), instead of FCFS. Does the answer change?

Answer: No. The same basic argument still works.

Design Example 2 – Sometimes "Improvements" Do Nothing

Consider the batch system shown in Figure 1.3. There are always $N = 6$ jobs in this system (this is called the multiprogramming level). As soon as a job completes service, a new job is started (this is called a "closed" system). Each job must go through the "service facility." At the service facility, with probability $1/2$ the job goes to server 1, and with probability $1/2$ it goes to server 2. Server 1 services jobs at an average rate of 1 job every 3 seconds. Server 2 also services jobs at an average rate of 1 job every 3 seconds. The distribution on the service times of the jobs is irrelevant for this problem. Response time is defined as usual as the time from when a job first arrives at the service facility (at the fork) until it completes service.

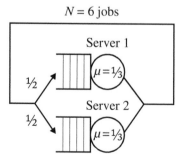

Figure 1.3. A closed batch system.

Question: You replace server 1 with a server that is twice as fast (the new server services jobs at an average rate of 2 jobs every 3 seconds). Does this "improvement" affect the average response time in the system? Does it affect the throughput? (Assume that the routing probabilities remain constant at $1/2$ and $1/2$.)

Answer: Not really. Both the average response time and throughput are hardly affected. This is explained in Chapter 7.

Question: Suppose that the system had a higher multiprogramming level, N. Does the answer change?

Answer: No. The already negligible effect on response time and throughput goes to zero as N increases.

Question: Suppose the system had a lower value of N. Does the answer change?

Answer: Yes. If N is sufficiently low, then the "improvement" helps. Consider, for example, the case $N = 1$.

Question: Suppose the system is changed into an open system, rather than a closed system, as shown in Figure 1.4, where arrival times are independent of service completions. Now does the "improvement" reduce mean response time?

Answer: Absolutely!

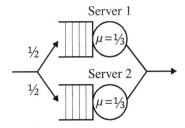

Figure 1.4. An open system.

Design Example 3 – One Machine or Many?

You are given a choice between one fast CPU of speed s, or n slow CPUs each of speed s/n (see Figure 1.5). Your goal is to minimize mean response time. To start, assume that jobs are *non-preemptible* (i.e., each job must be run to completion).

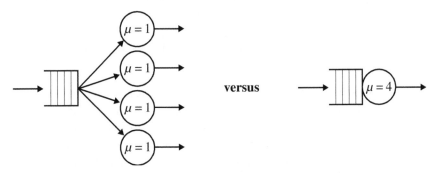

Figure 1.5. Which is better for minimizing mean response time: many slow servers or one fast server?

Question: Which is the better choice: one fast machine or many slow ones?

Hint: Suppose that I tell you that the answer is, "It depends on the workload." What aspects of the workload do you think the answer depends on?

Answer: It turns out that the answer depends on the variability of the job size distribution, as well as on the system load.

Question: Which system do you prefer when job size variability is high?

Answer: When job size variability is high, we prefer many slow servers because we do not want short jobs getting stuck behind long ones.

Question: Which system do you prefer when load is low?

Answer: When load is low, not all servers will be utilized, so it seems better to go with one fast server.

These observations are revisited many times throughout the book.

Question: Now suppose we ask the same question, but jobs are *preemptible*; that is, they can be stopped and restarted where they left off. When do we prefer many slow machines as compared to a single fast machine?

Answer: If your jobs are preemptible, you could always use a single fast machine to simulate the effect of n slow machines. Hence a single fast machine is at least as good.

The question of many slow servers versus a few fast ones has huge applicability in a wide range of areas, because anything can be viewed as a resource, including CPU, power, and bandwidth.

For an example involving power management in data centers, consider the problem from [69] where you have a fixed power budget P and a server farm consisting of n servers. You have to decide how much power to allocate to each server, so as to minimize overall mean response time for jobs arriving at the server farm. There is a function that specifies the relationship between the power allocated to a server and the speed (frequency) at which it runs – generally, the more power you allocate to a server, the faster it runs (the higher its frequency), subject to some maximum possible frequency and some minimum power level needed just to turn the server on. To answer the question of how to allocate power, you need to think about whether you prefer many slow servers (allocate just a little power to every server) or a few fast ones (distribute all the power among a small number of servers). In [69], queueing theory is used to optimally answer this question under a wide variety of parameter settings.

As another example, if bandwidth is the resource, we can ask when it pays to partition bandwidth into smaller chunks and when it is better not to. The problem is also interesting when performance is combined with price. For example, it is often cheaper (financially) to purchase many slow servers than a few fast servers. Yet in some cases, many slow servers can consume more total power than a few fast ones. All of these factors can further influence the choice of architecture.

Design Example 4 – Task Assignment in a Server Farm

Consider a server farm with a central dispatcher and several hosts. Each arriving job is immediately dispatched to one of the hosts for processing. Figure 1.6 illustrates such a system.

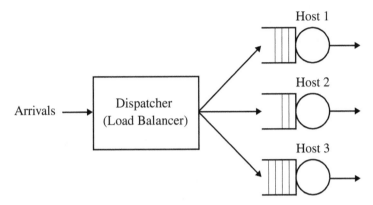

Figure 1.6. A distributed server system with a central dispatcher.

Server farms like this are found everywhere. Web server farms typically deploy a front-end dispatcher like Cisco's Local Director or IBM's Network Dispatcher. Super-computing sites might use LoadLeveler or some other dispatcher to balance load and assign jobs to hosts.

For the moment, let's assume that all the hosts are identical (homogeneous) and that all jobs only use a single resource. Let's also assume that once jobs are assigned to a host, they are processed there in FCFS order and are non-preemptible.

There are many possible *task assignment policies* that can be used for dispatching jobs to hosts. Here are a few:

Random: Each job flips a fair coin to determine where it is routed.

Round-Robin: The ith job goes to host $i \bmod n$, where n is the number of hosts, and hosts are numbered $0, 1, \ldots, n - 1$.

Shortest-Queue: Each job goes to the host with the fewest number of jobs.

Size-Interval-Task-Assignment (SITA): "Short" jobs go to the first host, "medium" jobs go to the second host, "long" jobs go to the third host, etc., for some definition of "short," "medium," and "long."

Least-Work-Left (LWL): Each job goes to the host with the least total remaining work, where the "work" at a host is the sum of the sizes of jobs there.

Central-Queue: Rather than have a queue at each host, jobs are pooled at one central queue. When a host is done working on a job, it grabs the first job in the central queue to work on.

Question: Which of these task assignment policies yields the lowest mean response time?

Answer: Given the ubiquity of server farms, it is surprising how little is known about this question. If job size variability is low, then the LWL policy is best. If job size variability is high, then it is important to keep short jobs from getting stuck behind long ones, so a SITA-like policy, which affords short jobs isolation from long ones, can be far better. In fact, for a long time it was believed that SITA is always better than LWL when job size variability is high. However, it was recently discovered (see [90]) that SITA can be far worse than LWL even under job size variability tending to infinity. It turns out that other properties of the workload, including load and fractional moments of the job size distribution, matter as well.

Question: For the previous question, how important was it to know the size of jobs? For example, how does LWL, which requires knowing job size, compare with Central-Queue, which does not?

Answer: Actually, most task assignment policies do not require knowing the size of jobs. For example, it can be proven by induction that LWL is equivalent to Central-Queue. Even policies like SITA, which by definition are based on knowing the job size, can be well approximated by other policies that do not require knowing the job size; see [82].

Question: Now consider a different model, in which jobs are preemptible. Specifically, suppose that the servers are Processor-Sharing (PS) servers, which time-share among all the jobs at the server, rather than serving them in FCFS order. Which task assignment policy is preferable now? Is the answer the same as that for FCFS servers?

Answer: The task assignment policies that are best for FCFS servers are often a disaster under PS servers. For PS servers, the Shortest-Queue policy is near optimal ([79]), whereas that policy is pretty bad for FCFS servers if job size variability is high.

There are many open questions with respect to task assignment policies. The case of server farms with PS servers, for example, has received almost no attention, and even the case of FCFS servers is still only partly understood. There are also many other task assignment policies that have not been mentioned. For example, *cycle stealing* (taking advantage of a free host to process jobs in some other queue) can be combined with many existing task assignment policies to create improved policies. There are also other metrics to consider, like minimizing the variance of response time, rather than mean response time, or maximizing fairness. Finally, task assignment can become even more complex, and more important, when the workload changes over time.

Task assignment is analyzed in great detail in Chapter 24, after we have had a chance to study empirical workloads.

Design Example 5 – Scheduling Policies

Suppose you have a *single* server. Jobs arrive according to a Poisson process. Assume anything you like about the distribution of job sizes. The following are some possible service orders (scheduling orders) for serving jobs:

First-Come-First-Served (FCFS): When the server completes a job, it starts working on the job that arrived earliest.

Non-Preemptive Last-Come-First-Served (LCFS): When the server completes a job, it starts working on the job that arrived last.

Random: When the server completes a job, it starts working on a random job.

Question: Which of these non-preemptive service orders will result in the lowest mean response time?

Answer: Believe it or not, they all have the same mean response time.

Question: Suppose we change the non-preemptive LCFS policy to a Preemptive-LCFS policy (PLCFS), which works as follows: Whenever a new arrival enters the system, it immediately preempts the job in service. How does the mean response time of this policy compare with the others?

Answer: It depends on the variability of the job size distribution. If the job size distribution is at least moderately variable, then PLCFS will be a huge improvement. If the job size distribution is hardly variable (basically constant), then PLCFS policy will be up to a factor of 2 worse.

We study many counterintuitive scheduling theory results toward the very end of the book, in Chapters 28 through 33.

More Design Examples

There are many more questions in computer systems design that lend themselves to a queueing-theoretic solution.

One example is the notion of a *setup cost*. It turns out that it can take both significant time and power to turn *on* a server that is *off*. In designing an efficient power management policy, we often want to leave servers *off* (to save power), but then we have to pay the setup cost to get them back on when jobs arrive. Given performance goals, both with respect to response time and power usage, an important question is whether it pays to turn a server off. If so, one can then ask exactly how many servers should be left on. These questions are discussed in Chapters 15 and 27.

There are also questions involving optimal scheduling when jobs have priorities (e.g., certain users have paid more for their jobs to have priority over other users' jobs, or some jobs are inherently more vital than others). Again, queueing theory is very useful in designing the right priority scheme to maximize the value of the work completed.

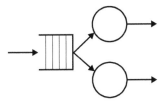

Figure 1.7. Example of a difficult problem: The M/G/2 queue consists of a single queue and two servers. When a server completes a job, it starts working on the job at the head of the queue. Job sizes follow a general distribution, G.

However, queueing theory (and more generally analytical modeling) is *not* currently all-powerful! There are lots of very simple problems that we can at best only analyze approximately. As an example, consider the simple two-server network shown in Figure 1.7, where job sizes come from a general distribution. No one knows how to derive mean response time for this network. Approximations exist, but they are quite poor, particularly when job size variability gets high [76]. We mention many such open problems in this book, and we encourage readers to attempt to solve these!

CHAPTER 2

Queueing Theory Terminology

2.1 Where We Are Heading

Queueing theory is the study of queueing behavior in networks and systems. Figure 2.1 shows the solution process.

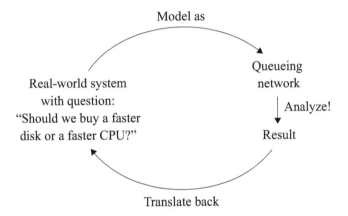

Figure 2.1. Solution process.

In Chapter 1, we looked at examples of the power of queueing theory as a design tool. In this chapter, we start from scratch and define the terminology used in queueing theory.

2.2 The Single-Server Network

A **queueing network** is made up of **servers**.

The simplest example of a queueing network is the **single-server network**, as shown in Figure 2.2. The discussion in this section is limited to the single-server network with First-Come-First-Served (FCFS) service order. You can think of the server as being a CPU.

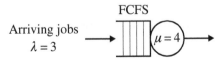

Figure 2.2. Single-server network.

There are several parameters associated with the single-server network:

Service Order This is the order in which jobs will be served by the server. Unless otherwise stated, assume First-Come-First-Served (FCFS).

Average Arrival Rate This is the average rate, λ, at which jobs arrive to the server (e.g., $\lambda = 3$ jobs/sec).

Mean Interarrival Time This is the average time between successive job arrivals (e.g., $1/\lambda = \frac{1}{3}$ sec).

Service Requirement, Size The "size" of a job is typically denoted by the random variable S. This is the time it would take the job to run on this server if there were no other jobs around (no queueing). In a queueing model, the size (a.k.a. service requirement) is typically associated with the server (e.g., this job will take 5 seconds on this server).

Mean Service Time This is the expected value of S, namely the average time required to service a job on this CPU, where "service" does not include queueing time. In Figure 2.2, $\mathbf{E}[S] = \frac{1}{4}$ sec.

Average Service Rate This is the average rate, μ, at which jobs are served (e.g., $\mu = 4$ jobs/sec $= \frac{1}{\mathbf{E}[S]}$).

Observe that this way of speaking is different from the way we normally talk about servers in conversation. For example, nowhere have we mentioned the absolute speed of the CPU; rather we have only defined the CPU's speed in terms of the set of jobs that it is working on.

In normal conversation, we might say something like the following:

- The average arrival rate of jobs is 3 jobs per second.
- Jobs have different service requirements, but the average number of cycles required by a job is 5,000 cycles per job.
- The CPU speed is 20,000 cycles per second.

That is, an average of 15,000 cycles of work arrive at the CPU each second, and the CPU can process 20,000 cycles of work a second.

In the queueing-theoretic way of talking, we would never mention the word "cycle." Instead, we would simply say

- The average arrival rate of jobs is 3 jobs per second.
- The average rate at which the CPU can service jobs is 4 jobs per second.

This second way of speaking suppresses some of the detail and thus makes the problem a little easier to think about. You should feel comfortable going back and forth between the two.

We consider these common **performance metrics** in the context of a single-server system:

Response Time, Turnaround Time, Time in System, or Sojourn Time (T) We define a job's response time by $T = t_{\text{depart}} - t_{\text{arrive}}$, where t_{depart} is the time when the job leaves the system, and t_{arrive} is the time when the job arrived to the system. We are interested in $\mathbf{E}\,[T]$, the mean response time; $\mathbf{Var}(T)$, the variance in response time; and the tail behavior of T, $\mathbf{P}\,\{T > t\}$.

Waiting Time or Delay (T_Q) This is the time that the job spends in the queue, not being served. It is also called the "time in queue" or the "wasted time." Notice that $\mathbf{E}\,[T] = \mathbf{E}\,[T_Q] + \mathbf{E}\,[S]$. Under FCFS service order, waiting time can be defined as the time from when a job arrives to the system until it first receives service.

Number of Jobs in the System (N) This includes those jobs in the queue, plus the one being served (if any).

Number of Jobs in Queue (N_Q) This denotes only the number of jobs waiting (in queue).

There are some immediate observations that we can make about the single-server network. First, observe that as λ, the mean arrival rate, increases, all the performance metrics mentioned earlier increase (get worse). Also, as μ, the mean service rate, increases, all the performance metrics mentioned earlier decrease (improve).

We require that $\lambda \leq \mu$ (we always assume $\lambda < \mu$).

Question: If $\lambda > \mu$ what happens?

Answer: If $\lambda > \mu$ the queue length goes to infinity over time.

Question: Can you provide the intuition?

Answer: Consider a large time t. Then, if $N(t)$ is the number of jobs in the system at time t, and $A(t)$ (respectively, $D(t)$) denotes the number of arrivals (respectively, departures) by time t, then we have:

$$E[N(t)] = E[A(t)] - E[D(t)] \geq \lambda t - \mu t = t(\lambda - \mu).$$

(The inequality comes from the fact that the expected number of departures by time t is actually smaller than μt, because the server is not always busy). Now observe that if $\lambda > \mu$, then $t(\lambda - \mu) \to \infty$, as $t \to \infty$.

Throughout the book we assume $\lambda < \mu$, which is needed for stability (keeping queue sizes from growing unboundedly). Situations where $\lambda \geq \mu$ are touched on in Chapter 9.

Question: Given the previous stability condition ($\lambda < \mu$), suppose that the interarrival distribution and the service time distribution are *Deterministic* (i.e., both are constants). What is T_Q? What is T?

Answer: $T_Q = 0$, and $T = S$.

Therefore queueing (waiting) results from *variability* in service time and/or interarrival time distributions. Here is an example of how variability leads to queues: Let's discretize time. Suppose at each time step, an arrival occurs with probability $p = 1/6$. Suppose at each time step, a departure occurs with probability $q = 1/3$. Then there is a non-zero probability that the queue will build up (temporarily) if several arrivals occur without a departure.

2.3 Classification of Queueing Networks

Queueing networks can be classified into two categories: **open networks** and **closed networks**. Stochastic processes books (e.g., [149, 150]) usually limit their discussion to open networks. By contrast, the systems performance analysis books (e.g., [117, 125]) almost exclusively discuss closed networks. Open networks are introduced in Section 2.4. Closed networks are introduced in Section 2.6.

2.4 Open Networks

An open queueing network has external arrivals and departures. Four examples of open networks are illustrated in this section.

Example: The Single-Server System

This was shown in Figure 2.2.

Example: Network of Queues with Probabilistic Routing

This is shown in Figure 2.3. Here server i receives external arrivals ("outside arrivals") with rate r_i. Server i also receives internal arrivals from some of the other servers. A packet that finishes service at server i is next routed to server j with probability p_{ij}. We can even allow the probabilities to depend on the "class" of the packet, so that not all packets have to follow the same routing scheme.

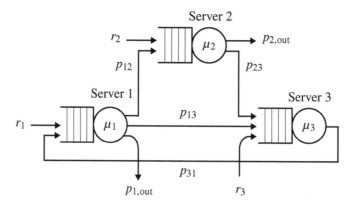

Figure 2.3. Network of queues with probabilistic routing.

Application: In modeling packet flows in the Internet, for example, one could make the class of the packet (and hence its route) depend on its source and destination IP addresses. In modeling delays, each wire might be replaced by a server that would be used to model the wire latency. The goal might be to predict mean round-trip times for packets on a particular route, given the presence of the other packets. We solve this problem in Chapter 18.

Example: Network of Queues with Non-Probabilistic Routing

This is shown in Figure 2.4. Here all jobs follow a predetermined route: CPU to disk 1 to disk 2 to disk 1 to disk 2 to disk 1 and out.

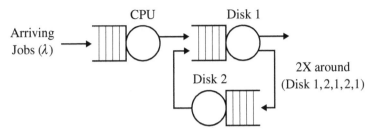

Figure 2.4. Network of queues with non-probabilistic routing.

Example: Finite Buffer

An example of a single-server network with finite buffer is shown in Figure 2.5. Any arrival that finds no room is dropped.

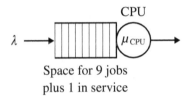

Figure 2.5. Single-server network with finite buffer capacity.

2.5 More Metrics: Throughput and Utilization

We have already seen four performance metrics: $\mathbf{E}[N]$, $\mathbf{E}[T]$, $\mathbf{E}[N_Q]$, and $\mathbf{E}[T_Q]$. Although these were applied to a single-server system, they can also be used to describe performance in a multi-server, multi-queue system. For example, $\mathbf{E}[T]$ would denote the mean time a job spends in the whole system, including all time spent in various queues and time spent receiving service at various servers, whereas $\mathbf{E}[T_Q]$ refers to just the mean time the job "wasted" waiting in various queues. If we want to refer to just the ith queue in such a system, we typically write $\mathbf{E}[N_i]$ to denote the expected number of jobs both queueing and in service at server i, and $\mathbf{E}[T_i]$ to denote the expected time a job spends queueing and in service at server i.

Now we introduce two new performance metrics: throughput and utilization. Throughput is arguably the performance metric most used in conversation. Everyone wants higher throughput! Let's see why.

Question: How does maximizing throughput relate to minimizing response time? For example, in Figure 2.6, which system has higher throughput?

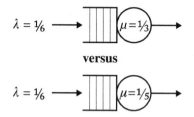

Figure 2.6. Comparing throughput of two systems.

Answer: We will see soon.

Let's start by defining utilization.

Device Utilization (ρ_i) is the *fraction of time device i is busy*. Note our current definition of utilization applies only to a single device (server). When the device is implied, we simply write ρ (omitting the subscript).

Suppose we watch a device i for a long period of time. Let τ denote the length of the observation period. Let B denote the total time during the observation period that the device is non-idle (busy). Then

$$\rho_i = \frac{B}{\tau}.$$

Device Throughput (X_i) is the *rate of completions at device i* (e.g., jobs/sec). The throughput (X) of the system is the rate of job completions in the system.

Let C denote the total number of jobs completed at device i during time τ. Then

$$X_i = \frac{C}{\tau}.$$

So how does X_i relate to ρ_i? Well,

$$\frac{C}{\tau} = \left(\frac{C}{B}\right) \cdot \frac{B}{\tau}.$$

Question: So what is $\frac{C}{B}$?

Answer: Well, $\frac{B}{C} = \mathbf{E}\left[S\right]$. So $\frac{C}{B} = \frac{1}{\mathbf{E}[S]} = \mu_i$.

So we have

$$X_i = \mu_i \cdot \rho_i.$$

Here is another way to derive this expression by conditioning:

$$\begin{aligned}
X_i &= \text{Mean rate of completion at server } i \\
&= \mathbf{E}\left[\text{Rate of completion at server } i \mid \text{server } i \text{ is busy}\right] \cdot \mathbf{P}\left\{\text{server } i \text{ is busy}\right\} \\
&\quad + \mathbf{E}\left[\text{Rate of completion at server } i \mid \text{server } i \text{ is idle}\right] \cdot \mathbf{P}\left\{\text{server } i \text{ is idle}\right\} \\
&= \mu_i \cdot \mathbf{P}\left\{\text{server } i \text{ is busy}\right\} + 0 \\
&= \mu_i \cdot \rho_i
\end{aligned}$$

Or, equivalently,

$$\rho_i = X_i \cdot \mathbf{E}\,[S]\,.$$

This latter formulation has a name: *the Utilization Law*.

Example: Single-Server Network: What Is the Throughput?

In Figure 2.7 we have a single-server system.

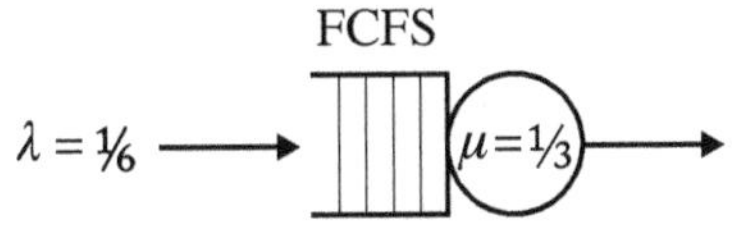

Figure 2.7. Single-server model.

Question: What is X?

Answer: $X = \rho \cdot \mu$. But what is ρ? In Chapter 6, we will prove that $\rho = \frac{\lambda}{\mu}$. For now here is a hand-wavy but intuitive way to see this, but *not* a proof!!

$$
\begin{aligned}
\rho &= \text{Fraction of time server is busy} \\
&= \frac{\text{Average service time required by a job}}{\text{Average time between arrivals}} \\
&= \frac{1/\mu}{1/\lambda} \\
&= \frac{\lambda}{\mu}.
\end{aligned}
$$

So, this leaves us with

$$X = \rho \cdot \mu = \frac{\lambda}{\mu} \cdot \mu = \lambda.$$

So the throughput does not depend on the service rate whatsoever!

In particular, in the example shown in Figure 2.6, repeated again in Figure 2.8, both systems have the same throughput of $1/6$ jobs/sec. In the case of the faster processor, the response time drops and the queue length drops, but X does not change. Therefore lower response time is *not* related to higher throughput.

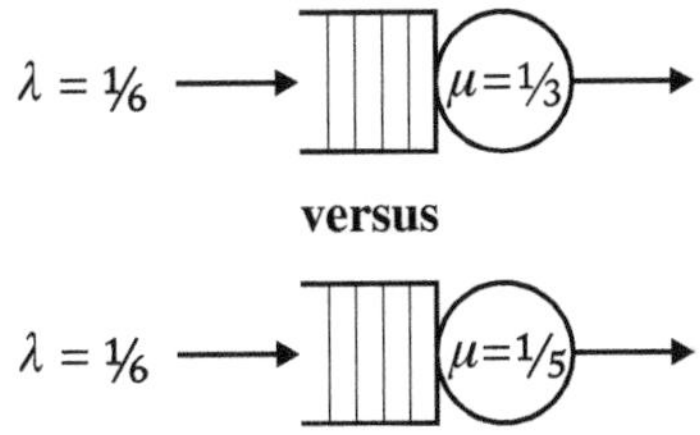

Figure 2.8. Same model, but different values of μ. Throughput, X, is the same in both.

Question: Explain why X does not change.

Answer: No matter how high we make μ, the completion rate is still bounded by the arrival rate: "rate in = rate out." Changing μ affects the *maximum possible X*, but not the *actual* X. Note that because we assume a stable system, then, for large t, the number of arrivals during t is approximately the number of completions during t.

Example: Probabilistic Network of Queues: What is the Throughput?

For Figure 2.3, r_i denotes the average outside arrival rate into server i, and μ_i denotes the average service rate at server i.

Question: What is the system throughput, X, in Figure 2.3?

Answer: $X = \sum_i r_i$.

Question: What is the throughput at server i, X_i?

Answer: Let λ_i denote the total arrival rate into server i. Then $X_i = \lambda_i$. But to get λ_i we need to solve these simultaneous equations:

$$\lambda_i = r_i + \sum_j \lambda_j P_{ji} \tag{2.1}$$

Question: How are the r_i's constrained in these equations?

Answer: For the network to reach "equilibrium" (flow into server = flow out of server), we must have $\lambda_i < \mu_i, \forall i$, and this constrains the r_i's (see Exercise 2.1).

Example: Network of Queues with Non-Probabilistic Routing: What is the Throughput?

Question: What is X in Figure 2.4?

Answer: $X = \lambda$.

Question: What are X_{Disk1} and X_{Disk2}?

Answer: $X_{\text{Disk1}} = 3\lambda$ and $X_{\text{Disk2}} = 2\lambda$.

Example: Finite Buffer: What is the Throughput?

For Figure 2.5, the outside arrival rate is λ and the service rate is μ.

Question: What is X?

Answer: $X = \rho\mu$. But we need stochastic analysis to determine ρ because it is no longer simply λ/μ. Observe that $X < \lambda$ because some arrivals get dropped.

2.6 Closed Networks

Closed queueing networks have no external arrivals or departures. They can be classified into two categories as shown in Figure 2.9.

Closed networks

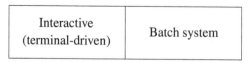

Figure 2.9. Closed network categories.

2.6.1 *Interactive (Terminal-Driven) Systems*

An example of an interactive (terminal-driven) system is shown in Figure 2.10. Terminals represent users who each send a job to the "central subsystem" and then wait for a response. The central subsystem is a network of queues. A user cannot submit her next job before her previous job returns. Thus, the number of jobs in the system is fixed (equal to the number of terminals). This number is sometimes called the **load** or **MPL** (multiprogramming level), not to be confused with device utilization.

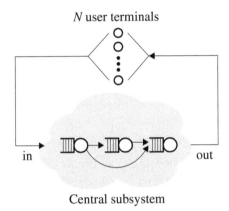

Figure 2.10. Interactive system.

There is a **think time**, Z, which is a random variable representing the time at each terminal between receiving the result of one job and sending out the next job. Note that the number of jobs in the central subsystem is at most the number of terminals, because some users might be in the "thinking" state.

An example of an interactive system such as the one shown in Figure 2.10 is a data-entry application. N users each sit at terminals filling out the entries on their screens. Several fields of the screen must be filled out, and then the whole screen is submitted to the central subsystem for appropriate processing and database update. A new screen cannot be filled out until the previous update is performed. The "think time," Z, is the time to key data to the screen.

An individual user (terminal) oscillates between the think state and the submitted state as shown in Figure 2.11.

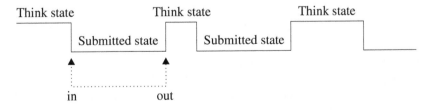

Figure 2.11. The user alternates between thinking and waiting for the submitted job to return.

Question: How would you define the response time for the interactive system?

Answer: Response time is the time it takes a job to go between "in" and "out" in Figures 2.10 and 2.11. We denote the average time to get from "in" to "out" by $\mathbf{E}$ [Response Time] or $\mathbf{E}[R]$ to differentiate it from $\mathbf{E}[T]$, which is defined as

$$\mathbf{E}[T] = \mathbf{E}[R] + \mathbf{E}[Z]$$

Important: Although "response time" in open systems is denoted by the random variable (r.v.) T, for closed interactive systems, we refer to T as the *system time* (or "time in system") and reserve the r.v. R for *response time*.

Goal: The goal in an interactive system is to find a way to allow as many users as possible to get onto the system at once, so they can all get their work done, while keeping $\mathbf{E}[R]$ low enough. Note that interactive systems are very different from open systems in that a small change in N has a profound effect on the system behavior.

The typical questions asked by systems designers are:

- Given the original system, how high can I make N while keeping $\mathbf{E}[R]$ below some threshold? That is, how does $\mathbf{E}[R]$ rise with N?
- Assume a fixed multiprogramming level, N. Given that we can make changes to the central subsystem (i.e., make certain devices faster), which changes will improve $\mathbf{E}[R]$ the most?

Question: Say we are modeling performance at a website. Would you model the website as a closed interactive system or an open system?

Answer: The jury is still out. There are research papers of both types. On the one hand, once a user clicks on a link (submits a job), he typically waits to receive the result before clicking on another link. Thus users behave as if the website is a closed system. On the other hand, a website may have a huge number of users, each of whom is very transient in his or her use of the website. In this respect, the website might behave more like an open system.

Schroeder et al. [165] proposes the idea of a "partly-open" system. Here users arrive from outside as in an open system, but make k requests to the system when they arrive, where each request can only be made when the previous request completes (as in a closed system).

2.6.2 Batch Systems

An example of a batch system is shown in Figure 2.12. A batch system looks like an interactive system with a think time of zero. However, the goals are somewhat different for batch systems. In a batch system, typically one is running many jobs overnight. As soon as one job completes, another one is started. So there are always N jobs in the central subsystem. The MPL is usually predetermined and fixed. For example the MPL might be the number of jobs that fit into memory.

N user terminals

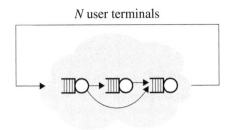

Central subsystem

Figure 2.12. Batch system.

Goal: For a batch system, the goal is to obtain high *throughput*, so that as many jobs as possible are completed overnight.

The typical question asked by systems designers is, "How can we improve the central subsystem so as to maximize throughput?"

Note that we are typically constrained by some fixed maximum MPL (because only so many jobs fit into memory or for some other reason). Thus the only method we have for increasing throughput is changing the central subsystem, either by changing the routing or by speeding up some device. Observe that in the batch system we are not concerned with response times because the jobs are running overnight.

Question: What does X mean in a closed system?

Answer: X is the number of jobs crossing "out" per second. Note that "in" = "out" for the batch system.

2.6.3 *Throughput in a Closed System*

Let's look at some examples.

Example: Single Server

Figure 2.13 shows a closed network consisting of a single server.

MPL = N

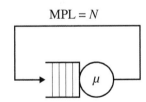

Figure 2.13. Single-server closed network.

Question: What is the throughput, X, in Figure 2.13?

Answer: $X = \mu$.

Observe that this is *very different* from the case of the open network where throughput was independent of service rate!

Question: What is the mean response time, $\mathbf{E}[R]$, in Figure 2.13?

Answer: For a closed batch system, $\mathbf{E}[R] = \mathbf{E}[T]$, namely the response time and time in system are the same. For Figure 2.13, $\mathbf{E}[T] = N/\mu$, because every "arrival" waits behind $N - 1$ jobs and then runs.

Note that X and $\mathbf{E}[R]$ are inversely related!

Example: Tandem Servers

Now consider the example of a more complicated closed network, as shown in Figure 2.14.

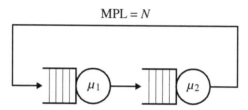

MPL $= N$

Figure 2.14. Tandem servers closed network.

Question: What is the throughput?

Answer: We would like to say $X = \min(\mu_1, \mu_2) \ldots$

Question: Why is this previous answer not necessarily correct?

Answer: The previous answer is correct if we know that the slower server is always busy, but that is not necessarily the case. Imagine $N = 1$. Then it is certainly not the case that the slower server is always busy.

Question: OK, but what happens when $N = 2$. Now it appears that there is always at least one job at the slow server, doesn't it?

Answer: Nope, the slower server is still not always busy. What we're missing here is the fact that sometimes the slow server is faster than the fast server – because these service rates are just averages! So do we in fact need to take the job size distribution into account to get the exact answer? Does the job size distribution really affect the answer very much?

We will answer these questions soon enough... For now, let's sum up the differences between the behavior of open and closed networks and why we need to consider both.

2.7 Differences between Closed and Open Networks

Open Systems
- Throughput, X, is independent of the μ_i's
- X is not affected by doubling the μ_i's.
- Throughput and response time are *not* related.

Closed Systems

- X depends on μ_i's.
- If we double all the μ_i's while holding N constant, then X changes.
- In fact we see in Chapter 6 that for closed systems,

$$\text{Higher throughput} \iff \text{Lower avg. response time.}$$

2.7.1 A Question on Modeling

Here is a final question: A few years ago I got a call from some folks at IBM. They were trying to model their blade server as a single-server queue. They knew the arrival rate into the server, λ, in jobs/sec. However they were wondering how to get $\mathbf{E}[S]$, the mean job size.

Question: How do you obtain $\mathbf{E}[S]$ in practice for your single-server system?

Answer: At first glance, you might reason that because $\mathbf{E}[S]$ is the mean time required for a job in isolation, you should just send a single job into the system and measure its response time, repeating that experiment a hundred times to get an average. This makes sense in theory, but does not work well in practice, because cache conditions and other factors are very different for the scenario of just a single job compared with the case when the system has been loaded for some time.

A better approach is to recall that $\mathbf{E}[S] = \frac{1}{\mu}$, so it suffices to think about the service rate of the server in jobs/second. To get μ, assuming an open system, we can make λ higher and higher, which will increase the completion rate, until the completion rate levels off at some value, which will be rate μ.

An even better idea is to put our server into a closed system, with zero think time. This way the server is guaranteed to always be occupied with work. Now, if we measure the completion rate at the server (jobs completing per second), then that will give us μ for the server. $\mathbf{E}[S]$ is then the reciprocal of μ.

2.8 Related Readings

Especially helpful in understanding closed queueing networks are Lazowska (pp. 58–59) [117] and Menascé (pp. 84–87) [125]. Both of these are wonderful books.

There is surprisingly very little known in the literature on how closed systems compare to open systems. For example, consider a closed interactive single-server system with load ρ, versus the corresponding open system with load ρ. How do these compare to each other with respect to their mean response time? How does variability in service time affect closed systems versus open ones? These questions and many others are considered in [186] and [24], as well as in Exercises 7.2, 7.5, 13.7, and 13.8. Another question is how the scheduling policy (service order) at the server affects closed systems versus open systems. This question was not really discussed until 2006 [165]. For a more recent discussion of the open versus closed topic, we recommend the book by Y.C. Tay [173].

In this chapter, we have mentioned several times that ensuring that the arrival rate is less than the service rate ($\lambda < \mu$) is *necessary* for stability. This condition will also be *sufficient* to ensure stability of the networks we consider in this book. However, it is not generally a *sufficient* condition for stability in more complex queueing networks. To understand why, we recommend the papers of Maury Bramson (see [29]).

2.9 Exercises

2.1 Maximum Outside Arrival Rate

For the network-of-queues with probabilistic routing given in Figure 2.3, suppose that each server serves at an average rate of 10 jobs/sec; that is, $\mu_i = 10, \forall i$. Suppose that $r_2 = r_3 = 1$. Suppose that $p_{12} = p_{2,\text{out}} = 0.8$, $p_{23} = p_{13} = 0.2$, $p_{1,\text{out}} = 0$, and $p_{31} = 1$. What is the maximum allowable value of r_1 to keep this system stable?

2.2 Slowdown

(a) Jobs arrive at a server that services them in FCFS order:

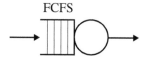

The average arrival rate is $\lambda = \frac{1}{2}$ job/sec. The job sizes (service times) are independently and identically distributed according to random variable S where

$$S = \begin{cases} 1 & \text{with probability 3/4} \\ 2 & \text{otherwise} \end{cases}.$$

You have measured the mean response time: $\mathbf{E}\left[T\right] = \frac{29}{12}$.

Based on this information, compute the mean slowdown, $\mathbf{E}\left[\text{Slowdown}\right]$, where the slowdown of job j is defined as $\text{Slowdown}(j) = \frac{T(j)}{S(j)}$, where $T(j)$ is the response time of job j and $S(j)$ is the size of job j.

(b) If the service order in part (a) had been Shortest-Job-First (SJF), would the same technique have worked for computing mean slowdown?

2.3 Scheduling Orders

(a) For a single-server CPU, where jobs arrive according to some process, let SRPT denote the *preemptive* scheduling policy that always serves the job with the currently Shortest-Remaining-Processing-Time (assume one knows this information). It is claimed that for any *arrival sequence*, consisting of the arrival time and size of every job, SRPT scheduling minimizes mean response time over that arrival sequence. Prove or disprove this claim.

(b) The slowdown of a job is defined as the job's response time divided by its service requirement. (i) Mean slowdown is thought by many to be a more important performance metric than mean response time. Why do you think this is? (ii) It seems intuitive that the SRPT scheduling policy should minimize mean slowdown. Prove or disprove this hypothesis.

PART II

Necessary Probability Background

Probability is an important part of analytical modeling. Part II provides all the probability that we will need throughout this book. Chapter 3 provides a quick review of undergraduate probability. Chapter 4 reviews two methods for generating random variables, which will be important in simulating queues. Finally, Chapter 5 discusses more advanced topics, like sample paths, convergence of sequences of random variables, and different types of averages, such as time averages and ensemble averages. These concepts are important and are referred to throughout the book; however they are also difficult, and it is reasonable that a reader might want to skim Chapter 5 during a first reading and return to the chapter for a more in-depth reading after covering Markov chains in Chapters 8 and 9.

CHAPTER 3

Probability Review

In this book, we assume a knowledge of undergraduate probability, including both discrete and continuous random variables. The first three chapters (about 180 pages) of Sheldon Ross's book, *Introduction to Probability Models* [150], provide excellent coverage of these topics, and we encourage readers to look there. In this chapter we provide a brief review of the specific probabilistic concepts that we will need in this book, by way of some simple illustrative examples. We start with a discussion of probability on events and then move on to random variables. Working through these examples, plus the exercises at the end of this chapter, should suffice as a review of undergraduate probability for the purposes of this book.

3.1 Sample Space and Events

Probability is typically defined in terms of some **experiment**. The **sample space**, Ω, of the experiment is the set of all possible outcomes of the experiment.

> **Definition 3.1** An *event*, E, is any subset of the sample space, Ω.

For example, in an experiment where two dice are rolled, each outcome (a.k.a. sample point) is denoted by the pair (i, j), where i is the first roll and j is the second roll. There are 36 sample points. We can consider the event

$$E = \{ (1, 3) \text{ or } (2, 2) \text{ or } (3, 1) \}$$

that the sum of the dice rolls is 4.

In general, the sample space may be *discrete*, meaning that the number of outcomes is finite, or at least countably infinite, or *continuous*, meaning that the number of outcomes is uncountable.

One can talk of unions and intersections of events, because they are also sets (e.g., $E \cup F$, $E \cap F$, and E^C, where E and F are events and E^C, the complement of E, denotes the set of points in Ω but not in E).

Question: For the dice-rolling experiment, consider events E_1 and E_2 defined on Ω in Figure 3.1. Do you think that E_1 and E_2 are independent?

Answer: No, they are not independent. We get to this later when we define independence. We say instead that E_1 and E_2 are mutually exclusive.

$$
\Omega = \left\{
\begin{array}{cccccc}
(1,1) & (1,2) & (1,3) & (1,4) & (1,5) & (1,6) \\
(2,1) & (2,2) & (2,3) & (2,4) & (2,5) & (2,6) \\
(3,1) & (3,2) & (3,3) & (3,4) & (3,5) & (3,6) \\
(4,1) & (4,2) & (4,3) & (4,4) & (4,5) & (4,6) \\
(5,1) & (5,2) & (5,3) & (5,4) & (5,5) & (5,6) \\
(6,1) & (6,2) & (6,3) & (6,4) & (6,5) & (6,6)
\end{array}
\right.
$$

E_1 E_2

Figure 3.1. Illustration of two events in sample space Ω.

Definition 3.2 If $E_1 \cap E_2 = \emptyset$, then E_1 and E_2 are ***mutually exclusive***.

Definition 3.3 If $E_1, E_2, \ldots, E_n$ are events such that $E_i \cap E_j = \emptyset, \forall i, j$, and such that $\bigcup_{i=1}^{n} E_i = F$, then we say that events $E_1, E_2, \ldots, E_n$ ***partition*** set F.

3.2 Probability Defined on Events

Probability is defined on events.

$$\mathbf{P}\{E\} = \text{probability of event } E \text{ occurring.}$$

We can think of each sample point as having some probability of occurring, and the probability that event E occurs is the sum of the probabilities of the sample points in E. For example, in the two-dice example, each sample point (an ordered pair of numbers) occurs with a probability of $\frac{1}{36}$.

Importantly the probability of Ω, where Ω is the sample space, is defined to be 1.

Definition 3.4 The probability of the union of two events is defined as follows:

$$\mathbf{P}\{E \cup F\} = \mathbf{P}\{E\} + \mathbf{P}\{F\} - \mathbf{P}\{E \cap F\}$$

This should make sense if we think of events as sets as shown in Figure 3.2. Observe that the subtraction of the $\mathbf{P}\{E \cap F\}$ term is necessary so that those sample points are not counted twice.

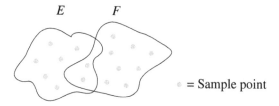

$\bullet$ = Sample point

Figure 3.2. Venn diagram.

Theorem 3.5 $\mathbf{P}\{E \cup F\} \leq \mathbf{P}\{E\} + \mathbf{P}\{F\}$.

Proof This follows immediately from Definition 3.4.   ■

Question: When is Theorem 3.5 an equality?

Answer: When E and F are mutually exclusive.

Question: Suppose your experiment involves throwing a dart, which is *equally likely* to land anywhere in the interval $[0, 1]$. What is the probability that the dart lands at exactly 0.3?

Answer: The probability of landing at exactly 0.3 is defined to be 0. To see this, suppose that the probability were strictly greater than 0, say $\epsilon > 0$. Then the probability of landing at 0.5 would also be ϵ, as would the probability of landing at any rational point. But these different landing outcomes are mutually exclusive events, so their probabilities add. Thus the probability of landing in the interval $[0, 1]$ would be greater than 1, which is not allowed, because $\mathbf{P}\{\Omega\} = 1$. While the probability of landing at exactly 0.3 is defined to be 0, the probability of landing in the interval $[0, 0.3]$ is defined to be 0.3.

3.3 Conditional Probabilities on Events

Definition 3.6 The *conditional probability of event E given event F* is written as $\mathbf{P}\{E \mid F\}$ and is given by the following, where we assume $\mathbf{P}\{F\} > 0$:

$$\mathbf{P}\{E \mid F\} = \frac{\mathbf{P}\{E \cap F\}}{\mathbf{P}\{F\}} \tag{3.1}$$

$\mathbf{P}\{E \mid F\}$ should be thought of as the probability that event E occurs, given that we have narrowed our sample space to points in F. To see this, consider Figure 3.3, where $\mathbf{P}\{E\} = \frac{8}{42}$ and $\mathbf{P}\{F\} = \frac{10}{42}$.

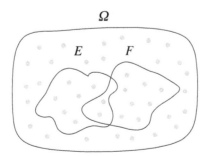

Figure 3.3. Sample space with 42 sample points.

If we imagine that we narrow our space to the 10 points in F, then the probability of being in set E, given we are in set F, should be 2 out of 10. Indeed,

$$\mathbf{P}\{E \mid F\} = \frac{2}{10} = \frac{\frac{2}{42}}{\frac{10}{42}} = \frac{\mathbf{P}\{E \cap F\}}{\mathbf{P}\{F\}}.$$

Example: Table 3.1 shows my sandwich choices each day. We define the "first half of the week" to be Monday through Wednesday (inclusive), and the "second half of the week" to be Thursday through Sunday (inclusive).

Table 3.1. *My sandwich choices*

Mon	Tue	Wed	Thu	Fri	Sat	Sun
Jelly	Cheese	Turkey	Cheese	Turkey	Cheese	None

Question: What is $\mathbf{P}\{\text{Cheese} \mid \text{Second half of week}\}$?

Answer: This is asking for the fraction of days in the second half of the week when I eat a cheese sandwich. The answer is clearly 2 out of 4, or $\frac{2}{4}$. Alternatively, we can use (3.1) as follows:

$$\mathbf{P}\{\text{Cheese} \mid \text{Second half of week}\} = \frac{\mathbf{P}\{\text{Cheese \& Second half}\}}{\mathbf{P}\{\text{Second half}\}} = \frac{\frac{2}{7}}{\frac{4}{7}} = \frac{2}{4}.$$

3.4 Independent Events and Conditionally Independent Events

Definition 3.7 Events E and F are ***independent*** if

$$\mathbf{P}\{E \cap F\} = \mathbf{P}\{E\} \cdot \mathbf{P}\{F\}.$$

Question: If E and F are independent, what is $\mathbf{P}\{E \mid F\}$?

Answer: Assuming $\mathbf{P}\{F\} > 0$, we have

$$\mathbf{P}\{E \mid F\} = \frac{\mathbf{P}\{E \cap F\}}{\mathbf{P}\{F\}} \overset{\text{indpt}}{=} \frac{\mathbf{P}\{E\} \cdot \mathbf{P}\{F\}}{\mathbf{P}\{F\}} = \mathbf{P}\{E\}.$$

That is, $\mathbf{P}\{E\}$ is not affected by whether F is true or not.

Question: Can two mutually exclusive (non-null) events ever be independent?

Answer: No. In this case, $\mathbf{P}\{E \mid F\} = 0 \neq \mathbf{P}\{E\}$.

Question: Suppose one is rolling two dice. Which of these pairs of events are independent?
  1. $E_1 =$ "First roll is 6" and $E_2 =$ "Second roll is 6"
  2. $E_1 =$ "Sum of the rolls is 7" and $E_2 =$ "Second roll is 4"

Answer: They are both independent!

Question: Suppose we had defined: $E_1 =$ "Sum of the rolls is 8" and $E_2 =$ "Second roll is 4." Are they independent now?

Answer: No.

A different notion of independence that comes up frequently in problems (see for example, Exercise 3.20) is that of conditional independence.

Definition 3.8 Two events E and F are said to be ***conditionally independent*** given event G, where $\mathbf{P}\{G\} > 0$, if

$$\mathbf{P}\{E \cap F \mid G\} = \mathbf{P}\{E \mid G\} \cdot \mathbf{P}\{F \mid G\}.$$

Independence does not imply conditional independence and vice versa.

3.5 Law of Total Probability

Observe that the set E can be expressed as

$$E = (E \cap F) \cup \left(E \cap F^C\right).$$

That is, E is the union of the set $E \cap F$ and the set $E \cap F^C$, because any point in E is either also in F or also *not* in F.

Now observe that $E \cap F$ and $E \cap F^C$ are mutually exclusive. Thus,

$$
\begin{aligned}
\mathbf{P}\{E\} &= \mathbf{P}\{E \cap F\} + \mathbf{P}\{E \cap F^C\} \\
&= \mathbf{P}\{E \mid F\}\mathbf{P}\{F\} + \mathbf{P}\{E \mid F^C\}\mathbf{P}\{F^C\}
\end{aligned}
$$

where $\mathbf{P}\{F^C\} = 1 - \mathbf{P}\{F\}$.

Theorem 3.9 is a generalization.

Theorem 3.9 (Law of Total Probability) *Let* $F_1, F_2, \ldots, F_n$ *partition the state space* Ω. *Then,*

$$\mathbf{P}\{E\} = \sum_{i=1}^{n} \mathbf{P}\{E \cap F_i\}$$

$$= \sum_{i=1}^{n} \mathbf{P}\{E \mid F_i\} \cdot \mathbf{P}\{F_i\}.$$

Proof

$$E = \bigcup_{i=1}^{n} (E \cap F_i).$$

Now, because the events $E \cap F_i, i = 1, \ldots, n$, are mutually exclusive, we have that

$$\mathbf{P}\{E\} = \sum_{i=1}^{n} \mathbf{P}\{E \cap F_i\} = \sum_{i=1}^{n} \mathbf{P}\{E \mid F_i\} \cdot \mathbf{P}\{F_i\}. \qquad \blacksquare$$

Question: Suppose we are interested in the probability that a certain type of transaction fails. We know that if there is a caching failure, then the transaction will fail with probability $5/6$. We also know that if there is a network failure then the transaction will fail with probability $1/4$. Suppose that the network fails with probability $1/100$, and the cache fails with probability $1/100$. Is this enough to tell us the probability that the transaction will fail?

Answer: It is tempting to write

(WRONG)

$$\mathbf{P}\{\text{transaction fails}\} = \mathbf{P}\{\text{transaction fails} \mid \text{caching failure}\} \cdot \frac{1}{100}$$

$$+ \mathbf{P}\{\text{transaction fails} \mid \text{network failure}\} \cdot \frac{1}{100}$$

$$= \frac{5}{6} \cdot \frac{1}{100} + \frac{1}{4} \cdot \frac{1}{100}.$$

Question: What is wrong with that solution?

Answer: The two events we conditioned on – a network failure and a caching failure – do not necessarily partition the space. The sum of the probabilities of these events is clearly < 1. Furthermore, there may be a non-zero probability that *both* failures occur.

One needs to be very careful that the events are both (i) mutually exclusive and (ii) sum to the whole sample space.

3.6 Bayes Law

Sometimes, one needs to know $\mathbf{P}\{F \mid E\}$, but all one knows is the reverse direction: $\mathbf{P}\{E \mid F\}$. Is it possible to get $\mathbf{P}\{F \mid E\}$ from $\mathbf{P}\{E \mid F\}$? It turns out that it is, assuming that we also know $\mathbf{P}\{E\}$ and $\mathbf{P}\{F\}$.

Theorem 3.10 (Bayes Law)

$$\mathbf{P}\{F \mid E\} = \frac{\mathbf{P}\{E \mid F\} \cdot \mathbf{P}\{F\}}{\mathbf{P}\{E\}}$$

Proof

$$\mathbf{P}\{F \mid E\} = \frac{\mathbf{P}\{E \cap F\}}{\mathbf{P}\{E\}} = \frac{\mathbf{P}\{E \mid F\} \cdot \mathbf{P}\{F\}}{\mathbf{P}\{E\}} \qquad \blacksquare$$

The Law of Total Probability can be combined with Bayes Law as follows: Let $F_1, F_2, \ldots, F_n$ partition Ω. Then we can write: $\mathbf{P}\{E\} = \sum_{j=1}^{n} \mathbf{P}\{E \mid F_j\} \cdot \mathbf{P}\{F_j\}$. This yields the following:

Theorem 3.11 (Extended Bayes Law) *Let $F_1, F_2, \ldots, F_n$ partition Ω. Then*

$$\mathbf{P}\{F \mid E\} = \frac{\mathbf{P}\{E \mid F\} \cdot \mathbf{P}\{F\}}{\mathbf{P}\{E\}} = \frac{\mathbf{P}\{E \mid F\} \cdot \mathbf{P}\{F\}}{\sum_{j=1}^{n} \mathbf{P}\{E \mid F_j\} \mathbf{P}\{F_j\}}$$

Example: A test is used to diagnose a rare disease. The test is only 95% accurate, meaning that, in a person who has the disease it will report "positive" with probability 95% (and negative otherwise), and in a person who does not have the disease, it will report "negative" with probability 95% (and positive otherwise). Suppose that 1 in 10,000 children get the disease.

Question: A mom brings in her child to be tested. Given that the test comes back positive, how worried should the mom be?

Answer:

$$\mathbf{P}\left\{\text{Child has disease} \mid \text{Test positive}\right\}$$

$$= \frac{\mathbf{P}\left\{\text{Test Positive} \mid \text{Disease}\right\} \cdot \mathbf{P}\left\{\text{Disease}\right\}}{\mathbf{P}\left\{\text{Test positive} \mid \text{Disease}\right\} \cdot \mathbf{P}\left\{\text{Disease}\right\} + \mathbf{P}\left\{\text{Test positive} \mid \text{Healthy}\right\} \cdot \mathbf{P}\left\{\text{Healthy}\right\}}$$

$$= \frac{0.95 \cdot \frac{1}{10000}}{0.95 \cdot \frac{1}{10000} + 0.05 \cdot \frac{9999}{10000}}$$

$$= 0.0019$$

Thus the probability that the child has the disease is only about 2 out of 1,000.

3.7 Discrete versus Continuous Random Variables

Consider an experiment, such as rolling two dice. Suppose that we are interested in the sum of the two rolls. That sum could range anywhere from 2 to 12, with each of these events having a different probability. A random variable, X, associated with this experiment, is a way to represent the value of the experiment (in this case the sum of the rolls). Specifically, when we write X, it is understood that X has many instances, ranging from 2 to 12 and that different instances occur with different probabilities (e.g., $\mathbf{P}\left\{X = 3\right\} = \frac{2}{36}$).

> **Definition 3.12** A *random variable* (r.v.) is a real-valued function of the outcome of an experiment.

> **Definition 3.13** A *discrete random variable* can take on at most a countably infinite number of possible values, whereas a *continuous random variable* can take on an uncountable set of possible values.

Question: Which of these random variables is discrete and which is continuous?

1. The sum of the rolls of two dice
2. The number of arrivals at a website by time t
3. The time until the next arrival at a website
4. The CPU requirement of an HTTP request

Answer: The first of these can take on only a finite number of values – those between 2 and 12 – so it clearly is a discrete r.v. The number of arrivals at a website can take on the values: $0, 1, 2, 3, \ldots$ namely a countable set; hence this is discrete as well. Time, in general, is modeled as a continuous quantity, even though there is a non-zero granularity in our ability to measure time via a computer. Thus quantities three and four above are continuous r.v.'s.

We use capital letters to denote random variables. For example, we might define X to be a random variable equal to the sum of two dice. Then,

$$\mathbf{P}\left\{X = 7\right\} = \mathbf{P}\left\{(1, 6) \text{ or } (2, 5) \text{ or } (3, 4), \ldots, \text{ or } (6, 1)\right\} = \frac{1}{6}.$$

Important: *Because the "outcome of the experiment" is just an event, all the theorems that we learned about events apply to random variables as well.* In particular, the Law of Total Probability holds. For example, if N denotes the number of arrivals at a website by time t, then $N > 10$ is an event. We can then use conditioning on events to get

$$\mathbf{P}\left\{N > 10\right\} = \mathbf{P}\left\{N > 10 \mid \text{weekday}\right\} \cdot \frac{5}{7} + \mathbf{P}\left\{N > 10 \mid \text{weekend}\right\} \cdot \frac{2}{7}.$$

All of this will become more concrete once we study examples of common random variables next.

3.8 Probabilities and Densities

3.8.1 Discrete: Probability Mass Function

Discrete random variables take on a countable number of values, each with some probability.

Definition 3.14 Let X be a discrete r.v. Then the ***probability mass function (p.m.f.)***, $p_X(\cdot)$ of X, is defined as follows:

$$p_X(a) = \mathbf{P}\left\{X = a\right\}, \text{where} \sum_x p_X(x) = 1$$

The ***cumulative distribution function*** of X is defined as

$$F_X(a) = \mathbf{P}\left\{X \leq a\right\} = \sum_{x \leq a} p_X(x).$$

We also write

$$\overline{F}_X(a) = \mathbf{P}\left\{X > a\right\} = \sum_{x > a} p_X(x) = 1 - F_X(a).$$

Common discrete distributions include the Bernoulli, the Binomial, the Geometric, and the Poisson, all of which are discussed next.

Bernoulli(p) represents the result of a single coin flip, where the coin has probability p of coming up heads (we map this event to the value 1) and $1 - p$ of coming up tails (we map this event to the value 0). If X is a r.v. drawn from the Bernoulli(p) distribution, then we write: $X \sim$ Bernoulli(p) and define X as follows:

$$X = \begin{cases} 1 & \text{w/ prob } p \\ 0 & \text{otherwise} \end{cases}$$

The p.m.f. of r.v. X is defined as follows:

$$p_X(1) = p$$
$$p_X(0) = 1 - p$$

The p.m.f. is depicted in Figure 3.4.

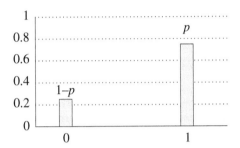

Figure 3.4. Probability mass function of Bernoulli(p) distribution, with $p = 0.76$.

Binomial(n, p) builds on Bernoulli(p). Given a coin with probability p of coming up heads (success), we flip the coin n times (these are independent flips). If $X \sim$ Binomial(n, p), then X represents the number of heads (successes) when flipping a Bernoulli(p) coin n times. Observe that X can take on discrete values: $0, 1, 2, \ldots, n$.

The p.m.f. of r.v. X is defined as follows:

$$p_X(i) = \mathbf{P}\{X = i\}$$
$$= \binom{n}{i} p^i (1-p)^{n-i}, \text{ where } i = 0, 1, 2, \ldots, n$$

The p.m.f. is shown in Figure 3.5.

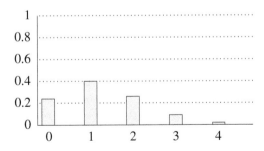

Figure 3.5. Probability mass function of the Binomial(n, p) distribution, with $n = 4$ and $p = 0.3$.

Geometric(p) also builds on Bernoulli(p). Again we have a coin with probability p of coming up heads (success). We now flip it until we get a success; these are independent trials, each Bernoulli(p). If $X \sim$ Geometric(p), then X represents the number of flips until we get a success.

The p.m.f. of r.v. X is defined as follows:

$$p_X(i) = \mathbf{P}\{X = i\} = (1 - p)^{i-1} p, \text{ where } i = 1, 2, 3, \ldots$$

The p.m.f. is shown in Figure 3.6.

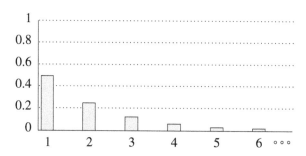

Figure 3.6. Probability mass function of the Geometric(p) distribution, with $p = 0.5$.

Question: Let's review. Suppose you have a room of n disks. Each disk independently dies with probability p each year. How are the following quantities distributed?

1. The number of disks that die in the first year
2. The number of years until a particular disk dies
3. The state of a particular disk after one year

Answer: The distributions are: 1. Binomial(n, p), 2. Geometric(p), 3. Bernoulli(p).

Poisson(λ) is another discrete distribution that is very common in computer systems analysis. We define Poisson(λ) via its p.m.f. Although the p.m.f. does not appear to have any meaning at present, we will show many interesting properties of this distribution in Chapter 11. The Poisson distribution occurs naturally when looking at a mixture of a very large number of independent sources, each with a very small individual probability. It can therefore be a reasonable approximation for the number of arrivals to a website or a router per unit time.

If $X \sim \text{Poisson}(\lambda)$, then

$$p_X(i) = \frac{e^{-\lambda} \lambda^i}{i!}, \text{ where } i = 0, 1, 2, \ldots$$

The p.m.f. for the Poisson(λ) distribution is shown in Figure 3.7.

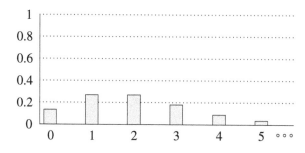

Figure 3.7. Probability mass function of the Poisson(λ) distribution with $\lambda = 2$.

You may have noticed that the Poisson distribution does not look all that different from the Binomial distribution. It turns out, as shown in Exercise 3.12, that if n is large and p is small, then Binomial(n, p) is actually very close to Poisson(np).

3.8.2 *Continuous: Probability Density Function*

Continuous r.v.'s take on an uncountable number of values. The range of a continuous r.v. can be thought of as an interval or collection of intervals on the real line. The probability that a continuous r.v., X, is equal to any particular value is zero. We define probability for a continuous r.v. in terms of a density function.

> **Definition 3.15** The ***probability density function (p.d.f.)*** of a continuous r.v. X is a non-negative function $f_X(\cdot)$ where
> $$\mathbf{P}\{a \leq X \leq b\} = \int_a^b f_X(x)dx \quad \text{and where} \quad \int_{-\infty}^{\infty} f_X(x)dx = 1.$$

Definition 3.15 is illustrated in Figure 3.8.

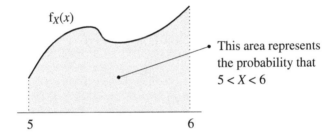

Figure 3.8. Area under the curve represents the probability that r.v. X is between 5 and 6, namely $\int_5^6 f_X(x)dx$.

Question: Does $f_X(x)$ have to be < 1 for all x?

Answer: No, $f_X(x) \neq \mathbf{P}\{X = x\}$.

To interpret the density function, $f(\cdot)$, think of
$$f_X(x)dx \doteq \mathbf{P}\{x \leq X \leq x + dx\}.$$

Question: Which of these are valid p.d.f.'s?
$$f_X(x) = \begin{cases} .5x^{-.5} & \text{if } 0 < x < 1 \\ 0 & \text{otherwise} \end{cases}$$
$$f_X(x) = \begin{cases} 2x^{-2} & \text{if } 0 < x < 1 \\ 0 & \text{otherwise} \end{cases}$$
$$f_X(x) = \begin{cases} x^{-2} & \text{if } 1 < x < \infty \\ 0 & \text{otherwise} \end{cases}$$

Answer: Only the first and third p.d.f.'s integrate to 1, so only they are valid.

Definition 3.16 The *cumulative distribution function (c.d.f.)* of a continuous r.v. X is the function $F(\cdot)$ defined by

$$F_X(a) = \mathbf{P}\{-\infty < X \leq a\} = \int_{-\infty}^{a} f_X(x)dx.$$

We also write:

$$\overline{F}(a) = 1 - F_X(a) = \mathbf{P}\{X > a\}.$$

Question: We know how to get $F_X(x)$ from $f_X(x)$. How do we get $f_X(x)$ from $F_X(x)$?

Answer: By the Fundamental Theorem of Calculus,

$$f_X(x) = \frac{d}{dx}\int_{-\infty}^{x} f(t)dt = \frac{d}{dx}F_X(x).$$

There are many common continuous distributions. Below we briefly define just a few: the Uniform, Exponential, and the Pareto distributions.

Uniform(a,b), often written $U(a, b)$, models the fact that any interval of length δ between a and b is equally likely. Specifically, if $X \sim U(a, b)$, then

$$f_X(x) = \begin{cases} \dfrac{1}{b-a} & \text{if } a \leq x \leq b \\ 0 & \text{otherwise} \end{cases}.$$

Question: For $X \sim U(a, b)$, what is $F_X(x)$?

Answer:

$$F_X(x) = \int_{a}^{x} \frac{1}{b-a}dx = \frac{x-a}{b-a}$$

Figure 3.9 depicts $f_X(x)$ and $F_X(x)$ graphically.

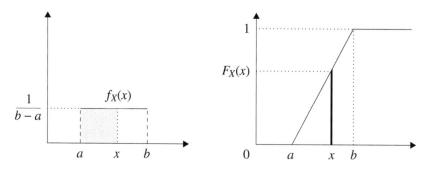

Figure 3.9. The p.d.f., $f(x)$, and c.d.f., $F(x)$, functions for Uniform(a, b). The shaded region in the left graph has an area equal to the height of the darkened segment in the right graph.

Exp(λ) denotes the Exponential distribution, whose probability density function drops off exponentially. We say that a random variable X is distributed Exponentially with rate λ, written $X \sim \mathrm{Exp}(\lambda)$, if

$$f_X(x) = \begin{cases} \lambda e^{-\lambda x} & x \geq 0 \\ 0 & x < 0 \end{cases}.$$

The graph of the p.d.f. is shown in Figure 3.10. The c.d.f., $F_X(x) = \mathbf{P}\{X \leq x\}$, is given by

$$F_X(x) = \int_{-\infty}^{x} f(y)dy = \begin{cases} 1 - e^{-\lambda x} & x \geq 0 \\ 0 & x < 0 \end{cases}.$$

$$\overline{F}_X(x) = 1 - F_X(x) = e^{-\lambda x}, \ x \geq 0$$

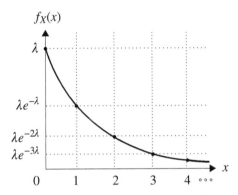

Figure 3.10. Exponential probability density function.

Observe that both $f_X(x)$ and $\overline{F}(x)$ drop off by a *constant* factor, $e^{-\lambda}$, with each unit increase of x. This fact will be important in proving the "memoryless" property of the Exponential distribution, described in Chapter 11.

Pareto(α) is a distribution with a power-law tail, meaning that its density decays as a polynomial in $1/x$ rather than exponentially, as in $\mathrm{Exp}(\lambda)$. The parameter α is often referred to as the "tail parameter." It is generally assumed that $0 < \alpha < 2$. As we see later, this range of α gives the Pareto infinite variance (variance is defined in Section 3.9). If $X \sim \mathrm{Pareto}(\alpha)$, then

$$f_X(x) = \begin{cases} \alpha x^{-\alpha-1} & x \geq 1 \\ 0 & \text{otherwise} \end{cases}.$$

$$F_X(x) = 1 - x^{-\alpha}.$$
$$\overline{F}_X(x) = x^{-\alpha}.$$

Although the Pareto distribution has a ski-slope shape, like that of the Exponential, its tail decreases much more slowly (compare $\overline{F}(x)$ for the two distributions). The Pareto distribution is said to have a "heavy tail" or a "fat tail," where a lower α corresponds to a fatter tail. This is all covered in Chapter 20.

An important continuous distribution that we have not mentioned is the **Normal**, a.k.a. Gaussian, distribution. The discussion of the Normal distribution requires first understanding expectation and variance, so we defer it until Section 3.14.

3.9 Expectation and Variance

The *mean* of a distribution, also known as its *expectation*, follows immediately from the probability mass function (or density function, in the case of continuous distributions) for the distribution. For r.v. X, we write $\mathbf{E}[X]$ to denote its mean. This is defined in the following table.

Discrete case	Continuous case
$\mathbf{E}[X] = \sum_x x \cdot p_X(x)$	$\mathbf{E}[X] = \int_{-\infty}^{\infty} x \cdot f_X(x)dx$

For the case of a discrete r.v., X, its expectation can be viewed as a sum of the possible outcomes, each weighted by its probability.

$$\mathbf{E}[X] = \sum_x x \mathbf{P}\{X = x\}$$

To see this, consider the following example.

Example: Average Cost of Lunch

What is the average cost of my lunch?

Monday	Tuesday	Wednesday	Thursday	Friday	Saturday	Sunday
$7	$7	$5	$5	$5	$0	$2

$$\text{Avg} = \frac{7 + 7 + 5 + 5 + 5 + 0 + 2}{7}$$

$$|||$$

$$\mathbf{E}[\text{Cost}] = \frac{2}{7}(7) + \frac{3}{7}(5) + \frac{1}{7}(2) + \frac{1}{7}(0)$$

Each possible value – 7, 5, 2, and 0 – is weighted by its probability.

Question: If $X \sim \text{Bernoulli}(p)$, what is $\mathbf{E}[X]$?

Answer: $\mathbf{E}[X] = 0 \cdot (1 - p) + 1 \cdot (p) = p$.

Question: Suppose a coin has probability $\frac{1}{3}$ of coming up heads. In expectation, how many times do I need to toss the coin to get a head?

Answer: This is simply $\mathbf{E}[X]$, where $X \sim \text{Geometric}(p)$, with $p = \frac{1}{3}$. Assuming $X \sim \text{Geometric}(p)$, we have

$$
\begin{aligned}
\mathbf{E}[X] &= \sum_{n=1}^{\infty} n(1-p)^{n-1}p \\
&= p \cdot \sum_{n=1}^{\infty} n \cdot q^{n-1} \quad \text{where } q = (1-p) \\
&= p \cdot \sum_{n=1}^{\infty} \frac{d}{dq}(q^n) \\
&= p \cdot \frac{d}{dq} \sum_{n=1}^{\infty} q^n \\
&= p \cdot \frac{d}{dq}\left(\frac{q}{1-q}\right) \\
&= \frac{p}{(1-q)^2} \\
&= \frac{1}{p}.
\end{aligned}
$$

So when $p = \frac{1}{3}$, the expected number of flips is 3.

Question: If $X \sim \text{Poisson}(\lambda)$, what is $\mathbf{E}[X]$?

Answer:

$$
\begin{aligned}
\mathbf{E}[X] &= \sum_{i=0}^{\infty} i\frac{e^{-\lambda}\lambda^i}{i!} \\
&= \sum_{i=1}^{\infty} i\frac{e^{-\lambda}\lambda^i}{i!} \\
&= \lambda e^{-\lambda} \sum_{i=1}^{\infty} \frac{\lambda^{i-1}}{(i-1)!} \\
&= \lambda e^{-\lambda} \sum_{k=0}^{\infty} \frac{\lambda^k}{k!} \\
&= \lambda e^{-\lambda} e^{\lambda} \\
&= \lambda.
\end{aligned}
$$

Question: If $X \sim \text{Exp}(\lambda)$, what is $\mathbf{E}[X]$?

Answer:

$$
\mathbf{E}[X] = \int_{-\infty}^{\infty} x f_X(x)dx = \int_{0}^{\infty} x\lambda e^{-\lambda x}dx = \frac{1}{\lambda} \quad \text{(integration by parts)}.
$$

Observe that whereas the λ parameter for the Poisson distribution is also its mean, for the Exponential distribution, the λ parameter is the reciprocal of the mean. We will refer to λ as the "rate" of the Exponential. For example, if the time until the next arrival is Exponentially distributed with rate 3 arrivals per second, then the expected time until the next arrival is $\frac{1}{3}$ seconds.

We can also think about *higher moments* of a random variable X. The ith moment of r.v. X, denoted by $\mathbf{E}[X^i]$, is defined as follows:

Discrete case	Continuous case
$\mathbf{E}[X^i] = \sum_x x^i \cdot p_X(x)$	$\mathbf{E}[X^i] = \int_{-\infty}^{\infty} x^i \cdot f_X(x)dx$

More generally, we can talk about the *expectation of a function $g(\cdot)$ of a random variable X*. This is defined as follows for a discrete r.v. X:

$$\mathbf{E}[g(X)] = \sum_x g(x) \cdot p_X(x)$$

and as follows for a continuous r.v. X:

$$\mathbf{E}[g(X)] = \int_{-\infty}^{\infty} g(x)f_X(x)dx$$

Question: Suppose X is defined as follows:

$$X = \begin{cases} 0 & \text{w/ prob. } 0.2 \\ 1 & \text{w/ prob. } 0.5 \\ 2 & \text{w/ prob. } 0.3 \end{cases}$$

What is $\mathbf{E}[X]$ and what is $\mathbf{E}[2X^2 + 3]$?

Answer:

$$\mathbf{E}[X] = (0)(.2) + (1)(.5) + (2)(.3).$$

$$\mathbf{E}[2X^2 + 3] = \left(2 \cdot 0^2 + 3\right)(.2) + \left(2 \cdot 1^2 + 3\right)(.5) + \left(2 \cdot 2^2 + 3\right)(.3).$$

You may have noticed that $\mathbf{E}[2X^2 + 3] = 2\mathbf{E}[X^2] + 3$. This is no coincidence and is due to Linearity of Expectation to be discussed in Section 3.13.

Definition 3.17 The *variance* of a r.v. X, written as $\mathbf{Var}(X)$, is the expected squared difference of X from its mean (i.e., the square of how much we expect X to differ from its mean, $\mathbf{E}[X]$). This is defined as follows:

$$\mathbf{Var}(X) = \mathbf{E}\left[(X - \mathbf{E}[X])^2\right]$$

and can be equivalently expressed as follows:

$$\mathbf{Var}(X) = \mathbf{E}[X^2] - (\mathbf{E}[X])^2$$

(The derivation of why these expressions are equivalent will be obvious after we cover Linearity of Expectation in Section 3.13.)

Question: If $X \sim \text{Bernoulli}(p)$, what is $\mathbf{Var}(X)$?

Answer:

$$\mathbf{E}[X] = p$$

$$\mathbf{Var}(X) = \mathbf{E}\left[(X - p)^2\right] = p(1-p)^2 + (1-p)(0-p)^2 = p(1-p)$$

Question: What is the variance of $X \sim \text{Uniform}(a, b)$?

Answer:

$$\mathbf{E}[X] = \int_a^b x \frac{1}{b-a} dx = \frac{1}{b-a} \cdot \frac{(b^2 - a^2)}{2} = \frac{a+b}{2}$$

$$\mathbf{Var}(X) = \mathbf{E}\left[\left(X - \frac{a+b}{2}\right)^2\right] = \int_a^b \left(X - \frac{a+b}{2}\right)^2 \cdot \frac{1}{b-a} dx = \frac{(b-a)^2}{12}$$

Table 3.2 shows the p.m.f. (or p.d.f.) and the mean and variance for many common distributions.

Table 3.2. *Discrete and continuous distributions*

Distribution	p.m.f. $p_X(x)$	Mean	Variance
Bernoulli(p)	$p_X(0) = 1 - p$; $p_X(1) = p$	p	$p(1-p)$
Binomial(n, p)	$p_X(x) = \binom{n}{x} p^x (1-p)^{n-x}$, $x = 0, 1, \ldots, n$	np	$np(1-p)$
Geometric(p)	$p_X(x) = (1-p)^{x-1} p$, $\quad x = 1, 2, \ldots$	$\frac{1}{p}$	$\frac{1-p}{p^2}$
Poisson(λ)	$p_X(x) = e^{-\lambda} \cdot \frac{\lambda^x}{x!}$, $\quad x = 0, 1, 2, \ldots$	λ	λ

Distribution	p.d.f. $f_X(x)$	Mean	Variance
Exp(λ)	$f_X(x) = \lambda e^{-\lambda x}$	$\frac{1}{\lambda}$	$\frac{1}{\lambda^2}$
Uniform(a, b)	$f_X(x) = \frac{1}{b-a}$, $\quad$ if $a \leq x \leq b$	$\frac{b+a}{2}$	$\frac{(b-a)^2}{12}$
Pareto$(\alpha), 0 < \alpha < 2$	$f_X(x) = \alpha x^{-\alpha-1}$, $\quad$ if $x > 1$	$\begin{cases} \infty & \text{if } \alpha \leq 1 \\ \frac{\alpha}{\alpha-1} & \text{if } \alpha > 1 \end{cases}$	∞
Normal(μ, σ^2)	$f_X(x) = \frac{1}{\sqrt{2\pi}\sigma} e^{-\frac{1}{2}\left(\frac{x-\mu}{\sigma}\right)^2}$, $-\infty < x < \infty$	μ	σ^2

3.10 Joint Probabilities and Independence

We are often interested in probability statements concerning two or more r.v.'s simultaneously. For example, we might want to know the probability that two disks will both crash within some time interval. The behavior of the two disks might be correlated or not. As another example, computer systems performance is often measured in terms of the energy-delay product [68], namely the product of the energy used by the system and the delay experienced by users. Energy and delay typically are correlated with each other, and one can imagine a joint distribution between these two random variables. In this section and the next, we present the definitions needed to formally express these ideas.

Definition 3.18 The *joint probability mass function* between discrete r.v.'s X and Y is defined by

$$p_{X,Y}(x,y) = \mathbf{P}\{X = x \,\&\, Y = y\}.$$

This is typically written as $\mathbf{P}\{X = x, Y = y\}$. Similarly, $f_{X,Y}(x,y)$ represents the *joint probability density function* between continuous r.v.'s X and Y, where

$$\int_c^d \int_a^b f_{X,Y}(x,y)dxdy = \mathbf{P}\{a < X < b \,\,\&\,\, c < Y < d\}$$

Question: What is the relationship between $f_X(x)$ and $f_{X,Y}(x,y)$?

Answer: Applying the Law of Total Probability, we have

$$f_X(x) = \int_{-\infty}^{\infty} f_{X,Y}(x,y)dy \quad \text{and} \quad f_Y(y) = \int_{-\infty}^{\infty} f_{X,Y}(x,y)dx.$$

Likewise,

$$p_X(x) = \sum_y p_{X,Y}(x,y) \quad \text{and} \quad p_Y(y) = \sum_x p_{X,Y}(x,y).$$

Similarly to the way we defined two events E and F as being independent, we can likewise define two r.v.'s as being independent.

Definition 3.19 We say that discrete r.v.'s X and Y are *independent*, written $X \perp Y$, if

$$p_{X,Y}(x,y) = p_X(x) \cdot p_Y(y).$$

Likewise, we say that continuous r.v.'s X and Y are independent if

$$f_{X,Y}(x,y) = f_X(x) \cdot f_Y(y), \quad \forall x,y.$$

Theorem 3.20 *If* $X \perp Y$, *then* $\mathbf{E}[XY] = \mathbf{E}[X] \cdot \mathbf{E}[Y]$.

Proof

$$
\begin{aligned}
\mathbf{E}[XY] &= \sum_x \sum_y xy \cdot \mathbf{P}\{X = x, Y = y\} \\
&= \sum_x \sum_y xy \cdot \mathbf{P}\{X = x\}\mathbf{P}\{Y = y\} \quad \text{(by definition of } \perp) \\
&= \sum_x x\mathbf{P}\{X = x\} \cdot \sum_y y\mathbf{P}\{Y = y\} \\
&= \mathbf{E}[X]\mathbf{E}[Y]
\end{aligned}
$$

The same argument works for continuous r.v.'s.   ■

The same proof shows that if $X \perp Y$, then

$$\mathbf{E}\left[g(X)f(Y)\right] = \mathbf{E}\left[g(X)\right] \cdot \mathbf{E}\left[f(Y)\right]$$

for arbitrary functions g and f.

Question: If $\mathbf{E}\left[XY\right] = \mathbf{E}\left[X\right]\mathbf{E}\left[Y\right]$, does that imply that $X \perp Y$?

Answer: No, see Exercise 3.10.

3.11 Conditional Probabilities and Expectations

Just as we studied conditional probabilities of events – that is, the probability that one event occurs, given that another has occurred – we can also extend this to conditional probabilities in random variables. We start with the discrete case and then move on to the continuous case. The following example will help motivate the idea.

Example: Hair Color

Suppose we divide the people in the class into Blondes (color value 1), Red-heads (color value 2), Brunettes (color value 3), and Black-haired people (color value 4). Let's say that 5 students are Blondes, 2 are Red-heads, 17 are Brunettes, and 14 are Black-haired. Let X be a random variable whose value is hair color. Then the probability mass function for X looks like this:

$$p_X(1) = \mathbf{P}\left\{\text{Blonde}\right\} = 5/38$$
$$p_X(2) = \mathbf{P}\left\{\text{Red}\right\} = 2/38$$
$$p_X(3) = \mathbf{P}\left\{\text{Brown}\right\} = 17/38$$
$$p_X(4) = \mathbf{P}\left\{\text{Black}\right\} = 14/38$$

Now let's say that a person has *light-colored* hair if the hair color is either Blonde or Red. Let's say that a person has *dark-colored* hair if the hair color is either Brown or Black. Let A denote the event that a person's hair color is light.

$$\mathbf{P}\left\{A\right\} = 7/38 \quad \text{and} \quad \mathbf{P}\left\{A^C\right\} = 31/38$$

Definition 3.21 Let X be a discrete r.v. with p.m.f. $p_X(\cdot)$ defined over a countable space. Let A be an event. Then $p_{X|A}(\cdot)$ is the **conditional p.m.f.** of X given event A. We define

$$p_{X|A}(x) = \mathbf{P}\left\{X = x \mid A\right\} = \frac{\mathbf{P}\left\{(X = x) \cap A\right\}}{\mathbf{P}\left\{A\right\}}.$$

More formally, if Ω denotes the sample space and ω represents a sample point in the sample space, and $\{\omega : X(\omega) = x\}$ is the set of sample points that result in X having value x, then

$$p_{X|A}(x) = \mathbf{P}\left\{X = x \mid A\right\} = \frac{\mathbf{P}\left\{\{\omega : X(\omega) = x\} \cap A\right\}}{\mathbf{P}\left\{A\right\}}.$$

A conditional probability thus involves narrowing down the probability space. For example,

$$p_{X|A}(\text{Blonde}) = \frac{\mathbf{P}\{(X = \text{Blonde}) \cap A\}}{\mathbf{P}\{A\}} = \frac{\frac{5}{38}}{\frac{7}{38}} = \frac{5}{7}.$$

Likewise $p_{X|A}(\text{Red}) = 2/7$.

As another example,

$$p_{X|A}(\text{Brown}) = \frac{\mathbf{P}\{(X = \text{Brown}) \cap A\}}{\mathbf{P}\{A\}} = \frac{0}{\frac{7}{38}} = 0.$$

Likewise $p_{X|A}(\text{Black}) = 0$.

Question: If we sum $p_{X|A}(x)$ over all x, what do we get?

Answer:

$$\sum_x p_{X|A}(x) = \sum_x \frac{\mathbf{P}\{(X = x) \cap A\}}{\mathbf{P}\{A\}} = \frac{\mathbf{P}\{A\}}{\mathbf{P}\{A\}} = 1.$$

Thus $p_{X|A}(x)$ is a valid p.m.f.

Definition 3.22 For a discrete r.v. X, the *conditional expectation of X given event A* is as follows:

$$\mathbf{E}[X \mid A] = \sum_x x p_{X|A}(x) = \sum_x x \cdot \frac{\mathbf{P}\{(X = x) \cap A\}}{\mathbf{P}\{A\}}$$

Question: For our example, viewing Blonde as having value 1 and Red-haired as having value 2, what is $\mathbf{E}[X \mid A]$?

Answer:

$$\mathbf{E}[X \mid A] = 1 \cdot \frac{5}{7} + 2 \cdot \frac{2}{7} = \frac{9}{7}.$$

We can also consider the case where the event, A, is an instance of a random variable. For example, A might be the event $Y = y$. It is then common to write the conditional p.m.f. of X given the event $Y = y$ as

$$p_{X|Y}(x|y) = \mathbf{P}\{X = x \mid Y = y\} = \frac{\mathbf{P}\{X = x \,\&\, Y = y\}}{\mathbf{P}\{Y = y\}} = \frac{p_{X,Y}(x,y)}{p_Y(y)},$$

and

$$\mathbf{E}[X \mid Y = y] = \sum_x x \cdot p_{X|Y}(x|y).$$

Example of Conditioning on Random Variables

Two discrete random variables X and Y taking the values $\{0, 1, 2\}$ have a joint probability mass function given by Table 3.3.

Table 3.3. *Joint probability mass function, $p_{X,Y}(x, y)$*

$Y = 2$	0	$\frac{1}{6}$	$\frac{1}{8}$
$Y = 1$	$\frac{1}{8}$	$\frac{1}{6}$	$\frac{1}{8}$
$Y = 0$	$\frac{1}{6}$	$\frac{1}{8}$	0
	$X = 0$	$X = 1$	$X = 2$

Question: Compute the conditional expectation $\mathbf{E}\left[X \mid Y = 2\right]$.

Answer:

$$\mathbf{E}\left[X \mid Y = 2\right] = \sum_x x \cdot p_{X|Y}(x|2)$$

$$= \sum_x x \cdot \mathbf{P}\left\{X = x \mid Y = 2\right\}$$

$$= 0 \cdot \frac{\mathbf{P}\left\{X = 0 \,\&\, Y = 2\right\}}{\mathbf{P}\left\{Y = 2\right\}} + 1 \cdot \frac{\mathbf{P}\left\{X = 1 \,\&\, Y = 2\right\}}{\mathbf{P}\left\{Y = 2\right\}}$$

$$+ 2 \cdot \frac{\mathbf{P}\left\{X = 2 \,\&\, Y = 2\right\}}{\mathbf{P}\left\{Y = 2\right\}}$$

$$= 1 \cdot \frac{\frac{1}{6}}{\frac{7}{24}} + 2 \cdot \frac{\frac{1}{8}}{\frac{7}{24}} = \frac{10}{7}.$$

For a continuous, real-valued, r.v. X, the conditional p.d.f. of X given event A is analogous to that for the discrete case, except that A is now a subset of the real line, where we define $\mathbf{P}\left\{X \in A\right\}$ to be the probability that X has value within the subset A.

Definition 3.23 Let X be a continuous r.v. with p.d.f. $f_X(\cdot)$ defined over the reals. Let A be a subset of the real line with $\mathbf{P}\left\{X \in A\right\} > 0$. Then $f_{X|A}(\cdot)$ is the *conditional p.d.f.* of X given event A. We define

$$f_{X|A}(x) = \begin{cases} \frac{f_X(x)}{\mathbf{P}\{X \in A\}} & \text{if } x \in A \\ 0 & \text{otherwise} \end{cases}.$$

As with the discrete case, the conditional p.d.f. is zero outside the conditioning set A. Within A, the conditional p.d.f. has exactly the same shape as the unconditional one, except that it is scaled by the constant factor $\frac{1}{\mathbf{P}\{X \in A\}}$, so that $f_{X|A}(x)$ integrates to 1.

Definition 3.24 Let X be a continuous r.v. with p.d.f. $f_X(\cdot)$ defined over the reals. Let A be a subset of the real line with $\mathbf{P}\left\{X \in A\right\} > 0$. The *conditional expectation of X given A*, written $\mathbf{E}\left[X \mid A\right]$, is defined by

$$\mathbf{E}\left[X \mid A\right] = \int_{-\infty}^{\infty} x f_{X|A}(x) dx = \int_A x f_{X|A}(x) dx = \frac{1}{\mathbf{P}\left\{X \in A\right\}} \int_A x f_X(x) dx.$$

Example: Pittsburgh Supercomputing Center

The Pittsburgh Supercomputing Center (PSC) runs large parallel jobs for scientists from all over the country. To charge users appropriately, jobs are grouped into different bins based on the number of CPU hours they require, each with a different price. Suppose that job durations are Exponentially distributed with *mean* 1,000 processor-hours. Further suppose that all jobs requiring less than 500 processor-hours are sent to bin 1, and all remaining jobs are sent to bin 2.

Question: Consider the following questions:
- **(a)** What is $\mathbf{P}$ {Job is sent to bin 1}?
- **(b)** What is $\mathbf{P}$ {Job duration < 200 | job is sent to bin 1}?
- **(c)** What is the conditional density of the duration X, $f_{X|Y}(t)$, where Y is the event that the job is sent to bin 1?
- **(d)** What is $\mathbf{E}$ [Job duration | job is in bin 1]?

Answer: Start by recalling that for $X \sim \text{Exp}\left(\frac{1}{1000}\right)$ we have

$$f_X(t) = \begin{cases} \frac{1}{1000} e^{-\frac{t}{1000}} & \text{if } t > 0 \\ 0 & \text{otherwise} \end{cases}.$$

$$F_X(t) = \mathbf{P}\{X \leq t\} = 1 - e^{-\frac{1}{1000}t}.$$

Then:
- **(a)** $F_X(500) = 1 - e^{-\frac{500}{1000}} = 1 - e^{-\frac{1}{2}} \approx 0.39$
- **(b)** $\frac{F_X(200)}{F_X(500)} = \frac{1 - e^{-\frac{1}{5}}}{1 - e^{-\frac{1}{2}}} \approx 0.46$
- **(c)**

$$f_{X|Y}(t) = \begin{cases} \dfrac{f_X(t)}{F(500)} = \dfrac{\frac{1}{1000} e^{-\frac{t}{1000}}}{1 - e^{-\frac{1}{2}}} & \text{if } t < 500 \\ 0 & \text{otherwise} \end{cases}$$

- **(d)**

$$\mathbf{E}\,[\,\text{Job duration} \mid \text{job in bin 1}\,] = \int_{-\infty}^{\infty} t f_{X|Y}(t)dt$$

$$= \int_0^{500} t \frac{\frac{1}{1000} e^{-\frac{t}{1000}}}{1 - e^{-\frac{1}{2}}} dt \approx 229$$

Question: Why is the expected size of jobs in bin 1 less than 250?

Answer: Consider the shape of the Exponential p.d.f. Now truncate it at 500, and scale everything by a constant needed to make it integrate to 1. There is still more weight on the smaller values, so the expected value is less than the midpoint.

Question: How would the answer to question (d) change if the job durations were distributed Uniform$(0, 2000)$, still with mean 1,000?

Answer: Logically, given that the job is in bin 1 and the distribution is uniform, we should find that the expected job duration is 250 hours. Here is an algebraic argument:

$$\mathbf{E}\,[\,\text{Job duration} \mid \text{job in bin 1}\,] = \int_{-\infty}^{\infty} t f_{X|Y}(t)dt = \int_0^{500} t \frac{\frac{1}{2000}}{\frac{500}{2000}} dt = 250$$

3.12 Probabilities and Expectations via Conditioning

Recall from the Law of Total Probability that, if $F_1, \ldots, F_n$ partition the sample space Ω, then

$$\mathbf{P}\{E\} = \sum_{i=1}^{n} \mathbf{P}\{E \mid F_i\} \mathbf{P}\{F_i\}.$$

This extends to random variables, because "$X = k$" is an event.

The **Law of Total Probability for Discrete Random Variables** says

$$\mathbf{P}\{X = k\} = \sum_{y} \mathbf{P}\{X = k \mid Y = y\} \mathbf{P}\{Y = y\}$$

(A similar statement can be made for continuous random variables.)

This is a *huge* tool! It allows us to break a problem into a number of simpler problems. The trick, as usual, is knowing what to condition on.

Example: Which Exponential Happens First?

Derive $\mathbf{P}\{X_1 < X_2\}$ where $X_1 \perp X_2$ and $X_1 \sim \text{Exp}(\lambda_1)$ and $X_2 \sim \text{Exp}(\lambda_2)$.

Question: What do you condition on?

Answer: We choose to condition on the value of X_2, where we use $f_2(\cdot)$ to denote the p.d.f. for X_2:

$$\mathbf{P}\{X_1 < X_2\} = \int_{-\infty}^{\infty} \mathbf{P}\{X_1 < X_2 \mid X_2 = k\} \cdot f_2(k) dk$$

$$= \int_{0}^{\infty} \mathbf{P}\{X_1 < k\} \cdot \lambda_2 e^{-\lambda_2 k} dk$$

$$= \int_{0}^{\infty} \left(1 - e^{-\lambda_1 k}\right)\left(\lambda_2 e^{-\lambda_2 k}\right) dk$$

$$= \frac{\lambda_1}{\lambda_1 + \lambda_2}$$

Theorem 3.25 *For discrete random variables,*

$$\mathbf{E}[X] = \sum_{y} \mathbf{E}[X \mid Y = y] \mathbf{P}\{Y = y\}.$$

Similarly for continuous random variables,

$$\mathbf{E}[X] = \int \mathbf{E}[X \mid Y = y] f_Y(y) dy.$$

Proof We present the proof for the discrete case:

$$\mathbf{E}[X] = \sum_x x \mathbf{P}\{X = x\}$$

$$= \sum_x x \sum_y \mathbf{P}\{X = x \mid Y = y\} \mathbf{P}\{Y = y\}$$

$$= \sum_x \sum_y x \mathbf{P}\{X = x \mid Y = y\} \mathbf{P}\{Y = y\}$$

$$= \sum_y \sum_x x \mathbf{P}\{X = x \mid Y = y\} \mathbf{P}\{Y = y\}$$

$$= \sum_y \mathbf{P}\{Y = y\} \sum_x x \mathbf{P}\{X = x \mid Y = y\}$$

$$= \sum_y \mathbf{P}\{Y = y\} \mathbf{E}[X \mid Y = y] \qquad \blacksquare$$

This proof generalizes to

$$\mathbf{E}[g(X)] = \sum_y \mathbf{E}[g(X) \mid Y = y] \mathbf{P}\{Y = y\},$$

which is very important when we need to compute the variance of X or higher moments.

Example: Geometric

Suppose we want to use conditioning to *easily* compute the mean of the Geometric distribution with parameter p. That is, we seek $\mathbf{E}[N]$, where N is the number of flips required to get the first head.

Question: What do we condition on?

Answer: We condition on the value of the first flip, Y, as follows:

$$\mathbf{E}[N] = \mathbf{E}[N \mid Y = 1] \mathbf{P}\{Y = 1\} + \mathbf{E}[N \mid Y = 0] \mathbf{P}\{Y = 0\}$$

$$= 1p + (1 + \mathbf{E}[N])(1 - p)$$

$$p\mathbf{E}[N] = p + (1 - p)$$

$$\mathbf{E}[N] = \frac{1}{p}$$

Note how much simpler this derivation is than our original derivation of the mean of a Geometric!

3.13 Linearity of Expectation

The following is one of the most powerful theorems of probability.

Theorem 3.26 (Linearity of Expectation) *For random variables X and Y,*

$$\mathbf{E}\left[X + Y\right] = \mathbf{E}\left[X\right] + \mathbf{E}\left[Y\right].$$

Question: Does Theorem 3.26 require $X \perp Y$?

Answer: No! Recall that we *do* need independence for simplifying $\mathbf{E}\left[XY\right]$, but not for $\mathbf{E}\left[X + Y\right]$.

Proof Here is a proof in the case where X and Y are continuous. The discrete case is similar: Just replace $f_{X,Y}\left(x, y\right)$ with $p_{X,Y}\left(x, y\right)$.

$\mathbf{E}\left[X + Y\right]$

$$= \int_{y=-\infty}^{\infty} \int_{x=-\infty}^{\infty} (x + y) f_{X,Y}\left(x, y\right) dx dy$$

$$= \int_{y=-\infty}^{\infty} \int_{x=-\infty}^{\infty} x f_{X,Y}\left(x, y\right) dx dy + \int_{y=-\infty}^{\infty} \int_{x=-\infty}^{\infty} y f_{X,Y}\left(x, y\right) dx dy$$

$$= \int_{x=-\infty}^{\infty} \int_{y=-\infty}^{\infty} x f_{X,Y}\left(x, y\right) dy dx + \int_{y=-\infty}^{\infty} \int_{x=-\infty}^{\infty} y f_{X,Y}\left(x, y\right) dx dy$$

$$= \int_{x=-\infty}^{\infty} x \int_{y=-\infty}^{\infty} f_{X,Y}\left(x, y\right) dy dx + \int_{y=-\infty}^{\infty} y \int_{x=-\infty}^{\infty} f_{X,Y}\left(x, y\right) dx dy$$

$$= \int_{x=-\infty}^{\infty} x f_X\left(x\right) dx + \int_{y=-\infty}^{\infty} y f_Y\left(y\right) dy$$

$$= \mathbf{E}\left[X\right] + \mathbf{E}\left[Y\right] \qquad \blacksquare$$

This identity can simplify many proofs. Consider the following example:

Example: Binomial

$X \sim \text{Binomial}(n, p)$. What is $\mathbf{E}\left[X\right]$?

Question: If we simply use the definition of the Binomial, what expression do we have for $\mathbf{E}\left[X\right]$?

Answer: $\mathbf{E}\left[X\right] = \sum_{i=0}^{n} i \binom{n}{i} p^i (1 - p)^{n-i}$. This expression appears daunting.

Question: Can we think of Binomial(n, p) as a sum of random variables?

Answer: Let

$$X = \text{number of successes in } n \text{ trials} = X_1 + X_2 + \cdots + X_n$$

where

$$X_i = \begin{cases} 1 & \text{if trial } i \text{ is successful} \\ 0 & \text{otherwise} \end{cases}$$

$$\mathbf{E}[X_i] = p.$$

Then

$$\mathbf{E}[X] = \mathbf{E}[X_1] + \mathbf{E}[X_2] + \cdots + \mathbf{E}[X_n] = n\mathbf{E}[X_i] = np.$$

This result should make sense, because n coin flips, each with probability p of coming up heads, should result in an average of np heads.

The X_i's above are called **indicator random variables** because they take on values 0 or 1. In the previous example, the X_i's were i.i.d. (independent and identically distributed). However, even if the trials were not independent, we would have

$$\mathbf{E}[X] = \mathbf{E}[X_1] + \cdots + \mathbf{E}[X_n].$$

The following example makes this clear.

Example: Hats

At a party, n people throw their hats into the middle of a circle. Each closes his or her eyes and picks a random hat. Let X denote the number of people who get back their own hat. Our goal is to determine $\mathbf{E}[X]$.

Question: How can we express X as a sum of indicator random variables?

Answer: $X = I_1 + I_2 + \cdots + I_n$, where

$$I_i = \begin{cases} 1 & \text{if the } i\text{th person gets their own hat} \\ 0 & \text{otherwise} \end{cases}.$$

Observe that although the I_i's have the same distribution (by symmetry), they are *not* independent of each other! Nevertheless, we can still use Linearity of Expectation to say

$$\begin{aligned} \mathbf{E}[X] &= \mathbf{E}[I_1] + \mathbf{E}[I_2] + \cdots + \mathbf{E}[I_n] \\ &= n\mathbf{E}[I_i] \\ &= n\left(\frac{1}{n} \cdot 1 + \frac{n-1}{n} \cdot 0\right) \\ &= 1. \end{aligned}$$

Observe that Linearity of Expectation can also be used to show that

$$\mathbf{E}[X^2 + Y^2] = \mathbf{E}[X^2] + \mathbf{E}[Y^2].$$

Nonetheless this *does not* imply that Linearity of Expectation holds for variance. For that, we require an independence assumption, as in the following theorem.

Theorem 3.27 *Let X and Y be random variables where $X \perp Y$. Then*

$$\mathbf{Var}(X + Y) = \mathbf{Var}(X) + \mathbf{Var}(Y).$$

Proof

$$\begin{aligned}
\mathbf{Var}(X+Y) &= \mathbf{E}\left[(X+Y)^2\right] - \left(\mathbf{E}\left[(X+Y)\right]\right)^2 \\
&= \mathbf{E}\left[X^2\right] + \mathbf{E}\left[Y^2\right] + 2\mathbf{E}\left[XY\right] \\
&\quad - \left(\mathbf{E}\left[X\right]\right)^2 - \left(\mathbf{E}\left[Y\right]\right)^2 - 2\mathbf{E}\left[X\right]\mathbf{E}\left[Y\right] \\
&= \mathbf{Var}(X) + \mathbf{Var}(Y) \\
&\quad \underbrace{+2\mathbf{E}\left[XY\right] - 2\mathbf{E}\left[X\right]\mathbf{E}\left[Y\right]}_{\text{equals 0 if } X \perp Y}
\end{aligned}$$
∎

3.14 Normal Distribution

A very important and ubiquitous continuous distribution is the Normal distribution.

Definition 3.28 A continuous r.v. X is said to be *Normal*(μ, σ^2) or *Gaussian*(μ, σ^2) if it has p.d.f. $f_X(x)$ of the form

$$f_X(x) = \frac{1}{\sqrt{2\pi}\sigma} e^{-\frac{1}{2}\left(\frac{x-\mu}{\sigma}\right)^2}, \qquad -\infty < x < \infty$$

where $\sigma > 0$. The parameter μ is called the *mean*, and the parameter σ is called the *standard deviation*.

Definition 3.29 A Normal$(0, 1)$ r.v. Y is said to be a *standard Normal*. Its c.d.f. is denoted by

$$\Phi(y) = F_Y(y) = \mathbf{P}\{Y \le y\} = \frac{1}{\sqrt{2\pi}} \int_{-\infty}^{y} e^{-t^2/2} dt.$$

The Normal(μ, σ^2) p.d.f. has a "bell" shape and is clearly symmetric around μ, as shown in Figure 3.11. The fact that $f_X(x)$ in Definition 3.28 is actually a density function can be seen by integrating it via a change into polar coordinates (trust me, you do not want to see the gory details [176]).

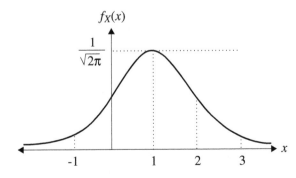

Figure 3.11. Normal$(1, 1)$ p.d.f.

Theorem 3.30 *Let $X \sim Normal(\mu, \sigma^2)$, then $\mathbf{E}[X] = \mu$ and $\mathbf{Var}(X) = \sigma^2$.*

Proof   Because $f_X(x)$ is symmetric around μ, it is obvious that $\mathbf{E}[X] = \mu$.

$$\mathbf{Var}(X) = \int_{-\infty}^{\infty} (x - \mu)^2 f_X(x) dx$$

$$= \frac{1}{\sqrt{2\pi}\sigma} \int_{-\infty}^{\infty} (x - \mu)^2 e^{-\frac{1}{2}((x-\mu)/\sigma)^2} dx$$

$$= \frac{\sigma^2}{\sqrt{2\pi}} \int_{-\infty}^{\infty} y^2 e^{-y^2/2} dy \qquad \text{by change of variables } y = (x - \mu)/\sigma \text{ and}$$
$$\qquad\qquad\qquad\qquad\qquad\qquad dx = \sigma dy$$

$$= \frac{\sigma^2}{\sqrt{2\pi}} \int_{-\infty}^{\infty} y \cdot \left(y e^{-y^2/2}\right) dy$$

$$= \frac{\sigma^2}{\sqrt{2\pi}} \left(-y e^{-y^2/2}\right)\Big]_{-\infty}^{\infty} + \frac{\sigma^2}{\sqrt{2\pi}} \int_{-\infty}^{\infty} e^{-y^2/2} dy \quad \text{by integration by parts}$$

$$= \frac{\sigma^2}{\sqrt{2\pi}} \int_{-\infty}^{\infty} e^{-y^2/2} dy$$

$$= \sigma^2$$

The last line was obtained by using the fact that

$$\frac{1}{\sqrt{2\pi}} \int_{-\infty}^{\infty} e^{-y^2/2} dy = 1$$

because the integrand is the density function of the standard Normal.   ■

3.14.1 *Linear Transformation Property*

The Normal distribution has a very particular property known as the "Linear Transformation Property," which says that if X is a Normal r.v., and you take a linear function of X, then that new r.v. will also be distributed as a Normal. Note that this property is *not* true for other distributions that we have seen, such as the Exponential.

Theorem 3.31 (Linear Transformation Property) *Let $X \sim Normal(\mu, \sigma^2)$. Let $Y = aX + b$, where $a > 0$ and b are scalars. Then $Y \sim Normal(a\mu + b, a^2\sigma^2)$.*

Proof   It is easy to show that $\mathbf{E}[Y] = a\mathbf{E}[X] + b = a\mu + b$ and $\mathbf{Var}(Y) = a^2\mathbf{Var}(X) = a^2\sigma^2$. All that remains is to show that $f_Y(y)$ is Normally distributed. We relate the c.d.f. of Y to the c.d.f. of X as follows:

$$F_Y(y) = \mathbf{P}\{Y \le y\} = \mathbf{P}\{aX + b \le y\} = \mathbf{P}\left\{X \le \frac{y - b}{a}\right\} = F_X\left(\frac{y - b}{a}\right)$$

We now differentiate both sides with respect to y:

$$\frac{d}{dy}F_Y(y) = \frac{d}{dy}\int_{-\infty}^{y} f_Y(t)dt = f_Y(y)$$

$$\frac{d}{dy}F_X\left(\frac{y-b}{a}\right) = \frac{d}{dy}\int_{-\infty}^{\frac{y-b}{a}} f_X(t)dt = f_X\left(\frac{y-b}{a}\right)\cdot\frac{d}{dy}\left(\frac{y-b}{a}\right)$$

$$= f_X\left(\frac{y-b}{a}\right)\cdot\frac{1}{a}$$

Thus we have shown that

$$f_Y(y) = \frac{1}{a}f_X\left(\frac{y-b}{a}\right).$$

Evaluating this, we have

$$f_Y(y) = \frac{1}{a}f_X\left(\frac{y-b}{a}\right)$$

$$= \frac{1}{a\sqrt{2\pi}\sigma}e^{-\left(\frac{y-b}{a}-\mu\right)^2/2\sigma^2}$$

$$= \frac{1}{\sqrt{2\pi}(a\sigma)}e^{-(y-b-a\mu)^2/2a^2\sigma^2}$$

$$= \frac{1}{\sqrt{2\pi}(a\sigma)}e^{-(y-(b+a\mu))^2/2a^2\sigma^2}.$$

So $f_Y(y)$ is a Normal p.d.f. with mean $a\mu + b$ and variance $a^2\sigma^2$. ∎

Unfortunately, we do not know how to integrate the density of the Normal from 0 to y symbolically. To compute the c.d.f. of a Normal distribution, we must therefore use a table of numerically integrated results for $\Phi(y)$, such as that given in [200].[1] A subset of the table is given next for reference:

y	0.5	1.0	1.5	2.0	2.5	3.0
$\Phi(y)$	0.6915	0.8413	0.9332	0.9772	0.9938	0.9987

Question: Looking at the table you see, for example, that $\Phi(1) = 0.8413$. What does this tell us about the probability that the standard Normal is within one standard deviation of its mean?

---

[1] In practice no one ever goes to the table anymore, because there are approximations that allow you to compute the values in the table to within seven decimal places; see for example [131].

Answer: We are given that $\mathbf{P}\{Y < 1\} = 0.84$. We want to know $\mathbf{P}\{-1 < Y < 1\}$.

$$
\begin{aligned}
\mathbf{P}\{-1 < Y < 1\} &= \mathbf{P}\{Y < 1\} - \mathbf{P}\{Y < -1\} \\
&= \mathbf{P}\{Y < 1\} - \mathbf{P}\{Y > 1\} \quad \text{(by symmetry)} \\
&= \mathbf{P}\{Y < 1\} - (1 - \mathbf{P}\{Y < 1\}) \\
&= 2\mathbf{P}\{Y < 1\} - 1 \\
&= 2\Phi(1) - 1 \\
&\doteq 2 \cdot 0.84 - 1 \\
&= 0.68
\end{aligned}
$$

So with probability 68%, we are within one standard deviation of the mean.

Likewise, we can use the same argument to show that with probability 95%, we are within two standard deviations of the mean, and with probability 99.7%, we are within three standard deviations of the mean, etc.

Question: The previous results were expressed for a standard Normal. What if we do not have a standard Normal?

Answer: We can convert a non-standard Normal into a standard Normal using the Linear Transformation Property. Here is how it works:

$$
X \sim \text{Normal}(\mu, \sigma^2) \iff Y = \frac{X - \mu}{\sigma} \sim \text{Normal}(0, 1)
$$

So

$$
\mathbf{P}\{X < k\} = \mathbf{P}\left\{\frac{X - \mu}{\sigma} < \frac{k - \mu}{\sigma}\right\} = \mathbf{P}\left\{Y < \frac{k - \mu}{\sigma}\right\} = \Phi\left(\frac{k - \mu}{\sigma}\right).
$$

Theorem 3.32 *If $X \sim Normal(\mu, \sigma^2)$, then the probability that X deviates from its mean by less than k standard deviations is the same as the probability that the standard Normal deviates from its mean by less than k.*

Proof Let $Y \sim \text{Normal}(0, 1)$. Then,

$$
\mathbf{P}\{-k\sigma < X - \mu < k\sigma\} = \mathbf{P}\left\{-k < \frac{X - \mu}{\sigma} < k\right\} = \mathbf{P}\{-k < Y < k\} \qquad \blacksquare
$$

Theorem 3.32 illustrates why it is often easier to think in terms of standard deviations than in absolute values.

Question: Proponents of IQ testing will tell you that human intelligence (IQ) has been shown to be Normally distributed with mean 100 and standard deviation 15. What fraction of people have an IQ greater than 130 ("the gifted cutoff")?

Answer: We are looking for the fraction of people whose IQ is more than two standard deviations *above* the mean. This is the same as the probability that the standard Normal exceeds its mean by more than two standard deviations, which is $1 - \Phi(2) = 0.023$. Thus only about 2% of people have an IQ above 130.

3.14.2 *Central Limit Theorem*

Consider sampling the heights of all the individuals in the state and taking that average. The Central Limit Theorem (CLT), which we define soon, says that this average will tend to be Normally distributed. This would be true even if we took the average of a large number of i.i.d. random variables, where the random variables come from a distribution that is decidedly non-Normal, say a Uniform distribution. It is this property that makes the Normal distribution so important!

We now state this more formally. Let $X_1, X_2, X_3, \ldots, X_n$ be independent and identically distributed r.v.'s with some mean μ and variance σ^2. Note: We are *not* assuming that these are Normally distributed r.v.'s. In fact we are not even assuming that they are necessarily continuous r.v.'s – they may be discrete r.v.'s.

Let

$$S_n = X_1 + X_2 + \cdots + X_n. \tag{3.2}$$

Question: What are the mean and standard deviation of S_n?

Answer: $\mathbf{E}[S_n] = n\mu$ and $\mathbf{Var}(S_n) = n\sigma^2$. Thus the standard deviation is $\sigma\sqrt{n}$.

Let

$$Z_n = \frac{S_n - n\mu}{\sigma\sqrt{n}}.$$

Question: What are the mean and standard deviation of Z_n?

Answer: Z_n has mean 0 and standard deviation 1.

Theorem 3.33 (Central Limit Theorem (CLT)) *Let $X_1, X_2, \ldots, X_n$ be a sequence of i.i.d. r.v.'s with common mean μ and variance σ^2, and define*

$$Z_n = \frac{X_1 + \cdots + X_n - n\mu}{\sigma\sqrt{n}}.$$

Then the c.d.f. of Z_n converges to the standard normal c.d.f.; that is,

$$\lim_{n \to \infty} \mathbf{P}\{Z_n \leq z\} = \Phi(z) = \frac{1}{\sqrt{2\pi}} \int_{-\infty}^{z} e^{-x^2/2} dx$$

for every z.

Proof Our proof makes use of transforms, so we defer the proof of CLT to Chapter 25, Exercise 25.15. ∎

Question: What is the distribution of S_n in (3.2)?

Answer: By the Linear Transformation Property, $S_n \sim \text{Normal}(n\mu, n\sigma^2)$.

The Central Limit Theorem is extremely general and explains many natural phenomena that result in Normal distributions. The fact that CLT applies to any sum of i.i.d. r.v.'s allows us to prove that the Binomial(n, p) distribution, which is a sum of i.i.d. Bernoulli(p) r.v.'s, converges to a Normal distribution when n is high. When we study the Poisson distribution in more depth in Chapter 11, we will see that the Poisson(λ) distribution can also be viewed as a sum of i.i.d. r.v.'s; hence the Poisson(λ) distribution is also well approximated by a Normal distribution with mean λ and variance λ.

We now illustrate the use of the Normal distribution in approximating the distribution of a complicated sum.

Example: Normal Approximation of a Sum

Imagine that we are trying to transmit a signal. During the transmission, there are a hundred sources independently making low noise. Each source produces an amount of noise that is Uniformly distributed between $a = -1$ and $b = 1$. If the total amount of noise is greater than 10 or less than -10, then it corrupts the signal. However, if the absolute value of the total amount of noise is under 10, then it is not a problem.

Question: What is the approximate probability that the absolute value of the total amount of noise from the 100 signals is less than 10?

Answer: Let X_i be the noise from source i. Observe that $\mu_{X_i} = 0$. Observe that $\sigma_{X_i}^2 = \frac{(b-a)^2}{12} = \frac{1}{3}$ and $\sigma_{X_i} = \frac{1}{\sqrt{3}}$. Let $S_{100} = X_1 + X_2 + \cdots + X_{100}$.

$$\mathbf{P}\{-10 < S_{100} < 10\} = \mathbf{P}\left\{\frac{-10}{\sqrt{100/3}} < \frac{S_{100} - 0}{\sqrt{100/3}} < \frac{10}{\sqrt{100/3}}\right\}$$

$$\approx 2\Phi\left(\frac{10}{\sqrt{33.33}}\right) - 1$$

$$= 2(0.9572) - 1$$

$$= 0.9144$$

Hence the approximate probability of the signal getting corrupted is less than 10%. In practice, this approximation is excellent.

3.15 Sum of a Random Number of Random Variables

In many applications one often needs to add up a number of i.i.d. random variables, where the number of these variables is itself a random variable. Specifically, we are talking about the quantity S in the following expression. Let $X_1, X_2, X_3, \ldots$ be i.i.d. random variables. Let

$$S = \sum_{i=1}^{N} X_i, \quad N \perp X_i$$

where N is a non-negative, integer-valued random variable.

We now review how to derive quantities like $\mathbf{E}[S]$ and $\mathbf{E}[S^2]$, which we will need throughout the book.

Question: Why can't we directly apply Linearity of Expectation?

Answer: Linearity equations only apply when N is a constant.

Question: Does this give you any ideas?

Answer: Let's condition on the value of N, and then apply Linearity of Expectation.

$$
\begin{aligned}
\mathbf{E}[S] = \mathbf{E}\left[\sum_{i=1}^{N} X_i\right] &= \sum_n \mathbf{E}\left[\sum_{i=1}^{N} X_i \,\Big|\, N = n\right] \cdot \mathbf{P}\{N = n\} \\
&= \sum_n \mathbf{E}\left[\sum_{i=1}^{n} X_i\right] \cdot \mathbf{P}\{N = n\} \\
&= \sum_n n\mathbf{E}[X] \cdot \mathbf{P}\{N = n\} \\
&= \mathbf{E}[X] \cdot \mathbf{E}[N] \quad\quad\quad\quad\quad\quad\quad (3.3)
\end{aligned}
$$

Question: Can we use the same trick to get $\mathbf{E}[S^2]$?

Answer: The difficulty with conditioning on N is that we end up with a big sum that we need to square, and it is not obvious how to do that. Consider the following:

$$
\begin{aligned}
\mathbf{E}[S^2] &= \sum_n \mathbf{E}[S^2 \mid N = n] \cdot \mathbf{P}\{N = n\} \\
&= \sum_n \mathbf{E}\left[\left(\sum_{i=1}^{n} X_i\right)^2\right] \cdot \mathbf{P}\{N = n\}
\end{aligned}
$$

A better idea is to first derive $\mathbf{Var}(S \mid N = n)$ and then use that to get $\mathbf{E}[S^2 \mid N = n]$. Observe that, by Theorem 3.27,

$$
\mathbf{Var}(S \mid N = n) = n\mathbf{Var}(X).
$$

Observe also that

$$
\begin{aligned}
n\mathbf{Var}(X) = \mathbf{Var}(S \mid N = n) &= \mathbf{E}[S^2 \mid N = n] - (\mathbf{E}[S \mid N = n])^2 \\
&= \mathbf{E}[S^2 \mid N = n] - (n\mathbf{E}[X])^2.
\end{aligned}
$$

From the previous expression, we have that

$$
\mathbf{E}[S^2 \mid N = n] = n\mathbf{Var}(X) + n^2 (\mathbf{E}[X])^2.
$$

It follows that

$$\mathbf{E}\left[S^2\right] = \sum_n \mathbf{E}\left[S^2 \mid N = n\right] \cdot \mathbf{P}\left\{N = n\right\}$$

$$= \sum_n \left(n\mathbf{Var}(X) + n^2\left(\mathbf{E}\left[X\right]\right)^2\right)\mathbf{P}\left\{N = n\right\}$$

$$= \mathbf{E}\left[N\right]\mathbf{Var}(X) + \mathbf{E}\left[N^2\right]\left(\mathbf{E}\left[X\right]\right)^2.$$

Furthermore,

$$\mathbf{Var}(S) = \mathbf{E}\left[S^2\right] - \left(\mathbf{E}\left[S\right]\right)^2$$

$$= \mathbf{E}\left[N\right]\mathbf{Var}(X) + \mathbf{E}\left[N^2\right]\left(\mathbf{E}\left[X\right]\right)^2 - \left(\mathbf{E}\left[N\right]\mathbf{E}\left[X\right]\right)^2$$

$$= \mathbf{E}\left[N\right]\mathbf{Var}(X) + \mathbf{Var}(N)\left(\mathbf{E}\left[X\right]\right)^2.$$

We have proven Theorem 3.34:

Theorem 3.34 *Let $X_1, X_2, X_3, \ldots$ be i.i.d. random variables. Let*

$$S = \sum_{i=1}^{N} X_i, \quad N \perp X_i.$$

Then

$$\mathbf{E}\left[S\right] = \mathbf{E}\left[N\right]\mathbf{E}\left[X\right],$$

$$\mathbf{E}\left[S^2\right] = \mathbf{E}\left[N\right]\mathbf{Var}(X) + \mathbf{E}\left[N^2\right]\left(\mathbf{E}\left[X\right]\right)^2,$$

$$\mathbf{Var}(S) = \mathbf{E}\left[N\right]\mathbf{Var}(X) + \mathbf{Var}(N)\left(\mathbf{E}\left[X\right]\right)^2.$$

The variance trick was pretty cool. You may be wondering how we would get the third moment, $\mathbf{E}\left[S^3\right]$, if we ever needed it, given that the variance trick will not work there. The answer is to use transform analysis (generating functions), which will easily provide any moment of S. This topic is covered in Chapter 25.

3.16 Exercises

3.1 Expectation Brainteaser
A friend told me that during his first year in school he was never in a class with less than 90 students. He said that almost all of his friends had the same experience. The dean, however, insists that the mean freshman class size is 30 students. How can this be? Explain with a simple numerical example what is going on.

3.2 Nerdy Ned
Nerdy Ned asks out a new girl every day. With probability $\frac{1}{100}$ the girl says "yes," and with probability $\frac{99}{100}$ the girl says "no." What is the probability that it takes Ned more than 100 days to get a girlfriend?

3.3 Variance
Use Linearity of Expectation to prove that $\mathbf{Var}(X) = \mathbf{E}\left[X^2\right] - \mathbf{E}\left[X\right]^2$.

3.4 Chain Rule for Conditioning

Let $E_1, E_2, \ldots, E_n$ be n events, each with positive probability. Prove that

$$\mathbf{P}\left\{\bigcap_{i=1}^{n} E_i\right\} = \mathbf{P}\left\{E_1\right\} \cdot \mathbf{P}\left\{E_2 \mid E_1\right\} \cdot \mathbf{P}\left\{E_3 \mid E_1 \cap E_2\right\} \cdots \mathbf{P}\left\{E_n \mid \bigcap_{i=1}^{n-1} E_i\right\}.$$

3.5 Assessing Risk

Queueville Airlines knows that on average 5% of the people making flight reservations do not show up. (They model this information by assuming that each person independently does not show up with probability of 5%.) Consequently, their policy is to sell 52 tickets for a flight that can only hold 50 passengers. What is the probability that there will be a seat available for every passenger who shows up?

3.6 Practice with Conditional Expectation

For the joint p.m.f. in Table 3.3, compute $\mathbf{E}\left[X \mid Y \neq 1\right]$.

3.7 How Does Variance Scale?

Consider the following two random variables:

$$X = \begin{cases} 3 & \text{w/prob } \frac{1}{3} \\ 2 & \text{w/prob } \frac{1}{3} \\ 1 & \text{w/prob } \frac{1}{3} \end{cases} \qquad Y = \begin{cases} 30 & \text{w/prob } \frac{1}{3} \\ 20 & \text{w/prob } \frac{1}{3} \\ 10 & \text{w/prob } \frac{1}{3} \end{cases}$$

(a) Y is a scaled version of X. Do X and Y have the same variance?

(b) Intuitively, if we think of X as representing measurements in seconds, and Y as representing measurements in tenths of seconds, then we would like to feel that X and Y have the same variance. A common metric in computer systems is the squared coefficient of variation, where the squared coefficient of variation of X is written as C_X^2 and is defined as $C_X^2 = \frac{\mathbf{Var}(X)}{\mathbf{E}[X]^2}$. This can be viewed as a normalized variance. How do C_X^2 and C_Y^2 compare?

3.8 Understanding Variance and Risk

Let c be an integer where $c > 1$. We are given c independent instances of the r.v. X: call these $X_1, X_2, \ldots, X_c$.

(a) Which has lower variance: $\mathbf{Var}(X_1 + X_2 + \cdots + X_c)$ or $\mathbf{Var}(cX)$? Compute each of these.

(b) The selling point of mutual funds is that they are less risky than buying a single stock. Explain this statement.

3.9 Identities

Let A and B be independent random variables. Prove or disprove the following statement:

$$\mathbf{E}\left[A/B\right] = \mathbf{E}\left[A\right]/\mathbf{E}\left[B\right]$$

3.10 Expectation of Product

Prove or disprove the following claim: If

$$\mathbf{E}\left[XY\right] = \mathbf{E}\left[X\right] \cdot \mathbf{E}\left[Y\right],$$

then X and Y are independent r.v.'s.

3.11 Variance of the Binomial

Let $X \sim$ Binomial(n, p). Use Theorem 3.27 to easily derive **Var**(X).

3.12 Poisson Approximation to Binomial

Prove that the Binomial(n, p) distribution is well approximated by the Poisson(np) distribution when n is large and p is small. [Hint: Start with the probability mass function for the Binomial(n, p) distribution. Set $p = \lambda/n$. Expand out all the terms. Take limits and show you get a Poisson(λ) distribution, where $\lambda = np$.]

3.13 Probability Bounds

You are told that the average file size in a database is $6K$.

(a) Explain why it follows (from the definition of expectation) that fewer than half of the files can have size $> 12K$.

(b) You are now given the additional information that the minimum file size is $3K$. Derive a tighter upper bound on the percentage of files that have size $> 12K$.

3.14 Quality of Service

A company pays a fine if the time to process a request exceeds 7 seconds. Processing a request consists of two tasks: (a) retrieving the file – which takes some time X that is Exponentially distributed with mean 5, and (b) parsing the file – which takes some time Y that is independent of X and is distributed Uniform$(1, 3)$, with mean 2. Given that the mean time to process a request is clearly 7 seconds, the company views the fine as unfair, because it will have to pay the fine on half its requests. Is this right? What is the actual fraction of time that the fine will have to be paid, and how much does this differ from $1/2$?

3.15 Positive Correlation

We say that events A and B are *positively correlated* if

$$\mathbf{P}\{A \mid B\} > \mathbf{P}\{A\}. \tag{3.4}$$

Prove or disprove that (3.4) implies

$$\mathbf{P}\{B \mid A\} > \mathbf{P}\{B\}. \tag{3.5}$$

3.16 Covariance

The *covariance* of any two random variables X and Y, denoted by cov(X, Y), is defined by

$$\mathrm{cov}(X, Y) = \mathbf{E}\left[(X - \mathbf{E}[X])(Y - \mathbf{E}[Y])\right].$$

(a) Prove that cov$(X, Y) = \mathbf{E}[XY] - \mathbf{E}[X]\mathbf{E}[Y]$.

(b) If $X \perp Y$, what can we say about cov(X, Y)?

(c) Let X and Y be indicator random variables, where

$$X = \begin{cases} 1 & \text{if event } A \text{ occurs} \\ 0 & \text{o.w.} \end{cases}$$

and

$$Y = \begin{cases} 1 & \text{if event } B \text{ occurs} \\ 0 & \text{o.w.} \end{cases}.$$

Prove that if events A and B are positively correlated (see Exercise 3.15), then $\text{cov}(X, Y) > 0$, whereas if A and B are negatively correlated, then $\text{cov}(X, Y) < 0$. *Note:* This notion can be extended to general random variables X and Y, not just indicator random variables.

3.17 Normal Approximation

Bill Gater invites 1,000 friends to a dinner. Each is asked to make a contribution. The contributions are i.i.d. Poisson-distributed random variables with mean $1,000 each. Bill hopes to raise $1,000,000.

Your job is to compute the probability that Bill raises $< \$999,000$.
(a) Compute this using the Normal approximation from this chapter.
(b) Now write an *exact* expression for this probability, and then use your calculator or a small program to evaluate the expression.

3.18 Joint Distributions

Your TAs, Eric and Timmy, have agreed to meet between 2 and 3 pm to design the next homework. They are rather busy and are not quite sure when they can arrive, so assume that each of their arrival times is independent and uniformly distributed over the hour. Each agrees to wait 15 minutes for the other TA, after which he will leave. What is the probability that Eric and Timmy will be able to meet?

3.19 Bayesian Reasoning for Weather Prediction

In the hope of having a dry outdoor wedding, John and Mary decide to get married in the desert, where the average number of rainy days per year is 10. Unfortunately, the weather forecaster is predicting rain for tomorrow, the day of John and Mary's wedding. Suppose that the weather forecaster is not perfectly accurate: If it rains the next day, 90% of the time the forecaster predicts rain. If it is dry the next day, 10% of the time the forecaster still (incorrectly) predicts rain. Given this information, what is the probability that it will rain during John and Mary's wedding?

3.20 Bayesian Reasoning for Health Care Testing

A pharmaceutical company has developed a potential vaccine against the H1N1 flu virus. Before any testing of the vaccine, the developers assume that with probability 0.5 their vaccine will be effective and with probability 0.5 it will be ineffective. The developers do an initial laboratory test on the vaccine. This initial lab test is only partially indicative of the effectiveness of the vaccine, with an accuracy of 0.6. Specifically, if the vaccine is effective, then this laboratory test will return "success" with probability 0.6, whereas if the vaccine is ineffective, then this laboratory test will return "failure" with probability 0.6.
(a) What is the probability that the laboratory test returns "success"?
(b) What is the probability that the vaccine is effective, given that the laboratory test returned "success"?

(c) The developers decide to add a second experiment (this one on human beings) that is more indicative than the original lab test and has an accuracy of 0.8. Specifically, if the vaccine is effective, then the human being test will return "success" with probability 0.8. If the vaccine is ineffective, then the human being test will return "failure" with probability 0.8. What is the probability that the vaccine is effective, given that both the lab test and the human being test came up "success"? How useful was it to add this additional test? Assume that the two tests (human test and lab test) are conditionally independent on the vaccine being effective or ineffective.

3.21 Dating Costs: Deriving Expectation and Variance via Conditioning

A man, in search of a wife, tries two approaches: generous and cheapskate. When the man tries the generous approach, he ends up spending $1,000 on his date, who will, eventually, with probability 0.95 break up with him, but with probability 0.05 marry him. When the man tries the cheapskate approach, he spends $50 on his date, who will eventually break up with him. So far in his life, the man has only experienced failure, so he cannot tell which approach works better. He therefore decides to choose an approach (generous or cheapskate) at random.

(a) Assuming the man starts searching today, what is his expected cost to find a wife?

(b) Compute the variance on the amount of money the man ends up spending to find a wife.

3.22 Variance of the Geometric

Let $X \sim \text{Geometric}(p)$. Prove that $\mathbf{Var}(X) = \frac{1-p}{p^2}$. [Hint: Use conditioning.]

3.23 Good Chips versus Lemons

A chip supplier produces 95% good chips and 5% lemons. The good chips fail with probability 0.0001 each day. The lemons fail with probability 0.01 each day. You buy a random chip. Let T be the time until your chip fails. Compute $\mathbf{E}[T]$ and $\mathbf{Var}(T)$.

3.24 Alternative Definition of Expectation[2]

(a) Let X: non-negative, discrete, integer-valued random variable. Prove

$$\mathbf{E}[X] = \sum_{x=0}^{\infty} \mathbf{P}\{X > x\}$$

(b) Let X: non-negative, continuous random variable. Prove

$$\mathbf{E}[X] = \int_{x=0}^{\infty} \mathbf{P}\{X > x\}\, dx$$

(c) Let X: non-negative, continuous random variable. Does this quantity have a nicer name?

$$\int_{x=0}^{\infty} x\mathbf{P}\{X > x\}\, dx$$

---

[2] *Warning:* The result of this exercise will be invoked throughout the book.

3.25 Expectation via Conditioning

Stacy's fault-tolerant system only crashes if there are $k = 10$ *consecutive* failures. If every minute a failure occurs independently with probability $p = \frac{1}{10}$, what is the expected number of minutes until Stacy's system crashes. (Express generally in terms of k and p.) [Hint: Write a recurrence relation.]

3.26 Napster – Brought to You by the RIAA

As a present for my brother, I decided to create a collection of all the songs from his favorite band. I needed to download the band's 50 songs. Unfortunately, whenever I typed in the band name, I was sent a *random* song from the band. Let D denote the number of downloads required to get all 50 songs.

(a) What is $\mathbf{E}[D]$? Give a closed-form approximation.

(b) What is $\mathbf{Var}(D)$? (No need for closed-form here.)

3.27 Fractional Moments

Given the ugliness of the Normal distribution, I am happy to say that it never comes up in my research... until a few days ago! Here's the story: I had a random variable $X \sim \text{Exp}(1)$ and I needed to compute $\mathbf{E}\left[X^{\frac{1}{2}}\right]$. Figure out why I needed a Normal distribution to do this and what answer I finally got. Here are some hints: Start by applying integration by parts. Then make the right change of variables. If you do it right, the standard Normal should pop out. Remember that the Exponential ranges from 0 to ∞, whereas the Normal ranges from $-\infty$ to ∞.

CHAPTER 4

Generating Random Variables
for Simulation

In Chapter 3 we reviewed the most common discrete and continuous random variables. This chapter shows how we can use the density function or cumulative distribution function for a distribution to generate instances of that distribution. For example, we might have a system in which the interarrival times of jobs are well modeled by an Exponential distribution and the job sizes (service requirements) are well modeled by a Normal distribution. To simulate the system, we need to be able to generate instances of Exponential and Normal random variables. This chapter reviews the two basic methods used in generating random variables. Both these methods assume that we already have a generator of Uniform(0,1) random variables, as is provided by most operating systems.[1,2]

4.1 Inverse-Transform Method

This method assumes that (i) we know the c.d.f. (cumulative distribution function), $F_X(x) = \mathbf{P}\{X \leq x\}$, of the random variable X that we are trying to generate, and (ii) that this distribution is easily invertible, namely that we can get x from $F_X(x)$.

4.1.1 *The Continuous Case*

Idea: We would like to map each instance of a uniform r.v. generated by our operating system – that is, $u \in U(0,1)$ – to some x, which is an instance of the random variable X, where X has c.d.f. F_X. We assume WLOG that X ranges from 0 to ∞. Let's suppose there is some mapping that takes each u and assigns it a unique x. Such a mapping is illustrated by $g^{-1}(\cdot)$ in Figure 4.1.

Question: Can you figure out what the mapping $g^{-1}(\cdot)$ in Figure 4.1 should be?

Hint: Think about what property we want for our output. What should be the probability of outputting a value between 0 and x?

Answer: A value in $(0, x)$ should be output with probability $F_X(x)$.

Question: What is the actual probability that $g^{-1}(\cdot)$ outputs a value in $(0, x)$?

---

[1] Actually, most operating systems provide a random integer between 1 and $N = 2^{32} - 1$. This is easy to convert into a Uniform(0,1) by just dividing by N.

[2] One cannot always trust the random number generator provided by one's operating system. It is worth reading the literature to understand how to best "seed" the random number generator and what guarantees it provides. See for example, [31].

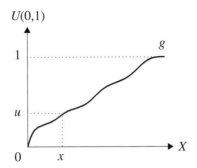

Figure 4.1. Illustration of mapping $g(\cdot)$.

Answer: Because $g^{-1}(\cdot)$ only maps values in $(0, u)$ to values in $(0, x)$, the probability of outputting a value in $(0, x)$ is the probability that the uniform instance is in $(0, u)$.

Question: And what is the probability that the uniform instance is in $(0, u)$?

Answer: u.

So we want that

$$u = \mathbf{P}\left\{0 < U < u\right\} = \mathbf{P}\left\{0 < X < x\right\} = F_X(x).$$

That is, we want

$$u = F_X(x) \quad \text{or equivalently} \quad x = F_X^{-1}(u). \tag{4.1}$$

Question: So what was the $g(\cdot)$ function in Figure 4.1?

Answer: $g(\cdot) = F(\cdot)$, the cumulative distribution function.

Inverse-Transform Method to generate r.v. X:

1. Generate $u \in U(0, 1)$.
2. Return $X = F_X^{-1}(u)$.

Example: Generate $X \sim \text{Exp}(\lambda)$

For the $\text{Exp}(\lambda)$ distribution,

$$F(x) = 1 - e^{-\lambda x}.$$

So by (4.1) we want

$$x = F^{-1}(u)$$
$$\Longrightarrow F(x) = u$$
$$\Longrightarrow 1 - e^{-\lambda x} = u$$
$$\Longrightarrow -\lambda x = \ln(1 - u)$$
$$\Longrightarrow x = -\frac{1}{\lambda}\ln(1 - u).$$

Given $u \in U(0, 1)$, setting $x = -\frac{1}{\lambda}\ln(1 - u)$ produces an instance of $X \sim \text{Exp}(\lambda)$.

4.1.2 *The Discrete Case*

The discrete case follows the same basic idea as the continuous case (see Figure 4.2). This time, we want to generate a discrete r.v. X such that

$$X = \begin{cases} x_0 & \text{with prob } p_0 \\ x_1 & \text{with prob } p_1 \\ \dots \\ x_k & \text{with prob } p_k \end{cases}.$$

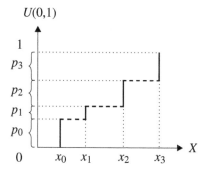

Figure 4.2. Generating a discrete random variable with 4 values.

Solution:

1. Arrange $x_0, \dots, x_k$ s.t. $x_0 < x_1 < \dots < x_k$.
2. Generate $u \in U(0,1)$.
3. If $0 < u \le p_0$, then output x_0.
   If $p_0 < u \le p_0 + p_1$, then output x_1.
   If $p_0 + p_1 < u \le p_0 + p_1 + p_2$, then output x_2.
   If $\sum_{i=0}^{\ell-1} p_i < u \le \sum_{i=0}^{\ell} p_i$, then output x_ℓ, where $0 \le \ell \le k$.

Notice that again our $g(\cdot)$ function is $F_X(\cdot)$, the cumulative distribution function.

This sounds easy enough, but it is not always practical. If X can take on many values, then we have to compute many partial sums: $\sum_{i=0}^{\ell} p_i$ for all $0 \le \ell \le k$. For this method to be practical, we therefore need closed-form expressions for $\sum_{i=0}^{\ell} p_i$ for all ℓ. Equivalently, we need a closed form for $F_X(x) = \mathbf{P}\{X \le x\}$ for any x. Then we could do the same thing as in the continuous case, as in (4.1): generate $u \in U(0,1)$, and return $x = F_X^{-1}(u)$. Thus, as in the continuous case, we need to both have a closed-form expression for the cumulative distribution function and also know how to invert this function.

4.2 Accept-Reject Method

The Inverse-Transform method required knowing the cumulative distribution function, $F_X(\cdot)$. However, there are many cases where we do not know the c.d.f., $F_X(\cdot)$, but only know the p.d.f., $f_X(\cdot)$. For example, suppose we want to generate a random variable from the Normal distribution, whose c.d.f. is not known. We thus need a new method.

The Accept-Reject method involves generating instances of the desired random variable, but throwing away (rejecting) some of the generated instances until the desired p.d.f (or p.m.f.) is met. It is easiest to explain the method for the case of a discrete r.v. first.

4.2.1 *Discrete Case*

The Accept-Reject method requires the following structure:

Given: Efficient method for generating random variable Q with probability mass function $\{q_j, \ j\text{:discrete}\}$, where $q_j = \mathbf{P}\{Q = j\}$.

Output: Random variable P with probability mass function $\{p_j, \ j\text{:discrete}\}$, where $p_j = \mathbf{P}\{P = j\}$.

Requirement: For all j, we must have $q_j > 0 \iff p_j > 0$. That is, P and Q take on the same set of values.

Example: Suppose we want to generate

$$P = \begin{cases} 1 & \text{with prob } p_1 = 0.36 \\ 2 & \text{with prob } p_2 = 0.24 \\ 3 & \text{with prob } p_3 = 0.40 \end{cases}.$$

We know how to generate

$$Q = \begin{cases} 1 & \text{with prob } q_1 = 0.33 \\ 2 & \text{with prob } q_2 = 0.33 \\ 3 & \text{with prob } q_3 = 0.33 \end{cases}.$$

Any ideas? We are looking for a method where we generate an instance of Q, and then we either choose to accept the value or reject it. If we accept it, that becomes the value of P.

Idea #1: Suppose we generate an instance j of Q and accept it with probability p_j?

Question: What are the disadvantages to this approach?

Answer: The obvious disadvantage is the time needed to output a value of P. Suppose the number of possible values is n, and n is high. Then $q_j = \frac{1}{n}$, and most p_j's will be very low – certainly it could be the case that all p_j's are approximately $\frac{1}{n}$ but not exactly. In this case, the time needed to output a value is on the order of n.

Another disadvantage of Idea #1 is that in general Q may not have a uniform distribution, so we need to normalize the acceptance probabilities.

Idea #2: Suppose we generate an instance j of Q and accept it with probability $\frac{p_j}{q_j}$? That is, with probability $\frac{p_j}{q_j}$, we return $P = j$, and with probability $1 - \frac{p_j}{q_j}$, we flip again.

Question: What is the intuition behind Idea #2?

Answer: Suppose Q is not uniform, and Q has an especially low probability of generating j. Then we will make up for that by having a higher than p_j probability of accepting j when it is generated.

Question: What is wrong with Idea #2?

Answer: It requires that $p_j \leq q_j, \forall j$, which cannot be true if $P \neq Q$.

But we can work with Idea #2. We just need a normalizing constant. Let c be a constant such that

$$\frac{p_j}{q_j} \leq c, \ \forall j \text{ s.t. } p_j > 0.$$

Observe $c > 1$.

Accept-Reject Algorithm to generate discrete r.v. P:

   1. Find r.v. Q s.t. $q_j > 0 \Leftrightarrow p_j > 0$.
   2. Generate an instance of Q, and call it j.
   3. Generate r.v. $U \in (0, 1)$.
   4. If $U < \frac{p_j}{cq_j}$, return $P = j$ and stop; else return to step 2.

We will now prove that the Accept-Reject algorithm does in fact result in a P with the appropriate distribution.

We want to prove that

$$\mathbf{P}\left\{ P \text{ ends up being set to } j \text{ (as opposed to some other value)} \right\} = p_j.$$

Now observe that

$$\mathbf{P}\left\{ P \text{ ends up being set to } j \right\} = \frac{\text{Fraction of time } j \text{ is generated and accepted}}{\text{Fraction of time any value is accepted}}.$$

Fraction of time j is generated and accepted

$$= \mathbf{P}\left\{ j \text{ is generated} \right\} \cdot \mathbf{P}\left\{ j \text{ is accepted given } j \text{ is generated} \right\}$$

$$= q_j \cdot \frac{p_j}{cq_j} = \frac{p_j}{c}.$$

Fraction of time any value is accepted

$$= \sum_j \text{Fraction of time } j \text{ is generated and is accepted}$$

$$= \sum_j \frac{p_j}{c} = \frac{1}{c}.$$

So,

$$\mathbf{P}\left\{P \text{ ends up being set to } j\right\} = \frac{\frac{p_j}{c}}{\frac{1}{c}} = p_j$$

as desired.

Question: On average, how many values of Q are generated before one is accepted?

Answer: c. (The fraction of time any value is accepted is $\frac{1}{c}$.)

In our example,

$$c = \max\left(\frac{0.36}{0.33}, \frac{0.24}{0.33}, \frac{0.40}{0.33}\right) = 1.2.$$

Thus we only need 1.2 iterations on average.

4.2.2 *Continuous Case*

The Accept-Reject method works the same way for continuous random variables, except that we now use probability density functions, rather than probability mass functions.

Given: We know how to generate Y with probability density function $f_Y(t)$.

Goal: To generate X with p.d.f. $f_X(t)$.

Requirement: For all t,

$$f_Y(t) > 0 \iff f_X(t) > 0.$$

Accept-Reject Algorithm to generate continuous r.v. X:

1. Find continuous r.v. Y s.t. $f_Y(t) > 0 \Leftrightarrow f_X(t) > 0$. Let c be a constant such that
$$\frac{f_X(t)}{f_Y(t)} \le c, \ \forall t \text{ s.t. } f_X(t) > 0.$$

2. Generate an instance t of Y.
3. With probability $\frac{f_X(t)}{c \cdot f_Y(t)}$, return $X = t$ (i.e. "accept t" and stop). Else reject t and return to step 2.

Simple Example

Suppose we want to generate a r.v. X with p.d.f.:

$$f_X(t) = 20t(1-t)^3, \quad 0 < t < 1$$

If you plot this function, it looks like Figure 4.3. Observe that X has positive p.d.f. only in the interval $(0, 1)$. Thus we want to choose a Y that is easy to generate and also has positive p.d.f. only in $(0, 1)$.

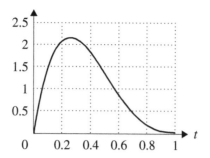

Figure 4.3. Plot of $f_X(t)$.

Question: Any ideas for what $f_Y(t)$ should be?

Answer: Consider simply $f_Y(t) = 1$, where $0 < t < 1$.

Question: Suppose we now apply the Accept-Reject method. What will c be?

Answer: c should not be too bad – just over 2 based on the plot. To determine c precisely, we want to determine

$$\max_t \left\{ \frac{f_X(t)}{f_Y(t)} \right\} = \max_t \left\{ 20t(1-t)^3 \right\}.$$

Taking the derivative with respect to t, and setting it equal to zero, we have

$$\frac{d}{dt}(20t(1-t)^3) = 0 \Leftrightarrow t = \frac{1}{4}.$$

So the maximum value is obtained when $t = \frac{1}{4}$:

$$\frac{f_X\left(\frac{1}{4}\right)}{f_Y\left(\frac{1}{4}\right)} = 20\left(\frac{1}{4}\right)\left(\frac{3}{4}\right)^3 = \frac{135}{64} = c. \tag{4.2}$$

Observe how easy it was to make a good guess for $f_Y(t)$ just by looking at the plot of $f_X(t)$.

Example: Generating Normal Random Variable

For the previous example we could have used the Inverse-Transform method. Now let's try an example where we cannot apply the Inverse-Transform method.

Goal: Generate $N \sim \text{Normal}(0,1)$.

Idea: It will be enough to generate $X = |N|$ and then multiply N by -1 with probability 0.5.

So how do we generate such an X? A plot of X is shown in Figure 4.4. Let $f_X(t)$ be the p.d.f of X:

$$f_X(t) = \frac{2}{\sqrt{2\pi}} e^{-\frac{t^2}{2}}, \quad 0 < t < \infty$$

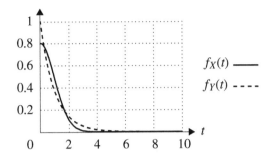

Figure 4.4. Solid line shows $f_X(t)$. Dashed line shows proposed $f_Y(t)$.

Question: The idea is now to think of a random variable Y that we know how to generate, such that $f_Y(t)$ (the p.d.f. of Y) fits $f_X(t)$ reasonably well. Can you think of such a Y?

Answer: Let $Y \sim \text{Exp}(1)$.

$$f_Y(t) = e^{-t}, \quad 0 < t < \infty$$

Observe that $f_X(t)$ is not too much higher than $f_Y(t)$, according to Figure 4.4.

Question: How many iterations are needed on average?

Answer: We need to determine c.

$$\frac{f_X(t)}{f_Y(t)} = \frac{2}{\sqrt{2\pi}} e^{-\frac{t^2}{2}+t} = \sqrt{\frac{2}{\pi}} e^{t-\frac{t^2}{2}}$$

So, the maximum value occurs when $t - \frac{t^2}{2}$ is maximized.

$$0 = \frac{d}{dt}\left(t - \frac{t^2}{2}\right) = 1 - t \quad \Rightarrow \quad t = 1$$

So,

$$c = \frac{f_X(1)}{f_Y(1)} = \sqrt{\frac{2e}{\pi}} \approx 1.3.$$

Thus we only need 1.3 iterations on average!

4.2.3 *Some Harder Problems*

Consider a Poisson r.v. with mean λ.

$$p_i = \mathbf{P}\{X = i\} = \frac{e^{-\lambda}\lambda^i}{i!}$$

Observe that there are an infinite number of p_i's. There is no closed form for $F(i) = \mathbf{P}\{X \leq i\}$ so the Inverse-Transform method will not work.

It looks like we should be able to apply the Accept-Reject method, but it is hard to find the right distribution to match up to (for more discussion see [116], p. 503).

In Chapter 11, we see that the Poisson distribution can be viewed as counting the number of instances of an Exponentially distributed random variable that occur by a fixed time. This gives us another way of generating Poisson random variables – by generating many instances of an Exponential random variable.

4.3 Readings

A lot more is known about simulating random variables than we have described in this chapter. Some particularly well-written texts are [148] (see Chs. 4 and 5) and [116] (see Ch. 8).

4.4 Exercises

4.1 Generating Random Variables for Simulation (from [148]).

Give an algorithm for generating a r.v. having the following density function

$$f(x) = 30(x^2 - 2x^3 + x^4), \quad \text{where } 0 \leq x \leq 1.$$

4.2 Inverse-Transform Method

Explain how to generate values from a continuous distribution with density function $f(t) = \frac{5}{4}t^{-2}$, where $1 < t < 5$, given $u \in U(0,1)$.

4.3 Simulation of M/M/1

This problem asks you to simulate a single M/M/1 queue. Do not worry; you do not need to know what this notation means – everything you need to know is explained in this problem. Use any programming language you like.

The job sizes are distributed according to $\text{Exp}(\mu)$, where $\mu = 1$. The interarrival times between jobs are i.i.d. according to $\text{Exp}(\lambda)$.

Consider three cases: $\lambda = 0.5$, $\lambda = 0.7$, and $\lambda = 0.9$. Your goal is to measure the mean response time $\mathbf{E}[T]$ for each load level (each value of λ). Do this by averaging independent samples.

Let one "run" of the simulator consist of running the system from the empty state for 2,000 arrivals, and then record the response time experienced by arrival number 2,001. Perform $n = 200$ (independent) runs, each of which will generate one "sample," and then determine the mean of the $n = 200$ samples.

CHAPTER 5

Sample Paths, Convergence, and Averages

If you are a theoretician, you probably are already starting to get uncomfortable with the way we use the word "average" without carefully defining it and, in particular, with the way we define the load ρ by seemingly dividing two averages ($\rho = \frac{1/\mu}{1/\lambda} = \frac{\lambda}{\mu}$). Everything we have said is correct, but we would like to prove this, rather than just assuming it. This chapter sets up the groundwork to allow us to make such claims about averages.

Before we can talk about averages, we first need to discuss convergence of random variables. In this chapter, we define the convergence of random variables and state some limit theorems. We then define two types of averages: ensemble averages and time averages. These are needed for the next chapter on Little's Law, which will allow us to formally relate mean response time to the mean number of jobs in the system and to properly define the load, ρ.

This chapter is more theoretically oriented and abstract than the rest of this book. It is not necessary for the reader to follow everything in this chapter to understand later chapters. A reader might wish to skim the chapter to pick up the basic terminology and then come back later for a more in-depth reading.

Although this chapter is somewhat formal, we are still just grazing the surface of this material. If you really want to understand the concepts in depth, we recommend reading a measure-theory book such as Halmos's book [80].

5.1 Convergence

Recall from high school the standard definition of convergence of a sequence of numbers:

Definition 5.1 A sequence $\{a_n : n = 1, 2, \ldots\}$ converges to b as $n \to \infty$, written

$$a_n \longrightarrow b, \text{ as } n \to \infty$$

or equivalently,

$$\lim_{n \to \infty} a_n = b$$

if $\forall \epsilon > 0, \exists n_0(\epsilon)$, such that $\forall n > n_0(\epsilon)$, we have $|a_n - b| < \epsilon$.

This is very easy to think about because the a_i's are constants. It says that a sequence converges to b if, for any given "degree of convergence," ϵ, one can find some index point in the sequence (call that point $n_0(\epsilon)$) such that, beyond that point, all elements of the sequence are within ϵ of b.

We now need a similar definition for random variables. The point to remember is that *a random variable becomes a constant for each possible outcome of an experiment.* We refer to the outcome of the experiment as a *sample path.* For example, consider a random variable, Z, equal to the larger of two rolls of a die. Given a particular sample path, $\omega = (4, 6)$, we know that the value of Z is exactly 6.

As another example, consider a sequence of random variables: $\{Y_n : n = 1, 2, \ldots\}$, where Y_n denotes the average of the first n coin flips. Here again, these are all variables. Now consider a *sample path*, ω, consisting of an infinite sequence of coin flips (e.g. $\omega = 01101001011\ldots$). If we evaluate the sequence of random variables on ω, we have a sequence of constants: $\{Y_n(\omega) : n = 1, 2, \ldots\} = \{0, \frac{1}{2}, \frac{2}{3}, \frac{1}{2}, \frac{3}{5}, \ldots\}$.

Definition 5.2 The sequence of random variables $\{Y_n : n = 1, 2, \ldots\}$ *converges almost surely* to μ, written

$$Y_n \xrightarrow{a.s.} \mu, \text{ as } n \to \infty$$

or equivalently, the sequence *converges with probability 1*, written

$$Y_n \longrightarrow \mu, \text{ as } n \to \infty \text{ w.p. } 1$$

if

$$\forall k > 0, \mathbf{P}\left\{\lim_{n \to \infty} |Y_n - \mu| > k\right\} = 0.$$

The $\mathbf{P}\{\ldots\}$ in the previous expression is over the set of sample paths. More precisely we might write

$$\forall k > 0, \mathbf{P}\left\{\omega : \lim_{n \to \infty} |Y_n(\omega) - \mu| > k\right\} = 0$$

(although no one actually writes this).

To understand Definition 5.2, consider the sequence of random variables, $\{Y_n : n = 1, 2, \ldots\}$, evaluated on a particular sample path, ω_0, yielding the sequence of constants, $\{Y_n(\omega_0) : n = 1, 2, \ldots\}$. Now look at the *limit* of this sequence of constants and ask whether it deviates from μ by more than k. We say that the *sample path ω_0 behaves well* if the sequence of constants, $\{Y_n(\omega_0) : n = 1, 2, \ldots\}$, converges to μ (meaning it is within k of μ for all $k > 0$ as $n \to \infty$) and that it *behaves badly* otherwise. Likewise, the sample path ω_1 behaves well if the sequence of constants, $\{Y_n(\omega_1) : n = 1, 2, \ldots\}$, converges to μ.

Question: What does $\mathbf{P}\{\omega : \lim_{n \to \infty} |Y_n(\omega) - \mu| > k\}$ represent?

Answer: This represents the mass (probability) of sample paths that behave badly in that, for each such bad sample path, ω, the limit of the sequence $\{Y_n(\omega) : n = 1, 2, \ldots\}$ is not μ or does not exist.

Almost sure convergence occurs when, on almost all sample paths, the sequence of random variables will, after some point, start behaving well and continue behaving well from that point on. That is, almost all sample paths ω have the property that the sequence $\{Y_n(\omega) : n = 1, 2, \ldots\}$ converges to μ. The mass comprising sample paths that do not have this property has probability zero – meaning, there may be some sample paths that do not have this property, but these paths have a total "mass" of zero. Figure 5.1 shows an illustration of almost sure convergence.

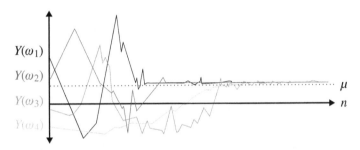

Figure 5.1. Illustration of the concept of almost sure convergence. The dotted line indicates μ. $Y(\omega_1)$ is shorthand for the sequence of constants: $\{Y_n(\omega_1) : n = 1, 2, \ldots\}$. All four sample paths shown, after some point, behave well – meaning that the sequence of constants, created by evaluating $\{Y_n : n = 1, 2, \ldots\}$ on that sample path, converges to μ.

Question: In the case where Y_n represents the average of the first n coin flips, what do we expect the sequence $\{Y_n(\omega) : n = 1, 2, \ldots\}$ to converge to?

Answer: Assuming a fair coin, $\frac{1}{2}$.

Question: Why can't we say that this convergence holds for all sample paths?

Answer: There are always some sample paths, such as the coin flips $1111\ldots$, that do not average to $\frac{1}{2}$ no matter how far out we look. Luckily the total measure made up by such sample paths is zero.

Question: How many badly behaving sample paths are there? A finite number? Countably many? Uncountably many?

Answer: Actually there are uncountably many such bad paths, each occurring with probability zero and summing to a measure of zero.

Question: How can we determine that there are uncountably many bad paths?

Answer: Let's refer to the sequence 110 as a "red car" and to the sequence 101 as a "blue car." Now any sequence made up of red and blue cars is clearly bad (because it has twice as many 1's as 0's). However, there are an uncountable number of possible sequences of red and blue cars, because there are an uncountable number of binary sequences (by Cantor's diagonalization argument).

We now present another definition of convergence of random variables that is sometimes used.

Definition 5.3 The sequence of random variables $\{Y_n : n = 1, 2, \ldots\}$ *converges in probability* to μ, written

$$Y_n \xrightarrow{P} \mu, \text{ as } n \to \infty$$

if

$$\forall k > 0, \lim_{n \to \infty} \mathbf{P}\{|Y_n - \mu| > k\} = 0.$$

The $\mathbf{P}\{\ldots\}$ in Definition 5.3 is over the set of possible sample paths, ω. More precisely we might write

$$\forall k > 0, \lim_{n \to \infty} \mathbf{P}\{\omega : |Y_n(\omega) - \mu| > k\} = 0 \qquad (5.1)$$

(although no one actually writes this).

To understand Definition 5.3, again consider the sequence of random variables, $\{Y_n : n = 1, 2, \ldots\}$, evaluated on a particular sample path, ω_0. This time, however, look only at the nth constant in the resulting sequence of constants, $Y_n(\omega_0)$. If that nth constant, $Y_n(\omega_0)$, deviates from μ by more than k, we say that *the sample path ω_0 behaves badly for Y_n*. Let's repeat the experiment for a different sample path, ω_1. Consider the sequence $\{Y_n(\omega_1) : n = 1, 2, \ldots\}$. Again look only at the nth constant, $Y_n(\omega_1)$, and ask whether $Y_n(\omega_1)$ deviates from μ by more than k. If so, then the sample path ω_1 behaves badly for Y_n.

Question: What does $\mathbf{P}\{\omega : |Y_n(\omega) - \mu| > k\}$ represent?

Answer: The probability comprising sample paths that behave badly for the nth r.v., Y_n. This is a number between 0 and 1.

Question: What does $\mathbf{P}\{\omega : |Y_{n+1}(\omega) - \mu| > k\}$ represent?

Answer: The probability comprising sample paths that behave badly for the $n + 1$th r.v., Y_{n+1}.

Note that Y_n and Y_{n+1} may behave badly on different sample paths. We are only interested in the *mass* (probability) of sample paths that are bad for Y_n, the mass that are bad for Y_{n+1}, the mass of those that are bad for Y_{n+2}, etc.

Question: What is $\lim_{n \to \infty} \mathbf{P}\{\omega : |Y_n(\omega) - \mu| > k\}$?

Answer: This is the limit of a sequence of probabilities: the probability comprising sample paths that are bad for Y_n, the probability comprising sample paths that are bad for Y_{n+1}, the probability comprising sample paths that are bad for Y_{n+2}, etc. If this limit, $\lim_{n \to \infty} \mathbf{P}\{\omega : |Y_n(\omega) - \mu| > k\}$, exists and is zero for all $k > 0$, then we say that the sequence of random variables $\{Y_n : n = 1, 2, \ldots\}$ converges in probability to μ.

Question: Given the definition of a limit of a sequence of constants, how could we expand the definition of convergence in probability to replace the limit in there?

Answer:

$$\forall k > 0, \forall \epsilon > 0, \exists n_0(\epsilon) \; s.t. \; \forall n > n_0(\epsilon), \; |\mathbf{P}\{\omega : |Y_n(\omega) - \mu| > k\}| < \epsilon.$$

Question: Which is stronger: almost sure convergence or convergence in probability?

Answer: Almost sure convergence implies convergence in probability. Here is the intuition: Given almost sure convergence, we know that (almost) all sample paths eventually do the right thing, each from some $n_0(\omega)$ point onward. Thus, looking out at higher and higher n, we see that the number of sample paths behaving badly past that point gets smaller and smaller. From this it seems intuitive that the *mass* of sample paths behaving badly gets smaller and smaller as we look at further out values of n. Note that this is only intuition, because the total number of sample paths also grows with n. Thus it is hard to immediately claim that the *probability* comprising paths behaving badly decreases for all n values.

Question: Explain how a sequence $\{Y_n\}$ might converge in probability but *not* almost surely.

Answer: Even if $\{Y_n\}$ converges in probability, it could still be the case that *no* sample path has the property that from some point onward it behaves well. For example, each sample path may have occasional spikes; however, these spikes get further and further apart for large n. Thus for no sample path ω does $\{Y_n(\omega) : n = 1, 2, \ldots\}$ converge. However, for any fixed n the fraction of sample paths ω under which $Y_n(\omega)$ is far from μ is small – and gets smaller as we increase n. This is illustrated in Figure 5.2.

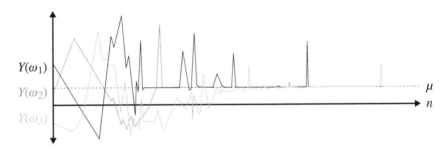

Figure 5.2. Illustration of the convergence in probability without almost sure convergence. Again, the dotted line indicates μ.

5.2 Strong and Weak Laws of Large Numbers

Theorem 5.4 (Weak Law of Large Numbers) *Let $X_1, X_2, X_3, \ldots$ be i.i.d. random variables with mean $\mathbf{E}[X]$. Let*

$$S_n = \sum_{i=1}^{n} X_i \quad and \quad Y_n = \frac{S_n}{n}.$$

Then

$$Y_n \xrightarrow{P} \mathbf{E}[X], \text{ as } n \to \infty.$$

This is read as "Y_n converges in probability to $\mathbf{E}[X]$," which is shorthand for the following:

$$\forall k > 0, \lim_{n \to \infty} \mathbf{P}\{|Y_n - \mathbf{E}[X]| > k\} = 0.$$

Theorem 5.5 (Strong Law of Large Numbers) *Let* $X_1, X_2, X_3, \ldots$ *be i.i.d. random variables with mean* $\mathbf{E}[X]$*. Let*

$$S_n = \sum_{i=1}^{n} X_i \quad \text{and} \quad Y_n = \frac{S_n}{n}.$$

Then

$$Y_n \xrightarrow{a.s.} \mathbf{E}[X], \text{ as } n \to \infty.$$

This is read as "Y_n converges almost surely to $\mathbf{E}[X]$" or "Y_n converges to $\mathbf{E}[X]$ with probability 1," which is shorthand for the following:

$$\forall k > 0, \mathbf{P}\left\{\lim_{n \to \infty} |Y_n - \mathbf{E}[X]| \geq k\right\} = 0.$$

Question: Going back to the example where the X_i's are all $0/1$ random variables with mean $\frac{1}{2}$, what is the Strong Law of Large Numbers saying?

Answer: Each sample path is an infinite sequence of coin flips. The Strong Law says that for "almost every" sample path, if we average the coin flips far out enough along the path, we will get convergence to $\frac{1}{2}$ from that point onward. As we have discussed, even if there are uncountably many bad paths that do not behave this way, the mass comprising those paths is zero, when compared to all the well-behaved sample paths.

The proof of the Weak Law of Large Numbers is derived in Exercise 5.1. The proof of the Strong Law is much more involved (as are many proofs regarding almost all sample paths). There are several different proofs; one of the simpler versions is given in Ross [149], pp. 56–58.

5.3 Time Average versus Ensemble Average

You may think that the concept of an "average" is quite clear. However, in stochastic processes there are multiple types of averages. Two of these types are the *time average* and the *ensemble average*.

To keep this discussion from becoming too abstract, we will repeatedly return to the following simple example: a single FCFS queue in which at every second a new job is added to the queue with probability p and at every second the job in service (if there is one) is completed with probability q, where $q > p$. Let $N(v) =$ number of jobs in the system at time v.

5.3.1 *Motivation*

Once upon a time there were two students in my class, Tim and Enzo (see Figure 5.3). Tim was very tall and long, and he looked very much like a time-line. Enzo was more 2-dimensional looking (if they both look a little like robots, remember that this is a computer science department). Both Tim and Enzo were trying to simulate their FCFS queue to determine the average number of jobs in the system.

Figure 5.3. Tim and Enzo.

Tim, who saw the world as a time-line, generated *one* very long sequence of coin flips (a single process), which he used to simulate the queue over a very, very long period of time, as shown in Figure 5.4. During the running of this queue, Tim logged the number of jobs in the system each second, obtaining a million samples. Then he took the average over all the million samples in his log to get the "average number of jobs."

Enzo took a more 2-dimensional approach. Instead of averaging over one long simulation of length 1,000,000, he generated 1,000 shorter simulations, each of length 1,000. For each simulation, he would wait until his simulation had run for $t = 1,000$ seconds, and then he would sample the queue at exactly time t, obtaining *one* value for $N(t)$, the number of jobs at time t. Enzo then restarted the experiment from scratch (with a

Figure 5.4. Tim and Enzo's different simulation approaches.

new random seed) and again simulated the queue until time t, when he sampled the number of jobs, obtaining *one more* value. Enzo continued to restart his experiment a thousand times. Each time, he would run his simulation until time t and obtain *one more* sample for the number of jobs. After obtaining a thousand samples, he averaged these to get the "average number of jobs."

Question: Who is "right"? Tim or Enzo?

Answer: We will soon see ...

5.3.2 *Definition*

Definition 5.6

$$\overline{N}^{\text{Time Avg}} = \lim_{t \to \infty} \frac{\int_0^t N(v)dv}{t}.$$

Definition 5.7

$$\overline{N}^{\text{Ensemble}} = \lim_{t \to \infty} \mathbf{E}\left[N(t)\right] = \sum_{i=0}^{\infty} i p_i$$

where

$$p_i = \lim_{t \to \infty} \mathbf{P}\left\{N(t) = i\right\}$$
$$= \text{mass of sample paths with value } i \text{ at time } t.$$

5.3.3 *Interpretation*

When we talk about a time average we implicitly have in mind a particular sample path ω over which we are taking the time average. Thus a more precise definition might be as follows:

Definition 5.8

$$\overline{N}^{\text{Time Avg}}(\omega) = \lim_{t \to \infty} \frac{\int_0^t N(v, \omega)dv}{t},$$

where $N(v, \omega)$ represents the number of jobs in the system at time v under sample path ω.

Thus the time average, $\overline{N}^{\text{Time Avg}}$, is defined by observing a *single* sample path over a long period of time, t, as shown in Figure 5.5. During this long period of time, we monitor the number of jobs in the system, and then we take the average over time. The important point here is that we are looking at a single process – *one sequence of coin flips*, ω. Consider the example of the single server. The queue might start empty ($N(0, \omega) = 0$). Then at time 1, there might be an arrival but no departure ($N(1, \omega) = 1$). At time 2, there might again be an arrival but no departure ($N(2, \omega) = 2$). At time 3, there might again be an arrival but no departure ($N(3, \omega) = 3$). Now at time 4, there might be no arrival and a departure ($N(4, \omega) = 2$), etc. The average number of jobs in the system by time 4 for this process is $(0 + 1 + 2 + 3 + 2)/5 = 8/5$. We could continue looking at this process up to time t for some huge time t in the future and ask what is the average number of jobs in the system for this process by time t. If t is really large, we hope that the average number of jobs in the system for this sample path, ω, converges. We then call this limit the *time average* number of jobs in the system along sample path ω.

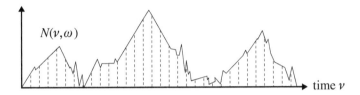

Figure 5.5. Time average for sample path ω.

Yet the time average number may seem suspicious because we are only looking at a *single* sequence of coin flips. Perhaps this was a particularly unusual sequence?

The ensemble average, $\overline{N}^{\text{Ensemble}}$, is what we more typically mean when we talk about the average number of jobs in the system, $\mathbf{E}[N]$. This represents the expected number of jobs in the system when the system is in steady state. (*Note:* the term "steady state" will only be formally defined when we get to Markov chains. For now consider steady state to be some point in time where the effects of the initial starting state are long gone.) The ensemble average takes into account *all possible sequences of coin flips* – all sample paths, as shown in Figure 5.6. Consider again the example of the single server. Again the system might start empty ($N(0) = 0$). Considering all possible events during the first time step, we see that at time 1 there is some probability that the system is still empty and there is some probability that the system contains one job. Thus we can compute $\mathbf{E}[N(1)]$, the expected number of jobs at time 1. Now at time 2, again considering all possible sequences of coin flips and their likelihoods, we can again see that there is some probability that the system is empty, some probability that the system contains 1 job, and some probability that the system contains 2 jobs. We can thus compute $\mathbf{E}[N(2)]$, the expected number of jobs in the system at time 2. Likewise, for any time t we can compute $\mathbf{E}[N(t)]$. If we choose t large enough ($t \to \infty$), under typical conditions there will be some limiting probability that the system contains 0 jobs, p_0, and some limiting probability that the system contains 1 job, p_1, and some limiting probability that the system contains 2 jobs, p_2, and some limiting probability that the system contains i jobs, for any i, p_i. The expectation of these, $\sum_{i=0}^{\infty} i p_i$, is exactly what we mean by $\overline{N}^{\text{Ensemble}}$.

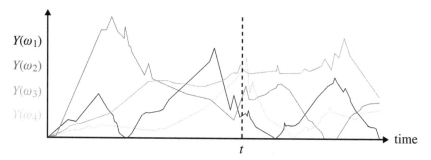

Figure 5.6. Ensemble average.

Question: Which type of average is Tim? Which type is Enzo?

Answer: Tim is measuring a time average, whereas Enzo is measuring the ensemble average.

Remark: As a practical matter, both Tim and Enzo need to be concerned about initial conditions, but in different ways. Enzo needs to be sure his initial conditions have attenuated sufficiently before his measurement point, whereas Tim needs to make sure the portion of his simulation that is affected by initial conditions is sufficiently small.

5.3.4 *Equivalence*

How does $\overline{N}^{\text{Time Avg}}$ compare with $\overline{N}^{\text{Ensemble}}$?

Theorem 5.9 *For an "ergodic" system (see Definition 5.10), the ensemble average exists and, with probability 1,*

$$\overline{N}^{\text{Time Avg}} = \overline{N}^{\text{Ensemble}}.$$

That is, for (almost) all sample paths, the time average along that sample path converges to the ensemble average.

This theorem is discussed in greater detail and proven in Chapter 9. The intuition, however, is very simple. To explain the intuition, we first need to explain the term "ergodic."

Question: First, do you have any *intuition* about what conditions might be required to make the time average equal to the ensemble average?

Definition 5.10 An *ergodic* system is one that is positive recurrent, aperiodic, and irreducible.

These terms are all defined precisely in Chapter 9, but we explain the ideas now. We start with **irreducibility**. Irreducibility says that a process should be able to get from any state to any other state (think of the state as the number of jobs in the system). This is important for ensuring that the choice of initial state does not matter.

The **positive recurrent** property is the most important condition with respect to understanding the equivalence between the time average and the ensemble average: Given an irreducible system, in which we can get to any state, the system is positive recurrent if for any state i, the state is revisited infinitely often, and the mean time between visits to state i (renewals) is finite. Furthermore, every time that we visit state i the system will probabilistically restart itself.

Question: Give an example of what it means for the process to probabilistically restart itself.

Answer: Every time that the system empties (0 jobs), the process starts anew in state 0. We call this a "restart." In a positive recurrent system, the system empties infinitely often. This includes all systems that we will study.

Consider our example of a queue, where a new job is created at each time step with probability p and a job is removed with probability $q > p$. We start out with zero jobs in the system. We now start flipping coins, and the number of jobs in the system goes up and down. At some point, the number of jobs in the system returns to zero. At this point, we can imagine the same statistical process starting over again. And the next time the number of jobs in the system returns to zero, it will start over again. *Thus a single long run of the system (Tim's view) actually appears to be an infinite number of statistically independent runs (Enzo's view).*

The **aperiodicity** condition is important in making sure that the ensemble average exists. Aperiodicity refers to the fact that the system state (number of jobs in the system) should not be tied in some particular way to the time step; for example, it should not be the case that the system is always in state 0 for even time steps and state 1 for odd time steps; otherwise, the particular t that Enzo picked for stopping the system might sway his result.

Question: Explain intuitively why an ergodic system should have the property that the time average equals the ensemble average.

Answer: Consider the time average over a single long run of the system as shown in Figure 5.7. This run can be thought of as a chain of many independent but statistically identical runs, each called a "renewal." Let X_1 represent the time average over just

Figure 5.7. Single process restarting itself.

the first renewal, let X_2 represent the time average over just the second renewal, etc. Then the overall time average is the average of $X_1, X_2, \ldots$. But these are i.i.d. So, by the Strong Law of Large Numbers (SLLN), the average of these converges with probability 1 to the *expected* time average over a single renewal, where the expectation is an *ensemble* average (taken over all sample paths).

5.3.5 *Simulation*

What does all this say about how we do simulation? Tim's method of sampling a single process over a very long period of time and averaging those samples results in $\overline{N}^{\text{Time Avg}}$. Enzo's method of generating many independent processes and taking their average at some far-out time t yields $\overline{N}^{\text{Ensemble}}$. If these yield the same result, should we go for the easier method?

Question: The ensemble average seems more costly to compute, because we need new random seeds. Why bother with the ensemble average if it comes out to the same thing as the time average?

Answer: The main reason is that the ensemble average can be obtained in parallel, by running simulations on different cores or different machines. Another reason for using the ensemble average is that the independent data points allow us to generate confidence intervals, which allow us to bound the deviation in our result.

Question: Why in both the definitions of ensemble average and time average is it so important that the system be run for a "long" time?

Answer: We want to get to the point where the initial state has no effect: We want to reach "steady state." This will all become more clear when we get to Markov chain theory.

5.3.6 *Average Time in System*

So far, we have talked about the average number of jobs in the system. We can also define two versions of the average time in system as follows:

$$\overline{T}^{\text{Time Avg}} = \lim_{t \to \infty} \frac{\sum_{i=1}^{A(t)} T_i}{A(t)},$$

where T_i is the time in system of the ith arrival and $A(t)$ is the number of arrivals by time t. Again the time average is assumed to be associated with a single sample path.

$$\overline{T}^{\text{Ensemble}} = \lim_{i \to \infty} \mathbf{E}\left[T_i\right],$$

where $\mathbf{E}\left[T_i\right]$ is the average time in system of the ith job, where the average is taken over all sample paths.

5.4 Related Readings

The following books provide more detail on the information covered in this chapter: Karlin and Taylor (pp. 474–89) [105], and Gross and Harris (pp. 38–45) [75].

5.5 Exercise

5.1 Weak Law of Large Numbers

Let X_1, X_2, X_3, ..., be i.i.d. random variables with finite mean $\mathbf{E}[X]$ and finite variance σ^2. Your goal is to prove the Weak Law of Large Numbers:

$$\forall \epsilon, \quad \lim_{n \to \infty} \mathbf{P}\left\{ \left| \frac{S_n}{n} - \mathbf{E}[X] \right| > \epsilon \right\} = 0$$

where $S_n = \sum_{i=1}^{n} X_i$.

(a) Start out by proving Markov's Inequality, which says: If X is non-negative then

$$\mathbf{P}\{X > t\} \leq \frac{\mathbf{E}[X]}{t}, \quad \forall t > 0.$$

(b) Now use Markov's Inequality to prove Chebyshev's Inequality, which says: Let Y be a random variable with finite mean $\mathbf{E}[Y]$ and finite variance σ_Y^2. Then

$$\mathbf{P}\{|Y - \mathbf{E}[Y]| \geq t\} \leq \frac{\sigma_Y^2}{t^2}.$$

(c) Finally use Chebyshev's Inequality to prove the Weak Law of Large Numbers.

The Predictive Power of Simple Operational Laws: "What-If" Questions and Answers

Part III is about operational laws. Operational laws are very powerful because they apply to any system or part of a system. They are both simple and exact. A very important feature of operational laws is that they are "distribution independent." This means, for example, that the laws do not depend on the distribution of the job service requirements (job sizes), just on their mean. Likewise the results do not depend on the distribution of the job interarrival times, just on the mean arrival rate. The fact that the results do not require the Markovian assumptions that we will see in Part IV, coupled with the fact that using operational laws is so easy, makes these laws very popular with system builders.

The most important operational law that we will study is Little's Law, which relates the mean number of jobs in any system to the mean response time experienced by arrivals to that system. We will study Little's Law and several other operational laws in Chapter 6.

In Chapter 7 we will see how to put together several operational laws to prove asymptotic bounds on system behavior (specifically, mean response time and throughput) for closed systems. Asymptotic bounds will be proven both in the limit as the multiprogramming level approaches infinity and in the limit as the multiprogramming level approaches 1. These asymptotic bounds will be very useful in allowing us to answer "what-if" questions of the form, "Is it preferable to increase the speed of the CPU by a factor of 2, or to increase the speed of the I/O device by a factor of 3, or does neither really make a difference?"

CHAPTER 6

Little's Law and Other Operational Laws

Little's Law is probably the single most famous queueing theory result. It states that the average number of jobs in the system is equal to the product of the average arrival rate into the system and the average time a job spends in the system. It also holds when the system consists of just the "queues" in the system. Little's Law applies to both open and closed systems, and we explain it in both cases.

6.1 Little's Law for Open Systems

Let's first consider open systems, as shown in Figure 6.1.

Theorem 6.1 (Little's Law for Open Systems) *For any ergodic[1] open system we have that*

$$\mathbf{E}\left[N\right] = \lambda \mathbf{E}\left[T\right]$$

where $\mathbf{E}\left[N\right]$ is the expected number of jobs in the system, λ is the average arrival rate into the system, and $\mathbf{E}\left[T\right]$ is the mean time jobs spend in the system.

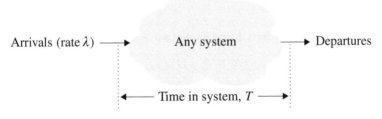

Figure 6.1. Setup for Little's Law.

It is important to note that Little's Law makes no assumptions about the arrival process, the service time distributions at the servers, the network topology, the service order, or anything!

At this point it may be hard to appreciate Little's Law. Its usefulness stems from the fact that when we study Markov chains, we see many techniques for computing $\mathbf{E}\left[N\right]$. Applying Little's Law will then immediately yield $\mathbf{E}\left[T\right]$.

---

[1] The term ergodic was defined briefly in Section 5.3. In Section 6.4 we elaborate on its purpose in Theorems 6.1 and 6.2.

6.2 Intuitions

This section contains some intuitions to help you remember Little's Law. They are *not* proofs! We will prove Little's Law in Section 6.4.

It should seem intuitive that $\mathbf{E}[T]$ and $\mathbf{E}[N]$ are proportional. Consider the example of a fast-food restaurant [18]. It gets people out fast (low $\mathbf{E}[T]$) and also does not require much waiting room (low $\mathbf{E}[N]$). By contrast, a slow-service restaurant gets people out slowly (high $\mathbf{E}[T]$) and therefore needs a lot more seating room ($\mathbf{E}[N]$). Thus $\mathbf{E}[T]$ should be directly proportional to $\mathbf{E}[N]$.

Here is the way I always remember Little's Law (intuition only): Think about a single FCFS queue, as shown in Figure 6.2. A customer arrives and sees $\mathbf{E}[N]$ jobs in the system. The expected time for each customer to complete is $1/\lambda$ (not $1/\mu$), because the average rate of completions is λ (see Section 2.5). Hence the expected time until the customer leaves is $\mathbf{E}[T] \approx \frac{1}{\lambda} \cdot \mathbf{E}[N]$.

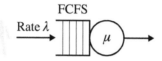

Figure 6.2. Little's Law applied to a single server.

6.3 Little's Law for Closed Systems

In a closed system, $\mathbf{E}[N]$ is fixed at N, the multiprogramming level. Thus, for a closed system, the statement of Little's Law is as follows:

> **Theorem 6.2 (Little's Law for Closed Systems)** *Given any ergodic closed system,*
>
> $$N = X \cdot \mathbf{E}[T],$$
>
> *where N is a constant equal to the multiprogramming level, X is the throughput (i.e., the rate of completions for the system), and $\mathbf{E}[T]$ is the mean time jobs spend in the system.*

Figure 6.3 shows a batch system and an interactive (terminal-driven) system. Note that for the interactive system (right), the time in system, T, is the time to go from "out" to "out," whereas response time, R, is the time from "in" to "out." Specifically, for a *closed interactive system*, we define $\mathbf{E}[T] = \mathbf{E}[R] + \mathbf{E}[Z]$, where $\mathbf{E}[Z]$ is the average think time, $\mathbf{E}[T]$ is the average time in system, and $\mathbf{E}[R]$ is the average response time. The notation is a little overloaded, in that for open systems and closed batch systems, we refer to $\mathbf{E}[T]$ as mean response time, whereas for closed interactive systems $\mathbf{E}[T]$ represents the mean time in system and $\mathbf{E}[R]$ is the mean response time, since response time does not include thinking.

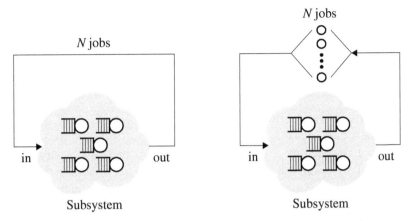

Figure 6.3. Closed systems: A batch system (left) and an interactive system (right).

Recall from Chapter 2 that, for an *open system*, throughput and mean response time are uncorrelated. By contrast, Little's Law tells us that, for a *closed* system, X and $\mathbf{E}[T]$ are inversely related, as are X and $\mathbf{E}[R]$. *Thus in a closed system, improving response time results in improved throughput and vice versa.*

6.4 Proof of Little's Law for Open Systems

We are now ready to prove Little's Law. This section focuses on open systems (see Figure 6.4). The next section concentrates on closed systems.

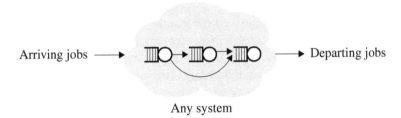

Figure 6.4. Open system.

6.4.1 *Statement via Time Averages*

Theorem 6.3 is a statement of Little's Law as you will see it in the literature. As you see, Little's Law is actually stated as a relationship between time averages (see Section 5.3).

Let

$$\lambda = \lim_{t \to \infty} \frac{A(t)}{t} \quad \text{and} \quad X = \lim_{t \to \infty} \frac{C(t)}{t},$$

where $A(t)$ is the number of arrivals by time t and $C(t)$ is the number of system completions (departures) by time t. Observe that it is typically the case that $\lambda = X$ (one could have $\lambda > X$ if some arrivals get dropped, or if some jobs get stuck and never complete for some reason).

Theorem 6.3 (Little's Law for Open Systems Restated)   *Given any system where* $\overline{N}^{\text{Time Avg}}$, $\overline{T}^{\text{Time Avg}}$, λ, *and* X *exist and where* $\lambda = X$, *then*

$$\overline{N}^{\text{Time Avg}} = \lambda \cdot \overline{T}^{\text{Time Avg}}.$$

Observe that Little's Law is stated as an equality between *time averages*, not *ensemble averages*. Little's Law says that the time-average number in system for sample path ω is equal to λ times the time-average time in system for that sample path. However, we know that if we assume that the system is also *ergodic*, then the time average converges to the ensemble average with probability 1; namely, on almost every sample path, the time average on that sample path will be equal to the ensemble average over all paths (see Section 5.3). Thus, assuming ergodicity, we can apply Little's Law in an ensemble-average sense, which we will do.

Consider the requirements in Theorem 6.3. They are all subsumed by the assumption that the system is *ergodic*, for if the system is ergodic then the above limits all exist and furthermore the average arrival rate and completion rate are equal, because the system empties infinitely often. Furthermore, if we assume that the system is ergodic, then the time average is equal to the ensemble (or "true") average. Thus it is sufficient to require that the system is ergodic for Little's Law, as stated in Theorem 6.1, to hold.

6.4.2 Proof

Proof (***Theorem 6.3***)   Let T_i denote the time that the ith arrival to the system spends in the system, as shown in Figure 6.5. Now, for any time t, consider the area, $\mathcal{A}$, contained within all the rectangles in Figure 6.5, up to time t (this includes most of the rectangle labeled T_5). We first view this area, $\mathcal{A}$, by summing *horizontally* and then, equivalently, view it again by summing *vertically*.

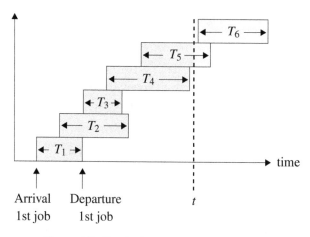

Figure 6.5. Graph of arrivals in an open system.

The horizontal view consists of summing up the T_i's as follows: We observe that

$$\sum_{i \in C(t)} T_i \leq \mathcal{A} \leq \sum_{i \in A(t)} T_i$$

where $\sum_{i \in C(t)} T_i$ denotes the sum of the time in system of those jobs that have completed by time t, and $\sum_{i \in A(t)} T_i$ denotes the sum of the time in system of those jobs that have arrived by time t.

The vertical view of $\mathcal{A}$ adds up the number of jobs in system at any moment in time, $N(s)$, where s ranges from 0 to t. Thus,

$$\mathcal{A} = \int_0^t N(s) ds.$$

Combining these two views, we have

$$\sum_{i \in C(t)} T_i \leq \int_0^t N(s) ds \leq \sum_{i \in A(t)} T_i.$$

Dividing by t throughout, we get

$$\frac{\sum_{i \in C(t)} T_i}{t} \leq \frac{\int_0^t N(s) ds}{t} \leq \frac{\sum_{i \in A(t)} T_i}{t}$$

or, equivalently,

$$\frac{\sum_{i \in C(t)} T_i}{C(t)} \cdot \frac{C(t)}{t} \leq \frac{\int_0^t N(s) ds}{t} \leq \frac{\sum_{i \in A(t)} T_i}{A(t)} \cdot \frac{A(t)}{t}.$$

Taking limits as $t \to \infty$,

$$\lim_{t \to \infty} \frac{\sum_{i \in C(t)} T_i}{C(t)} \cdot \lim_{t \to \infty} \frac{C(t)}{t} \leq \overline{N}^{\text{Time Avg}} \leq \lim_{t \to \infty} \frac{\sum_{i \in A(t)} T_i}{A(t)} \cdot \lim_{t \to \infty} \frac{A(t)}{t}$$

$$\Rightarrow \overline{T}^{\text{Time Avg}} \cdot X \leq \overline{N}^{\text{Time Avg}} \leq \overline{T}^{\text{Time Avg}} \cdot \lambda.$$

Yet we are given that X and λ are equal. Therefore,

$$\overline{N}^{\text{Time Avg}} = \lambda \cdot \overline{T}^{\text{Time Avg}}.$$

■

Question: Are we assuming FCFS service order in this argument?

Answer: No, this argument does not depend on service order. Observe that the second arrival departs *after* the third arrival departs.

Question: Are we assuming anywhere that this is a single-server system?

Answer: No, this argument holds for any system.

6.4.3 *Corollaries*

> **Corollary 6.4 (Little's Law for Time in Queue)** *Given any system where* $\overline{N}_Q^{\text{Time Avg}}$, $\overline{T}_Q^{\text{Time Avg}}$, λ, *and* X *exist and where* $\lambda = X$, *then*
>
> $$\overline{N}_Q^{\text{Time Avg}} = \lambda \cdot \overline{T}_Q^{\text{Time Avg}},$$
>
> *where* N_Q *represents the number of jobs in queue in the system and* T_Q *represents the time jobs spend in queues.*

Question: How would you prove Corollary 6.4?

Answer: Same proof as for Theorem 6.3, except that now instead of drawing T_i, we draw $T_Q(i)$, namely the time the ith arrival to the system spends in queues (wasted time). Note that $T_Q(i)$ may not be a solid rectangle. It may be made up of several rectangles because the ith job might be in queue for a while, then in service, then waiting in some other queue, then in service, again, etc.

> **Corollary 6.5 (Utilization Law)** *Consider a single device* i *with average arrival rate* λ_i *jobs/sec and average service rate* μ_i *jobs/sec, where* $\lambda_i < \mu_i$. *Let* ρ_i *denote the long-run fraction of time that the device is busy. Then*
>
> $$\rho_i = \frac{\lambda_i}{\mu_i}.$$

We refer to ρ_i as the "device utilization" or "device load." Observe that, given ergodicity, ρ_i represents both the long-run fraction of time that device i is busy and also the limiting probability (ensemble average) that device i is busy.

Question: Do you see how to use Little's Law to prove this corollary? What should we define the "system" to be?

Proof Let the "system" consist of just the service facility *without* the associated queue, as shown in the shaded box of Figure 6.6. Now the number of jobs in the "system" is always just 0 or 1.

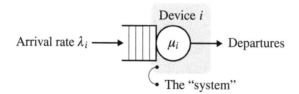

Figure 6.6. Using Little's Law to prove the Utilization Law.

Question: What is the expected number of jobs in the system as we have defined it?

Answer: The number of jobs in the system is 1 when the device is busy (this happens with probability ρ_i) and is 0 when the device is idle (this happens with probability

$1 - \rho_i$). Hence the *expected* number of jobs in the system is ρ_i. So, applying Little's Law, we have

$$\rho_i = \text{Expected number jobs in service facility for device } i$$
$$= (\text{Arrival rate into service facility}) \cdot (\text{Mean time in service facility})$$
$$= \lambda_i \cdot \mathbf{E}\,[\text{Service time at device } i]$$
$$= \lambda_i \cdot \frac{1}{\mu_i}. \qquad \blacksquare$$

We often express the Utilization Law as

$$\boxed{\rho_i = \lambda_i \mathbf{E}\,[S_i] = X_i \mathbf{E}\,[S_i]}$$

where ρ_i, λ_i, X_i, and $\mathbf{E}\,[S_i]$ are the load, average arrival rate, average throughput, and average service requirement at device i, respectively.

Question: Suppose we are only interested in "red" jobs, where "red" denotes some type of jobs. Can we apply Little's Law to just "red" jobs? Prove it.

Answer: Yes.

$$\boxed{\mathbf{E}\,[\text{Number of red jobs in system}] = \lambda_{\text{red}} \cdot \mathbf{E}\,[\text{Time spent in system by red jobs}]}$$

The proof is exactly the same as before, but only the T_i's corresponding to the red jobs are included in Figure 6.5.

6.5 Proof of Little's Law for Closed Systems

6.5.1 *Statement via Time Averages*

As in the previous section, we begin with a restatement of Little's Law for closed systems. As before we define

$$X = \lim_{t \to \infty} \frac{C(t)}{t}$$

where $C(t)$ is the number of system completions by time t.

This time, however, there are no exogenous arrivals. We thus define

$$\lambda = \lim_{t \to \infty} \frac{A(t)}{t}$$

where $A(t)$ is the number of jobs that *are generated* by time t.

Theorem 6.6 (Little's Law for Closed Systems Restated) *Given any closed system (either interactive or batch) with multiprogramming level N and given that $\overline{T}^{\text{Time Avg}}$ and X exist and that $\lambda = X$, then*

$$N = X \cdot \overline{T}^{\text{Time Avg}}.$$

6.5.2 *Proof*

It is important to note that T in Theorem 6.6 corresponds to the total time in system, namely the time to go from "out" to "out" in Figure 6.3, which includes both response time (R) and think time (Z). Thus, as soon as one T_i completes, another immediately starts, as shown in Figure 6.7.

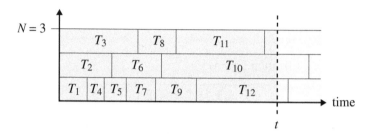

Figure 6.7. Graph of job system times in closed system with $N = 3$.

Proof   Figure 6.7 shows the time in system for arrivals. Observe that a new job cannot arrive until one departs. Thus there are always N jobs in the system. At any time t, the area made up by all rectangles up to time t is Nt, which can be bounded above and below as follows:

$$\sum_{i \in C(t)} T_i \leq N \cdot t \leq \sum_{i \in A(t)} T_i$$

$$\Rightarrow \frac{\sum_{i \in C(t)} T_i}{t} \leq N \leq \frac{\sum_{i \in A(t)} T_i}{t}$$

$$\Rightarrow \frac{\sum_{i \in C(t)} T_i}{C(t)} \cdot \frac{C(t)}{t} \leq N \leq \frac{\sum_{i \in A(t)} T_i}{A(t)} \cdot \frac{A(t)}{t}$$

Taking limits as $t \to \infty$,

$$\lim_{t \to \infty} \frac{\sum_{i \in C(t)} T_i}{C(t)} \cdot \lim_{t \to \infty} \frac{C(t)}{t} \leq N \leq \lim_{t \to \infty} \frac{\sum_{i \in A(t)} T_i}{A(t)} \cdot \lim_{t \to \infty} \frac{A(t)}{t}$$

$$\Rightarrow \overline{T}^{\text{Time Avg}} \cdot X \leq N \leq \lambda \cdot \overline{T}^{\text{Time Avg}}.$$

But X and λ are equal. Therefore

$$N = X \cdot \overline{T}^{\text{Time Avg}}. \qquad \blacksquare$$

6.6 Generalized Little's Law

Note that the relationships presented so far have all been between the *mean* time in system, $\mathbf{E}[T]$, and the *mean* number of jobs in system, $\mathbf{E}[N]$. You might be wondering if Little's Law can be generalized to relate higher moments as well, such as a relationship between $\mathbf{E}[T^2]$ and $\mathbf{E}[N^2]$. Some research papers have been successful at proving relationships between higher moments under certain very restrictive conditions, generally requiring that jobs leave in the order that they arrive, as in a single FCFS queue, see [33, 19]. Although we later derive a relationship between the higher moments of T and N for a single-server M/G/1 queue (see Chapter 26), it is typically very difficult to get higher moments of T for more general multi-queue systems.

6.7 Examples Applying Little's Law

The versatility of Little's Law lies in two properties: First, Little's Law is *distribution independent*. This means that it depends only on mean quantities (e.g., the mean interarrival time or the mean service time), not on whether the service times are Exponentially distributed or Uniformly distributed, nor on whether the arrival process is Poisson or something else. Second, Little's Law applies to any system or *piece of a system*, as we demonstrate in the following examples.

Example 1: Refer to Figure 6.8

We have an interactive system with $N = 10$ users, as shown in Figure 6.8. We are told that the expected think time is $\mathbf{E}[Z] = 5$ seconds and that the expected response time is $\mathbf{E}[R] = 15$ seconds. Note that the response time is the time it takes a job to get from "in" to "out" in Figure 6.8.

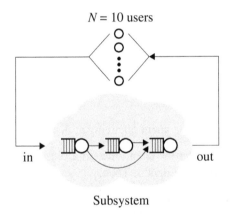

Figure 6.8. An interactive system.

Question: What is the throughput, X, of the system?

Answer: Using Little's Law for closed systems, we have

$$N = X \cdot \mathbf{E}[T] = X(\mathbf{E}[Z] + \mathbf{E}[R])$$
$$\Rightarrow X = \frac{N}{\mathbf{E}[R] + \mathbf{E}[Z]} = \frac{10}{5 + 15} = 0.5 \text{ jobs/sec.}$$

The application of Little's Law to closed systems is often referred to as the **Response Time Law for Closed Systems**:

$$\boxed{\mathbf{E}[R] = \tfrac{N}{X} - \mathbf{E}[Z]}$$

Example 2: Refer to Figure 6.9

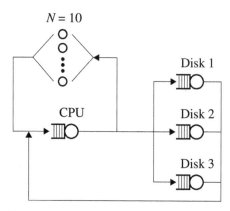

Figure 6.9. A more complex interactive system.

We are given the system in Figure 6.9 and the following information:

- The throughput of disk 3 is 40 requests/sec ($X_{disk3} = 40$).
- The service time of an average request at disk 3 is 0.0225 sec ($\mathbf{E}\left[S_{disk3}\right] = .0225$).
- The average number of jobs in the system consisting of disk 3 and its queue is 4 ($\mathbf{E}\left[N_{disk3}\right] = 4$).

Question: What is the utilization of disk 3?

Answer:

$$\rho_{disk3} = X_{disk3} \cdot \mathbf{E}\left[S_{disk3}\right] = 40 \cdot (0.0225) = 90\%.$$

Question: What is the mean time spent queueing at disk 3?

Answer: Let T_{disk3} denote the time spent queueing plus serving at disk 3. Let T_Q^{disk3} denote the time spent queueing at disk 3. Then,

$$\mathbf{E}\left[T_{disk3}\right] = \frac{\mathbf{E}\left[N_{disk3}\right]}{X_{disk3}} = \frac{4}{40} = .1 \text{ sec.}$$

$$\mathbf{E}\left[T_Q^{disk3}\right] = \mathbf{E}\left[T_{disk3}\right] - \mathbf{E}\left[S_{disk3}\right] = 0.1 \text{ sec} - 0.0225 \text{ sec} = 0.0775 \text{ sec.}$$

Question: Find $\mathbf{E}$ [Number of requests queued at disk 3].

Answer:

$$\begin{aligned}
\mathbf{E}\left[N_Q^{disk3}\right] &= \mathbf{E}\left[N_{disk3}\right] - \mathbf{E}\text{ [Number requests serving at disk 3]} \\
&= \mathbf{E}\left[N_{disk3}\right] - \rho_{disk3} \\
&= 4 - 0.9 \\
&= 3.1 \text{ requests.}
\end{aligned}$$

Alternatively, we could have obtained this same answer from

$$\mathbf{E}\left[N_Q^{\text{disk3}}\right] = \mathbf{E}\left[T_Q^{\text{disk3}}\right] \cdot X_{\text{disk3}} = 0.775 \cdot 40 = 3.1 \text{ requests.}$$

Next we are told that

- $\mathbf{E}$ [Number of ready users (not thinking)] $= 7.5$.
- Number of terminals N is 10.
- $\mathbf{E}$ [Think time] $= \mathbf{E}\left[Z\right] = 5$ sec.

Question: What is the system throughput?

Answer: Looking at the whole system, we have

$$X = \frac{N}{\mathbf{E}\left[R\right] + \mathbf{E}\left[Z\right]} = \frac{10}{\mathbf{E}\left[R\right] + 5}$$

but we do not know $\mathbf{E}\left[R\right]$. Looking only at the non-thinking part of the system, we have

$$\mathbf{E}\left[R\right] = \frac{\mathbf{E}\left[N_{\text{not-thinking}}\right]}{X} = \frac{7.5}{X}$$

but we do not know X. Solving these two equations simultaneously yields $X = .5$ requests per second and $\mathbf{E}\left[R\right]$ is 15 seconds.

Question: Is there a way to get system throughput using only one equation?

Answer: Yes, we could instead apply Little's Law to the thinking region only. The throughput of the thinking region is still X, and the mean time spent in the thinking region is $\mathbf{E}\left[Z\right]$. Hence,

$$\mathbf{E}\left[N_{\text{thinking}}\right] = X \cdot \mathbf{E}\left[Z\right]$$
$$2.5 = X \cdot 5$$
$$X = 0.5.$$

Example 3: Refer to Figure 6.10

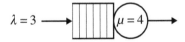

Figure 6.10. A finite buffer.

Figure 6.10 shows a single FCFS queue with a capacity limitation of 7 jobs (there is room for 1 job to serve and buffer space for 6 more waiting jobs). Arrivals that find a full buffer are dropped.

Question: What does Little's Law look like for this system?

Answer: The problem is that $\lambda \neq X$ as required by Little's Law. However, the *effective arrival rate*, meaning the rate of those jobs that get through, is

$\lambda(1 - \mathbf{P}\{7 \text{ jobs in system}\})$, which is equal to the completion rate, as required. So

$$\mathbf{E}[N] = \lambda \cdot (1 - \mathbf{P}\{7 \text{ jobs in system}\}) \cdot \mathbf{E}[T].$$

6.8 More Operational Laws: The Forced Flow Law

The **Forced Flow Law** relates system throughput to the throughput of an individual device as follows:

$$X_i = \mathbf{E}[V_i] \cdot X$$

where X denotes the system throughput, X_i denotes the throughput at device i, and V_i denotes the number of visits to device i per job.

V_i is often referred to as the *visit ratio* for device i (see Figure 6.11).

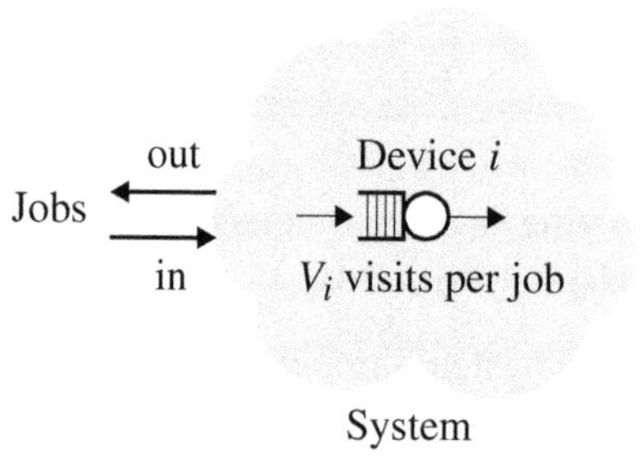

Figure 6.11. A single device within a larger system. (In a closed system the "in" and "out" arrows would be connected.)

The Forced Flow Law should seem intuitive: For every system completion, there are on average $\mathbf{E}[V_i]$ completions at device i. Hence the rate of completions at device i is $\mathbf{E}[V_i]$ times the rate of system completions.[2]

---

[2] A more formal argument would go like this: Consider Figure 6.11. Suppose we observe the system for some large observation period t. Let $C(t)$ denote the number of system completions during time t and let $C_i(t)$ denote the number of completions at device i during time t. Let $V_i^{(j)}$ be the number of visits that the jth job entering the system makes to device i. Then,

$$C_i(t) \approx \sum_{j \in C(t)} V_i^{(j)}$$

$$\frac{C_i(t)}{t} \approx \frac{\sum_{j \in C(t)} V_i^{(j)}}{t}$$

$$\frac{C_i(t)}{t} \approx \frac{\sum_{j \in C(t)} V_i^{(j)}}{C(t)} \cdot \frac{C(t)}{t}$$

$$\lim_{t \to \infty} \frac{C_i(t)}{t} \approx \lim_{t \to \infty} \frac{\sum_{j \in C(t)} V_i^{(j)}}{C(t)} \cdot \lim_{t \to \infty} \frac{C(t)}{t}$$

$$X_i = \mathbf{E}[V_i] \cdot X.$$

Note that approximation signs are used here because $C(t)$ actually provides a lower bound on the sum, whereas $A(t)$ would provide an upper bound. To be precise, we should use both the upper and lower bounds, but this becomes irrelevant once we take the limit as $t \to \infty$.

Example of Forced Flow Law

Question: Suppose we are given the network shown in Figure 6.12. What are the visit ratios? That is, what are $\mathbf{E}\,[V_a]$, $\mathbf{E}\,[V_b]$, and $\mathbf{E}\,[V_{\text{cpu}}]$?

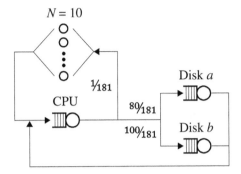

Figure 6.12. Calculating the visit ratios.

Answer: Although it may seem obvious for this example, let's work it out formally because later exercises may be more complicated.

Looking at the figure, we see

$$C_a = C_{\text{cpu}} \cdot 80/181$$
$$C_b = C_{\text{cpu}} \cdot 100/181$$
$$C = C_{\text{cpu}} \cdot 1/181$$
$$C_{\text{cpu}} = C_a + C_b + C.$$

Dividing through by C (the number of system completions) yields the visit ratios. So we get

$$\mathbf{E}\,[V_a] = \mathbf{E}\,[V_{\text{cpu}}] \cdot 80/181$$
$$\mathbf{E}\,[V_b] = \mathbf{E}\,[V_{\text{cpu}}] \cdot 100/181$$
$$1 = \mathbf{E}\,[V_{\text{cpu}}] \cdot 1/181$$
$$\mathbf{E}\,[V_{\text{cpu}}] = \mathbf{E}\,[V_a] + \mathbf{E}\,[V_b] + 1.$$

Solving this system of simultaneous equations yields

$$\mathbf{E}\,[V_{\text{cpu}}] = 181$$
$$\mathbf{E}\,[V_a] = 80$$
$$\mathbf{E}\,[V_b] = 100.$$

6.9 Combining Operational Laws

Simple Example

Suppose we have an interactive system with the following characteristics:

- 25 terminals ($N = 25$)
- 18 seconds average think time ($\mathbf{E}\,[Z] = 18$)
- 20 visits to a specific disk per interaction on average ($\mathbf{E}\,[V_{\text{disk}}] = 20$)

- 30% utilization of that disk ($\rho_{\text{disk}} = .3$)
- 0.025 sec average service time per visit to that disk ($\mathbf{E}\left[S_{\text{disk}}\right] = .025$)

That is all the information we have. We are not told anything else about the rest of the system.

Question: What is the mean response time, $\mathbf{E}\left[R\right]$?

Answer:

1. $\mathbf{E}\left[R\right] = \dfrac{N}{X} - \mathbf{E}\left[Z\right]$, but we still need X.

2. $X = \dfrac{X_{\text{disk}}}{\mathbf{E}\left[V_{\text{disk}}\right]}$, but we still need X_{disk}.

3. $X_{\text{disk}} = \dfrac{\rho_{\text{disk}}}{\mathbf{E}\left[S_{\text{disk}}\right]}$, both of which we know.

Working backward, we calculate

$$X_{\text{disk}} = \frac{\rho_{\text{disk}}}{\mathbf{E}\left[S_{\text{disk}}\right]} = 12 \text{ requests/sec}$$

$$\Rightarrow X = \frac{X_{\text{disk}}}{\mathbf{E}\left[V_{\text{disk}}\right]} = .6 \text{ interactions/sec}$$

$$\Rightarrow \mathbf{E}\left[R\right] = \frac{N}{X} - \mathbf{E}\left[Z\right] = 23.7 \text{ sec.}$$

Harder Example

This is a case study taken from Lazowska et al., p. 49 [117]. We are told the following information only:

- It is an interactive system.
- The central subsystem consists of a CPU and three disks.
- Swapping *may* occur between interactions, causing a user to lose her memory partition. Thus a request *sometimes* has to queue up in the memory queue to get back its memory partition before entering the central subsystem, but sometimes can skip this queue.

Figure 6.13 is a sketch of what the system looks like based on this information. Observe that some jobs have to wait in the "get memory queue," whereas others already have the prerequisite memory allocated and can skip over this part and go directly to the central subsystem. We are not given information as to the fraction of jobs that go each way.

Here are the measurements that were collected about this system:

- number of time-sharing users ($N = 23$)
- average think time per user ($\mathbf{E}\left[Z\right] = 21$ seconds)
- system throughput ($X = 0.45$ interactions per second)
- average number of requests trying to get memory ($\mathbf{E}\left[N_{\text{getting memory}}\right] = 11.65$)
- average number of visits to the CPU per interaction ($\mathbf{E}\left[V_{\text{cpu}}\right] = 3$)
- average service demand per visit to the CPU ($\mathbf{E}\left[S_{\text{cpu}}\right] = .21$ seconds)

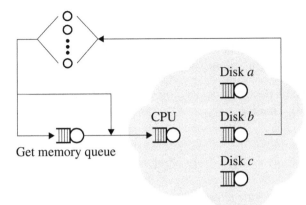

Figure 6.13. A system with a memory queue.

Question: What is the average amount of time that elapses between getting a memory partition and completing the interaction?

Answer: This question asks us for the expected time that jobs spend in the central subsystem. There are several ways to answer it. Here is one:

$$\mathbf{E}\,[\text{Time in central subsystem}] = \mathbf{E}\,[\text{Response Time}] - \mathbf{E}\,[\text{Time to get memory}]$$

It is true that not every job has to go get memory, but you can think of $\mathbf{E}$[Time to get memory] as the *expected* time to go from the point right before the split in the figure to right after the join in the figure.

Now by the Response Time Law,

$$\mathbf{E}\,[\text{Response Time}] = \frac{N}{X} - \mathbf{E}\,[Z] = \frac{23}{0.45} - 21 = 30.11 \text{ sec.}$$

Furthermore,

$$\mathbf{E}\,[\text{Time to get memory}] = \frac{\mathbf{E}\,[\text{Number getting memory}]}{X} = \frac{11.65}{0.45} = 25.88 \text{ sec.}$$

Thus,

$$\mathbf{E}\,[\text{Time in central subsystem}] = \mathbf{E}\,[\text{Response Time}] - \mathbf{E}\,[\text{Time to get memory}]$$
$$= 30.11 - 25.88$$
$$= 4.23 \text{ sec.}$$

Question: What is the CPU utilization?

Answer:

$$\rho_{\text{cpu}} = X_{\text{cpu}} \cdot \mathbf{E}\,[S_{\text{cpu}}] = X \cdot \mathbf{E}\,[V_{\text{cpu}}] \cdot \mathbf{E}\,[S_{\text{cpu}}] = 0.45 \cdot 3 \cdot 0.21 = 0.28.$$

6.10 Device Demands

We end with one final law, called the Bottleneck Law. This law is very important in answering "what-if" type questions about systems, which come up in the next chapter.

Define D_i to be the total service demand on device i for all visits of a single job (i.e., a single interaction). That is,

$$D_i = \sum_{j=1}^{V_i} S_i^{(j)},$$

where $S_i^{(j)}$ is the service time required by the jth visit of the job to server i.

We immediately see by (3.3) that

$$\mathbf{E}\left[D_i\right] = \mathbf{E}\left[V_i\right] \cdot \mathbf{E}\left[S_i\right],$$

provided that V_i and the $S_i^{(j)}$'s are independent. That is, we are assuming that the number of visits a job makes to device i is not affected by its service demand at the device.

We will soon discuss the importance of these D_i's. First, let's observe how easy D_i typically is to measure. Suppose we had to measure the V_i's. This would be *hard*, because we would have to keep track of a particular job and count its visits to device i. If device i is time-shared among jobs, it would be even harder. Luckily, we do not have to do this!

Question: How would you determine $\mathbf{E}\left[D_i\right]$ in practice?

Answer: Consider a long observation period. Observe that

$$\mathbf{E}\left[D_i\right] = \frac{B_i}{C},$$

where B_i is the busy time at device i for the duration of our observation period and C is the number of *system* completions during this observation period. These are very easy measurements to get.

The importance of $\mathbf{E}\left[D_i\right]$ lies in the following law, which we call the **Bottleneck Law**:

$$\boxed{\rho_i = X \cdot \mathbf{E}\left[D_i\right]}$$

Question: Can you explain the Bottleneck Law intuitively?

Answer: X is the jobs/sec arriving into the whole system. Each of those outside arrivals into the system contributes $\mathbf{E}\left[D_i\right]$ seconds of work for device i. So device i is busy for $X \cdot \mathbf{E}\left[D_i\right]$ seconds out of every second (e.g., device i might be busy for half a second out of every second). Thus $X \cdot \mathbf{E}\left[D_i\right]$ represents the utilization of device i.

Here is a proof of the Bottleneck Law:

$$\rho_i = X_i \cdot \mathbf{E}\left[S_i\right] = X \cdot \mathbf{E}\left[V_i\right] \cdot \mathbf{E}\left[S_i\right] = X \cdot \mathbf{E}\left[D_i\right].$$

Example

As a simple example, consider a system with an outside arrival rate of 3 jobs/second. Suppose that each job, on average, visits the disk 10 times. Suppose that each visit to the disk takes 0.01 second on average. Then, the per-job demand on the disk is .1 seconds, and the utilization of the disk is .3.

6.11 Readings and Further Topics Related to Little's Law

Little's Law was invented by J.D.C. Little in 1961, [121]. The following books are useful in providing examples of the application of Little's Law and other operational laws, as explained in this chapter and Chapter 7: Jain (pp. 547–67) [104], Lazowska et al. (pp. 40–95) [117], Bertsekas & Gallager (pp. 152–57) [18], and Menascé et al. (pp. 84–89) [125].

The proof of Little's Law can be generalized to allow for more general notions of the time in system, T, and the number in system, N. One of the generalizations is known in the literature as $H = \lambda G$, where H takes the place of $\overline{N}$ and G takes the place of $\overline{T}$. The $H = \lambda G$ law and its further generalizations are described in great detail in a gem of a book by El-Taha and Stidham [51], Ch. 6. Another generalization is the Rate Conservation Law (RCL); see [126, 103, 167, 183].

Finally, as mentioned earlier, there have been many attempts to prove relationships between higher moments of T and N. The *Distributional Little's Law* holds only under certain very restrictive conditions, generally requiring that jobs leave in the order that they arrive, as in a single FCFS queue. Some relevant references are [33, 19]. Exercises 26.4 and 26.5 derive the Distributional Little's Law for an M/G/1 FCFS queue and illustrate its application to more complex systems.

6.12 Exercises

6.1 Professors and Students

A professor practices the following strategy with respect to taking on new Ph.D. students. On even-numbered years, she takes on 2 new students. On odd-numbered years, she takes on 1 new student. Assuming the average time to graduate is 6 years, how many students on average will the professor have? Prove your answer using an operational law.

6.2 Simplified Power Usage in Server Farms

Given that power is expensive, it is common practice to leave servers on only when they are being used and to turn them off whenever they are not in use. Assume that the following power-aware algorithm is used: When a job arrives, it instantly turns on a fresh server (assume zero setup cost). When the job completes service, it instantly turns off that server. Assume that there is always a server available for every job (i.e., there is no queueing). Your goal is to derive the time-average rate at which power is used in our system. Assume that when a server is on, it consumes power at a rate of $\mathcal{P} = 240$ watts. Assume $\lambda = 10$

jobs arrive per second and that the service requirement of jobs is Uniformly distributed ranging from 1 second to 9 seconds.

(Note: This is a highly simplified model. We will study much more complex models in Chapter 27.)

6.3 Measurements Gone Wrong

After spending months carefully building his closed batch data storage system, David comes to see his advisor with the following description and measurements: The MPL for the system is fixed at 19 jobs. David explains that 90% of jobs find the data they need in the cache, and hence their expected response time is only 1 second. However, 10% end up having to go to the database, where their expected response time is 10 seconds. David's advisor asks one question: "How many jobs do you see on average at the database?" When David answers "5," his advisor says he needs to go back to the drawing board. What went wrong?

6.4 More Practice Manipulating Operational Laws

For the interactive system in Figure 6.14, suppose that we are given the following information:

mean user think time = 5 seconds
expected service time at device i = .01 seconds
utilization of device i = .3
utilization of CPU = .5
expected number of visits to device i per visit to CPU = 10
expected number of jobs in the central subsystem (the cloud shape) = 20
expected total time in system (including think time) per job = 50 seconds.

How many jobs are there in the queue portion of the CPU on average, $\mathbf{E}\left[N_Q^{\text{cpu}}\right]$?

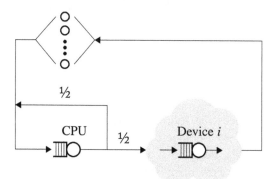

Figure 6.14. Figure for Exercise 6.4.

6.5 Little's Law for Closed Systems

Recall that the Response Time Law for a closed interactive system says that

$$\mathbf{E}\left[R\right] = \frac{N}{X} - \mathbf{E}\left[Z\right].$$

Thus it seems possible that $\mathbf{E}\left[R\right]$ might be negative! Prove that this can never happen. (If you are clever, your proof can be only two lines.)

6.6 Little's Law for Mean Slowdown

Recall that Little's Law relates the mean response time to the mean number of jobs in any ergodic system. It is interesting to ask whether a similar law can be proven that relates mean slowdown to the mean number of jobs in the system. We do not have an answer. However, you should be able to derive the following bound in the case of a *single FCFS queue*:

$$\mathbf{E}\left[\text{Slowdown}\right] \leq \frac{\mathbf{E}\left[N\right]}{\lambda} \cdot \mathbf{E}\left[\frac{1}{S}\right]$$

where S represents job size, N represents the number of jobs in the system, and λ is the average arrival rate into the queue.

6.7 More on SRPT

The SRPT scheduling policy is important because it minimizes mean response time. In Exercise 2.3, we saw that SRPT does *not* minimize mean slowdown. Runting suggests that the problem with SRPT is that it picks jobs with the shortest remaining time, whereas to minimize mean slowdown we want to choose jobs that have both short remaining time and also small original size. Runting proposes that we use the *RS algorithm*, which computes the product of a job's current remaining size (R) and its (original) size (S), and then runs that job whose product (RS) is smallest. Is Runting right?

(a) Explain the intuition behind the RS algorithm for minimizing mean slowdown.

(b) Prove or disprove that the RS algorithm minimizes mean slowdown on every arrival sequence. If it minimizes mean slowdown, provide a proof. If it does not minimize mean slowdown, provide a counterexample.

RS is also known as SPTP and is analyzed in [100].

CHAPTER 7

Modification Analysis: "What-If" for Closed Systems

In the last chapter we learned about several operational laws. Operational laws are laws that hold independently of any assumptions about the distribution of arrivals or the distribution of service times (job sizes). They are extremely useful and simple to apply. Operational laws may be applied to open and closed systems, although they often are most powerful when applied to closed systems.

In this chapter we do the following:

1. We use our operational laws to prove some very cool *asymptotic bounds* for closed systems. *Note:* These asymptotic bounds apply *only* to *closed* systems.
2. We use our newly developed asymptotic bounds to do *modification analysis* on closed systems. In modification analysis we ask "what-if" questions about which design changes will result in performance improvements for the closed system.
3. Finally, we return to the question of how closed systems differ from open systems.

After this chapter, you can don a suit and call yourself a systems consultant :-)

7.1 Review

So far we have seen several operational laws. They all follow immediately from the derivation of Little's Law.

Little's Law for an Open System This holds for *any* ergodic open system and states that

$$\mathbf{E}\left[N\right] = \lambda \cdot \mathbf{E}\left[T\right],$$

where λ is the average outside arrival rate into the system, also equal to the (average) throughput rate of the system, X. Here $\mathbf{E}\left[N\right]$ is the expected number of jobs in the system, and $\mathbf{E}\left[T\right]$ is the expected time a job spends in the system.

We saw several variations on this law, including

$$\mathbf{E}\left[N_Q\right] = \lambda \cdot \mathbf{E}\left[T_Q\right],$$

which relates the number of jobs that are waiting (in queues) to the mean time jobs spend waiting, and

$$\mathbf{E}\left[N_{\text{red}}\right] = \lambda_{\text{red}} \cdot \mathbf{E}\left[T_{\text{red}}\right],$$

which applies Little's Law to just the "red-colored" jobs.

Little's Law for a Closed Batch System (Zero Think Time) This holds for *any* ergodic closed batch system and states that

$$N = X \cdot \mathbf{E}\,[T]\,,$$

where N is the multiprogramming level of the system.

Response Time Law for Closed Interactive Systems This law holds for any ergodic closed interactive (terminal-driven) system and states that

$$\mathbf{E}\,[R] = \frac{N}{X} - \mathbf{E}\,[Z]\,,$$

where N is the multiprogramming level (number of users), X is the throughput, $\mathbf{E}\,[Z]$ denotes the mean time spent thinking, and $\mathbf{E}\,[R]$ is the expected response time.

Utilization Law This applies to a single server i and states that

$$\rho_i = \frac{\lambda_i}{\mu_i} = \lambda_i \mathbf{E}\,[S_i]\,,$$

where ρ_i is the utilization of the server, λ_i is the average arrival rate into the server (this is also the server's throughput rate, X_i), and $\mu_i = \frac{1}{\mathbf{E}[S_i]}$ is the mean service rate at the server.

Forced Flow Law This law relates system throughput to the throughput of an individual device i:

$$X_i = \mathbf{E}\,[V_i] \cdot X,$$

where X denotes the system throughput, X_i denotes the throughput at device i, and $\mathbf{E}\,[V_i]$ denotes the expected number of visits to device i per job.

Bottleneck Law This law involves D_i, the total service demand on device i for all visits of a single job. Over a long observation period T, $D_i = B_i/C$, where B_i is the total time during T that device i is busy and C is the total number of *system* completions during time T. The Bottleneck Law states that

$$\rho_i = X \cdot \mathbf{E}\,[D_i]\,.$$

7.2 Asymptotic Bounds for Closed Systems

We will now see that, by knowing the D_i's alone, we are able to both:

1. Estimate X and $\mathbf{E}\,[R]$ as a function of the multiprogramming level, N (this section).
2. Determine which changes to the system will be worthwhile and which will not (next section).

Let m be the number of devices in our system. Let

$$D = \sum_{i=1}^{m} \mathbf{E}\,[D_i]$$

and let

$$D_{\max} = \max_i \{ \mathbf{E}[D_i] \}.$$

We will assume an interactive system ($\mathbf{E}[Z] \neq 0$). One can always set $\mathbf{E}[Z] = 0$ to get a batch system.

Theorem 7.1 *For any closed interactive system with N terminals,*
$$X \leq \min \left(\frac{N}{D + \mathbf{E}[Z]}, \frac{1}{D_{\max}} \right).$$
$$\mathbf{E}[R] \geq \max \left(D, N \cdot D_{\max} - \mathbf{E}[Z] \right).$$
Importantly, the first term in each clause ($\frac{N}{D + \mathbf{E}[Z]}$ or D) is an asymptote for small N, and the second term ($\frac{1}{D_{\max}}$ or $N \cdot D_{\max} - \mathbf{E}[Z]$) is an asymptote for large N.

Proof   First, we derive the large N asymptotes:

1.
$$\forall i, X \cdot \mathbf{E}[D_i] = \rho_i \leq 1$$
$$\Rightarrow \forall i, X \leq 1/\mathbf{E}[D_i]$$
$$\Rightarrow X \leq 1/D_{\max}. \tag{7.1}$$

For *large* N, the $D_{\max}$ server is always busy ($\rho_{\max} \approx 1$), so $X = 1/D_{\max}$. Thus $1/D_{\max}$ is an asymptote for large N.

2.
$$\mathbf{E}[R] = N/X - \mathbf{E}[Z] \geq N \cdot D_{\max} - \mathbf{E}[Z],$$

where the inequality comes from (7.1) and thus forms a tight bound for large N.

Next, we derive the small N asymptotes:

1. Let $\mathbf{E}[R(N)]$ denote the mean response time when the multiprogramming level is N. Then,

$$\mathbf{E}[R(N)] \geq \mathbf{E}[R(1)] = D^1, \tag{7.2}$$

where the above expression is a tight asymptote for low N (when there is no congestion).

Question: Why is $\mathbf{E}[R(1)] = D$? Are we saying all devices must be visited by every job?

Answer: No, We are not saying that all devices must be visited by every job, but that an average job has an expected amount of time at each device because some fraction of all jobs go to each device.

---

[1] For all the systems that we will look at, $\mathbf{E}[R(1)] = D$. However, one can imagine some systems where $\mathbf{E}[R(1)] \neq D$. For example, suppose that a job can utilize two devices at the same exact time. Then $\mathbf{E}[R(1)]$ might be less than $D = \sum D_i$. In this case, we want to make sure that we use $\mathbf{E}[R(1)]$, in Theorem 7.1, **not** D.

2.

$$X = \frac{N}{\mathbf{E}\,[R] + \mathbf{E}\,[Z]}$$

$$\leq \frac{N}{D + \mathbf{E}\,[Z]},$$

where the inequality comes from (7.2) and thus forms a tight bound for small N.

∎

The power of this theorem lies in the fact that the bounds are *asymptotes*. That is, for large N or small N, the curve comes very close to touching these lines.

It is possible to get even tighter estimates (upper and lower bound on X and $\mathbf{E}\,[R]$ by using the Balanced Bounds technique, described in Lazowska et al.'s book [117] (Section 5.4).

A Simple Example of Bounds

Let's examine a system like the one in Figure 7.1. Suppose

- $\mathbf{E}\,[Z] = 18$
- $\mathbf{E}\,[D_{\text{CPU}}] = 5$ sec
- $\mathbf{E}\,[D_{\text{disk a}}] = 4$ sec
- $\mathbf{E}\,[D_{\text{disk b}}] = 3$ sec

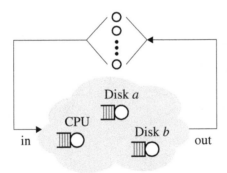

Figure 7.1. Closed system example.

Our goal is to determine X and $\mathbf{E}\,[R]$ as a function of the multiprogramming level N. From this information, we see that

- $D = 5 + 4 + 3 = 12$ seconds
- $D_{\text{max}} = 5$ (the CPU is the bottleneck device)

Thus $X \leq \min\{N/30, 1/5\}$, and $\mathbf{E}\,[R] \geq \max\{12, 5N - 18\}$. This is illustrated in Figures 7.2(a) and 7.2(b), which give us a good estimate of the performance of the system as a function of N. Observe that the point at which the asymptotes cross is denoted by N^*.

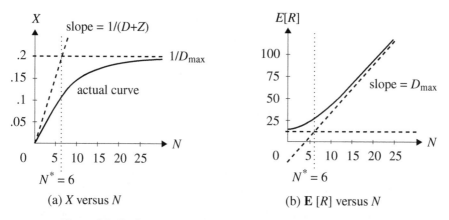

(a) X versus N (b) $\mathbf{E}[R]$ versus N

Figure 7.2. Performance as a function of multiprogramming level, N.

7.3 Modification Analysis for Closed Systems

We start with some motivation for where we are going.

A Simple, but Counterintuitive Example

Consider the very simple closed network shown in Figure 7.3(a). Let's suppose that N is high for this system. In this network both servers have service rate $\mu = 1/3$. Now consider the "improvement" to the system shown in Figure 7.3(b), where one of the servers has been replaced with a faster server of service rate $\mu = 1/2$.

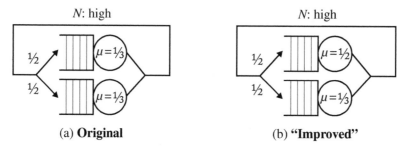

(a) **Original**   (b) **"Improved"**

Figure 7.3. A simple system and the "improved" system.

Question: How much does the throughput improve in going from Figure 7.3(a) to Figure 7.3(b)? How much does the mean response time improve?

Answer: Neither throughput nor mean response time changes! This is because we are only looking at the high N regime, which is dominated by $D_{\max}$, and $D_{\max}$ has not changed. Yes, this is counterintuitive. We examine this result more carefully in Exercise 7.2.

For now, let's continue with our discussion . . .

Important Observations

Looking at the asymptotic bounds, we make the following observations:

- The knee of the X and $\mathbf{E}[R]$ curves occurs at some point N, which we denote by N^*, where $N^* = \frac{D + \mathbf{E}[Z]}{D_{\max}}$.

  Question: What does N^* represent?

  Answer: N^* represents the point beyond which there must be some queueing in the system ($\mathbf{E}[R] > D$).

- For fixed $N > N^*$, to get more throughput, one must decrease $D_{\max}$. To get lower response time, one must similarly decrease $D_{\max}$. Other changes will be largely ineffective.

- To expand on the previous item, let us suppose we decrease some other D_i, like $D_{\text{next\_to\_max}}$. What happens? The heavy load asymptote in both X and $\mathbf{E}[R]$ does not change, so performance for $N \gg N^*$ does not change. Performance for $N \ll N^*$ will improve a little because D will drop. For the graph of X versus N, when D decreases, the light-load asymptote will get a little steeper (better). For the graph of $\mathbf{E}[R]$ versus N, when D decreases, the light-load asymptote will get a little lower (better).

Question: What happens if $\mathbf{E}[Z]$ goes to zero (the batch case)?

Answer: N^* decreases, meaning that the domination of $D_{\max}$ occurs with fewer jobs in the system.

Summary: To summarize, the device corresponding to $D_{\max}$ is the **bottleneck device**. The bottleneck device is the *key limiting factor* to improving system performance. Improving other devices will have little effect. The first step in improving system performance is to identify the bottleneck device.

7.4 More Modification Analysis Examples

Simple Example

Refer to the system in Figure 7.4, with $N = 20$, and $\mathbf{E}[Z] = 5$. Now consider the following two systems:

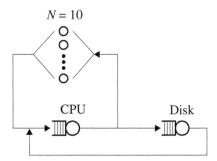

Figure 7.4. Simple closed system.

1. **System A** looks like Figure 7.4 with $D_{\text{cpu}} = 4.6$ and $D_{\text{disk}} = 4.0$.
2. **System B** looks like Figure 7.4 with $D_{\text{cpu}} = 4.9$ and $D_{\text{disk}} = 1.9$ (a slightly slower CPU and a much faster disk).

Question: Which system has higher throughput?

Answer: $N_A^* = \frac{D + \mathbf{E}[Z]}{D_{\max}} = \frac{13.6}{4.6} < 3$ and $N_B^* = \frac{11.8}{4.9} < 3$. So $N \gg N^*$ for both systems. Thus System A wins, because it has a lower $D_{\max}$.

Harder Example

The following measurements were obtained for an interactive system[2]:

- $T = 650$ seconds (the length of the observation interval)
- $B_{cpu} = 400$ seconds
- $B_{slowdisk} = 100$ seconds
- $B_{fastdisk} = 600$ seconds
- $C = C_{cpu} = 200$ jobs
- $C_{slowdisk} = 2{,}000$ jobs
- $C_{fastdisk} = 20{,}000$ jobs
- $\mathbf{E}[Z] = 15$ seconds
- $N = 20$ users

The above are typically easy-to-measure quantities.

In this example, we examine four possible improvements (modifications) – hence the name "modification analysis."

1. **Faster CPU:** Replace the CPU with one that is twice as fast.
2. **Balancing slow and fast disks:** Shift some files from the fast disk to the slow disk, balancing their demand.
3. **Second fast disk:** Buy a second fast disk to handle half the load of the busier existing fast disk.
4. **Balancing among three disks plus faster CPU:** Make all three improvements together: Buy a second fast disk, balance the load across all three disks, and also replace the CPU with a faster one.

To evaluate these modifications, we need to derive the following quantities. Note that we sometimes drop the expectation symbols around a random variable when it is obvious that they are implied.

- $D_{cpu} = B_{cpu}/C = 400$ sec$/200$ jobs $= 2.0$ sec/job
- $D_{slowdisk} = B_{slowdisk}/C = 100$ sec$/200$ jobs $= 0.5$ sec/job
- $D_{fastdisk} = B_{fastdisk}/C = 600$ sec$/200$ jobs $= 3.0$ sec/job
- $\mathbf{E}[V_{cpu}] = C_{cpu}/C = 200$ visits$/200$ jobs $= 1$ visit/job
- $\mathbf{E}[V_{slowdisk}] = C_{slowdisk}/C = 2{,}000$ visits$/200$ job $= 10$ visits/job
- $\mathbf{E}[V_{fastdisk}] = C_{fastdisk}/C = 20{,}000$ visits$/200$ job $= 100$ visits/job
- $\mathbf{E}[S_{cpu}] = B_{cpu}/C_{cpu} = 400$ sec$/200$ visits $= 2.0$ sec/visit
- $\mathbf{E}[S_{slowdisk}] = B_{slowdisk}/C_{slowdisk} = 100$ sec$/2{,}000$ visits $= .05$ sec/visit
- $\mathbf{E}[S_{fastdisk}] = B_{fastdisk}/C_{fastdisk} = 600$ sec$/20{,}000$ visits $= .03$ sec/visit

---

[2] Just as most fairy tales start with "once upon a time," most performance analysis problems begin with "the following measurements were obtained."

Now let's examine the four possible modifications:

1. **Faster CPU:** Originally, $D_{\max} = 3$ sec/job, $D = 5.5$, $N^* = \frac{20.5}{3} \approx 7 \ll N$. $D_{\text{cpu}} \to 1$ sec/job does not change $D_{\max} = 3$ sec/job. Notice that N^* hardly changes at all. The fast disk is the bottleneck. We can never get more than 1 job done every 3 seconds on average.

2. **Balancing slow and fast disks:** Shift some files from the fast disk to the slow disk, balancing their demand. To do this we need that

$$V_{\text{slow}} + V_{\text{fast}} = 110 \text{ as originally}$$

but $S_{\text{slow}} \cdot V_{\text{slow}} = S_{\text{fast}} \cdot V_{\text{fast}}$ because we are balancing the demand.

Solving this system of linear equations yields the new demands $D_{\text{slow}} = D_{\text{fast}} = 2.06$. Now, $D_{\max} = 2.06$ sec/job, although D increases slightly because some files have been moved from the fast disk to the slow disk.

3. **Second fast disk:** We keep $D_{\text{slow}} = 0.5$, the same as before. However, we buy a second fast disk to handle half the load of the original fast disk. So now

$$D_{\text{fast1}} = D_{\text{fast2}} = 1.5 \text{ sec/job.}$$

Thus our new $D_{\max}$ is 2.0 sec/job (the CPU becomes the bottleneck).

4. **Balancing among three disks plus faster CPU:** We now make the CPU faster *and* balance load across all three disks, so

$$V_{\text{slow}} + V_{\text{fast1}} + V_{\text{fast2}} = 110.$$
$$S_{\text{slow}} \cdot V_{\text{slow}} = S_{\text{fast1}} \cdot V_{\text{fast1}} = S_{\text{fast2}} \cdot V_{\text{fast2}}.$$

Solving these simultaneous equations yields: $D_{\text{disk1}} = D_{\text{disk2}} = D_{\text{disk3}} = 1.27$. So $D_{\max} = 1.27$, since we cut D_{cpu} to 1 already.

A graph of the results is shown in Figure 7.5. Assuming N is not too small, we conclude the following:

- Change 1 is insignificant.
- Changes 2 and 3 are about the same, which is interesting because change 2 was achieved without any hardware expense.
- Change 4 yields the most dramatic improvement.

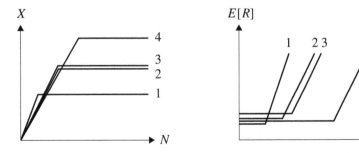

Figure 7.5. Throughput and response time versus N, showing the effects of four possible improvements from the harder example, where the improvements are labeled 1, 2, 3, and 4.

Concluding Remarks

The salient features of modification analysis are that (i) it is easy and computationally feasible; (ii) it does not rely on any assumptions about the distribution of the service time, the interarrival time, or the scheduling order used for serving jobs; and (iii) although it only yields bounds, if N is sufficiently far from N^* these bounds are all we need to analyze proposed changes.

7.5 Comparison of Closed and Open Networks

The asymptotic bounds in this chapter were for closed networks.

Question: Why don't they make sense for open networks?

Answer: Because they are not *asymptotic* bounds in the open case. For open networks, it is still true that $X \leq 1/D_{\max}$. For example, if jobs require 3 seconds of service on average, there is no way that we can complete more than 1 job every 3 seconds on average. However, we already know that $X = \lambda$, so $1/D_{\max}$ is an upper bound on X, but not necessarily a tight upper bound. Thus, our corresponding bound on $\mathbf{E}[R]$ for large N is also not tight.

However, the lessons of this chapter will still be true in the open network case if the outside arrival rate is high enough that X is close to $1/D_{\max}$: Alleviate the bottleneck device!

As an interesting example of the difference between closed and open networks, consider Figure 7.3. In the closed network shown, it did not help to speed up only one of the two devices (under probabilistic routing). However, consider the same network now in the form of an open network. The mean response time, $\mathbf{E}[T]$, will certainly improve by speeding up just one of the two devices.

7.6 Readings

A few years ago, one of the smart, industrious students studying this material in my class, Eno Thereska, decided that operational laws might actually be important for real computer systems design (unimaginable!). So he got together with another smart student who had also taken the class, Dushyanth Narayanan, and they wrote a paper [175] on self-predicting storage systems. This led to a series of papers, all dealing with predictions possible via operational laws, and eventually to Eno's Ph.D. thesis on how operational laws can be applied to storage performance prediction [174]. Eno and Dushyanth continue to leverage operational laws today.

That's it! Time to throw on that suit and go make some money!

7.7 Exercises

7.1 Outside Arrival Rates – Open Networks
Consider an open network consisting of two devices. Packets arrive to device 1 from outside with rate r_1 jobs/sec. Packets arrive to device 2 from outside with

rate $r_2 = 10$ jobs/sec. Assume 30% of the packets completing service at device 1 will next queue up at device 2 (the rest leave the system). Assume 50% of the packets completing service at device 2 will next queue up at device 1 (the rest leave the system). The mean service time at device 1 is $\mathbf{E}[S_1] = .1$ sec. The mean service time at device 2 is $\mathbf{E}[S_2] = .05$ sec.

(a) In this network, how high can we make r_1?

(b) When r_1 is maximized, what is the utilization of device 2?

7.2 Open versus Closed

Consider the system in Figure 7.6. Suppose that server 2 is replaced by one exactly twice as fast.

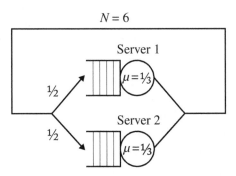

Figure 7.6. The system prior to improvement.

(a) Does this replacement result in significant improvement in the mean response time of the network? Explain via operational laws.

(b) Explain your answer to (a) by showing a time-line of where the jobs are at each step, both before and after the replacement. To do this you will need to make the problem deterministic, so you should assume that the service time at each server is a constant and that jobs alternately go to server 1 and 2. This is not meant to be a proof, just an explanation of what is going on. Make sure that you extend your time-line long enough that the average response time becomes clear.

(c) Given that the replacement has been made, is there any further modification you would propose to improve the mean response time in the closed system that does not involve spending more money? By how much would your modification improve performance?

(d) If the above system were an open system, would the replacement improve the mean response time? Prove your answer. (*Note:* we do not expect you to know how to determine mean response time in an open system yet, but you can still come up with a proof.)

7.3 Modification Analysis

Marty is running his database as a closed interactive system with $N = 50$ users. Each user submits a screenful of data to the database (her "job") to process, waits until she gets back an answer from the system, spends $\mathbf{E}[Z] = 10$ seconds entering a new screenful of data (think time), and then submits that new job to the database. This process repeats ad infinitum.

Marty realizes that his system's CPU utilization and his disk utilization are both high. He considers two modifications to his database to increase throughput. The first is to buy a second CPU (new CPUs on the market run at *twice* the speed of old ones) and divide the CPU load among the old CPU and the new one according to some optimal split. The second is to buy a second disk (new disks on the market run at *three times* the speed of old ones) and divide the disk load among the old disk and the new one according to some optimal split.

You obtain the following measurements of Marty's original system:

- $C = 100$ (number of jobs that completed during the observation period)
- $C_{\text{CPU}} = 300$ (number of completions at the CPU during observation)
- $C_{\text{disk}} = 400$ (number of completions at the disk during observation)
- $B_{\text{CPU}} = 600$ sec (time that the CPU was busy during observation)
- $B_{\text{disk}} = 1,200$ sec (time that the disk was busy during observation)

Your job is to answer two questions:

1. Assuming that the new disk and new CPU are equally priced, which should Marty buy to increase throughput?
2. Assuming that he chooses to buy the new disk (CPU), how should he optimally split requests between the old disk (CPU) and the new one? Work this out for whichever device you chose.

7.4 More Practice with Modification Analysis – from [117]

Consider an interactive system with a CPU and two disks. The following measurement data was obtained by observing the system:

- observation interval = 17 minutes
- mean think time = 12 seconds
- number of complete transactions during observation interval = 1,600
- number of completions at CPU = 1,600
- number of fast disk accesses = 32,000
- number of slow disk accesses = 12,000
- CPU busy time = 1,080 seconds
- fast disk busy time = 400 seconds
- slow disk busy time = 600 seconds

(a) Give asymptotic bounds on throughput and response time as a function of the number of terminals.

(b) Now consider the following modifications to the system:
   1. Move all files to the fast disk.
   2. Replace the slow disk by a second fast disk.
   3. Increase the CPU speed by 50% (with the original disks).
   4. Increase the CPU speed by 50% and balance the disk load across the two fast disks.

   For each of these four modifications, compute and graph the effects on the original system. Explain in words the effect when the multiprogramming level, N, is small and when N is large.

7.5 Proportional Power – based on [69]

In the world of power distribution, one reasonable approximation is that the power that is allocated to a machine is proportional to the speed at which that machine can run. In this problem we assume that, if a machine is allocated power w, then that machine processes jobs at speed w jobs/sec.

Consider a closed batch system with two servers and N users, where N is assumed to be high. Assume that each job, with probability p, is routed to server 1 for processing and, with probability $1 - p$, is routed to server 2. It may help to look at Figure 7.6 here.

You are given a total power budget W, which you need to distribute between the two machines. You can *choose* any way of dividing the power budget W between the two machines, and you can also *choose* any value you want for p, the routing probability.

(a) What choice for dividing W and for picking p will maximize the throughput of your system?

(b) Suppose that N was small. Would your answer still be the same? If so, explain why. If not, derive the optimal strategy.

7.6 Minimizing Mean Slowdown

In Exercise 6.7, we saw that the RS algorithm does not minimize mean slowdown on every arrival sequence. We have also seen that the SRPT algorithm does not minimize mean slowdown. In this problem either find an algorithm that minimizes mean slowdown or prove that no online algorithm can minimize mean slowdown on every arrival sequence (an online algorithm is one that does not know future arrivals).

From Markov Chains to Simple Queues

Part IV introduces both discrete-time Markov chains (referred to as DTMCs) and continuous-time Markov chains (referred to as CTMCs). These allow us to model systems in much greater detail and to answer distributional questions, such as "What is the probability that there are k jobs queued at server i?" Markov chains are extremely powerful. However, only certain problems can be modeled via Markov chains. These are problems that exhibit the *Markovian* property, which allows the future behavior to be independent of all past behavior.

Chapter 8 introduces DTMCs and the Markovian property. We purposely defer the more theoretical issues surrounding ergodicity, including the existence of a limiting distribution and the equivalence between time averages and ensemble averages, to Chapter 9. Less theoretically inclined readers may wish to skim Chapter 9 during a first reading. Chapter 10 considers some real-world examples of DTMCs in computing today, including Google's PageRank algorithm and the Aloha (Ethernet) protocol. This chapter also considers more complex DTMCs that occur naturally and how generating functions can be used to solve them.

Next we transition to CTMCs. Chapter 11 discusses the Markovian property of the Exponential distribution and the Poisson process, which make these very applicable to CTMCs. Chapter 12 shows an easy way to translate all that we learned for DTMCs to CTMCs. Chapter 13 applies CTMC theory to analyzing the M/M/1 single-server queue and also covers the PASTA property.

CTMCs will be used extensively in Part V to analyze multi-server systems.

CHAPTER 8

Discrete-Time Markov Chains

Let's review what we already know how to do at this point.

Closed Systems

For closed systems, we can approximate and bound the values of throughput, X, and the expected response time, $\mathbf{E}[R]$. The approximations we have developed are independent of the distribution of service times of the jobs, but require that the system is *closed*. When the multiprogramming level, N, is much higher than N^*, we have a tight bound on X and $\mathbf{E}[R]$. Also, when $N = 1$, we have a tight bound. However, for intermediate values of N, we can only approximate X and $\mathbf{E}[R]$.

Open Systems

For open systems, we cannot do very much at all yet. Consider even a single queue. If we knew $\mathbf{E}[N]$, then we could calculate $\mathbf{E}[T]$, but we do not yet know how to compute $\mathbf{E}[N]$.

Markov chain analysis is a tool for deriving the above performance metrics and in fact deriving a lot more. It will enable us to determine not only the mean number of jobs, $\mathbf{E}[N_i]$, at server i of a queueing network, but also the full distribution of the number of jobs at the server.

All the chapters in Parts IV and V will exploit the power of Markov chain analysis. It is important, however, to keep in mind that not all systems can readily be modeled using Markov chains. We will see that, in queueing networks where the service times at a server are Exponentially distributed and the interarrival times of jobs are also Exponentially distributed, the system can often be exactly modeled by a Markov chain. This is true because the Exponential distribution has the Markovian property (a.k.a. memoryless property), meaning that the remaining time until a service completes or a new job arrives is independent of how long we have waited so far. Properties of the Exponential distribution are covered in Chapter 11. The same holds for Geometrically distributed interarrival times and service times, where jobs arrive or complete with some fixed probability at each time step, independent of the past. All of this will become more clear after we define discrete-time Markov chains in this chapter.

By contrast, other workload distributions do not have the Markovian property, and thus are harder to model via a Markov chain. In many cases, however, even these non-Markovian workloads can be approximated by *mixtures* of Exponential distributions, and hence still lend themselves to Markov chain analysis, as explained in Chapter 21.

Markov chains are extremely powerful and are used to model problems in computer science, statistics, physics, biology, operations research, and business – you name it! They are used extensively in machine learning, computer science theory, and in all areas of computer system modeling (analysis of networking protocols, memory management protocols, server performance, capacity provisioning, disk protocols, etc.). Markov chains are also very common in operations research, including supply-chain management and inventory management.

As we study Markov chains, be on the lookout for Markov chains in your own work and the world around you. They are everywhere!

8.1 Discrete-Time versus Continuous-Time Markov Chains

We now cover Markov chains in depth, starting with Discrete-Time Markov Chains (DTMCs). In a DTMC, the world is broken up into synchronized time steps. An event (arrival or departure) can only occur at the end of a time step. This property makes DTMCs a little odd for modeling computer systems. However, there are many other problems that are well modeled by DTMCs.

In Continuous-Time Markov Chains (CTMCs) events can happen at any moment in time. This makes CTMCs convenient for modeling systems.

Note: Solving Markov chains typically requires solving large systems of simultaneous equations. We therefore recommend that readers take the time to familiarize themselves with the three M's: Matlab, Mathematica, and Maple. The latter two are particularly useful in that they allow symbolic computation.

8.2 Definition of a DTMC

A *stochastic process* is simply a sequence of random variables.

Definition 8.1 A *DTMC* (discrete-time Markov chain) is a stochastic process $\{X_n, n = 0, 1, 2, \ldots\}$, where X_n denotes the state at (discrete) time step n and such that, $\forall n \geq 0$, $\forall i, j$, and $\forall i_0, \ldots, i_{n-1}$,

$$\mathbf{P}\{X_{n+1} = j \mid X_n = i, X_{n-1} = i_{n-1}, \ldots, X_0 = i_0\} = \mathbf{P}\{X_{n+1} = j \mid X_n = i\}$$
$$= P_{ij} \text{ (by stationarity),}$$

where P_{ij} is independent of the time step and of past history.

The first equality in the definition of a DTMC indicates the application of the Markovian property.

Definition 8.2 The *Markovian Property* states that the conditional distribution of any future state X_{n+1}, given past states $X_0, X_1, \ldots, X_{n-1}$, and given the present state X_n, is independent of past states and depends only on the present state X_n.

The second equality in the definition of a DTMC follows from the "stationary" property, which indicates that the transition probability is independent of time.

Definition 8.3 The *transition probability matrix* associated with any DTMC is a matrix, $\mathbf{P}$, whose (i, j)th entry, P_{ij}, represents the probability of moving to state j on the next transition, given that the current state is i.

Observe that the transition probability matrix, $\mathbf{P}$, might have infinite order, if there are infinitely many states. Also observe that by definition, $\sum_j P_{ij} = 1$, $\forall i$, because, given that the DTMC is in state i, it must next transition to some state j.

We begin this chapter by focusing on DTMCs with a **finite number of states**, M. Later in the chapter, we generalize to DTMCs with an infinite number of states.

In this chapter, we do *not* discuss issues of ergodicity. Specifically, we do not dwell on questions of the existence of limiting probabilities. We simply assume that there exists some limiting probability of being in each state of the chain (to be defined soon), and we defer all discussion of the existence of these limits to Chapter 9.

8.3 Examples of Finite-State DTMCs

We start with a few examples of some simple Markov chains to illustrate the key concepts. More involved and interesting examples are saved for the exercises.

8.3.1 *Repair Facility Problem*

A machine is either working or in the repair center. If it is working today, then there is a 95% chance that it will be working tomorrow. If it is in the repair center today, then there is a 40% chance that it will be working tomorrow. We are interested in questions like "what fraction of time does my machine spend in the repair shop?"

Question: Describe the DTMC for the repair facility problem.

Answer: There are two states, "Working" and "Broken," where "Broken" denotes that the machine is in repair. The transition probability matrix is

$$\mathbf{P} = \begin{array}{c} W \\ B \end{array} \begin{array}{cc} W & B \\ \begin{bmatrix} 0.95 & 0.05 \\ 0.40 & 0.60 \end{bmatrix} \end{array}.$$

The Markov chain diagram is shown in Figure 8.1.

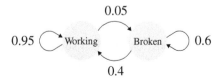

Figure 8.1. Markov chain for repair facility problem.

Question: Now suppose that after the machine remains broken for 4 days, the machine is replaced with a new machine. How does the DTMC diagram change?

Answer: The revised DTMC is shown in Figure 8.2.

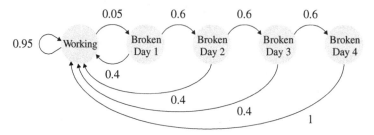

Figure 8.2. Markov chain for repair facility problem with 4-day limit.

8.3.2 *Umbrella Problem*

An absent-minded professor has two umbrellas that she uses when commuting from home to office and back. If it rains and an umbrella is available in her location, she takes it. If it is not raining, she always forgets to take an umbrella. Suppose that it rains with probability p each time she commutes, independently of prior commutes. Our eventual goal is to determine the fraction of commutes during which the professor gets wet.[1]

Question: What is the state space?

Hint: You can model this with three states!

Answer: The states track the number of umbrellas available at the current location, regardless of what this current location is. The DTMC is shown in Figure 8.3.

The transition probability matrix is $\mathbf{P} = \begin{bmatrix} 0 & 0 & 1 \\ 0 & 1-p & p \\ 1-p & p & 0 \end{bmatrix}$.

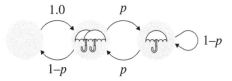

Figure 8.3. DTMC for umbrella problem.

8.3.3 *Program Analysis Problem*

A program has three types of instructions: CPU instructions (C), Memory instructions (M), and User interaction instructions (U). In analyzing the program, we note that

---

[1] The umbrella example is borrowed from Bertsekas & Gallager [18].

a C instruction with probability 0.7 is followed by another C instruction, but with probability 0.2 is followed by an M instruction and with probability 0.1 is followed by a U instruction. We also note that an M instruction with probability 0.1 is followed by another M instruction, but with probability 0.8 is followed by a C instruction, and with probability 0.1 is followed by a U instruction. Finally, a U instruction, with probability 0.9 is followed by a C instruction, and with probability 0.1 is followed by an M instruction.

In the exercises for this chapter and the next, we answer questions like, "What is the fraction of C instructions?" and "What is the mean length of the instruction sequence between consecutive M instructions?" For now, we simply note that the program can be represented as a Markov chain with the transition probability matrix, **P**:

$$
\mathbf{P} = \begin{array}{c} \\ C \\ M \\ U \end{array}
\begin{array}{ccc} C & M & U \\ \left[\begin{array}{ccc} 0.7 & 0.2 & 0.1 \\ 0.8 & 0.1 & 0.1 \\ 0.9 & 0.1 & 0 \end{array}\right] \end{array}
$$

8.4 Powers of P: n-Step Transition Probabilities

Let $\mathbf{P}^n = \mathbf{P} \cdot \mathbf{P} \cdots \mathbf{P}$, multiplied n times. We will use the notation P_{ij}^n to denote $\left(\mathbf{P}^n\right)_{ij}$.

Question: What does P_{ij}^n represent?

Answer: To answer this, we first consider two examples.

Umbrella Problem

Consider the umbrella problem from before where the chance of rain on any given day is $p = 0.4$. We then have

$$
\mathbf{P} = \begin{bmatrix} 0 & 0 & 1 \\ 0 & 0.6 & 0.4 \\ 0.6 & 0.4 & 0 \end{bmatrix}, \quad
\mathbf{P}^5 = \begin{bmatrix} .06 & .30 & .64 \\ .18 & .38 & .44 \\ .38 & .44 & .18 \end{bmatrix}, \quad
\mathbf{P}^{30} = \begin{bmatrix} .230 & .385 & .385 \\ .230 & .385 & .385 \\ .230 & .385 & .385 \end{bmatrix}.
$$

Observe that all the rows become the *same*! Note also that, for all the above powers, each row sums to 1.

Repair Facility Problem

Now, consider again the simple repair facility problem, with general transition probability matrix **P**:

$$
\mathbf{P} = \begin{bmatrix} 1-a & a \\ b & 1-b \end{bmatrix}, \quad 0 < a < 1, \quad 0 < b < 1
$$

You should be able to prove by induction that

$$\mathbf{P}^n = \begin{bmatrix} \frac{b+a(1-a-b)^n}{a+b} & \frac{a-a(1-a-b)^n}{a+b} \\ \frac{b-b(1-a-b)^n}{a+b} & \frac{a+b(1-a-b)^n}{a+b} \end{bmatrix}.$$

$$\lim_{n\to\infty} \mathbf{P}^n = \begin{bmatrix} \frac{b}{a+b} & \frac{a}{a+b} \\ \frac{b}{a+b} & \frac{a}{a+b} \end{bmatrix}.$$

Question: Again, all rows are the same. Why? What is the meaning of the row?

Hint: Consider a DTMC in state i. Suppose we want to know the probability that it will be in state j two steps from now. To go from state i to state j in two steps, the DTMC must have passed through some state k after the first step. Below we condition on this intermediate state k:

For an M-state DTMC, as shown in Figure 8.4,

$$P_{ij}^2 = \sum_{k=0}^{M-1} P_{ik} \cdot P_{kj}$$

$$= \text{Probability that after 2 steps we will be in state } j, \text{ given that}$$

we are in state i now.

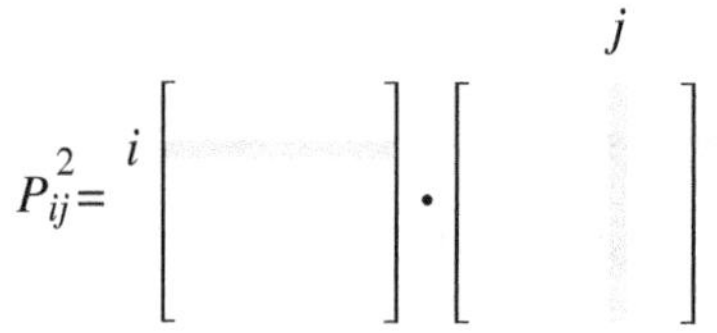

Figure 8.4. P_{ij}^2.

Likewise, the n-wise product can be viewed as

$$P_{ij}^n = \sum_{k=0}^{M-1} P_{ik}^{n-1} P_{kj}$$

$$= \text{Probability of being in state } j \text{ in } n \text{ steps, given we are in state } i \text{ now.}$$

Limiting Probabilities

We now move on to looking at the limit. Consider the (i,j)th entry of the power matrix $\mathbf{P}^n$ for large n:

$$\lim_{n\to\infty} P_{ij}^n = \left(\lim_{n\to\infty} \mathbf{P}^n \right)_{ij}$$

This quantity represents the limiting probability of being in state j infinitely far into the future, given that we started in state i.

Question: So what is the limiting probability of having 0 umbrellas?

Answer: According to $\mathbf{P}^{30}$, it is 0.23.

Question: The fact that the rows of $\lim_{n \to \infty} \mathbf{P}^n$ are all the same is interesting because it says what?

Answer: It says that the starting state (i) does not matter.

Definition 8.4 Let

$$\pi_j = \lim_{n \to \infty} P_{ij}^n.$$

π_j represents the **limiting probability** that the chain is in state j (independent of the starting state i). For an M-state DTMC, with states $0, 1, \ldots, M - 1$,

$$\vec{\pi} = (\pi_0, \pi_1, \ldots, \pi_{M-1}), \quad \text{where} \quad \sum_{i=0}^{M-1} \pi_i = 1$$

represents the **limiting distribution** of being in each state.

Important Note: As defined, π_j is a limit. Yet it is not at all obvious that the limit π_j exists! It is also not obvious that $\vec{\pi}$ represents a distribution (i.e., $\sum_i \pi_i = 1$), although this latter part turns out to be easy to see (Exercise 8.2). For the rest of this chapter, we assume that the limiting probabilities exist. In Chapter 9 we look at the existence question in detail.

Question: So what is the limiting probability that the professor gets wet?

Answer: The professor gets wet if both (i) the state is 0, that is there are zero umbrellas in the current location; and (ii) it is raining. So the limiting probability that the professor gets wet on any given day is $\pi_0 \cdot p = (0.23)(0.4) = .092$.

Question: Can you see why the limiting probability of having 1 umbrella is equal to the limiting probability of having 2 umbrellas?

Answer: This is a little tricky. Notice that if we are only looking at the DTMC from the perspective of 1 versus 2 umbrellas, then the chain becomes symmetric. The collapsed chain is shown in Figure 8.5.

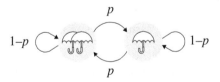

Figure 8.5. Compressed umbrella problem.

8.5 Stationary Equations

Question: Based only on what we have learned so far, how do we determine $\pi_j = \lim_{n \to \infty} P_{ij}^n$?

Answer: We take the transition probability matrix $\mathbf{P}$ and raise it to the nth power for some large n and look at the jth column, any row.

Question: Multiplying $\mathbf{P}$ by itself many times sounds quite onerous. Also, it seems one might need to perform a very large number of multiplications if the Markov chain is large. Is there a more efficient way?

Answer: Yes, by solving stationary equations, given in Definition 8.5.

Definition 8.5 A probability distribution $\vec{\pi} = (\pi_0, \pi_1, \ldots, \pi_{M-1})$ is said to be *stationary* for the Markov chain if

$$\vec{\pi} \cdot \mathbf{P} = \vec{\pi} \quad \text{and} \quad \sum_{i=0}^{M-1} \pi_i = 1.$$

These equations are referred to as the **stationary equations**. Definition 8.5 says that $\vec{\pi}$ is stationary if

$$\sum_{i=0}^{M-1} \pi_i P_{ij} = \pi_j, \ \forall j \quad \text{and} \quad \sum_{i=0}^{M-1} \pi_i = 1. \tag{8.1}$$

Question: What does the left-hand-side (LHS) of the first equation in (8.1) represent?

Answer: The LHS represents the probability of being in state j one transition from now, given that the current probability distribution on the states is $\vec{\pi}$. So equation (8.1) says that if we start out distributed according to $\vec{\pi}$, then one step later our probability of being in each state will still follow distribution $\vec{\pi}$. Thus from then on we will always have the same probability distribution on the states. Hence we call the distribution "stationary."

8.6 The Stationary Distribution Equals the Limiting Distribution

The following theorem relates the *limiting distribution* to the *stationary distribution* for a finite-state DTMC. Specifically, the theorem says that for a finite-state DTMC, the stationary distribution obtained by solving (8.1) is unique and represents the limiting probabilities of being in each state, assuming these limiting probabilities exist.

Theorem 8.6 (Stationary distribution = Limiting distribution) *Given a finite-state DTMC with M states, let*

$$\pi_j = \lim_{n \to \infty} P_{ij}^n > 0$$

be the limiting probability of being in state j and let

$$\vec{\pi} = (\pi_0, \pi_1, \ldots, \pi_{M-1}), \quad \text{where} \quad \sum_{i=0}^{M-1} \pi_i = 1$$

be the limiting distribution. Assuming that the limiting distribution exists, then $\vec{\pi}$ is also a stationary distribution and no *other stationary distribution exists.*

Proof We will prove two things about the limiting distribution $\vec{\pi}$.

1. We will prove that $\{\pi_j, \ j = 0, 1, 2, \ldots, M - 1\}$ is a stationary distribution. Hence at least one stationary distribution exists.
2. We will prove that any stationary distribution must be equal to the limiting distribution.

Throughout, $\{\pi_j, \ j = 0, 1, 2, \ldots, M - 1\}$ is used to refer to the limiting distribution.

Part 1: Proof that $\{\pi_j, \ j = 0, 1, 2, \ldots, M - 1\}$ is a stationary distribution:

$$\pi_j = \lim_{n \to \infty} P_{ij}^{n+1} = \lim_{n \to \infty} \sum_{k=0}^{M-1} P_{ik}^n \cdot P_{kj} = \sum_{k=0}^{M-1} \lim_{n \to \infty} P_{ik}^n P_{kj} = \sum_{k=0}^{M-1} \pi_k P_{kj}$$

Hence $\vec{\pi}$ satisfies the stationary equations.

Part 2: Proof that any stationary distribution must equal the limiting distribution:

Let $\vec{\pi}'$ be any stationary probability distribution. As usual, $\vec{\pi}$ represents the limiting probability distribution. We will prove that $\vec{\pi}' = \vec{\pi}$, and specifically that $\pi_j' = \pi_j$.

Let's assume that we start at time 0 with distribution $\vec{\pi}'$. Then

$$\pi_j' = \mathbf{P}\{X_0 = j\} = \mathbf{P}\{X_n = j\} \text{ because } \vec{\pi}' \text{ is stationary.}$$

So

$$\begin{aligned}
\pi_j' &= \mathbf{P}\{X_n = j\}, \quad \forall n \\
&= \sum_{i=0}^{M-1} \mathbf{P}\{X_n = j \mid X_0 = i\} \cdot \mathbf{P}\{X_0 = i\}, \quad \forall n \\
&= \sum_{i=0}^{M-1} P_{ij}^n \pi_i', \quad \forall n.
\end{aligned}$$

So

$$\pi_j' = \lim_{n \to \infty} \pi_j' = \lim_{n \to \infty} \sum_{i=0}^{M-1} P_{ij}^n \pi_i' = \sum_{i=0}^{M-1} \lim_{n \to \infty} P_{ij}^n \pi_i' = \sum_{i=0}^{M-1} \pi_j \pi_i' = \pi_j \sum_{i=0}^{M-1} \pi_i' = \pi_j.$$

$\blacksquare$

Note that we were allowed to pull the limit into the summation sign in both parts because we had finite sums (M is finite).

One more thing: In the literature you often see the phrase "Consider a stationary Markov chain," or "Consider the following Markov chain in steady state..."

> **Definition 8.7** A Markov chain for which the limiting probabilities exist is said to be ***stationary*** or in ***steady state*** if the initial state is chosen according to the stationary probabilities.

Summary: Finding the Limiting Probabilities in a Finite-State DTMC:

By Theorem 8.6, given the limiting distribution $\{\pi_j,\ j = 0, 1, 2, \ldots, M-1\}$ exists, we can obtain it by solving the stationary equations

$$\vec{\pi} \cdot \mathbf{P} = \vec{\pi} \quad \text{and} \quad \sum_{i=0}^{M-1} \pi_i = 1$$

where $\vec{\pi} = (\pi_0, \pi_1, \ldots, \pi_{M-1})$.

8.7 Examples of Solving Stationary Equations

8.7.1 *Repair Facility Problem with Cost*

Consider again the repair facility problem represented by the finite-state DTMC shown here:

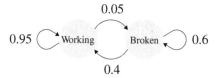

We are interested in the following type of question.

Question: The help desk is trying to figure out how much to charge me for maintaining my machine. They figure that it costs them $300 every day that my machine is in repair. What will my annual repair bill be?

To answer this question, we first derive the limiting distribution $\vec{\pi} = (\pi_W, \pi_B)$ for this chain. We solve the stationary equations to get $\vec{\pi}$ as follows:

$$\vec{\pi} = \vec{\pi} \cdot \mathbf{P}, \text{ where } \mathbf{P} = \begin{pmatrix} .95 & .05 \\ .4 & .6 \end{pmatrix}$$

$$\pi_W + \pi_B = 1$$

This translates to the following equations:

$$\pi_W = \pi_W \cdot .95 + \pi_B \cdot .4$$
$$\pi_B = \pi_W \cdot .05 + \pi_B \cdot .6$$
$$\pi_W + \pi_B = 1$$

Question: What do you notice about the first two equations above?

Answer: They are identical! In general, if $\vec{\pi} = \vec{\pi} \cdot \mathbf{P}$ results in M equations, only $M - 1$ of these will be linearly independent. Fortunately, the last equation above (the normalization condition) is there to help us out. Solving, we get $\pi_W = \frac{8}{9}$ and $\pi_B = \frac{1}{9}$.

By Theorem 8.6, the stationary distribution also represents the limiting probability distribution. Thus my machine is broken 1 out of every 9 days on average. The expected daily cost is $\frac{1}{9} \cdot 300 = \$33.33$ (with an annual cost of more than \$12,000).

8.7.2 *Umbrella Problem*

Consider again the umbrella problem with probability p of rain each day. Before, we raised the transition probability matrix $\mathbf{P}$ to the nth power to get the limiting probabilities, in the case where $p = 0.4$. Now let's use the stationary equations to obtain the limiting probabilities for general p.

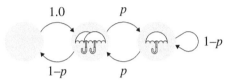

We solve the following stationary equations to get the limiting probabilities:

$$\pi_0 = \pi_2 \cdot (1 - p)$$
$$\pi_1 = \pi_1 \cdot (1 - p) + \pi_2 \cdot p$$
$$\pi_2 = \pi_0 \cdot 1 + \pi_1 \cdot p$$
$$\pi_0 + \pi_1 + \pi_2 = 1$$

Their solution is

$$\pi_0 = \frac{1 - p}{3 - p}. \qquad \pi_1 = \frac{1}{3 - p}. \qquad \pi_2 = \frac{1}{3 - p}.$$

Question: Suppose the probability of rain is $p = 0.6$. What fraction of days does the professor get soaked?

Answer: The professor gets wet if she has zero umbrellas and it is raining: $\pi_0 \cdot p = \frac{0.4}{2.4} \cdot 0.6 = 0.1$. Not too bad!

8.8 Infinite-State DTMCs

So far we have only talked about *finite*-state DTMCs with M states. Now we move on to infinite-state DTMCs. For a Markov chain with an infinite number of states, one can still imagine a transition probability matrix, $\mathbf{P}$, although the matrix has infinite order. We denote the limiting probability distribution on the states by

$$\vec{\pi} = (\pi_0, \pi_1, \pi_2, \dots) \quad \text{where} \quad \pi_j = \lim_{n \to \infty} P_{ij}^n \quad \text{and} \quad \sum_{j=0}^{\infty} \pi_j = 1.$$

Infinite-state Markov chains are common in modeling systems where the number of customers or jobs is unbounded, and thus the state space is unbounded.

8.9 Infinite-State Stationarity Result

We have seen that for a finite-state DTMC, if the limiting distribution exists, then the limiting distribution and stationary distribution are equivalent (Theorem 8.6). The same result holds for infinite-state DTMCs.

> **Theorem 8.8 (Stationary distribution = Limiting distribution)** *Given an infinite-state DTMC, let*
>
> $$\pi_j = \lim_{n \to \infty} P_{ij}^n > 0$$
>
> *be the limiting probability of being in state j and let*
>
> $$\vec{\pi} = (\pi_0, \pi_1, \pi_2, \ldots) \quad where \quad \sum_{i=0}^{\infty} \pi_i = 1$$
>
> *be the limiting distribution. Assuming that the limiting distribution exists, then $\vec{\pi}$ is also a stationary distribution and* no other *stationary distribution exists.*

Proof We will prove two things about this limiting distribution, assuming it exists.

1. We will prove that $\{\pi_j, \ j = 0, 1, 2, \ldots\}$ is a stationary distribution. Hence at least one stationary distribution exists.
2. We will prove that any stationary distribution must be equal to the limiting distribution.

Part 1: Proof that $\{\pi_j, j = 0, 1, 2, \ldots\}$ is a stationary distribution:

$$\pi_j = \lim_{n \to \infty} P_{ij}^{n+1} = \lim_{n \to \infty} \sum_{k=0}^{\infty} P_{ik}^n \cdot P_{kj} \tag{8.2}$$

Question: If we could interchange the limit and sum at this point, what would we know about π_j?

Answer: We would know that π_j is a stationary distribution – we would be done with Part 1.

Unfortunately, we cannot in general interchange the limit and sum when the sum is infinite. So what we need to do in these types of proofs is convert the infinite sum to a finite sum, make the switch, and then convert back to an infinite sum . . . carefully.

$$\pi_j = \lim_{n \to \infty} P_{ij}^{n+1}$$

$$= \lim_{n \to \infty} \sum_{k=0}^{\infty} P_{ik}^n P_{kj}$$

$$\geq \lim_{n \to \infty} \sum_{k=0}^{M} P_{ik}^n P_{kj}, \quad \forall M$$

$$= \sum_{k=0}^{M} \lim_{n \to \infty} P_{ik}^n P_{kj}, \quad \forall M$$

$$= \sum_{k=0}^{M} \pi_k P_{kj}, \quad \forall M$$

So

$$\forall M, \ \pi_j \geq \sum_{k=0}^{M} \pi_k P_{kj}$$

$$\Rightarrow \pi_j \geq \lim_{M \to \infty} \sum_{k=0}^{M} \pi_k P_{kj}$$

$$\Rightarrow \pi_j \geq \sum_{k=0}^{\infty} \pi_k P_{kj}.$$

We are almost there. We would like to prove that the above inequality is actually an equality. Suppose, by contradiction, $\exists l$ such that

$$\pi_l > \sum_{k=0}^{\infty} \pi_k P_{kl}.$$

Let's consider $\sum_{j=0}^{\infty} \pi_j$:

$$\sum_{j=0}^{\infty} \pi_j > \sum_{j=0}^{\infty} \left(\sum_{k=0}^{\infty} \pi_k P_{kj} \right) = \sum_{k=0}^{\infty} \sum_{j=0}^{\infty} \pi_k P_{kj} = \sum_{k=0}^{\infty} \pi_k \cdot 1 = 1$$

Yet this says that the sum of the limiting probabilities is strictly greater than 1, which is impossible and hence a contradiction. So we have shown that

$$\pi_j = \sum_{k=0}^{\infty} \pi_k P_{kj}. \tag{8.3}$$

Part 2: Proof that any stationary distribution must equal the limiting distribution:

Let $\vec{\pi}'$ be any stationary probability distribution. As usual, $\vec{\pi}$ represents the limiting probability distribution. Our goal is to prove that $\pi_j' = \pi_j, \forall j$.

Let's assume that we start at time 0 with distribution $\vec{\pi}'$. Then

$$\pi_j' = \mathbf{P}\{X_0 = j\} = \mathbf{P}\{X_n = j\} \text{ because } \pi_j' \text{ is stationary.}$$

So

$$\pi_j' = \mathbf{P}\{X_n = j\}$$

$$= \sum_{i=0}^{\infty} \mathbf{P}\{X_n = j \mid X_0 = i\} \cdot \mathbf{P}\{X_0 = i\}$$

$$= \sum_{i=0}^{\infty} P_{ij}^n \pi_i'$$

$$= \sum_{i=0}^{M} P_{ij}^n \pi_i' + \sum_{i=M+1}^{\infty} P_{ij}^n \pi_i' \quad \text{(for any integer } M\text{)}.$$

Observing that $0 \leq P_{ij}^n \leq 1$, we now apply the sandwich theorem to the above equation, which will allow us to prove that π_j' is bounded above and below by π_j.

$$\sum_{i=0}^{M} P_{ij}^n \pi_i' \leq \quad \pi_j' \quad \leq \sum_{i=0}^{M} P_{ij}^n \pi_i' + \sum_{i=M+1}^{\infty} \pi_i'$$

$$\lim_{n\to\infty} \sum_{i=0}^{M} P_{ij}^n \pi_i' \leq \lim_{n\to\infty} \pi_j' \leq \lim_{n\to\infty} \sum_{i=0}^{M} P_{ij}^n \pi_i' + \lim_{n\to\infty} \sum_{i=M+1}^{\infty} \pi_i'$$

$$\sum_{i=0}^{M} \pi_j \pi_i' \leq \quad \pi_j' \quad \leq \sum_{i=0}^{M} \pi_j \pi_i' + \sum_{i=M+1}^{\infty} \pi_i'$$

$$\pi_j \sum_{i=0}^{M} \pi_i' \leq \quad \pi_j' \quad \leq \pi_j \sum_{i=0}^{M} \pi_i' + \sum_{i=M+1}^{\infty} \pi_i'$$

$$\lim_{M\to\infty} \pi_j \sum_{i=0}^{M} \pi_i' \leq \lim_{M\to\infty} \pi_j' \leq \lim_{M\to\infty} \pi_j \sum_{i=0}^{M} \pi_i' + \lim_{M\to\infty} \sum_{i=M+1}^{\infty} \pi_i'$$

$$\pi_j \leq \quad \pi_j' \quad \leq \pi_j$$

Thus we have shown that $\pi_j' = \pi_j$ as desired. ∎

8.10 Solving Stationary Equations in Infinite-State DTMCs

We have seen that to obtain the limiting probability distribution $\vec{\pi}$, assuming that it exists, we only need to solve the stationary equations. Yet there are an infinite number of stationary equations! Let's see how we solve them.

Consider the example of an **unbounded queue** (see Figure 8.6). Imagine jobs (or customers) arriving at a server. These jobs queue up at the server. The server works on the job at the head of the queue, and when it finishes that job, it moves on to the next job. This server never drops jobs, but just allows them to queue.

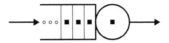

Figure 8.6. Illustration of a server with unbounded buffer.

Suppose at every time step, with probability $p = \frac{1}{40}$ one job arrives, and independently, with probability $q = \frac{1}{30}$ one job departs. Note that during a time step, we might have both an arrival and a transmission, or neither.

We will be interested in answering questions like, *what is the average number of jobs in the system?*

To answer this question, we model the problem as a DTMC with an infinite number of states: $0, 1, 2, \ldots$, representing the number of jobs at the router. Let $r = p(1 - q) = \frac{29}{1200}$ and $s = q(1 - p) = \frac{39}{1200}$, where $r < s$. Figure 8.7 shows the Markov chain for our problem.

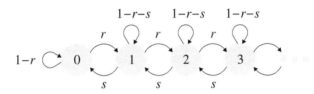

Figure 8.7. DTMC for a server with unbounded queue.

Here the transition probability matrix is infinite!

$$
\mathbf{P} = \begin{pmatrix}
1 - r & r & 0 & 0 & \cdots \\
s & 1 - r - s & r & 0 & \cdots \\
0 & s & 1 - r - s & r & \cdots \\
0 & 0 & s & 1 - r - s & \cdots \\
\vdots & \vdots & \vdots & \vdots & \vdots
\end{pmatrix}
$$

The stationary equations look like this:

$$\pi_0 = \pi_0(1 - r) + \pi_1 s$$
$$\pi_1 = \pi_0 r + \pi_1(1 - r - s) + \pi_2 s$$
$$\pi_2 = \pi_1 r + \pi_2(1 - r - s) + \pi_3 s$$
$$\pi_3 = \pi_2 r + \pi_3(1 - r - s) + \pi_4 s$$

$$\vdots$$

$$\pi_0 + \pi_1 + \pi_2 + \pi_3 + \cdots = 1$$

Question: How are we going to solve this infinite number of equations?

Hint: Observe that the first equation can be rewritten as

$$\pi_1 = \frac{r}{s}\pi_0.$$

Can you use this to express π_2 in terms of π_0?

Answer: If we substitute the above expression for π_1 into the second stationary equation, we can express π_2 in terms of π_0 as well:

$$\pi_2 = \left(\frac{r}{s}\right)^2 \pi_0$$

We can now substitute the expression for π_2 into the third stationary equation, to express π_3 in terms of π_0 as well:

$$\pi_3 = \left(\frac{r}{s}\right)^3 \pi_0$$

We can now make a general "guess":

$$\pi_i = \left(\frac{r}{s}\right)^i \pi_0$$

Question: How do we verify that this guess is correct?

Answer: To verify your guess, you need to show that it satisfies the stationary equations:

$$\pi_i = \pi_{i-1}r + \pi_i(1 - r - s) + \pi_{i+1}s$$
$$\left(\frac{r}{s}\right)^i \pi_0 = \left(\frac{r}{s}\right)^{i-1} \pi_0 r + \left(\frac{r}{s}\right)^i \pi_0(1 - r - s) + \left(\frac{r}{s}\right)^{i+1} \pi_0 s \quad \checkmark$$

Question: OK, but we still do not know π_0. How can we determine π_0?

Answer: To determine π_0, we make use of the fact that $\sum_i \pi_i = 1$.

This says that

$$\pi_0 \cdot \left(1 + \frac{r}{s} + \left(\frac{r}{s}\right)^2 + \left(\frac{r}{s}\right)^3 + \cdots\right) = 1$$
$$\pi_0 \cdot \left(\frac{1}{1 - \frac{r}{s}}\right) = 1$$
$$\pi_0 = 1 - \frac{r}{s}.$$

So

$$\pi_i = \left(\frac{r}{s}\right)^i \cdot \left(1 - \frac{r}{s}\right).$$

Question: What is the average number of jobs at the server?

Answer: Let N denote the number of jobs at the server. Then

$$\mathbf{E}\,[N] = \pi_0 \cdot 0 + \pi_1 \cdot 1 + \pi_2 \cdot 2 + \pi_3 \cdot 3 + \ldots$$

Question: Can we get a closed-form expression for $\mathbf{E}\,[N]$?

Answer: Yes! It will help to define

$$\rho = \frac{r}{s}$$

for shorthand. Then $\pi_i = \rho^i(1 - \rho)$.

$$\begin{aligned}
\mathbf{E}\,[N] &= 1\rho(1 - \rho) + 2\rho^2(1 - \rho) + 3\rho^3(1 - \rho) + \ldots \\
&= (1 - \rho)\rho\left(1 + 2\rho + 3\rho^2 + 4\rho^3 + \ldots\right) \\
&= (1 - \rho)\rho\frac{d}{d\rho}\left(1 + \rho + \rho^2 + \rho^3 + \rho^4 + \ldots\right) \\
&= (1 - \rho)\rho\frac{d}{d\rho}\left(\frac{1}{1 - \rho}\right) \\
&= (1 - \rho)\rho \cdot \frac{1}{(1 - \rho)^2} \\
&= \frac{\rho}{1 - \rho} \qquad\qquad (8.4)
\end{aligned}$$

Wow! That is a really simple formula. We will see this again ...

For our example $\rho = \frac{29}{39}$ and $\mathbf{E}\,[N] = 2.9$. So on average there are about 3 jobs in the system.

8.11 Exercises

8.1 Solving for Limiting Distribution
Consider the program analysis problem from Section 8.3.3. Determine the limiting distribution, (π_C, π_M, π_U), by solving the stationary equations.

8.2 Powers of Transition Matrix
Given any finite-state transition matrix, $\mathbf{P}$, prove that for any integer n, $\mathbf{P}^n$ maintains the property that each row sums to 1.

8.3 Doubly Stochastic Matrix
A doubly stochastic matrix is one in which the entries in each row sum up to 1 and the entries in each column sum up to 1. Suppose you have a finite-state Markov chain whose limiting probabilities exist and whose transition matrix is doubly stochastic. What can you prove about the stationary distribution of this Markov chain?

8.4 Gambling Game

Dafna starts out with zero dollars. Every day she gains a dollar with probability p, stays put with probability s, or loses all her money (goes broke) with probability b, where $p + s + b = 1$. Dafna plays the game forever. Use a DTMC to determine the stationary probability that Dafna has i dollars. What happens to your solution when $s = 0$? What is Dafna's long-run expected money?

8.5 Randomized Chess

In chess, a rook can move either horizontally within its row (left or right) or vertically within its column (up or down) any number of squares. In an 8×8 chess board, imagine a rook that starts at the lower left corner of a chess board. At each move, a bored child decides to move the rook to a random legal location (assume that the "move" cannot involve staying still). Let T denote the time until the rook first lands in the upper right corner of the board. Compute $\mathbf{E}\left[T\right]$ and $\mathbf{Var}(T)$.

8.6 Threshold Queue

We define a threshold queue with parameter T as follows: When the number of jobs is $< T$, then the number of jobs decreases by 1 with probability 0.4 and increases by 1 with probability 0.6 at each time step. However, when the number of jobs increases to $> T$, then the reverse is true, and the number of jobs increases by 1 with probability 0.4 and decreases by 1 with probability 0.6 at each time step, as shown in Figure 8.8.

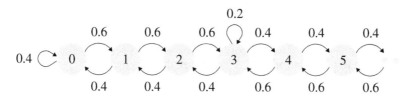

Figure 8.8. Markov chain for threshold queue with $T = 3$.

(a) Assume that the limiting probabilities exist. Use the stationary equations to derive the limiting probability distribution as a function of T, for arbitrary threshold T.

(b) Compute the mean number of jobs, $\mathbf{E}\left[N\right]$, in a threshold queue as a function of T.

(c) What happens to $\mathbf{E}\left[N\right]$ when $T = 0$? Does this answer make sense?

8.7 Naval Battle Analysis

In the game Axis & Allies, the outcome of a two-sided naval battle is decided by repeated rolling of dice. Until all ships on at least one side are destroyed, each side rolls one (six-sided) die for each of its existing ships. The die rolls determine casualties inflicted on the opponent; these casualties are removed from play and cannot fire (roll) in subsequent rounds. There are two types of ships: battleships and destroyers. For a battleship, a die roll of four or lower is scored as a "hit." For a destroyer, a die roll of three or lower is scored as a "hit."

It takes two hits (not necessarily in the same round) to destroy a battleship and only one hit to destroy a destroyer (side note: battleships are twice as expensive as destroyers). The defender gets to decide to which ship to allocate the hit; we assume the defender chooses intelligently. If two destroyers engage a battleship in a naval battle, what is the probability that the destroyers win? How about the battleship? [Hint: You will need to raise a matrix to a large power.]

CHAPTER 9

Ergodicity Theory

9.1 Ergodicity Questions

At this point, in our discussion of DTMCs, we have defined the notion of a *limiting probability of being in state j*:

$$\pi_j = \lim_{n \to \infty} (\mathbf{P}^n)_{ij},$$

typically written $\pi_j = \lim_{n \to \infty} P_{ij}^n$, where the limiting distribution is

$$\vec{\pi} = (\pi_0, \pi_1, \pi_2, \pi_3, \ldots) \quad \text{with} \quad \sum_{i=0}^{\infty} \pi_i = 1.$$

We have also defined the notion of a *stationary distribution*, $\vec{\pi}$, as a distribution that satisfies

$$\vec{\pi} \cdot \mathbf{P} = \vec{\pi} \quad \text{and} \quad \sum_{i=0}^{\infty} \pi_i = 1$$

or, equivalently,

$$\pi_j = \sum_{i=0}^{\infty} \pi_i P_{ij} \quad \text{and} \quad \sum_{i=0}^{\infty} \pi_i = 1.$$

We also proved two theorems (Theorem 8.6 for finite-state chains and Theorem 8.8 for infinite-state chains) that said that, assuming the limiting distribution exists, then the limiting distribution is a stationary distribution and no other stationary distribution exists. These theorems are key because they allow us to simply solve the stationary equations to get the limiting distribution.

Question: Is $\pi_j = \lim_{n \to \infty} P_{ij}^n$ a time average or an ensemble average?

Answer: Ensemble. When we raise matrix $\mathbf{P}$ to the nth power, we are averaging over all sample paths of length n (i.e., all possible choices for the first hop, 2nd hop, 3rd hop, etc.). π_j is defined to be the limiting probability of being in state j. By contrast, we can define p_j to be the time-average fraction of time spent in state j, averaged over one infinitely long sample path.

In the previous chapter we looked at how to find π_j, assuming it exists. However, we did not spend much time on questions like the following:

1. Under what conditions does the limiting distribution exist?
2. How does the limiting probability of being in state j, π_j, compare with the long-run time-average fraction of time spent in state j, p_j?

3. What can we say about the mean time between visits to state j, and how is this related to π_j?

This entire chapter is devoted to these and other theoretical questions, all related to the notion of *ergodicity* (you can look ahead to Definition 9.24, where ergodicity is defined). We end with a brief discussion of time-reversibility, which gives a faster method for computing limiting probabilities in the case of certain Markov chains.

Unsurprisingly, most of the questions just presented are simpler to think about in the context of a finite-state Markov chain. Hence, we start in Section 9.2 by discussing these issues for a finite-state chain. After that, we move on to infinite-state chains.

This is a highly theoretical chapter. The reader may wish to forgo the proofs during a first reading and return later for a more in-depth reading.

9.2 Finite-State DTMCs

9.2.1 *Existence of the Limiting Distribution*

We dive right into the question of existence of the limiting distribution, with a few examples.

Question: What is an example of a valid two-state transition matrix for which π_j does not exist?

Answer:

$$\mathbf{P} = \begin{bmatrix} 0 & 1 \\ 1 & 0 \end{bmatrix}$$

The problem is that this chain is *periodic*; specifically, a given state is only visited every *other* time step. Observe that $\pi_j = \lim_{n \to \infty} P_{jj}^n$ does not exist, although $\lim_{n \to \infty} P_{jj}^{(2n)}$ does exist.

Question: What is the time average, p_j, for the above chain?

Answer: The above chain is a valid DTMC, so there has to be some fraction of time spent in each state. In this case, the time averages are obvious: $p_0 = \frac{1}{2} = p_1$.

Question: Does this chain have a stationary distribution?

Answer: Yes, the stationary distribution *does* exist. To see this, let's set up the stationary equations $\vec{\pi} \cdot P = \vec{\pi}$:

$$\pi_0 = \pi_1$$
$$\pi_1 = \pi_0$$
$$\pi_0 + \pi_1 = 1$$

Solving these, we get $\vec{\pi} = \left(\frac{1}{2}, \frac{1}{2}\right) = (p_1, p_2)$.

Examples like this one illustrate why we need to pay attention to the conditions under which all these kinds of averages agree. Let's consider another example.

Question: Does the following transition matrix have limiting probabilities?

$$\mathbf{P} = \begin{bmatrix} 0 & 0 & 1/2 & 1/2 \\ 1 & 0 & 0 & 0 \\ 0 & 1 & 0 & 0 \\ 0 & 1 & 0 & 0 \end{bmatrix}$$

Answer: No, this too is periodic – it is just a little harder to see.

Definition 9.1 The *period* of state j is the greatest common divisor (GCD) of the set of integers n, such that $P_{jj}^n > 0$. A state is *aperiodic* if it has period 1. A chain is said to be aperiodic if all of its states are aperiodic.

So aperiodicity is clearly necessary for the limiting probabilities to exist. However in an aperiodic Markov chain, it could still turn out that the limiting probabilities depend on the start state, whereas we want $\pi_j = \lim_{n\to\infty} P_{ij}^n$ to be the same for all i.

If we also want the limiting probabilities to be independent of the start state, we need one more condition, known as *irreducibility*, which says that from any state one can get to any other state.

Definition 9.2 State j is *accessible* from state i if $P_{ij}^n > 0$ for some $n > 0$. States i and j *communicate* if i is accessible from j and vice versa.

Definition 9.3 A Markov chain is *irreducible* if all its states communicate with each other.

Question: Why is irreducibility needed for the limiting probabilities to be independent of the start state?

Answer: Without irreducibility, one might, for example, have the situation where the Markov chain consists of two disconnected components – thus the limiting probabilities would depend on which component contains the start state.

Question: What is a simple transition matrix that is *not* irreducible?

Answer: The identity matrix.

Question: Do you think that aperiodicity and irreducibility are enough to guarantee the existence of the limiting distribution?

Answer: As we see in Theorem 9.4, for a finite-state DTMC, aperiodicity and irreducibility are all that is needed to ensure that the limiting probabilities exist, are positive, sum to 1, and are independent of the starting state. This is very convenient, because it is often easy to argue that a DTMC is aperiodic and irreducible.

Theorem 9.4 *Given an aperiodic, irreducible, finite-state DTMC with transition matrix $\mathbf{P}$, as $n \to \infty$, $\mathbf{P}^n \to \mathbf{L}$, where $\mathbf{L}$ is a limiting matrix all of whose rows are the same vector, $\vec{\pi}$. The vector $\vec{\pi}$ has all positive components, summing to 1.*

Proof We are trying to show that $\mathbf{P}^n$ converges to a matrix where all rows are the same. Specifically, we are trying to show that, for any j, the jth column of $\mathbf{P}^n$ converges to a vector of all constants.

Let $\vec{e}$ represent the column vector of the same dimension as $\mathbf{P}$, whose jth component is 1 and whose remaining components are all 0. That is

$$\vec{e} = \begin{pmatrix} 0 \\ \vdots \\ 0 \\ 1 \\ 0 \\ \vdots \\ 0 \end{pmatrix}.$$

We are trying to show that

$$\mathbf{P}^n \cdot \vec{e}$$

converges to a vector all of whose components are the same.

The idea is to view $\mathbf{P}^n \vec{e} = \mathbf{P}(\ldots(\mathbf{P}(\mathbf{P}(\mathbf{P}\vec{e}))))$.

Consider the innermost product $\mathbf{P}\vec{e}$. Because $\mathbf{P}$ is a matrix of probabilities, where each row sums to 1, the effect of multiplying $\vec{e}$ by $\mathbf{P}$ is to replace each component of $\vec{e}$ by a value that is a *weighted average* of all the components. In particular, the effect is to bring all the components of $\vec{e}$ closer together. That is, the difference between the maximum component and the minimum component should decrease.

Here is an example of the effect of successive multiplications by $\mathbf{P}$:

$$\mathbf{P}\vec{e} = \begin{pmatrix} \frac{1}{2} & \frac{1}{3} & \frac{1}{6} \\ \frac{1}{3} & \frac{1}{3} & \frac{1}{3} \\ \frac{1}{4} & \frac{3}{4} & 0 \end{pmatrix} \cdot \begin{pmatrix} 0 \\ 1 \\ 0 \end{pmatrix} = \begin{pmatrix} \frac{1}{3} \\ \frac{1}{3} \\ \frac{3}{4} \end{pmatrix}$$

$$\mathbf{P}(\mathbf{P}\vec{e}) = \begin{pmatrix} \frac{1}{2} & \frac{1}{3} & \frac{1}{6} \\ \frac{1}{3} & \frac{1}{3} & \frac{1}{3} \\ \frac{1}{4} & \frac{3}{4} & 0 \end{pmatrix} \cdot \begin{pmatrix} \frac{1}{3} \\ \frac{1}{3} \\ \frac{3}{4} \end{pmatrix} = \begin{pmatrix} .40 \\ .47 \\ .33 \end{pmatrix}$$

Let M_n denote the maximum component of $\mathbf{P}^n \vec{e}$ and let m_n denote the minimum component of $\mathbf{P}^n \vec{e}$.

We now *claim* that

$$M_n - m_n \leq (1 - 2s)(M_{n-1} - m_{n-1}) \tag{9.1}$$

where s is the smallest element in $\mathbf{P}$.

To see why (9.1) is true, consider the vector $\vec{y} = \mathbf{P}^{n-1}\vec{e}$. By our definition, the maximum component of $\vec{y}$ is M_{n-1} and the minimum is m_{n-1}. Now, if we multiply $\vec{y}$ by $\mathbf{P}$

(obtaining $\mathbf{P}\vec{y} = \mathbf{P}^n\vec{e}$), we are replacing each component of $\vec{y}$ by a weighted average of all the components of $\vec{y}$.

Question: What is an upper bound on the largest possible component in $\mathbf{P} \cdot \vec{y}$?

Answer: The largest possible weighted average is obtained if all but one of the elements of $\vec{y}$ are M_{n-1}, with the remaining one being m_{n-1}, where m_{n-1} is weighted by the smallest value, s. An upper bound on the largest possible component of $\mathbf{P} \cdot \vec{y}$ is

$$s \cdot m_{n-1} + (1 - s) \cdot M_{n-1}.$$

Question: What is a lower bound on the smallest possible component in $\mathbf{P} \cdot \vec{y}$?

Answer: In the smallest weighted average, all but one of the elements of $\vec{y}$ are m_{n-1}, with the remaining one being M_{n-1}, where M_{n-1} is weighted by the smallest value, s. Thus a lower bound on the smallest possible component of $\mathbf{P} \cdot \vec{y}$ is

$$(1 - s) \cdot m_{n-1} + s \cdot M_{n-1}.$$

Thus an upper bound on the greatest difference between the components in $\mathbf{P}\vec{y}$ is

$$s \cdot m_{n-1} + (1 - s) \cdot M_{n-1} - (1 - s) \cdot m_{n-1} - s \cdot M_{n-1}$$
$$= (1 - 2s)(M_{n-1} - m_{n-1}).$$

This proves our claim in (9.1). Finally, because $s \leq \frac{1}{2}$ (when $M \geq 2$), we see that the difference between the maximum and minimum elements of $\mathbf{P}^n \vec{e}$ continues to decrease as we continue to multiply by $\mathbf{P}$, until eventually all elements are the same.

The proof would now be complete except for a small hole...

Question: Can you see the hole?

Answer: If $s = 0$, then the above argument does not result in convergence, because $(1 - 2s) = 1$.

Question: How can this be fixed?

Hint: Even if $\mathbf{P}$ contains some zero elements, what do we know about $\mathbf{P}^n$ for high enough n, given that $\mathbf{P}$ is aperiodic and irreducible?

Answer: Because $\mathbf{P}$ is aperiodic and irreducible, there exists some n_0 such that, $\forall n \geq n_0$, $\mathbf{P}^n$ has all positive elements. This follows from the Euclidean number property. [Here is a sketch: For any (j, j) entry, by aperiodicity, there are some powers x and y such that $\mathbf{P}^x$ and $\mathbf{P}^y$ have a positive (j, j) entry, where $GCD(x, y) = 1$. Hence, by the Euclidean number property, $\exists n_0(j, j)$ s.t., $\forall n \geq n_0(j, j)$, n can be expressed as a linear combination of x and y with non-negative coefficients; hence, $\forall n \geq n_0(j, j)$, there is a path of length n from j to j, and thus the (j, j)th entry of $\mathbf{P}^n$ is positive. Now repeat this argument for all (j, j) pairs (there are only a finite number). Finally, consider two arbitrary states i and j, where $i \neq j$. By irreducibility there is some x s.t. there is a path from i to j of length x. However, since we also know that

$\forall n \geq n_0(i,i)$ there is a path of length n from i to i, it follows that $\forall n \geq n_0(i,i) + x$ there is a path of length n from i to j. Define $n_0(i,j) = n_0(i,i) + x$. Finally, define n_0 to be the maximum of all $n_0(i,j)$ values, over all i and j. Now, for all $n \geq n_0$, $\mathbf{P}^n$ has all positive elements.]

To complete the proof, we now define $\mathbf{P}' = \mathbf{P}^{n_0}$. Then

$$\mathbf{P}^n \vec{e} = (\mathbf{P}^{n_0})^{n/n_0} = (\mathbf{P}')^{n/n_0}.$$

Now repeat the argument in (9.1), except that the decrease by a factor of $(1 - 2s) < 1$ occurs only every n_0 multiplications of $\mathbf{P}$. However, because $n/n_0 \to \infty$ as $n \to \infty$, we still have an infinite number of these decreases, meaning that

$$(\mathbf{P}')^{n/n_0} \to \mathbf{L}, \quad \text{as } n \to \infty.$$

To finish off the proof of the theorem, we note that by Exercise 8.2, all powers of $\mathbf{P}$ have the property that the components of each row sum to 1. Furthermore, because $\mathbf{P}^{n_0}$ has all positive elements, and because multiplying by $\mathbf{P}$ only creates weighted averages, then $\mathbf{P} \cdot \mathbf{P}^{n_0}$ still has all positive elements and so forth as we continue to multiply by $\mathbf{P}$. Hence the limiting matrix $\mathbf{L}$ will still have all positive elements and will have the property that the components of each row sum to 1. $\blacksquare$

Summary: We have proven that for any aperiodic, irreducible, finite-state Markov chain, the limiting probabilities exist.

9.2.2 *Mean Time between Visits to a State*

Consider the mean time between visits to state j. It seems that this quantity should be related to the limiting probability of being in state j. Let's see how.

Consider an *irreducible* finite-state Markov chain with M states and transition matrix $\mathbf{P}$.

> **Definition 9.5** Let m_{ij} denote the expected number of time steps needed to first get to state j, given we are currently at state i. Likewise, let m_{jj} denote the expected number of steps between visits to state j.

In Exercise 9.16, we will prove from first principles that m_{jj} is finite. Theorem 9.6 relates m_{jj} to π_j.

> **Theorem 9.6** *For an irreducible, aperiodic finite-state Markov chain with transition matrix* $\mathbf{P}$,
>
> $$m_{jj} = \frac{1}{\pi_j}$$
>
> *where m_{jj} is the mean time between visits to state j and $\pi_j = \lim_{n \to \infty} (\mathbf{P}^n)_{ij}$.*

Proof By conditioning on the first step, we have

$$m_{ij} = P_{ij} \cdot 1 + \sum_{k \neq j} P_{ik}(1 + m_{kj})$$

$$= 1 + \sum_{k \neq j} P_{ik} m_{kj} \tag{9.2}$$

Likewise

$$m_{jj} = P_{jj} \cdot 1 + \sum_{k \neq j} P_{jk}(1 + m_{kj})$$

$$= 1 + \sum_{k \neq j} P_{jk} m_{kj} \tag{9.3}$$

Let's express (9.2) and (9.3) using matrix notation. All the matrices in this proof are of the same order as $\mathbf{P}$, namely $M \times M$. Imagine a matrix $\mathbf{M}$ whose (i, j)th entry is m_{ij}. For purposes of the proof, it will be convenient to express $\mathbf{M}$ as a sum of two matrices $\mathbf{M} = \mathbf{D} + \mathbf{N}$, where $\mathbf{D}$ is a matrix whose entries are all zero, except for its diagonal entries: $d_{jj} = m_{jj}$, and $\mathbf{N}$ is a matrix whose diagonal entries are all zero, but where $N_{ij} = m_{ij}, \forall i \neq j$. Finally, let $\mathbf{E}$ be a matrix with *all* entries 1. Then by (9.2) and (9.3), we can write[1]

$$\mathbf{M} = \mathbf{E} + \mathbf{PN}. \tag{9.4}$$

Rewriting (9.4), we have

$$\mathbf{N} + \mathbf{D} = \mathbf{E} + \mathbf{PN}.$$

$$(\mathbf{I} - \mathbf{P}) \cdot \mathbf{N} = \mathbf{E} - \mathbf{D}.$$

Let $\vec{\pi}$ denote the limiting probability distribution. We know that $\vec{\pi}$ exists because we have aperiodicity and irreducibility. Multiplying both sides by $\vec{\pi}$, we have

$$\vec{\pi} \cdot (\mathbf{I} - \mathbf{P}) \cdot \mathbf{N} = \vec{\pi} (\mathbf{E} - \mathbf{D}). \tag{9.5}$$

Question: What do we know about the left-hand side of (9.5)?

Hint: Remember that $\vec{\pi}$ is also a stationary distribution.

Answer:

$$\vec{\pi} \mathbf{P} = \vec{\pi}$$

$$\Rightarrow \vec{\pi}(\mathbf{I} - \mathbf{P}) = \vec{0}$$

$$\Rightarrow \vec{\pi}(\mathbf{I} - \mathbf{P})\mathbf{N} = \vec{0}$$

---

[1] To see this, observe that by (9.4),

$$\forall i \neq j, \quad m_{ij} = 1 + \sum_{k} P_{ik} N_{kj} = 1 + \sum_{k \neq j} P_{ik} N_{kj} = 1 + \sum_{k \neq j} P_{ik} m_{kj} \quad \text{which matches (9.2).}$$

$$m_{jj} = 1 + \sum_{k} P_{jk} N_{kj} = 1 + \sum_{k \neq j} P_{jk} N_{kj} = 1 + \sum_{k \neq j} P_{jk} m_{kj} \quad \text{which matches (9.3).}$$

Thus, we have from (9.5)

$$\vec{0} = \vec{\pi}(\mathbf{E} - \mathbf{D})$$
$$\Rightarrow \vec{\pi}\mathbf{E} = \vec{\pi}\mathbf{D}$$
$$\Rightarrow (1, 1, \ldots, 1) = (\pi_0 m_{00}, \pi_1 m_{11}, \ldots, \pi_{M-1} m_{M-1,M-1})$$
$$\Rightarrow \pi_i m_{ii} = 1, \quad \forall i. \qquad \blacksquare$$

9.2.3 *Time Averages*

So far, we have seen that, for a finite-state Markov chain, the limiting distribution, $\vec{\pi} = (\pi_0, \pi_1, \ldots, \pi_{M-1})$, when it exists, is equal to the unique stationary distribution. We have also seen that $\pi_j = \frac{1}{m_{jj}}$, where m_{jj} is the mean time (number of steps) between visits to state j. We now consider p_j, the fraction of time that the Markov chain spends in state j, along a given sample path.

Question: What would you guess is the relationship between π_j and p_j, assuming that the limiting distribution exists?

Answer: It seems pretty natural to believe that $\pi_j = p_j$. We prove this formally later in Theorem 9.28, where we show that $p_j = \frac{1}{m_{jj}}$ with probability 1 (i.e., for almost every sample path). Because we also know that $\pi_j = \frac{1}{m_{jj}}$, it follows that, with probability 1, $p_j = \pi_j$.

The formal argument requires renewal theory, which is described in Section 9.5. However, intuitively, it should make sense that if the average time between visits to state j is m_{jj}, then, during a long period of time t, we visit state j approximately $x = \frac{t}{m_{jj}}$ times. Hence the proportion of time spent in state j during time t is $\frac{x}{t} = \frac{t}{m_{jj}} \cdot \frac{1}{t} = \frac{1}{m_{jj}}$.

9.3 Infinite-State Markov Chains

We now turn to infinite-state Markov chains. These are far more difficult to reason about than finite-state Markov chains, and it will take some time to even develop the terminology we need to discuss them.

Consider the three infinite-state DTMCs shown in Figure 9.1.

Question: Which of these chains are aperiodic and irreducible?

Answer: All of them.

Question: For *finite-state* DTMCs that are aperiodic and irreducible, does a limiting distribution always exist?

Answer: Yes, by Theorem 9.4.

Question: Does a limiting distribution exist for all the chains in Figure 9.1?

Answer: We will see that a limiting distribution exists only for the first chain. For the first chain, there is a well-defined limiting probability of being in each state, and

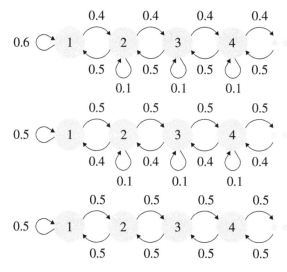

Figure 9.1. Examples of positive recurrent, transient, and null-recurrent chains (looking from top to bottom).

these probabilities sum to 1. For the other two chains, we will show that the limiting probability of being in each state is 0, and the limiting probabilities do not sum to 1; hence there does not exist a limiting distribution. The first chain has a property called "positive recurrent." The second chain is what we call "transient," and the third chain is "null recurrent." We explain all these terms in this chapter and how they relate to the existence of limiting distributions.

Question: Intuitively, what is the problem with the second and third chains in Figure 9.1?

Answer: The second chain can be viewed as an ocean, where the shore is at state 1. There is a drift away from shore. Given this drift, it is not obvious that we keep returning back to shore. There could be some point after which we never return to the shore. This same argument holds for any state k that we call the "shore." In the case of the third chain, it seems that we should return to each state, but it is not obvious how long it will take to return. If the time between visits to a state is infinite, then it seems that the limiting probability of being in the state should be zero.

9.3.1 Recurrent versus Transient

Definition 9.7 f_j = probability that a chain starting in state j ever returns to state j.

Definition 9.8 A state j is either recurrent or transient:
- If $f_j = 1$, then j is a **recurrent** state.
- If $f_j < 1$, then j is a **transient** state.

Question: What is the distribution of the number of visits to a transient state j?

Answer: Every time we visit state j we have probability $1 - f_j$ of never visiting it again. Hence the number of visits is distributed Geometrically with mean $1/(1 - f_j)$.

> **Theorem 9.9** *With probability* 1*, the number of visits to a* **recurrent** *state is infinite. With probability* 1*, the number of visits to a* **transient** *state is finite.*

Proof If a state j is recurrent, then starting in state j, with probability 1 we will visit j again. Thus, repeating this argument, we see that with probability 1 state j will be visited an infinite number of times. In contrast, if state j is transient, then every time we visit state j, there is some probability $(1 - f_j)$ that we will never again visit j. Thus, with probability 1 state j will be visited a finite number of times. ∎

> **Theorem 9.10**
>
> $$\mathbf{E}\left[\# \text{ visits to state } i \text{ in } s \text{ steps} \mid \text{start in state } i\right] = \sum_{n=0}^{s} P_{ii}^n \qquad (9.6)$$
>
> $$\mathbf{E}\left[\text{Total } \# \text{ visits to state } i \mid \text{start in state } i\right] = \sum_{n=0}^{\infty} P_{ii}^n \qquad (9.7)$$

Proof
$$\mathbf{E}\left[\text{Number visits to state } i \text{ in } s \text{ steps} \mid X_0 = i\right]$$
$$= \mathbf{E}\left[\sum_{n=0}^{s} I_n \mid X_0 = i\right], \text{ where } I_n = \begin{cases} 1 & \text{if } X_n = i \\ 0 & \text{o.w.} \end{cases}$$
$$= \sum_{n=0}^{s} \mathbf{E}\left[I_n \mid X_0 = i\right]$$
$$= \sum_{n=0}^{s} \mathbf{P}\left\{X_n = i \mid X_0 = i\right\}$$
$$= \sum_{n=0}^{s} P_{ii}^n$$

The above proves (9.6). To get (9.7), we take the limit as $s \to \infty$. ∎

So, combining Theorems 9.9 and 9.10, we have the following theorem.[2]

> **Theorem 9.11** *If state i is recurrent, then $\sum_{n=0}^{\infty} P_{ii}^n = \infty$.*
> *If state i is transient, then $\sum_{n=0}^{\infty} P_{ii}^n < \infty$.*

---

[2] Theorem 9.11 is an application of the Borel-Cantelli lemma [57].

Theorem 9.12 *If state i is recurrent and i communicates with j, $(i \longleftrightarrow j)$, then j is recurrent.*

We start with the intuition for Theorem 9.12. Consider Figure 9.2. We know that we come back to i infinitely many times. By the definition of "communicates," every time we are in i, we have some probability of taking the road to j, and once we are in j, we have some probability of taking the road to i. So, for every visit to i, there's some non-zero probability that we'll also visit j. Therefore the number of visits to j is proportional to the number of visits to i. Because the number of visits to i is infinite, so is the number of visits to j.

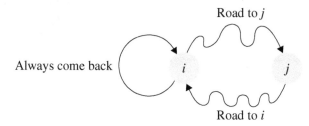

Figure 9.2. Proof of Theorem 9.12.

Now for the formal proof.

Proof We know that i communicates with j. Thus, there exists an m such that $P_{ji}^m > 0$ and there exists n such that $P_{ij}^n > 0$.

Now

$$P_{jj}^{m+s+n} \geq P_{ji}^m P_{ii}^s P_{ij}^n. \tag{9.8}$$

The right-hand side of (9.8) represents only some of the ways to go from j to j in $m + n + s$ steps, whereas the left-hand side represents all the ways. Summing both sides of (9.8) over s, we have

$$\sum_s P_{jj}^{m+s+n} \geq \sum_s P_{ji}^m P_{ii}^s P_{ij}^n = P_{ji}^m P_{ij}^n \sum_s P_{ii}^s = \infty,$$

where the last step is due to the fact that state i is recurrent.

So

$$\sum_{t=0}^{\infty} P_{jj}^t \geq \sum_{t=m+n}^{\infty} P_{jj}^t = \sum_{s=0}^{\infty} P_{jj}^{m+n+s} = \infty.$$

Therefore state j is recurrent.   ∎

Theorem 9.13 *If state i is transient and i communicates with j, $(i \longleftrightarrow j)$, then j is transient.*

Proof This follows directly from the previous Theorem 9.12. Suppose by contradiction that state j is recurrent. Then because j and i communicate, i is recurrent as well, which is a contradiction to the assumption. ∎

We have thus seen that *in an irreducible Markov chain, either all states are transient, or all are recurrent.*

Theorem 9.14 *For a transient Markov chain,*

$$\lim_{n \to \infty} P_{ij}^n = 0, \quad \forall j.$$

Proof As we have seen, in a transient Markov chain there is some point after which we never visit state j again. So the probability of being in state j after n steps is zero as $n \to \infty$. This holds for every state j. ∎

Theorem 9.15 *If for a Markov chain*

$$\pi_j = \lim_{n \to \infty} P_{ij}^n = 0, \quad \forall j,$$

then

$$\sum_{j=0}^{\infty} \pi_j = 0$$

so the limiting distribution does not exist.

Proof This follows because we are adding a countable number of 0's, which equals 0. ∎

Corollary 9.16 *For a transient Markov chain the limiting distribution does not exist.*

Proof This follows immediately from Theorems 9.14 and 9.15. ∎

In situations where the limiting probabilities are all 0, it seems hard to imagine that a stationary distribution exists. Theorem 9.17 states that, in agreement with our intuition, no stationary distribution exists.

Theorem 9.17 *Given an aperiodic, irreducible chain. Suppose that the limiting probabilities are all zero. That is, $\pi_j = \lim_{n \to \infty} P_{ij}^n = 0, \forall j$. Then the stationary distribution does not exist.*

Proof This proof follows very closely the structure of the proof of Theorem 8.8. Let $\vec{\pi}'$ be any stationary probability distribution. As usual, $\vec{\pi}$ represents the limiting probability distribution. We are given that $\pi_j = \lim_{n \to \infty} P_{ij}^n = 0, \forall j$.

Our goal is to prove that $\pi_j' = 0, \forall j$. Observe that

$$\pi_j' = \mathbf{P}\left\{X_0 = j\right\} = \mathbf{P}\left\{X_n = j\right\} \text{ because } \pi_j' \text{ is stationary.}$$

So

$$\pi'_j = \mathbf{P}\{X_n = j\}$$

$$= \sum_{i=0}^{\infty} \mathbf{P}\{X_n = j \mid X_0 = i\} \cdot \mathbf{P}\{X_0 = i\}$$

$$= \sum_{i=0}^{\infty} P_{ij}^n \pi'_i$$

$$= \sum_{i=0}^{M} P_{ij}^n \pi'_i + \sum_{i=M+1}^{\infty} P_{ij}^n \pi'_i \quad \text{(for any integer } M\text{)}.$$

We now prove that π'_j is bounded above by 0. By the previous equation,

$$\pi'_j \leq \sum_{i=0}^{M} P_{ij}^n \pi'_i + \sum_{i=M+1}^{\infty} \pi'_i$$

$$\lim_{n \to \infty} \pi'_j \leq \lim_{n \to \infty} \sum_{i=0}^{M} P_{ij}^n \pi'_i + \lim_{n \to \infty} \sum_{i=M+1}^{\infty} \pi'_i$$

$$\pi'_j \leq \sum_{i=0}^{M} \pi_j \pi'_i + \sum_{i=M+1}^{\infty} \pi'_i$$

$$\pi'_j \leq 0 + \sum_{i=M+1}^{\infty} \pi'_i$$

Now taking the limit as $M \to \infty$, the final summation becomes zero, so $\pi'_j \leq 0$ as desired. ∎

9.3.2 Infinite Random Walk Example

Consider the random walk shown in Figure 9.3, where at each step a gambler either gains a dollar (with probability p) or loses a dollar (with probability $q = 1 - p$).

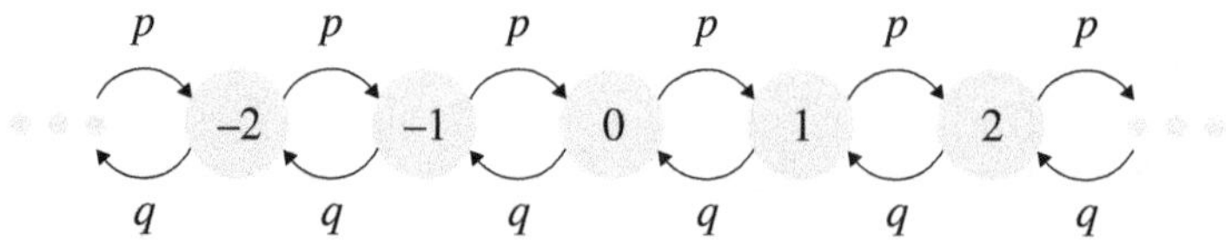

Figure 9.3. Random walk.

Because all states communicate, it follows from Theorems 9.12 and 9.13 that either all states are transient or all are recurrent. Hence to determine whether the chain is recurrent or transient, it suffices to look at state 0.

To determine whether state 0 is transient or recurrent, we invoke Theorem 9.11. Let

$$V = \sum_{n=1}^{\infty} P_{00}^n$$

denote the expected number of visits to state 0. If V is finite, then state 0 is transient. Otherwise it is recurrent.

Since one cannot get from 0 to 0 in an odd number of steps, it follows that

$$V = \sum_{n=1}^{\infty} P_{00}^{2n} = \sum_{n=1}^{\infty} \binom{2n}{n} p^n q^n \tag{9.9}$$

We now simplify this equation using Lavrov's lemma.

Lemma 9.18 (due to Misha Lavrov) *For $n \geq 1$,*

$$\frac{4^n}{2n+1} < \binom{2n}{n} < 4^n \tag{9.10}$$

Proof By simple binomial expansion,

$$\sum_{k=0}^{2n} \binom{2n}{k} = (1+1)^{2n} = 2^{2n} = 4^n$$

Since $\binom{2n}{n}$ is the largest term in the sum, it follows that it is bigger than the average term, $4^n/(2n+1)$. However it is also smaller than the total sum, 4^n. ∎

Substituting (9.10) into (9.9), we get that

$$\sum_{n=1}^{\infty} \frac{4^n}{2n+1} p^n q^n < V < \sum_{n=1}^{\infty} 4^n p^n q^n \tag{9.11}$$

If we substitute $p = q = \frac{1}{2}$ into the left-hand side of (9.11), we get that

$$V > \sum_{n=1}^{\infty} \frac{4^n}{2n+1} \cdot \frac{1}{4^n} = \sum_{n=1}^{\infty} \frac{1}{2n+1} = \infty \tag{9.12}$$

If instead we assume $p \neq q$ and consider the right-hand side of (9.11), we get that

$$V < \sum_{n=1}^{\infty} (4pq)^n < \infty \quad \text{(since } 4pq < 1) \tag{9.13}$$

Thus by (9.12) and (9.13) we see that $V = \sum_{n=1}^{\infty} P_{00}^n$ is infinite if and only if $p = \frac{1}{2}$. So the chain is recurrent if and only if $p = \frac{1}{2}$.

We have thus proven Theorem 9.19.

Theorem 9.19 *The random walk shown in Figure 9.3 is recurrent only when $p = \frac{1}{2}$ and is transient otherwise.*

Question: Recall that we defined f_0 as the probability that the chain ever returns to state 0. What do we know about f_0 for the random walk example?

Answer: We know that when $p = \frac{1}{2}$, we should have $f_0 = 1$. However, when $p \neq \frac{1}{2}$, it should be the case that $f_0 < 1$.

Lemma 9.20 *For the random walk shown in Figure 9.3, in the case where the chain is transient with rightward drift ($p > q$), we have that $f_0 = 2q < 1$.*

Proof This follows by conditioning. Let f_{ij} denote the probability that we ever get to state j given that we start in state i. Thus, $f_{00} = f_0$. Then $f_0 = qf_{-1,0} + pf_{1,0}$.

We will argue two things:

1. $f_{-1,0} = 1$
2. $f_{1,0} = \frac{q}{p}$

Together these result in

$$f_0 = qf_{-1,0} + pf_{1,0} = q + p \cdot \frac{q}{p} = 2q.$$

That $f_{-1,0} = 1$ should be clear from the fact that the chain has a rightward drift, so eventually we must get to state 0. It can also be seen by conditioning on the first step as follows:

$$f_{-1,0} = qf_{-2,0} + p = q\left(f_{-1,0}\right)^2 + p$$

and observing that $f_{-1,0} = 1$ is a solution to the above equation, because $q + p = 1$.

The fact that $f_{1,0} = q/p$ can be seen by conditioning on the first step as follows:

$$f_{1,0} = q \cdot 1 + p \cdot f_{2,0} = q + p \cdot \left(f_{1,0}\right)^2$$

and observing that $f_{1,0} = q/p$ is a solution to the above equation, because $q + p = 1$. ∎

9.3.3 *Positive Recurrent versus Null Recurrent*

Question: Is knowing that a chain is aperiodic, irreducible, and recurrent enough to guarantee the existence of the limiting distribution?

Answer: No. What is required is "positive recurrence."

Definition 9.21 Recurrent Markov chains fall into two types: ***positive recurrent*** and ***null recurrent***. In a positive-recurrent MC, the mean time between recurrences (returning to same state) is finite. In a null-recurrent MC, the mean time between recurrences is infinite.

The following theorem is proven in Exercise 9.16.

Theorem 9.22 *If state i is positive recurrent and $i \longleftrightarrow j$, then j is positive recurrent. If state i is null recurrent and $i \longleftrightarrow j$, then j is null recurrent.*

Null-recurrent chains seem like an oxymoron: For a null-recurrent state j, the mean time between visits to state j is ∞, and yet state j is visited an infinite number of times.

An example of a null-recurrent chain is the random walk shown in Figure 9.3 with $p = \frac{1}{2}$. In the previous example we proved that this chain is recurrent. We now show that the mean time between visits to state 0 is infinite. Hence state 0 is null recurrent, and, since all states communicate, by Theorem 9.22 all states are null recurrent.

Theorem 9.23 *For the symmetric random walk shown in Figure 9.3 with $p = \frac{1}{2}$, the mean number of time steps between visits to state 0 is infinite.*

Proof The theorem can be proven in several ways. We present a very short argument here, but illustrate two more proofs in Exercises 9.11 and 9.13.[3] We use the notation $m_{i,j}$ to denote the mean number of time steps until we visit state j, given that we are currently at state i. Our goal is to prove that m_{00} is infinite.

We present a proof by contradiction. Assume that m_{00} is finite. Then it follows that $m_{1,0}$ must be finite as well. This follows from the fact that

$$m_{00} = \frac{1}{2}m_{1,0} + \frac{1}{2}m_{-1,0} + 1.$$

Hence we cannot have $m_{1,0}$ being infinity.

Now that we know that $m_{1,0}$ is finite, we compute it by conditioning on the next state

$$m_{1,0} = 1 + \frac{1}{2} \cdot 0 + \frac{1}{2}m_{2,0}. \tag{9.14}$$

Now observe that

$$m_{2,0} = 2m_{1,0} \tag{9.15}$$

because the mean time to go from 2 to 0 is the mean time to go from 2 to 1 plus the mean time to go from 1 to 0; and $m_{2,1} = m_{1,0}$ because the chain is location-invariant.

Hence (9.14) reduces to

$$m_{1,0} = 1 + \frac{1}{2} \cdot 0 + \frac{1}{2}m_{2,0}$$
$$= 1 + \frac{1}{2} \cdot 2m_{1,0} \quad \text{(by 9.15)}$$
$$m_{1,0} = 1 + m_{1,0}.$$

However, this contradicts the fact that $m_{1,0}$ is finite. ∎

---

[3] The proof here is due to a student in my class, Ameya Velingker.

9.4 Ergodic Theorem of Markov Chains

Definition 9.24 An *ergodic* DTMC is one that has all three desirable properties: aperiodicity, irreducibility, and positive recurrence.[4]

Remark: For a finite-state DTMC, positive recurrence is a consequence of irreducibility. This fact is proven in Exercise 9.16. Hence, for finite-state chains, aperiodicity and irreducibility suffice for ergodicity.

The Ergodic Theorem of Markov Chains (Theorem 9.25) tells us that for any ergodic DTMC, the limiting probabilities exist and are positive. Furthermore, for any state i, the limiting probability of being in state i is equal to the reciprocal of the mean time between visits to state i.

The Ergodic Theorem of Markov Chains is saying the same thing that we saw in Theorems 9.4 and 9.6. However, those theorems were restricted to *finite*-state chains. The fact that we now allow for infinite-state chains makes the proof much more technical, and thus we defer the proof to Section 9.10.

Theorem 9.25 (Ergodic Theorem of Markov Chains) *Given a recurrent, aperiodic, irreducible DTMC, $\pi_j = \lim_{n \to \infty} P_{ij}^n$ exists and*

$$\pi_j = \frac{1}{m_{jj}}, \quad \forall j.$$

For a positive recurrent, aperiodic, irreducible DTMC, $\pi_j > 0, \forall_j$.

Proof Deferred to Section 9.10.   ∎

Question: The second sentence in Theorem 9.25 follows immediately from the first one. Why is this?

Answer: For a positive-recurrent chain, m_{jj} is finite, so $\frac{1}{m_{jj}} > 0$.

Remark: It may not seem obvious that the π_j's as defined by Theorem 9.25 actually sum up to 1, when m_{jj} is finite. This fact will be proven shortly in Corollary 9.30.

Let us now consider what Theorem 9.25 says about a null-recurrent Markov chain.

---

[4] Note that in some books, *ergodicity* is defined as the equivalence of the ensemble- and and time-average probabilities, where the three properties of aperiodicity, irreducibility, and positive recurrence are then consequences of this equivalence.

Theorem 9.26 *For an aperiodic, null-recurrent Markov chain, the limiting probabilities are all zero and the limiting distribution and stationary distribution do not exist.*

Proof   For a null-recurrent chain, the mean time between visits to each state is infinite ($m_{ii} = \infty$). Hence, by Theorem 9.25, all the limiting probabilities are zero. Thus, by Theorem 9.15, a limiting distribution does not exist, and by Theorem 9.17, neither does the stationary distribution. ∎

We now state a single theorem that summarizes all that we have seen so far regarding limiting distributions and stationary distributions.

Theorem 9.27 (Summary Theorem)   *An irreducible, aperiodic DTMC belongs to one of the following two classes:*
Either
   (i) *All the states are transient, or all are null recurrent. In this case $\pi_j = \lim_{n \to \infty} P_{ij}^n = 0$, $\forall j$, and there does NOT exist a stationary distribution.*
or
   (ii) *All states are positive recurrent. Then the limiting distribution $\vec{\pi} = (\pi_0, \pi_1, \pi_2, \ldots)$ exists, and there is a positive probability of being in each state. Here*

$$\pi_j = \lim_{n \to \infty} P_{ij}^n > 0, \quad \forall i$$

   is the limiting probability of being in state j. In this case $\vec{\pi}$ is a stationary distribution, and no other stationary distribution exists. Also, π_j is equal to $\frac{1}{m_{jj}}$, where m_{jj} is the mean number of steps between visits to state j.

Proof   We know by Theorems 9.22 and 9.13 that transience, null recurrence, and positive recurrence are class properties, meaning that in an irreducible Markov chain all the states are of the same one type.

If all states are transient, then by Theorem 9.14 all the limiting probabilities are zero, and by Theorem 9.15, these limiting probabilities add up to 0, so no limiting distribution exists.

If all states are null recurrent, then by Theorem 9.26 all the limiting probabilities are zero, and again by Theorem 9.15, no limiting distribution exists.

Whenever the limiting probabilities are all zero, it follows by Theorem 9.17 that the stationary probabilities are all zero as well, so no stationary distribution exists.

If all states are positive recurrent, then by Theorem 9.25, the limiting probabilities are all positive and equal to $\frac{1}{m_{jj}}$, and by Corollary 9.30 (coming up soon) they sum to 1, so the limiting distribution exists. Furthermore, by Theorems 8.6 and 8.8, the limiting distribution is also equal to the unique stationary distribution. ∎

> **Important Remark:** What is nice about this summary theorem is that it tells us that we never have to actually determine whether our DTMC is positive recurrent. It suffices to simply check for irreducibility and aperiodicity and then solve the stationary equations. If these stationary equations yield a distribution, then that distribution is also the limiting probability distribution.

So life is good when our DTMC is irreducible and aperiodic. One question that you might be wondering about is what happens when our DTMC is either not irreducible or is periodic. Can we still solve the stationary equations? If the solution still exists, what does it represent? Section 9.8 answers these questions. We see, for example, that for periodic chains, when the solution to the stationary equations exists, it does not represent the limiting distribution, but rather it represents the long-run time-average fraction of time spent in each state. Time averages are the topic of our next section.

9.5 Time Averages

Question: Recall that $\pi_j = \lim_{n \to \infty} P_{ij}^n$ is an ensemble average. How might we define p_j, the time-average fraction of time spent in state j (i.e., the "long-run" proportion of time spent in state j)?

Answer: Let $N_j(t)$ be the number of times that the Markov chain enters state j by time t (t transitions). The time-average fraction of time that the Markov chain spends in state j is then

$$p_j = \lim_{t \to \infty} \frac{N_j(t)}{t} = \text{Time-average fraction of time in state } j.$$

Observe that p_j is actually defined as an average over a single sample path, ω. What we would like to say is (i) that this average converges with probability 1 (meaning it converges along "almost" all the sample paths), (ii) that it always converges to the same quantity, and (iii) that this quantity is positive. Theorem 9.28 tells us that when the chain is positive recurrent and irreducible, all these good things happen.

> **Theorem 9.28**   *For a positive recurrent, irreducible Markov chain, with probability 1,*
>
> $$p_j = \lim_{t \to \infty} \frac{N_j(t)}{t} = \frac{1}{m_{jj}} > 0,$$
>
> *where m_{jj} is the (ensemble) mean number of time steps between visits to state j.*

Importantly, the existence of p_j does *not* require aperiodicity.

Before we prove Theorem 9.28, let's discuss some of its consequences.

Question: Where have we seen the term $\frac{1}{m_{jj}}$ before?

Answer: This is the same expression that was equal to the limiting probability π_j; see Theorem 9.27(ii). This observation leads to Corollary 9.29.

Corollary 9.29 *For an ergodic DTMC, with probability 1,*

$$p_j = \pi_j = \frac{1}{m_{jj}}$$

where $p_j = \lim_{t \to \infty} \frac{N_j(t)}{t}$ and $\pi_j = \lim_{n \to \infty} P_{ij}^n$ and m_{jj} is the (ensemble) mean number of time steps between visits to state j.

Corollary 9.30 *For an ergodic DTMC, the limiting probabilities sum to 1 (i.e., $\sum_{j=0}^{\infty} \pi_j = 1$).*

Proof This is an immediate consequence of the fact that $p_j = \pi_j$ from Corollary 9.29: Because the p_j's sum up to 1 (as the Markov chain must be in some state at every moment of time), it follows that the π_j's must likewise sum up to 1. ∎

The remainder of this section is devoted to proving Theorem 9.28. We start with some preliminary theorems that we will need to invoke. Theorem 9.31 reviews the Strong Law of Large Numbers (SLLN) from Theorem 5.5.

Theorem 9.31 (SLLN) *Let $X_1, X_2, \ldots$ be a sequence of independent, identically distributed random variables each with mean $\mathbf{E}[X]$. Let $S_n = \sum_{i=1}^{n} X_i$. Then with probability 1,*

$$\lim_{n \to \infty} \frac{S_n}{n} = \mathbf{E}[X].$$

With SLLN in hand, we are ready to define a renewal process.

Definition 9.32 A *renewal process* is any process for which the times between events are i.i.d. random variables with a distribution F.

An example of a renewal process is shown in Figure 9.4. Let $N(t)$ denote the number of events by time t. Then, we have the following theorem.

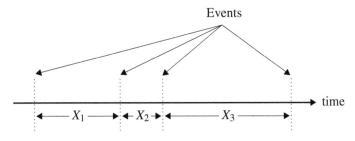

Figure 9.4. A renewal process. $X_i \sim F$, for all i.

Theorem 9.33 (Renewal Theorem) *For a renewal process, if $\mathbf{E}[X]$ is the mean time between renewals, we have*

$$\lim_{t \to \infty} \frac{N(t)}{t} = \frac{1}{\mathbf{E}[X]} \text{ with probability 1.} \qquad (9.16)$$

Proof The basic idea in this proof is to apply SLLN, which gives us the convergence on all sample paths (w.p.1). Let S_n be the time of the nth event. Then we have, $\forall t$,

$$S_{N(t)} \leq t < S_{N(t)+1}$$

$$\frac{S_{N(t)}}{N(t)} \leq \frac{t}{N(t)} < \frac{S_{N(t)+1}}{N(t)}.$$

But,

$$\frac{S_{N(t)}}{N(t)} = \frac{\sum_{i=1}^{N(t)} X_i}{N(t)} \longrightarrow \mathbf{E}[X] \text{ as } t \to \infty \text{ w.p.1. (SLLN)}$$

Likewise,

$$\frac{S_{N(t)+1}}{N(t)} = \frac{S_{N(t)+1}}{N(t)+1} \cdot \frac{N(t)+1}{N(t)} \longrightarrow \mathbf{E}[X] \text{ as } t \to \infty \text{ w.p.1. (SLLN)}$$

So, by the sandwich theorem, we have that

$$\frac{t}{N(t)} \longrightarrow \mathbf{E}[X] \text{ w.p.1.}$$

$$\Rightarrow \frac{N(t)}{t} \longrightarrow \frac{1}{\mathbf{E}[X]} \text{ as } t \to \infty \text{ w.p.1.} \qquad \blacksquare$$

Proof (Theorem 9.28) To prove Theorem 9.28, we simply apply the Renewal theorem, where we consider each time that the Markov chain enters state j to be a renewal. Because the Markov chain is irreducible, we know that it will eventually reach state j. Because the chain is positive recurrent, we know that $m_{jj} < \infty$, where m_{jj} is the mean number of steps between visits to state j. From the Renewal theorem we know

$$p_j = \lim_{t \to \infty} \frac{N_j(t)}{t} = \frac{1}{m_{jj}} \text{ w.p.1,}$$

and since $m_{jj} < \infty$, we have that $p_j > 0$. $\qquad \blacksquare$

9.6 Limiting Probabilities Interpreted as Rates

So far we have seen that, for an *ergodic* Markov chain,

$$\pi_i = \text{limiting probability Markov chain is in state } i$$

$$= \text{long-run proportion of time process is in state } i.$$

Now we observe that

$$\pi_i P_{ij} = \text{``rate'' of transitions from state } i \text{ to state } j.$$

To see this, observe that the DTMC is in state i for π_i fraction of all time steps. Furthermore, P_{ij} fraction of those time steps will result in the chain next moving to j. Hence, for $\pi_i P_{ij}$ fraction of all time steps, the DTMC is in state i, and its next step is to go to state j. Thus, if we look over t time steps (let t be large), then $\pi_i P_{ij} t$ transitions will have their start point in i and their end point in j. Dividing by t, we see that the *rate* of transitions (number of transitions per time step) that have their start point in i and their end point in j is $\pi_i P_{ij}$.

Question: What does $\sum_j \pi_i P_{ij}$ represent?

Answer: This is the total rate of transitions out of state i, including possibly returning right back to state i (if there are self-loops in the chain).

Question: What does $\sum_j \pi_j P_{ji}$ represent?

Answer: This is the total rate of transitions into state i, from any state, including possibly from state i (if there are self-loops in the chain).

Recall the stationary equation for state i:

$$\pi_i = \sum_j \pi_j P_{ji}$$

We also know that $\pi_i = \pi_i \sum_j P_{ij} = \sum_j \pi_i P_{ij}$.

Thus we have

$$\pi_i = \sum_j \pi_i P_{ij} = \sum_j \pi_j P_{ji}. \tag{9.17}$$

Yet this says that the stationary equations are simply relating the total rate of transitions out of state i with the total rate of transitions into state i:

$$\text{Total rate leaving state } i = \text{Total rate entering state } i$$

Question: Why does it make sense that the total rate of transitions leaving state i should equal the total rate of transitions entering state i?

Answer: Every time a transition leaves state i, we cannot have another transition leave state i until some transition enters state i. Hence the *number* of transitions leaving state i is within 1 of the number of transitions entering state i. Now the *rate* of transitions leaving state i is the total number of transitions over a long period of time, t, divided by that time t. Since t is large, the difference of 1 in the number of transitions leaving state i and the number entering state i vanishes when divided by t, and hence the rates are equal.

We can also rewrite the stationary equations, equivalently, as follows by *ignoring* self-loops:

$$\sum_{j \neq i} \pi_i P_{ij} = \sum_{j \neq i} \pi_j P_{ji} \tag{9.18}$$

Equation (9.18) follows by subtracting $\pi_i P_{ii}$ from both sides of the stationary equation (9.17). The set of equations (9.18) over all states i are often referred to as

balance equations because they equate the rate that we leave state i to go to a state other than i, with the rate that we enter state i from a state other than i. As you can see, balance equations are mathematically equivalent to stationary equations – hence we can always simply ignore the self-loops and write balance equations. Balance equations can also be applied to a set of states as well as to a single state. For example, if a Markov chain is divided into two sets of states – call these S and S^c (here S^c denotes the complement of S) – then we can equate the rate of transitions (the "flux") from S to S^c with the rate of transitions from S^c to S.

Question: Why does it make sense that the total flux from S to S^c should equal that from S^c to S?

Answer: The argument is identical to what we observed for a single state. Every time a transition takes us from S to S^c, we have left the states in S. We therefore cannot have another transition from S to S^c until we reenter the states in S, but this requires a transition from S^c to S.

9.7 Time-Reversibility Theorem

You might be wondering at this point whether we can simplify the stationary/balance equations even further. In some cases we can. The following theorem is useful because it simplifies the balance equations. We will revisit time-reversibility later in the book.

Theorem 9.34 (Time-reversible DTMC) *Given an aperiodic, irreducible Markov chain, if there exist x_1, x_2, x_3, ... s.t., $\forall i, j$,*

$$\sum_i x_i = 1 \quad and \quad x_i P_{ij} = x_j P_{ji},$$

then

1. *$\pi_i = x_i$ (the x_i's are the limiting probabilities).*
2. *We say that the Markov chain is time-reversible.*

Proof
$$x_i P_{ij} = x_j P_{ji}$$

$$\Rightarrow \sum_i x_i P_{ij} = \sum_i x_j P_{ji}$$

$$\Rightarrow \sum_i x_i P_{ij} = x_j \sum_i P_{ji}$$

$$\Rightarrow \sum_i x_i P_{ij} = x_j$$

Now, because we also know that $\sum_i x_i = 1$, we know that the x_j's satisfy the stationary equations. Hence, because by Theorem 9.27 the solution to the stationary equations is unique, we know that $x_j = \pi_j$, the limiting probability of being in state j. ∎

This leads to the following simpler algorithm for determining the π_j's:

1. First try time-reversibility equations (between pairs of states):
   $x_i P_{ij} = x_j P_{ji}, \quad \forall i, j$ and $\sum_i x_i = 1$.
2. If you find x_i's that work, that is great! Then we are done: $\pi_i = x_i$.
3. If not, we need to return to the regular stationary (or balance) equations.

The exercises at the end of this chapter help elucidate which chains are time-reversible and which are not.

Example: Three Types of Equations

Consider the Markov chain depicted in Figure 9.5.

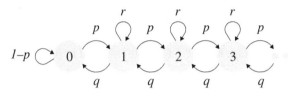

Figure 9.5. A very familiar Markov chain.

Regular Stationary Equations:

$$\pi_i = \pi_{i-1}p + \pi_i r + \pi_{i+1}q \quad \text{and} \quad \sum_i \pi_i = 1$$

These are messy to solve.

Balance Equations:

$$\pi_i(1 - r) = \pi_{i-1}p + \pi_{i+1}q \quad \text{and} \quad \sum_i \pi_i = 1$$

These are a little nicer, because we are ignoring self-loops, but still messy to solve.

Time-Reversibility Equations:

$$\pi_i p = \pi_{i+1}q \quad \text{and} \quad \sum_i \pi_i = 1$$

These are *much simpler* to solve.

9.8 When Chains Are Periodic or Not Irreducible

From the Summary Theorem (Theorem 9.27) we know that if a DTMC is both irreducible and aperiodic, and if we can find a solution to the stationary equations, then that solution is the unique limiting distribution for the Markov chain. However, what can be said when we have a chain that is not irreducible or is not aperiodic? What does the solution to the stationary equations (or the time-reversibility equations) represent in this case? This section answers these questions.

9.8.1 *Periodic Chains*

We show that analyzing periodic chains is not a problem. Specifically, we show in Theorem 9.36 that for any periodic, irreducible positive-recurrent chain the stationary distribution, $\vec{\pi}$, still exists. However $\vec{\pi}$ does not represent the limiting distribution, but rather the long-run time-average proportion of time spent in each state. We also prove a Summary Theorem for irreducible, periodic chains, Theorem 9.37, which is reminiscent of the Summary Theorem for irreducible, aperiodic chains (Theorem 9.27). Theorem 9.37 states that for an irreducible, periodic chain, if a stationary distribution, $\vec{\pi}$, exists, then the chain must be positive recurrent; hence, by Theorem 9.36, it follows that $\vec{\pi}$ is also the time-average distribution.

We start with a lemma.[5]

Lemma 9.35 *In an irreducible DTMC, all states have the same period.*

Proof Suppose states i and j communicate, where the period of i is p and the period of j is q. Since i and j communicate, there is a path of length, say, d_1, from i to j and some path of length, say, d_2, from j to i. Joining these gives a loop from i back to i of length $d_1 + d_2$. The period, p, is the GCD of all loops, so in particular

$$p \mid (d_1 + d_2)$$

(i.e., p divides $(d_1 + d_2)$). Now consider any loop from j back to j (note that the loop may or may not contain i). Let's say that the length of this loop is x. Now take the path from i to j of length d_1, then follow the loop of length x, then take the path from j to i of length d_2. This entire journey from i to i has length $d_1 + d_2 + x$; hence

$$p \mid (d_1 + d_2 + x).$$

Subtracting the previous two lines, we have that

$$p \mid x$$

However this is true for all loops from j to j. Therefore, p also divides the GCD of the lengths of all these loops. Thus $p \mid q$.

By a symmetric argument $q \mid p$, so it must be the case that $p = q$. ∎

Theorem 9.36 *In an irreducible, positive-recurrent DTMC with period $d < \infty$, the solution $\vec{\pi}$ to the stationary equations*

$$\vec{\pi} \cdot \mathbf{P} = \vec{\pi} \quad and \quad \sum_i \pi_i = 1$$

exists, is unique, and represents the time-average proportion of time spent in each state.

The majority of this section will be devoted to proving Theorem 9.36. We will follow this outline:

1. We start by finding a convenient way to label the states of a periodic chain in terms of "residue classes."
2. We prove that the distribution of time averages is a stationary distribution.
3. We show that any stationary distribution equals the time-average distribution.

---

[5] The algebraic argument in this section was proposed by PhD students, Sherwin Doroudi and Misha Lavrov.

Labeling the States of Periodic Chains

Imagine a chain where every state has period d.

Question: Pick a state, i. Does state i get visited once every d steps? If not, can we at least say that there is some positive probability that state i will be visited every d steps?

Answer: No. Consider a state i whose period is 2. There may be a path from i to i that takes 4 steps and another path that takes 6 steps. There is zero probability of going from i to i in 2 steps, yet the period is 2, as shown in the coloring of Figure 9.6.

Figure 9.6. Chain has period 2, as illustrated in the alternating coloring of the states.

What *is* clear is that the time between visits to any state i can never be *less than* d time steps. Now every state has period d, and we must be somewhere at each time step, and the chain is irreducible (so we eventually get to each state). It follows that we can *partition* the states into d "residue classes," with names: $0, 1, 2, \ldots, d-1$, where from a state in class 0, we can only next transition to a state in class 1, from a state in class 1 we can only next transition to a state in class 2, $\ldots$, and from a state in class $d-1$ we can only next transition to a state in class 0. Every state is in exactly one class and thus will be visited at most once every d steps. For a more mathematically rigorous definition of residue classes see Exercise 9.15.

Question: Given a chess board and a knight, if the "state" of the knight is the square that it is currently on, how many residue classes do we have?

Answer: The knight alternates between black squares and white ones, and every state can return to itself in 2 steps. Hence we have 2 residue classes: 0 and 1.

The first step of the proof is to relabel all states based on their residue classes, so that their names are as follows:

$$0_1, 0_2, 0_3, \ldots, 1_1, 1_2, 1_3, \ldots, 2_1, 2_2, 2_3, \ldots, (d-1)_1, (d-1)_2, (d-1)_3, \ldots$$

More succinctly, we will refer to the states as $(\vec{0}, \vec{1}, \vec{2}, \ldots, \overrightarrow{d-1})$.

Question: Once states are relabeled in this way, what is the form of the transition matrix $\mathbf{P}$? Where are its non-zero elements?

Answer:

$$
\mathbf{P} = \begin{array}{c} \\ \vec{0} \\ \vec{1} \\ \vec{2} \\ \vdots \\ \overrightarrow{d-1} \end{array}
\begin{array}{c} \overset{\vec{0}}{} \quad \overset{\vec{1}}{} \quad \overset{\vec{2}}{} \quad \overset{\ldots}{} \quad \overset{\overrightarrow{d-1}}{} \\
\begin{bmatrix}
0 & \mathbf{A}_{0,1} & 0 & 0 & 0 \\
0 & 0 & \mathbf{A}_{1,2} & 0 & 0 \\
0 & 0 & 0 & \mathbf{A}_{2,3} & 0 \\
0 & 0 & 0 & 0 & \ddots \\
\mathbf{A}_{d-1,0} & 0 & 0 & 0 & 0
\end{bmatrix}
\end{array}
\qquad (9.19)
$$

Question: What can we say about the matrices $\mathbf{A}_{i,i+1}$?

Answer: These matrices each have rows that sum to 1 (they are *stochastic*). This follows from the fact that $\mathbf{P}$ is stochastic.

Question: Are all the elements in $\mathbf{A}_{i,i+1}$ positive?

Answer: Not necessarily – there may not be a direct connection between every element of $\vec{i}$ and $\overrightarrow{i+1}$.

Now consider the dth power of $\mathbf{P}$.

Question: What does $\mathbf{P}^d$ look like? How can we express it in terms of the $\mathbf{A}_{i,i+1}$ matrices?

Answer:

$$
\mathbf{P}^d = \begin{array}{c} \\ \vec{0} \\ \vec{1} \\ \vec{2} \\ \vdots \\ \overrightarrow{d-1} \end{array}
\begin{bmatrix}
\mathbf{D}_{0,0} & 0 & 0 & 0 & 0 \\
0 & \mathbf{D}_{1,1} & 0 & 0 & 0 \\
0 & 0 & \mathbf{D}_{2,2} & 0 & 0 \\
0 & 0 & 0 & \ddots & 0 \\
0 & 0 & 0 & 0 & \mathbf{D}_{d-1,d-1}
\end{bmatrix}
\tag{9.20}
$$

where

$$
\begin{aligned}
\mathbf{D}_{0,0} &= \mathbf{A}_{0,1} \cdot \mathbf{A}_{1,2} \cdot \mathbf{A}_{2,3} \cdots \mathbf{A}_{d-1,0} \\
\mathbf{D}_{1,1} &= \mathbf{A}_{1,2} \cdot \mathbf{A}_{2,3} \cdots \mathbf{A}_{d-1,0} \cdot \mathbf{A}_{0,1} \\
\mathbf{D}_{2,2} &= \mathbf{A}_{2,3} \cdots \mathbf{A}_{d-1,0} \cdot \mathbf{A}_{0,1} \cdot \mathbf{A}_{1,2} \\
\mathbf{D}_{i,i} &= \mathbf{A}_{i,i+1} \cdot \mathbf{A}_{i+1,i+2} \cdots \mathbf{A}_{i-2,i-1} \cdot \mathbf{A}_{i-1,i}
\end{aligned}
\tag{9.21}
$$

Question: Is $\mathbf{D}_{i,i}$ stochastic? What does $\mathbf{D}_{i,i}$ represent? Is it irreducible? aperiodic? positive recurrent?

Answer: $\mathbf{D}_{i,i}$ is stochastic because it is the product of stochastic matrices, see Exercise 8.2. The matrix represents the probability of moving between each state in $\vec{i}$ to each of the other states in $\vec{i}$ in d steps. $\mathbf{D}_{i,i}$ is irreducible since $\mathbf{P}$ is irreducible, and all paths from states in $\vec{i}$ to states in $\vec{i}$ have length that is a multiple of d. To see that $\mathbf{D}_{i,i}$ is aperiodic, assume not. Then the period of $\mathbf{D}_{i,i}$ is at least 2. But this contradicts the fact that all states in $\vec{i}$ have period d. Finally, since the original chain is positive recurrent, we know that $\mathbf{D}_{i,i}$ is as well.

Showing that the Time-Average Distribution is a Stationary Distribution

Using the above labeling, consider the time-average distribution, $\vec{p}$:

$$
\vec{p} = (p_{0_1}, p_{0_2}, p_{0_3}, \ldots, p_{1_1}, p_{1_2}, p_{1_3}, \ldots, p_{(d-1)_1}, p_{(d-1)_2}, p_{(d-1)_3}, \ldots)
$$

where

$$
\sum_{i=0}^{d-1} \sum_{j} p_{i_j} = 1
$$

Here p_{i_j} represents the long-run proportion of time spent in state i_j. In shorthand, we will write $\vec{p} = (p_{\vec{0}}, p_{\vec{1}}, \ldots, p_{\overrightarrow{d-1}})$.

Question: What do we know about $\sum_j p_{i_j}$?

Answer: Since $\vec{i}$ is only visited once every d steps, $\sum_j p_{i_j} = \frac{1}{d}$. Let

$$q_{\vec{i}} = d \cdot p_{\vec{i}} \tag{9.22}$$

Observe that $\sum_j q_{i_j} = 1$.

Question: What does $q_{\vec{i}}$ represent? What does it mean in relation to $\mathbf{D_{i,i}}$?

Answer: Imagine observing the chain *only* every d steps when it hits states in $\vec{i}$. Then $q_{\vec{i}}$ represents the time-average proportion of time spent in each state of $\vec{i}$ during those observations and $\mathbf{D_{i,i}}$ represents the probability transition matrix, where its (x, y)th entry is the probability that from state i_x we will next transition to i_y (at the next observation time).

Since $\mathbf{D_{i,i}}$ is ergodic, it follows that it has a unique stationary distribution, that is equal both to the limiting distribution and the time-average distribution. Thus $\forall i$, $q_{\vec{i}}$ is the unique solution to the stationary equations:

$$q_{\vec{i}} \cdot \mathbf{D_{i,i}} = q_{\vec{i}} \quad \text{and} \quad \sum_j q_{i_j} = 1 \tag{9.23}$$

From (9.23) it is tempting to start thinking about $(p_{\vec{0}}, p_{\vec{1}}, \ldots, p_{\overrightarrow{d-1}})$ being a stationary distribution for $\mathbf{D} = \mathbf{P}^d$. However that's *not* where we want to go! What we want to prove is that $(p_{\vec{0}}, p_{\vec{1}}, \ldots, p_{\overrightarrow{d-1}})$ is a stationary distribution for $\mathbf{P}$. To do this, we need to get back to the $\mathbf{A_{i,i+1}}$ matrices, rather than the $\mathbf{D_{i,i}}$ matrices.

From (9.23) and (9.21), we have that:

$$
\begin{aligned}
q_{\vec{i}} \cdot \mathbf{A_{i,i+1}} &= (q_{\vec{i}}\mathbf{D_{i,i}}) \, \mathbf{A_{i,i+1}} \\
&= q_{\vec{i}} \cdot (\mathbf{A_{i,i+1}}\mathbf{A_{i+1,i+2}} \cdots \mathbf{A_{i-1,i}}) \cdot \mathbf{A_{i,i+1}} \\
&= (q_{\vec{i}}\mathbf{A_{i,i+1}}) \cdot (\mathbf{A_{i+1,i+2}} \cdots \mathbf{A_{i,i+1}}) \\
&= (q_{\vec{i}}\mathbf{A_{i,i+1}}) \cdot \mathbf{D_{i+1,i+1}} \tag{9.24}
\end{aligned}
$$

Let

$$\vec{r} = q_{\vec{i}} \cdot \mathbf{A_{i,i+1}}$$

Question: What do we know about the sum of the elements in $\vec{r}$?

Answer: Since the elements of $q_{\vec{i}}$ sum to 1, and since $\mathbf{A_{i,i+1}}$ is stochastic and thus preserves sums of vectors, we have that the sum of elements of $\vec{r}$ is 1.

From (9.24) we thus have that:

$$\vec{r} = \vec{r} \cdot \mathbf{D_{i+1,i+1}} \quad \text{and} \quad \sum_j r_j = 1$$

Thus $\vec{r}$ is a stationary distribution for $\mathbf{D_{i+1,i+1}}$. But $q_{\overrightarrow{i+1}}$ is the unique stationary distribution for $\mathbf{D_{i+1,i+1}}$.

Hence it follows that:

$$\vec{r} = q_{\overrightarrow{i+1}}$$
$$\Rightarrow q_{\vec{i}} \cdot \mathbf{A_{i,i+1}} = q_{\overrightarrow{i+1}}$$

$$\Rightarrow (q_{\vec{0}}, q_{\vec{1}}, \ldots, q_{\overrightarrow{d-1}}) \cdot \mathbf{P} = (q_{\vec{0}}, q_{\vec{1}}, \ldots, q_{\overrightarrow{d-1}}) \quad \text{where} \quad \sum_i \sum_j q_{i_j} = d$$

$$\Rightarrow (p_{\vec{0}}, p_{\vec{1}}, \ldots, p_{\overrightarrow{d-1}}) \cdot \mathbf{P} = (p_{\vec{0}}, p_{\vec{1}}, \ldots, p_{\overrightarrow{d-1}}) \quad \text{where} \quad \sum_i \sum_j p_{i_j} = 1$$

Hence we see that $\vec{p}$ satisfies the stationary equations for the original chain with transition matrix $\mathbf{P}$.

Showing That the Solution to the Stationary Distribution Is Unique

Consider a stationary distribution $\vec{s} = (s_{\vec{0}}, s_{\vec{1}}, \ldots, s_{\overrightarrow{d-1}})$. We will show that $\vec{s} = \vec{p}$.

$$\vec{s} \cdot \mathbf{P} = \vec{s} \quad \text{and} \quad \sum_j s_j = 1$$

$$\Rightarrow \vec{s} \cdot \mathbf{P}^d = \vec{s}$$

$$\Rightarrow \vec{s} \cdot \mathbf{D} = \vec{s}$$

$$\Rightarrow s_{\vec{i}} \cdot \mathbf{D}_{\mathbf{i},\mathbf{i}} = s_{\vec{i}}$$

Furthermore,

$$\sum_j s_{i_j} = \frac{1}{d}$$

since we only visit states in $\vec{i}$ once every d steps.

But by (9.23) and (9.22), $p_{\vec{i}}$ is the unique solution to:

$$p_{\vec{i}} \cdot \mathbf{D}_{\mathbf{i},\mathbf{i}} = p_{\vec{i}} \quad \text{and} \quad \sum_j p_{i_j} = \frac{1}{d}$$

Hence

$$p_{\vec{i}} = s_{\vec{i}}, \quad \forall i.$$

> **Theorem 9.37 (Summary Theorem for Periodic Chains)**   *Given an irreducible DTMC with period $d < \infty$, if a stationary distribution $\vec{\pi}$ exists for the chain, then the chain must be positive recurrent.*

Proof   The proof uses much of the proof of Theorem 9.36. We partition all states into d residue classes. We denote by $\vec{i}$ the states with residue i and denote by $\pi_{\vec{i}}$ those components of $\vec{\pi}$ that correspond to states with residue i.

We define $\mathbf{D}_{\mathbf{i},\mathbf{i}}$ as in this section. Via the same arguments as used in this section, we can argue that $\mathbf{D}_{\mathbf{i},\mathbf{i}}$ is irreducible and aperiodic. (However we don't know that $\mathbf{D}_{\mathbf{i},\mathbf{i}}$ is positive recurrent.)

Since $\vec{\pi}$ is stationary, we have that

$$\vec{\pi} \cdot \mathbf{P} = \vec{\pi}.$$

It therefore follows that

$$\vec{\pi} \cdot \mathbf{P}^d = \vec{\pi}.$$

Looking at (9.20), we see that, $\forall i$,

$$\pi_{\vec{i}} \cdot \mathbf{D_{i,i}} = \pi_{\vec{i}} \,.$$

We can now conclude that we have a stationary solution to $\mathbf{D_{i,i}}$, once we multiply $\pi_{\vec{i}}$ by some appropriate normalizing constant to make sure its probabilities sum to 1.

At this point, we have shown that $\mathbf{D_{i,i}}$ is aperiodic and irreducible and has a stationary solution. Thus, from Theorem 9.27, it follows that $\mathbf{D_{i,i}}$ must be positive recurrent, for every i. But now, since all the $\mathbf{D_{i,i}}$'s are positive recurrent, it must be the case that the original Markov chain was positive recurrent as well. ∎

9.8.2 *Chains that Are Not Irreducible*

Given an aperiodic, positive-recurrent chain that is *not* irreducible, there is still a notion of "limiting probabilities." However two things are no longer true: First, it is no longer the case that the limiting probability of being in state j is necessarily independent of the starting state i. Thus, we can't define $\pi_j = \lim_{n \to \infty} P_{ij}^n$, independent of i, as in Theorem 9.27. Second, it is no longer the case that the limiting probability of every state j is positive, as we had in Theorem 9.27, since some states may not be reachable, or there may be an "absorbing" state (or states), from which one never leaves. While the entire chain is not irreducible, the chain can still be subdivided into irreducible components (sometimes individual states), where an irreducible component may function as its own ergodic chain. In Section 10.1.2, we consider some examples of chains that are not irreducible and illustrate the above points.

9.9 Conclusion

What you should take away from this chapter is that, given ergodicity, there are many equivalent representations of limiting probabilities. We can think of the limiting probability of being in state j as either the average fraction of time spent in state j, the stationary probability of being in state j, the reciprocal of the mean time between visits to state j, or even the rate of transitions out of state j. Depending on the occasion, you may find it preferable to use one representation over another. Figure 9.7 illustrates some of these equivalences.

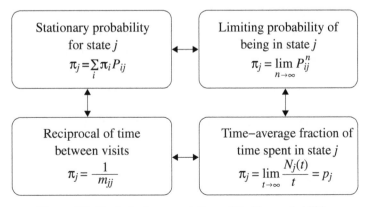

Figure 9.7. Equivalent representations of limiting probabilities.

You should also take away the fact that there are many techniques for determining the limiting probabilities, including raising the probability transition matrix $\mathbf{P}$ to high powers, solving stationary equations (or equivalently balance equations), or trying to solve time-reversibility equations. Although some techniques are simple (e.g., solving time-reversibility equations), they will not always work.

9.10 Proof of Ergodic Theorem of Markov Chains*

This section is devoted to proving Theorem 9.25, adapting material in Karlin and Taylor [105], (Ch. 4).

Our goal is to show that the sequence $\{P_{ii}^n, n = 1, 2, 3, \ldots\}$ converges to $\frac{1}{m_{ii}}$. Our plan is to define an upper and lower bound on the sequence of P_{ii}^n and then show that our upper and lower bounds are actually the same, both equaling $\frac{1}{m_{ii}}$.

We begin with the following definition:

Definition 9.38 Define f_{ii}^k to be the probability of first returning to state i after the kth transition, where we define f_{ii}^0 to be zero. Define P_{ii}^k to represent the probability of being in state i after the kth transition, given that we started in state i, where we define $P_{ii}^0 = 1$. Finally, we define

$$m_{ii} = \mathbf{E}\,[\text{Number time steps to return to state } i] = \sum_{k=0}^{\infty} k f_{ii}^k$$

which follows by conditioning on the time of the first return to state i.

We now review definitions of $\lim\sup$ and $\lim\inf$ and present several preliminary lemmas on the limiting behavior of P_{ii}^n. We then express Theorem 9.25 more precisely as Theorem 9.43. Finally, we prove Theorem 9.43.

Definition 9.39 Consider a sequence $\{a_n\}$.
1. We say $\lim_{n \to \infty} a_n = b$ if $\forall \epsilon > 0, \exists n_0(\epsilon)$ s.t. $|a_n - b| < \epsilon, \forall n \geq n_0(\epsilon)$.
2. We say $\lim\sup_{n \to \infty} a_n = b$ if $\forall \epsilon > 0, \exists n_0(\epsilon)$ s.t., $\forall n \geq n_0(\epsilon)$,
   (a) $a_n < b + \epsilon$, and
   (b) b is the smallest value for which the above is true.
3. We say $\lim\inf_{n \to \infty} a_n = b$ if $\forall \epsilon > 0, \exists n_0(\epsilon)$ s.t., $\forall n \geq n_0(\epsilon)$,
   (a) $a_n > b - \epsilon$, and
   (b) b is the largest value for which the above is true.

The following are three immediate consequences of the definition of $\lim\sup$. Similar consequences exist for $\lim\inf$.

---

* This section can be skipped without disturbing the flow of the book.

Lemma 9.40 *From* $\limsup\limits_{n\to\infty} a_n = b$ *it follows that*

1. $\forall \epsilon > 0$, *the sequence* $\{a_n\}$ *exceeds the value* $b - \epsilon$ *infinitely many times.*
2. *There exists an infinite subsequence of* $\{a_n\}$, *denoted by* $\{a_{n_j}\}$ *where* $n_1 < n_2 < n_3 < \ldots$, *s.t.* $\lim_{j\to\infty} a_{n_j} = b$.
3. *If there is an infinite subsequence of* $\{a_m\}$, *denoted by* $\{a_{m_j}\}$ *where* $m_1 < m_2 < m_3 < \ldots$, *and if* $\lim_{j\to\infty} a_{m_j} \neq b$ *(or does not exist), then there exists* $b' < b$ *such that there are an infinite number of elements of* $\{a_{m_j}\}$ *that are below* b'.

Proof

1. This follows from the fact that there cannot be a "last time" that $\{a_n\}$ exceeds $b - \epsilon$; otherwise $b - \epsilon$ would be the $\limsup$, rather than b.
2. We need to show that for any ϵ, there is some point on the subsequence after which all elements are in the range of $b \pm \epsilon$. We define our subsequence to meet these requirements as follows: First, by the definition of $\limsup$, we know that there is some n_0 s.t. $\forall n > n_0$, we have $a_n < b + \epsilon$. Furthermore by (1.), we know that there are infinitely many elements of $\{a_n\}$ with $n > n_0$, where $a_n > b - \epsilon$. We now consider all those elements as our subsequence, S. If we now pick a smaller ϵ', we can just look further out in S to a point where again all elements are less than $b + \epsilon'$, while still being assured that by (1.) there will be an infinite subsequence of $\{a_n\}$ exceeding $b - \epsilon'$ and also contained within S.
3. Suppose that the subsequence $\{a_{m_j}\}$ has a limit, but that limit is not b. Let that limit be b''. We know that $b'' < b$. Then define b' to lie between b'' and b. By the fact that $\lim_{j\to\infty}\{a_{m_j}\} = b''$, we know that it has an infinite number of elements less than b'. Now suppose that the subsequence $\{a_{m_j}\}$ does not have a limit. In this case, there exists some ϵ such that there is no point after which all the elements of $\{a_{m_j}\}$ are above $b - \epsilon$. Thus, if we define $b' = b - \epsilon$, then we know that at any point there is always "yet another" element of $\{a_{m_j}\}$ that lies below b', and hence there are an infinite number of elements of $\{a_{m_j}\}$ below b'.

■

Lemma 9.41 *Given a recurrent Markov chain, let* $\{f_{ii}^k\}$ *and* $\{P_{ii}^k\}$ *be the sequences specified in Definition 9.38. Let* $\lambda \equiv \limsup\limits_{k\to\infty} P_{ii}^k$. *By Lemma 9.40.2 there exists a subsequence* $\{P_{ii}^{n_j}\}$, $n_1 < n_2 < \ldots$, *for which* $\lim\limits_{j\to\infty} P_{ii}^{n_j} = \lambda$. *Given a* $c > 0$ *such that* $f_{ii}^c > 0$, *then*

$$\lim_{j\to\infty} P_{ii}^{n_j - c \cdot d} = \lambda \quad \text{for all integers } d \geq 0.$$

Lemma 9.42 *Given a recurrent Markov chain, let $\mu \equiv \liminf\limits_{k\to\infty} P_{ii}^k$. By the analogue of Lemma 9.40.2 there exists a subsequence $\{P_{ii}^{m_j}\}$, $m_1 < m_2 < \ldots$, for which $\lim\limits_{j\to\infty} P_{ii}^{m_j} = \mu$. Given a $c > 0$ such that $f_{ii}^c > 0$, then*

$$\lim_{j\to\infty} P_{ii}^{m_j - c \cdot d} = \mu \quad \text{for all integers } d \geq 0.$$

We now present a proof of Lemma 9.41. The proof of Lemma 9.42 follows via a very similar argument.

Proof (Lemma 9.41) We first prove that $\lim\limits_{j\to\infty} P_{ii}^{n_j - c} = \lambda$, by using the given condition $f_{ii}^c > 0$. Only at the very end of the proof do we consider d.

Suppose, to the contrary, that $\lim\limits_{j\to\infty} P_{ii}^{n_j - c} \neq \lambda$. Then it follows by Lemma 9.40.3 that there exists $\lambda' < \lambda$ such that $P_{ii}^{n_j - c} < \lambda'$ for an infinite number of j.

Let $\epsilon = \left[f_{ii}^c (\lambda - \lambda') \right] / 3$. We determine N such that

$$\sum_{k=N}^{\infty} f_{ii}^k < \epsilon. \tag{9.25}$$

(We know that $\sum_{k=0}^{\infty} f_{ii}^k = 1$, so we are simply looking at the tail of this distribution.) Let j be chosen so large that $n_j \geq N$ and

$$P_{ii}^{n_j} > \lambda - \epsilon \quad \left(\text{possible because } \lim_{j\to\infty} P_{ii}^{n_j} = \lambda \right), \tag{9.26}$$

$$P_{ii}^{n_j - c} < \lambda' < \lambda \quad \text{(determination of } \lambda'\text{)}, \tag{9.27}$$

$$P_{ii}^n < \lambda + \epsilon \quad \forall n \geq n_j - N \quad \text{(Definition 9.39.2a)}. \tag{9.28}$$

By conditioning on the time of first return, we get the following equation:

$$P_{ii}^n = \sum_{k=0}^{n} f_{ii}^k P_{ii}^{n-k} \quad \forall n > 0 \tag{9.29}$$

Then,

$$P_{ii}^{n_j} = \sum_{k=0}^{n_j} f_{ii}^k P_{ii}^{n_j - k} \quad \text{(by 9.29)}$$

$$\leq \sum_{k=0}^{N} f_{ii}^k P_{ii}^{n_j - k} + \sum_{k=N+1}^{n_j} f_{ii}^k \quad \left(\text{because } P_{ii}^k \leq 1 \right)$$

$$< \sum_{k=0}^{N} f_{ii}^k P_{ii}^{n_j - k} + \epsilon \quad \text{(by 9.25)}$$

$$= \sum_{k=0, k \neq c}^{N} f_{ii}^{k} P_{ii}^{n_j - k} + f_{ii}^{c} P_{ii}^{n_j - c} + \epsilon$$

$$< \sum_{k=0, k \neq c}^{N} f_{ii}^{k} (\lambda + \epsilon) + f_{ii}^{c} \lambda' + \epsilon$$

$(P_{ii}^{n_j - k} < \lambda + \epsilon$ by 9.28; and $P_{ii}^{n_j - c} < \lambda'$ by 9.27)

$$= \left(\sum_{k=0}^{N} f_{ii}^{k} - f_{ii}^{c} \right) (\lambda + \epsilon) + f_{ii}^{c} \cdot \lambda' + \epsilon$$

$$\leq (1 - f_{ii}^{c}) (\lambda + \epsilon) + f_{ii}^{c} \lambda' + \epsilon$$

$$= \lambda + 2\epsilon - f_{ii}^{c} (\lambda + \epsilon - \lambda')$$

$$< \lambda + 2\epsilon - f_{ii}^{c} (\lambda - \lambda')$$

$$= \lambda - \epsilon \quad \text{(by definition of } \epsilon \text{ and the fact that } f_{ii}^{c} > 0)$$

Thus, $P_{ii}^{n_j} < \lambda - \epsilon$. Yet this contradicts (9.26), and so $\lim_{j \to \infty} P_{ii}^{n_j - c} = \lambda$.

By induction, we find that, for any integer $d \geq 0$,

$$\lim_{j \to \infty} P_{ii}^{n_j - c \cdot d} = \lambda. \tag{9.30}$$

∎

Theorem 9.43 *Given a recurrent, aperiodic Markov chain, let $\left\{ f_{ii}^{k} \right\}$ and $\left\{ P_{ii}^{k} \right\}$ be the sequences specified in Definition 9.38. Then $\lim_{n \to \infty} P_{ii}^{n}$ exists, and*

$$\lim_{n \to \infty} P_{ii}^{n} = \frac{1}{\sum_{k=0}^{\infty} k f_{ii}^{k}} \equiv \frac{1}{m_{ii}}.$$

Proof Let

$$r_n = f_{ii}^{n+1} + f_{ii}^{n+2} + \cdots = \mathbf{P} \left\{ \text{Time to return to } i \text{ exceeds } n \right\}.$$

Observe $m_{ii} = \mathbf{E} \left[\text{Time to return to } i \right] = \sum_{k=0}^{\infty} k f_{ii}^{k} = \sum_{n=0}^{\infty} r_n$.

Consider the quantity

$$\sum_{k=0}^{n} r_k P_{ii}^{n-k} = \sum_{k=0}^{n} r_{n-k} P_{ii}^{k}$$

Question: What is the value of this sum?

Answer: This sum equals 1, for all n. To see this, suppose that we start in state i at time 0. We now ask, "What is the last time we visit state i before time n?" Observe that this could be any time step between 0 and n, inclusive. There certainly must exist some last time, because we are already in state i at time 0. The quantity $P_{ii}^{k} r_{n-k}$ represents the probability that the last time that we visited state i up to and including time n was at time k. We now sum $P_{ii}^k r_{n-k}$ from $k = 0$ to $k = n$, representing the full domain of the probability distribution; hence,

$$\sum_{k=0}^{n} r_k P_{ii}^{n-k} = \sum_{k=0}^{n} r_{n-k} P_{ii}^k = 1. \tag{9.31}$$

We would like to take the limit on relation (9.31) in such a way that P_{ii}^{n-k} can be moved out of the sum as a constant. We will look for subsequences of P_{ii}^n for relatively large n where we can do this by looking at partial sums of Equation (9.31), and exploiting Lemmas 9.41 and 9.42.

Let

$$\lambda = \limsup_{n \to \infty} P_{ii}^n.$$
$$\mu = \liminf_{n \to \infty} P_{ii}^n.$$

Clearly $\mu \le \lambda$. We will show that $\mu \ge \lambda$. This will establish that $\pi_i = \lim_{n \to \infty} P_{ii}^n = \lambda = \mu$.

Let $n_1 < n_2 < \ldots$ denote the indices of a subsequence of $\{P_{ii}^n\}$ for which $\lim_{j \to \infty} P_{ii}^{n_j} = \lambda$. This subsequence must exist by Lemma 9.40.2. Likewise, let $m_1 < m_2 < \ldots$ denote the indices of a subsequence of $\{P_{ii}^m\}$ for which $\lim_{j \to \infty} P_{ii}^{m_j} = \mu$. This subsequence must exist by the analogue to Lemma 9.40.2.

Using Equation (9.31), and because $r_n \ge 0$ and $0 \le P_{ii}^n \le 1$ for all n, we obtain, for any finite M and fixed j such that $n_j, m_j > N + M > 0$,

$$\sum_{k=0}^{n_j - M} r_k P_{ii}^{n_j - M - k} = 1 = \sum_{k=0}^{m_j - M} r_k P_{ii}^{m_j - M - k}$$

$$\sum_{k=0}^{N} r_k P_{ii}^{n_j - M - k} + \sum_{k=N+1}^{n_j - M} r_k \cdot 0 \le 1 \le \sum_{k=0}^{N} r_k P_{ii}^{m_j - M - k} + \sum_{k=N+1}^{m_j - M} r_k \cdot 1. \tag{9.32}$$

To take the limits with the desired effect, we apply Lemmas 9.41 and 9.42 and find that, if $f_{ii}^1 > 0$, then $\lim_{j \to \infty} P_{ii}^{n_j - M - k} = \lambda$ and $\lim_{j \to \infty} P_{ii}^{m_j - M - k} = \mu$, where $M = 0$. We will shortly argue that even if $f_{ii}^1 = 0$, so long as the chain is aperiodic we can fix finite $M > 0$ and still apply Lemmas 9.41 and 9.42.

Evaluating the inequality chain in Equation (9.32) first as $j \to \infty$ and then as $N \to \infty$ gives

$$\lambda \sum_{k=0}^{N} r_k \le \quad 1 \quad \le \mu \sum_{k=0}^{N} r_k + \sum_{k=N+1}^{\infty} r_k \quad \text{(as } j \to \infty)$$

$$\lambda \sum_{k=0}^{\infty} r_k \le \quad 1 \quad \le \quad \mu \sum_{k=0}^{\infty} r_k \quad \text{(as } N \to \infty)$$

$$\lambda \quad \le \frac{1}{\sum_{k=0}^{\infty} r_k} \le \quad \mu.$$

Yet, by definition of $\lim \sup$ and $\lim \inf$, $\mu \leq \lambda$. Thus $\mu = \lambda$, which means that $\lim_{n \to \infty} P_{ii}^n$ exists and its value is

$$\pi_i = \lim_{n \to \infty} P_{ii}^n = \frac{1}{\sum_{k=0}^{\infty} r_k} = \frac{1}{\sum_{k=0}^{\infty} k f_{ii}^k} \tag{9.33}$$

We now consider the remaining case: $f_{ii}^1 = 0$. However, because the chain is aperiodic, the greatest common divisor of those c for which $f_{ii}^c > 0$ is 1.

Consider the set of $\{c_i\}$ such that $f_{ii}^{c_i} > 0$, where we know, by aperiodicity, that the greatest common divisor of the $\{c_i\}$ is 1. Now consider any linear combination of the c_i's: $p = \sum_i c_i d_i$, where $d_i > 0$. Then we can show by induction on Lemmas 9.41 and 9.42 that

$$\lim_{j \to \infty} P_{ii}^{n_j - p} = \lambda \quad \text{and} \quad \lim_{j \to \infty} P_{ii}^{m_j - p} = \mu.$$

Applying the Euclidean number property, we know that there exists an M where any $n > M$ can be expressed as a positive linear combination of a set of $\{c_i\}$ whose greatest common divisor is 1.

Therefore, there exists a sufficiently large M such that

$$\lim_{j \to \infty} P_{ii}^{n_j - M - d} = \lambda \quad \text{and} \quad \lim_{j \to \infty} P_{ii}^{m_j - M - d} = \mu, \quad \forall \text{ integers } d \geq 0.$$

At this point we have proved our theorem when $\pi_j = \lim_{n \to \infty} P_{jj}^n$. We now invoke the irreducibility assumption, which allows us to reach state j from any initial state i, hence completing the proof of the theorem. ∎

9.11 Exercises

9.1 Irreducibility, Aperiodicity, and Positive Recurrence

For each of the following transition matrices, state whether the chain is (i) irreducible, (ii) aperiodic, or (iii) positive recurrent. [Note: If the period is not defined, then the chain is *not* aperiodic.]

(a) $\begin{pmatrix} \frac{1}{4} & \frac{1}{4} & \frac{1}{2} \\ 0 & 0 & 1 \\ 1 & 0 & 0 \end{pmatrix}$ (b) $\begin{pmatrix} 0 & 1 & 0 \\ 0 & 1 & 0 \\ 1 & 0 & 0 \end{pmatrix}$ (c) $\begin{pmatrix} \frac{1}{3} & 0 & \frac{2}{3} \\ \frac{1}{4} & \frac{3}{4} & 0 \\ 0 & 0 & 1 \end{pmatrix}$

9.2 Practice with Balance Equations and Time-Reversibility Equations

Consider the following Markov chains:

$$\mathbf{P}^{(1)} = \begin{pmatrix} 0 & 2/3 & 0 & 1/3 \\ 1/3 & 0 & 2/3 & 0 \\ 0 & 1/3 & 0 & 2/3 \\ 2/3 & 0 & 1/3 & 0 \end{pmatrix}$$

$$\mathbf{P}^{(2)} = \begin{pmatrix} 1/3 & 2/3 & 0 & 0 \\ 1/3 & 0 & 2/3 & 0 \\ 0 & 1/3 & 0 & 2/3 \\ 0 & 0 & 1/3 & 2/3 \end{pmatrix}$$

(a) Draw the corresponding Markov chains for $\mathbf{P}^{(1)}$ and $\mathbf{P}^{(2)}$.

(b) Solve for the time-average fraction of time spent in each state for both $\mathbf{P}^{(1)}$ and $\mathbf{P}^{(2)}$. First try to use the time-reversibility equations, and if they do not work, then use the balance equations.

(c) Was $\mathbf{P}^{(1)}$ time-reversible? Was $\mathbf{P}^{(2)}$ time-reversible?

(d) For those chain(s) that were time-reversible, explain why it makes sense that for all states i, j in the chain, the rate of transitions from i to j should equal the rate of transitions from j to i.

9.3 Data Centers, Backhoes, and Bugs

Data centers alternate between "working" and "down." There are many reasons why data centers can be down, but for the purpose of this problem we mention only two reasons: (i) a backhoe accidentally dug up some cable, or (ii) a software bug crashed the machines. Suppose that a data center that is working today will be down tomorrow due to backhoe reasons with probability $\frac{1}{6}$, but will be down tomorrow due to a software bug with probability $\frac{1}{4}$. A data center that is down today due to backhoe reasons will be up tomorrow with probability 1. A data center that is down today due to a software bug will be up tomorrow with probability $\frac{3}{4}$.

(a) Draw a DTMC for this problem.

(b) Is your DTMC ergodic? Why or why not?

(c) Is your DTMC time-reversible? Why or why not?

(d) What fraction of time is the data center working?

(e) What is the expected number of days between backhoe failures?

9.4 Ergodicity Summary

You are given an *aperiodic*, *irreducible* DTMC, with $n > 1$ states.

Put a check mark in *ALL* boxes that are valid (possible). Note that some rows may be empty, whereas others may have multiple check marks. (We started you off by filling in some boxes.)

	Chain is Positive Recurrent	Chain is Transient	Chain is Null Recurrent
$f_j = 1$	✓		
$f_j = 0$			
$0 < f_j < 1$			
$m_{jj} = \infty$			
$m_{jj} < \infty$	✓		
$\sum_{n=0}^{\infty} P_{jj}^n = \infty$			
$\sum_{n=0}^{\infty} P_{jj}^n < \infty$			
$0 < \pi_j < 1$			
$\pi_j = 0$			
$\pi_j = 1$			
$\pi_j < 0$			

Glossary:

m_{jj} = mean number of steps to return to j given we're in state j

P_{ii}^n = probability that the chain is in state i in n steps given the chain is currently in state i

f_j = probability that a chain starting in state j ever returns to state j

π_j = limiting probability of being in state j

Warning: Read the directions carefully! Every word is meaningful.

9.5 Time between Visits

Given an ergodic DTMC, let m_{ij} denote the mean number of steps to get from state i to state j. Sherwin makes the following conjecture:

$$m_{jj} \leq m_{ji} + m_{ij} \tag{9.34}$$

Either prove or disprove Sherwin's conjecture.

9.6 Pricing Model

You are the market maker for GOGO. You have no clue whether GOGO stock will rise or fall, but you are obligated to buy or sell single shares from customers at all times. However, you do get to set the share price.

To control the size of your position (number of shares of GOGO you own), when you are long (i.e., own) GOGO, you set the price so that with probability $p < \frac{1}{2}$, your next trade is a buy, and with probability $q = 1 - p$ your next trade is a sell. In contrast, if you are short (i.e., owe) GOGO, you set the price so that with probability p, your next trade is a sell, and with probability q your next trade is a buy.

Your position is represented by the bidirectional chain in Figure 9.8, with a negative state indicating how many shares you owe and a positive state indicating how many shares you own.

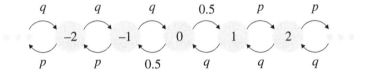

Figure 9.8. Bidirectional chain for pricing.

(a) Given this pricing, what does your position tend to revert to?
(b) Derive the time-average fraction of time spent in each state.
(c) Why weren't you asked to find the limiting probabilities?
(d) What is the expected (absolute value) size of your position?

9.7 Expected Time until k Failures

This is a repeat of Exercise 3.25, where we want to derive the expected number of minutes until there are k consecutive failures in a row, assuming that a failure occurs independently every minute with probability p. However this time, the problem should be solved by finding the limiting probability of some Markov chain. Please include a picture of your Markov chain. [Hint: You will have to think a bit to see how to convert from the limiting probabilities of the DTMC to what you really want.]

9.8 Walks on Undirected Weighted Graphs

This problem comes up in many areas. Consider any undirected graph with weights, where $w_{ij} = w_{ji}$ is the weight on edge (i, j). Consider a particle that moves from node to node in the graph in the following manner: A particle residing at node i will next move to node j with probability P_{ij} where

$$P_{ij} = \frac{w_{ij}}{\Sigma_j w_{ij}}.$$

(Draw a picture to help yourself visualize this.) What is the long-run proportion of time that the particle is in state i? [Hint: To answer this question, it will help to write out the time-reversibility equations, rather than the stationary equations. You will need to guess a solution to these equations.]

9.9 Randomized Chess

This problem concerns the behavior of various chess pieces as they move randomly around the board. If you are not familiar with chess, all you need to know for this problem is the following. The game is played on a board divided into 64 squares (8×8) that alternate from white to black. There are many different types of pieces that each move in a different way. The three pieces in this exercise are the king, bishop, and knight. The king can move one square in any direction (including the diagonal). The bishop can move any number of squares, but only in the diagonal directions. Finally, the knight moves in an L-shape. That is, the knight moves two squares to either side (left or right) and one square up or down. Or, the knight can move two squares up or down and one square to the side (left or right).

(a) You are given an empty 8×8 chessboard with a lone king placed in one corner. At each time step, the king will make a uniformly random legal move. Is the corresponding Markov chain for this process (i) irreducible? (ii) aperiodic?

(b) What if a bishop is used instead?

(c) What if a knight is used instead?

(d) Now take advantage of Exercise 9.8 on undirected weighted graphs and time-reversibility to calculate the expected time for the king to return to the corner. Think about how hard this would be without time-reversibility. [Hint: the calculation should be very simple.]

(e) Do the same for the bishop.

(f) Do the same for the knight.

9.10 Threshold Queue Revisited

In Exercise 8.6, we defined a threshold queue, depicted by the chain in Figure 9.9.

(a) Argue that the Markov chain is aperiodic and irreducible.

(b) Argue that the Markov chain is positive recurrent.

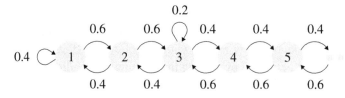

Figure 9.9. Threshold chain where threshold point is $T = 3$.

9.11 Symmetric Random Walk

[Proposed by PhD student, Srivatsan Narayanan] This problem presents a combinatorial proof of Theorem 9.23 that uses Catalan numbers. Given the symmetric random walk shown in Figure 9.10, we know that, if we start at state 0, then, with probability 1, we will return to state 0. Prove that $m_{00} = \infty$, where m_{00} denotes the mean time between visits to state 0.

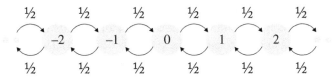

Figure 9.10. Symmetric random walk.

(a) Let T_{00} be a random variable denoting the time of the *first* return to state 0. If we knew the probability mass function for T_{00}, how would we use that to get m_{00}?

(b) Assume WLOG that the first step is to the right (from 0 to 1). Then the last step before returning to state 0 must be to the left (from 1 to 0). If $T_{00} = n$, how can we characterize the middle $n - 2$ steps?

(c) The Catalan number $C(k)$ represents the number of strings of length $2k$ such that there are k 0's and k 1's, such that no prefix of the strings contains more 0's than 1's. Express $\mathbf{P}\{T_{00} = n\}$ in terms of an expression involving a Catalan number. It may help to start by observing that $\mathbf{P}\{T_{00} = n\} = \mathbf{P}\{T_{00} = n \mid \text{First step is right}\}$.

(d) It is well known that

$$C(k) = \frac{1}{k+1}\binom{2k}{k}.$$

Use this fact and Lemma 9.18 to derive a lower bound on $\mathbf{P}\{T_{00} = n\}$. Then use that lower bound in (a) to show that $m_{00} = \infty$.

9.12 Stopping Times and Wald's Equation

A positive integer-valued random variable N is said to be a *stopping time* for a sequence: $X_1, X_2, X_3, \ldots$ if the event $\{N = n\}$ is independent of $X_{n+1}, X_{n+2}, \ldots$ That is, the stopping time, N, can depend on everything seen so far, but not on the future.

(a) Consider a sequence of coin flips. Let N denote the time until we see 5 heads total. Is N a stopping time? How about the time until we see 5 consecutive heads?

(b) Consider a gambler who starts with zero dollars and in each game is equally likely to win a dollar or lose a dollar. Let X_i denote the result of the ith game. The gambler stops whenever he is 2 dollars ahead. Let N be the stopping time in terms of number of games. Write a mathematical expression for N, involving a sum.

(c) Let X_i be i.i.d. random variables, and let Y denote a positive integer-valued random variable that is independent of the X_i's. What do we know about $\mathbf{E}\left[\sum_{i=1}^{Y} X_i\right]$?

(d) Let X_i be i.i.d. random variables with finite mean. Let N be a stopping time for the sequence $X_1, X_2, X_3, \ldots$ Assume $\mathbf{E}[N] < \infty$. Then **Wald's equation** says that

$$\mathbf{E}\left[\sum_{i=1}^{N} X_i\right] = \mathbf{E}[N]\,\mathbf{E}[X]. \tag{9.35}$$

Importantly, N is *not* independent of the X_i's. Prove Wald's equation. [Hint: (i) It may help to define an indicator random variable $I_n = 1$ if and only if $N \geq n$ and then consider the product $X_n I_n$. (ii) The fact that the X_i's have finite mean will allow you to move an expectation into an infinite summation.]

9.13 Another Derivation of the Symmetric Random Walk

Wu suggests a different proof of Theorem 9.23 based on Wald's equation (9.35). Given the symmetric random walk shown in Figure 9.11, we know that, because the chain is recurrent, if we start at any state, then with probability 1 we will return to that state. Our goal is to prove that $m_{11} = \infty$, where m_{11} denotes the mean time between visits to state 1.

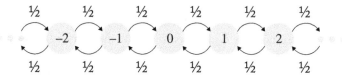

Figure 9.11. Symmetric random walk.

(a) Prove that $m_{11} > 0.5 m_{01}$. It thus suffices to show that $m_{01} = \infty$.

(b) Let T_{01} denote the time until we first hit state 1, given that we start at state 0. Note that T_{01} is well defined because the symmetric random walk is recurrent. Explain why T_{01} is a stopping time.

(c) If X_n is the state at time step n, what is $X_{T_{01}}$?

(d) Express $X_{T_{01}}$ as a sum of i.i.d. r.v.'s. Assuming that $\mathbf{E}\left[T_{01}\right]$ is finite, show that Wald's equation leads to a contradiction. Hence $m_{01} = \mathbf{E}\left[T_{01}\right] = \infty$.

9.14 Recurrent versus Transient

This problem involves the DTMC shown in Figure 9.12. Assume throughout this problem that $q = 1 - p$.

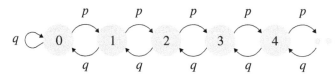

Figure 9.12. Markov chain for Exercise 9.14.

(a) For what values of p is this chain recurrent? For what values of p is it transient? Give an argument for each case based on the expected number of visits to each state. You might choose to compute $\sum_n P_{00}^n$ or to leverage any of the other ideas and arguments from this chapter.

(b) In the case where the chain is transient, compute

$$f_0 = \mathbf{P}\left\{\text{Ever return to state 0 given start there}\right\}$$

as a function of p.

(c) Assume that $p < q$. Let T_{00} denote the time to go from state 0 to state 0. Derive $\mathbf{E}\left[T_{00}\right]$. What does this tell us about $\pi_0 = \lim_{n \to \infty} P_{00}^n$?

(d) Assume $p < q$. Use the stationary equations to derive all the limiting probabilities.

(e) Again assume $p < q$. Is the chain time reversible? Why or why not?

9.15 Residue Classes in Periodic Chains

In Section 9.8, we partitioned the states of an irreducible DTMC with period d into "residue classes." This problem defines residue classes more rigorously. Let i be an arbitrary state. Define i to have residue class 0. For every other state j, define its residue class as the length of any path from i to j, taken modulo d (by irreducibility, there exists at least one such path).

(a) Show that the notion of residue classes is well-defined, by proving that the lengths of any two paths from i to j are equivalent modulo d.

(b) Prove that from a state in residue class k we can only go to a state in residue class $k + 1$.

9.16 Finite-State DTMCs

(a) Prove the following theorem:

> *Theorem: For a finite state, irreducible DTMC, all states are positive recurrent.*

In your proof, you may make use of the following two class properties, which are proved in (b):

- Theorem: Null recurrence is a class property (i.e., if i: null recurrent and i communicates with j then j: null recurrent).
- Theorem: Positive recurrence is a class property (i.e., if i: positive recurrent and i communicates with j then j: positive recurrent).

(b) Prove the preceding two class property theorems. Your proof should work for infinite-state Markov chains as well.

CHAPTER 10

Real-World Examples: Google, Aloha, and Harder Chains*

This chapter discusses applications of DTMCs in the real world. Section 10.1 describes Google's PageRank algorithm, and Section 10.2 analyzes the Aloha Ethernet protocol. Both problems are presented from the perspective of open-ended research problems, so that they serve as a lesson in modeling. Both are also good examples of ergodicity issues that come up in real-world problems. Finally, in Section 10.3, we consider DTMCs that arise frequently in practice but for which it is difficult to "guess a solution" for the limiting probabilities. We illustrate how generating functions can be used to find the solution for such chains.

10.1 Google's PageRank Algorithm

10.1.1 *Google's DTMC Algorithm*

Most of you probably cannot remember a search engine before google.com. When Google came on the scene, it quickly wiped out all prior search engines. The feature that makes Google so good is not the web pages that it finds, but the *order* in which it ranks them.

Consider a search on some term; for example, "koala bears." Thousands of web pages include the phrase "koala bears," ranging from the San Diego zoo koala bear home page, to anecdotes on the mating preferences of Australian lesbian koala bears, to a koala bear chair. The value of a good search engine is to rank these pages so that the page we need will most likely fall within the "top 10," thus enabling us to quickly find our information. Of course, how can a search engine know exactly which of the thousand pages will be most relevant to us?

A common solution is to rank the pages in order of the number of links to that page (often called *backlinks* of the page), starting with the page that has the highest number of pointers into it. We refer to this strategy as **citation counting**.

Citation counting is a very commonly used measure of importance. For example, many tenure decisions are determined not by your number of publications, but by the number of citations to your publications.

Question: Suppose that we could determine the number of backlinks of each page (number of links pointing to the page). Why would that *not* necessarily be a good measure of the importance of the page?

---

* This chapter can be skipped without disturbing the flow of the book.

Answer:

1. Not all links are equal. If a page has a link to it from the Yahoo web page, that link should be counted much more than if a page has a link to it from Joe Schmo's web page.

2. The citation counting scheme is easily tricked. Suppose I want my web page to have a high rank. I simply create a thousand pages that each point to my web page. Now my web page has a thousand pointers into it, so it should be ranked highly. (Hmmm . . . not a bad way to handle the tenure citation issue too . . .).

OK, so citation counting is not the best of schemes. While it is insufficient to just count the number of pages pointing into a page, we might do better by weighting each pointer by the number of pages pointing into it.

Question: Why is this system also easy to fool?

Answer: Now, to make my web page rank highly, I again create a thousand dummy web pages and have them all point to each other as well as to my page. That is, I create a clique of size 1,000. Now my web page has a high number of backlinks, all of which also have a high number of backlinks.

Google's Solution: Google's solution is to define page rank recursively: "A page has high rank if the sum of the ranks of its backlinks is high." Observe that this covers both the case when a page has many backlinks and when a page has a few highly ranked backlinks.

Question: It is easy to say that "a page has high rank if the sum of the ranks of its backlinks is high," but how does that help us figure out the rank of a page?

Answer: The "aha" that the Google founders made was to realize that the recursive definition is actually saying

$$\pi_j = \sum_{i=1}^{n} \pi_i P_{ij}.$$

That is, the only way for page j to have high limiting probability is if the i's pointing into j have high limiting probability. Remind you of anything?

The rank of a page is thus just its limiting probability in a Markov chain.

Google's PageRank Algorithm:

1. Create a DTMC transition diagram where there is one state for each web page and there is an arrow from state i to state j if page i has a link to page j.

2. If page i has $k > 0$ outgoing links, then set the probability on each outgoing arrow from state i to be $1/k$.

3. Solve the DTMC to determine limiting probabilities. Pages are then ranked based on their limiting probabilities (higher probability first).

This simple algorithm was the original basis behind the entire Google company!

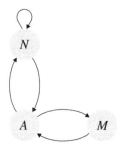

Figure 10.1. Links between web pages.

Example

Suppose the entire web consists of the three pages shown in Figure 10.1. Then the corresponding DTMC transition diagram is shown in Figure 10.2.

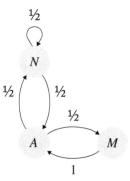

Figure 10.2. Corresponding DTMC transition diagram.

We now solve the balance equations:

$$\pi_A = \frac{1}{2}\pi_N + \pi_M$$

$$\frac{1}{2}\pi_N = \frac{1}{2}\pi_A$$

$$\pi_M = \frac{1}{2}\pi_A$$

$$1 = \pi_A + \pi_M + \pi_N$$

This results in: $\pi_A = \pi_N = \frac{2}{5}$; $\pi_M = \frac{1}{5}$.

Intuition behind the Google Algorithm: Imagine that each page initially has one unit of importance. At each round, each page shares whatever importance it has among its successors. Pages with a lot of incoming links will receive lots of importance (will be visited frequently in the DTMC).

10.1.2 *Problems with Real Web Graphs*

Unfortunately, PageRank does not work well on all web graphs. Consider the following two examples.

Example: Dead End or Spider Trap

Consider Figure 10.1, where this time there is either no outgoing link from page M (in this case M is called a "dead end") or there is a self-loop at state M (in this case M is called a "spider trap").

In either case Figure 10.3 shows the corresponding DTMC transition diagram.

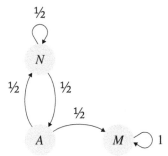

Figure 10.3. DTMC for a web graph with a dead end or spider trap at M.

The balance equations are

$$\frac{1}{2}\pi_N = \frac{1}{2}\pi_A$$

$$0 \cdot \pi_M = \frac{1}{2}\pi_A$$

$$\pi_A = \frac{1}{2}\pi_N$$

$$\pi_A + \pi_N + \pi_M = 1.$$

The solution to these equations is $\pi_M = 1, \pi_N = 0 = \pi_A$. These are also the limiting probabilities (note that the start state does not matter).

Somehow this solution is very unsatisfying. Just because person M chooses to be anti-social and not link to anyone else, it should not follow that person M is the only important person on the web. Our solution does not match our intuitive view of surfing a web graph.

Example: Two Spider Traps

Now imagine that both M and N are anti-social and link only to themselves. The resulting DTMC transition diagram is shown in Figure 10.4.

The corresponding balance equations are:

$$0 \cdot \pi_N = \frac{1}{2} \cdot \pi_A$$

$$0 \cdot \pi_M = \frac{1}{2} \cdot \pi_A$$

$$\pi_A = 0$$

$$\pi_A + \pi_N + \pi_M = 1.$$

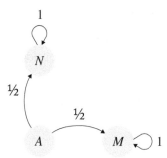

Figure 10.4. DTMC for a web graph with two spider traps.

Observe that there are an infinite number of possible solutions. This is because the limiting probabilities depend on the start state.

Again the solution is very unsatisfying.

10.1.3 *Google's Solution to Dead Ends and Spider Traps*

Google's solution to dead ends and spider traps is to "tax" each page some fraction of its "importance" and then distribute that taxed importance equally among all pages in the web graph. This "tax" keeps the DTMC from getting trapped in a dead end or spider trap.

Figure 10.5 shows the effect of applying a 30% tax on the DTMC of Figure 10.3. First, every existing transition is multiplied by 70%. Then, for each state s in an n-state chain, we add a transition of weight $\frac{30\%}{n}$ from state s to every other state, including itself. Thus in the three-state chain in Figure 10.3, we add a transition of weight 10% from each state to every other state.

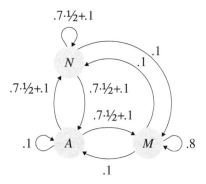

Figure 10.5. DTMC transition diagram for Figure 10.3 after 30% tax.

Observe that the spider trap is now no longer a problem, and we can easily solve for the limiting probabilities:

$$\pi_A = .19; \quad \pi_M = .55; \quad \pi_N = .26$$

The problem now is that these limiting probabilities are highly dependent on the amount of tax.

The readings at the end of the chapter describe experiments with other taxation ideas; for example, where the tax is distributed among just one or two pages.

10.1.4 *Evaluation of the PageRank Algorithm*

PageRank is intended to give an indication of the popularity of a page – the fraction of times that page is referenced as compared with other pages. This works well when the graph is irreducible, but is problematic when there are spider traps or dead ends. The taxation solution for solving the spider trap problem seems ad hoc. If the tax is too small, then we still end up with too high a limiting probability at the spider trap state (as in $\pi_M = 0.55$ in Section 10.1.3). Thus we need to use a high tax. Yet a high tax seems totally unrealistic, because it leads to every state being of equal weight.

In practice it seems that when you come to a page with links only back to itself, you usually back up (hit the "BACK" key). Perhaps we can combine the idea of taxation with the idea of backing up. That is, we apply a high tax to each page, but the tax is distributed only among the *predecessors* of the page, not among all pages of the web. This idea is explored in [53].

10.1.5 *Practical Implementation Considerations*

You might be wondering how in practice Google goes about solving the DTMC for the limiting probabilities, given that it is a huge (finite) DTMC. Solving such a large number of simultaneous equations seems difficult.

Question: Is there another approach to obtain the limiting probabilities?

Answer: Yes, we can take powers of $\mathbf{P}$, the transition probability matrix. This turns out to be faster when the transition probability matrix is large and sparse and only an approximate solution is needed. This is the approach employed by Google.

10.2 Aloha Protocol Analysis

The slotted Aloha protocol is the progenitor of the Ethernet protocol. Ethernet is a datalink-level protocol allowing multiple users to transmit a data frame along a single wire in a switchless LAN as shown in Figure 10.6. Only one user (host) can use the wire at a time. However, because the multiple users are working independently, it

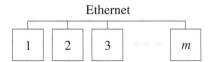

Figure 10.6. Ethernet with m hosts.

could turn out that more than one user tries to send a packet at once. In that case, a "collision" occurs, and all messages are corrupted and must be resent. Of course, if we had centralized control, we could ensure that the users take turns sending packets. However, we want to make this work *without* centralized control.

Ethernet uses CSMA/CD (Carrier Sense Multiple Access/Collision Detection). What is important in CSMA/CD is that, although the users basically submit independently of each other,[1] when their messages do collide, they are able to detect the collision (they do this by seeing that their data frames are garbled), and then they know that they need to resend. The key idea in CSMA/CD is that the retransmissions of the data need to occur at random times, so as to minimize the chance of repeated collisions.

In this section we use DTMCs to begin to analyze various protocols for how to handle the retransmissions. We start by looking at the Slotted Aloha protocol and studying the problems with this earlier protocol.

We will only go part of the way toward solving this problem during this chapter, but this discussion will give you a feel for how to model such problems with Markov chains and will also help make concepts of ergodicity more concrete.

10.2.1 *The Slotted Aloha Protocol*

The Slotted Aloha protocol is defined as follows: Time is divided into discrete time steps or "slots." There are m transmitting hosts. At each time step, each of the m hosts independently transmits a new message (frame) with probability p (assume $p < \frac{1}{m}$).

If exactly 1 message (frame) is transmitted in a slot, the transmission is deemed "successful" and the message leaves the system. However, if more than 1 message is transmitted during a slot, the transmission is deemed "unsuccessful." In this case *none* of those messages leave the system. Every message involved in an "unsuccessful transmission" is then *retransmitted* at every step with probability q, until it successfully leaves the system. To keep things stable, we may need to make q very small; for the time being, assume that q is a very small constant. Note that, regardless of the backlog of messages, each of the m hosts continues to transmit *new* messages with probability p at each step.

10.2.2 *The Aloha Markov Chain*

Question: Given values of m, p, and $q \ll p$, what does the Markov chain for the Slotted Aloha protocol look like?

Hint: It may not be obvious what we need to track. Each of the m hosts independently transmits a message at each time step with probability p, so there is no need to track that. What we need to track is the number of messages that need retransmission (i.e., the messages that have been through at least one collision).

---

[1] This is not entirely true, because users do "listen" to the wire before sending, although listening is not sufficient to avoid all collisions.

Answer: Before we begin, observe that the number of *new* messages transmitted during a time slot is distributed Binomially with parameters m and p. Therefore, the probability of generating k new messages is

$$p_k = \binom{m}{k} p^k (1-p)^{m-k}, \forall k = 0, 1, \ldots, m.$$

Likewise, when there are n messages in the previously collided pile, the probability of k retransmissions occurring is q_k^n where,

$$q_k^n = \binom{n}{k} q^k (1-q)^{n-k}, \forall k = 0, 1, \ldots, n.$$

We define the *state* at time step t to be the number of messages *remaining* in the system at the end of time step t. We now describe the transition probabilities for the states.

First, consider state 0 (no messages remaining in the system). The probability of remaining at state 0 is the probability that there are no new transmissions or there is exactly 1 new transmission (which gets out of the system). For a state transition to occur from 0 to $j > 1$, we need j new transmissions. There cannot be more than m new transmissions. Thus the probability of moving from state 0 to state $j > m$ is zero. Also, it is logically impossible to go from state 0 to state 1. Hence we have

$$P_{0,0} = (1-p)^m + mp(1-p)^{m-1}.$$
$$P_{0,1} = 0.$$
$$P_{0,j} = \binom{m}{j} p^j (1-p)^{m-j}, \forall j = 2, \ldots, m.$$
$$P_{0,j} = 0, \forall j > m.$$

Now consider state k, $k > 0$ (i.e., there are k unsuccessful messages left in the system at the end of the time step, waiting to be retransmitted). Because at most 1 message gets through at every time step, transitions from k to state $j \leq k - 2$ cannot occur. Further, a maximum of only m new messages can be generated. Therefore, the state cannot increase by more than m. The possible transitions are thus as follows:

- $k \to k - 1$: No new transmissions and 1 retransmission. The retransmitted message gets out of the system. Probability: $(1-p)^m kq(1-q)^{k-1}$.
- $k \to k$: There are several ways this can happen:
    1. One new transmission and no retransmissions:
       Probability: $mp(1-p)^{m-1}(1-q)^k$.
    2. No new transmission and no retransmissions:
       Probability: $(1-p)^m (1-q)^k$.
    3. No new transmission and at least 2 retransmissions:
       Probability: $(1-p)^m \left(1 - (1-q)^k - kq(1-q)^{k-1}\right)$.
- $k \to k + 1$: One new transmission and *at least* 1 retransmission. As a result, collision occurs, and the number of messages increases by 1.
  Probability: $mp(1-p)^{m-1} \left(1 - (1-q)^k\right)$.

- $k \to k + j$, $j = 2, \ldots, m$: There are j new transmissions. The number of re-transmissions does not matter, because collision occurs anyway.
  Probability: $\binom{m}{j} p^j (1 - p)^{m-j}$.

To summarize,

$$P_{k,j} = 0, \quad \forall j \leq k - 2.$$
$$P_{k,k-1} = (1 - p)^m kq(1 - q)^{k-1}.$$
$$P_{k,k} = m(1 - q)^k p(1 - p)^{m-1} + \left(1 - kq(1 - q)^{k-1}\right)(1 - p)^m.$$
$$P_{k,k+1} = mp(1 - p)^{m-1}\left(1 - (1 - q)^k\right).$$
$$P_{k,k+j} = \binom{m}{j} p^j (1 - p)^{m-j}, \quad \forall j = 2, \ldots, m.$$
$$P_{k,j} = 0, \quad \forall j > k + m.$$

These probabilities describe the system completely.

10.2.3 *Properties of the Aloha Markov Chain*

Question: Is this chain aperiodic and irreducible?

Answer: Yes.

Question: Does the Aloha protocol work?

Hint: Is the Markov chain ergodic (positive recurrent and aperiodic and irreducible), or is it transient, or is it null recurrent?

Answer: Let $P_{\text{back}}^{(k)}$ represent the probability of transitioning to a lower numbered state, given we are in state k. Let $P_{\text{forw}}^{(k)} = 1 - P_{\text{back}}^{(k)}$. Then,

$$P_{\text{back}}^{(k)} = \sum_{j=0}^{k-1} P_{k,j} = P_{k,k-1} = kq(1 - q)^{k-1}(1 - p)^m.$$

It can be seen that for a given constant q and p,

$$\lim_{k \to \infty} P_{\text{back}}^{(k)} = \lim_{k \to \infty} k(1 - p)^m q(1 - q)^{k-1} = \infty \cdot 0$$
$$= q(1 - p)^m \lim_{k \to \infty} \frac{k}{(1 - q)^{1-k}} = \frac{\infty}{\infty}$$
$$= q(1 - p)^m \lim_{k \to \infty} \frac{\frac{d}{dk}[k]}{\frac{d}{dk}[(1 - q)^{1-k}]}$$
$$= q(1 - p)^m \lim_{k \to \infty} \frac{1}{(1 - q)^{1-k} \cdot \ln(1 - q) \cdot (-1)}$$
$$= 0.$$

$$\lim_{k \to \infty} P_{\text{forw}}^{(k)} = 1 - \lim_{k \to \infty} P_{\text{back}}^{(k)} = 1.$$

$$\lim_{k \to \infty} P_{k,k} = \lim_{k \to \infty} \left(m(1-q)^k p(1-p)^{m-1} + \left(1 - kq(1-q)^{k-1}\right)(1-p)^m \right)$$

$$= \lim_{k \to \infty} \left(m(1-q)^k p(1-p)^{m-1} + (1-p)^m \right)$$

$$- \lim_{k \to \infty} \left(kq(1-q)^{k-1}(1-p)^m \right)$$

$$= (1-p)^m + \lim_{k \to \infty} P_{\text{back}}^{(k)}$$

$$= (1-p)^m < 1.$$

Thus as k increases, the probability of going to lower states tends to zero, and the probability of staying at the same state tends to a small constant, $(1-p)^m$; with high probability, tending to $1 - (1-p)^m$, we move to higher states. Consider a state k, for k large. Once the state is visited, the probability of returning back to the state goes to zero, because, almost surely, the chain proceeds ahead and never returns back.

Question: If you make q really, really small, does the Aloha protocol work then?

Answer: No, for any constant q the chain is transient.

Here's some more intuition: Consider the expected number of transmissions during a slot, given that the DTMC is in state k. The expected number of new transmissions is mp. The expected number of retransmissions is kq. Now, if the expected total number of transmissions ($\mathbf{E}[N] = mp + kq$) exceeds 1, then the state either stays the same or gets worse. Assume a fixed q. When k gets higher than $\frac{1}{q}$, then $\mathbf{E}[N] > 1$. Thus we expect that the number of simultaneous transmissions for each state from that point on exceeds 1.

Unsurprisingly to us queueing theorists, the original Aloha protocol implementation was subject to occasional unexplained freezes, in which all messages were dropped. However, the protocol was improved and became the basis behind today's Ethernet protocol.

10.2.4 *Improving the Aloha Protocol*

Question: Can you see a different way to set q so as to make the chain ergodic?

Answer: We want to ensure that the expected number of transmissions during a slot is less than 1. That is, we want to ensure that, for all states k,

$$mp + kq < 1.$$

This could perhaps be achieved by making q decreasing in k (e.g., $q < \frac{1-mp}{k}$), or going even further and making q geometrically decreasing in k, such as $q \propto \alpha/k^n$ where $\alpha < (1-mp)$ and $n > 1$, or even where $q \propto \beta^{-k}$, for some $\beta > 1$.

Question: Is there any drawback to making q small?

Answer: If q is small, the probability of retransmission is very low, and unsuccessful messages are likely to remain in the system for a long time. As $q \to 0$, the mean delay for retransmission goes to infinity; hence the mean time to send a message goes to infinity too. The goal is therefore to look for an optimal value for q that is just low enough to ensure that the Markov chain is ergodic, without being so low as to cause the mean time for a transmission to skyrocket.

The actual Ethernet protocol is based on the idea of *exponential backoff*, where each host waits some random time after each collision before resubmitting and where the mean of that "waiting time" increases exponentially as a function of the number of collisions experienced so far [114].

10.3 Generating Functions for Harder Markov Chains

Solving DTMCs is not always easy. In the case of a finite-state DTMC, we at least know that the number of simultaneous balance equations is finite. Hence, given enough computing power, we should in theory be able to solve for limiting probabilities. (Of course, in practice, there are some singularity problems that may arise when the chains are too big or the probabilities are too small.)

However, for an infinite-state DTMC, it is not at all obvious that one can even solve the chain. It is often the case that the balance equations take the form of recurrence relations, as in the recurrence from Section 8.10:

$$\pi_{i+1}(r+s) = \pi_i \cdot r + \pi_{i+2} \cdot s \tag{10.1}$$

or equivalently

$$\pi_{i+2} = \pi_{i+1}\left(\frac{r}{s}+1\right) - \pi_i \cdot \frac{r}{s}.$$

So far, we have been able to "guess" the solution for all the recurrences that we have looked at, and the solution was often simple. For example, the solution to (10.1) is

$$\pi_i = \rho^i \pi_0 \qquad \text{where } \rho = \frac{r}{s}.$$

However, in general the recurrence relation is not always so easy to solve. Consider for example, a very simple looking recurrence relation:

$$f_i = f_{i-1} + f_{i-2} \tag{10.2}$$

Question: Do you recognize the relation?

Answer: It is the Fibonacci sequence.

Although (10.2) seems even simpler than (10.1), it turns out to be impossible to solve by just unraveling the recurrence or "guessing" the solution – please try it!

In this section, we see how to derive a closed-form expression for f_n, the nth Fibonacci number, using a four-step method involving generating functions (that we will introduce shortly). This method may seem overly complex. However, for many Markov chains that come up in practice (see for example Exercise 10.7), there is no clear way to "guess" a solution, and using generating functions is the easiest way to solve these chains for their limiting distribution.

10.3.1 *The z-Transform*

The generating function that we choose to use is a called a *z-transform*. This is one type of generating function. We discuss transforms in much more depth in Chapter 25, but for this chapter you will not need more than the definition.

> **Definition 10.1** Given a sequence $\{f_0, f_1, f_2, \ldots\}$, define
>
> $$F(z) = \sum_{i=0}^{\infty} f_i z^i.$$
>
> $F(z)$ is the *z-transform of the sequence*.

In the Markov chains that we look at, f_i takes the place of $\pi_i = \mathbf{P}\{\text{State is } i\}$, and our goal is to derive a closed-form expression for f_i.

10.3.2 *Solving the Chain*

We illustrate the method on a recurrence relation of this form:

$$f_{i+2} = b f_{i+1} + a f_i \tag{10.3}$$

where we assume f_0 and f_1 are given and a and b are constants. However, the method can obviously be applied more generally.

Step 1: Represent $F(z)$ as a ratio of polynomials.

The goal in Step 1 is to represent $F(z)$ as a ratio of two polynomials in z. From (10.3), we have

$$f_{i+2} = b f_{i+1} + a f_i.$$

$$f_{i+2} z^{i+2} = b f_{i+1} z^{i+2} + a f_i z^{i+2}.$$

$$\sum_{i=0}^{\infty} f_{i+2} z^{i+2} = b \sum_{i=0}^{\infty} f_{i+1} z^{i+2} + a \sum_{i=0}^{\infty} f_i z^{i+2}.$$

$$F(z) - f_1 z - f_0 = bz \sum_{i=0}^{\infty} f_{i+1} z^{i+1} + a z^2 \sum_{i=0}^{\infty} f_i z^i.$$

$$F(z) - f_1 z - f_0 = bz \left(F(z) - f_0 \right) + a z^2 F(z).$$

$$\left(1 - bz - a z^2 \right) F(z) = f_1 z + f_0 - bz f_0.$$

$$F(z) = \frac{f_0 + z \left(f_1 - b f_0 \right)}{1 - bz - a z^2}. \tag{10.4}$$

Step 2: Rewrite $F(z)$ via partial fractions.

The goal in Step 2 is to apply partial fractions to $F(z)$. If $F(z) = \frac{N(z)}{D(z)}$, then we want to write

$$F(z) = \frac{A}{h(z)} + \frac{B}{g(z)},$$

where $D(z) = h(z)\, g(z)$ and h, g are (hopefully) linear.

Lemma 10.2 *If $D(z) = az^2 + bz + 1$, then*

$$D(z) = \left(1 - \frac{z}{r_0}\right)\left(1 - \frac{z}{r_1}\right)$$

where r_0 and r_1 are the (real) roots of $D(z)$.

Proof To see that the two ways of writing $D(z)$ are equivalent, we note that the two quadratic expressions have the same two roots, r_0 and r_1, and furthermore have the same constant term, 1. ∎

In our case, see (10.4), $D(z) = -az^2 - bz + 1$, so

$$(r_0, r_1) = \left(\frac{-b - \sqrt{b^2 + 4a}}{2a}, \frac{-b + \sqrt{b^2 + 4a}}{2a}\right). \tag{10.5}$$

$$D(z) = h(z) \cdot g(z)$$

$$h(z) = 1 - \frac{z}{r_0}$$

$$g(z) = 1 - \frac{z}{r_1}$$

We now use $N(z) = f_0 + z\,(f_1 - f_0 b)$ from (10.4) to solve for A and B:

$$F(z) = \frac{A}{1 - \frac{z}{r_0}} + \frac{B}{1 - \frac{z}{r_1}} \tag{10.6}$$

$$= \frac{A\left(1 - \frac{z}{r_1}\right) + B\left(1 - \frac{z}{r_0}\right)}{\left(1 - \frac{z}{r_0}\right)\left(1 - \frac{z}{r_1}\right)}$$

$$= \frac{(A + B) + z\left(-\frac{A}{r_1} - \frac{B}{r_0}\right)}{\left(1 - \frac{z}{r_0}\right)\left(1 - \frac{z}{r_1}\right)} = \frac{N(z)}{D(z)} = \frac{f_0 + z(f_1 - f_0 b)}{D(z)} \tag{10.7}$$

Matching the z-coefficients in the numerators of (10.7), we have

$$A + B = f_0$$

$$-\frac{A}{r_1} - \frac{B}{r_0} = f_1 - f_0 b$$

which solves to

$$B = \frac{r_0 f_0 + (f_1 - f_0 b) r_0 r_1}{r_0 - r_1}. \tag{10.8}$$

$$A = f_0 - B. \tag{10.9}$$

Step 3: Rewrite $F(z)$ via series expansion.

Returning to (10.6), and using the fact that $\frac{1}{1-\alpha z} = \sum_{i=0}^{\infty} (\alpha z)^i$, we have

$$\frac{A}{1 - \frac{z}{r_0}} = A \sum_{i=0}^{\infty} \left(\frac{z}{r_0} \right)^i \quad \text{and} \quad \frac{B}{1 - \frac{z}{r_1}} = B \sum_{i=0}^{\infty} \left(\frac{z}{r_1} \right)^i.$$

Thus, the geometric series expansion of $F(z)$ can be rewritten as follows:

$$F(z) = \sum_{i=0}^{\infty} f_i z^i = A \sum_{i=0}^{\infty} \left(\frac{z}{r_0} \right)^i + B \sum_{i=0}^{\infty} \left(\frac{z}{r_1} \right)^i \tag{10.10}$$

Step 4: Match terms to obtain f_n.

Finally, we match the z-coefficients in (10.10) to obtain the f_n's:

$$f_n = \frac{A}{r_0^n} + \frac{B}{r_1^n}$$

Summary

We have proven that the solution to a recurrence relation of the form

$$f_{n+2} = b \cdot f_{n+1} + a \cdot f_n$$

given f_0 and f_1 is given by

$$f_n = \frac{A}{r_0^n} + \frac{B}{r_1^n}$$

where A and B are obtained from (10.9) and (10.8) and r_0 and r_1 are obtained from (10.5).

In Exercise 10.5, you will apply these steps to derive a closed-form expression for the nth Fibonacci number.

10.4 Readings and Summary

This chapter has explored a couple of open-ended modeling problems illustrating the ergodicity properties that we covered in Chapter 9 in the context of real-world problems. There is much more information about both problems available on the web. The exercises at the end of the chapter provide more examples of modeling and ergodicity. For Google's PageRank algorithm, we recommend several early research papers: [139, 109, 53].

10.5 Exercises

10.1 Caching

If you think about it, web browsing is basically a Markov chain – the page you will go to next depends on the page you are currently at. Suppose our web server has three pages, and we have the following transition probabilities:

$$P_{1,1} = 0 \qquad P_{1,2} = x \qquad P_{1,3} = 1 - x$$
$$P_{2,1} = y \qquad P_{2,2} = 0 \qquad P_{2,3} = 1 - y$$
$$P_{3,1} = 0 \qquad P_{3,2} = 1 \qquad P_{3,3} = 0$$

where $P_{i,j}$ represents the probability that I will next ask for page j, given that I am currently at page i. Assume that $0 < x < y < \frac{1}{2}$.

Web browsers cache pages so that they can be quickly retrieved later. We will assume that the cache has enough memory to store two pages. Whenever a request comes in for a page that is not cached, the browser will store that page in the cache, replacing the page *least likely* to be referenced next based on the current request. For example, if my cache contained pages $\{2,3\}$ and I requested page 1, the cache would now store $\{1,3\}$ (because $x < 1 - x$).

(a) Find the proportion of time that the cache contains the following pages:
(i) $\{1,2\}$ (ii) $\{2,3\}$ (iii) $\{1,3\}$.

(b) Find the proportion of requests that are for cached pages.

10.2 DTMC for Stock Evaluation

A stock has an equilibrium price P, where P is an integer. The stock price fluctuates each day according to the DTMC shown in Figure 10.7. Note that, for ease of analysis, we assume that the stock price can go negative.

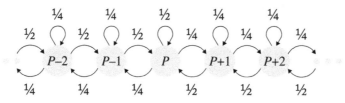

Figure 10.7. DTMC for the stock price.

(a) What is the fraction of time that the stock is priced at P?

(b) Let I denote the difference between the stock price and P. What is the expectation of the absolute value of I?

10.3 Time to Empty

Consider a router where, at each time step, the number of packets increases by 1 with probability 0.4 and decreases by 1 with probability 0.6. We are interested in the time required for the router to empty. The Markov chain depicting the number of packets is shown in Figure 10.8. Let $T_{1,0}$ denote the time to get

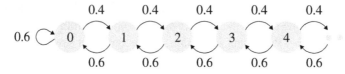

Figure 10.8. Number of packets at router.

from state 1 to state 0. (a) Compute $\mathbf{E}\,[T_{1,0}]$. (b) Compute $\mathbf{Var}(T_{1,0})$. [Hint: The variance computation is a little tricky. Be careful not to lump together distinct random variables.]

10.4 Time to Empty – Extra Strength
Consider the same setup as in Exercise 10.3. This time, we use $T_{n,0}$ to denote the time to get from state n to state 0. (a) Compute $\mathbf{E}\,[T_{n,0}]$. (b) Compute $\mathbf{Var}(T_{n,0})$.

10.5 Fibonacci Sequence
The Fibonacci sequence is defined by $f_0 = 0$, $f_1 = 1$, $f_{n+2} = f_{n+1} + f_n$. Use the generating function technique from this chapter to derive f_n, the nth term of the Fibonacci sequence.

10.6 Simple Random Walk: Solution via Generating Functions
Figure 10.9 shows a simple random walk, where $r < s$. Follow the generating function approach in this chapter to solve for the limiting probabilities of this random walk using the z-transform, $\Pi(z) = \sum_{i=0}^{\infty} \pi_i z^i$. [*Note:* To get the initial probability, π_0, observe that $\Pi(z)|_{z=1} = 1$. You will also need to use the balance equation for state 0 to get π_1.]

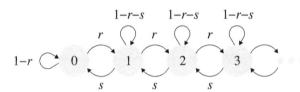

Figure 10.9. DTMC for random walk.

10.7 Processor with Failures
Consider the DTMC shown in Figure 10.10. This kind of chain is often used to model a processor with failures. The chain tracks the number of jobs in the system. At any time step, either the number of jobs increases by 1 (with probability p), or decreases by 1 (with probability q), or a processor failure occurs (with probability r), where $p + q + r = 1$. In the case of a processor failure, all jobs in the system are lost. Derive the limiting probability, π_i, of there being i jobs in the system. [Hint: Use the generating function approach from this chapter.]

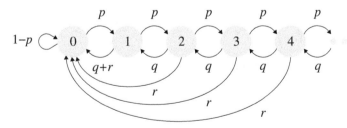

Figure 10.10. DTMC for processor with failures.

CHAPTER 11

Exponential Distribution and the Poisson Process

We finished discussing Discrete-Time Markov Chains (DTMCs) in Chapter 10 and are now heading toward Continuous-Time Markov Chains (CTMCs). DTMCs are totally synchronized, in that the state only changes at discrete time steps, whereas in CTMCs the state can change at any time. This makes CTMCs more realistic for modeling computer systems, where events can occur at any time. In preparation for CTMCs, we need to discuss the Exponential distribution and the Poisson arrival process.

11.1 Definition of the Exponential Distribution

We say that a random variable X is distributed Exponentially with rate λ,

$$X \sim \text{Exp}(\lambda)$$

if X has the probability density function:

$$f(x) = \begin{cases} \lambda e^{-\lambda x} & x \geq 0. \\ 0 & x < 0. \end{cases}$$

The graph of the probability density function is shown in Figure 11.1.

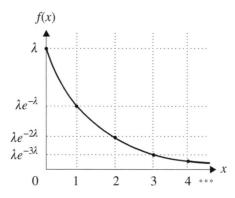

Figure 11.1. Exponential p.d.f., $f(x)$.

The cumulative distribution function, $F(x) = \mathbf{P}\{X \leq x\}$, is given by

$$F(x) = \int_{-\infty}^{x} f(y)dy = \begin{cases} 1 - e^{-\lambda x} & x \geq 0. \\ 0 & x < 0. \end{cases}$$

$$\overline{F}(x) = e^{-\lambda x}, \ x \geq 0.$$

206

Observe that both $f(x)$ and $\overline{F}(x)$ drop off by a *constant* factor, $e^{-\lambda}$, with each unit increase of x.

The Exponential distribution has mean:

$$\mathbf{E}[X] = \int_{-\infty}^{\infty} x f(x) dx = \frac{1}{\lambda}.$$

The second moment of $X \sim \text{Exp}(\lambda)$ is

$$\mathbf{E}[X^2] = \int_{-\infty}^{\infty} x^2 f(x) dx = \frac{2}{\lambda^2}.$$

The variance is

$$\mathbf{Var}(X) = \mathbf{E}[X^2] - (\mathbf{E}[X])^2 = \frac{1}{\lambda^2}.$$

Question: Why is λ referred to as the "rate" of the distribution?

Answer: Because the mean of the distribution is $1/\lambda$ and "rate" is typically viewed as the reciprocal of the "mean."

Question: What is the squared coefficient of variation of $\text{Exp}(\lambda)$?

Answer: The squared coefficient of variation of random variable X is defined as

$$C_X^2 = \frac{\mathbf{Var}(X)}{\mathbf{E}[X]^2}.$$

This can be thought of as the "scaled" or "normalized" variance. When $X \sim \text{Exp}(\lambda)$, $C_X^2 = 1$.

11.2 Memoryless Property of the Exponential

A random variable X is said to be **memoryless** if

$$\mathbf{P}\{X > s + t \mid X > s\} = \mathbf{P}\{X > t\}, \quad \forall s, t \geq 0.$$

Question: Prove that $X \sim \text{Exp}(\lambda)$ is memoryless.

Answer:

$$\mathbf{P}\{X > s + t \mid X > s\} = \frac{\mathbf{P}\{X > s + t\}}{\mathbf{P}\{X > s\}} = \frac{e^{-\lambda(s+t)}}{e^{-\lambda s}} = e^{-\lambda t} = \mathbf{P}\{X > t\}.$$

To understand this, think of X as being the lifetime of, say, a lightbulb. The expression says that the probability that the lightbulb survives for at least another t seconds before burning out, given that the lightbulb has survived for s seconds already, is the same as the probability that the lightbulb survives at least t seconds, *independent of s*.

Question: Does this seem realistic for a lightbulb?

Answer: Who knows?

Question: What are some real-life examples whose lifetimes can be modeled by an X such that $\mathbf{P}\{X > s + t \mid X > s\}$ goes down as s goes up?

Answer: A car's lifetime. The older a car is, the less likely that it will survive another, say, $t = 6$ years.

Distributions for which $\mathbf{P}\{X > s + t \mid X > s\}$ goes down as s goes up are said to have **increasing failure rate**. The device is more and more likely to fail as time goes on.

Question: What are some real-life examples whose lifetimes can be modeled by an X such that $\mathbf{P}\{X > s + t \mid X > s\}$ goes up as s goes up?

Answer: One example is UNIX job CPU lifetimes; see [85]. The more CPU a job has used up so far, the more CPU it is likely to use up. Another example is computer chips. If they are going to fail, they will do so early. That is why chip manufacturers test chips for a while before selling them.

Distributions for which $\mathbf{P}\{X > s + t \mid X > s\}$ goes up as s goes up are said to have **decreasing failure rate**. The device is less likely to fail as time goes on.

More precisely, the **failure rate function r(t)** (a.k.a. hazard rate function) is defined as follows: Let X be a continuous random variable with probability density function $f(t)$ and cumulative distribution function $F(t) = \mathbf{P}\{X < t\}$. Then

$$r(t) \equiv \frac{f(t)}{\overline{F}(t)}.$$

To interpret this expression, consider the probability that a t-year-old item will fail during the next dt seconds:

$$\mathbf{P}\{X \in (t, t + dt) \mid X > t\} = \frac{\mathbf{P}\{X \in (t, t + dt)\}}{\mathbf{P}\{X > t\}}$$
$$\approx \frac{f(t) \cdot dt}{\overline{F}(t)}$$
$$= r(t) \cdot dt$$

Thus $r(t)$ represents the instantaneous failure rate of a t-year-old item.

Definition 11.1 When $r(t)$ is strictly decreasing in t, we say that the distribution $f(t)$ has **decreasing failure rate**; if $r(t)$ is strictly increasing in t, we say that the distribution has **increasing failure rate**.

Observe that in general $r(t)$ is not necessarily going to always decrease with t or increase with t – it might behave differently for different t.

Question: Suppose $r(t)$ is constant. What do you know about $f(t)$?

Answer: In Exercise 11.4, we prove that $f(t)$ *must* be the Exponential p.d.f.

Bank Example

Question: If the time a customer spends in a bank is Exponentially distributed with mean 10 minutes, what is $\mathbf{P}$ {Customer spends $>$ 5 min in bank}?

Answer: $e^{-5 \cdot 1/10} = e^{-1/2}$.

Question: What is $\mathbf{P}$ {Customer spends $>$ 15 min in bank total $\mid$ he is there after 10 min}?

Answer: Same as previous answer.

The reason why the Exponential distribution is so convenient to work with is that history does not matter!

Question: Suppose $X \sim \text{Exp}(\lambda)$. What is $\mathbf{E}[X \mid X > 20]$?

Answer: The Exponential distribution "starts over" at 20, or at any other point. Hence, $\mathbf{E}[X \mid X > 20] = 20 + \mathbf{E}[X] = 20 + \frac{1}{\lambda}$.

Post Office Example

Suppose that a post office has two clerks. Customer B is being served by one clerk, and customer C is being served by the other clerk, when customer A walks in. All service times are Exponentially distributed with mean $\frac{1}{\lambda}$.

Question: What is $\mathbf{P}$ {A is the last to leave}?

Answer: $\frac{1}{2}$. Note that either B or C will leave first. WLOG, let us say B leaves first. Then C and A will have the same distribution on their remaining service time. It does not matter that C has been served for a while.

It can be proven that the Exponential distribution is the *only* continuous-time memoryless distribution.

Question: What is the only discrete-time memoryless distribution?

Answer: The Geometric distribution.

11.3 Relating Exponential to Geometric via δ-Steps

We find it very helpful when reasoning about Exponential random variables to instead think about Geometric random variables, for which we have more intuition. We like to think of the Exponential distribution as the "continuous counterpart" of the Geometric distribution by making the following analogy: Recall that the Geometric distribution can be viewed as the *number* of flips needed to get a "success." The distribution of the remaining number of flips is independent of how many times we have flipped so far. The same holds for the Exponential distribution, which is the *time* until "success."

To unify the Geometric and Exponential distributions, we introduce the notion of a "δ-step proof." Throughout the next few chapters, we will use this way of thinking to come up with quick intuitions and arguments.[1] The idea is to imagine each unit of time as divided into n pieces, each of size $\delta = \frac{1}{n}$, and suppose that a trial (flip) occurs every δ time period, rather than at unit times.

Let

$$X \sim \text{Exp}(\lambda).$$

We now define a random variable Y, where Y is Geometrically distributed with probability $p = \lambda\delta$ of getting a head, for some small $\delta \to 0$. However, rather than flipping every unit time step, we flip every δ-step. That is,

$$Y \sim \text{Geometric}(p = \lambda\delta \mid \text{flip every } \delta\text{-step}).$$

Observe that Y denotes the *number* of flips until success. Now define $\widetilde{Y}$ to be the *time* until success under Y:

$$\widetilde{Y} = \text{Time associated with } Y$$

Observe that as $\delta \to 0$ (or $n \to \infty$), $\widetilde{Y}$ becomes a positive, real-valued random variable, because success can occur at any time.

Question: What is $\mathbf{E}\left[\widetilde{Y}\right]$? How is $\widetilde{Y}$ distributed?

Answer: The mean of $\widetilde{Y}$ is $\frac{1}{\lambda}$.

$$\mathbf{E}\left[\widetilde{Y}\right] = (\text{avg. number trials until success}) \cdot (\text{time per trial})$$

$$= \frac{1}{\delta\lambda} \cdot \delta = \frac{1}{\lambda}$$

To understand the distribution of $\widetilde{Y}$, we observe that $\widetilde{Y} > t$ if all the trials up to at least time t have been failures (i.e., we have had at least t/δ failures).

$$\mathbf{P}\left\{\widetilde{Y} > t\right\} = \mathbf{P}\left\{\text{at least } \frac{t}{\delta} \text{ failures}\right\}$$

$$= (1 - \delta\lambda)^{\frac{t}{\delta}}$$

$$= [(1 - \delta\lambda)^{\frac{1}{\delta}}]^t$$

$$= \left[\left(1 - \frac{1}{\frac{1}{\delta\lambda}}\right)^{\frac{1}{\delta\lambda} \cdot \lambda}\right]^t$$

$$\longrightarrow [(e^{-1})^\lambda]^t, \text{ as } \delta \to 0$$

$$= e^{-\lambda t}$$

This says that $\widetilde{Y} \sim \text{Exp}(\lambda)$.

---

[1] I concocted this notion of a δ-step proof as a PhD student, struggling with messy integrals. The δ-step proofs helped me reason about properties of the Exponential distribution and Poisson process. They also helped me leverage my understanding of DTMCs to quickly reason about CTMCs (see Chapter 12).

We have thus seen that *an Exponential random variable with rate λ represents the time to a successful event, given that an event occurs every δ-step and is successful with probability $\lambda\delta$, where $\delta \to 0$.* This is depicted in Figure 11.2.

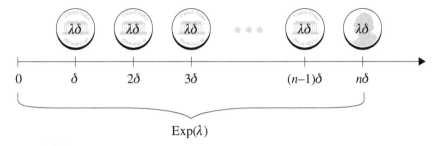

Figure 11.2. Geometric depiction of the $Exp(\lambda)$ distribution. Time is divided into steps of duration δ, and a coin (with probability $\lambda\delta$ of "heads") is flipped only at each δ-step.

11.4 More Properties of the Exponential

Before we continue, here is a useful definition:

Definition 11.2

$$f = o(\delta) \quad \text{if} \quad \lim_{\delta \to 0} \frac{f}{\delta} = 0.$$

For example, $f = \delta^2$ is $o(\delta)$ because $\frac{\delta^2}{\delta} \to 0$ as $\delta \to 0$. Basically, a function is $o(\delta)$ if it goes to zero faster than δ, as $\delta \to 0$.[2]

We now illustrate how to combine the $o(\delta)$ notation with the discretized view of an Exponential to prove a few properties of the Exponential distribution.

Theorem 11.3 *Given $X_1 \sim Exp(\lambda_1)$, $X_2 \sim Exp(\lambda_2)$, $X_1 \perp X_2$,*

$$\mathbf{P}\{X_1 < X_2\} = \frac{\lambda_1}{\lambda_1 + \lambda_2}.$$

Proof (Traditional Algebraic Proof)

$$\mathbf{P}\{X_1 < X_2\} = \int_0^\infty \mathbf{P}\{X_1 < X_2 \mid X_2 = x\} \cdot f_2(x)dx$$

$$= \int_0^\infty \mathbf{P}\{X_1 < x\} \cdot \lambda_2 e^{-\lambda_2 x}dx$$

---

[2] This definition may seem a little odd, if one is used to theoretical computer science where "big-O" and "little-o" notation are defined in terms of some $n \to \infty$, not as $\delta \to 0$.

$$= \int_0^\infty (1 - e^{-\lambda_1 x})(\lambda_2 e^{-\lambda_2 x}) dx$$

$$= \int_0^\infty \lambda_2 e^{-\lambda_2 x} dx - \lambda_2 \int_0^\infty e^{-(\lambda_1 + \lambda_2)x} dx$$

$$= 1 - \frac{\lambda_2}{\lambda_1 + \lambda_2}$$

$$= \frac{\lambda_1}{\lambda_1 + \lambda_2} \qquad \blacksquare$$

Here is the more intuitive proof, by analogy with the Geometric distribution:

Proof (Intuitive Geometric Proof) Success of type 1 occurs with probability $\lambda_1 \delta$ on each δ-step. Independently, success of type 2 occurs with probability $\lambda_2 \delta$ on each δ-step. The problem is really asking the following: Given that a success of type 1 or type 2 has occurred, what is the probability that it is a success of type 1?

$$\mathbf{P}\{\text{type 1} \mid \text{type 1 or type 2}\} = \frac{\mathbf{P}\{\text{type 1}\}}{\mathbf{P}\{\text{type 1 or type 2}\}}$$

$$= \frac{\lambda_1 \delta}{\lambda_1 \delta + \lambda_2 \delta - (\lambda_1 \delta)(\lambda_2 \delta)}$$

$$= \frac{\lambda_1 \delta}{\lambda_1 \delta + \lambda_2 \delta - o(\delta)}$$

$$= \frac{\lambda_1}{\lambda_1 + \lambda_2 - \frac{o(\delta)}{\delta}}$$

$$= \frac{\lambda_1}{\lambda_1 + \lambda_2} \text{ as } \delta \to 0 \qquad \blacksquare$$

Example

There are two potential failure points for our server: the power supply and the disk. The lifetime of the power supply is Exponentially distributed with mean 500 days, and the lifetime of the disk is independently Exponentially distributed with mean 1,000 days.

Question: What is the probability that the system failure, when it occurs, is caused by the power supply?

Answer: $\frac{\frac{1}{500}}{\frac{1}{500} + \frac{1}{1000}}$.

Theorem 11.4 *Given $X_1 \sim Exp(\lambda_1)$, $X_2 \sim Exp(\lambda_2)$, $X_1 \perp X_2$.*
Let

$$X = \min(X_1, X_2).$$

Then

$$X \sim Exp(\lambda_1 + \lambda_2).$$

Proof (Traditional Algebraic Proof)

$$\mathbf{P}\{X > t\} = \mathbf{P}\{\min(X_1, X_2) > t\}$$
$$= \mathbf{P}\{X_1 > t \text{ and } X_2 > t\}$$
$$= \mathbf{P}\{X_1 > t\} \cdot \mathbf{P}\{X_2 > t\}$$
$$= e^{-\lambda_1 t} \cdot e^{-\lambda_2 t}$$
$$= e^{-(\lambda_1 + \lambda_2)t} \qquad \blacksquare$$

Here is an alternative argument by analogy with the Geometric distribution:

Proof (Intuitive Geometric Proof)

1. A trial occurs every δ-step.
2. The trial is "successful of type 1" with probability $\lambda_1 \delta$.
3. The trial is "successful of type 2" independently with probability $\lambda_2 \delta$.
4. We are looking for the time until there is a success of either type. A trial is "successful" (either type) with probability

$$\lambda_1 \delta + \lambda_2 \delta - (\lambda_1 \delta) \cdot (\lambda_2 \delta) = \delta \left(\lambda_1 + \lambda_2 - \frac{o(\delta)}{\delta} \right).$$

5. Thus the time until we get a "success" is Exponentially distributed with rate

$$\lambda_1 + \lambda_2 + \frac{o(\delta)}{\delta},$$

and as $\delta \to 0$ this gives the desired result. $\qquad \blacksquare$

Question: In the server from the previous example, what is the time until there is a failure of either the power supply or the disk?

Answer: Exponential with rate $\left(\frac{1}{500} + \frac{1}{1,000} \right)$.

11.5 The Celebrated Poisson Process

The Poisson process is the most widely used model for arrivals into a system for two reasons:

1. The Markovian properties of the Poisson process make it analytically tractable.
2. In many cases, it is an excellent model. For example,
   (a) In communications networks, such as the telephone system, it is a good model for the sequence of times at which telephone calls are originated. Although the calls of a single user do not look like a Poisson process, the aggregate over many users does.
   (b) Many physical phenomena behave in a Poisson fashion, such as the sequence of gamma ray emissions from a radioactive substance.

The Poisson process appears often in nature when we are observing the *aggregate* effect of a large number of individuals or particles operating independently. The reason for this is explained by the Limiting Theorem (due to Palm '43, Khinchin '60, and described in [105] pp. 221–228). This theorem states that if you merge n (assume that n is very large) identical and independently distributed arrival processes, each with an arrival rate $\frac{\lambda}{n}$, where each of the arrival processes is a renewal process with an *arbitrary* fixed interarrival distribution F, then the aggregate arrival process approaches a Poisson process with rate λ.

When considering questions on resource allocation, task assignment, scheduling, and the like, we find that, whereas the job size distribution has a large effect on mean response times, the arrival process of jobs typically has much less of an effect. Specifically, assuming a Poisson arrival process for arrivals allows us to analytically predict response times, and these predictions are often not too far from results based on trace-driven simulation.

Before we define a Poisson process, we need a little terminology.

Consider a sequence of events:

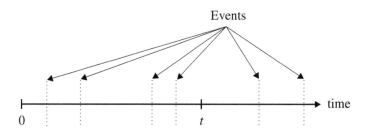

Define $N(t), t \geq 0$ as the number of events that occurred by time t.

Definition 11.5 An event sequence has ***independent increments*** if the numbers of events that occur in disjoint time intervals are independent. Specifically, for all $t_0 < t_1 < t_2 < \ldots < t_n$, the random variables

$$N(t_1) - N(t_0), N(t_2) - N(t_1), \ldots, N(t_n) - N(t_{n-1})$$

are independent.

Example

Let us look at three event processes:

1. births of children
2. people entering a building
3. goals scored by a particular soccer player

Question: Do these event processes have independent increments?

Answer:

1. No. Birth rate depends on population, which increases with births.
2. Yes.
3. Maybe. Depends on whether we believe in slumps!

Definition 11.6 The event sequence has *stationary increments* if the number of events during a time period depends only on the length of the time period and not on its starting point. That is, $N(t + s) - N(s)$ has the same distribution for all s.

Definition 1 of the Poisson Process:

A **Poisson process having rate** λ is a sequence of events such that

1. $N(0) = 0$.
2. The process has independent increments.
3. The number of events in any interval of length t is Poisson distributed with mean λt. That is, $\forall s, t \geq 0$,

$$\mathbf{P}\{N(t + s) - N(s) = n\} = \frac{e^{-\lambda t}(\lambda t)^n}{n!} \quad n = 0, 1, \ldots$$

Question: Why is λ called the "rate" of the process?

Answer: Observe that $\mathbf{E}[N(t)] = \lambda t$, so $\frac{\mathbf{E}[N(t)]}{t} = \lambda$.

Question: Why only "independent increments" ?

Answer: The third item in the definition implies stationary increments, because the number of events within an interval of length t depends only on t.

Observe that the assumption of stationary and independent increments is equivalent to asserting that, at any point in time, the process *probabilistically restarts itself*; that is, the process from any point onward is independent of all that occurred previously (by independent increments) and also has the same distribution as the original process (by stationary increments). Simply put, a Poisson process has no memory. This leads us to the second definition of the Poisson process.

Definition 2 of the Poisson Process:

A **Poisson process with rate** λ is a sequence of events such that the interarrival times are i.i.d. Exponential random variables with rate λ and $N(0) = 0$.

Question: Which definition of a Poisson process would you use when trying to simulate a Poisson process: Definition 1 or Definition 2?

Answer: Definition 2.

Definition 1 ⇒ Definition 2

Let $T_1, T_2, \ldots, T_n, \ldots$ be the *interarrival* times of a sequence of events. We need to show that $T_i \sim \text{Exp}(\lambda)$, $\forall i$. By Definition 1,

$$\mathbf{P}\{T_1 > t\} = \mathbf{P}\{N(t) = 0\} = \frac{e^{-\lambda t}(\lambda t)^0}{0!} = e^{-\lambda t}.$$

Next,

$$\mathbf{P}\left\{T_{n+1} > t \;\middle|\; \sum_{i=1}^{n} T_i = s\right\} = \mathbf{P}\left\{0 \text{ events in } (s, s+t) \;\middle|\; \sum_{i=1}^{n} T_i = s\right\}$$

$$= \mathbf{P}\{0 \text{ events in } (s, s+t)\},$$

by independent increments

$$= e^{-\lambda t}, \text{ by stationary increments.}$$

Definition 2 ⇒ Definition 1

Feller [58], p. 11, has a rigorous algebraic proof that Definition 2 ⇒ Definition 1. The idea is to show that the sum of n i.i.d. $\text{Exp}(\lambda)$ random variables has a Gamma, $\Gamma(n, \lambda)$, distribution. Feller then uses the $\Gamma(n, \lambda)$ distribution to show that the number of arrivals by time t has a Poisson distribution.

Rather than going through this tedious algebraic proof, we instead provide an argument by analogy with the Geometric distribution: $N(t)$ refers to the number of arrivals by time t. Our goal is to prove that $N(t) \sim \text{Poisson}(\lambda t)$. Think of an "arrival" as being a "success." $\text{Exp}(\lambda)$ interarrival times correspond to flipping a coin every δ-step, where a flip is a success (i.e., arrival) with probability $\lambda\delta$.

$$N(t) = \text{Number of successes (arrivals) by time } t$$

$$\sim \text{Binomial}(\text{\# flips, probability of success of each flip})$$

$$\sim \text{Binomial}\left(\frac{t}{\delta}, \lambda\delta\right)$$

Observe above that as $\delta \to 0$, $\frac{t}{\delta}$ becomes very large and $\lambda\delta$ becomes very small.

Question: Now what do you know about $\text{Binomial}(n, p)$ for large n and tiny p?

Answer: Recall from Exercise 3.12 that

$$\text{Binomial}(n, p) \to \text{Poisson}(np), \quad \text{as } n \to \infty \text{ and } p \to 0.$$

So as $\delta \to 0$,

$$N(t) \sim \text{Poisson}\left(\frac{t}{\delta} \cdot \lambda\delta\right) = \text{Poisson}(\lambda t).$$

Definition 3 of the Poisson Process:

A **Poisson process having rate** λ is a sequence of events such that
1. $N(0) = 0$.
2. The process has stationary and independent increments.
3. $\mathbf{P}\{N(\delta) = 1\} = \lambda\delta + o(\delta)$.
4. $\mathbf{P}\{N(\delta) \geq 2\} = o(\delta)$.

We have shown that Definition 1 $\Leftrightarrow$ Definition 2. To show that all three definitions are equivalent, we now show that Definition 1 $\Leftrightarrow$ Definition 3.

Definition 1 $\Rightarrow$ Definition 3

This is taken from [127], p. 245:

$$
\mathbf{P}\{N(\delta) = 1\} = \frac{e^{-\lambda\delta}(\lambda\delta)^1}{1!}
$$

$$
= \lambda\delta \left[1 - \lambda\delta + \frac{(\lambda\delta)^2}{2!} - \cdots \right]
$$

$$
= \lambda\delta - \lambda^2(\delta)^2 + \frac{\lambda^3(\delta)^3}{2} - \cdots
$$

$$
= \lambda\delta + o(\delta)
$$

$$
\mathbf{P}\{N(\delta) = i\} = \frac{e^{-\lambda\delta}(\lambda\delta)^i}{i!}
$$

$$
= \frac{(\lambda\delta)^i}{i!} \left(1 - \lambda\delta + \frac{(\lambda\delta)^2}{2!} - \cdots \right) = \frac{\lambda^i \delta^i}{i!} + o(\delta^i)
$$

So

$$
\mathbf{P}\{N(\delta) \geq 2\} = \sum_{i=2}^{\infty} \mathbf{P}\{N(\delta) = i\} = \sum_{i=2}^{\infty} \left(\frac{\lambda^i \delta^i}{i!} + o(\delta^i) \right) = o(\delta).
$$

Definition 3 $\Rightarrow$ Definition 1

A slightly approximate argument is provided in [149], Ch. 2, which is very intuitive and which we repeat here.

To show that $N(t) \sim \text{Poisson}(\lambda t)$,

- Subdivide $[0, t]$ into increments of length $\delta \to 0$.
- $\mathbf{P}\{\text{Any interval has } \geq 2 \text{ events}\}$

$$
\leq (\# \text{ of intervals}) \cdot \mathbf{P}\{\text{Single interval has } \geq 2 \text{ events}\}
$$

$$
= \frac{t}{\delta} \cdot o(\delta)
$$

$$
= t \cdot \frac{o(\delta)}{\delta} \to 0, \text{ as } \delta \to 0.
$$

- So now we can think of each δ-size interval as having 1 event with probability $\lambda\delta + o(\delta)$ and otherwise having 0 events (note this is just an approximation).

- But now we see that $N(t)$, the number of events by time t is simply

$$N(t) \sim \text{Binomial}\left(\frac{t}{\delta}, \lambda\delta + o(\delta)\right)$$

$$\rightarrow \text{Poisson}\left(\frac{t}{\delta}(\lambda\delta + o(\delta))\right) \text{ as } \delta \rightarrow 0$$

$$= \text{Poisson}\left(\lambda t + t\frac{o(\delta)}{\delta}\right) \rightarrow \text{Poisson}(\lambda t).$$

11.6 Merging Independent Poisson Processes

Theorem 11.7   *Given two independent Poisson processes, where process 1 has rate λ_1 and process 2 has rate λ_2, the merge of process 1 and process 2 is a single Poisson process with rate $(\lambda_1 + \lambda_2)$.*

Proof   Process 1 has $\text{Exp}(\lambda_1)$ interarrival times. Process 2 has $\text{Exp}(\lambda_2)$ interarrival times. The time until the first event from either process 1 or process 2 is the time until the minimum of $\text{Exp}(\lambda_1)$ and $\text{Exp}(\lambda_2)$, which is distributed $\text{Exp}(\lambda_1 + \lambda_2)$. Likewise, the time until the second event is also distributed $\text{Exp}(\lambda_1 + \lambda_2)$, etc. Thus by Definition 2 of the Poisson process we have a Poisson process with rate $\lambda_1 + \lambda_2$.   ■

Alternative Proof   Let $N_i(t)$ denote the number of events in process i by time t.

$$N_1(t) \sim \text{Poisson}(\lambda_1 t)$$
$$N_2(t) \sim \text{Poisson}(\lambda_2 t)$$

Yet the sum of two independent Poisson random variables is still Poisson with the sum of the means, so

$$\underbrace{N_1(t) + N_2(t)}_{\text{merged process}} \sim \text{Poisson}(\lambda_1 t + \lambda_2 t).$$

■

11.7 Poisson Splitting

Theorem 11.8   *Given a Poisson process with rate λ, suppose that each event is classified "type A" with probability p and "type B" with probability $1 - p$. Then type A events form a Poisson process with rate $p\lambda$, type B events form a Poisson process with rate $(1 - p)\lambda$, and these two processes are independent. Specifically,* *if $N_A(t)$ denotes the number of type A events by time t, and $N_B(t)$ denotes the number of type B events by time t, then*

$$\mathbf{P}\{N_A(t) = n, N_B(t) = m\} = \mathbf{P}\{N_A(t) = n\} \cdot \mathbf{P}\{N_B(t) = m\}$$

$$= e^{-\lambda tp}\frac{(\lambda tp)^n}{n!} \cdot e^{-\lambda t(1-p)}\frac{(\lambda t(1-p))^m}{m!}.$$

This is one of those theorems that is very difficult to prove if you just stick to the idea of Exponential interarrival times. It is really not clear why the times between the type A events end up being *Exponentially* distributed with rate λp as opposed to something else. Consider the original Poisson process and a sequence of coin flips with bias p. When the coin flip comes up "heads" (this happens with probability p), then the event is classified "type A." If we now consider a sequence of just the type A events, we might imagine that the time between type A events would be $\text{Exp}(\lambda)$, for a time period during which the coin flips had a streak of "heads," and then there might be a large interarrival time consisting of some sum of $\text{Exp}(\lambda)$'s during the time period when the coin flips had a streak of "tails," after which we return to an interarrival time of $\text{Exp}(\lambda)$. It is not at all clear why the interarrival times between type A events are actually $\text{Exp}(\lambda p)$.

However, this theorem is very easy to understand by analogy with the Geometric distribution. We first provide intuition for the theorem, by making use of the Geometric δ-step arguments. We then provide a rigorous proof of the theorem.

Intuition – by Analogy with the Geometric Distribution

The original process has $\text{Exp}(\lambda)$ interarrival times, which is equivalent to tossing a coin every $\delta \to 0$ steps, where the coin comes up "success" with probability $\lambda\delta$. We refer to this $\lambda\delta$ coin as the "first" coin. Each success (head) of the first coin is labeled as a *type A success* with probability p. Thus we can imagine a second coin being flipped, where the second coin has probability p of success. Only if *both* the first and second coins are successes do we have a type A success. But this is equivalent to flipping just a single coin with probability $\lambda\delta p$ of success. The time between type A successes is then distributed $\text{Exp}(\lambda p)$. This proof is illustrated in Figure 11.3 and can be repeated for type B events.

Proof This proof is taken from [150], p. 258. What makes this proof precise is that (1) it uses no approximations and (2) it explicitly proves independence. Let

$$N(t) = \text{Number of events by time } t \text{ in the original process}$$
$$N_A(t) = \text{Number of type A events by time } t$$
$$N_B(t) = \text{Number of type B events by time } t$$

The idea is to compute the joint probability that there are n events of type A and m events of type B by time t, $\mathbf{P}\{N_A(t) = n, N_B(t) = m\}$, and then to use this to compute

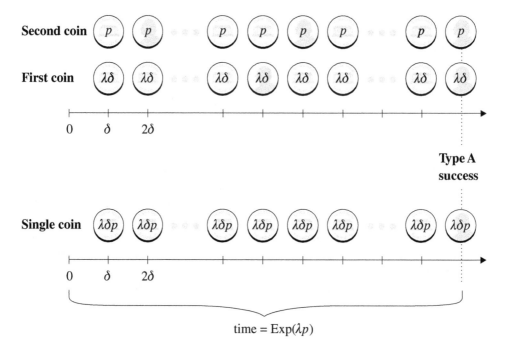

Figure 11.3. A "type A success" only occurs if both the $\lambda\delta$-coin and the p-coin are heads.

$\mathbf{P}\left\{N_A(t) = n\right\}$ and $\mathbf{P}\left\{N_B(t) = m\right\}$, so that we can verify the independence of the two processes.

$$\mathbf{P}\{N_A(t) = n, N_B(t) = m\}$$

$$= \sum_{k=0}^{\infty} \mathbf{P}\left\{N_A(t) = n, N_B(t) = m \mid N(t) = k\right\} \cdot \mathbf{P}\left\{N(t) = k\right\}$$

$$= \mathbf{P}\left\{N_A(t) = n, N_B(t) = m \mid N(t) = n + m\right\} \cdot \mathbf{P}\left\{N(t) = n + m\right\}$$

(because this is the only non-zero term in the above sum)

$$= \mathbf{P}\left\{N_A(t) = n, N_B(t) = m \mid N(t) = n + m\right\} \cdot e^{-\lambda t}\frac{(\lambda t)^{n+m}}{(n+m)!}$$

$$= \binom{n+m}{n} p^n (1-p)^m e^{-\lambda t}\frac{(\lambda t)^{n+m}}{(n+m)!}$$

$$= \frac{(m+n)!}{n!m!}p^n (1-p)^m e^{-\lambda t}\frac{(\lambda t)^{n+m}}{(n+m)!}$$

$$= e^{-\lambda tp}\frac{(\lambda tp)^n}{n!} \cdot e^{-\lambda t(1-p)}\frac{(\lambda t(1-p))^m}{m!} \tag{11.1}$$

Now to compute $\mathbf{P}\{N_A(t) = n\}$, we simply sum the joint probability, (11.1), over all values of m, as follows:

$$\mathbf{P}\{N_A(t) = n\} = \sum_{m=0}^{\infty} \mathbf{P}\{N_A(t) = n, N_B(t) = m\}$$

$$= e^{-\lambda t p} \frac{(\lambda t p)^n}{n!} \sum_{m=0}^{\infty} e^{-\lambda t(1-p)} \frac{(\lambda t(1-p))^m}{m!}$$

$$= e^{-\lambda t p} \frac{(\lambda t p)^n}{n!}$$

In a similar fashion we can show that

$$\mathbf{P}\{N_B(t) = m\} = e^{-\lambda t(1-p)} \frac{(\lambda t(1-p))^m}{m!}.$$

Hence by (11.1), we have that

$$\mathbf{P}\{N_A(t) = n, N_B(t) = m\} = \mathbf{P}\{N_A(t) = n\} \cdot \mathbf{P}\{N_B(t) = m\}, \quad (11.2)$$

showing that the processes are independent.

Now because the other conditions in Definition 1 such as independent increments are also obviously satisfied, we have that $\{N_A(t), t \geq 0\}$ forms a Poisson process with rate λp and $\{N_B(t), t \geq 0\}$ forms an independent Poisson process with rate $\lambda(1 - p)$. ∎

11.8 Uniformity

Theorem 11.9 *Given that one event of a Poisson process has occurred by time t, that event is equally likely to have occurred anywhere in $[0, t]$.*

Proof Let T_1 denote the time of the one event.

$$\mathbf{P}\{T_1 < s \mid N(t) = 1\} = \frac{\mathbf{P}\{T_1 < s \text{ and } N(t) = 1\}}{\mathbf{P}\{N(t) = 1\}}$$

$$= \frac{\mathbf{P}\{1 \text{ event in } [0, s] \text{ and } 0 \text{ events in } [s, t]\}}{\frac{e^{-\lambda t}(\lambda t)^1}{1!}}$$

$$= \frac{\mathbf{P}\{1 \text{ event in } [0, s]\} \cdot \mathbf{P}\{0 \text{ events in } [s, t]\}}{e^{-\lambda t} \cdot \lambda t}$$

$$= \frac{e^{-\lambda s} \cdot \lambda s \cdot e^{-\lambda(t-s)} \cdot (\lambda(t - s))^0}{e^{-\lambda t} \cdot \lambda t}$$

$$= \frac{s}{t}$$

∎

Generalization: If k events of a Poisson process occur by time t, then the k events are distributed independently and uniformly in $[0, t]$. This is proven in [149], pp. 36–38.

11.9 Exercises

11.1 Memorylessness
Let $X \sim \text{Exp}(\lambda)$. What is $\mathbf{E}[X \mid X > 10]$? Solve this in two ways:
(a) by integrating the conditional p.d.f.
(b) by a two-line argument via the memoryless property of Exponential distribution.

11.2 Memorylessness Continued
Given $X \sim \text{Exp}(1)$, what is $\mathbf{E}[X^2 \mid X > 10]$?

11.3 Doubling Exponentials
Suppose that job sizes are Exponentially distributed with rate μ. If job sizes all double, what can we say about the distribution of job sizes now? Prove it.

11.4 Failure Rate
Let X be a continuous random variable with probability density function $f(t)$ and cumulative distribution function $F(t) = \mathbf{P}\{X < t\}$. We define the failure rate of X to be $r(t)$, where

$$r(t) \equiv \frac{f(t)}{\overline{F}(t)}.$$

Thus $r(t)dt$ represents the probability that a t-year-old item will fail in the next dt seconds.
(a) Prove that for the Exponential distribution, the failure rate is a constant.
(b) Prove that the Exponential distribution is the only distribution with constant failure rate.

11.5 Practice with Definition of Poisson Process
(a) Consider a stream of packets arriving according to a Poisson process with rate $\lambda = 50$ packets/sec. Suppose each packet is of type "green" with probability 5% and of type "yellow" with probability 95%. Given that 100 green packets arrived during the previous second, (i) what is the expected number of yellow packets that arrived during the previous second? (ii) what is the probability that 200 yellow packets arrived during the previous second?
(b) Red packets arrive according to a Poisson process with rate $\lambda_1 = 30$ packets/sec. Black packets arrive according to a Poisson process with rate $\lambda_2 = 10$ packets/sec. Assume the streams are statistically multiplexed into one stream. Suppose we are told that 60 packets arrived during the second. What is the probability that exactly 40 of those were red?
(c) Suppose packets arrive according to a Poisson process with rate λ, and you are told that by time 30 seconds 100 packets have arrived. What is the probability that 20 packets arrived during the first 10 seconds?

11.6 Number of Arrivals of a Poisson Process during a Service

In this chapter, we considered, $N(t)$, the number of Poisson(λ) arrivals during a time t. In queueing, one often needs to know A_S, the number of Poisson(λ) arrivals during S, where S is a continuous random variable denoting, say, the service time of a job. Derive $\mathbf{E}[A_S]$ and $\mathbf{Var}(A_S)$.

11.7 Malware and Honeypots

A new malware is out in the Internet! Our goal is to estimate its spread/damage by time t, assuming it starts at time 0. Assume that the Internet hosts get infected by this malware according to a Poisson process with parameter λ, where λ is *not known*. Thrasyvoulos installs a Honeypot security system to detect whether hosts are infected. Unfortunately there is a *lag time* between when a computer is infected by the malware and the Honeypot detects the damage. Assume that this lag time is distributed Exp(μ). Suppose that Thrasyvoulos's Honeypot system has detected $N_1(t)$ infected hosts by time t. Thrasyvoulos worries that, because of the lag, the number of infected hosts is actually much higher than $N_1(t)$. The goal of the problem is to understand how many *additional* hosts, $N_2(t)$, are expected to also be infected at time t.

(a) Suppose that an infection happens at time s, where $0 < s < t$. What is the probability that the infection is detected by time t?

(b) Consider an arbitrary infection that happens before time t. What is the (unconditional) probability, p, that the infection is detected by the Honeypot by time t?

(c) How can we use our knowledge of $N_1(t)$ to estimate λ?

(d) Use your estimate of λ to determine the expected value of $N_2(t)$.

[*Note:* None of the above solutions requires more than a couple lines.]

11.8 Sum of Geometric Number of Exponentials[3]

Let $N \sim$ Geometric(p). Let $X_i \sim$ Exp(μ). Let $S_N = \sum_{i=1}^{N} X_i$. Your goal is to prove that S_N is Exponentially distributed and derive the rate of S_N. Prove this fact using δ-step arguments. [*Note:* In Chapter 25 you will see how to prove this same result using transforms.]

11.9 Reliability Theory: Max of Two Exponentials

Redundancy is often built into systems so that if a device (say a disk) fails there is no catastrophe. In these settings, we are often concerned with the expected time until *both* disks fail, which is the time until a catastrophe occurs. This can be viewed as the "max" of two random variables.

(a) Let $X_1 \sim$ Exp(λ). Let $X_2 \sim$ Exp(λ). Suppose $X_1 \perp X_2$. What is $\mathbf{E}[\max(X_1, X_2)]$?

(b) Let $X_1 \sim$ Exp(λ_1). Let $X_2 \sim$ Exp(λ_2). Suppose $X_1 \perp X_2$. What is $\mathbf{E}[\max(X_1, X_2)]$?

11.10 Exponential Downloads

You need to download two files: file 1 and file 2. File 1 is available via source A or source B. File 2 is available only via source C. The time to download

---

[3] Warning: The result of Exercise 11.8 will be used many times throughout the book.

file 1 from source A is Exponentially distributed with rate 1. The time to download file 1 from source B is Exponentially distributed with rate 2. The time to download file 2 from source C is Exponentially distributed with rate 3. You decide to download from *all three* sources simultaneously, in the hope that you get both file 1 and file 2 as soon as possible. Let T denote the time until you get *both* files.

(a) What is $\mathbf{E}[T]$?

(b) What is $\mathbf{P}\{T < t\}$?

11.11 Reliability Theory: Max of Many Exponentials

Let $X_1, X_2, X_3, \ldots, X_n$ be i.i.d. Exponentially distributed random variables all with rate λ. Let

$$Z = \max(X_1, X_2, \ldots, X_n).$$

(a) What is $\mathbf{E}[Z]$?

(b) Roughly, what does $\mathbf{E}[Z]$ look like as a function of n and λ when n is high?

(c) Derive the distribution of Z.

11.12 Conditional Distribution

Let $X \sim \text{Exp}(\lambda_X)$ and $Y \sim \text{Exp}(\lambda_Y)$, where $X \perp Y$. Let $Z = \min(X, Y)$. Prove that

$$(X \mid X < Y) \sim Z.$$

That is, show that $\mathbf{P}\{X > t \mid X < Y\} = \mathbf{P}\{Z > t\}$.

CHAPTER 12

Transition to Continuous-Time Markov Chains

12.1 Defining CTMCs

Recall the definition of a DTMC (repeated from Definition 8.1):

Definition 12.1 A *DTMC* (Discrete-Time Markov Chain) is a stochastic process $\{X_n, n = 0, 1, 2, \ldots\}$, where X_n denotes the state at (discrete) time step n and such that, $\forall n \geq 0, \forall i, j$, and $\forall i_0, \ldots, i_{n-1}$,

$$\mathbf{P}\{X_{n+1} = j \mid X_n = i, X_{n-1} = i_{n-1}, \ldots, X_0 = i_0\} = \mathbf{P}\{X_{n+1} = j \mid X_n = i\}$$
$$= P_{ij} \text{ (by stationarity)},$$

where P_{ij} is independent of the time step and of past history.

Notice the three properties of Definition 12.1:

1. Transitions are always made at discrete time steps, $n = 0, 1, 2, \ldots$
2. The past does not matter. Only the present state matters. In particular, it does not matter how long the Markov chain was sitting in state i already. This is the Markovian Property (M.P.).
3. Transition probabilities are "stationary," meaning that they are independent of time step n.

Continuous-Time Markov Chains (CTMCs) are the continuous-time analogue of DTMCs. Thus we keep properties 2 and 3 of DTMCs. However, we replace property 1 with: "transitions between states can happen at any time."

Definition 12.2 A *Continuous-Time Markov Chain (CTMC)* is a continuous-time stochastic process $\{X(t), t \geq 0\}$ s.t., $\forall s, t \geq 0$ and $\forall i, j, x(u)$,

$$\mathbf{P}\{X(t + s) = j \mid X(s) = i, X(u) = x(u), 0 \leq u \leq s\}$$
$$= \mathbf{P}\{X(t + s) = j \mid X(s) = i\} \text{ (by M.P.)}$$
$$= \mathbf{P}\{X(t) = j \mid X(0) = i\} = P_{ij}(t) \text{ (stationarity)}.$$

We assume throughout that the state space is countable.

Now consider the quantity τ_i, defined next.

Definition 12.3 Define τ_i to be the time until the CTMC leaves state i, given that the CTMC is currently in state i.

By the Markovian and stationary properties of the CTMC, the probability that the CTMC leaves state i in the next t seconds is independent of how long the CTMC has already been in state i. That is,

$$\mathbf{P}\left\{\tau_i > t + s \mid \tau_i > s\right\} = \mathbf{P}\left\{\tau_i > t\right\}.$$

Question: What does this say about τ_i?

Answer: This says that τ_i is memoryless. But this means τ_i is Exponentially distributed!

This means that we can define a CTMC as follows:

> **Definition 12.4 CTMC – VIEW 1:** A CTMC is a stochastic process with the property that every time it enters state i, the following hold:
>   1. The amount of time the process spends in state i before making a transition is Exponentially distributed with some rate (call it ν_i).
>   2. When the process leaves state i, it will next enter state j with some probability (call it p_{ij}) independent of the time spent at state i.

VIEW 1 of a CTMC is depicted in Figure 12.1. In this view, we stay in state i for time $\tau_i \sim \text{Exp}(\nu_i)$. When we leave i, we transition to j with probability p_{ij}, where $\sum_j p_{ij} = 1$.

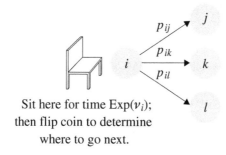

Sit here for time $\text{Exp}(\nu_i)$;
then flip coin to determine
where to go next.

Figure 12.1. VIEW 1 of a CTMC.

Observe that p_{ij}, the probability that when we leave i we next go to state j, is a constant. It is independent of time, t, by stationarity. It is independent of the time spent in state i, τ_i, by the Markovian property.

Consider the moment just before we leave state i. At this moment, the time we have spent in state i is irrelevant: That is all history (Markovian assumption). All that is relevant is that we are at state i at this moment s. The particular time s is irrelevant as well (stationarity assumption).

There is an alternative way to view CTMCs (we call it VIEW 2) that is more practical.

Definition 12.5 CTMC – VIEW 2: Let $X_j \sim \text{Exp}(\nu_i p_{ij})$ represent the time to transition from i to j, $\forall j \neq i$. Let $\tau_i = \min_j\{X_j\}$ be the time until the Markov chain leaves state i. Let the next state be m where $m = \operatorname*{argmin}_j\{X_j\}$, i.e., X_m was the $\min_j\{X_j\}$.

This definition may seem confusing. Here is what VIEW 2 is really saying (see Figure 12.2): Think of yourself as sitting in state i (home) on a Saturday night and waiting to receive a phone call that will tell you where to move next. There are three possible transitions that you can take: to j, to k, or to l (these are the names of the three dates who might call). You have three phones. The first is a direct line to state j so j can call you and invite you over. The second is a direct line to state k. The third is a direct line to state l. You will go to whomever calls you first – you are desperate! The time until you receive a phone call from state j is a random variable $X_j \sim \text{Exp}(\nu_i p_{ij})$. Independently, the time until you receive a phone call from state k is a random variable $X_k \sim \text{Exp}(\nu_i p_{ik})$. The time until you receive a phone call from state l is a random variable $X_l \sim \text{Exp}(\nu_i p_{il})$. All of X_j, X_k, X_l are taking place simultaneously. As soon as you get any phone call, you leave state i and go to the party who called you, and the process starts all over again at that state.

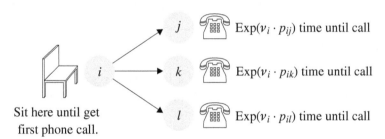

Figure 12.2. VIEW 2 of a CTMC.

It is not at all obvious that VIEW 1 is equivalent to VIEW 2.

Proof That VIEW 2 $\Rightarrow$ VIEW 1

Using VIEW 2, consider the time spent in state i, namely τ_i.

$$\tau_i = \min_j\{X_j\} \sim \text{Exp}\left(\sum_j \nu_i p_{ij}\right) = \text{Exp}(\nu_i).$$

Furthermore, the probability that from state i we transition to state m is:

$$\mathbf{P}\left\{X_m = \min_j\{X_j\}\right\} = \frac{\nu_i p_{im}}{\displaystyle\sum_j \nu_i p_{ij}} = p_{im}. \qquad \blacksquare$$

Heuristic Proof That VIEW 1 $\Rightarrow$ VIEW 2

Using VIEW 1, we describe the Markov chain as sitting in state i for $\text{Exp}(\nu_i)$ time. After that a "direction coin" is flipped. With probability p_{ij} the direction coin points to j. With probability p_{ik} the direction coin points to k. With probability p_{il} the direction coin points to l. To make this more concrete, let's assume $p_{ij} = \frac{1}{2}$, $p_{ik} = \frac{1}{3}$, $p_{il} = \frac{1}{6}$.

Now let's translate the above into its Geometric analogue: The Markov chain (MC) sits in state i flipping a coin every δ steps. The coin has probability $\nu_i \delta$ of success. The MC waits for a success. As soon as it gets a success, it flips the direction coin to determine the type of its success.

This description is equivalent to the following: The MC sits in state i flipping a coin every δ steps. With probability $\nu_i \cdot \frac{1}{2}\delta$, the coin is a "success type j." With probability $\nu_i \cdot \frac{1}{3}\delta$, the coin is a "success type k." With probability $\nu_i \cdot \frac{1}{6}\delta$, the coin is a "success type l." With probability $1 - \nu_i \delta$, the coin is not a success. The Markov chain waits for a success (of any type) and heads to the appropriate next destination (based on the type of the success).

Considering those coin flips solely from the perspective of whether they lead to a success of type j, we see that the time until a success of type j is $\text{Exp}(\nu_i p_{ij})$. Likewise, independently and in parallel, we see that the time until a success of type k is $\text{Exp}(\nu_i p_{ik})$. And again, independently and in parallel, we see that the time until a success of type l is $\text{Exp}(\nu_i p_{il})$.

But this is exactly VIEW 2.   ■

Remark: The heuristic proof can be made a little more rigorous by including the $o(\delta)$ probabilities that two success types happen on a given δ time step. We have not included this detail because it washes out in the end as you will see in later examples.

Example

Let us model the single-server network shown in Figure 12.3 as a CTMC. Here the state is the number of jobs in the system.

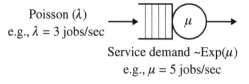

Poisson (λ)
e.g., $\lambda = 3$ jobs/sec

Service demand $\sim\text{Exp}(\mu)$
e.g., $\mu = 5$ jobs/sec

Figure 12.3. A single-server network.

Using VIEW 2, we arrive at the equivalent picture shown in Figure 12.4 about which we make the following remarks:

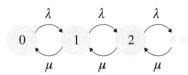

Figure 12.4. VIEW 2 of the same single-server network.

- λ and μ are *not* probabilities (we can have $\lambda = 3$, $\mu = 5$).
- An event is something that *changes* our state.
- Suppose we are in state i, where $i \geq 1$. Then the next event is either an arrival or a departure.
- Let X_A denote the time to the next arrival. Then $X_A \sim \text{Exp}(\lambda)$ regardless of how long we have been in the current state. Let X_D denote the time to the next departure. Then $X_D \sim \text{Exp}(\mu)$ regardless of how long we have been in the current state. X_A and X_D are independent of each other.
- The previous two events are happening in parallel. One of these, the arrival or the departure, will occur first. So τ_i, the time until we leave state i, has the following distribution: $\tau_i \sim \text{Exp}(\lambda + \mu)$. Thus, $\nu_i = \lambda + \mu$.
- The probability that when we leave state i we will next go to state $i + 1$ is $\mathbf{P}\{X_A < X_D\} = \frac{\lambda}{\lambda+\mu}$.

12.2 Solving CTMCs

Let $\pi_j = \lim_{t\to\infty} P_{ij}(t) =$ limiting probability of being in state j. How do we determine the π_j's?

Different books have different ways of leading the reader to the right method. Ross [149] (see Section 4.8 and then Section 5.5) goes through semi-Markov chains. Trivedi [179] goes through Kolmogorov equations. Gallager [66] goes through semi-Markov chain theory and embedded Markov chains.

We go through a more intuitive argument for obtaining the limiting probabilities. For ease of readability, we continue to refer to the previous very simple chain example, but everything generalizes to more complex CTMCs, as we discuss later.

1. *Suppose you had a DTMC.* Then you would know how to obtain the π_i's: Simply check for aperiodicity and irreducibility, and then try to solve the stationary equations, as explained in Theorem 9.27. If a solution to the stationary equations exists, that solution is the limiting probability. If no solution to the stationary equations exists, then all the limiting probabilities are zero.

2. *But we do not have a DTMC*; we have a CTMC.

3. *However, we can model the CTMC via a DTMC.* In the CTMC, if we are in state i,
   - Time to next arrival $\sim \text{Exp}(\lambda)$

- Time to next departure $\sim \text{Exp}(\mu)$
- Time until first of these occurs (i.e., leave state i) $\sim \text{Exp}(\lambda + \mu)$.

We can model this situation by flipping two coins simultaneously every δ-step, where $\delta \to 0$, as shown in Figure 12.5.

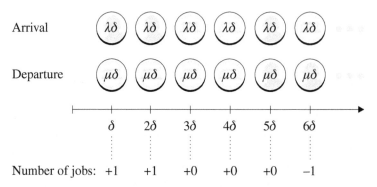

Figure 12.5. Flipping two coins simultaneously each δ-step, one with probability $\lambda\delta$ of heads and the other with probability $\mu\delta$ of heads.

The first coin represents arrivals. When the first coin is flipped at each δ-step, it has probability $\lambda\delta$ of returning "arrival" and probability $1 - \lambda\delta$ of returning nothing.

The second coin represents departures. When the second coin is flipped at each δ-step, it has probability $\mu\delta$ of returning "departure" and probability $1 - \mu\delta$ of returning nothing.

A "flip" refers to the result of the two coins. Expanding out the four cases yields

- With probability $\lambda\delta(1 - \mu\delta)$, the flip returns "arrival and no departure."
- With probability $(1 - \lambda\delta)\mu\delta$, the flip returns "departure and no arrival."
- With probability $\lambda\delta\mu\delta$, the flip returns "arrival and departure."
- With probability $(1 - \text{all of the above})$, the flip returns "no arrival and no departure."

But this looks just like a *DTMC* that makes a transition every δ steps with the *probabilities* shown in Figure 12.6.

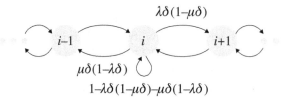

Figure 12.6. The equivalent DTMC.

4. ***Thus the solution to the original CTMC in Figure 12.4 equals the solution to the DTMC in Figure 12.6*** where transitions occur at every δ-step. Let's see if we can clean up this DTMC.

We can rewrite

$$\lambda\delta(1 - \mu\delta) \longrightarrow \lambda\delta + o(\delta)$$
$$\mu\delta(1 - \lambda\delta) \longrightarrow \mu\delta + o(\delta)$$
$$\lambda\delta\mu\delta \longrightarrow o(\delta)$$
$$(1 - \text{all of the above}) \longrightarrow 1 - \lambda\delta - \mu\delta + o(\delta),$$

which allows us to represent the DTMC as in Figure 12.7. Observe that the edges are just probabilities, and transitions occur on every δ-step. Observe also that if the DTMC is in state i, with high probability it will still be in state i at the next δ-step.

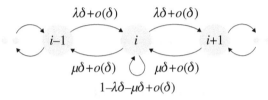

Figure 12.7. The equivalent DTMC with small factors hidden.

5. *Let's solve this DTMC, while taking the limit as $\delta \longrightarrow 0$*. It simplifies the math to observe that we can ignore self-loops in a DTMC and write balance equations (recall Section 9.6). We then divide by δ, take the limit as $\delta \to 0$, and solve.

$$\text{Rate leave state } 0 = \text{Rate enter state } 0$$
$$\pi_0 \left(\lambda\delta + o(\delta)\right) = \pi_1 \left(\mu\delta + o(\delta)\right)$$
$$\pi_0 \left(\lambda + \frac{o(\delta)}{\delta}\right) = \pi_1 \left(\mu + \frac{o(\delta)}{\delta}\right)$$
$$\lim_{\delta \to 0} \pi_0 \left(\lambda + \frac{o(\delta)}{\delta}\right) = \lim_{\delta \to 0} \pi_1 \left(\mu + \frac{o(\delta)}{\delta}\right)$$
$$\pi_0 \cdot \lambda = \pi_1 \cdot \mu$$
$$\Rightarrow \pi_1 = \frac{\lambda}{\mu}\pi_0$$

$$\text{Rate leave state } 1 = \text{Rate enter state } 1$$
$$\pi_1 \left(\lambda\delta + o(\delta) + \mu\delta + o(\delta)\right) = \pi_0 \left(\lambda\delta + o(\delta)\right) + \pi_2 \left(\mu\delta + o(\delta)\right)$$
$$\lim_{\delta \to 0} \pi_1 \left(\frac{\lambda\delta}{\delta} + \frac{o(\delta)}{\delta} + \frac{\mu\delta}{\delta}\right) = \lim_{\delta \to 0} \pi_0 \left(\frac{\lambda\delta}{\delta} + \frac{o(\delta)}{\delta}\right) + \pi_2 \left(\frac{\mu\delta}{\delta} + \frac{o(\delta)}{\delta}\right)$$
$$\pi_1(\lambda + \mu) = \pi_0(\lambda) + \pi_2(\mu)$$
$$\frac{\lambda}{\mu}\pi_0(\lambda + \mu) = \lambda\pi_0 + \mu\pi_2$$
$$\Rightarrow \pi_2 = \left(\frac{\lambda}{\mu}\right)^2 \pi_0$$

$$\text{Rate leave state 2} = \text{Rate enter state 2}$$

$$\pi_2 \left(\lambda\delta + o(\delta) + \mu\delta + o(\delta) \right) = \pi_1(\lambda\delta + o(\delta)) + \pi_3(\mu\delta + o(\delta))$$

$$\cdots$$

$$\pi_2(\lambda + \mu) = \pi_1(\lambda) + \pi_3(\mu)$$

$$\Rightarrow \pi_3 = \left(\frac{\lambda}{\mu} \right)^3 \pi_0$$

etc.

6. *Look at the format of the equations we are left with for the DTMC.* These look just like what we would imagine "balance equations" should look like for the original CTMC:

$$\pi_0(\lambda) = \pi_1(\mu) \tag{12.1}$$

$$\pi_1(\lambda + \mu) = \pi_0(\lambda) + \pi_2(\mu) \tag{12.2}$$

$$\pi_2(\lambda + \mu) = \pi_1(\lambda) + \pi_3(\mu) \tag{12.3}$$

Consider these in light of our original CTMC, redrawn in Figure 12.8. In the balance equations shown in (12.1), (12.2), (12.3), λ and μ are *not* probabilities, but they behave as if they are with respect to creating the equations.

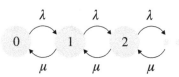

Figure 12.8. Our original CTMC.

7. *So it seems that to solve a CTMC, all one has to do is write out the balance equations for the CTMC and solve them.* That will result in the same answer as solving the δ-step DTMC, which is equivalent to the CTMC. Note that we have only shown that this statement is true for this particular example. In the next section we discuss more general chains.

8. To find limiting probabilities via balance (or stationary) equations, we still need to ensure that the DTMC is irreducible and aperiodic so that we can apply the theory of DTMCs (Theorem 9.27). To do so, it suffices to check that the Markov chain is irreducible (aperiodicity is not an issue in the continuous case).

12.3 Generalization and Interpretation

The argument we just presented for translating from a CTMC to a DTMC was applied to one specific example. Figure 12.9 provides some intuition for why this argument works for a general CTMC.

Assume we start with a general CTMC. Consider a single state i as shown in Figure 12.9. The arcs pointing out of state i represent Exponential rates. We can model the CTMC as a DTMC where transitions happen every δ-step. The transition probabilities are shown in Figure 12.9. There is a self-loop at state i that contains the remaining probability of leaving state i. Observe that in the DTMC interpretation, there is some probability that when we are in state i, more than one of our coins will come up a success during a particular flip (single δ-step). However, the probability of such an event is just $o(\delta)$. It does not matter how we choose to interpret such an event because the $o(\delta)$ washes out. We will react to the event of more than one success in a single δ-step by simply staying at state i. Now we solve the DTMC by writing out the balance equations for the DTMC. The limiting probabilities we obtain for the DTMC are also the limiting probabilities of the original CTMC. Observe that in the DTMC shown in Figure 12.9, if we are in state i, on most δ-step transitions, we simply return to state i. This exactly models the CTMC where we sit in state i for a while.

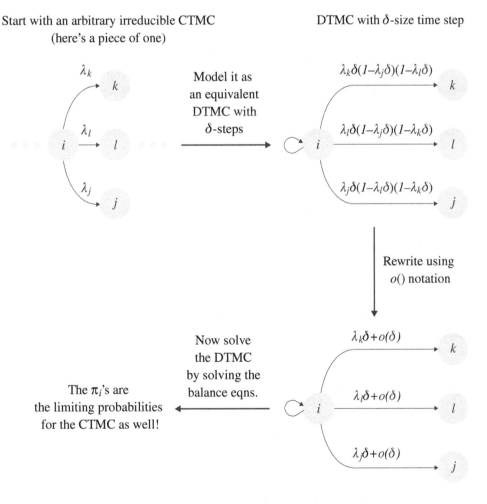

Figure 12.9. The solution of an arbitrary CTMC using our method.

The point to take away from this is that in practice we do not need to go through the translation to a DTMC with δ-steps. Just think that part and write down the balance equations for the CTMC directly, from which we can solve for the π_i's.

12.3.1 *Interpreting the Balance Equations for the CTMC*

We have been referring to the equations we obtain at the end of the translation as "balance equations." This name is in fact appropriate because they balance the rate at which jobs leave state j in the CTMC with the rate at which jobs enter state j in the CTMC, for each state j. Here is the standard notation for CTMCs:

$$\pi_j \nu_j = \sum_i \pi_i q_{ij} \tag{12.4}$$

The left-hand side (LHS) of (12.4) is the product of the limiting probability of being in state j, π_j, and the rate the MC leaves state j given that it is in state j, ν_j. Thus the LHS represents the total rate of transitions leaving state j.

The ith term in the summand of the RHS represents the product of the limiting probability of being in state i, π_i, and the rate the MC leaves state i to go to state j given that it is in state i, q_{ij}. Thus the ith term in the summand of the RHS represents the rate of transitions leaving state i to go to state j. The RHS therefore represents the total rate of transitions entering state j from any state.

Observe that $q_{ij} = \nu_i \cdot p_{ij}$. Hence we can equivalently write:

$$\pi_j \sum_i q_{ji} = \sum_i \pi_i q_{ij}$$

12.3.2 *Summary Theorem for CTMCs*

Because CTMCs can basically be viewed as DTMCs in which the time step goes to zero, all the ergodicity theory that we developed for DTMCs carries over to CTMCs. In particular, we have the following summary theorem, analogous to Theorem 9.27.

Theorem 12.6 (Summary Theorem for CTMCs) *Given an irreducible CTMC, suppose* $\exists$ π_i's *s.t.* $\forall j$,

$$\pi_j \nu_j = \sum_i \pi_i q_{ij} \quad and \quad \sum_i \pi_i = 1.$$

Then the π_i's *are the limiting probabilities for the CTMC, and the CTMC is ergodic.*

12.4 Exercises

12.1 Converting a CTMC to a DTMC
In this chapter we saw how to model any CTMC as a DTMC where the time step in the DTMC is of length δ. Draw the corresponding DTMC for the CTMC

in Figure 12.10. Then write out the DTMC balance equations, take the limit as $\delta \to 0$, and show the resulting CTMC balance equations. You need not solve them.

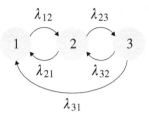

Figure 12.10. A simple CTMC.

12.2 Potential Pitfall: Balance $\neq$ Stationary for CTMC

Recall that for DTMCs, balance equations are equivalent to stationary equations (see Sections 9.6 and 9.7). For a CTMC, the balance equations yield the limiting probabilities, while the stationary equations are meaningless, unless we first translate to a DTMC. We illustrate this point for the CTMC in Figure 12.10.

(a) Write all the balance equations for the CTMC:

$$\pi_j \nu_j = \sum_i \pi_i q_{ij} \quad \text{where} \quad \sum_i \pi_i = 1$$

(b) Write all the (meaningless) stationary equations for the CTMC:

$$\pi_j = \sum_i \pi_i q_{ij} \quad \text{where} \quad \sum_i \pi_i = 1$$

Observe that these do not match the balance equations.

(c) Convert the CTMC to a DTMC, as in Exercise 12.1. Now write the balance equations and the stationary equations for the DTMC. Explain why these are equivalent.

CHAPTER 13

M/M/1 and PASTA

13.1 The M/M/1 Queue

The simplest queueing model consists of a single server in which the service times are i.i.d. Exponential random variables with mean $1/\mu$, and the customers (jobs) arrive into the system according to a Poisson process with rate λ. Such a system is referred to as an M/M/1 queueing system and is shown in Figure 13.1.

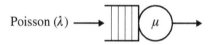

Poisson (λ) ⟶

Figure 13.1. The M/M/1 queueing system.

M/M/1 is Kendall notation and describes the queueing system architecture. The first slot characterizes the distribution of the interarrival times for the arrival process. The "M" in this first slot stands for "memoryless" and says that the interarrival times are Exponentially distributed. The second slot characterizes the distribution of the service times. The "M" in this slot says that the service times of jobs are "memoryless," namely Exponentially distributed. The third slot indicates the number of servers in the system. For now this is 1, but we will see more complicated examples later. A fourth slot is typically used to indicate an upper bound on the capacity of the system in terms of the total space available to hold jobs. Sometimes, however, the fourth slot is used to indicate the scheduling discipline used for the system. The absence of a fourth field indicates that the queue is unbounded and that the scheduling policy is FCFS. Kendall notation is by no means sufficient to fully describe the characteristics of all queueing systems. For example, systems where jobs move from one queue to another are not represented by Kendall notation, but it is a reasonable start for describing single-queue systems.

The number of customers in an M/M/1 system forms a continuous-time Markov chain (CTMC) where the state of the system corresponds to the number of customers in the system. Figure 13.2 shows the transition rate diagram for the M/M/1 system.

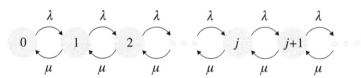

Figure 13.2. CTMC for the M/M/1 queueing system.

The structure of this chain is referred to as a **birth-death process**, with the λ's denoting the "births" and the μ's denoting the "deaths." In general, in a birth-death process, transitions are only defined between consecutive states, but the rates of the births (or deaths) do not have to be homogeneous.

The limiting probabilities for the states of the M/M/1 CTMC may be obtained by solving the balance equations. Recall that the balance equations equate the rate at which the system leaves state j with the rate at which the system enters state j.

Question: What is the rate of transitions leaving state 1 to go to state 2?

Answer: $\pi_1 \lambda$. Observe that λ represents the rate of transitions (number of transitions per second) that move from any state i to the next higher state, $i + 1$. If we multiply by π_1, we are limiting ourselves to only those upward transitions that occur when the chain is in state 1.

Here are the full balance equations:

State	Balance equation	Simplified equation
$0:$	$\pi_0 \lambda = \pi_1 \mu$	$\Rightarrow \pi_1 = \dfrac{\lambda}{\mu} \pi_0$
$1:$	$\pi_1 (\lambda + \mu) = \pi_0 \lambda + \pi_2 \mu$	$\Rightarrow \pi_2 = \left(\dfrac{\lambda}{\mu}\right)^2 \pi_0$
$2:$	$\pi_2 (\lambda + \mu) = \pi_1 \lambda + \pi_3 \mu$	$\Rightarrow \pi_3 = \left(\dfrac{\lambda}{\mu}\right)^3 \pi_0$
$i:$	$\pi_i (\lambda + \mu) = \pi_{i-1} \lambda + \pi_{i+1} \mu$	$\Rightarrow$???

We guess that

$$\pi_i = \left(\frac{\lambda}{\mu}\right)^i \pi_0.$$

We check that this is correct by substituting back into the balance equation for state i, as follows:

$$\left(\frac{\lambda}{\mu}\right)^i \pi_0 (\lambda + \mu) = \left(\frac{\lambda}{\mu}\right)^{i-1} \pi_0 \lambda + \left(\frac{\lambda}{\mu}\right)^{i+1} \pi_0 \mu$$

$$\frac{\lambda^{i+1}}{\mu^i} + \frac{\lambda^i}{\mu^{i-1}} \overset{\vee}{=} \frac{\lambda^i}{\mu^{i-1}} + \frac{\lambda^{i+1}}{\mu^i}$$

Next we determine π_0 such that the equation $\sum_{i=0}^{\infty} \pi_i = 1$ is satisfied:

$$\sum_{i=0}^{\infty} \pi_i = 1$$

$$\Rightarrow \sum_{i=0}^{\infty} \left(\frac{\lambda}{\mu} \right)^i \pi_0 = 1$$

$$\Rightarrow \pi_0 \left(\frac{1}{1 - \frac{\lambda}{\mu}} \right) = 1$$

$$\Rightarrow \pi_0 = 1 - \frac{\lambda}{\mu}$$

Therefore, substituting back into the equation for π_i we obtain

$$\pi_i = \left(\frac{\lambda}{\mu} \right)^i \left(1 - \frac{\lambda}{\mu} \right) = \rho^i (1 - \rho)$$

$$\pi_0 = 1 - \frac{\lambda}{\mu} = 1 - \rho$$

where $\rho = \lambda/\mu$ is the server utilization. It should make sense that π_0, the probability that the system is idle, equals $1 - \rho$.

Observe that the condition $\rho < 1$ must be met if the system is to be stable in the sense that the number of customers in the system does not grow without bound. For this condition to be true, we must have $\lambda < \mu$.

The mean number of customers in the system can be derived by conditioning on the state:

$$\mathbf{E}[N] = \sum_{i=0}^{\infty} i \pi_i$$

$$= \sum_{i=1}^{\infty} i \pi_i$$

$$= \sum_{i=1}^{\infty} i \rho^i (1 - \rho)$$

$$= \rho(1 - \rho) \sum_{i=1}^{\infty} i \rho^{i-1}$$

$$= \rho(1 - \rho) \frac{d}{d\rho} \left[\sum_{i=0}^{\infty} \rho^i \right]$$

$$= \rho(1 - \rho)\frac{d}{d\rho}\left[\frac{1}{1-\rho}\right]$$

$$= \rho(1 - \rho)\frac{1}{(1-\rho)^2}$$

$$= \frac{\rho}{1-\rho}.$$

Figure 13.3 plots the equation $\mathbf{E}[N] = \rho/(1-\rho)$. Observe that for $\rho < 0.5$ or even $\rho < 0.6$, the mean number of customers in the system hardly goes up. However after that point, it goes up a lot. Also, the impact of increasing ρ from 0.8 to 0.9 is much greater than the impact of increasing ρ from 0.7 to 0.8.

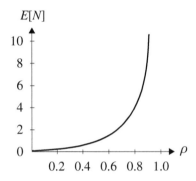

Figure 13.3. Plot of the expected number of customers in the M/M/1 system vs. ρ.

In Exercise 13.12, we will prove that the variance of the number of customers in the system is given by

$$\mathbf{Var}(N) = \frac{\rho}{(1-\rho)^2}.$$

This grows even more sharply than the mean number of jobs.

The mean time in the system and mean time in queue are found using Little's Law:

$$\mathbf{E}[T] = \frac{\mathbf{E}[N]}{\lambda} = \frac{1}{\mu - \lambda}$$

$$\mathbf{E}[T_Q] = \mathbf{E}[T] - \frac{1}{\mu} = \frac{\rho}{\mu - \lambda}$$

13.2 Examples Using an M/M/1 Queue

Example: Practice with the Formulas

Question: Given an M/M/1 server, what is the maximum allowable arrival rate of jobs if the mean job size (service demand) is 3 minutes and the mean waiting time ($\mathbf{E}[T_Q]$) must be kept under 6 minutes?

Answer: We are given that $\mu = 1/3$ jobs/minute. We are also given that the expected time in the system must be less than 9 minutes ($\mathbf{E}[T] = \mathbf{E}[T_Q] + \mathbf{E}[S]$).

Therefore,

$$\frac{1}{\mu - \lambda} \leq 9$$

$$\Rightarrow \lambda \leq \mu - \frac{1}{9} = \frac{2}{9} \text{ jobs/min.}$$

Example: Increasing Arrival and Service Rates Proportionally

Given an M/M/1 system (with $\lambda < \mu$), suppose that we increase the arrival rate λ and the service rate μ by a factor of k each.

Question: How are the following affected?

- utilization, ρ?
- throughput, X?
- mean number in the system, $\mathbf{E}[N]$?
- mean time in system, $\mathbf{E}[T]$?

Answer: We are given that

$$\lambda_{\text{new}} = k\lambda.$$

$$\mu_{\text{new}} = k\mu.$$

This yields

$$\rho_{\text{new}} = \frac{k\lambda}{k\mu} = \frac{\lambda}{\mu} = \rho_{\text{old}}.$$

$$X_{\text{new}} = \lambda_{\text{new}} = k\lambda_{\text{old}}.$$

$$\mathbf{E}[N_{\text{new}}] = \frac{\rho_{\text{new}}}{1 - \rho_{\text{new}}} = \frac{\rho_{\text{old}}}{1 - \rho_{\text{old}}} = \mathbf{E}[N_{\text{old}}].$$

$$\mathbf{E}[T_{\text{new}}] = \frac{1}{\mu_{\text{new}} - \lambda_{\text{new}}} = \frac{1}{k(\mu - \lambda)} = \frac{1}{k}\mathbf{E}[T_{\text{old}}].$$

Thus the system utilization is unchanged. The throughput is increased by a factor of k. The mean number of jobs in the system is unchanged. The mean response time drops by a factor of k.

These results should help explain the following quote from Bertsekas and Gallager [18]:

> *A transmission line k times as fast will accommodate k times as many packets at k times smaller average delay per packet.*

This is a very general result that also holds for any distribution on the service times and even applies to networks of queues.

Question: Why?

Answer: By speeding up both arrivals and service times by a factor of k, we are basically just speeding up our "clock speed" by a factor of k. That is, we can imagine a system where we make no changes, except for making the time scale a factor of k smaller. Now the number of packets an arriving packet sees ahead of it is the same under both time scales, but response time becomes a factor of k smaller when time is scaled. This is the reasoning we used in the example on the Federation versus the Klingons from Chapter 1.

Example: Statistical Multiplexing vs. Frequency-Division Multiplexing

Suppose m independent Poisson packet streams, each with an arrival rate of λ/m packets per second, are transmitted over a communication line. The transmission time for each packet is Exponentially distributed with mean $\frac{1}{\mu}$. We wish to analyze the performance of two different approaches to multiplexing the use of the communication line.

Statistical Multiplexing (SM): This approach merges the m streams into a single stream. Because the merge of m Poisson streams is still a Poisson stream, the resulting system may be modeled as a simple M/M/1 queueing system as shown in Figure 13.4.

Figure 13.4. The statistical multiplexing model.

Frequency-Division Multiplexing (FDM): This approach leaves the m streams separated and divides the transmission capacity into m equal portions as shown in Figure 13.5.

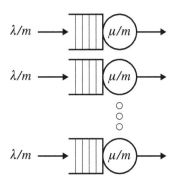

Figure 13.5. The frequency-division multiplexing model.

Question: How do the two methods compare with respect to mean response time?

Answer: The expected time in the system for SM is simply

$$\mathbf{E}\left[T^{\text{SM}}\right] = \frac{1}{\mu - \lambda}.$$

The expected time in the system for FDM is

$$\mathbf{E}\left[T^{\text{FDM}}\right] = \frac{1}{\mu/m - \lambda/m} = \frac{m}{\mu - \lambda}.$$

Thus the response time is m times greater under FDM.

Question: Why would one ever use FDM?

Answer: Frequency-division multiplexing guarantees a specific service rate to each stream. Statistical multiplexing is unable to provide any such guarantee. More importantly, suppose the original m streams were very regular (i.e., the interarrival times were less variable than Exponential, say closer to Deterministic than Exponential). By merging the streams, we introduce lots of variability into the arrival stream. This leads to problems if an application requires a low variability in delay (e.g., voice or video).

Warning: This is one of those results we may overturn later when we discuss higher variability job sizes.

13.3 PASTA

In later examples we will often be interested in the state of the system *as seen from the perspective of an arrival.*

To motivate this discussion, consider that you are running a simulation of some system. You want to determine the fraction of time that the system has n jobs. To do this, you consider each arrival into the system and ask whether it sees n jobs or not. You then track the fraction of arrivals that witnessed n jobs when arriving into the system. The question is whether this method gives you the right answer.

We'll assume an *ergodic* continuous-time system. Let $\pi_n = p_n$ be the limiting probability that there are n jobs in the system (or equivalently the long-run fraction of time that there are n jobs in the system). Let a_n be the limiting probability that an arrival sees n jobs in the system (or equivalently the long-run fraction of arrivals that see n jobs). Let d_n be the limiting probability that a departure leaves behind n jobs in the system when it departs (or equivalently the long-run fraction of departures that leave behind n jobs).

Question: Is $a_n = p_n$?

Answer: No, according to Claim 13.1.

Claim 13.1 a_n *is not necessarily equal to* p_n.[1]

---

[1] *Note:* Although the average number of jobs in the system is not necessarily the same as the average number seen by an arrival, the average time in system (response time) is by definition the same as the average response time experienced by an arrival. Similarly, the probability that the response time exceeds x is by definition the probability that an arrival spends more than x seconds in the system.

Proof   By example. Consider a single queue whose customers have an interarrival time distributed Uniformly between 1 and 2 (i.e., $\sim U(1, 2)$). Assume that all service times are constant with a value of 1. Then, $a_0 = 1$ and $d_0 = 1$ because a customer will complete service before the next customer arrives. However, $p_0 \neq 1$ because the system is not always empty.   ■

Question: Is $a_n = d_n$?

Answer: Yes, according to Claim 13.2.

Claim 13.2   *Assuming that customers arrive one at a time and are served one at a time, then $a_n = d_n$.*

Proof   An arrival sees n customers already in the system whenever the number of customers in the system goes from n to $n + 1$. A departure leaves n customers in the system whenever the number of customers in the system goes from $n + 1$ to n.

Because customers arrive one at a time and depart one at a time, these events happen an equal number of times (within 1). Because all states are recurrent, each of these events happens an infinite number of times. Thus the proportion of arrivals that find n customers in the system is equal to the proportion of departures that leave n customers in the system, given that the overall arrival rate equals the overall departure rate.   ■

We are now ready for PASTA – "Poisson Arrivals See Time Averages" (see Figure 13.6). PASTA states that $a_n = p_n$, and by Claim 13.2, $d_n = p_n$, when the arrivals follow a Poisson process. We state this as Claim 13.3.

Figure 13.6. PASTA makes us happy.

Claim 13.3   *If the arrival process to the system is a Poisson process, then $a_n = p_n$.*[2]

Proof   Viewing p_n and a_n as limiting probabilities, we have

$$p_n = \lim_{t \to \infty} \mathbf{P}\left\{N(t) = n\right\}.$$

$$a_n = \lim_{t \to \infty} \mathbf{P}\left\{N(t) = n \mid \text{an arrival occurred just after time } t\right\}.$$

---

[2] Sometimes the following requirement is appended: "Assume that interarrival times and service times are independent." This is necessary only for the perverse scenario described in the question at the very end of this section.

We show that $a_n = p_n$. Let $A(t, t + \delta)$ be the event that an arrival occurred just after time t. Then,

$$
\begin{aligned}
a_n &= \lim_{t \to \infty} \lim_{\delta \to 0} \mathbf{P}\left\{N(t) = n \mid A(t, t + \delta)\right\} \\
&= \lim_{t \to \infty} \lim_{\delta \to 0} \frac{\mathbf{P}\left\{N(t) = n, A(t, t + \delta)\right\}}{\mathbf{P}\left\{A(t, t + \delta)\right\}} \\
&= \lim_{t \to \infty} \lim_{\delta \to 0} \frac{\mathbf{P}\left\{A(t, t + \delta) \mid N(t) = n\right\} \mathbf{P}\left\{N(t) = n\right\}}{\mathbf{P}\left\{A(t, t + \delta)\right\}} \quad (*) \\
&= \lim_{t \to \infty} \lim_{\delta \to 0} \frac{\mathbf{P}\left\{A(t, t + \delta)\right\} \mathbf{P}\left\{N(t) = n\right\}}{\mathbf{P}\left\{A(t, t + \delta)\right\}} \quad (**) \\
&= \lim_{t \to \infty} \mathbf{P}\left\{N(t) = n\right\} \\
&= p_n.
\end{aligned}
$$
∎

The key step where the Poisson process assumption is used is in going between lines (*) and (**).

Remark: All you need to make this proof go through is the fact that $A(t, t + \delta)$ is independent of $N(t)$.

Question: Why would this proof *not* go through for the example of the Uniform arrival process with Deterministic job service times?

Answer: Consider the case where interarrival times are distributed $U(1, 2)$ and job service times are Deterministic, equal to 1. In this case, we cannot move from (*) to (**) in the PASTA proof because knowing $N(t)$ affects whether there will be an arrival in the next δ seconds. In particular if $N(t) = 1$, then there will *not* be an arrival in the next δ seconds. By contrast, for the Poisson arrival process, an arrival occurs during $(t, t + \delta)$ with probability $\lambda\delta + o(\delta)$ independent of $N(t)$. The fact that an arrival occurs tells us nothing about $N(t)$ and vice versa.

Question: Why might we need to make the further assumption (stated in the footnote to Claim 13.3) that the interarrival times and service times are independent? Isn't Poisson arrivals already saying this?

Answer: Imagine the perverse situation where you have Poisson arrivals, but the service times are correlated to the interarrival times of the arrivals. Specifically, suppose that the service time of the nth arrival is always set to equal half the interarrival time between packets n and $n + 1$. In this case, an arrival would find the system empty; however, the time-average number of packets in the system would be $\frac{1}{2}$. Note that this situation is purely hypothetical because it is not possible to know the interarrival times between packets until the next arrival occurs.

Application to Simulation

PASTA is useful in system simulations. If we are simulating a Poisson arrival process to some system and would like to know the mean number of jobs in the system, or the fraction of time the system has n jobs, or something of that type, then it suffices to average over what *arrivals* see at the moment they enter the system. By contrast, if the arrival process is not Poisson, it is very dangerous to average over what arrivals see, because that may not be the true time average for the system.

13.4 Further Reading

PASTA can be stated much more generally, applying to more than just the number of jobs in the system. For further reading on PASTA, we recommend Wolff [195], pp. 293–96.

13.5 Exercises

13.1 Bathroom queue

It is well known that women spend twice as long in the restroom on average as men.[3] That said, the waiting time, T_Q, in the women's line seems much longer than twice that in the men's line. Is this an illusion or reality? Model the women's line as an M/M/1 queue with arrival rate λ and service rate μ. Model the men's line as an M/M/1 queue with arrival rate λ and service rate 2μ. Derive the ratio

$$\frac{\mathbf{E}\left[T_Q\right]^{\text{women}}}{\mathbf{E}\left[T_Q\right]^{\text{men}}}$$

as a function of the load $\rho = \frac{\lambda}{\mu}$ in the women's queue. What is the lowest value of this ratio? What is the highest?

13.2 Server Farm

In the server farm shown in Figure 13.7, jobs arrive according to a Poisson process with rate λ and are probabilistically split between two servers, with p fraction of the jobs going to server 1, which has service rate μ_1, and $q = 1 - p$ fraction going to server 2, which has service rate μ_2. Assume that job sizes are Exponentially distributed. Derive an expression for the mean response time, $\mathbf{E}\left[T\right]$, experienced by arrivals to the server farm.

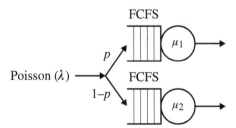

Figure 13.7. Server farm from Exercise 13.2.

---

[3] Women spend 89 ± 7 seconds, compared to men's 39 ± 6 seconds [62].

13.3 M/M/1 Simulation

This problem is a slight twist on Exercise 4.3. Your job is to simulate an M/M/1 queue. You can write your simulator in any programming language. See Chapter 4 for techniques for generating the needed random variables. The mean job size is 10. The mean arrival rate is λ. Adjust λ as needed to create the following three loads – $\rho = 0.5$, $\rho = 0.7$, and $\rho = 0.9$ – and run your simulator under each load to measure mean response time. Compare your results with the steady-state mean response time derived in this chapter.

13.4 M/M/1 Number in Queue

For an M/M/1 queue with load ρ, prove that

$$\mathbf{E}\left[N_Q\right] = \frac{\rho^2}{1 - \rho}. \tag{13.1}$$

13.5 M/M/1/FCFS with Finite Capacity

Your system consists of a single CPU with finite buffer capacity. Jobs arrive according to a Poisson process with rate λ jobs/sec. The job sizes are Exponentially distributed with mean $1/\mu$ seconds. Jobs are serviced in FCFS order. Let $N - 1$ denote the maximum number of jobs that your system can hold in the queue. Thus, including the job serving, there are a maximum of N jobs in the system at any one time (this is called an M/M/1/N queue). If a job arrives when there are already N jobs in the system, then the arriving job is rejected.

Your DARPA proposal requires that you reduce the loss probability in your system. To do this you could either ask for money to double the buffer size, or, alternatively, you could ask for money to double the speed of the CPU so that jobs get processed faster, thereby lowering the probability that there are N jobs in the system. Assuming both proposals have the same cost, which do you choose? (Asking for both makes you seem greedy.)

These are the specific questions you should answer:
(a) Draw the CTMC.
(b) Derive the limiting probabilities.
(c) What is the utilization of the system?
(d) What is the fraction of jobs turned away (loss probability)? Use the word PASTA in your explanation.
(e) What is the rate at which jobs are turned away?
(f) Derive a closed-form expression for $\mathbf{E}\left[\text{Number in system}\right]$.
(g) Determine a closed-form expression for $\mathbf{E}\left[T\right]$ for only those jobs that enter the system.
(h) Suppose that $N = 5$, and $\rho = \frac{\lambda}{\mu} = .4$. Which would have the greater effect on lowering loss probability: doubling the buffer size or doubling the CPU speed?
(i) Answer the same question as (h) except now $N = 5$, and $\rho = \frac{\lambda}{\mu} = .8$.
(j) Explain intuitively why (h) and (i) resulted in different answers.

13.6 Admission Control

Consider the M/M/1 with finite capacity from Exercise 13.5. Now consider those jobs that are turned away (because there are already N jobs in the system). Is the stream of arrivals that are turned away a Poisson process? Why or why not?

13.7 Open versus Closed Networks

Consider the closed batch network shown in Figure 13.8(a) and the single-server open network shown in Figure 13.8(b). In (a), N is often called the "multiprogramming level" or "load." In (b), the load is $\rho = \frac{\lambda}{\mu}$.

Under what criterion does (a) have higher $\mathbf{E}[T]$ than (b)? Express your criterion in terms of N and ρ only. Also try to explain your finding.

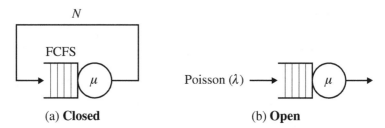

(a) **Closed**   (b) **Open**

Figure 13.8. Open and closed systems.

13.8 More Open versus Closed Systems

Figure 13.9 shows a closed queueing network and an open one. Job sizes are Exponentially distributed, where the service rate is shown for each server, and p denotes a probability.

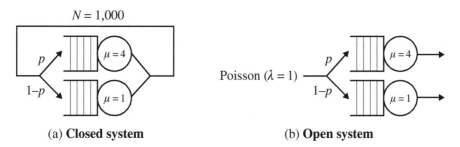

(a) **Closed system**   (b) **Open system**

Figure 13.9. Figure for Exercise 13.8.

(i) For the closed system, what value of p minimizes mean response time, $\mathbf{E}[T]$?

(ii) Derive an expression for $\mathbf{E}[T]$ for the open system.

(iii) Does the value of p that you found in (i) minimize $\mathbf{E}[T]$ in the open system? If yes, give a proof. If no, give a counterexample.

(iv) Under the optimal p for the closed system, what is the (approximate) throughput X for the closed system?

(v) Under the optimal p for the open system, what is X for the open system?

13.9 M/M/1/2

Consider an M/M/1/2 (see Exercise 13.5) with arrival rate λ, service rate μ, and finite capacity of 2. Derive $\mathbf{E}[T_{1,0}]$, the mean time to go from having one job in the system until the system is empty.

13.10 Busy Period in M/M/1[4]

A busy period, B, is the time from when the system has 1 job until the system is first empty. (Obviously, the number of jobs may go up and down a lot in going from state 1 to state 0.) Your goal is to derive $\mathbf{E}[B]$ for an M/M/1.

(a) Draw the CTMC for the M/M/1 with arrival rate λ and service rate μ.

(b) Write a recurrence relation for $\mathbf{E}[B]$ by conditioning on the next state that the CTMC moves to after leaving state 1.

(c) Solve the recurrence relation for $\mathbf{E}[B]$. What does the expression for $\mathbf{E}[B]$ remind you of?

13.11 Response time distribution for M/M/1[4]

In this problem, you are asked to derive the distribution of response time for an M/M/1 queue with arrival rate λ and service rate μ. To do this, think about the response time experienced by an arrival, "job x." Think about the number of jobs that job x sees in the system, and the work associated with each of these jobs. Then express job x's response time in terms of these quantities.

(a) At the time when job x arrives, what is the service requirement (job size) for each job in the queue? What is the *remaining* service requirement for the job in service, if there is one?

(b) Let N denote the total number of jobs in the system that job x sees when it arrives. What is $\mathbf{P}\{N = n\}$? Use PASTA.

(c) Consider a new distribution N' where N' is the number of jobs in the system seen by job x, plus itself. What is $\mathbf{P}\{N' = n\}$?

(d) The distribution N' has a name. What is the name of the distribution of N' and what is the appropriate parameter?

(e) If S_i denotes the service requirement of the ith job in the M/M/1, we can express the response time of job x as a sum involving some of the random variables above. Write this sum.

(f) Fully specify the distribution of response time of job x along with its parameter(s). [Hint: you will need to utilize a result from the exercises in Chapter 11.]

13.12 Variance of the Number of Jobs in an M/M/1

Let N denote the number of jobs in an M/M/1 with load ρ. Prove that

$$\mathbf{Var}(N) = \frac{\rho}{(1-\rho)^2}.$$

[Hint: It may help to make use of Exercise 3.22.]

13.13 Back to the Server Farm

Consider again the server farm from Exercise 13.2. Use what you learned in Exercise 13.11 to derive expressions for

(a) the tail behavior of response time, $\mathbf{P}\{T > t\}$

(b) variance of response time, $\mathbf{Var}(T)$.

---

[4] *Warning:* This result will be used many times throughout the book.

13.14 Threshold Queue

We define a threshold queue with parameter T as follows: When the number of jobs is $< T$, then jobs arrive according to a Poisson process with rate λ and their service time is Exponentially distributed with rate μ, where $\lambda > \mu$ (i.e., the queue is running in overload). However, when the number of jobs is $> T$, then jobs arrive with Exponential rate μ and are served with Exponential rate λ.

Figure 13.10 shows the CTMC for the case of $T = 2$. Compute $\mathbf{E}[N]$, the mean number of jobs in the system, as a function of T. As a check, evaluate your answer when $T = 0$. Note that when $T = 0$, we have $\rho = \mu/\lambda$.

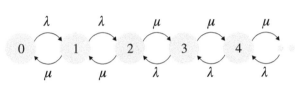

Figure 13.10. Threshold queue with $T = 2$.

Server Farms and Networks: Multi-server, Multi-queue Systems

Part V involves the analysis of multi-server and multi-queue systems.

We start in Chapter 14 with the M/M/k server farm model, where k servers all work "cooperatively" to handle incoming requests from a single queue. We derive simple closed-form formulas for the distribution of the number of jobs in the M/M/k. We then exploit these formulas in Chapter 15 to do capacity provisioning for the M/M/k. Specifically, we answer questions such as, "What is the minimum number of servers needed to guarantee that only a small fraction of jobs are delayed?" We derive simple answers to these questions in the form of square-root staffing rules. In these two chapters and the exercises therein, we also consider questions pertaining to resource allocation, such as whether a single fast server is superior to many slow servers, and whether a single central queue is superior to having a queue at each server.

We then move on to analyzing networks of queues, consisting of multiple servers, each with its own queue, with probabilistic routing of packets (or jobs) between the queues. In Chapter 16 we build up the fundamental theory needed to analyze networks of queues. This includes time-reversibility and Burke's theorem. In Chapter 17, we apply our theory to Jackson networks of queues. We prove that these have product form, and we derive the limiting distribution of the number of packets at each queue. Our proofs introduce the concept of Local Balance, which we use repeatedly in derivations throughout the book. In Chapter 18, we generalize our analysis to allow for classed networks, where the route of a packet can depend on its class (type). Chapter 19 extends the analysis to closed networks of queues. In the exercises in Chapters 17, 18, and 19, we derive further extensions, including networks of servers with load-dependent service rate, where the speed of the server can depend on the number of jobs in the queue, and networks of M/M/k queues, where each service station is a server farm.

Throughout Part V, to facilitate analysis, we assume Markovian distributions, including Exponentially distributed service times and Poisson arrival processes. Later in Part VI, we explore more general analysis that does not require Markovian assumptions.

CHAPTER 14

Server Farms: M/M/k and M/M/k/k

In today's high-volume world, almost no websites, compute centers, or call centers consist of just a single server. Instead a "server farm" is used. The server farm is a collection of servers that work together to handle incoming requests. Each request might be routed to a different server, so that servers "share" the incoming load. From a practical perspective, server farms are often preferable to a single "super-fast" server because of their low cost (many slow servers are cheaper than a single fast one) and their flexibility (it is easy to increase/decrease capacity as needed by adding/removing servers). These practical features have made server farms ubiquitous.

In this chapter, we study server farms where there is a *single queue* of requests and where each server, when free, takes the next request off the queue to work on. Specifically, there are no queues at the individual servers. We defer discussion of models with queues at the individual servers to the exercises and later chapters.

The two systems we consider in this chapter are the M/M/k system and the M/M/k/k system. In both, the first "M" indicates that we have memoryless interarrival times, and the second "M" indicates memoryless service times. The third field denotes that k servers *share* a common pool of arriving jobs. For the M/M/k system, there is no capacity constraint, and this common pool takes the form of an unbounded FCFS queue, as shown later in Figure 14.3, where each server, when free, grabs the job at the head of the queue to work on. For the M/M/k/k system shown in Figure 14.1, there is a capacity constraint of k jobs. This means that there is no room for a queue. If a job arrives to find all k servers busy, then the job is dropped.

Because the analysis of the M/M/k/k is easier, we begin with that, in Section 14.2, and then go on to the M/M/k, in Section 14.3. Before we discuss these systems, it will be helpful to revisit the concept of time-reversibility, this time for CTMCs rather than DTMCs. We do this in Section 14.1.

14.1 Time-Reversibility for CTMCs

We start by reviewing terminology used in CTMCs.

Question: Can you properly define the following terms: q_{ij}, $\pi_i q_{ij}$, ν_i, $\nu_i P_{ij}$?

Answer: Recall that q_{ij} is the rate of transitions from state i to state j, given that the CTMC is in state i. That is, q_{ij} is the label on the arrow from i to j in the Markov transition diagram for the CTMC. If π_i is the limiting probability that the CTMC is in state i, then $\pi_i q_{ij}$ is the rate of transitions from state i to state j. Likewise $\pi_j q_{ji}$ is the rate of transitions from state j to state i.

Recall also that ν_i is the total rate of transitions leaving i, given that we are in state i, and $\nu_i P_{ij}$ denotes the rate of transitions leaving state i and going to state j, given that we are in state i, i.e., $\nu_i P_{ij} = q_{ij}$. Thus $\pi_i \nu_i$ denotes the rate of transitions leaving state i, and $\pi_i \nu_i P_{ij}$ denotes the rate of transitions leaving i and going to j.

Recall the useful time-reversibility theorem for DTMCs, Theorem 9.34, which said that, for an aperiodic and irreducible DTMC, if we can find x_i's such that

$$\sum_i x_i = 1 \quad \text{and} \quad x_i P_{ij} = x_j P_{ji}, \quad \forall i, j$$

then these x_i's are the limiting probabilities. We now prove a counterpart to this theorem for CTMCs.

Definition 14.1 A CTMC is **time-reversible** if, for all states i and j, the rate of transitions from state i to state j equals the rate of transitions from state j to state i (i.e., $\pi_i q_{ij} = \pi_j q_{ji}$, where $\sum_i \pi_i = 1$).

Lemma 14.2 *Given an irreducible CTMC, suppose we can find x_i's such that*

$$\sum_i x_i = 1 \quad \text{and} \quad x_i q_{ij} = x_j q_{ji}, \quad \forall i, j$$

where q_{ij} is the rate of transitions from state i to state j given that the MC is in state i. Then,
   1. *The x_i's are the limiting probabilities of the CTMC.*
   2. *The CTMC is time-reversible.*

Proof   What we need to prove here is that the x_i's are the π_i's (the limiting probabilities). We are given that, $\forall i, j$,

$$x_i q_{ij} = x_j q_{ji}.$$

Thus,

$$\sum_i x_i q_{ij} = x_j \sum_i q_{ji}$$

$$\sum_i x_i q_{ij} = x_j \sum_i \nu_j P_{ji}$$

$$\sum_i x_i q_{ij} = x_j \nu_j \sum_i P_{ji}$$

$$\sum_i x_i q_{ij} = x_j \nu_j.$$

Since these are the balance equations for the CTMC, by Theorem 12.6 it then follows that the x_i's must be the π_i's. Thus it further follows that

$$\pi_i q_{ij} = \pi_j q_{ji}, \quad \forall i, j$$

hence the CTMC is time-reversible.   ∎

Question: What is an example of a CTMC that is *not* time-reversible?

Answer: Consider a chain that has an arc from state i to state j labeled q_{ij}, but no arc from state j to state i. Then the rate of going from state i to state j is $\pi_i q_{ij}$, but the rate of going from state j to state i is zero.

Question: Recall that the M/M/1 chain is a birth-death process. Are all birth-death processes time-reversible?

Answer: Yes. Here's a proof: First observe that during any period of time, t, the number of transitions from state i to state $i + 1$ is within 1 of the number of transitions from state $i + 1$ to state i. The reason for this is that you cannot repeat going from i to $i + 1$ without first going back to i again – and the only way to go back to state i is to make a transition from $i + 1$ to i. Thus the long-run rate of transitions (number of transitions divided by time) from state i to state $i + 1$ is equal to the rate of transitions from $i + 1$ to i (as time gets big, that "difference of 1" can be ignored).

As in the case of DTMCs, it is often helpful to write the time-reversibility equations and see if a solution to these can be found. If so, that solution also represents the limiting distribution. If not, then one needs to go back to the balance equations. Fortunately, we will see that the CTMCs for the M/M/k/k and the M/M/k are both birth-death processes, and hence the time-reversibility equations will be solvable.

14.2 M/M/k/k Loss System

The M/M/k/k queueing system is also called the **k-server loss system.** Jobs arrive according to a Poisson process, with some average arrival rate, λ. Job sizes are Exponentially distributed with rate μ. There are k servers that can each hold one job. The system only has capacity for k jobs total; if an arrival shows up and sees all k servers already busy with a job, the arrival is dropped.

The M/M/k/k loss system originally arose from the early phone switching systems that could handle at most k calls simultaneously, as shown in Figure 14.1. An incoming call request could be picked up and serviced by any one of the k circuits. However, if none of the k circuits was free, the phone call request was dropped. The duration of a phone call was assumed to be Exponentially distributed.

Another application for the k-server loss system is a system that maintains virtual connections between nodes A and B in a network. Only k virtual connections are allowed. Each incoming request for a virtual connection is given one; however, if all k virtual connections are in use, the request is rejected.

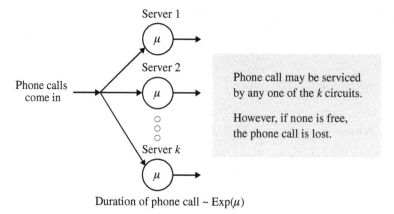

Duration of phone call ~ Exp(μ)

Figure 14.1. The k-server loss system: M/M/k/k.

The **key question** in these types of systems is, "What is the fraction of jobs that are lost?" This fraction is known as the **blocking probability**, P_{block}. We determine the blocking probability by modeling the M/M/k/k queueing system as a CTMC.

Question: What should the state space be?

Answer: The state represents the number of busy servers in the system. The CTMC is shown in Figure 14.2.

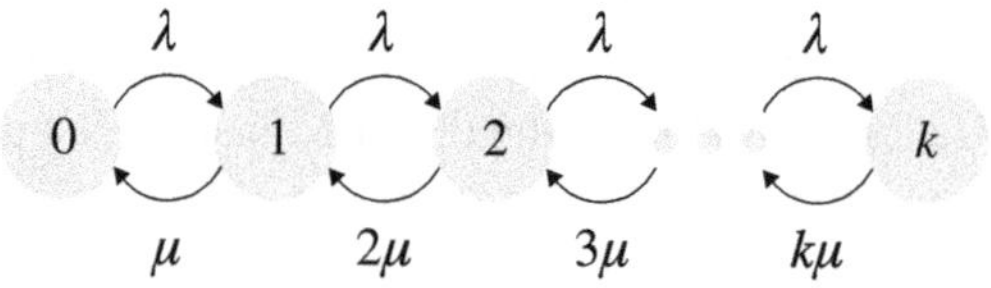

Figure 14.2. An M/M/k/k queueing system modeled using a CTMC. The state represents the number of busy servers.

We solve the time-reversibility equations to determine the limiting probabilities for the states as shown in Table 14.1.

Table 14.1. *Time-reversibility equations for the M/M/k/k*

State	Time-reversibility equation	Simplified equation
0	$\pi_0 \lambda = \pi_1 \mu$	$\pi_1 = \frac{\lambda}{\mu} \pi_0$
1	$\pi_1 \lambda = \pi_2 2\mu$	$\pi_2 = \left(\frac{\lambda}{\mu}\right)^2 \frac{1}{2!} \pi_0$
2	$\pi_2 \lambda = \pi_3 3\mu$	$\pi_3 = \left(\frac{\lambda}{\mu}\right)^3 \frac{1}{3!} \pi_0$
$k-1$	$\pi_{k-1} \lambda = \pi_k k\mu$	$\pi_k = \left(\frac{\lambda}{\mu}\right)^k \frac{1}{k!} \pi_0$

We guess that

$$\pi_i = \left(\frac{\lambda}{\mu}\right)^i \frac{1}{i!} \pi_0. \tag{14.1}$$

We can verify that this is correct by substituting back into the time-reversibility equation for π_i. Finally, we determine π_0 such that the equation $\sum_{i=0}^{k} \pi_i = 1$ is satisfied:

$$\sum_{i=0}^{k} \pi_i = 1$$

$$\sum_{i=0}^{k} \left(\frac{\lambda}{\mu}\right)^i \frac{1}{i!} \pi_0 = 1$$

$$\Rightarrow \pi_0 = \frac{1}{\sum_{i=0}^{k} \left(\frac{\lambda}{\mu}\right)^i \frac{1}{i!}}$$

Therefore, substituting back into equation (14.1), we obtain

$$\pi_i = \frac{\left(\frac{\lambda}{\mu}\right)^i / i!}{\sum_{j=0}^{k} \left(\frac{\lambda}{\mu}\right)^j \frac{1}{j!}}.$$

The blocking probability, P_{block}, is the probability that an arrival finds all k servers busy. By PASTA, this is the limiting probability that the chain is in state k. Thus,

$$P_{\text{block}} = \pi_k = \frac{\left(\frac{\lambda}{\mu}\right)^k / k!}{\sum_{j=0}^{k} \left(\frac{\lambda}{\mu}\right)^j \frac{1}{j!}}. \tag{14.2}$$

Equation (14.2) is called the Erlang-B formula.

Question: There is an easy way to remember the formula for P_{block} by relating it to the Poisson distribution. Can you see what it is?

Hint: Multiply both the numerator and denominator by $e^{-\frac{\lambda}{\mu}}$.

Lemma 14.3 Let $X \sim Poisson\left(\frac{\lambda}{\mu}\right)$. Then

$$P_{\text{block}} = \frac{e^{-\frac{\lambda}{\mu}} \cdot \left(\frac{\lambda}{\mu}\right)^k / k!}{\sum_{j=0}^{k} e^{-\frac{\lambda}{\mu}} \cdot \left(\frac{\lambda}{\mu}\right)^j \frac{1}{j!}} = \frac{\mathbf{P}\{X = k\}}{\mathbf{P}\{X \le k\}} \tag{14.3}$$

The applicability of the Erlang-B formula stems from the fact that it is *independent of the service time distribution*. That is, this same formula arises when the service demand has a mean of $\frac{1}{\mu}$ with any probability distribution. This is known as an **insensitivity result**, because the result depends only on the mean of the distribution. Insensitivity results are always quite striking when they occur, because it is much more typical that queueing behavior is highly influenced by the distribution of the service time. Insensitivity results often occur in situations where *there is no queue*. We will see several other insensitivity results during the course of this book.

14.3 M/M/k

Figure 14.3 illustrates the M/M/k queueing system. As in the fixed-capacity system, the k servers draw from the same pool of incoming jobs, except that this time the pool has infinite space. Whenever a server becomes free, it takes the next job from the pool. The "pool" is just an FCFS queue with unbounded capacity.

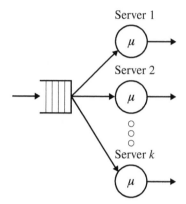

Figure 14.3. An M/M/k queueing system.

We can model the number of jobs in the M/M/k queueing system as a CTMC as shown in Figure 14.4.

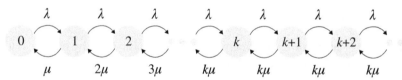

Figure 14.4. An M/M/k queueing system modeled using a CTMC.

We write the time-reversibility equations as shown in Table 14.2.

Table 14.2. *Time-reversibility equations for the M/M/k*

State	Time-reversibility equation	Simplified equation
0	$\pi_0 \lambda = \pi_1 \mu$	$\pi_1 = \frac{\lambda}{\mu} \pi_0$
1	$\pi_1 \lambda = \pi_2 2\mu$	$\pi_2 = \left(\frac{\lambda}{\mu}\right)^2 \frac{1}{2!} \pi_0$
2	$\pi_2 \lambda = \pi_3 3\mu$	$\pi_3 = \left(\frac{\lambda}{\mu}\right)^3 \frac{1}{3!} \pi_0$
$k-1$	$\pi_{k-1} \lambda = \pi_k k\mu$	$\pi_k = \left(\frac{\lambda}{\mu}\right)^k \frac{1}{k!} \pi_0$
k	$\pi_k \lambda = \pi_{k+1} k\mu$	$\pi_{k+1} = \left(\frac{\lambda}{\mu}\right)^{k+1} \frac{1}{k!} \frac{1}{k} \pi_0$
$k+1$	$\pi_{k+1} \lambda = \pi_{k+2} k\mu$	$\pi_{k+2} = \left(\frac{\lambda}{\mu}\right)^{k+2} \frac{1}{k!} \frac{1}{k^2} \pi_0$

Therefore,

$$\pi_i = \begin{cases} \left(\frac{\lambda}{\mu}\right)^i \frac{1}{i!}\pi_0 & \text{if } i \leq k \\[2ex] \left(\frac{\lambda}{\mu}\right)^i \frac{1}{k!}\left(\frac{1}{k}\right)^{i-k}\pi_0 & \text{if } i > k \end{cases}.$$

Let's express these equations in terms of the system utilization.

Question: But what is the system utilization?

Answer: For an M/M/k, the system utilization is defined as

$$\rho = \frac{\lambda}{k\mu}$$

where λ is the arrival rate into the system in jobs/sec, and $k\mu$ represents the total service capacity of the system in jobs/sec.

Note: In a typical system, the term "system utilization" is not well defined because different devices may be running at different utilizations. The term "utilization" is thus typically reserved for a single device. An M/M/k queue is an exception in that system utilization is well defined because, by symmetry, the utilization (load) is the same at all servers. Specifically, consider the fraction of time that a particular server is busy. That server, by symmetry, sees an arrival rate of $\frac{\lambda}{k}$ and experiences a service rate of μ. Hence the utilization at that server is $\frac{\lambda}{k\mu}$. But this is also the utilization at every server.

Let R denote the expected number of busy processors.

Question: What is R?

Answer: $R = \lambda/\mu$. To see this, consider that each server is busy with probability $\frac{\lambda}{k\mu}$ and there are k servers. Thus the expected number of jobs in service is

$$R = \mathbf{E}\left[\text{number in service}\right] = k \cdot \frac{\lambda}{k\mu} = \frac{\lambda}{\mu}. \tag{14.4}$$

Observe that R can also be viewed as the minimal *resource requirement* (i.e., the minimum number of servers required to handle the arrival rate). For example, if the average arrival rate is $\lambda = 30$ jobs/sec, and the service rate of each server is $\mu = 5$ jobs/sec, then we have a minimal resource requirement of $R = \lambda/\mu = 30/5 = 6$ servers needed just to maintain stability.

These definitions are used throughout the book, so we state them again for reference:

Definition 14.4 For an M/M/k with average arrival rate λ and service rate μ, the *system utilization* or *load* is denoted by ρ, where

$$\rho = \frac{\lambda}{k\mu}.$$

The *resource requirement* is denoted by R, where

$$R = \frac{\lambda}{\mu}.$$

R can also be viewed as the minimum number of servers needed to keep the system stable, or as the expected number of servers that are busy, or as the expected number of jobs in service.

Using ρ, we rewrite the equations for π_i as follows:

$$\pi_i = \begin{cases} \frac{(k\rho)^i}{i!}\pi_0 & \text{if } i \leq k \\ \frac{\rho^i}{k!}k^k \pi_0 & \text{if } i > k \end{cases}$$

Finally, we need to determine π_0:

$$\pi_0 + \sum_{i=1}^{k-1} \pi_i + \sum_{i=k}^{\infty} \pi_i = 1$$

$$\pi_0 \left[1 + \sum_{i=1}^{k-1} \frac{(k\rho)^i}{i!} + \sum_{i=k}^{\infty} \frac{\rho^i}{k!}k^k \right] = 1$$

$$\pi_0 \left[\sum_{i=0}^{k-1} \frac{(k\rho)^i}{i!} + \frac{k^k}{k!}\frac{\rho^k}{1-\rho} \right] = 1$$

$$\Rightarrow \pi_0 = \left[\sum_{i=0}^{k-1} \frac{(k\rho)^i}{i!} + \frac{(k\rho)^k}{k!(1-\rho)} \right]^{-1}$$

Probability That an Arriving Job Has to Queue

Having found the stationary probabilities, we now find the **probability that an arriving job has to queue, P_Q**. Observe that P_Q is the probability that an arrival finds all k servers busy.

$$P_Q = \mathbf{P}\{\text{An arrival finds all servers busy}\}$$

$$= \mathbf{P}\{\text{An arrival sees} \geq k \text{ jobs in system}\}$$

$$= \text{Limiting probability that there are} \geq k \text{ jobs in system} \quad \text{(by PASTA)}$$

$$= \sum_{i=k}^{\infty} \pi_i$$

$$= \frac{k^k}{k!}\pi_0 \sum_{i=k}^{\infty} \rho^i$$

$$= \frac{(k\rho)^k \pi_0}{k!(1-\rho)} \quad \text{where } \pi_0 = \left[\sum_{i=0}^{k-1} \frac{(k\rho)^i}{i!} + \frac{(k\rho)^k}{k!(1-\rho)} \right]^{-1} \quad (14.5)$$

Equation (14.5) is the famous Erlang-C formula.

It is interesting to compare the probability that an arrival finds all servers busy in an M/M/k, P_Q, with the probability that an arrival finds all servers busy in an M/M/k/k, P_{block}.

Question: Intuitively, which system will have a higher probability that all k servers are busy?

Answer: The M/M/k system will.

Question: Why?

Answer: In the M/M/k system, jobs can arrive during the time that the k servers are busy. These jobs do not disappear but rather queue up, thus creating more work for later and thus affecting the future probability that the system is busy.

Theorem 14.5 relates the blocking probability for the M/M/k/k to the queueing probability for the M/M/k.

Theorem 14.5 *Let P_{block} denote the blocking probability for the M/M/k/k and P_Q the queueing probability for the M/M/k. Let ρ denote the load (system utilization) for the M/M/k. Then*

$$P_{\text{block}} = \frac{(1 - \rho)P_Q}{1 - \rho P_Q}. \tag{14.6}$$

Proof Observing that the M/M/k/k chain is contained within the M/M/k chain, we have

$$
\begin{aligned}
P_{\text{block}}^{\text{M/M/k/k}} &= \mathbf{P}\left\{N = k \mid N \leq k\right\}^{\text{M/M/k}} \\
&= \frac{\mathbf{P}\left\{N = k\right\}^{\text{M/M/k}}}{\mathbf{P}\left\{N \leq k\right\}^{\text{M/M/k}}} \\
&= \frac{\mathbf{P}\left\{N \geq k\right\}^{\text{M/M/k}} - \mathbf{P}\left\{N > k\right\}^{\text{M/M/k}}}{1 - \mathbf{P}\left\{N > k\right\}^{\text{M/M/k}}} \\
&= \frac{P_Q - \rho P_Q}{1 - \rho P_Q}
\end{aligned}
$$

where the last line follows from the fact that, beyond state k, the M/M/k looks like an M/M/1 with load ρ, hence $\mathbf{P}\left\{N > k\right\}^{\text{M/M/k}} = \rho \cdot \mathbf{P}\left\{N \geq k\right\}^{\text{M/M/k}}$. ∎

Expected Number in the Queue

We can now calculate the expected number in the queue portion of the M/M/k:

$$
\begin{aligned}
\mathbf{E}\left[N_Q\right]^{\text{M/M/k}} &= \sum_{i=k}^{\infty} \pi_i (i - k) \\
&= \pi_0 \sum_{i=k}^{\infty} \frac{\rho^i k^k}{k!} \cdot (i - k)
\end{aligned}
$$

$$= \pi_0 \frac{\rho^k k^k}{k!} \sum_{i=k}^{\infty} \rho^{i-k} \cdot (i-k)$$

$$= \pi_0 \frac{\rho^k k^k}{k!} \sum_{i=0}^{\infty} \rho^i \cdot i$$

$$= \pi_0 \frac{\rho^k k^k}{k!} \cdot \rho \cdot \frac{1}{(1-\rho)^2}$$

$$= P_Q \frac{\rho}{1-\rho}$$

Question: Explain why

$$\mathbf{E}[N_Q] = P_Q \frac{\rho}{1-\rho}.$$

Answer:

$$\mathbf{E}[N_Q] = \mathbf{E}[N_Q \mid \text{queueing}] \cdot \mathbf{P}\{\text{queueing}\}$$
$$+ \mathbf{E}[N_Q \mid \text{no queueing}] \cdot \mathbf{P}\{\text{no queueing}\}.$$

But

$$\mathbf{E}[N_Q \mid \text{no queueing}] = 0.$$

So

$$\mathbf{E}[N_Q] = \mathbf{E}[N_Q \mid \text{queueing}] \cdot P_Q.$$

Now consider the CTMC for the M/M/k, given that there is queueing. That CTMC looks identical to the CTMC for an M/M/1, where the M/M/1 has arrival rate λ and service rate $k\mu$. Specifically, $\mathbf{E}[N_Q \mid \text{queueing}]$ for the M/M/k is just the expected number of jobs in *system* for an M/M/1 queue, where the M/M/1 queue has load $\rho = \frac{\lambda}{k\mu}$ and mean number of jobs $\frac{\rho}{1-\rho}$. So,

$$\mathbf{E}[N_Q] = \frac{\rho}{1-\rho} \cdot P_Q. \tag{14.7}$$

Finishing up, we can derive the remaining performance metrics for the M/M/k easily as follows:

$$\mathbf{E}[T_Q] = \frac{1}{\lambda} \cdot \mathbf{E}[N_Q] = \frac{1}{\lambda} \cdot P_Q \cdot \frac{\rho}{1-\rho} \tag{14.8}$$

$$\mathbf{E}[T] = \mathbf{E}[T_Q] + \frac{1}{\mu} = \frac{1}{\lambda} \cdot P_Q \cdot \frac{\rho}{1-\rho} + \frac{1}{\mu} \tag{14.9}$$

$$\mathbf{E}[N] = \lambda \cdot \mathbf{E}[T] = P_Q \cdot \frac{\rho}{1-\rho} + k\rho \tag{14.10}$$

As a check, observe that

$$\mathbf{E}[\text{Number being served}] = \mathbf{E}[N] - \mathbf{E}[N_Q] = k\rho = \frac{\lambda}{\mu} = R.$$

This is the expected result from (14.4).

14.4 Comparison of Three Server Organizations

Consider the following three different server organizations, all having arrival rate λ, total service rate $k\mu$, and load $\rho = \frac{\lambda}{k\mu}$, shown in Figure 14.5. Under frequency-division multiplexing (FDM), traffic is split into k separate channels. Under the M/M/k, the traffic is lumped together, but the service capacity is split. Under the M/M/1, nothing is split. We want to determine which of these configurations is best for minimizing mean response time.

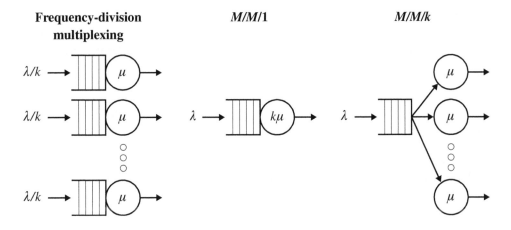

Figure 14.5. Frequency-division multiplexing, M/M/1, and M/M/k, all with load $\rho = \frac{\lambda}{k\mu}$.

Question: Which is better in terms of mean response time: FDM or the M/M/1?

Answer: Obviously the M/M/1. Each job experiences a k times higher arrival rate under the M/M/1, but also a k times higher service rate. Thus we expect the mean response time to be k times lower for the M/M/1. Computing these response times, we have:

$$\mathbf{E}\,[T]^{\text{FDM}} = \frac{1}{\mu - \frac{\lambda}{k}} = \frac{k}{k\mu - \lambda}. \tag{14.11}$$

$$\mathbf{E}\,[T]^{\text{M/M/1}} = \frac{1}{k\mu - \lambda}. \tag{14.12}$$

By comparing equations (14.11) and (14.12), it is obvious that M/M/1 is k times better than FDM.

Question: How does the M/M/1 system compare with the M/M/k system?

Answer: Recall that for the M/M/k, from (14.9)

$$\mathbf{E}\,[T]^{\text{M/M/k}} = \frac{1}{\lambda} \cdot P_Q \cdot \frac{\rho}{1 - \rho} + \frac{1}{\mu}$$

where $\rho = \frac{\lambda}{k\mu}$, and P_Q is the probability an arrival is forced to queue.

To compare the M/M/k with the M/M/1, consider

$$\frac{\mathbf{E}\left[T\right]^{\text{M/M/k}}}{\mathbf{E}\left[T\right]^{\text{M/M/1}}} = \frac{\frac{1}{\lambda} \cdot P_Q \cdot \frac{\rho}{1-\rho} + \frac{1}{\mu}}{\frac{1}{\lambda} \cdot \frac{\rho}{1-\rho}}$$

$$= P_Q^{\text{M/M/k}} + \frac{\lambda}{\mu} \cdot \frac{1-\rho}{\rho}$$

$$= P_Q^{\text{M/M/k}} + k(1 - \rho). \qquad (14.13)$$

Now consider two cases.

Case 1: $\rho \approx 0$

As the load drops, the probability of queueing drops, so $P_Q^{\text{M/M/k}} \approx 0$, and expression (14.13) is approximately $0 + k = k$. Thus, the M/M/1 is k times faster than M/M/k.

Question: Explain intuitively why this makes sense.

Answer: In the M/M/k, under light load, most servers are idle. The few servers that are busy serve the jobs they get at rate μ. By contrast, in the M/M/1, with the same light load, every job gets served with rate $k\mu$. Thus jobs complete more quickly in the M/M/1.

Case 2: $\rho \approx 1$

With the load high, $P_Q^{\text{M/M/k}} \approx 1$, and so expression (14.13) is approximately 1. Thus, the M/M/k and M/M/1 have the same response time.

Question: Explain why this makes sense.

Answer: Because the load is high, there are always jobs in the queue. Thus, the state of the CTMC for the M/M/k is always greater than k. This portion of the CTMC looks like Figure 14.6. Thus the M/M/k under high load behaves just like an M/M/1 with arrival rate λ and service rate $k\mu$.

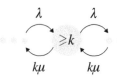

Figure 14.6. M/M/k queue under high load.

14.5 Readings

We stated that the k-server loss system exhibits an interesting insensitivity property, whereby the distribution of the number of jobs in the loss system depends only on the *mean* job size, not on its distribution. For a unique and interesting proof of the insensitivity property for this system and several others, we refer the reader to [178], pp. 202–09.

14.6 Exercises

14.1 Comparison of Three Server Organizations

Repeat the comparison of three server organizations from Section 14.4. This time, however, assume $k = 2$ and derive exact closed-form formulas for $\mathbf{E}\left[T\right]$ for each of the three architectures shown in Figure 14.5.

14.2 Scherr's Thesis 1965

Once upon a time, back in 1965, an MIT student named Allan Scherr needed to analyze the Compatible Time-Sharing System (CTSS). CTSS was an early time-sharing system in which user programs were swapped in and out of main memory with only one complete program in memory at a time. Because there was no overlap of program execution and swapping, Scherr modeled the sum of the program execution time and swapping time as the CPU service time, S. He modeled the CTSS as a simple interactive system with N terminals and one CPU as shown in Figure 14.7. For Scherr's system, N was 60, the mean CPU service time was $\mathbf{E}[S] = 0.8$ seconds, and the mean user think time was $\mathbf{E}[Z] = 35$ seconds. To determine the mean response time of the system, $\mathbf{E}[R]$, Scherr made the *false* assumption that Z and S were Exponentially distributed random variables. This assumption allowed him to set up a CTMC and solve for the mean response time of the system. Everyone was surprised when the mean response time that Scherr got via his analysis was in fact very close to the measured mean response time of the system, given all his simplifications, so Scherr got a PhD and won a bunch of awards. His thesis is online. Don't you wish it was still 1965?

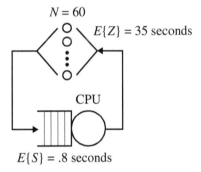

Figure 14.7. Scherr's CTSS model.

(a) Solve Scherr's problem as he did, by making the Exponential assumptions and setting up a CTMC. Determine the limiting probabilities (can you apply the time-reversibility equations?). Write out an expression for $\mathbf{E}[R]$. Now plug in Scherr's numbers and determine $\mathbf{E}[R]$ (you will need to write a small program to do the sum).

(b) Now use operational analysis (see Chapters 6 and 7), which is *distribution-independent*, to obtain asymptotic bounds for $\mathbf{E}[R]$ in Scherr's problem (remember to determine N^*).

If you have done it all right, you may be wondering at this point why Scherr himself did not use operational analysis. Turns out operational analysis did not exist until the early 1970s.

14.3 M/M/2/3

Figure 14.8 shows a 2-server system with a waiting room that can hold only 1 job. Any arrival that sees 3 jobs already in the system is dropped. Jobs arrive from outside according to a Poisson process with rate $\lambda = 1$. Whenever a server finishes serving a job, it grabs the job from the waiting area, if there is one. Job sizes are Exponentially distributed with rate $\mu = 1$.

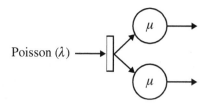

Figure 14.8. The M/M/2/3 system.

(a) Draw a CTMC where the state represents the total number of jobs in the system.

(b) Suppose that there are exactly 2 jobs in the system. What is the probability that a job arrives before a job completes?

(c) Use your CTMC to determine the probability that the system is idle (both servers are idle).

(d) What is the throughput of the system?

(e) What is $\mathbf{E}[N]$, the expected number of jobs in the system?

(f) What is $\mathbf{E}[T]$, the expected response time (for those jobs not dropped)?

(g) Consider the process of arrivals to the system that are not dropped. Is this a Poisson process? Why or why not?

14.4 The Infinite Help Desk (M/M/∞)

Imagine that you could call up a company for customer service and never get the message, "We're sorry; all of our service representatives are busy with other customers . . . " This can be modeled by a queueing system with an *infinite* number of servers.

Concretely, consider the M/M/∞ queueing system, where interarrival times are Exponential with rate λ and the service times are Exponential with rate μ, but where there are an infinite number of servers ($k = \infty$).

(a) Draw a state diagram for the continuous-time Markov chain of this system.

(b) Derive the limiting probabilities. You need to get a closed-form expression here that is simple and easy to recognize.

(c) From the limiting probabilities, derive a closed-form expression for the expected number of jobs in the system, $\mathbf{E}[N]$.

(d) Applying Little's Law gives you $\mathbf{E}[T]$. Does $\mathbf{E}[T]$ make sense? Explain.

14.5 M/M/2 with Heterogeneous Servers

Consider a variant of the M/M/2 queue where the service rates of the two processors are not identical. Denote the service rate of the first processor by μ_1 and the service rate of the second processor by μ_2, where $\mu_1 > \mu_2$. In the case of heterogeneous servers, the rule is that when both servers are idle, the faster server is scheduled for service before the slower one. Define the utilization, ρ, for this system to be $\rho = \frac{\lambda}{\mu_1 + \mu_2}$.

Set up a CTMC and determine the mean number of jobs in the system and the mean response time. You should get

$$\mathbf{E}[N] = \frac{1}{A(1-\rho)^2} \qquad (14.14)$$

where

$$A = \frac{\mu_1 \mu_2 (1 + 2\rho)}{\lambda(\lambda + \mu_2)} + \frac{1}{1 - \rho}. \tag{14.15}$$

14.6 Is Load Balancing Good? + More on Closed vs. Open Systems

Consider the server farm shown in Figure 14.9. The arrival stream is a Poisson process with rate λ, and job sizes are Exponentially distributed. Each job with probability p is sent to Host 1, which has service rate μ_1, and with probability $1 - p$ is sent to Host 2, which has service rate μ_2. There is a queue at each host.

(a) Assume $\mu_1 = \mu_2$. Either prove or disprove that $\mathbf{E}[T_Q]$ and $\mathbf{E}[T]$ are always minimized when p is chosen to balance the load.

(b) Now assume $\mu_1 \neq \mu_2$. Either prove or disprove that $\mathbf{E}[T_Q]$ and $\mathbf{E}[T]$ are always minimized when p is chosen to balance the load.

(c) Continue to assume $\mu_1 \neq \mu_2$, but now suppose that we have a closed system with zero think time and large MPL, N, where Figure 14.9 represents the central subsystem in the closed system. Either prove or disprove that $\mathbf{E}[T_Q]$ and $\mathbf{E}[T]$ are always minimized when p is chosen to balance the load.

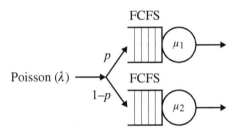

Figure 14.9. Distributed server system.

14.7 Throwing Away Servers

Suppose your computer center currently consists of a single server of speed μ. Jobs arrive according to a Poisson process with rate λ, and their service times are Exponentially distributed.

Suppose the current response time is considered intolerable by the users. A second, faster server, running at speed $\alpha\mu$ (for $\alpha > 1$), is purchased and added to the system in a heterogeneous M/M/2 structure with a single queue as in Exercise 14.5. Denote the load (utilization) of the M/M/2 system by ρ. Denote the mean response time of the M/M/2 system by $\mathbf{E}[T]$.

(a) Use the result in (14.14) from Exercise 14.5 to derive a formula for $\mathbf{E}[T]$, the mean response time of the M/M/2 system with heterogeneous servers.

(b) A hotshot consultant walks in and makes the radical proposal of disconnecting the original server entirely (i.e., simply letting the faster server run by itself). Clearly this makes sense with respect to power, but the consultant claims this is also a win for $\mathbf{E}[T]$. For \$400/hr, what is the consultant thinking? Come up with an instance, in terms of λ, μ_2, and μ_1 for which the consultant is right. Also, explain intuitively what is happening. [If you find this problem interesting, you can think about a general criterion under which the consultant would be right ... Throwing away servers is fun!]

14.8 Comparison of Multi-server Architectures with Heterogeneous Servers
This problem asks you to apply (14.14), but does not require you to have solved Exercise 14.5. Consider four different server configurations. In all of these the outside arrival process is Poisson with rate λ. Also the service time at Host 1 (respectively, Host 2) is Exponentially distributed with rate μ_1 (respectively, μ_2), where $\mu_1 = \alpha\mu_2$, $\alpha \geq 1$.

(1) An M/M/2 heterogeneous server system.

(2) A server farm consisting of two hosts, each with its own queue. Every incoming job is immediately dispatched to Host 1 (with probability p) or to Host 2 (with probability $1 - p$). The probabilities p and $1 - p$ are chosen so as to *balance load* at the two hosts.

(3) A server farm consisting of two hosts, each with its own queue. Every incoming job is immediately dispatched to Host 1 (with probability p) or to Host 2 (with probability $1 - p$). The probabilities p and $1 - p$ are chosen so as to *minimize mean response time*.

(4) A server farm consisting of two hosts, each with its own queue. Every incoming job is immediately dispatched to Host 1 (with probability p) or to Host 2 (with probability $1 - p$), where we set $p = 1$.

Observe that

$$\rho = \frac{\lambda}{\mu_1 + \mu_2} = \frac{\lambda}{\alpha\mu_2 + \mu_2}.$$

Now consider the following table:

	$\rho = \text{low} = 0.25$	$\rho = \text{high} = 0.75$
Two identical hosts:	Fill in ...	Fill in ...
$\mu_1 = \mu_2 = 1$	(use $\lambda = 0.5$)	(use $\lambda = 1.5$)
Host 1 is faster:	Fill in ...	Fill in ...
$\mu_1 = 4$, $\mu_2 = 1$	(use $\lambda = 1.25$)	(use $\lambda = 3.75$)

Your job is to fill in each entry of this table with a ranking of the four server configurations in order from greatest mean response time to least mean response time; for example,

$$T_{\text{config1}} > T_{\text{config2}} = T_{\text{config3}} > T_{\text{config4}}.$$

You may use ">" or "=" signs, but may *not* use ambiguous signs like $\geq$.

Note: For configuration (4) observe that the correspondence between ρ and λ does not make sense. Thus when evaluating configuration (4) please just use the λ value.

It will help if you first try to think about the problem using intuition. Feel free to use Mathematica to compare your expressions.

CHAPTER 15

Capacity Provisioning for Server Farms

If servers were free, then every server farm would have an infinite number of servers, and no job would ever have to wait in a queue. Unfortunately, servers are not free to buy, and they are also not free to operate. Running servers consumes lots of power, and even leaving a server on, but idle, still consumes nearly 60% of the power consumed by a busy server [15]. Given these costs, it pays to spend some time thinking about how many servers one really needs. This subject is called *capacity provisioning*.

Observe that we can actually already, in theory, answer the question of how many servers we need to achieve a given Quality of Service (QoS) goal, based on the formulas we derived in Chapter 14. In that chapter, we considered the M/M/k server farm model and derived expressions for the distribution of the number of jobs in the system, the probability of queueing, P_Q, and the expected response time, $\mathbf{E}[T]$. Given a QoS constraint on $\mathbf{E}[T]$ or P_Q, we can iterate over these formulas and deduce the exact number of servers, k, needed to achieve the desired constraint.

However, iterating over a formula is time consuming and also does not provide any intuitions for the result. The purpose of this chapter is to formulate intuitions and rules of thumb for understanding how many servers we need to achieve a certain QoS goal, and what the impact is of increasing the number of servers.

As usual, we build up to the question with discussions aimed at honing our intuition. We start in Section 15.1 by trying to get a better understanding of what load means in a multi-server system. We find that, in an M/M/k, having high load does not necessarily imply high delay. In Section 15.2, we introduce the concept of a server farm with an infinite number of servers, the M/M/∞. Although this does not exist in the real world, this hypothetical system will simplify many future proofs and will give us a first cut at a capacity provisioning rule. The chapter culminates in the famous "square-root staffing rule," described and proved in Section 15.3, which will provide a very good approximation for the number of servers needed in an M/M/k as a function of QoS goals. In the exercises we explore additional QoS goals, such as the 95th percentile of response time.

15.1 What Does Load Really Mean in an M/M/k?

A common rule of thumb for a single-server M/M/1 system is that the utilization, ρ, should be kept below 0.8. If ρ gets higher (e.g., $\rho = 0.95$), delays explode. For example, with $\rho = 0.8$, $\mathbf{E}[N]$ for an M/M/1 is 4, whereas for $\rho = 0.95$, $\mathbf{E}[N] = 19$. In this section we ask whether this rule of thumb of $\rho < 0.8$ makes sense for a multi-server M/M/k system as well.

Consider the formula from (14.8) for an M/M/k system:

$$\mathbf{E}\left[T_Q\right]^{\text{M/M/k}} = \frac{1}{\lambda} P_Q \frac{\rho}{1 - \rho} \tag{15.1}$$

Here $\rho = \frac{\lambda}{k\mu}$ represents the load or system utilization (see Definition 14.4). It is hard to get a feel for how $\mathbf{E}\left[T_Q\right]$ behaves, because there is a P_Q factor, which we also do not have a handle on yet. For convenience, let's therefore consider a slightly different metric that washes out the P_Q factor: $\mathbf{E}\left[T_Q\right]/P_Q$.

Question: What does $\mathbf{E}\left[T_Q\right]/P_Q$ represent?

Answer: Observe that

$$\begin{aligned}\mathbf{E}\left[T_Q\right] &= \mathbf{E}\left[T_Q \mid \text{delayed}\right] \cdot P_Q + \mathbf{E}\left[T_Q \mid \text{not delayed}\right] \cdot (1 - P_Q) \\ &= \mathbf{E}\left[T_Q \mid \text{delayed}\right] \cdot P_Q.\end{aligned}$$

Thus,

$$\frac{\mathbf{E}\left[T_Q\right]}{P_Q} = \mathbf{E}\left[T_Q \mid \text{delayed}\right].$$

Namely, $\mathbf{E}\left[T_Q\right]/P_Q$ represents the **expected waiting time of those customers who are delayed.**

Now observe from (15.1) that

$$\frac{\mathbf{E}\left[T_Q\right]}{P_Q} = \mathbf{E}\left[T_Q \mid \text{delayed}\right] = \frac{1}{\lambda} \cdot \frac{\rho}{1 - \rho} = \frac{1}{k\mu(1 - \rho)}. \tag{15.2}$$

Suppose that we now fix ρ to be some constant. Then we find that the expected waiting time of those customers who are delayed drops in direct proportion to the number of servers, k.

The **take-home message** is that *high values of system utilization, ρ, do not imply that customers will suffer, provided that there are sufficiently many servers.*

For example, we might have an average server utilization of $\rho = 0.95$ with 5 servers. In this case, the average wait for customers who are delayed is $\frac{1}{5\mu(.05)} = \frac{4}{\mu}$, namely 4 times a job size. By contrast, we could have the same average server utilization of $\rho = 0.95$ with 100 servers. In this case, the average wait experienced by customers who are delayed is only $\frac{1}{100\mu(.05)} = \frac{1}{5\mu}$, namely a fifth of a job size.

Question: Why does having more servers help, given that ρ, the average server utilization, stays the same?

Answer: Even if all servers still have utilization ρ, with more servers it is less likely that they are *all* busy at the same time. Hence it is more likely that an arrival finds a free server.

Question: Haven't we seen an analogous result for a single-server system?

Answer: Yes, even in an M/M/1, if we hold ρ constant, but increase both λ and μ by the same factor, then delay will drop indefinitely.

15.2 The M/M/∞

We start, in Section 15.2.1, by imagining a server farm with an infinite number of servers. Although this is somewhat unrealistic, it will lead us to a good first cut at an approximation for capacity provisioning, which we describe in Section 15.2.2.

15.2.1 Analysis of the M/M/∞

Imagine that you could call up the phone company for customer service, and never get the message, "We're sorry, but all of our service representatives are busy serving other customers . . . "

This dream situation can be modeled by a queueing system with an *infinite* number of servers, so that there is always a server to take your call. Such a system is called the M/M/∞ queueing system. The interarrival times are Exponential with rate λ, the service times are Exponential with rate μ, and there are an infinite number of servers.

We are interested in deriving the probability distribution of the number of jobs in such a system.

Question: What does the state diagram look like for the M/M/∞?

Answer: The Markov chain for the system is shown in Figure 15.1.

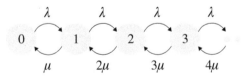

Figure 15.1. CTMC for the M/M/∞ system.

Question: You should be able to solve this for the limiting probabilities. Can you express the limiting probabilities via a *closed-form* expression that is simple and clearly recognizable as something you have seen before?

Answer: To derive the limiting probabilities, we set up the time-reversibility equations:

$$\pi_1 = \frac{\lambda}{\mu}\pi_0$$

$$\pi_2 = \frac{\lambda}{2\mu}\pi_1 = \frac{\lambda}{2\mu} \cdot \frac{\lambda}{\mu} \cdot \pi_0$$

$$\pi_3 = \frac{\lambda}{3\mu}\pi_2 = \frac{\lambda}{3\mu} \cdot \frac{\lambda}{2\mu} \cdot \frac{\lambda}{\mu} \cdot \pi_0$$

Based on this, a good guess for the limiting probabilities is

$$\pi_i = \left(\frac{\lambda}{\mu}\right)^i \cdot \frac{1}{i!} \cdot \pi_0.$$

You should recognize this distribution as being the Poisson distribution with mean $\frac{\lambda}{\mu}$, where

$$\pi_0 = e^{-\frac{\lambda}{\mu}}.$$

Question: From the limiting probabilities, derive a closed-form expression for the expected number of jobs in the system, $\mathbf{E}[N]$.

Answer:

$$\text{Number of jobs in the M/M/}\infty \sim \text{Poisson}\left(\frac{\lambda}{\mu}\right). \qquad (15.3)$$

The mean of this distribution is

$$\mathbf{E}[N] = \frac{\lambda}{\mu}.$$

Question: Applying Little's Law gives us $\mathbf{E}[T]$. Does $\mathbf{E}[T]$ make sense?

Answer: By Little's Law,

$$\mathbf{E}[T] = \frac{\mathbf{E}[N]}{\lambda} = \frac{1}{\mu}.$$

Thus the mean response time is just the mean service time. This makes sense, because jobs do not ever have to queue up!

Question: We have actually seen the M/M/∞ before when we discussed closed systems. Where was this?

Hint: What happens in a closed interactive system?

Answer: The think station in a closed interactive system is an M/M/∞, where the mean "service time" is the mean time spent thinking.

You may be worrying that the think time is not necessarily Exponentially distributed. However, this does not matter because the M/M/∞ is insensitive to the distribution of service time (see Exercise 15.7).

15.2.2 A First Cut at a Capacity Provisioning Rule for the M/M/k

Our goal is to understand how many servers, k, we need in an M/M/k so as to keep the probability of queueing, P_Q, below some level, say 20%.

Question: If the average arrival rate is λ, and the average service rate at each server is μ, what is the minimum number of servers, k, needed just to keep the system stable?

Answer: We need

$$\rho < 1$$

$$\Rightarrow \frac{\lambda}{k\mu} < 1$$

$$\Rightarrow k > \frac{\lambda}{\mu}.$$

Observe that $\frac{\lambda}{\mu}$ can be a fraction, in which case we would actually have to round up to the next integer.

We have seen this expression before in Definition 14.4, which we repeat here for reference.

Definition 15.1 (Repeated from Definition 14.4) For an M/M/k with average arrival rate λ and service rate μ, the ***resource requirement*** is denoted by **R**, where

$$R = \frac{\lambda}{\mu}.$$

R can be viewed as the minimum number of servers needed to keep the system stable, or as the expected number of servers that are busy, or as the expected number of jobs in service.

We now argue that, if R is a large number, then by using relatively few servers more than R, namely

$$k = R + \sqrt{R}$$

servers, we can get P_Q down below the 20% range. Our argument is based on the M/M/∞ queue.

Question: What is the probability of having more than $R + \sqrt{R}$ jobs in the M/M/∞?

Answer: As we saw in (15.3), the number of jobs in the M/M/∞ is Poisson distributed with mean R. Given that R is large, the Poisson(R) distribution is well approximated by a Normal(R, R) distribution (see Feller [57], p. 245). Hence, we are asking what is the probability that the Normal(R, R) distribution is more than one standard deviation above its mean. This is simply the probability that the standard Normal exceeds its mean by more than one standard deviation, namely $1 - \Phi(1)$, or about 16%.[1]

Thus, for an M/M/∞ the probability that we use more than $R + \sqrt{R}$ servers is only 16%. But the question we really wanted to answer was how many servers we need in an M/M/k, not an M/M/∞!

Question: Is the M/M/∞ result an upper bound or a lower bound on the M/M/k?

Answer: When a lot of work arrives, the M/M/∞ has more resources available for clearing this work than the M/M/k has (the work may have to queue in the M/M/k).

---

[1] Normal distributions are covered in Section 3.14.

Hence the fraction of time that the M/M/∞ has more than x servers busy is going to be lower than the fraction of time that the M/M/k has more than x servers busy. Hence 16% is a lower bound. In fact, as we see in the next section, when using $k = R + \sqrt{R}$ servers in the M/M/k, P_Q is about 20%.

15.3 Square-Root Staffing

In this section, we refine the $R + \sqrt{R}$ approximation developed in the previous section.

As before, we assume an M/M/k with average arrival rate λ and average server speed μ. The QoS goal that we set is that P_Q, the probability of queueing in the M/M/k, should be below some given value α (e.g., $\alpha = 20\%$). Our goal is to determine the minimal number of servers, k_α^*, needed to meet this QoS goal.

Note that bounding P_Q is really equivalent to bounding mean response time or mean queueing time, or similar metrics, because they are all simple functions of P_Q (e.g., from (14.9), we have $\mathbf{E}\left[T_Q\right] = \frac{1}{\lambda} \cdot P_Q \cdot \frac{\rho}{1-\rho}$).

Theorem 15.2 (Square-Root Staffing Rule) *Given an M/M/k with arrival rate λ and server speed μ and $R = \lambda/\mu$, where R is large, let k_α^* denote the least number of servers needed to ensure that $P_Q^{\mathrm{M/M/k}} < \alpha$. Then*

$$k_\alpha^* \approx R + c\sqrt{R},$$

where c is the solution to the equation,

$$\frac{c\Phi(c)}{\phi(c)} = \frac{1-\alpha}{\alpha} \tag{15.4}$$

where $\Phi(\cdot)$ denotes the c.d.f. of the standard Normal and $\phi(\cdot)$ denotes its p.d.f.

Remark: It is interesting to observe that the constant c in Theorem 15.2 does not depend on R or the arrival rate λ. Also, in practice, c is quite small. A good rule of thumb to remember is that when $\alpha = 0.2$, $c \approx 1$. Thus, to ensure that only 20% of jobs queue up, it suffices to use just $k = R + \sqrt{R}$ servers, where R is the number of servers needed to just maintain stability. Here are a few more values:

$\alpha = 0.8$	$\alpha = 0.5$	$\alpha = 0.2$	$\alpha = 0.1$
$c = 0.173$	$c = .506$	$c = 1.06$	$c = 1.42$

Remark: In Exercise 15.3, you will be asked to derive k_α^* both (i) via the approximation in Theorem 15.2 and (ii) exactly by evaluating the $P_Q^{\mathrm{M/M/k}}$ at different values of k. What you will find is that the approximation in Theorem 15.2 is exact or off by at most 1, even for very low R, like 1. This is surprising, because the proof of Theorem 15.2 assumes large R. Thus Theorem 15.2 even works well for staffing small server farms.

Proof (Square-Root Staffing) Our approach is to express P_Q in terms of P_{block} and determine a simple approximation for P_{block}. This may seem logically confusing, since P_Q refers to the M/M/k, while P_{block} is the blocking probability for the M/M/k/k (see Chapter 14). However, our approach is just an algebraic maneuver, since P_{block} is easy to derive and will thus quickly yield an approximation for P_Q. Recall from (14.6) that

$$P_{\text{block}} = \frac{(1-\rho)P_Q}{1-\rho P_Q}.$$

This allows us to express P_Q in terms of P_{block} as follows:

$$P_Q = \frac{P_{\text{block}}}{1-\rho+\rho P_{\text{block}}} = \frac{kP_{\text{block}}}{k-R+RP_{\text{block}}}. \tag{15.5}$$

We now turn to deriving P_{block}.

If we let X_R denote a random variable with Poisson distribution and mean R, then we can use (14.3) to express P_{block} as

$$P_{\text{block}} = \frac{\mathbf{P}\{X_R = k\}}{\mathbf{P}\{X_R \le k\}}.$$

These latter expressions involving X_R can be simply expressed if we use the fact that the Poisson distribution of mean R can be well approximated by the Normal distribution of the same mean and variance R, provided that R is large. Specifically, setting

$$k = R + c\sqrt{R},$$

we see that

$$\begin{aligned}
\mathbf{P}\{X_R \le k\} &= \mathbf{P}\left\{X_R \le R + c\sqrt{R}\right\} \\
&\approx \mathbf{P}\left\{\text{Normal}(R,R) \le R + c\sqrt{R}\right\} \\
&= \mathbf{P}\{\text{Normal}(0,1) \le c\} \\
&= \Phi(c).
\end{aligned}$$

$$\begin{aligned}
\mathbf{P}\{X_R = k\} &= \mathbf{P}\{X_R \le k\} - \mathbf{P}\{X_R \le k-1\} \\
&\approx \Phi(c) - \mathbf{P}\left\{X_R \le R + c\sqrt{R} - 1\right\} \\
&= \Phi(c) - \mathbf{P}\left\{X_R \le R + \sqrt{R}\left(c - \frac{1}{\sqrt{R}}\right)\right\} \\
&\approx \Phi(c) - \Phi\left(c - \frac{1}{\sqrt{R}}\right) \\
&\approx \frac{1}{\sqrt{R}}\phi(c) \quad \text{(again, we are assuming } R: \text{large).}
\end{aligned}$$

Thus we have

$$P_{\text{block}} = \frac{\mathbf{P}\{X_R = k\}}{\mathbf{P}\{X_R \le k\}} \approx \frac{\phi(c)}{\sqrt{R}\,\Phi(c)}. \tag{15.6}$$

Returning to the expression for P_Q in (15.5), and substituting in (15.6), as well as the fact that $k = R + c\sqrt{R}$, we now have

$$\begin{aligned}
P_Q &= \frac{k P_{\text{block}}}{k - R + R P_{\text{block}}} \\
&\approx \frac{(R + c\sqrt{R})\frac{\phi(c)}{\sqrt{R}\Phi(c)}}{R + c\sqrt{R} - R + R\frac{\phi(c)}{\sqrt{R}\Phi(c)}} \\
&= \frac{(\sqrt{R} + c)\frac{\phi(c)}{\Phi(c)}}{c\sqrt{R} + \sqrt{R}\frac{\phi(c)}{\Phi(c)}} \\
&= \frac{1 + \frac{c}{\sqrt{R}}}{1 + \frac{\Phi(c)}{\phi(c)} \cdot c}.
\end{aligned}$$

If we now assume that R is large so that $c << \sqrt{R}$, then

$$P_Q \approx \left(1 + \frac{\Phi(c)}{\phi(c)} c\right)^{-1}. \tag{15.7}$$

Now recall that our goal is to make $P_Q < \alpha$.

$$P_Q < \alpha$$

$$\iff \left(1 + \frac{\Phi(c)}{\phi(c)} c\right)^{-1} < \alpha$$

$$\iff \frac{\Phi(c)}{\phi(c)} c > \frac{1}{\alpha} - 1$$

The minimum value of c that satisfies the above is the solution to

$$\frac{\Phi(c)}{\phi(c)} c = \frac{1}{\alpha} - 1,$$

which is exactly equation (15.4).   ∎

15.4 Readings

The square-root staffing derivation is based on a beautifully written book by Tijms [178].

15.5 Exercises

15.1 Effect of Increased Number of Servers

Consider an M/M/k system, where the service rate at each server is $\mu = 1$. Fix system utilization at $\rho = 0.95$. Now increase the number of servers, k, as follows – 1, 2, 4, 8, 16, 32 – adjusting the arrival rate, λ, accordingly. For each number of servers, derive (i) the fraction of customers that are delayed and (ii) the expected waiting time for those customers who are delayed. We are just looking for numerical answers here. Feel free to write a math program to evaluate the needed summations. Explain the trend that you see.

15.2 Capacity Provisioning to Avoid Loss

In a call center with k operators, all calls that are not immediately answered by an operator are *dropped*. Calls arrive according to a Poisson process with rate λ and have Exponentially distributed service times with rate $\mu = 1$. For λ in the set $\{1, 2, 4, 8\}$, what should k be as a function of λ to ensure that fewer than 1% of calls are dropped? We are just looking for numerical solutions. Feel free to write a math program to evaluate the needed summations. When λ doubles, does the needed number of operators double?

15.3 Accuracy of Square-Root Staffing Rule

The point of this problem is to test the accuracy of the square-root staffing approximation given in Theorem 15.2. We want to determine the minimum number of servers, k^*, needed to staff our M/M/k call center, such that fewer than 20% of customers are delayed. Assume that job sizes are Exponentially distributed with mean $\frac{1}{\mu} = 1$. Consider the following cases for the resource requirement: $R = \frac{\lambda}{\mu} = 1, 5, 10, 50, 100, 250, 500, 1,000$. For each case, derive k^* according to the square-root staffing approximation given in Theorem 15.2, and then derive it from scratch using P_Q for the M/M/k. How close are the results?

15.4 95th Percentile of Response Time – M/M/1

While mean response time is a common performance metric, many system administrators prefer instead to measure the 95th percentile of response time, denoted by T_{95}. Formally, T_{95} is defined to be that x such that

$$\mathbf{P}\{T > x\} = 0.05.$$

Namely, only 5% of jobs have higher response time than T_{95}. Consider an M/M/1 with service rate $\mu = 1$ and load $\rho = \lambda$.

(a) How is response time, T, distributed in an M/M/1, in terms of ρ?
(b) How does $\mathbf{E}[T]$ scale with ρ?
(c) How does T_{95} grow with ρ? How does this compare with how $\mathbf{E}[T]$ grows with ρ?

15.5 95th Percentile of Time in Queue – M/M/k

In Exercise 15.4 we derived the 95th percentile of response time for the M/M/1. We now wish to follow a similar approach to derive the 95th percentile of the queueing time in the M/M/k, for those jobs that queue. Assume arrival rate λ, service rate μ at each of the k servers, and $\rho = \frac{\lambda}{k\mu} < 1$.

(a) Consider the queueing time of those jobs which queue, namely

$$[T_Q \mid \text{delayed}].$$

How is this quantity distributed?
(b) What is the 95th percentile of the queueing time of those jobs that queue, as a function of k, μ, and λ?

15.6 How to Split Capacity

For the server farm in Figure 15.2, jobs arrive according to a Poisson process with rate λ and are probabilistically split between two servers, with $p > \frac{1}{2}$ fraction going to server 1, and $q = 1 - p < \frac{1}{2}$ fraction going to server 2. If we have a total service capacity of μ for the two servers, how should we optimally split μ between the two servers, into μ_1 and μ_2, where $\mu = \mu_1 + \mu_2$, so as to minimize $\mathbf{E}[T]$? Assume job sizes are Exponentially distributed.

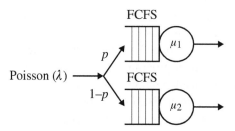

Figure 15.2. How should we split capacity μ between two servers?

(a) Let's start with some easy cases. What should the answer be if $p = 1$? How about if $p = \frac{1}{2}$?

(b) Returning to the general case of $p > \frac{1}{2}$, what is a lower bound on μ_1? How about on μ_2? After we allocate this minimum capacity to server 1 and server 2, what is the extra capacity left over?

(c) Of the "extra capacity" that remains, what fraction do you intuitively believe should be allocated to server 1?

(d) Prove that the optimal fraction of extra capacity going to server 1 is

$$\frac{\sqrt{p}}{\sqrt{p} + \sqrt{1 - p}}. \tag{15.8}$$

That is, the optimal value for μ_1 is $\mu_1^* = \lambda p + \frac{\sqrt{p}}{\sqrt{p}+\sqrt{1-p}}(\mu - \lambda)$.

(e) Provide intuition for at least the direction of the result.

15.7 Insensitivity of M/G/∞

The M/G/∞ system consists of a single FCFS queue, served by an infinite number of servers, where jobs arrive according to a Poisson process with rate λ and have generally distributed i.i.d. job service requirements with mean $\frac{1}{\mu}$. It turns out that the probability that there are k jobs in the M/G/∞ is insensitive to the distribution of G, depending on only the mean of G. Specifically,

$$\mathbf{P}\{\text{There are } k \text{ jobs in the M/G/∞}\} = \frac{e^{-\frac{\lambda}{\mu}}\left(\frac{\lambda}{\mu}\right)^k}{k!}. \tag{15.9}$$

This problem leads us through a heuristic derivation of this result, borrowed from [178], which provides a lot of intuition for the insensitivity result. (This argument can be made completely rigorous by using differential equations, see [178], pages 10–11.)

(a) Consider first the case where all jobs have the same Deterministic size $D = \frac{1}{\mu}$. Consider a time $t > D$. Derive the probability that there are k

customers at time t and show this agrees with (15.9). [Hint: What can you say about the arrival times of customers who are around at time t, given that all customers have fixed size D?]

(b) Now consider the case where there are ℓ classes of jobs. With probability p_i, an arrival is of class i. Jobs of class i have Deterministic size D_i. The average job size is still $\frac{1}{\mu}$, that is, $\sum_{i=1}^{\ell} p_i D_i = \frac{1}{\mu}$. Consider a time $t > \max_i D_i$. Derive the probability that there are k customers present at time t and show that this agrees with (15.9).

15.8 Pricing and Queueing

A software firm is designing a new cloud computing service and has hired you as a consultant to help price its service.

Users submit computing jobs to an M/M/1 (FCFS) server with arrival rate λ and service rate $\mu = 1$. The actual job size is unknown to both the user and the server until the job begins receiving service.

All users receiving service gain a monetary value worth $V - c \cdot T$ for each completed job, where $V > 1$ is a given constant value for all jobs, T is the response time of the job, and c is the cost of waiting per unit time. Without loss of generality, we will normalize our units to let $c = 1$, so a customer receives $V - T$ value from service.

At the time of arrival, a user must decide whether to allow his or her job to join the queue based on the following information: (i) The firm reveals the number of jobs already in the system, n, and (ii) the firm charges a fixed price of entry $\mathcal{P} > 0$. The user will allow the job to join if and only if the price of entry is no more than the value he or she expects to receive from the service. We can express this condition as

$$V - \mathbf{E}[T|N = n] \geq \mathcal{P}.$$

The firm wishes to set $\mathcal{P}$ to maximize its own earning rate:

$$\mathcal{R} = \lambda \mathcal{P} \cdot \mathbf{P} \{\text{an arrival joins the queue}\}$$

Because not all arrivals will join the queue, the queue will be stable, even for $\lambda > 1$. You may assume throughout this problem that V and $\mathcal{P}$ are integers.

(a) What is the greatest n for which arrivals are willing to join the queue (in terms of V and $\mathcal{P}$)?

(b) What is the earning rate $\mathcal{R}$ (in terms of λ, V, and $\mathcal{P}$)?

(c) Compute the optimal integer price $\mathcal{P}^*$ and the corresponding earning rate $\mathcal{R}$ for the following cases: (i) $V = 6$ and $\lambda = 0.1$; (ii) $V = 6$ and $\lambda = 0.9$; and (iii) $V = 6$ and $\lambda = 1.8$. (Create a table of $\mathcal{R}$ as a function of different $\mathcal{P}$ values.)

(d) Sherwin proposes that we can do better by charging a *state-dependent* price, $\mathcal{P}(n)$, when the state is n, where

$$\mathcal{P}(n) = \max\{1, \text{Highest price users will pay in state } n\}.$$

We charge 1 when users are unwilling to pay a positive integer price, effectively turning these users away and thereby ensuring that we always earn money for each job we serve. Define n_0 to be the lowest numbered state n for which users are unwilling to pay a positive price. Determine $\mathcal{P}(n)$ (in terms of n and V and n_0).

(e) Under state-dependent pricing, the earning rate becomes

$$\mathcal{R} = \lambda \sum_{n=0}^{n_0-1} \mathcal{P}(n) \cdot \mathbf{P}\{\text{an arrival joins the queue and pays } \mathcal{P}(n)\}.$$

Compute the earning rate $\mathcal{R}$ under state-dependent pricing for the cases given in part (c). How do your results compare to those in part (c)? Explain your findings intuitively.

Remark: It turns out that Sherwin's suggestion can sometimes be improved on by using a threshold policy whereby users are barred from entry once the queue length reaches a certain threshold [39].

15.9 Congestion Management

Consider this common congestion management scheme: Jobs are served in an M/M/1 queue, provided that the number of jobs is no more than T_{high}. Once the number of jobs hits T_{high}, a second server is immediately added, creating an M/M/2. The second server continues to be utilized until the number of jobs drops to T_{low}, at which point the second server is removed, and we are back to an M/M/1, and the process repeats. Assume that jobs arrive according to a Poisson process with rate λ and that job sizes are Exponentially distributed with rate μ. Assume that $T_{\text{low}} = 1$ and $T_{\text{high}} = t$, as shown in Figure 15.3. Derive an expression for the mean response time, $\mathbf{E}[T]$, as a function of t. Your expression does not need to be in closed form. Evaluate $\mathbf{E}[T]$ for $\lambda = 1.5$, $\mu = 1$, and $t = 4, 8, 16, 32, 64$. [*Note:* This problem is algebraically messy; using a math software package will help.]

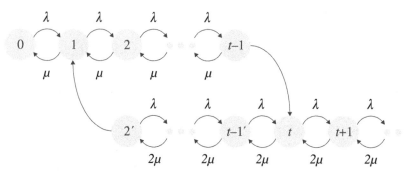

Figure 15.3. CTMC for Exercise 15.9.

15.10 M/M/1 with Setup Times

Consider an M/M/1 queue, where the server immediately shuts off when it is idle (e.g., to save power). When a job arrives and finds the server off there is a *setup time*, I, required to get the server back on. In this problem we assume $I \sim \text{Exp}(\alpha)$. Setup times are very important in capacity provisioning for systems, because they delay not only the job that finds the server off, but also subsequent jobs that arrive before the server is operational again. Interestingly, for an M/M/1 with an Exponentially distributed setup cost, one can prove the following result, relating the mean response time for an M/M/1 with setup to an M/M/1 without setup:

$$\mathbf{E}\left[T\right]^{\text{M/M/1/setup}} = \mathbf{E}\left[T\right]^{\text{M/M/1}} + \mathbf{E}\left[I\right] \tag{15.10}$$

Derive (15.10) by modeling the system via a Markov chain and solving for the limiting probabilities. *Warning:* While the chain looks simple, the fact that there are two rows makes it a lot harder to solve. This is a difficult problem. [*Note:* This problem will be revisited in Chapter 27 on power management in greater generality.]

CHAPTER 16

Time-Reversibility and Burke's Theorem

Many practical problems can be represented by a small finite-state CTMC. When this happens, one is always happy. A finite-state CTMC, whose transition rates are numbers (not variables), can always be solved, given enough computational power, because it simply translates to a finite set of linear simultaneous equations. When transition rates are arbitrary parameters (λ's and μ's and such), the chain might still be solvable via symbolic manipulation, provided that the number of equations is not too great. Section 16.1 provides additional practice with setting up and solving finite-state CTMCs.

Unfortunately, many systems problems involve unbounded queues that translate into infinite-state CTMCs. We have already seen the M/M/1 and the M/M/k, which involve just a single queue and are solvable, even though the number of states is infinite. However, as we move to queueing networks (systems with multiple queues), we see that we need to track the number of jobs in each queue, resulting in a chain that is infinite in more than one dimension. At first such chains seem entirely intractable. Fortunately, it turns out that a very large class of such chains is easily solvable in closed form. This chapter, starting with Section 16.2 on time-reversibility and leading into Section 16.3 on Burke's theorem, provides us with the foundations needed to develop the theory of queueing networks, which will be the topic of the next few chapters.

16.1 More Examples of Finite-State CTMCs

16.1.1 *Networks with Finite Buffer Space*

Imagine a small hair salon with only 2 chairs (see Figure 16.1). A customer first goes to chair 1, by the sink, where her hair is washed, and then to chair 2, by the mirror, where her hair is cut. There is no standing room in the salon (no queueing). Thus, a customer only enters the salon if chair 1 is empty, and if a customer is finished with chair 1 but chair 2 is still occupied, the customer waits in chair 1.

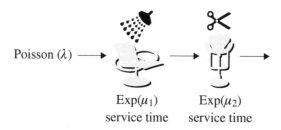

$$\text{Poisson } (\lambda) \longrightarrow$$

$$\text{Exp}(\mu_1) \qquad \text{Exp}(\mu_2)$$
$$\text{service time} \qquad \text{service time}$$

Figure 16.1. The hair salon.

This example may seem artificial, but in fact it is quite practical. It represents the situation where there are two routers in tandem, each with a finite capacity (in this case the finite buffer is of size 1 only, but it could be higher in general), and packets continue to occupy a buffer simply because the next buffer in the chain of routers is full.

We wish to answer these two questions:

1. What proportion of potential customers enter the salon?
2. What is the mean response time, $\mathbf{E}\,[T]$?

To answer these questions, we need to determine the state space.

Question: What is wrong with making the state be the number of customers in the system?

Answer: Doing so will not allow us to answer Question 1.

Question: How many customers can we have in each chair?

Answer: There can be 0 or 1 customers in each chair.

Question: How about this state space: $(0,0)$, $(0,1)$, $(1,0)$, $(1,1)$?

Answer: Not good enough: $(1,1)$ is ambiguous. Suppose we are in state $(1,1)$. With rate μ_2, where do we go? If $(1,1)$ represents the fact that there is one customer receiving service in chair 1 and one customer receiving service in chair 2, then with rate μ_2 we should go to state $(1,0)$. However, if $(1,1)$ represents the fact that there is one customer who has finished service in chair 1 and one customer still receiving service in chair 2, then with rate μ_2 we should go to state $(0,1)$.

Figure 16.2 shows the appropriate CTMC. State $(b,1)$ in the CTMC represents the state where there is a customer in both chairs, but the customer at chair 1 is finished and is blocked, waiting for chair 2.

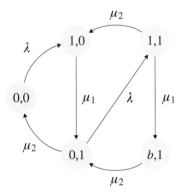

Figure 16.2. The hair salon state space.

We now write the balance equations for each state:

$$(0,0) \quad : \quad \pi_{0,0} \cdot \lambda = \pi_{0,1} \cdot \mu_2$$
$$(1,0) \quad : \quad \pi_{1,0} \cdot \mu_1 = \pi_{0,0} \cdot \lambda + \pi_{1,1} \cdot \mu_2$$

$$(0,1) \quad : \quad \pi_{0,1} \cdot (\mu_2 + \lambda) = \pi_{1,0} \cdot \mu_1 + \pi_{b,1} \cdot \mu_2$$
$$(1,1) \quad : \quad \pi_{1,1} \cdot (\mu_2 + \mu_1) = \pi_{0,1} \cdot \lambda$$
$$(b,1) \quad : \quad \pi_{b,1} \cdot \mu_2 = \pi_{1,1} \cdot \mu_1$$
$$\sum \pi_{i,j} \quad : \quad \pi_{0,0} + \pi_{1,0} + \pi_{0,1} + \pi_{1,1} + \pi_{b,1} = 1$$

We can now answer our questions, in terms of the limiting probabilities.

Question: What proportion of potential customers enter the salon?

Answer: An arrival enters the salon if she sees 0 customers in the first chair. By PASTA, the probability that an arrival sees 0 in the first chair is equal to the proportion of time there are 0 in the first chair, namely: $\pi_{0,0} + \pi_{0,1}$

Question: What is $\mathbf{E}[N]$?

Answer: $\mathbf{E}[N] = \pi_{1,0} + \pi_{0,1} + 2 \cdot (\pi_{1,1} + \pi_{b,1})$.

Question: What is $\mathbf{E}[T]$ for an entering customer?

Answer: $\mathbf{E}[T] = \frac{\mathbf{E}[N]}{\lambda_{\text{arrival}}} = \frac{\mathbf{E}[N]}{\lambda(\pi_{0,0} + \pi_{0,1})}$.

Importantly, in applying Little's Law, we use λ_{arrival}, which includes only those arrivals that actually make it through the network.

16.1.2 *Batch System with M/M/2 I/O*

Consider a system consisting of one CPU queue and one I/O queue, where the I/O queue is served by two disks, operating as an M/M/2 system, as shown in Figure 16.3. Our goal is to determine the exact throughput for this system (not approximations based on high N asymptotics).

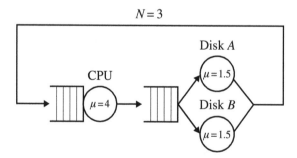

Figure 16.3. A batch system with M/M/2 I/O.

Question: Show the CTMC for this system.

Answer: Figure 16.4 shows the state space of the system.

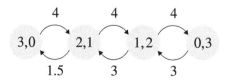

Figure 16.4. State space of a batch system with M/M/2 I/O.

State (i, j) represents the fact that there are i jobs in the CPU subsystem (including the CPU queue and server) and j jobs in the disk subsystem (including the disk queue and two disks). There are a total of $N = 3$ jobs in the whole system. The balance equations are as follows:

$$\pi_{3,0} \cdot 4 = \pi_{2,1} \cdot 1.5$$
$$\pi_{2,1} \cdot 5.5 = \pi_{3,0} \cdot 4 + \pi_{1,2} \cdot 3$$
$$\pi_{1,2} \cdot 7 = \pi_{2,1} \cdot 4 + \pi_{0,3} \cdot 3$$
$$\pi_{0,3} \cdot 3 = \pi_{1,2} \cdot 4$$
$$\pi_{3,0} + \pi_{2,1} + \pi_{1,2} + \pi_{0,3} = 1$$

Solving these, the steady-state probabilities are: $\pi_{3,0} = 0.08$, $\pi_{2,1} = 0.22$, $\pi_{1,2} = 0.3$, and $\pi_{0,3} = 0.4$.

Question: What is the throughput, X?

Answer: Every job passes through the CPU, so it suffices to look at X_{cpu}:

$$\rho_{\text{cpu}} = \pi_{3,0} + \pi_{2,1} + \pi_{1,2} = 0.6$$
$$X = X_{\text{cpu}} = \rho_{\text{cpu}} \cdot \mu_{\text{cpu}} = 0.6 \cdot 4 \text{ jobs/sec } = 2.4 \text{ jobs/sec}$$

Question: How does this compare with what we get from asymptotic calculations using only operational laws and assuming high N, as in Chapter 7?

Answer: For high N, we will have $X = 3$ jobs/sec, because at most 3 jobs can pass through the disk module each second.

Question: What is $\mathbf{E}\left[T_{\text{cpu}}\right]$?

Answer: $\mathbf{E}\left[T_{\text{cpu}}\right] = \frac{\mathbf{E}\left[N_{\text{cpu}}\right]}{X_{\text{cpu}}} = \frac{3 \cdot \pi_{3,0} + 2 \cdot \pi_{2,1} + 1 \cdot \pi_{1,2}}{2.4} = 0.41$ sec.

Question: What is $\rho_{\text{disk a}}$?

Answer: $\frac{1}{2} \cdot \pi_{2,1} + \pi_{1,2} + \pi_{0,3} = 0.8$.

16.2 The Reverse Chain

In the previous examples, the state space was finite, making the CTMC easy to solve. In open queueing systems, the state space is typically infinite, and it is often infinite in more than one dimension, because we need to track the "unbounded" number of jobs at each of several queues. To analyze such systems, we need to develop a new technique. This section and the next present this new technique.

Consider an ergodic CTMC in steady state. Now imagine we are watching the CTMC as it transitions between states:

$$\cdots \longrightarrow 3 \longrightarrow 5 \longrightarrow 1 \longrightarrow 2 \longrightarrow 1 \longrightarrow 3 \longrightarrow 4 \longrightarrow 1 \longrightarrow \cdots$$

Now consider the **reverse process** for the CTMC. That is, we watch the CTMC, but we look *backward* in time (think of watching a movie being played in reverse):

$$\cdots \longleftarrow 3 \longleftarrow 5 \longleftarrow 1 \longleftarrow 2 \longleftarrow 1 \longleftarrow 3 \longleftarrow 4 \longleftarrow 1 \longleftarrow \cdots$$

That is, the reverse process transitions from state 1 to 4 to 3 to 1 to 2 to 1, etc.

Claim 16.1   *The reverse process is also a CTMC.*

Proof   To see this, think of the CTMC via VIEW 1, as described in Chapter 12. The *forwards process* sits in state 3 for $\mathrm{Exp}(\nu_3)$ time and then flips a coin with probability $P_{3,5}$ of next going to 5. The process then sits in state 5 for $\mathrm{Exp}(\nu_5)$ time and again flips a coin to determine where to go next with probability $P_{5,1}$ of next going to state 1. The process then sits in state 1 for $\mathrm{Exp}(\nu_1)$ time.

If we look at just the coin flips (ignoring the time spent in each state), then the sequence of coin flips forms what is called an **embedded DTMC**.

Now consider the *reverse process*, transitioning over these same states. The reverse process also sits in state 1 for $\mathrm{Exp}(\nu_1)$ time. It then moves to state 5 where it sits for $\mathrm{Exp}(\nu_5)$ time and then moves to state 3 where it sits for $\mathrm{Exp}(\nu_3)$ time. So we already see that each time the reverse process visits state i, it also sits in state i for $\mathrm{Exp}(\nu_i)$ time. To show that the reverse process is a CTMC, all that remains is to show that there are *probabilities* defining the reverse process's transitions between states.

The probability that the reverse process moves from state 1 to state 5 is exactly the probability that the forwards process got to state 1 from state 5, rather than from some other state, given that the forwards process wound up in state 1. Let P_{ij}^* denote the probability that the reverse embedded DTMC moves from state i to state j, given that it is in state i. To finish this proof we do not need to explicitly compute P_{ij}^*; we just need to know that it is a valid probability, meaning that

$$\sum_j \mathbf{P}\{\text{Reverse process moves from state } i \text{ to state } j\} = 1,$$

which is obviously true given that the forward chain must have gotten to state i from some state.[1]   ∎

To keep from getting confused, we will tag all quantities associated with the reverse chain with an asterisk (*). So for example, we have seen that

$$\nu_j = \nu_j^*.$$

Question: How does π_j relate to π_j^*?

---

[1] We will not need to know this, but if you are curious about what P_{ij}^* looks like, you will find out in equation (16.2).

Answer: π_j represents the fraction of time that the forward CTMC chain is in state j. But this is equal to the fraction of time that the reverse chain is in state j. Thus,

$$\pi_j = \pi_j^*.$$

Let $\pi_i q_{ij}$ denote the rate of transitions from i to j in the forwards process, where π_i denotes the limiting probability of being in state i and q_{ij} denotes the rate of transitions from i to j, given we are in state i. Note here that

$$q_{ij} = \nu_i \cdot P_{ij}, \tag{16.1}$$

where ν_i is the total rate of transitions leaving state i, given that we are in state i.

Question: Is the rate of transitions from state i to state j in the reverse CTMC process the same as the rate of transitions from state i to state j in the forwards CTMC process?

Answer: No, $\pi_i^* q_{ij}^*$ is not necessarily equal to $\pi_i q_{ij}$ because q_{ij}^* is not necessarily equal to q_{ij}. For example, there may be zero rate of transitions from i to j in the forwards chain, and yet a positive rate of transitions from i to j in the reverse chain.

> **Claim 16.2** *The rate of transitions from i to j in the reverse CTMC process equals the rate of transitions from j to i in the forwards CTMC process. That is,*
>
> $$\pi_i^* q_{ij}^* = \pi_j q_{ji}.$$
>
> *This claim is always true and has nothing to do with time-reversibility.*

Proof Consider any observation period T. During T the number of transitions that the reverse process makes from i to j is exactly equal to the number of transitions that the forwards process makes from j to i. Thus the rates (number of transitions during T, divided by T) are also the same. ∎

An immediate corollary of Claim 16.2 combined with (16.1) is that[2]

$$P_{ij}^* = \frac{\pi_j \nu_j P_{ji}}{\pi_i \nu_i}. \tag{16.2}$$

---

[2] Here is an independent derivation of P_{ij}^*. Consider the embedded DTMC within our CTMC. Let π_i^{DTMC} be the limiting probability of being in state i for the embedded DTMC (note this is not the same as the limiting probability for the CTMC, π_i^{CTMC}). Observe that the rate of transitions from j to i in the forward embedded DTMC equals the rate of transitions from i to j in the reverse embedded DTMC. (This is true for every chain and has nothing to do with time-reversibility.) So

$$\pi_j^{\mathrm{DTMC}} P_{ji} = \pi_i^{*\mathrm{DTMC}} P_{ij}^*.$$

But because $\pi_i^{*\mathrm{DTMC}} = \pi_i^{\mathrm{DTMC}}$, we have

$$\pi_j^{\mathrm{DTMC}} P_{ji} = \pi_i^{\mathrm{DTMC}} P_{ij}^*,$$

which results in

$$P_{ij}^* = \frac{\pi_j^{\mathrm{DTMC}} P_{ji}}{\pi_i^{\mathrm{DTMC}}},$$

It turns out that we can say a lot more about the reverse chain *if* we know that the forwards chain is *time-reversible*.

Definition 16.3 A CTMC is ***time-reversible*** if, for all i, j:

$$\pi_i q_{ij} = \pi_j q_{ji} \quad \text{and} \quad \sum_i \pi_i = 1. \qquad (16.3)$$

In other words, a CTMC is time-reversible if for every pair of states i, j, the rate of transitions from i to j in the forwards process equals the rate of transitions from j to i in the forwards process. For example, the CTMC corresponding to a birth-death process is time-reversible, because the number of transitions from state i to state $i + 1$ is always within 1 of the number of transitions from state $i + 1$ to i, and hence the long-run *rate* of transitions from i to $i + 1$ equals the *rate* of transitions from $i + 1$ to i. Note that time-reversibility is defined as a property of the forwards process.

Claim 16.4 *If a CTMC is time-reversible, then its reverse chain is* statistically identical *to the forwards chain, meaning that the reverse chain can be described by the same CTMC as the forwards chain.*

Proof If the CTMC is time-reversible, then

$$
\begin{aligned}
\pi_i q_{ij} &= \pi_j q_{ji} \quad \text{(by definition of time-reversibility)} \\
&= \pi_i^* q_{ij}^* \quad \text{(by Claim 16.2)} \\
&= \pi_i q_{ij}^*.
\end{aligned}
$$

Therefore,

$$q_{ij} = q_{ij}^* \quad \text{for all } i, j.$$

Because these rates define the CTMC (think VIEW 2 of a CTMC from Chapter 12), the forwards and reverse chains are statistically identical. Note that this also implies $P_{ij} = P_{ij}^*$, because $q_{ij} = \nu_i P_{ij}$ and $\nu_i = \nu_i^*$. Thus the embedded DTMCs for the forwards and reverse processes are also identical. ■

16.3 Burke's Theorem

Theorem 16.5 (Burke) *Consider an M/M/1 system with arrival rate λ. Suppose the system starts in a steady state. Then the following are true:*

Now observe that there is a clear relation between π_i^{DTMC} (which spends time 1 during each visit to a state) and π_i^{CTMC} (which spends time $\text{Exp}(\nu_i)$ during each visit to state i); namely,

$$\pi_i^{\text{CTMC}} = \pi_i^{\text{DTMC}} \cdot \frac{1}{\nu_i} \cdot C,$$

where C is just a normalizing constant needed to get the limiting probabilities to sum to 1. Hence,

$$P_{ij}^* = \frac{\pi_j^{\text{DTMC}} P_{ji}}{\pi_i^{\text{DTMC}}} = \frac{\pi_j^{\text{CTMC}} \nu_j P_{ji}}{\pi_i^{\text{CTMC}} \nu_i}.$$

> **1.** *The departure process is Poisson(λ).*
> **2.** *At each time t, the number of jobs in the system at time t is independent of the sequence of departure times prior to time t.*

Part (1) of Theorem 16.5 says that the interdeparture times are Exponentially distributed with rate λ. It is not at all obvious that this should be the case. Clearly, while the server is busy, the interdeparture times are distributed $\mathrm{Exp}(\mu)$. But then the server is idle for $\mathrm{Exp}(\lambda)$ time, so the time until the following departure is $\mathrm{Exp}(\lambda) + \mathrm{Exp}(\mu)$. It is not obvious then why this should result in a departure process with $\mathrm{Exp}(\lambda)$ interdeparture times.

Part (2) of the theorem says that the number of jobs in the system at any time does not depend on the previous departure times or patterns. For example, knowing that there was recently a stream of closely spaced departures does not indicate that the number of jobs in the system currently is below average.

Proof

1. Observe that the departures in the forwards process occur at points of arrivals in the reverse process (see Figure 16.5). Now consider the points of arrivals in the reverse process. Because the M/M/1 is time-reversible, the reverse process is statistically identical to the forwards process by Claim 16.4. Thus the points of arrivals in the reverse process constitute a Poisson process with rate λ. So (by our previous observation) the points of departures in the forwards process also constitute a Poisson process with rate λ.

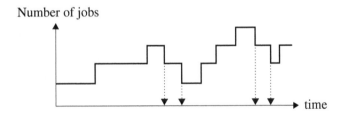

Figure 16.5. Departures in forwards process are arrivals in reverse process.

2. The sequence of departure times *prior* to time t in the forwards process is exactly the sequence of arrival times *after* time t in the reverse process. However, the future arrival pattern for the reverse process does not depend on the number of jobs at time t, because this process is a Poisson process. Therefore, looking at the forwards process, the number of jobs at time t is independent of the sequence of departures prior to time t. ∎

The claims in Burke's theorem also hold for an M/M/k system. The proofs are exactly the same.

Question: Give an example of a queueing network for which part (2) of Burke's theorem does *not* hold.

Answer: Consider a single-server network, where arrivals occur exactly at times 0, 2, 4, 6, . . . Suppose the service time is $U(0,2)$ (i.e., Uniformly distributed between 0 and 2). Let $N(t)$ be the number of jobs in the system at time t. Then $N(1)$ is either 0 or 1 and specifically depends on whether there was a departure during $(0,1)$.

16.4 An Alternative (Partial) Proof of Burke's Theorem

Having taught this material for many years, I have found that there are always some students who remain unconvinced about the first part of Burke's theorem, namely that the interdeparture times are distributed $\text{Exp}(\lambda)$. These students argue that the interdeparture times are either $\text{Exp}(\mu)$ (when the server is busy) or are of the form of $\text{Exp}(\lambda) + \text{Exp}(\mu)$ (when the server is idle); the term $\text{Exp}(\lambda) + \text{Exp}(\mu)$ comes from having to wait for an arrival and then to wait for that arrival to depart. It is not at all clear why having interdeparture times switch between these modes should form a Poisson(λ) departure process. This paradox is shown in Figure 16.6.

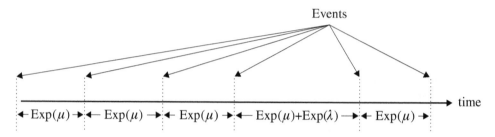

Figure 16.6. Interdeparture times in M/M/1.

For these frustrated students, I offer the following alternative explanation.

First observe that, for an M/M/1, the probability that a departure leaves behind a busy system is ρ, and the probability that a departure leaves behind an idle system is $1 - \rho$.

Question: Why is this?

Answer: As explained in Section 13.3, by PASTA, $a_n = p_n$, $\forall n$, implying that the probability that an arrival finds the system busy is the time-average fraction of time that the system is busy, namely ρ. However, for any ergodic system, $a_n = d_n$, so $d_n = p_n$, $\forall n$; hence the probability that a departure leaves behind a busy system is ρ.

Now, let's suppose that a departure just happened. We are interested in the quantity T, which is the time until the next departure. We would like to prove that $T \sim \text{Exp}(\lambda)$. Now, when the departure leaves, with probability ρ, it leaves behind a busy system, so $T \sim \text{Exp}(\mu)$, and with probability $1 - \rho$, it leaves behind an idle system, so $T \sim \text{Exp}(\lambda) + \text{Exp}(\mu)$.

Thus,

$$T \sim \begin{cases} \text{Exp}(\mu) & \text{w.p. } \rho \\ \text{Exp}(\mu) + \text{Exp}(\lambda) & \text{w.p. } 1 - \rho \end{cases}.$$

Question: Does the distribution of T look Exponential?

Answer: It does not seem so, but here is the argument. By conditioning on the value, t, of $\text{Exp}(\lambda)$,

$$\mathbf{P}\{T > x\} = \rho e^{-\mu x} + (1-\rho)\left(\int_{t=0}^{x} e^{-\mu(x-t)}\lambda e^{-\lambda t}dt + \int_{t=x}^{\infty} 1 \cdot \lambda e^{-\lambda t}dt\right)$$

$$= \rho e^{-\mu x} + (1-\rho)e^{-\mu x}\lambda \int_{t=0}^{x} e^{(\mu-\lambda)t}dt + (1-\rho)e^{-\lambda x}$$

$$= e^{-\mu x}\left(\rho + \frac{(1-\rho)\lambda\left(e^{(\mu-\lambda)x} - 1\right)}{\mu - \lambda} + (1-\rho)e^{(\mu-\lambda)x}\right)$$

$$= e^{-\mu x}\left(\rho + \rho e^{(\mu-\lambda)x} - \rho + (1-\rho)e^{(\mu-\lambda)x}\right)$$

$$= e^{-\mu x}\left(e^{(\mu-\lambda)x}\right)$$

$$= e^{-\lambda x}.$$

Hence the time between departures is in fact Exponentially distributed with rate λ.

Note that this proof is only a partial proof, compared with the proof in Section 16.3, because it does not argue *independence* of the interarrival times. Nonetheless it does shed some insight onto how the $\text{Exp}(\lambda)$ interdeparture times come about.

16.5 Application: Tandem Servers

We will now see how to apply Burke's theorem to obtain formulas that allow us to instantly analyze a large class of queueing networks. We start with a simple tandem system. We want to find the limiting probabilities of the tandem system, shown in Figure 16.7.

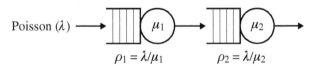

Figure 16.7. Tandem queues.

We can try to model the system by drawing the CTMC and solving the associated balance equations. We end up with an infinite-state CTMC, where each state is a pair (n_1, n_2) denoting the number of jobs at server 1 and the number at server 2. A piece of the CTMC is shown in Figure 16.8.

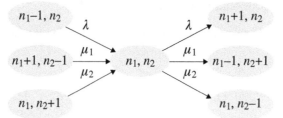

Figure 16.8. Portion of CTMC, assuming $n_1, n_2 \geq 1$.

The corresponding balance equations when $n_1 \geq 1$ and $n_2 \geq 1$ take the following form:

$$\pi_{n_1,n_2}(\lambda + \mu_1 + \mu_2) = \pi_{n_1-1,n_2} \cdot \lambda + \pi_{n_1+1,n_2-1} \cdot \mu_1 + \pi_{n_1,n_2+1} \cdot \mu_2$$

These balance equations look hard to solve.

On the other hand, we can apply Burke's theorem to find the solution to Figure 16.7 very easily. By part (1) of Burke's theorem, we know that the arrival stream into server 2 is Poisson(λ). If we view the two servers in isolation, they are both M/M/1 systems with arrival rates λ. Therefore,

$$\mathbf{P}\{n_1 \text{ jobs at server 1}\} = \rho_1^{n_1}(1 - \rho_1).$$
$$\mathbf{P}\{n_2 \text{ jobs at server 2}\} = \rho_2^{n_2}(1 - \rho_2).$$

Next, we show that the numbers of jobs at the two servers are independent. Let $N_1(t)$ denote the number of jobs at server 1 at time t. Let $N_2(t)$ denote the number of jobs at server 2 at time t. By part (2) of Burke's theorem, the sequence of departures from server 1 prior to time t is independent of $N_1(t)$. Because departures from server 1 are arrivals into server 2, we see that the sequence of arrivals into server 2 prior to time t is independent of $N_1(t)$. But $N_2(t)$ is completely determined by the sequence of arrivals into server 2 prior to time t. Therefore $N_2(t)$ is independent of $N_1(t)$ for all t.

Using these results, we can determine the limiting probabilities:

$$
\begin{aligned}
\pi_{n_1,n_2} &= \lim_{t\to\infty} \mathbf{P}\{N_1(t) = n_1 \quad \text{and} \quad N_2(t) = n_2\} \\
&= \lim_{t\to\infty} \mathbf{P}\{N_1(t) = n_1\} \cdot \mathbf{P}\{N_2(t) = n_2\} \\
&= \lim_{t\to\infty} \mathbf{P}\{N_1(t) = n_1\} \cdot \lim_{t\to\infty} \mathbf{P}\{N_2(t) = n_2\} \\
&= \mathbf{P}\{n_1 \text{ at server 1}\} \cdot \mathbf{P}\{n_2 \text{ at server 2}\} \\
&= \rho_1^{n_1}(1 - \rho_1)\rho_2^{n_2}(1 - \rho_2)
\end{aligned}
$$

To check our answer, we can substitute our expression for π_{n_1,n_2} back into the balance equations:

$$\pi_{n_1,n_2}(\lambda + \mu_1 + \mu_2) = \pi_{n_1-1,n_2}\lambda + \pi_{n_1+1,n_2-1}\mu_1 + \pi_{n_1,n_2+1}\mu_2$$

Try plugging it in... you will see it works. This therefore provides a second *proof* for why the number of jobs at server 1 and the number of jobs at server 2 are independent.

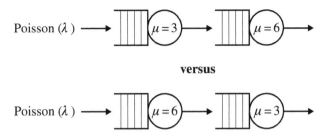

Figure 16.9. *Which of these is better?*

Question: Which of the systems in Figure 16.9 has better performance?

Answer: Both have the same performance. For both systems,

$$\mathbf{E}\left[N\right] = \mathbf{E}\left[N_1\right] + \mathbf{E}\left[N_2\right] = \frac{\rho_1}{1 - \rho_1} + \frac{\rho_2}{1 - \rho_2},$$

where $\rho_1 = \frac{\lambda}{3}$ and $\rho_2 = \frac{\lambda}{6}$.

16.6 General Acyclic Networks with Probabilistic Routing

Now consider any **acyclic** network of servers with probabilistic routing, as shown in Figure 16.10.

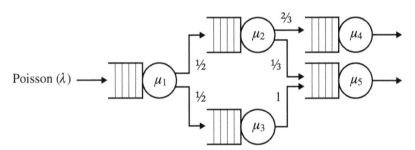

Figure 16.10. An acyclic network of servers.

Burke's theorem (Theorem 16.5) can be applied to find the limiting probabilities here in the same way as we applied Burke's theorem to the tandem system.

By part (1) of Burke's theorem, we see that, for each server, the arrival process into the server is a (merged and/or split) Poisson process. So each server, in isolation, can be viewed as an M/M/1 queue. Using part (2) of Burke's theorem and the same argument as for tandem queues, we can show that the numbers of jobs at the different servers are independent. Thus, assuming k servers we have

$$\pi_{n_1,n_2,\ldots,n_k} = \mathbf{P}\left\{n_1 \text{ jobs at server 1}\right\} \cdot \mathbf{P}\left\{n_2 \text{ jobs at server 2}\right\} \cdots \mathbf{P}\left\{n_k \text{ jobs at server } k\right\}$$
$$= \rho_1^{n_1}\left(1 - \rho_1\right) \cdot \rho_2^{n_2}\left(1 - \rho_2\right) \cdots \rho_k^{n_k}\left(1 - \rho_k\right).$$

Question: What is $\mathbf{P}\left\{N_1 = n_1\right\}$ in such an acyclic network with k servers?

Answer:

$$P\{N_1 = n_1\} = \sum_{n_2, n_3, \ldots, n_k} \pi_{n_1, n_2, \ldots, n_k}$$

$$= \sum_{n_2, n_3, \ldots, n_k} \rho_1^{n_1}(1 - \rho_1)\rho_2^{n_2}(1 - \rho_2) \cdots \rho_k^{n_k}(1 - \rho_k)$$

$$= \rho_1^{n_1}(1 - \rho_1).$$

16.7 Readings

With respect to the sections on the reverse chain and on time-reversibility, we highly recommend the following readings: [149] (Ch. 5, Section 6), and [18] (pp. 214–21). Burke's theorem was originally presented in [34].

16.8 Exercises

16.1 Practice with Finite-State Chains: Closed System Performance

For the closed interactive network in Figure 16.11, there are $N = 3$ users, think time is $Z \sim \text{Exp}(\lambda = 1)$, service time is $S \sim \text{Exp}(\mu = 2)$, and routing probabilities are as shown. For this network compute

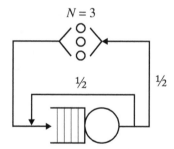

Figure 16.11. Closed queueing network from Exercise 16.1.

(a) the exact throughput, X.

(b) the exact mean response time, $\mathbf{E}[R]$, not including think time.

(c) the asymptotic throughput for high N using operational analysis from Chapter 7.

16.2 More Closed System Performance

For the closed interactive network in Figure 16.12, there are $N = 4$ users, think time is $Z \sim \text{Exp}(\lambda = 2)$, service time is $S \sim \text{Exp}(\mu = 4)$, and routing probabilities are as shown.

(a) Use operational laws to approximate throughput, X.

(b) Derive the exact throughput, X.

(c) Derive the exact mean response time, $\mathbf{E}[R]$, not including think time.

(d) What is the mean number of users that are thinking?

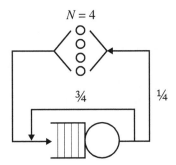

Figure 16.12. Closed queueing network from Exercise 16.2.

16.3 Chip Manufacturing Plant

At a chip manufacturing plant, wafers arrive according to a Poisson process with rate $\lambda = 1$. The wafers pass through three stations: a photoresist coating station, a circuit imprinting station, and an alkaline rinse station. Each station consists of two identical workers serving a single queue, as shown in Figure 16.13. For the purpose of this problem, assume that all service times are Exponentially distributed and that the service rate at station i is $\mu_i = i$, for $i = 1, 2, 3$. Derive the mean time from when a wafer arrives until a chip is created.

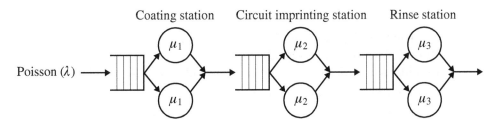

Figure 16.13. Sequence of M/M/2 stations in chip manufacturing.

16.4 Application of Square-Root Staffing to Chip Manufacturing

Figure 16.14 shows the 3 stations that wafers pass through in a chip manufacturing plant: a photoresist coating station, a circuit imprinting station, and an alkaline rinse station. Assume that all service times are Exponentially

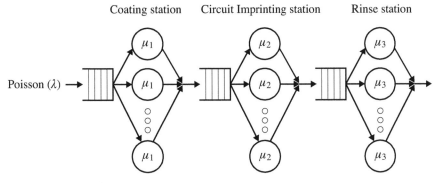

Figure 16.14. Sequence of stations in chip manufacturing.

distributed with rates shown, where $\mu_i = i$. Assume that wafers arrive according to a Poisson process with rate $\lambda = 10,000$ wafers per second. Use the square-root staffing rule from Chapter 15 to determine the minimum number of servers, k^*, needed at each station such that at every station fewer than 20% of wafers experience any delay.

16.5 Alternative Views of Time-Reversibility

Time-reversible chains have many beautiful properties. In this problem you will prove two of these.

(a) Prove that for any time-reversible CTMC, for any finite subset of states, S, the product of the transition rates along any cycle involving states in S equals the product of the transition rates along the same cycle in reverse order. Specifically, for any states $j_1, j_2, \ldots, j_n \in S$:

$$q_{j_1,j_2} \cdot q_{j_2,j_3} \cdot q_{j_3,j_4} \cdots q_{j_{n-1},j_n} \cdot q_{j_n,j_1}$$
$$= q_{j_1,j_n} \cdot q_{j_n,j_{n-1}} \cdot q_{j_{n-1},j_{n-2}} \cdots q_{j_2,j_1}.$$

(b) Prove that for a time-reversible CTMC, the rate of traversing any path equals the rate of traversing the same path in the reverse direction. Specifically, for any state j and any states $j_1, j_2, \ldots, j_n \in S$:

$$\pi_j \cdot q_{j,j_n} \cdot q_{j_n,j_{n-1}} \cdot q_{j_{n-1},j_{n-2}} \cdots q_{j_2,j_1}$$
$$= \pi_{j_1} \cdot q_{j_1,j_2} \cdot q_{j_2,j_3} \cdots q_{j_{n-1},j_n} \cdot q_{j_n,j}.$$

[Hint: Part (a) may be useful in proving this.]

16.6 Burke's Theorem for Finite Queues?

Consider the M/M/1/k single-server queue with finite capacity of k.

(a) Is this Markov chain time-reversible?

(b) Can we apply the proof of Burke's theorem to say that the departure process is a Poisson process? Explain.

CHAPTER 17

Networks of Queues and Jackson Product Form

We are now ready to consider a very general architecture called the "network of queues." This architecture allows for any number of servers, each with its own (unbounded) queue, and probabilistic routing between the servers. The architecture allows for cycles in the network and is very useful in modeling packet-routing computer networks or networks of manufacturing stations.

In this chapter, we consider the simplest such network of queues, called the *Jackson network*. In later chapters, we consider fancier versions. For example, in Chapter 18, the routing probabilities are allowed to depend on the "class" of the packets, which makes it even more applicable to packet-routing in the Internet. The point of this chapter is to prove the Jackson Product Form theorem, which provides us with an immediate simple closed-form solution for the limiting probabilities of any Jackson network.

17.1 Jackson Network Definition

A Jackson network is a very general form of queueing network. In a Jackson network, there are k servers, each with its own (unbounded) queue. Jobs at a server are served in FCFS order. The ith server has service rate $\text{Exp}(\mu_i)$. Each server may receive arrivals from *inside* and *outside* the network. The arrivals into the ith server from outside the network constitute a Poisson process with rate r_i. The routing of jobs is probabilistic. Specifically, every job that completes at server i will be transferred to server j with probability P_{ij}, or will exit the system with probability $P_{i,\text{out}} = 1 - \sum_j P_{ij}$. Figure 17.1 shows the general setup of a Jackson network.

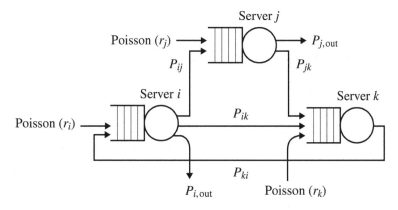

Figure 17.1. A simple Jackson network.

The **response time** of a job is defined as the time from when the job arrives to the network until it leaves the network, including possibly visiting the same server or different servers multiple times.

For each server i, we denote the *total* arrival rate into server i by λ_i.

Question: What is the total rate at which jobs leave server j?

Answer: λ_j is both the total rate at which jobs enter server j and at which they leave server j.

Question: What is the total rate at which jobs leave server j, going to server i?

Answer: $\lambda_j P_{ji}$.

The total arrival rate into server i is the sum of the *outside arrival rate* (rate of jobs arriving to server i from outside the network) and the *inside arrival rate* (rate of jobs arriving to server i from inside the network):

$$\underbrace{\lambda_i}_{\text{total arrival}} = \underbrace{r_i}_{\text{outside arrival}} + \underbrace{\sum_j \lambda_j P_{ji}}_{\text{internal transition}} . \qquad (17.1)$$

We can solve these simultaneous equations to obtain all the λ_i's. Equivalently, we can write

$$\underbrace{\lambda_i(1 - P_{ii})}_{\text{total arrival}} = \underbrace{r_i}_{\text{outside arrival}} + \underbrace{\sum_{j \neq i} \lambda_j P_{ji}}_{\text{internal transition}} \qquad (17.2)$$

where (17.2) is identical to (17.1), except that on both sides we are not including transitions from server i back to server i.

Note: **Be careful not to confuse servers with states.** Right now we are only talking about servers.

17.2 The Arrival Process into Each Server

At this point we see how to compute λ_i, the total arrival rate into server i. If we knew that the arrival process into each server was a Poisson process, then we could view each server as an M/M/1 queue and determine the distribution of the number of jobs at that server. This is the approach that we followed in the last chapter for acyclic networks.

Question: For acyclic networks, we saw that the arrival process into each server is a Poisson process. Can we still say that the arrival process into each server is a Poisson process if the network is not acyclic?

More specifically, consider the network in Figure 17.2. Here the output of a server feeds back into the same server. Is the arrival process into the server in Figure 17.2 a Poisson process?

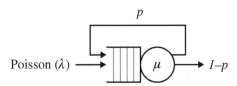

Figure 17.2. Network with feedback.

Answer: At first one might think the answer is yes. Here is the WRONG argument: We start with an M/M/1 with Poisson arrivals of rate λ. The departures of an M/M/1 are also a Poisson process of rate λ by Burke's theorem. Some fraction, $1 - p$ of those departures leaves, and the remaining fraction, p, gets fed back. This portion that gets fed back is also a Poisson process (by Poisson splitting) of rate λp. This gets merged with the outside arrival process, which is a Poisson process, and we know that the merge of two Poisson processes is still a Poisson process. Hence the total arrival process into the queue is a Poisson process.

Unfortunately, the above answer is wrong. To see this, consider the network in Figure 17.3.

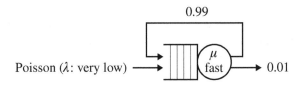

Figure 17.3. Illustrating why we do not see Poisson arrivals.

Suppose that the arrival rate, λ, is very low, so that the time between arrivals is typically very high. Now suppose there is an arrival at the server at time t. Then with high probability there will be another arrival to the server shortly. That is, it is much more likely that there is an arrival during $(t, t + \epsilon)$ than during some other ϵ-interval. Thus the arrival process into server i does not have independent increments. So it is not a Poisson process.

Question: What was wrong with the argument that said we were merging two Poisson processes and therefore should get a Poisson process?

Answer: The two Poisson processes that we were merging were not *independent* Poisson processes; therefore their merge was not a Poisson process.

Because the arrival process into this server is not a Poisson process, we cannot use the simplifications we used for solving tandem queues, where each server becomes an independent M/M/1.

17.3 Solving the Jackson Network

So let's go back to modeling the network with a CTMC and trying to solve the balance equations. The states of the network can be defined as a set of k-tuples

$$(n_1, n_2, \ldots, n_k),$$

in which the jth element in the tuple represents the number of jobs at server j (including both the queue and the server). We need to write the balance equation for each state. Remember the balance equation for each state is

Rate of jobs leaving the state = Rate entering the state.

Suppose the system is in state $(n_1, n_2, \ldots, n_k)$. To simplify the writing of balance equations, we will assume throughout the chapter that $n_i > 0$, $\forall i$. The case where some states have 0 jobs is left as an exercise.

The CTMC leaves state $(n_1, n_2, \ldots, n_k)$ when there is either (i) an outside arrival, or (ii) a service completion at any of the servers. Observe that both of these events happen with Exponential rates. The rate of transitions leaving the state $(n_1, n_2, \ldots, n_k)$ (and not returning to the state) is

$$\pi_{n_1, n_2, \ldots, n_k} \cdot \left[\sum_{i=1}^{k} r_i + \sum_{i=1}^{k} \mu_i (1 - P_{ii}) \right].$$

Now consider the rate at which the CTMC enters the state $(n_1, n_2, \ldots, n_k)$ (from some other state). State $(n_1, n_2, \ldots, n_k)$ is entered at moments where (i) there is an outside arrival, or (ii) there is a departure to outside, or (iii) there is an internal transition. Again these are Exponential rates. The rate of transitions entering the state is

$$\underbrace{\sum_{i=1}^{k} \pi_{n_1, \ldots, n_i - 1, \ldots, n_k} \cdot r_i}_{\text{outside arrival}} + \underbrace{\sum_{i=1}^{k} \pi_{n_1, \ldots, n_i + 1, \ldots, n_k} \cdot \mu_i P_{i,\text{out}}}_{\text{departure to outside}}$$

$$+ \quad \underbrace{\sum_{i=1}^{k} \sum_{j \neq i} \pi_{n_1, \ldots, n_i - 1, \ldots, n_j + 1, \ldots, n_k} \cdot \mu_j P_{ji}}_{\text{internal transition from server } j \text{ to server } i, \ j \neq i} \quad .$$

Therefore the balance equation for state $(n_1, \ldots, n_k)$ is

$$\pi_{n_1, n_2, \ldots, n_k} \cdot \left[\sum_{i=1}^{k} r_i + \sum_{i=1}^{k} \mu_i (1 - P_{ii}) \right]$$

$$= \sum_{i=1}^{k} \pi_{n_1, \ldots, n_i - 1, \ldots, n_k} \cdot r_i + \sum_{i=1}^{k} \pi_{n_1, \ldots, n_i + 1, \ldots, n_k} \cdot \mu_i P_{i,\text{out}}$$

$$+ \sum_{i=1}^{k} \sum_{j \neq i} \pi_{n_1, \ldots, n_i - 1, \ldots, n_j + 1, \ldots, n_k} \cdot \mu_j P_{ji}. \tag{17.3}$$

Of course (17.3) is the balance equation for just one particular state, $(n_1, \ldots, n_k)$. We need to write out the balance equation for *each* state.

Question: Why are there no λ_i's in the balance equation?

Answer: The *events* that change the state are only arrivals or service completions, all of which are Exponentially distributed. The λ_i's are not events; they denote average rates at which packets arrive and are thus used when discussing the network of *servers*, not the Markov chain with *states*.

Making a guess as to the limiting probabilities based on these complicated balance equations is impossible. Furthermore, it is going to get a lot messier in the next chapter when we move on to classed networks, where routing probabilities depend on class.

17.4 The Local Balance Approach

We need an approach to simplify the huge number of balance equations. Many popular books (e.g., [18, 149, 150]) at this point go into the "reverse chain argument." They try to guess what the reverse chain looks like and then use the limiting probabilities for the reverse chain. We do not want to take this approach because it is long and unintuitive, and how in the world can you start picturing what the reverse chain looks like when the forwards process is so complicated already?

Instead we are going to take a different approach based on the idea of **local balance**. This idea is not precisely defined and is just part of the "bag of tricks" that queueing theorists use. Although local balance is briefly mentioned in several texts (e.g., [151]), there is typically no algorithm provided for how to set up the local balance equations. That part is the "art," which is learned through trial and error. In the next few chapters, we will repeatedly show one particular way of using local balance that has worked very well for us when analyzing complex networks of queues.

The idea is to break down the left-hand side and right-hand side of the balance equation (17.3) into $k + 1$ matching components. If we can find a solution that maintains the equality for each matching component (local balance), then we know that it is a solution to the equation as a whole (global balance). Observe that satisfying local balance is a stronger condition than satisfying global balance. Because the local balance equations are so much simpler looking, it will be much easier to make a guess based on these equations and also to "check" that a guess satisfies these equations. Figure 17.4 shows the way to break down a balance equation into $k + 1$ distinct components. It is very important that you do it in *exactly this way*. There are many other ways of subdividing a balance equation that do not satisfy the local balance.

We want to find a solution that makes $A = A'$ and $B_i = B_i'$ true for all $1 \leq i \leq k$. Here A denotes the rate of leaving state $(n_1, n_2, \ldots, n_k)$ due to an outside arrival coming into the network. Here B_i denotes the rate of leaving state $(n_1, n_2, \ldots, n_k)$ due to a departure from server i. This departure may either go to some other server $j \neq i$ or may leave the network. Likewise A' denotes the rate of entering state $(n_1, n_2, \ldots, n_k)$

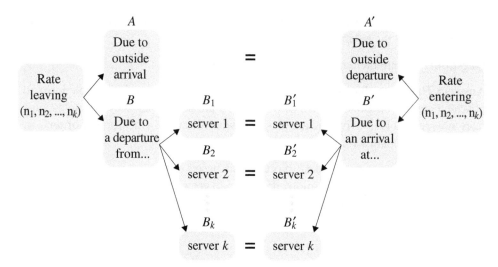

Figure 17.4. Local balance decomposition approach.

due to a job departing to outside the network. B_i' denotes the rate of entering state $(n_1, n_2, \ldots, n_k)$ due to an arrival at server i, where this arrival may either be coming from outside the network, or from another server $j \neq i$.

At this point we are not even sure whether a solution satisfying local balance exists. If we are lucky enough to find a solution that satisfies all the local balance equations, then we have global balance as well.

First we try to solve $A = A'$. To show $A = A'$, we need to show that

$$\sum_{i=1}^{k} \pi_{n_1, \ldots, n_i, \ldots, n_k} r_i = \sum_{i=1}^{k} \pi_{n_1, \ldots, n_i+1, \ldots, n_k} \mu_i P_{i,\text{out}}.$$

We need to make a guess for $\pi_{n_1, \ldots, n_k}$ and show that it satisfies this $A = A'$ equation. Here is how we come to our guess: Observe that the $\pi_{n_1, \ldots, n_i, \ldots, n_k}$ term in A and the $\pi_{n_1, \ldots, n_i+1, \ldots, n_k}$ term in A' only differ in the n_i spot. Let's suppose that

$$\pi_{n_1, \ldots, n_i, \ldots, n_k} \cdot c_i = \pi_{n_1, \ldots, n_i+1, \ldots, n_k},$$

where c_i is some constant depending on i.

Then rewriting the $A = A'$ equation, we have

$$\sum_{i=1}^{k} \pi_{n_1, \ldots, n_i, \ldots, n_k} r_i = \sum_{i=1}^{k} \pi_{n_1, \ldots, n_i+1, \ldots, n_k} \mu_i P_{i,\text{out}}.$$

$$\sum_{i=1}^{k} \pi_{n_1, \ldots, n_i, \ldots, n_k} r_i = \sum_{i=1}^{k} \pi_{n_1, \ldots, n_k} \cdot c_i \cdot \mu_i P_{i,\text{out}}.$$

$$\sum_{i=1}^{k} r_i = \sum_{i=1}^{k} (c_i \cdot \mu_i) P_{i,\text{out}}. \tag{17.4}$$

Question: Can you figure out what we would like c_i to be?

Answer: Observe that if

$$(c_i \cdot \mu_i) = \lambda_i,$$

then (17.4) is true because it would then say that

$$\sum_{i=1}^{k} r_i = \sum_{i=1}^{k} \lambda_i P_{i,\text{out}},$$

which simply says that the total rate of jobs entering the system from outside is the same as the total rate of jobs leaving the system (to go outside). This is obviously true in steady state.

Thus in our earlier guess, we want

$$c_i = \frac{\lambda_i}{\mu_i} = \rho_i.$$

Let's return to the process of making a guess for $\pi_{n_1,\ldots,n_k}$. We know that to satisfy $A = A'$ we would like to have

$$\pi_{n_1,\ldots,n_i,\ldots,n_k} \cdot \rho_i = \pi_{n_1,\ldots,n_i+1,\ldots,n_k}, \qquad \forall i.$$

Thus it seems a reasonable guess is that

$$\pi_{n_1,\ldots,n_i,\ldots,n_k} = C \rho_1^{n_1} \ldots \rho_k^{n_k},$$

where C is the usual normalizing constant.

Now we try to solve for $B_i = B_i'$. Here B_i is the rate of transitions leaving state $(n_1,\ldots,n_k)$ due to a departure from server i (not back to i), namely,

$$B_i = \pi_{n_1,\ldots,n_k} \cdot \mu_i (1 - P_{ii}).$$

B_i' is the rate of transitions entering $(n_1,\ldots,n_k)$ due to an arrival at server i. This includes outside arrivals into server i or internal arrivals from other servers. Therefore the expression for B_i' is

$$B_i' = \underbrace{\sum_{j \text{ s.t. } j \neq i} \pi_{n_1,\ldots,n_i-1,\ldots,n_j+1,\ldots,n_k} \cdot \mu_j P_{ji}}_{\text{internal transition from server } j \text{ to server } i \ (j \neq i)} + \underbrace{\pi_{n_1,\ldots,n_i-1,\ldots,n_k} \cdot r_i}_{\text{outside arrival}}.$$

Let's use our previous guess for $\pi_{n_1,\ldots,n_k}$ and check if it satisfies $B_i = B_i'$. Let

$$\pi_{n_1,\ldots,n_i,\ldots,n_k} = C \rho_1^{n_1} \rho_2^{n_2} \ldots \rho_k^{n_k}.$$

Now check that

$$B_i = B_i'$$

$$C\rho_1^{n_1}\rho_2^{n_2}\cdots\rho_k^{n_k}\mu_i(1-P_{ii}) = \sum_{j\neq i} C\rho_1^{n_1}\rho_2^{n_2}\cdots\rho_k^{n_k}\left(\frac{\rho_j}{\rho_i}\right)\mu_j P_{ji}$$

$$+ C\rho_1^{n_1}\rho_2^{n_2}\cdots\rho_k^{n_k}\left(\frac{1}{\rho_i}\right)r_i$$

$$\mu_i(1-P_{ii}) = \sum_{j\neq i}\frac{\rho_j\mu_j}{\rho_i}P_{ji} + \frac{r_i}{\rho_i}$$

$$\rho_i\mu_i(1-P_{ii}) = \sum_{j\neq i}\rho_j\mu_j P_{ji} + r_i$$

$$\lambda_i(1-P_{ii}) = \sum_{j\neq i}\lambda_j P_{ji} + r_i. \tag{17.5}$$

Question: Is Equation (17.5) true?

Answer: Yes, of course, this is exactly equation (17.2), the equation defining the outside arrival rates. So our guess for $\pi_{n_1,\ldots,n_k}$ also satisfies $B_i = B_i'$.

Lastly, we need to find the normalizing constant C:

$$\sum_{n_1,\ldots,n_k}\pi_{n_1,\ldots,n_k} = 1$$

$$C\sum_{n_1,\ldots,n_k}\rho_1^{n_1}\cdots\rho_k^{n_k} = 1$$

$$C\sum_{n_1}\rho_1^{n_1}\sum_{n_2}\rho_2^{n_2}\cdots\sum_{n_k}\rho_k^{n_k} = 1$$

$$C\left(\frac{1}{1-\rho_1}\right)\left(\frac{1}{1-\rho_2}\right)\cdots\left(\frac{1}{1-\rho_k}\right) = 1$$

Hence,

$$C = (1-\rho_1)(1-\rho_2)\cdots(1-\rho_k).$$

As a result,

$$\pi_{n_1,\ldots,n_k} = \rho_1^{n_1}(1-\rho_1)\rho_2^{n_2}(1-\rho_2)\cdots\rho_k^{n_k}(1-\rho_k). \tag{17.6}$$

This is an example of a **product form** solution for the limiting probabilities.

Question: What does the previous expression tell us about the distribution of the number of jobs at server 1?

Answer:

$$\mathbf{P}\{n_1 \text{ jobs at server } 1\} = \sum_{n_2,\ldots,n_k} \pi_{n_1,\ldots,n_k}$$

$$= \sum_{n_2,\ldots,n_k} \rho_1^{n_1}(1-\rho_1)\rho_2^{n_2}(1-\rho_2)\ldots\rho_k^{n_k}(1-\rho_k) = \rho_1^{n_1}(1-\rho_1).$$

Likewise,

$$\mathbf{P}\{n_i \text{ jobs at server } i\} = \rho_i^{n_i}(1-\rho_i).$$

That means all servers still behave like M/M/1 queues in terms of their stationary queue length distributions! This is really surprising because the arrival process into each server is *not* usually a Poisson process. Furthermore, by (17.6), the number of jobs at the different queues is *independent*. Specifically, we have now proven Theorem 17.1.

Theorem 17.1 *A Jackson network with k servers has product form, namely,*

$$\mathbf{P}\left\{\begin{array}{l} \text{State of network} \\ \text{is } (n_1, n_2, \ldots, n_k) \end{array}\right\} = \prod_{i=1}^{k} \mathbf{P}\{n_i \text{ jobs at server } i\} = \prod_{i=1}^{k} \rho_i^{n_i}(1-\rho_i).$$

Warning: So far, we have only proven product form for networks of queues that fit the Jackson model; that is, there is a probabilistic routing between servers, the outside arrivals are Poisson, the service times are Exponentially distributed, and jobs are served in FCFS order at each server.

Example: Web Server

Consider a web server that receives requests for files according to a Poisson arrival process, as shown in Figure 17.5. Each request requires alternating between the CPU and I/O some Geometrically distributed number of times as the file is segmented into packets and sent to the network.

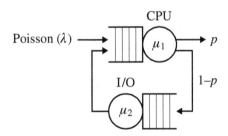

Figure 17.5. Example of a web server.

Question: What is π_{n_1,n_2} for Figure 17.5?

Answer: The system is a Jackson network. We first solve for λ_1 and λ_2:

$$\lambda_1 = \lambda + \lambda_2$$
$$\lambda_2 = (1-p)\lambda_1$$

Hence $\lambda_1 = \frac{\lambda}{p}$ and $\lambda_2 = \frac{\lambda}{p}(1-p)$. Thus,

$$\rho_1 = \frac{\lambda_1}{\mu_1} = \frac{\lambda}{p\mu_1}.$$

$$\rho_2 = \frac{\lambda_2}{\mu_2} = \frac{\lambda(1-p)}{p\mu_2}.$$

We can now substitute these values into

$$\pi_{n_1,n_2} = \rho_1^{n_1} \rho_2^{n_2} (1 - \rho_1)(1 - \rho_2).$$

Question: What is the average number of jobs in the system, $\mathbf{E}[N]$?

Answer:

$$\mathbf{P}\{n_1 \text{ jobs at server 1}\} = \rho_1^{n_1}(1 - \rho_1).$$

$$\mathbf{P}\{n_2 \text{ jobs at server 2}\} = \rho_2^{n_2}(1 - \rho_2).$$

$$\mathbf{E}[N_1] = \frac{\rho_1}{1-\rho_1}, \ \mathbf{E}[N_2] = \frac{\rho_2}{1-\rho_2}, \ \mathbf{E}[N] = \mathbf{E}[N_1] + \mathbf{E}[N_2].$$

17.5 Readings

Jackson networks and their product form solution were introduced in [102]. This paper was printed in Management Science's "Ten Most Influential Titles of *Management Science's* First Fifty Years."

17.6 Exercises

17.1 Practice Analyzing Jackson Networks

Figure 17.6 shows a queueing network with three FCFS servers. All servers have Exponentially distributed service times with rates as shown. Outside arrivals occur according to a Poisson process with rate $\lambda = 1$ packets/sec. The edges of the network indicate routing probabilities (assume 1 if none shown). What is the mean response time, $\mathbf{E}[T]$?

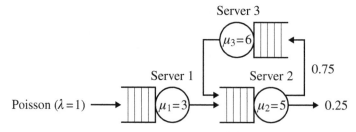

Figure 17.6. Queueing network from Exercise 17.1.

17.2 More Practice Analyzing Jackson Networks

A packet-switched Jackson network routes packets among two routers according to the routing probabilities shown in Figure 17.7. Notice that there are two points at which packets enter the network and two points at which they can depart.

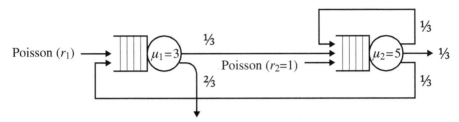

Figure 17.7. Jackson network from Exercise 17.2.

(a) What is the maximum allowable rate r_1 that the network can tolerate? Call this $r_1^{\max}$.

(b) Set $r_1 = 0.9 r_1^{\max}$. What is the mean response time for a packet entering at the router 1 queue?

17.3 Queue with Feedback

Figure 17.8 shows a simple queueing network. Jobs arrive according to a Poisson process with rate λ. When a job completes service, the job goes back into the queue with probability p and leaves the system with probability $1 - p$. Thus a single job may serve multiple times before leaving the system. Each time the job serves, its service time is a new Exponentially distributed random variable with rate μ.

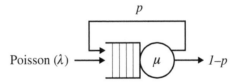

Figure 17.8. Network with feedback from Exercise 17.3.

Your goal is to derive the mean response time for a job in up to four different ways. A job's response time is the time from when the job first arrives until it finally leaves, including possibly multiple visits to the queue.

(1) To start, use the theory of Jackson networks from this chapter to derive an expression for the mean response time in terms of λ, μ, and p.

(2) Now again derive the mean response time, but this time do it by solving a CTMC that tracks the number of jobs in the system (draw only transitions that *change* the state).

(3) Tinglong makes the following suggestion: Why not view the whole network as a single M/M/1 where the arrival rate is $\hat{\lambda} = \frac{\lambda}{1-p}$ and the service rate is μ. Does Tinglong's solution result in the correct mean response time? Why or why not?

(4) Runting makes a different suggestion: Let $\mathbf{E}\left[T_{\text{visit}}\right]$ be the mean response time experienced by jobs during one visit to the server (including queueing plus service time). Then $\mathbf{E}\left[T\right] = \mathbf{E}\left[T_{\text{visit}}\right] \cdot \mathbf{E}\left[\text{Number visits}\right]$. Does Runting's suggestion work? Why or why not?

17.4 Network with Feedback

For the Jackson network in Figure 17.9, assume that $0 < p < q < 1$ and assume that r is chosen so as to not overload the network. Answer the following questions:

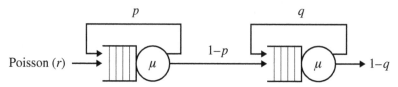

Figure 17.9. Network for Exercise 17.4.

(a) Determine the mean response time, $\mathbf{E}\left[T\right]$, as a function of r, μ, p, and q.

(b) If we interchange the order of the queues (i.e., the p and q are flipped), does $\mathbf{E}\left[T\right]$ increase, decrease, or stay the same?

17.5 Supercomputing Center

(This result was originally proved in [7].) In a supercomputing center, arriving jobs are parallel, typically running on several servers at once, as shown in Figure 17.10. Consider a supercomputing center with k servers and no waiting room, where outside arrivals occur according to a Poisson process with rate λ (think M/M/k/k). Assume that with probability p_i an arriving job is of "type i," which means that the job requires i servers simultaneously. If there are fewer than i servers free, the type i job is dropped. Otherwise the type i job grabs the i servers that it needs and holds these for $\text{Exp}(\mu_i)$ time, after which it releases all i servers at once.

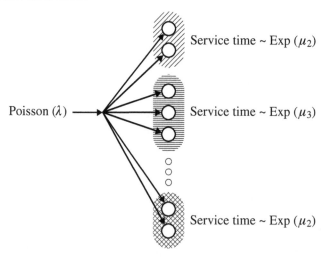

Figure 17.10. Supercomputing center with two jobs of type 2 and one job of type 3.

Let $(n_1, n_2, \ldots, n_k)$ be the state of the system, where n_i is the number of jobs of type i. Prove that

$$\pi_{n_1, n_2, \ldots, n_k} = \prod_{i=1}^{k} \frac{\rho_i^{n_i}}{n_i!} \cdot C,$$

where $\rho_i = \frac{\lambda_i}{\mu_i}$ and $\lambda_i = \lambda p_i$ and C is a normalizing constant.

17.6 Cloud Service Center

(This result was originally proved in [187].) A cloud service center consists of two server farms. The first server farm has CPU-powerful servers, and the second has I/O-powerful servers. Each incoming request (job) to the cloud service center asks for some number of CPU servers, i, and some number of I/O servers, j. Requests occur according to a Poisson process with rate λ, where a request is of type (i, j) with probability p_{ij}. If there are fewer than i free CPU servers or fewer than j free I/O servers, then a request of type (i, j) will be dropped. Otherwise, the request will grab all its requested servers and will hold these for time $\text{Exp}(\mu_{ij})$, after which it will release all the servers at once. This is illustrated in Figure 17.11.

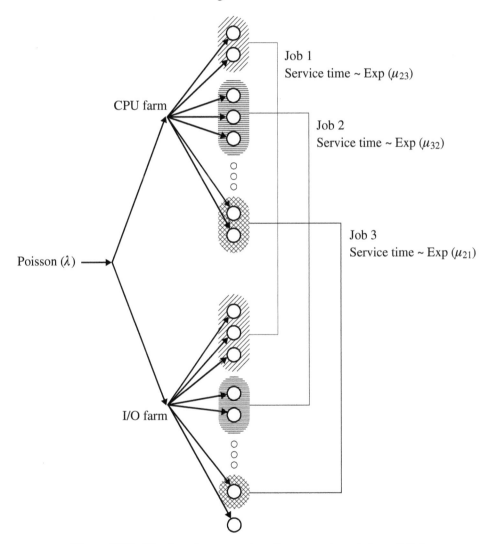

Figure 17.11. Cloud service center where three requests are being satisfied.

Let $(n_{11}, n_{12}, \ldots, n_{1k}, n_{21}, n_{22}, \ldots, n_{2k}, \ldots, n_{k1}, n_{k2}, \ldots, n_{kk})$ denote the state of the system, where n_{ij} is the number of jobs of type (i, j) in the system.

Prove that

$$\pi_{n_{11},n_{12},n_{13},\ldots,n_{kk}} = \prod_{i=1}^{k}\prod_{j=1}^{k}\frac{\rho_{ij}^{n_{ij}}}{n_{ij}!}\cdot C,$$

where $\rho_{ij} = \frac{\lambda_{ij}}{\mu_{ij}}$ and $\lambda_{ij} = \lambda p_{ij}$ and C is a normalizing constant.

CHAPTER 18

Classed Network of Queues

18.1 Overview

Throughout this chapter, when talking about a queueing network, we will use the vector,

$$(n_1, n_2, \ldots, n_k),$$

to denote that there are n_1 jobs at server 1 and n_2 jobs at server 2 and so on.

In the previous chapter, we saw that Jackson networks exhibit the "product form" property:

$$\mathbf{P}\left\{\begin{array}{c}\text{Distribution of jobs is} \\ (n_1, n_2, \ldots, n_k)\end{array}\right\} = \prod_{i=1}^{k}\mathbf{P}\left\{n_i \text{ jobs at server } i\right\} = \prod_{i=1}^{k}\rho_i^{n_i}(1-\rho_i)$$

The first equality represents the fact that the queues behave in an independent fashion. The second equality says that we can consider all the queues to behave as independent M/M/1 queues from a performance standpoint (although the arrival stream into each server is not actually Poisson).

In the next several chapters, as well as in the exercises at the end of this chapter, we will generalize the Jackson result to a much broader class of networks that exhibit product form. For example, we find in Chapter 19 that product form holds for *closed* Jackson networks as well as open Jackson networks (for closed networks, the product form requires a normalizing constant). We also find in that chapter's exercises that product form holds for Jackson-type networks where the service rate is allowed to depend on the number of jobs at the server; see Exercise 19.3. These are called *load-dependent* servers. In particular, each server could be an M/M/k station. We furthermore find that we can allow the routing probabilities, P_{ij}, (here i, j are servers, not states) to depend not just on i, j but also on the "class" of the packet or job. Such networks are called **classed networks** and are the topic of the current chapter. Finally, in Chapter 22, we prove product form results for networks of queues where the scheduling policy at the queues is no longer FCFS. Throughout, we use the method of local balance.

18.2 Motivation for Classed Networks

We provide three examples motivating the need for classed networks.

Motivating Example 1: Connection-Oriented Networks

Consider a network where each packet follows a particular route based on its type. A packet's type might, for example, be the concatenation of its source IP address and its destination IP address. For example, in the network shown in Figure 18.1 and the routes shown in Figure 18.2, type 1 packets always follow "route 1," meaning that they go to server 1, then server 2, then server 3. Type 2 packets always follow "route 2," meaning that they first go to server 3, then to server 2, then to server 4, then to server 5.

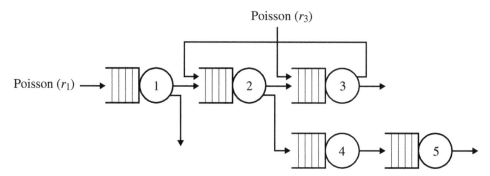

Figure 18.1. The network.

Assume we know the average outside arrival rate of packets along each route. A typical goal in such an example might be to determine $\mathbf{E}[T]$ for packets on route 2.

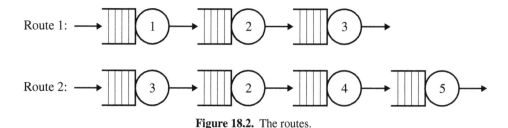

Figure 18.2. The routes.

Question: Why can't we model this network as a Jackson network?

Answer: The probability of going from server 2 to server 3 depends on the route. If the packet is of type 1, then the packet leaving server 2 always goes to server 3. However, if the packet is of type 2, then the packet leaving server 2 never goes to server 3.

So we would like the routing probability to be able to depend on the *type* of the packet.

Motivating Example 2: CPU-Bound and I/O-Bound Jobs

Consider a computer system with two different workloads. Suppose that *I/O-bound* jobs have a high probability of visiting the I/O device and a low probability of visiting the CPU. In contrast, *CPU-bound* jobs have a high probability of visiting the CPU and a low probability of visiting the I/O device.

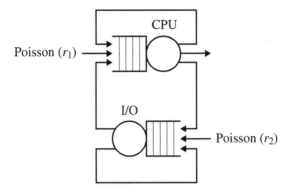

We need different routing probabilities for the CPU-bound and I/O-bound jobs.

Motivating Example 3: Service Facility with Repair Center

Jobs repeatedly visit some service facility. After each visit, with low probability the job needs to go to the repair center. If a job ever visits the repair center, it gets repaired and returns to the service facility; however, from then onward, there is a high probability that this job will have to go to the repair center again.

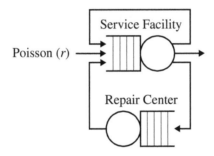

So again we want the routing probability to depend on the "type" of job. We would like to differentiate between two types of jobs: "good" and "bad." Good jobs have never visited the repair center, whereas bad jobs have visited the repair center.

Question: What else do we need?

Answer: We need to be able to change a job's type from "good" to "bad" once it visits the repair center.

Summary

In general, we would like our model to accommodate the following:

1. The outside arrival rate at server i, $r_i(c)$, should depend on the job class c.
2. The routing probabilities for moving from server i to server j should be allowed to depend on the job class c.
3. Jobs should be allowed to change classes after service.

To accommodate items (2.) and (3.), we use $P_{ij}^{(c_1)(c_2)}$ to denote the probability that a job of class c_1 at server i next moves to server j and changes class to c_2.

18.3 Notation and Modeling for Classed Jackson Networks

In this section we define **classed Jackson networks**. We assume an open queueing network with k servers and ℓ classes of packets. We define the following quantities:

$$r_i = \text{arrival rate to server } i \text{ from outside the network}$$

$$r_i(c) = \text{arrival rate of class } c \text{ jobs to server } i \text{ from outside the network}$$

$$\lambda_i = \text{total arrival rate to server } i, \text{ from both inside and outside}$$

$$= \text{total departure rate from server } i$$

$$\lambda_i(c) = \text{total arrival rate of class } c \text{ jobs to server } i$$

$$= \text{total departure rate of class } c \text{ jobs from server } i$$

$$P_{ij}^{(c)(c')} = \text{probability that job at server } i \text{ of class } c \text{ next moves to server } j \text{ and}$$

$$\text{becomes a class } c' \text{ job}$$

$$\mu_i = \text{service rate at server } i$$

$$\rho_i = \frac{\lambda_i}{\mu_i} = \text{utilization at server } i$$

$$c_i^{(j)} = \text{the class of the } j\text{th job in the queue at server } i$$

Observe that

$$r_i = \sum_{c=1}^{\ell} r_i(c).$$

$$\lambda_i = \sum_{c=1}^{\ell} \lambda_i(c).$$

Remark: It is important to note that, although the class of a packet determines the routing probability, it *does not* determine the service rate at a server. The service rate at server i is assumed to be μ_i for all packets. Although this is a drawback of the classed Jackson model, it is not as limiting as it may seem in that the routing probability can be used to force a certain class of packets to visit a server multiple times on average, thereby in effect creating a greater "service demand" at the server for that class.

Typically, we are given the outside arrival rates, $r_i(c)$, the per-class routing probabilities, $P_{ij}^{(c)(c')}$, and the service rates, μ_i, for all i, j, c, c', and we are asked to determine some metric like $\mathbf{E}[N_i]$, the mean number of jobs at server i.

Question: Can we solve for λ_j, the total arrival rate into server j, directly?

Answer: No. Here is an attempt:

$$\lambda_j = r_j + \sum_{i=1}^{k} \lambda_i P_{ij},$$

but P_{ij} is not defined.

However, we can compute $\lambda_j(c)$, the arrival rate of class c jobs into server j. It is determined by solving the following system of simultaneous equations:

$$\lambda_j(c) = r_j(c) + \sum_{i=1}^{k} \sum_{c'=1}^{\ell} \lambda_i(c') P_{ij}^{(c')(c)} \tag{18.1}$$

Then we get λ_j by summing the per-class rates as follows:

$$\lambda_j = \sum_{c=1}^{\ell} \lambda_j(c)$$

Question: We need to be able to derive limiting probabilities. What should the "states" of the CTMC look like?

Hint: What's wrong with using $(n_1, n_2, \ldots, n_k)$ where n_i denotes the number of jobs at server i?

Answer: This is not detailed enough information for our CTMC because, to know the probability of moving between states, we need to at least know the class of the job at the head of the queue at each server.

We define the *state* of the network to be

$$z = (z_1, z_2, \ldots, z_k),$$

where z_i is the state of server i. Specifically,

$$z_i = \left(c_i^{(1)}, c_i^{(2)}, \ldots, c_i^{(n_i)} \right),$$

where n_i denotes the number of packets at server i, and $c_i^{(1)}$ denotes the class of the 1st job at server i (the one serving), $c_i^{(2)}$ denotes the class of the 2nd job at server i, and $c_i^{(n_i)}$ denotes the class of the last job queued at server i.

Thus,

$$
\begin{aligned}
z &= (z_1, z_2, \ldots, z_k) \\
&= \left(\left(c_1^{(1)}, c_1^{(2)}, \ldots, c_1^{(n_1)} \right), \left(c_2^{(1)}, c_2^{(2)}, \ldots, c_2^{(n_2)} \right), \ldots, \left(c_k^{(1)}, c_k^{(2)}, \ldots, c_k^{(n_k)} \right) \right).
\end{aligned}
$$

18.4 A Single-Server Classed Network

To get a feel for classed networks, let's start by considering the case where the whole network consists of just a single server, say server 1. Server 1 represents a classed M/M/1 queue with ℓ classes of jobs (see Figure 18.3). Class c packets arrive with rate $\lambda_1(c)$, and we use λ_1 to denote the total arrival rate from all classes into server 1; that is, $\lambda_1 = \sum_c \lambda_1(c)$. All packets are served with rate μ_1. The class has no effect in this simple example, because all packets leave after serving (i.e., there is no routing).

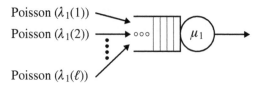

Figure 18.3. Single-server classed network.

We are interested in the limiting probability that the state of the system is $\left(c_1^{(1)}, c_1^{(2)}, \ldots, c_1^{(n_1)}\right)$; that is, the probability that there are n_1 jobs in the system and that their classes (in order from head to tail) are $c_1^{(1)}, c_1^{(2)}, \ldots, c_1^{(n_1)}$, respectively. Here $c_1^{(i)}$ denotes the class of the ith job queued at server 1.

Question: Can you guess what the limiting probability $\pi_{\left(c_1^{(1)}, c_1^{(2)}, \ldots, c_1^{(n_1)}\right)}$ looks like?

Answer: We know that the limiting probability must be related to the limiting probability that there are n_1 jobs in the system, which is $\rho_1^{n_1}(1 - \rho_1)$, where $\rho_1 = \frac{\lambda_1}{\mu_1}$. However, we also know that we need to include the particular classes of the jobs. Thus it seems plausible that

$$\pi_{\left(c_1^{(1)}, c_1^{(2)}, \ldots, c_1^{(n_1)}\right)} = \frac{\lambda_1\left(c_1^{(1)}\right) \lambda_1\left(c_1^{(2)}\right) \cdots \lambda_1\left(c_1^{(n_1)}\right)}{\mu_1^{n_1}} \cdot (1 - \rho_1). \quad (18.2)$$

Observe that, under the conjecture in (18.2),

$$\mathbf{P}\{n_1 \text{ jobs at server}\}$$

$$= \sum_{c_1^{(1)}=1}^{\ell} \sum_{c_1^{(2)}=1}^{\ell} \cdots \sum_{c_1^{(n_1)}=1}^{\ell} \pi_{\left(c_1^{(1)}, c_1^{(2)}, \ldots, c_1^{(n_1)}\right)}$$

$$= \sum_{c_1^{(1)}=1}^{\ell} \sum_{c_1^{(2)}=1}^{\ell} \cdots \sum_{c_1^{(n_1)}=1}^{\ell} \frac{\lambda_1\left(c_1^{(1)}\right) \lambda_1\left(c_1^{(2)}\right) \cdots \lambda_1\left(c_1^{(n_1)}\right)}{\mu_1^{n_1}} \cdot (1 - \rho_1)$$

$$= (1 - \rho_1) \sum_{c_1^{(1)}=1}^{\ell} \frac{\lambda_1\left(c_1^{(1)}\right)}{\mu_1} \cdot \sum_{c_1^{(2)}=1}^{\ell} \frac{\lambda_1\left(c_1^{(2)}\right)}{\mu_1} \cdots \sum_{c_1^{(n_1)}=1}^{\ell} \frac{\lambda_1\left(c_1^{(n_1)}\right)}{\mu_1}$$

$$= \frac{\lambda_1^{n_1}}{\mu_1^{n_1}}(1 - \rho_1)$$

$$= \rho_1^{n_1}(1 - \rho_1)$$

as desired.

We now prove that the guess in (18.2) satisfies the balance equations. We equate the rate that we leave the state $\left(c_1^{(1)}, c_1^{(2)}, \ldots, c_1^{(n_1)}\right)$ with the rate that we enter the state $\left(c_1^{(1)}, c_1^{(2)}, \ldots, c_1^{(n_1)}\right)$. Leaving the state happens when we are in the state $\left(c_1^{(1)}, c_1^{(2)}, \ldots, c_1^{(n_1)}\right)$ and have either an arrival or a departure. Entering the state occurs in one of two ways: Either we are in state $\left(c_1^{(1)}, c_1^{(2)}, \ldots, c_1^{(n_1-1)}\right)$ and we have an arrival of class $c_1^{(n_1)}$, which joins the end of the queue, *or* we are in state $\left(c, c_1^{(1)}, c_1^{(2)}, \ldots, c_1^{(n_1)}\right)$, where the job at the head of the queue is of class c, and we have a departure, so the job of class c leaves:

$$\text{Rate Leave} \ = \ \text{Rate Enter}$$

$$\pi_{\left(c_1^{(1)}, c_1^{(2)}, \ldots, c_1^{(n_1)}\right)}(\mu_1 + \lambda_1) = \pi_{\left(c_1^{(1)}, c_1^{(2)}, \ldots, c_1^{(n_1-1)}\right)}\lambda_1\left(c_1^{(n_1)}\right)$$

$$+ \sum_c \pi_{\left(c, c_1^{(1)}, c_1^{(2)}, \ldots, c_1^{(n_1)}\right)}\mu_1$$

Substituting in our "guess" from (18.2), we note that, for example,

$$\pi_{\left(c, c_1^{(1)}, c_1^{(2)}, \ldots, c_1^{(n_1)}\right)} = \frac{\lambda_1(c)}{\mu_1}\pi_{\left(c_1^{(1)}, c_1^{(2)}, \ldots, c_1^{(n_1)}\right)},$$

allowing us to reduce the rates of entering and leaving as follows:

$$\text{Rate Leave} \ = \ \text{Rate Enter}$$

$$\pi_{\left(c_1^{(1)}, c_1^{(2)}, \ldots, c_1^{(n_1)}\right)}(\mu_1 + \lambda_1) = \pi_{\left(c_1^{(1)}, c_1^{(2)}, \ldots, c_1^{(n_1-1)}\right)}\lambda_1\left(c_1^{(n)}\right)$$

$$+ \sum_c \pi_{\left(c, c_1^{(1)}, c_1^{(2)}, \ldots, c_1^{(n_1)}\right)}\mu_1$$

$$\pi_{\left(c_1^{(1)}, c_1^{(2)}, \ldots, c_1^{(n_1)}\right)}(\mu_1 + \lambda_1) = \frac{\mu_1}{\lambda_1\left(c_1^{(n_1)}\right)} \cdot \pi_{\left(c_1^{(1)}, c_1^{(2)}, \ldots, c_1^{(n_1)}\right)}\lambda_1\left(c_1^{(n_1)}\right)$$

$$+ \sum_c \frac{\lambda_1(c)}{\mu_1}\pi_{\left(c_1^{(1)}, c_1^{(2)}, \ldots, c_1^{(n_1)}\right)}\mu_1$$

$$\mu_1 + \lambda_1 = \frac{\mu_1}{\lambda_1\left(c_1^{(n_1)}\right)} \cdot \lambda_1\left(c_1^{(n_1)}\right) + \sum_c \frac{\lambda_1(c)}{\mu_1} \cdot \mu_1$$

$$\mu_1 + \lambda_1 = \mu_1 + \sum_c \lambda_1(c) \quad \checkmark$$

We have thus verified that the limiting probabilities for the *M/M/1 classed queue* are given by equation (18.2). We use this in the next section.

18.5 Product Form Theorems

Theorem 18.1 *The classed network of queues with k servers has product form, namely,*

$$\pi_{(z_1, z_2, \ldots, z_k)} = \prod_{i=1}^{k} \mathbf{P}\left\{state\ at\ server\ i\ is\ z_i\right\},$$

where $z_i = \left(c_i^{(1)}, c_i^{(2)}, \ldots, c_i^{(n_i)} \right)$, *and server i behaves like an* M/M/1 *classed queue. Specifically,*

$$\mathbf{P}\left\{ \text{state at server } i \text{ is } z_i \right\} = \frac{\lambda_i\left(c_i^{(1)} \right) \lambda_i\left(c_i^{(2)} \right) \cdots \lambda_i\left(c_i^{(n_i)} \right)}{\mu_i^{\,n_i}} \cdot (1 - \rho_i)$$

Proof   We use the concept of local balance, as explained in Chapter 17.

State z

$$\equiv (z_1, z_2, \ldots, z_k)$$
$$= \left(\left(c_1^{(1)}, c_1^{(2)}, \ldots, c_1^{(n_1)} \right), \left(c_2^{(1)}, c_2^{(2)}, \ldots, c_2^{(n_2)} \right), \ldots, \left(c_k^{(1)}, c_k^{(2)}, \ldots, c_k^{(n_k)} \right) \right)$$

We define (see Figure 18.4):

A = rate at which leave state z due to arrival from outside

B_i = rate at which leave state z due to departure from server i $(1 \le i \le k)$

A' = rate at which enter state z due to departure to outside

B_i' = rate at which enter state z due to arrival at server i $(1 \le i \le k)$

Note that

$$\text{Rate at which leave state } z = \sum_{i=1}^{k} B_i + A$$

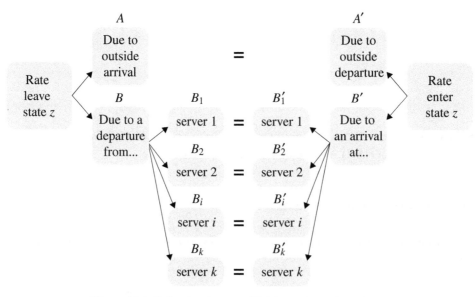

Figure 18.4. Balancing the rate of leaving and entering state z.

and

$$\text{Rate at which enter state } z = \sum_{i=1}^{k} B_i' + A'.$$

We will make the following guess, inspired by our analysis of the single-server classed network, see (18.2):

$$\pi_z = \pi_{(z_1, z_2, \ldots, z_k)} = \prod_{i=1}^{k} (1 - \rho_i) \frac{\lambda_i \left(c_i^{(1)} \right) \lambda_i \left(c_i^{(2)} \right) \cdots \lambda_i \left(c_i^{(n_i)} \right)}{\mu_i^{n_i}} \qquad (18.3)$$

where $\rho_i = \frac{\lambda_i}{\mu_i}$ and $\lambda_i = \sum_{c=1}^{\ell} \lambda_i(c)$.

It suffices to show that our guess satisfies $B_i = B_i'$ for all $1 \le i \le k$ and $A = A'$. We will now prove each of these statements.

To simplify notation, when denoting the state of the system, we will assume that the state at each server i is the usual $z_i = \left(c_i^{(1)}, c_i^{(2)}, \ldots, c_i^{(n_i)} \right)$, unless otherwise stated. Thus we will typically show only the state at those servers at which a job arrives or departs. To keep the number of cases down, we will for now ignore border cases where there are zero jobs at one or more queues. These cases can be handled very similarly to what is done here. One last remark: In the derivation of the unclassed Jackson networks (Theorem 17.1), we viewed the rate of leaving a state (or entering a state) as including only transitions that *change* the state, not transitions that return to the same state. However, in the following derivation, it is easier to broaden the definition of leaving the state (or entering) to include transitions back into the same state. None of this affects the validity of the balance equations.

To show $B_i = B_i'$ for all $1 \le i \le k$:

B_i = Rate at which leave state z due to departure from server i

$\quad = \pi_{(z_1, z_2, \ldots, z_k)} \cdot \mu_i$

Note that the service rate does not depend on the class of the job.

B_i' = Rate at which enter state z due to arrival at server i

$$= \pi_{\left(\ldots, \left(c_i^{(1)}, c_i^{(2)}, \ldots, c_i^{(n_i - 1)} \right), \ldots \right)} \cdot r_i \left(c_i^{(n_i)} \right)$$

$$+ \sum_{j=1}^{k} \sum_{c_j=1}^{\ell} \pi_{\left(\ldots, \left(c_i^{(1)}, c_i^{(2)}, \ldots, c_i^{(n_i - 1)} \right), \ldots, \left(c_j, c_j^{(1)}, \ldots, c_j^{(n_j)} \right), \ldots \right)} \cdot \mu_j P_{ji}^{(c_j)\left(c_i^{(n_i)} \right)}$$

$$= \pi_{(z_1, z_2, \ldots, z_k)} \cdot \frac{\mu_i}{\lambda_i \left(c_i^{(n_i)} \right)} \cdot r_i \left(c_i^{(n_i)} \right)$$

$$+ \sum_{j=1}^{k} \sum_{c_j=1}^{\ell} \pi_{(z_1, z_2, \ldots, z_k)} \cdot \frac{\mu_i}{\lambda_i \left(c_i^{(n_i)} \right)} \cdot \frac{\lambda_j(c_j)}{\mu_j} \cdot \mu_j P_{ji}^{(c_j)\left(c_i^{(n_i)} \right)}$$

$$= \pi_z \cdot \frac{\mu_i}{\lambda_i\left(c_i^{(n_i)}\right)} \cdot \left[r_i\left(c_i^{(n_i)}\right) + \sum_{j=1}^{k}\sum_{c_j=1}^{\ell} \lambda_j(c_j) P_{ji}^{(c_j)\left(c_i^{(n_i)}\right)} \right]$$

$$= \pi_z \cdot \frac{\mu_i}{\lambda_i\left(c_i^{(n_i)}\right)} \cdot \lambda_i\left(c_i^{(n_i)}\right) \quad \text{(by Equation (18.1))}$$

$$= \pi_z \cdot \mu_i$$

$$= B_i$$

To show $A = A'$:

$A = $ Rate at which leave state z due to outside arrival

$$= \pi_{(z_1, z_2, \ldots, z_k)} \cdot \sum_{i=1}^{k}\sum_{c=1}^{\ell} r_i(c)$$

$A' = $ Rate at which enter state z due to departure to outside

$$= \sum_{i=1}^{k}\sum_{c_i=1}^{\ell} \pi_{\left(\ldots,\left(c_i, c_i^{(1)}, \ldots, c_i^{(n_i)}\right),\ldots\right)} \cdot \mu_i P_{i,\text{out}}^{(c_i)(*)} \quad \text{(the } (*) \text{ denotes any class)}$$

$$= \pi_{(z_1, z_2, \ldots, z_k)} \cdot \sum_{i=1}^{k}\sum_{c_i=1}^{\ell} \frac{\lambda_i(c_i)}{\mu_i} \cdot \mu_i P_{i,\text{out}}^{(c_i)(*)}$$

$$= \pi_{(z_1, z_2, \ldots, z_k)} \cdot \sum_{i=1}^{k}\sum_{c_i=1}^{\ell} \lambda_i(c_i) P_{i,\text{out}}^{(c_i)(*)}$$

Now observe that

$$A = \pi_z \cdot \text{(total rate of entering the network from outside)}$$

$$A' = \pi_z \cdot \text{(total rate of leaving the network)}$$

Because the network is in equilibrium, the total average rate of entering the network must equal the total average rate of leaving the network; hence we have $A = A'$. $\checkmark$

Verify that the product form holds:

We would like to show that

$$\pi_{(z_1, z_2, \ldots, z_k)} = \prod_{i=1}^{k} \mathbf{P}\left\{\text{state at server } i \text{ is } z_i\right\},$$

given our guess from (18.3) that

$$\pi_{(z_1, z_2, \ldots, z_k)} = \prod_{i=1}^{k}(1 - \rho_i)\frac{\lambda_i\left(c_i^{(1)}\right)\lambda_i\left(c_i^{(2)}\right)\cdots\lambda_i\left(c_i^{(n_i)}\right)}{\mu_i^{n_i}}.$$

To compute $\mathbf{P}\{$state at server i is $z_i\}$, we simply sum (18.3) over all z_j, where $j \neq i$. Observe that summing over z_j involves *both* summing over all possible classes in the vector $\left(c_j^{(1)}, c_j^{(2)}, \ldots, c_j^{(n_j)}\right)$ and also summing over all possible values of n_j. This is illustrated in the following expressions:

$$\mathbf{P}\left\{\text{state at server } i \text{ is } z_i\right\}$$

$$= \sum_{z_j, j \neq i} \pi_{(z_1, z_2, \ldots, z_k)}$$

$$= (1 - \rho_i) \frac{\lambda_i\left(c_i^{(1)}\right) \cdots \lambda_i\left(c_i^{(n_i)}\right)}{\mu_i^{n_i}}$$

$$\times \prod_{j=1, j \neq i}^{k} \sum_{n_j=0}^{\infty} \sum_{c_j^{(1)}, \ldots, c_j^{(n_j)}} (1 - \rho_j) \frac{\lambda_j\left(c_j^{(1)}\right) \cdots \lambda_j\left(c_j^{(n_j)}\right)}{\mu_j^{n_j}}$$

$$= (1 - \rho_i) \frac{\lambda_i\left(c_i^{(1)}\right) \cdots \lambda_i\left(c_i^{(n_i)}\right)}{\mu_i^{n_i}} \prod_{j=1, j \neq i}^{k} \sum_{n_j=0}^{\infty} (1 - \rho_j) \frac{\lambda_j^{n_j}}{\mu_j^{n_j}}$$

$$= (1 - \rho_i) \frac{\lambda_i\left(c_i^{(1)}\right) \cdots \lambda_i\left(c_i^{(n_i)}\right)}{\mu_i^{n_i}} \prod_{j=1, j \neq i}^{k} 1$$

$$= (1 - \rho_i) \frac{\lambda_i\left(c_i^{(1)}\right) \cdots \lambda_i\left(c_i^{(n_i)}\right)}{\mu_i^{n_i}}$$

Hence we can rewrite (18.3) as

$$\pi_{(z_1, z_2, \ldots, z_k)} = \prod_{i=1}^{k} \mathbf{P}\left\{\text{state at server } i \text{ is } z_i\right\},$$

which is the definition of product form. ∎

Corollary 18.2 *In a classed network of queues, the number of jobs in each queue obeys the following distribution:*

$$\mathbf{P}\left\{\begin{array}{c} \text{Distribution of jobs is} \\ (n_1, n_2, \ldots, n_k) \end{array}\right\} = \prod_{i=1}^{k} \mathbf{P}\left\{n_i \text{ jobs at server } i\right\} = \prod_{i=1}^{k} \rho_i^{n_i}(1 - \rho_i)$$

Observe that Corollary 18.2 is identical to what we proved for the unclassed Jackson network.

Proof We again use the shorthand:

$$z_i = \left(c_i^{(1)}, c_i^{(2)}, \ldots, c_i^{(n_i)}\right)$$

$\mathbf{P}\left\{\text{Distribution of jobs is } (n_1, n_2, \ldots, n_k)\right\}$

$$= \sum_{c_1^{(1)} \ldots c_1^{(n_1)}, \ldots, c_k^{(1)} \ldots c_k^{(n_k)}} \mathbf{P}\left\{\begin{array}{l} \text{state at server 1 is } z_1, \\ \text{state at server 2 is } z_2, \\ \ldots \\ \text{state at server } k \text{ is } z_k \end{array}\right\}$$

$$\overset{\text{(Thm 18.1)}}{=} \sum_{c_1^{(1)} \ldots c_1^{(n_1)}, \ldots, c_k^{(1)} \ldots c_k^{(n_k)}} \prod_{i=1}^{k} \mathbf{P}\left\{\text{state at server } i \text{ is } z_i\right\}$$

$$= \prod_{i=1}^{k} \sum_{c_i^{(1)} \ldots c_i^{(n_i)}} \mathbf{P}\left\{\text{state at server } i \text{ is } \left(c_i^{(1)}, \ldots, c_i^{(n_i)}\right)\right\}$$

$$= \prod_{i=1}^{k} \sum_{c_i^{(1)} \ldots c_i^{(n_i)}} \frac{\lambda_i\left(c_i^{(1)}\right) \lambda_i\left(c_i^{(2)}\right) \ldots \lambda_i\left(c_i^{(n_i)}\right)}{\mu_i^{n_i}} \cdot (1 - \rho_i)$$

$$= \prod_{i=1}^{k} \rho_i^{n_i} \cdot (1 - \rho_i)$$

Thus, we have shown that

$$\mathbf{P}\left\{\text{Distribution of jobs is } (n_1, n_2, \ldots, n_k)\right\} = \prod_{i=1}^{k} \rho_i^{n_i} \cdot (1 - \rho_i). \qquad (18.4)$$

Summing both sides of (18.4) over all $i \neq j$, we have further shown that

$$\mathbf{P}\left\{n_j \text{ jobs at server } j\right\} = \rho_j^{n_j} (1 - \rho_j).$$

Hence we have shown that

$$\mathbf{P}\left\{\text{Distribution of jobs is } (n_1, n_2, \ldots, n_k)\right\} = \prod_{i=1}^{k} \mathbf{P}\left\{n_i \text{ jobs at server } i\right\}. \quad \blacksquare$$

18.6 Examples Using Classed Networks

In this section, we elaborate on some of the motivating examples mentioned in Section 18.2. Our first example only requires Corollary 18.2, whereas the other examples need the full power of Theorem 18.1.

18.6.1 Connection-Oriented ATM Network Example

Consider a connection-oriented network (not shown) with particular routes along which packets flow. The routes are shown in Figure 18.5.

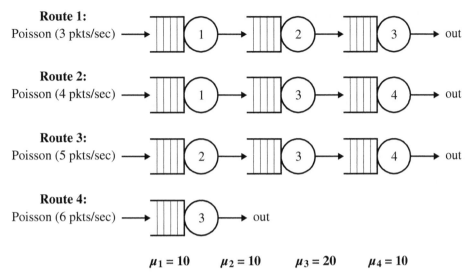

Figure 18.5. Routes for connection-oriented network.

Goal: We want to determine $\mathbf{E}\,[T]$ for packets on route 2.

Question: How can we express this problem as a classed network?

Answer: We want to associate the packets on each route with a particular class.

$$r_i(c) = \text{outside arrival rate into server } i \text{ of class } c \text{ packets}$$
$$P_{ij}^{(c)} = \text{probability that when a packet of class } c \text{ finishes at server } i,$$
$$\qquad \text{it next moves to server } j$$
$$\lambda_i(c) = \text{total arrival rate into server } i \text{ of class } c \text{ packets}$$

So, we have the following:

For class 1: $r_1(1) = 3;$ $\quad P_{12}^{(1)} = 1;$ $\quad P_{23}^{(1)} = 1;$ $\quad P_{3,\text{out}}^{(1)} = 1$

For class 2: $r_1(2) = 4;$ $\quad P_{13}^{(2)} = 1;$ $\quad P_{34}^{(2)} = 1;$ $\quad P_{4,\text{out}}^{(2)} = 1$

For class 3: $r_2(3) = 5;$ $\quad P_{23}^{(3)} = 1;$ $\quad P_{34}^{(3)} = 1;$ $\quad P_{4,\text{out}}^{(3)} = 1$

For class 4: $r_3(4) = 6;$ $\quad P_{3,\text{out}}^{(4)} = 1$

All other $r_i(c)$'s and $P_{ij}^{(c)}$'s are zero.

Now, we can solve for the $\lambda_i(c)$'s by solving these simultaneous equations:

$$\lambda_j(c) = r_j(c) + \sum_i \lambda_i(c) P_{ij}^{(c)}$$

However, in this case, the problem is so easy that we can determine the $\lambda_j(c)$'s by sight (it helps to read these from right to left):

$$\lambda_3(1) = \lambda_2(1) = \lambda_1(1) = r_1(1) = 3 \text{ jobs/sec}$$
$$\lambda_4(2) = \lambda_3(2) = \lambda_1(2) = r_1(2) = 4 \text{ jobs/sec}$$
$$\lambda_4(3) = \lambda_3(3) = \lambda_2(3) = r_2(3) = 5 \text{ jobs/sec}$$
$$\lambda_3(4) = r_3(4) = 6 \text{ jobs/sec}$$

Question: How do we determine the λ_i's?

Answer:

$$\lambda_j = \text{Total arrival rate into server } j = \sum_{c=1}^{\ell} \lambda_j(c).$$

$$\lambda_1 = \lambda_1(1) + \lambda_1(2) = 3 + 4 = 7 \text{ jobs/sec}$$
$$\lambda_2 = \lambda_2(1) + \lambda_2(3) = 3 + 5 = 8 \text{ jobs/sec}$$
$$\lambda_3 = \lambda_3(1) + \lambda_3(2) + \lambda_3(3) + \lambda_3(4) = 3 + 4 + 5 + 6 = 18 \text{ jobs/sec}$$
$$\lambda_4 = \lambda_4(2) + \lambda_4(3) = 4 + 5 = 9 \text{ jobs/sec}$$

Question: How do we determine the ρ_i's?

Answer:

$$\rho_i = \text{load at server } i = \frac{\lambda_i}{\mu_i}.$$

$$\rho_1 = \tfrac{7}{10}; \quad \rho_2 = \tfrac{8}{10}; \quad \rho_3 = \tfrac{18}{20}; \quad \rho_4 = \tfrac{9}{10}.$$

Question: What is $\mathbf{E}[T$ for route 2 packets$]$?

Answer: We first determine the expected time that is spent at each server by determining the expected number of packets at each server and applying Little's Law.

$$\mathbf{E}[N_i] = \text{Expected number of packets at server } i = \frac{\rho_i}{1 - \rho_i}.$$

$$\mathbf{E}[N_1] = \frac{0.7}{0.3} = \frac{7}{3}; \quad \mathbf{E}[N_2] = 4; \quad \mathbf{E}[N_3] = 9; \quad \mathbf{E}[N_4] = 9$$

$$\mathbf{E}[T_i] = \text{Expected time at server } i \text{ per visit} = \frac{\mathbf{E}[N_i]}{\lambda_i}$$

$$\mathbf{E}[T_1] = \frac{\mathbf{E}[N_1]}{\lambda_1} = \frac{7/3}{7} = \frac{1}{3} \text{ sec}$$

$$\mathbf{E}[T_2] = \frac{\mathbf{E}[N_2]}{\lambda_2} = \frac{4}{8} = \frac{1}{2} \text{ sec}$$

$$\mathbf{E}[T_3] = \frac{\mathbf{E}[N_3]}{\lambda_3} = \frac{9}{18} = \frac{1}{2} \text{ sec}$$

$$\mathbf{E}[T_4] = \frac{\mathbf{E}[N_4]}{\lambda_4} = \frac{9}{9} = 1 \text{ sec}$$

The total time a packet spends on route 2 is the sum of the times spent at each server that it visits.

$$\mathbf{E}\left[T \text{ for packets on route 2}\right] = \mathbf{E}\left[T_1\right] + \mathbf{E}\left[T_3\right] + \mathbf{E}\left[T_4\right] = \frac{11}{6} \text{ sec} \qquad \blacksquare$$

18.6.2 *Distribution of Job Classes Example*

In the previous example, we only needed Corollary 18.2. Sometimes we need the more powerful Theorem 18.1. Suppose, for example, that there are only two job types called class 1 and class 2, and we want to know the probability that there are exactly s jobs of class 1 and t jobs of class 2 at server i. Theorem 18.1 implies

$\mathbf{P}\left\{\text{Server } i \text{ has } s \text{ jobs of class 1 and } t \text{ jobs of class 2}\right\}$

$$= \binom{s+t}{s} \frac{\lambda_i(1)^s \lambda_i(2)^t}{\mu_i^{s+t}} \cdot (1 - \rho_i),$$

where $\rho_i = \frac{\lambda_i}{\mu_i}$ and $\lambda_i = \lambda_i(1) + \lambda_i(2)$.

Let's see if we can write this expression in a more intuitive way:

$\mathbf{P}\left\{\text{Server } i \text{ has } s \text{ jobs of class 1 and } t \text{ jobs of class 2}\right\}$

$$= \binom{s+t}{s} \frac{\lambda_i(1)^s \lambda_i(2)^t}{\mu_i^{s+t}} \cdot (1 - \rho_i)$$

$$= \binom{s+t}{s} \frac{\lambda_i(1)^s \lambda_i(2)^t}{\mu_i^{s+t} \rho_i^{s+t}} \cdot \rho_i^{s+t}(1 - \rho_i)$$

$$= \binom{s+t}{s} \frac{\lambda_i(1)^s \lambda_i(2)^t}{\lambda_i^{s+t}} \cdot \rho_i^{s+t}(1 - \rho_i)$$

$$= \binom{s+t}{s} \left(\frac{\lambda_i(1)}{\lambda_i}\right)^s \cdot \left(\frac{\lambda_i(2)}{\lambda_i}\right)^t \cdot \rho_i^{s+t}(1 - \rho_i)$$

$$= \left[\binom{s+t}{s} \left(\frac{\lambda_i(1)}{\lambda_i(1) + \lambda_i(2)}\right)^s \cdot \left(\frac{\lambda_i(2)}{\lambda_i(1) + \lambda_i(2)}\right)^t\right] \cdot \left[\rho_i^{s+t}(1 - \rho_i)\right] \quad (18.5)$$

We have written the result as a product of two factors (in brackets).

Question: What is the right factor in (18.5)?

Answer: The right factor is just the probability that there are $s + t$ jobs at server i.

Question: What is the left factor in (18.5)?

Answer: By definition the left factor of (18.5) must represent the probability that there are s jobs of type 1 and t jobs of type 2 at server i, given that there are $s + t$ jobs total at server i. In fact, setting

$$p = \frac{\lambda_i(1)}{\lambda_i(1) + \lambda_i(2)} = \frac{\lambda_i(1)}{\lambda_i} = \text{Fraction of type 1 arrivals at server } i,$$

we can rewrite the left factor of (18.5) as

$$\binom{s+t}{s} p^s (1-p)^t \tag{18.6}$$

If we now think of each job at server i as independently being of type 1 with probability p and type 2 otherwise, we see that (18.6) represents exactly what we want, namely the probability that there are s jobs of type 1 and t of type 2 at server i, given that there are $s + t$ jobs total at server i.

18.6.3 *CPU-Bound and I/O-Bound Jobs Example*

Here is a more complex example. Your system consists of two devices: a CPU device with Exponential service rate 2 jobs/sec and an I/O device with Exponential service rate 1 job/sec. There are two different types of jobs: *CPU-bound jobs* and *I/O-bound jobs*.

CPU-bound jobs arrive at the CPU from outside according to a Poisson process of rate 0.2 jobs/sec. After serving at the CPU, three things can happen to a CPU-bound job:

1. With probability 0.3, the job leaves the system.
2. With probability 0.65, the job returns to the CPU queue to repeat the process.
3. With probability 0.05, the job goes to the I/O device queue, serves there once, and immediately returns to the CPU queue to repeat the process.

The I/O-bound jobs arrive at the I/O from outside the network according to a Poisson process with rate 0.25 jobs/sec. After serving at the I/O, there are three things that can happen to an I/O-bound job:

1. With probability 0.4, the job leaves the system.
2. With probability 0.5, the job returns to the I/O queue to repeat the process.
3. With probability 0.1, the job goes to the CPU device queue. Each time the job serves at the CPU device, it has a 0.05 probability of returning to the CPU device and a 0.95 probability of returning to the I/O queue.

Our goal is to answer the following questions:

(a) What is the expected time in system of CPU-bound jobs?
(b) What is the average number of CPU-bound jobs at the CPU?

Solution: We model the routing of jobs between servers as shown in Figure 18.6. Let the CPU be device 1 and the I/O be device 2. Also, let C be the class of a CPU-bound job and I be the class of an I/O-bound job.

For the CPU-bound jobs,

$$\lambda_1^C = r_1^C + \lambda_1^C \cdot P_{1,1}^C + \lambda_2^C \cdot P_{2,1}^C$$
$$= 0.2 + 0.65\lambda_1^C + \lambda_2^C.$$
$$\lambda_2^C = r_2^C + \lambda_2^C \cdot P_{2,2}^C + \lambda_1^C \cdot P_{1,2}^C = 0.05\lambda_1^C.$$

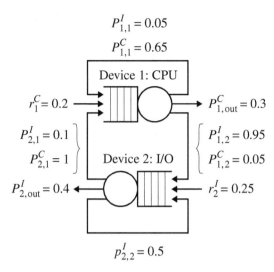

Figure 18.6. Class-based routing probabilities.

Solving these simultaneous equations, we get

$$\lambda_1^C = \frac{2}{3}, \quad \lambda_2^C = \frac{1}{30}.$$

Similarly for the I/O-bound jobs,

$$\lambda_1^I = r_1^I + \lambda_1^I \cdot P_{1,1}^I + \lambda_2^I \cdot P_{2,1}^I$$
$$= 0.05\lambda_1^I + 0.1\lambda_2^I.$$
$$\lambda_2^I = r_2^I + \lambda_2^I \cdot P_{2,2}^I + \lambda_1^I \cdot P_{1,2}^I$$
$$= 0.25 + 0.95\lambda_1^I + 0.5\lambda_2^I.$$

Again we solve these simultaneous equations and get

$$\lambda_1^I = \frac{5}{76}, \quad \lambda_2^I = \frac{5}{8}.$$

We now find the other parameters that we are interested in:

$$\lambda_1 = \lambda_1^C + \lambda_1^I = 0.7325$$
$$\lambda_2 = \lambda_2^C + \lambda_2^I = 0.6583$$
$$\rho_1 = \frac{\lambda_1}{\mu_1} = 0.3663$$
$$\rho_2 = \frac{\lambda_2}{\mu_2} = 0.6583$$
$$\mathbf{E}[N_1] = \frac{\rho_1}{1 - \rho_1} = 0.578$$
$$\mathbf{E}[N_2] = \frac{\rho_2}{1 - \rho_2} = 1.9265$$
$$\mathbf{E}[T_1] = \frac{\mathbf{E}[N_1]}{\lambda_1} = 0.7895$$
$$\mathbf{E}[T_2] = \frac{\mathbf{E}[N_2]}{\lambda_2} = 2.9265$$

(a) What is the expected time in system of CPU-bound jobs?

Let the expected time in system of CPU-bound jobs be $\mathbf{E}\left[T^C\right]$.

Method 1

$$\mathbf{E}\left[T^C\right] = 0.3\mathbf{E}\left[T \mid \text{leaves after visiting 1}\right]$$
$$+ 0.65\mathbf{E}\left[T \mid \text{loops back to 1}\right]$$
$$+ 0.05\mathbf{E}\left[T \mid \text{loops back to 1 via 2}\right]$$
$$= 0.3\mathbf{E}\left[T_1\right] + 0.65(\mathbf{E}\left[T_1\right] + \mathbf{E}\left[T^C\right]) + 0.05(\mathbf{E}\left[T_1\right] + \mathbf{E}\left[T_2\right] + \mathbf{E}\left[T^C\right])$$
$$\mathbf{E}\left[T^C\right] = 3.117$$

Method 2

$$\mathbf{E}\left[T^C\right] = \mathbf{E}\left[V_1^C\right] \cdot \mathbf{E}\left[T_1\right] + \mathbf{E}\left[V_2^C\right] \cdot \mathbf{E}\left[T_2\right]$$

We obtain $\mathbf{E}\left[V_1^C\right]$ and $\mathbf{E}\left[V_2^C\right]$ by solving these simultaneous equations:

$$\mathbf{E}\left[V_1^C\right] = 1 + 0.65\mathbf{E}\left[V_1^C\right] + 1.0\mathbf{E}\left[V_2^C\right]$$
$$\mathbf{E}\left[V_2^C\right] = 0.05\mathbf{E}\left[V_1^C\right]$$

(b) What is the average number of CPU-bound jobs at the CPU?

Question: We need to find $\mathbf{E}\left[N_1^C\right]$. How can we do this?

Hint: Use (18.5).

Answer: From (18.5) it follows that the expected number of CPU-bound jobs at server 1 is the expected number of jobs at server 1 multiplied by p, the fraction of those jobs that are CPU-bound jobs. That is,

$$\mathbf{E}\left[N_1^C\right] = \mathbf{E}\left[\text{Number jobs at CPU}\right] \cdot p = \frac{\rho_1}{1 - \rho_1} \cdot \frac{\lambda_1^C}{\lambda_1^C + \lambda_1^I}.$$

In case the above is not obvious, here is a full derivation:

$$\mathbf{E}\left[N_1^C\right] = \sum_{s=0}^{\infty} \mathbf{P}\left\{s \text{ jobs of type C at server 1}\right\} \cdot s$$
$$= \sum_{s=0}^{\infty} \sum_{n_1=s}^{\infty} \mathbf{P}\left\{s \text{ jobs of type C at server 1 and } n_1 \text{ jobs total}\right\} \cdot s$$

$$= \sum_{s=0}^{\infty} \sum_{n_1=s}^{\infty} \binom{n_1}{s} p^s (1-p)^{n_1-s} \cdot \rho_1^{n_1} (1-\rho_1) \cdot s \quad \text{by (18.5)}$$

$$= \sum_{n_1=0}^{\infty} \rho_1^{n_1} (1-\rho_1) \left(\sum_{s=0}^{n} \binom{n_1}{s} p^s (1-p)^{n_1-s} \cdot s \right)$$

$$= \sum_{n_1=0}^{\infty} \rho_1^{n_1} (1-\rho_1)(n_1 \cdot p) \quad \text{(mean of Binomial (n_1, p))}$$

$$= \mathbf{E}\left[N_1\right] \cdot p.$$

18.7 Readings

A nice example of using a classed Jackson network to solve a problem is provided in the SIGCOMM '99 best student paper [145].

18.8 Exercises

18.1 Classed Queueing Network

The server in Figure 18.7 processes jobs at an Exponential rate of $\mu = 10$ jobs/sec. There are two types of jobs being served at the FCFS server. Jobs of type 1 arrive according to a Poisson process with rate $r^{(1)} = 0.5$ jobs/sec. After each visit to the server, they require an additional visit with probability 0.75. Jobs of type 2 arrive according to a Poisson process with rate $r^{(2)} = 3$ jobs/sec. After each visit to the server, they require an additional visit with probability 0.5. What is the mean response time for jobs of type 1? Type 2?

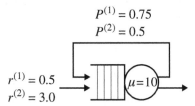

Figure 18.7. Classed queueing network.

18.2 Quick versus Slow Customers

Consider a single queue with a single service station with service time distributed Exponentially with mean 1. There are two types of customers:

1. "Quick customers" arrive according to a Poisson process with rate $\frac{1}{3}$, visit the server once, and leave.

2. "Slow customers" arrive according to a Poisson process with rate $\frac{1}{6}$ and visit the server a Geometric number of times with mean 3.

On average, how many quick customers and how many slow customers are in the system?

18.3 Jobs Needing Repair

A system consists of a service facility and a repair facility. The service time at both facilities is $\text{Exp}\left(\frac{1}{10}\right)$. Jobs arrive at the service facility according to a Poisson process with rate λ. After each visit to the service facility, the job either:

- leaves the system (probability 0.1)
- requires repair (probability 0.01)
- revisits the service facility (probability 0.89).

After completing repair, a job returns to the service facility, except that now, after each visit to the service facility, the job either:

- leaves the system (probability 0.1)
- requires repair (probability 0.5)
- revisits the service facility (probability 0.4).

Please answer the following questions about the system:

(a) What is the expected number of times that a job visits the service facility?

(b) What is the highest possible throughput, λ?

(c) Set $\lambda = \frac{1}{200}$. What is the expected time in system, $\mathbf{E}\left[T\right]$?

18.4 Class-Based Service Rates?

Consider a Jackson network with ℓ classes. Until now we have always assumed that the service rate is the same for each of the classes. Suppose you want to have the service rate depend on the class of the job (e.g., jobs of class c are served at rate $\mu(c)$). Can you solve balance equations for the case of a single server with class-dependent service rates? Why or why not? If you can, do it and determine the limiting probabilities: $\pi_{(c(1),\ldots,c(n))}$, where $c(i)$ denotes the class of the ith job in queue at the server.

18.5 Distribution of Job Classes

In Section 18.6.2, we considered a network with two classes of jobs and derived the probability that server i has s jobs of class 1 and t jobs of class 2, namely:

$\mathbf{P}\left\{\text{Server } i \text{ has } s \text{ jobs of class 1 and } t \text{ jobs of class 2}\right\}$

$$= \left[\binom{s+t}{s}\left(\frac{\lambda_i(1)}{\lambda_i(1)+\lambda_i(2)}\right)^s \cdot \left(\frac{\lambda_i(2)}{\lambda_i(1)+\lambda_i(2)}\right)^t\right] \cdot \left[\rho_i^{s+t}(1-\rho_i)\right].$$

(a) Generalize this expression to ℓ classes; namely, derive

$\mathbf{P}\{\text{Server } i \text{ has } m_1 \text{ jobs of class } 1, m_2 \text{ of class } 2, \ldots, m_\ell \text{ of class } \ell\}.$

(b) Provide an expression for the expected number of class 1 jobs at server i.

18.6 Not All Networks Have Product Form

Give an example of a 2-server network that does *not* have a product form limiting distribution. Analyze the limiting distribution of your network and prove that there exist n_1, n_2, such that

$\mathbf{P}\left\{n_1 \text{ jobs at server 1 } \& \ n_2 \text{ jobs at server 2}\right\}$

$\neq \mathbf{P}\left\{n_1 \text{ jobs at server 1}\right\} \cdot \mathbf{P}\left\{n_2 \text{ jobs at server 2}\right\}.$

CHAPTER 19

Closed Networks of Queues

Thus far, all of our analysis of networks of queues involved *open* queueing networks. We have witnessed the product form property for Jackson-type networks (those with probabilistic routing), which has allowed us to instantly derive the probability distribution of the number of jobs at each of the servers. It turns out that the same basic product form idea applies to *closed* queueing networks. The only difference is that additional work is involved in computing the normalizing constant for the case of closed networks, whereas it has a simple closed form for the case of open networks.

In this chapter, we briefly illustrate the product form analysis of closed queueing networks with probabilistic routing, also known as closed Jackson networks. To keep things simple, we stick to single-class networks, although everything that we say applies to multi-class networks as well. Also, we throughout assume a *batch* closed network, meaning zero think time (see Section 2.6.2). The extension to interactive closed networks is studied in the Exercise 19.3(4).

19.1 Motivation

Consider a closed system with multiple queues and probabilistic routing between the queues, as shown in the batch network in Figure 19.1. Our goal might be to determine the probability that there are 2 jobs at the third server.

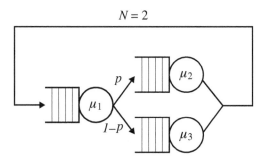

Figure 19.1. Example of a closed batch network.

For this example, the possible states are $(0, 0, 2)$, $(0, 2, 0)$, $(2, 0, 0)$, $(1, 0, 1)$, $(1, 1, 0)$, and $(0, 1, 1)$. The corresponding 6-state Markov chain results in a finite number of simultaneous equations, which can be solved to obtain the limiting probability of being in each state. In particular, we can obtain $\pi_{0,0,2}$, which is what we wanted. The Markov chain is shown in Figure 19.2.

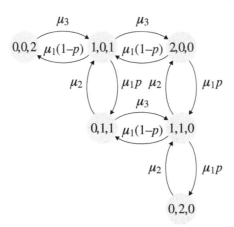

Figure 19.2. The corresponding CTMC.

In fact, any closed batch network is solvable, at least in theory, because we are dealing with a finite number of simultaneous equations. Provided that the total number of jobs, N, and the total number of servers/queues, k, are not too large, specific instances of the closed network (meaning chains with specific values of the μ_i's) should be tractable. Let's make this more concrete.

Question: Suppose there are k servers and N jobs total. What is the number of simultaneous balance equations that need to be solved for the CTMC?

Answer:

$$\text{Number of simultaneous equations} = \text{Number of states} = \binom{N+k-1}{k-1.}$$

Note: This expression represents all the ways of dividing the N jobs among k servers or, alternatively, of distributing $k-1$ "dividers" into $N+k-1$ slots, as shown in Figure 19.3.

☽ ☽ | ☽ ☽ ☽ | ☽ ☽ || ☽ ☽ ☽ ☽ ☽

Figure 19.3. Distributing a dozen balls into 5 bins (the 4th is empty).

The point of this chapter is to find a faster way to get to the limiting probabilities. We want to be able to express these limiting probabilities in closed form, as a function of the μ_i's and routing probabilities.

19.2 Product Form Solution

We consider a general closed batch Jackson-type network. This is characterized by the following properties. There are k servers, each with a FCFS queue. There is probabilistic routing between the servers: With probability P_{ij}, when a job leaves server i, it next goes to server j, as for example in Figure 19.4. There are no outside arrivals and no departures to the outside. There is a fixed multiprogramming level, N. That is, there are exactly N jobs in the network at any time. The state is $(n_1, n_2, \ldots, n_k)$, where n_i denotes the number of jobs at server i.

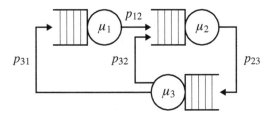

Figure 19.4. Closed batch Jackson network.

Question: It seems that a closed Jackson network is defined exactly like an open Jackson network, except for what?

Answer: For the closed network, $r_i = 0$ and $P_{i,\text{out}} = 0$ for all i.

Thus, the balance equations for closed networks are identical to the balance equations for the open networks, except that some of the terms (r_i's and $P_{i,\text{out}}$'s) are now set to zero. Thus it would seem that

$$\pi_{n_1,\ldots,n_k} = C\rho_1^{n_1}\rho_2^{n_2}\cdots\rho_k^{n_k} \tag{19.1}$$

might still work as a solution for the limiting probabilities. However, the set of balance equations in a closed network is a *subset* of the set of balance equations in the open network; some states are not allowed in the closed network because the number of jobs in the system do not sum up to N. Hence it is not obvious that the guess in (19.1) will work.

19.2.1 *Local Balance Equations for Closed Networks*

The local balance equations for a closed network equate B_i, the rate of leaving a state due to a departure from server i, with B_i', the rate of entering the state due to an arrival at server i. In both B_i and B_i', we will allow for transitions which take us back to the same state.

Question: Why don't we need to worry about $A = A'$?

Answer: There are no outside departures or arrivals.

We now need to check that the guess in (19.1) satisfies $B_i = B_i'$.

$$B_i \qquad\qquad\qquad\qquad\qquad\qquad B_i'$$

Rate leave state $(n_1, n_2, \ldots, n_k)$ $\qquad=\qquad$ Rate enter state $(n_1, n_2, \ldots, n_k)$
due to departure from server i $\qquad\qquad$ due to arrival at server i

$$\pi_{n_1,\ldots,n_k} \cdot \mu_i \quad = \quad \sum_{j=1}^{k} \pi_{n_1,\ldots,n_i-1,\ldots,n_j+1,\ldots,n_k} \cdot \mu_j \cdot P_{ji}$$

$$\mu_i \quad = \quad \sum_{j=1}^{k} \frac{\rho_j}{\rho_i} \mu_j \cdot P_{ji}$$

$$\lambda_i \quad = \quad \sum_{j=1}^{k} \lambda_j \cdot P_{ji}$$

The final line simply states that the total arrival rate into server i is the sum of the departure rates into server i from the other servers. This is obviously true, so we are done.

Question: Great, so we have verified that

$$\pi_{n_1,\ldots,n_k} = C\rho_1^{n_1} \rho_2^{n_2} \cdots \rho_k^{n_k}.$$

But what is ρ_i?

Answer: $\rho_i = \frac{\lambda_i}{\mu_i}$

Question: But how do we determine λ_i?

Answer: For open networks, we determined λ_i by solving k simultaneous equations:

$$\lambda_i = r_i + \sum_{j=1}^{k} \lambda_j P_{ji}$$

Question: Suppose we try solving these simultaneous equations for the case of a closed network. What goes wrong?

Answer: For closed networks, $r_i = 0$ so the k simultaneous equations only have $k-1$ linearly independent variables. So we cannot get a unique solution.

For example, consider the closed network of servers shown in Figure 19.5.

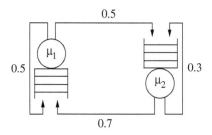

Figure 19.5. Simple example.

The simultaneous equations are

$$\lambda_1 = \lambda_2(0.7) + \lambda_1(0.5).$$
$$\lambda_2 = \lambda_1(0.5) + \lambda_2(0.3).$$

Both equations are the same. So $\lambda_2 = \frac{5}{7}\lambda_1$, but we do not know λ_1.

Another way to think about this is that we only know the λ_i's to within a constant factor. That is, we know

$$(c\lambda_1, c\lambda_2, \ldots, c\lambda_k)$$

but we do not know what c is. This turns out to be OK, however, because the c's get hidden into the normalizing constant in the limiting probabilities:

$$
\begin{aligned}
\pi_{n_1,\ldots,n_k} &= C\left(c\frac{\lambda_1}{\mu_1}\right)^{n_1}\left(c\frac{\lambda_2}{\mu_2}\right)^{n_2}\ldots\left(c\frac{\lambda_k}{\mu_k}\right)^{n_k} \\
&= Cc^N \rho_1^{n_1}\ldots\rho_k^{n_k} \\
&= C'\rho_1^{n_1}\ldots\rho_k^{n_k}
\end{aligned}
$$

What is important in this expression is that the final constant, C', is the same for any state of the CTMC. We summarize the procedure below.

Solving Closed Batch Jackson Networks:

1. Determine λ_i's. To do this, solve the simultaneous rate equations. You will have an infinite number of solutions that work. Pick any one solution (e.g., set $\lambda_1 = 1$).
2. Compute $\rho_i = \frac{\lambda_i}{\mu_i}$, for all i.
3. Set $\pi_{n_1,\ldots,n_k} = C'\rho_1^{n_1}\rho_2^{n_2}\ldots\rho_k^{n_k}$
4. Finally compute C'. To do this, use the fact that

$$\sum_{\substack{n_1,\ldots,n_k \\ \text{s.t.}\sum_i n_i = N}} C'\cdot\rho_1^{n_1}\rho_2^{n_2}\cdots\rho_k^{n_k} = 1$$

19.2.2 *Example of Deriving Limiting Probabilities*

Consider again the closed system shown in Figure 19.1, where $\mu_1 = 1, \mu_2 = 2, \mu_3 = 3$, and $p = \frac{1}{3}$.

We want to determine $\mathbf{E}$ [Number jobs at server 1]. The first thing to do is determine the ρ_i's. To do this we want to determine the λ_i's. This is done by solving the simultaneous rate equations:

$$
\begin{aligned}
\lambda_1 &= \lambda_2 + \lambda_3 \\
\lambda_2 &= \frac{1}{3}\cdot\lambda_1 \\
\lambda_2 &= \frac{2}{3}\cdot\lambda_1
\end{aligned}
$$

These equations are not linearly independent, so we arbitrarily set

$$\lambda_1 = 1.$$

This leaves us with

$$\lambda_2 = \frac{1}{3}$$

$$\lambda_3 = \frac{2}{3}.$$

We now compute $\rho_i = \frac{\lambda_i}{\mu_i}$ as follows, for $i = 1, 2, 3$:

$$\rho_1 = 1, \qquad \rho_2 = \frac{1}{6}, \qquad \rho_3 = \frac{2}{9}$$

Question: Are the above utilizations?

Answer: No. *These are not "real loads."* They do not mean anything in terms of load because they are based on a made-up value for λ_1.

To determine any performance metric, we first need to determine the limiting probabilities of the CTMC. We use the product form representation of the limiting probabilities:

$$\pi_{n_1,n_2,n_3} = C \cdot \rho_1^{n_1} \cdot \rho_2^{n_2} \cdot \rho_3^{n_3}$$

To use this formula we need to determine C. We consider all the possible states: (0,0,2), (0,2,0), (2,0,0), (1,0,1), (1,1,0), (0,1,1):

$$1 = \sum_{\text{all states}} \pi_{\text{state}}$$

$$= C \left(\rho_1^0 \rho_2^0 \rho_3^2 + \rho_1^0 \rho_2^2 \rho_3^0 + \rho_1^2 \rho_2^0 \rho_3^0 + \rho_1^1 \rho_2^0 \rho_3^1 + \rho_1^1 \rho_2^1 \rho_3^0 + \rho_1^0 \rho_2^1 \rho_3^1 \right)$$

$$= C \left(\left(\frac{2}{9} \right)^2 + \left(\frac{1}{6} \right)^2 + (1)^2 + \left(\frac{2}{9} \right) + \left(\frac{1}{6} \right) + \left(\frac{1}{6} \cdot \frac{2}{9} \right) \right)$$

$$= C \cdot 1.5031$$

So we are left with

$$C = \frac{1}{1.5031} = .6653.$$

Now we can use C and the ρ_i's to get the limiting probabilities:

$$\pi_{0,0,2} = C \cdot \rho_1^0 \rho_2^0 \rho_3^2 = 0.033$$
$$\pi_{0,2,0} = C \cdot \rho_1^0 \rho_2^2 \rho_3^0 = 0.018$$
$$\pi_{2,0,0} = C \cdot \rho_1^2 \rho_2^0 \rho_3^0 = 0.665$$
$$\pi_{1,0,1} = C \cdot \rho_1^1 \rho_2^0 \rho_3^1 = 0.148$$
$$\pi_{1,1,0} = C \cdot \rho_1^1 \rho_2^1 \rho_3^0 = 0.111$$
$$\pi_{0,1,1} = C \cdot \rho_1^0 \rho_2^1 \rho_3^1 = 0.025$$

Given the limiting probabilities, it is easy to determine any performance metric. For example,

$$\mathbf{E}\,[\text{Number at server 1}] = \pi_{1,0,1} + \pi_{1,1,0} + 2\pi_{2,0,0} = 1.589.$$
$$\text{Utilization of server } 1 = 1 - \pi_{0,0,2} - \pi_{0,2,0} - \pi_{0,1,1} = 0.924.$$

19.3 Mean Value Analysis (MVA)

The only difficulty in the previous approach for closed systems is that it requires computing C', the normalizing constant for the limiting probabilities. This involves summing

$$r = \binom{N+k-1}{k-1}$$

terms. Thus the number of terms we have to add up grows exponentially in N and k. (Note this is already a lot better than solving the original CTMC from scratch, where rather than just having to add r terms, we have to solve that many simultaneous equations.)

In practice, for a single-class closed network, summing these r terms to determine the normalizing constant is not usually a big deal. Typically the number of servers, k, is low. Now, if N is *also* low, then we can easily compute the normalizing constant. Otherwise, if N is high, operational bounds analysis will work very well.

Nonetheless, many people still find it cumbersome to have to determine this normalizing constant and there has been research into faster approaches for computing it [35]. We now present an alternative method for analyzing closed product form networks, which is very efficient and intuitive. This method is called *Mean Value Analysis* (MVA). The downside of MVA is that it does not provide more than mean metrics. That is, rather than providing the *distribution* of the number of jobs at each server, MVA provides only the *mean* number of jobs at each server.

MVA recursively relates the mean number of jobs at server j in a closed system where the total number of jobs is M, namely $\mathbf{E}\left[N_j^{(M)}\right]$, to the mean number of jobs at server j in the same system where the total number of jobs is $M-1$, namely $\mathbf{E}\left[N_j^{(M-1)}\right]$ (note that we have switched to writing M for the total number of jobs, rather than N, to avoid notation overload). This recursive relationship allows us to then start with a 1-job system ($M = 1$), which is easy to reason about; then use that to get the mean response time for the 2-job system; then use that to get the mean response time for the 3-job system; and so on, building up to the M-job system.

The recursive relationship between the M-job system and the $(M-1)$-job system is captured in the Arrival Theorem.

19.3.1 *The Arrival Theorem*

> **Theorem 19.1 (The Arrival Theorem)** *In a closed Jackson network with $M > 1$ total jobs, an arrival to server j witnesses a distribution of the number of jobs at each server equal to the steady-state distribution of the number of jobs at each server in the same network with $M - 1$ total jobs. In particular, the mean number of jobs that the arrival sees at server j is $\mathbf{E}\left[N_j^{(M-1)}\right]$.*

The Arrival Theorem may make some intuitive sense because the arrival is seeing a system that does not contain itself; hence it has $M - 1$ total jobs. However, it is not true for all networks.

Question: Provide an example of a closed network for which the Arrival Theorem is false.

Answer: Imagine a closed system consisting of two servers in tandem with $M = 2$ jobs, where the service time at each server is deterministically 1. Suppose that we start out with one job at each server. Then forever after, there will be exactly one job at each server (because jobs move in lock-step). Thus, an arrival, job j, into server 1 will always witness 0 jobs at server 1 and yet $\mathbf{E}\left[N_1^{(1)}\right] = \frac{1}{2}$.

The previous question/answer illustrates why the Arrival Theorem can be thought of as the "counterpart to PASTA" for closed systems: it requires job sizes to be Exponentially distributed.

In the rest of the section, we prove the Arrival Theorem and then show how to use it to derive $\mathbf{E}\left[T^{(M)}\right]$, the mean response time in a closed system with M jobs. Before we do this, however, we need to digress and recall the limiting probability for a closed Jackson network with M jobs. We use the superscript M to denote the fact that this is an M-job system.

Recall that

$$\pi_{n_1,n_2,\ldots,n_k}^{(M)} = C^{(M)} \left(\frac{\lambda_1^{(M)}}{\mu_1}\right)^{n_1} \cdot \left(\frac{\lambda_2^{(M)}}{\mu_2}\right)^{n_2} \cdots \left(\frac{\lambda_k^{(M)}}{\mu_k}\right)^{n_k} \tag{19.2}$$

whenever $\sum_{i=1}^{k} n_i = M$, and 0 otherwise. Here $\lambda_j^{(M)}$ denotes the total arrival rate into server j, given a closed system with M jobs, and $C^{(M)}$ is the appropriate normalizing constant for the M-job system. The problem is that the $\lambda_j^{(M)}$ term in (19.2) depends on M. For reasons that will become clear soon, it will be very helpful to replace this with a term that does not depend on M. Let's define a term that we call p_j, where

$$p_j = \frac{\lambda_j^{(M)}}{\lambda^{(M)}}. \tag{19.3}$$

Here $\lambda^{(M)} = \sum_{j=1}^{k} \lambda_j^{(M)}$ denotes the total arrival rate into all servers in the M-job system. Observe that p_j is just the fraction of total arrivals that are arrivals to server j (as opposed to some other server). Because p_j is a proportion rather than an absolute quantity, p_j is independent of M.[1]

We can now rewrite the limiting probabilities from (19.2) in terms of p_j as follows:

$$\pi_{n_1,n_2,\ldots,n_k}^{(M)} = C'^{(M)} \left(\frac{p_1}{\mu_1}\right)^{n_1} \cdot \left(\frac{p_2}{\mu_2}\right)^{n_2} \cdots \left(\frac{p_k}{\mu_k}\right)^{n_k}, \tag{19.5}$$

whenever $\sum_{i=1}^{k} n_i = M$, and 0 otherwise.

What is nice about the limiting probabilities given by (19.5) is that all the terms involving "M" have been subsumed into the constant.

We now prove the Arrival Theorem, after which we illustrate the derivation of $\mathbf{E}\left[T^{(M)}\right]$.

Proof (Arrival Theorem) We consider a job, job x, in an M-job system, that has just left server i and is headed to server j. We wish to determine the distribution of jobs at each server, as seen by job x. We will show that the probability that job x observes n_1 jobs at server 1, n_2 at server 2, n_3 at server 3, etc., where $\sum_{j=1}^{k} n_j = M - 1$ (we are not including the job itself), is exactly $\pi_{n_1,n_2,\ldots,n_k}^{(M-1)}$.

Our argument follows that of [150]. We start by observing that the probability that job x observes state $(n_1, n_2, \ldots, n_k)$, where $\sum_{j=1}^{k} n_j = M - 1$ is the same as the ratio of two rates: the rate of transitions from server i to server j which observe state $(n_1, n_2, \ldots, n_k)$ and the total rate of transitions from server i to server j.

$$\mathbf{P}\left\{\text{job } x \text{ observes } (n_1, n_2, \ldots, n_k), \text{ where } \sum_{j=1}^{k} n_j = M - 1\right\}$$

$$= \frac{\pi_{n_1,\ldots,n_i+1,\ldots,n_k}^{(M)} \mu_i P_{ij}}{\displaystyle\sum_{\substack{h_1,\ldots,h_k \\ \text{s.t.} \sum_\ell h_\ell = M - 1}} \pi_{h_1,\ldots,h_i+1,\ldots h_k}^{(M)} \mu_i P_{ij}}$$

$$= \frac{\pi_{n_1,\ldots,n_i+1,\ldots,n_k}^{(M)}}{\displaystyle\sum_{\substack{h_1,\ldots,h_k \\ \text{s.t.} \sum_\ell h_\ell = M - 1}} \pi_{h_1,\ldots,h_i+1,\ldots h_k}^{(M)}}$$

---

[1] To illustrate why p_j is independent of M, let V_j denote the number of visits to server j per job completion (independent of M), and let $X^{(M)}$ denote the total rate of job completions per second in a system with M jobs. Then

$$p_j = \frac{\lambda_j^{(M)}}{\lambda^{(M)}} = \frac{X^{(M)} V_j}{\sum_{j=1}^{k} X^{(M)} V_j} = \frac{V_j}{\sum_{j=1}^{k} V_j}, \tag{19.4}$$

which is clearly independent of M.

$$
= \frac{\frac{p_i}{\mu_i} \cdot \prod_{\ell=1}^{k} \left(\frac{p_\ell}{\mu_\ell}\right)^{n_\ell}}{\displaystyle\sum_{\substack{h_1,\ldots,h_k \\ \text{s.t.} \sum_\ell h_\ell = M-1}} \pi^{(M)}_{h_1,\ldots,h_i+1,\ldots h_k}} \quad \text{by (19.5)}
$$

$$
= C \prod_{\ell=1}^{k} \left(\frac{p_\ell}{\mu_\ell}\right)^{n_\ell}, \quad \text{where } C : \text{constant, independent of } n_1, n_2, \ldots, n_k
$$

$$
= \pi^{(M-1)}_{n_1,n_2,\ldots,n_k}.
$$

The last line follows from the fact that the probability over what job x sees is a "density" in the sense that, when we sum it over all possible $n_1, n_2, \ldots, n_k$, where $\sum_{\ell=1}^{k} n_\ell = M - 1$, we get 1. Hence the constant C above is the unique constant needed to make this density sum to 1. But that means that $C = C^{(M-1)}$, the unique constant needed to make the density in (19.5) sum to 1.

The above chain of equalities is true for all i, j, completing the proof. ∎

19.3.2 *Iterative Derivation of Mean Response Time*

We are now finally ready to express $\mathbf{E}\left[T_j^{(M)}\right]$ in terms of $\mathbf{E}\left[T_j^{(M-1)}\right]$. Once we have done this, we can then start with $\mathbf{E}\left[T_j^{(1)}\right]$ and use that to get $\mathbf{E}\left[T_j^{(2)}\right]$, which we will then use to get $\mathbf{E}\left[T_j^{(3)}\right]$, and so forth, until we have $\mathbf{E}\left[T_j^{(M)}\right]$.

Question: Pop quiz: What is $\mathbf{E}\left[T_j^{(1)}\right]$?

Answer: We are asking what is the mean response time at server j when the number of jobs in the system is 1. This is just the mean service time: $\frac{1}{\mu_j}$.

Invoking the Arrival Theorem, we have

$$
\mathbf{E}\left[T_j^{(M)}\right] = \frac{1}{\mu_j} + \frac{\mathbf{E}\left[\text{Number at server } j \text{ as seen by an arrival to } j\right]}{\mu_j}
$$

$$
= \frac{1}{\mu_j} + \frac{\mathbf{E}\left[N_j^{(M-1)}\right]}{\mu_j} \quad \text{(by the Arrival Theorem)}
$$

$$
= \frac{1}{\mu_j} + \frac{\lambda_j^{(M-1)}\mathbf{E}\left[T_j^{(M-1)}\right]}{\mu_j} \quad \text{(by Little's Law)}
$$

$$
= \frac{1}{\mu_j} + \frac{p_j \cdot \lambda^{(M-1)}\mathbf{E}\left[T_j^{(M-1)}\right]}{\mu_j} \quad \text{(by defn of } p_j \text{ in 19.3)}
$$

At this point, we have expressed $\mathbf{E}\left[T_j^{(M)}\right]$ in terms of $\mathbf{E}\left[T_j^{(M-1)}\right]$:

$$\mathbf{E}\left[T_j^{(M)}\right] = \frac{1}{\mu_j} + \frac{p_j \cdot \lambda^{(M-1)}\mathbf{E}\left[T_j^{(M-1)}\right]}{\mu_j} \tag{19.6}$$

However, we still have a $\lambda^{(M-1)}$ term in there.

Question: How do we get $\lambda^{(M-1)}$?

Hint: Use the fact that $\sum_{j=1}^{k}\mathbf{E}\left[N_j^{(M-1)}\right] = M-1$ and apply Little's Law.

Answer:

$$\begin{aligned}
M - 1 &= \sum_{j=1}^{k}\mathbf{E}\left[N_j^{(M-1)}\right] \\
&= \sum_{j=1}^{k}\lambda_j^{(M-1)}\mathbf{E}\left[T_j^{(M-1)}\right] \\
&= \sum_{j=1}^{k}p_j\lambda^{(M-1)}\mathbf{E}\left[T_j^{(M-1)}\right], \quad \text{by (19.3)} \\
&= \lambda^{(M-1)}\sum_{j=1}^{k}p_j\mathbf{E}\left[T_j^{(M-1)}\right].
\end{aligned}$$

From this expression we have that

$$\lambda^{(M-1)} = \frac{M-1}{\sum_{j=1}^{k}p_j\mathbf{E}\left[T_j^{(M-1)}\right]}. \tag{19.7}$$

Combining equations (19.6) and (19.7), we have the recurrence for $\mathbf{E}\left[T_j^{(M)}\right]$.

19.3.3 *An MVA Example*

Consider a closed system composed of 2 servers in tandem, where the second server is twice as fast as the first server, as shown in Figure 19.6. Given that the system has $M = 3$ jobs, how many of these are at server 1 and how many are at server 2 on average? To simplify calculations, we assume that the service rate at the first server is $\mu = 1$.

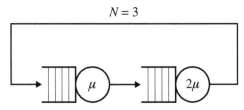

Figure 19.6. An MVA example. What is the expected number of jobs at each server?

Question: What do you expect the number of jobs at each server to be?

Answer: One might naively think that because the first server is half the speed of the second server, there should be twice as many jobs at the first server. This is not true. As we will see, the expected number of jobs at the first server is actually more than three times that at the second server.

Our goal is to determine $\mathbf{E}\left[N_1^{(3)}\right]$. We will get this by deriving $\mathbf{E}\left[T_1^{(3)}\right]$ via MVA and then applying Little's Law.

Question: What are p_1 and p_2?

Answer: Normally we would have to solve the simultaneous equations in (19.4) to get these, but in this case they are simple. Because the number of arrivals to server 1 is equal to the number of arrivals to server 2, we have that $p_1 = p_2 = \frac{1}{2}$.

We start by deriving $\mathbf{E}\left[T_1^{(1)}\right]$, $\mathbf{E}\left[T_2^{(1)}\right]$, and $\lambda^{(1)}$.

$$\mathbf{E}\left[T_1^{(1)}\right] = \frac{1}{\mu_1} = 1$$

$$\mathbf{E}\left[T_2^{(1)}\right] = \frac{1}{\mu_2} = \frac{1}{2}$$

$$\lambda^{(1)} = \frac{1}{\frac{1}{2} \cdot \left(1 + \frac{1}{2}\right)} = \frac{4}{3} \quad \text{by (19.7)}$$

From here we immediately move to $\mathbf{E}\left[T_1^{(2)}\right]$, $\mathbf{E}\left[T_2^{(2)}\right]$, and $\lambda^{(2)}$.

$$\mathbf{E}\left[T_1^{(2)}\right] = 1 + \frac{\frac{1}{2} \cdot \frac{4}{3} \cdot 1}{1} = \frac{5}{3} \quad \text{by (19.6)}$$

$$\mathbf{E}\left[T_2^{(2)}\right] = \frac{1}{2} + \frac{\frac{1}{2} \cdot \frac{4}{3} \cdot \frac{1}{2}}{2} = \frac{2}{3} \quad \text{by (19.6)}$$

$$\lambda^{(2)} = \frac{2}{\frac{1}{2} \cdot \left(\frac{5}{3} + \frac{2}{3}\right)} = \frac{12}{7} \quad \text{by (19.7)}$$

Next, we move to $\mathbf{E}\left[T_1^{(3)}\right]$, $\mathbf{E}\left[T_2^{(3)}\right]$, and $\lambda^{(3)}$.

$$\mathbf{E}\left[T_1^{(3)}\right] = 1 + \frac{\frac{1}{2} \cdot \frac{12}{7} \cdot \frac{5}{3}}{1} = \frac{17}{7} \quad \text{by (19.6)}$$

$$\mathbf{E}\left[T_2^{(3)}\right] = \frac{1}{2} + \frac{\frac{1}{2} \cdot \frac{12}{7} \cdot \frac{2}{3}}{2} = \frac{11}{14} \quad \text{by (19.6)}$$

$$\lambda^{(3)} = \frac{3}{\frac{1}{2} \cdot \left(\frac{17}{7} + \frac{11}{14}\right)} = \frac{28}{15} \quad \text{by (19.7)}$$

Finally, we derive $\mathbf{E}\left[N_1^{(3)}\right]$:

$$\mathbf{E}\left[N_1^{(3)}\right] = \mathbf{E}\left[T_1^{(3)}\right] \cdot \lambda_1^{(3)}$$

$$= \mathbf{E}\left[T_1^{(3)}\right] \cdot p_1 \cdot \lambda^{(3)}$$

$$= \frac{17}{7} \cdot \frac{1}{2} \cdot \frac{28}{15}$$

$$= \frac{34}{15}$$

As a check, we also derive $\mathbf{E}\left[N_2^{(3)}\right]$:

$$\mathbf{E}\left[N_2^{(3)}\right] = \mathbf{E}\left[T_2^{(3)}\right] \cdot \lambda_2^{(3)}$$

$$= \mathbf{E}\left[T_2^{(3)}\right] \cdot p_2 \cdot \lambda^{(3)}$$

$$= \frac{11}{14} \cdot \frac{1}{2} \cdot \frac{28}{15}$$

$$= \frac{11}{15}$$

Observe that $\mathbf{E}\left[N_1^{(3)}\right] + \mathbf{E}\left[N_2^{(3)}\right] = 3$ as expected. $\checkmark$

19.4 Readings

There has been a lot of work on obtaining the normalizing constants for closed queueing networks. Some good references are [94], [72], [40].

MVA was developed by Reiser and Lavenberg [147]. In this book we have chosen to only give a brief explanation of MVA and why it works. While our exposition was limited to single-class closed networks with no think time, the MVA method applies much more generally. A comprehensive discussion of the use of MVA for solving both single-class and multi-class product form networks is provided in [23]. The MVA method needs to be modified slightly to allow for think times as well as multiple classes. Some good references that explain these modifications are [125] and [5].

19.5 Exercises

19.1 Closed Jackson Network

Consider the very simple closed Jackson network given in Figure 19.7. Derive the expected number of jobs at server 1 in the case where the total number of jobs is (i) $M = 1$, (ii) $M = 2$, and (iii) $M = 3$. Do not use MVA.

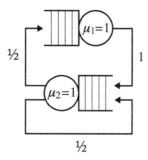

Figure 19.7. Jackson network for Exercise 19.1.

19.2 MVA

Repeat Exercise 19.1 using MVA to get your answers.

19.3 Networks with Load-Dependent Service Rates

This is a four-part question, with *dependent* parts, so please do these in order. Throughout, assume all packets come from a single class.

(1) The system consists of just a single (FCFS) server. Jobs arrive according to a Poisson process with rate λ. The service rate at the server is "load-dependent," meaning that when there are n jobs in the system, the job in service is served with rate $\mu(n)$. Systems with load-dependent service rate are used to model parallel processing applications. Determine the distribution of the number of jobs in the system.

(2) Now your system is a (single-class) open Jackson network of load-dependent servers. The state of the network is $(n_1, n_2, \ldots, n_k)$, where n_i denotes the number of jobs at server i. Let $\mu_i(n_i)$ denote the service rate at server i when there are n_i jobs at server i.

   i. Solve for the limiting probabilities, $\pi_{(n_1, n_2, \ldots, n_k)}$, using the local balance approach. These will not be in closed form.

   ii. Prove that the limiting probabilities have a product form solution; namely that

$$\pi_{(n_1, n_2, \ldots, n_k)} = \prod_{i=1}^{k} \mathbf{P}\left\{\text{Number of jobs at server } i \text{ is } n_i\right\}.$$

   iii. Check your solution by making the service rate constant at each server (i.e., $\mu_i(n_i) = \mu_i$, $\forall n_i$), and showing that you get the solution for ordinary open Jackson networks.

(3) Now your system is a Jackson network where each server is an M/M/m. Determine the limiting probabilities, $\pi_{(n_1, n_2, \ldots, n_k)}$.

(4) This chapter described the analysis of closed *batch* Jackson networks, but did not say anything about closed *interactive* Jackson networks. Assume that you can extend the analysis you have done in this problem to closed

batch Jackson networks, with load-dependent service rates. Explain in words how this would help you analyze a closed *interactive* Jackson network with Exponentially distributed think time with mean $\mathbf{E}\left[Z\right]$. Specifically, explain how you would derive mean response time and throughput for a closed interactive network.

Real-World Workloads: High Variability and Heavy Tails

Part VI discusses queueing analysis where the arrival process and/or service process are generally distributed.

We start with Chapter 20, where we study empirical job size distributions from computing workloads. These are often characterized by heavy tails, very high variance, and decreasing failure rate. Importantly, these are very different from the Markovian (Exponential) distributions that have enabled the Markov-chain-based analysis that we have done so far.

New distributions require new analysis techniques. The first of these, the method of phase-type distributions, is introduced in Chapter 21. Phase-type distributions allow us to represent general distributions as mixtures of Exponential distributions. This in turn enables the modeling of systems involving general distributions using Markov chains. However, the resulting Markov chains are very different from what we have seen before and often have no simple solution. We introduce matrix-analytic techniques for solving these chains numerically. Matrix-analytic techniques are very powerful. They are efficient and highly accurate. Unfortunately, they are still numerical techniques, meaning that they can only solve "instances" of the problem, rather than solving the problem symbolically in terms of the input variables.

In Chapter 22 we consider a new setting: networks of Processor-Sharing (PS) servers with generally distributed job sizes. These represent networks of computers, where each computer time-shares among several jobs. We again exploit the idea of phase-type distributions to analyze these networks, proving the BCMP product form theorem for networks with PS servers. The BCMP theorem provides a simple closed-form solution for a very broad class of networks of PS servers.

Another analysis technique, called the "tagged-job" technique, is introduced in Chapter 23. This technique provides us with a clean simple formula for the mean delay in an M/G/1 FCFS queue, known as the Pollaczek-Khinchin (P-K) formula. We also study extensions of the M/G/1 in the exercises, such as mean delay for the M/G/1 with failures and repairs, as well as the notion of a semi-Markov process that transitions between states, but allows for sitting in a state for a generally distributed time before transitioning. The P-K mean delay formula is so simple that it facilitates the analysis of whole server farms consisting of FCFS queues. Chapter 24 is an applications chapter, where we combine everything we have learned about FCFS queues and PS queues to design and analyze routing policies for general server farms.

Although the P-K formula is elegant and insightful, it does not provide us information about the variability of response time. To get higher moments of response time, we need transform analysis. Laplace transforms and z-transforms, as applied to queueing analysis, are introduced in Chapter 25. These are then applied to analyzing the M/G/1 queue in Chapter 26.

Chapter 27 is another applications chapter, this time looking at power management in servers, where there are tradeoffs between keeping the server on to reduce response time and turning it off to save on power. The problem is complicated by the fact that there is a "setup cost" for turning on a server. Transform analysis is extremely useful in analyzing systems with setup costs under generally distributed workloads – in fact, we do not know of any other solution technique for this problem.

CHAPTER 20

Tales of Tails: A Case Study of Real-World Workloads

We have alluded several times during this book to the fact that computing workloads have highly variable job sizes (service requirements), that are not well described by an Exponential distribution. This chapter is a story of my own experience in studying UNIX jobs in the mid-1990s, as a PhD student at U.C. Berkeley. Results of this research are detailed in [84, 85]. The story serves as both an introduction to empirical measurements of computer workloads and as a case study of how a deeper understanding of computer workloads can lead to improved computer system designs. The remaining chapters in the book address modeling and performance evaluation of systems with high-variability workloads.

20.1 Grad School Tales . . . Process Migration

In the mid-1990s, an important research area was CPU load balancing in a Network of Workstations (at U.C. Berkeley it was coined the "N.O.W. project"). The idea in *CPU load balancing* is that CPU-bound jobs might benefit from being *migrated* from a heavily loaded workstation to a more lightly loaded workstation in the network. CPU load balancing is still important in today's networks of servers. It is not free, however: Migration can be expensive if the job has a lot of "state" that has to be migrated with the job (e.g., lots of open files associated with the job), as is common for jobs that have been running for a while. When the state associated with the job is great, then the time to migrate the job to another machine is high, and hence it might not be worth migrating that job.

There are two types of migration used in load balancing techniques:

1. migration of newborn jobs only – also called *initial placement* or *remote execution*
2. migration of jobs that are already active (running) – also referred to as *active process migration*

In the mid-1990s it was generally accepted that migrating active processes was a bad idea, because of their high migration cost. Except for one or two experimental operating systems, like MOSIX [13], people only migrated newborn jobs.

Important terminology: When we talk about a job's **size** we mean its total CPU requirement. When we talk about a job's **age** we mean its total CPU usage thus far. A job's **lifetime** refers to its total CPU requirement (same thing as size). A job's **remaining lifetime** refers to its remaining CPU requirement.

Observe that what we really want to know is a job's remaining lifetime. If the job has a high remaining CPU requirement, then it may pay to migrate the job, even if the job has accumulated a lot of state, because the job will get to spend its long remaining lifetime on a lightly loaded machine.

Sadly, we do not know a job's remaining lifetime, just its current CPU age.

The common wisdom in the 1990s, backed up by many research papers, was that UNIX job CPU lifetimes were *Exponentially distributed.*

Question: What is the implication of UNIX job lifetimes being Exponentially distributed?

Answer: Exponential distributions exhibit a constant failure rate. That is, all jobs have the same remaining lifetime (and the same probability of requiring another second of CPU), regardless of their current age. Since newborn jobs and older (active) jobs have the *same* expected remaining lifetime, yet newborn jobs are much cheaper to migrate, it makes sense to migrate only the newborn jobs.

20.2 UNIX Process Lifetime Measurements

Refusing to believe that there were no benefits to active process migration, I decided to measure the distribution of job lifetimes.

I collected the CPU lifetimes of millions of jobs on a wide range of different machines, including instructional, research, and administrative machines, over the course of many months. Figure 20.1 shows the fraction of jobs whose size exceeds x, for all jobs whose size is greater than 1 second.

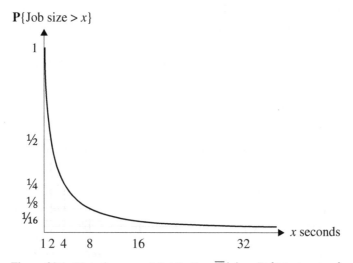

Figure 20.1. Plot of measured distribution, $\overline{F}(x) = \mathbf{P}\{\text{Job size} > x\}$.

At a first glance this plot looks like an Exponential distribution, $\overline{F}(x) = e^{-\lambda x}$. But on closer examination you can see that it is not Exponential.

Question: How can you tell that it is not Exponential?

Answer: For an Exponential distribution, the fraction of jobs remaining should drop by a constant factor with each unit increase in x (constant failure rate). In Figure 20.1, we see that the fraction of jobs remaining decreases by a slower and slower rate as we increase x (decreasing failure rate). In fact, looking at the graph, we see that if we start with jobs of CPU age 1 second, half of them make it to 2 seconds. Of those that make it to 2 seconds, half of those make it to 4 seconds. Of those that make it to 4 seconds, half of those make it to 8 seconds. Of those that make it to 8 seconds, half of those make it to 16 seconds, and so on.

To see the distribution more easily it helps to view it on a log-log plot as shown in Figure 20.2. The bumpy line shows the data, and the straight line is the best-fit curve.

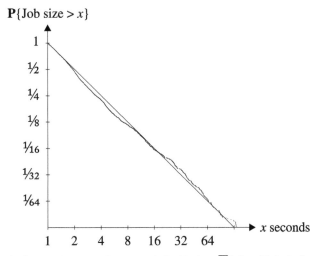

Figure 20.2. Log-log plot of measured distribution, $\overline{F}(x) = \mathbf{P}\,\{\text{Job size} > x\}$.

To see that the measured distribution is *not* an Exponential distribution, consider Figure 20.3, which shows the best-fit Exponential distribution in juxtaposition with the measured distribution from Figure 20.2.

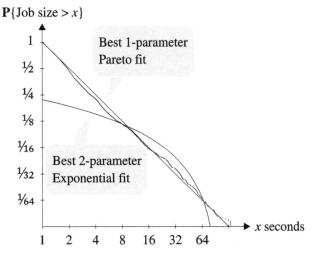

Figure 20.3. Plot of measured distribution on log-log axes along with best-fit Exponential distribution.

From Figure 20.2 it is apparent that the tail of the distribution of jobs with lifetimes longer than 1 second decays like $\frac{1}{x}$. That is,

$$\mathbf{P}\{\text{Job size} > x \mid \text{Job size} > 1\} = \frac{1}{x}.$$

At the time (mid-90s), I did not recognize this distribution and was suspicious of its simplicity, so I tried measuring different types of UNIX workloads. I also tried removing shells and daemon processes, as well as removing very short jobs. No matter what I tried, in all cases, I saw a straight line on a log-log plot, indicating the following distribution:

$$\overline{F}(x) = \frac{1}{x^{\alpha}}, \quad x \geq 1,$$

where α ranged from about 0.8 to about 1.2, in my measurements, across machines. Most commonly α was very close to 1, and the regression showed goodness of fit (R^2) values of more than 0.96.

20.3 Properties of the Pareto Distribution

It turns out that the distribution that I had measured has a name in economic theory. It is called the Pareto distribution, or "power-law distribution."

Definition 20.1 A distribution, $\overline{F}_X(x)$, such that
$$\overline{F}_X(x) = \mathbf{P}\{X > x\} = x^{-\alpha}, \quad \text{for } x \geq 1,$$
where $0 < \alpha < 2$ is called a **Pareto(α) distribution**.

Question: What is the failure rate of the Pareto distribution?

Answer:

$$\overline{F}(x) = \mathbf{P}\{X > x\} = x^{-\alpha}, \qquad x \geq 1$$
$$\Rightarrow F(x) = \mathbf{P}\{X < x\} = 1 - x^{-\alpha}, \qquad x \geq 1$$
$$\Rightarrow f(x) = \frac{dF(x)}{dx} = \alpha x^{-\alpha-1}, \qquad x \geq 1$$
$$\Rightarrow r(x) = \frac{f(x)}{\overline{F}(x)} = \frac{\alpha x^{-\alpha-1}}{x^{-\alpha}} = \frac{\alpha}{x}, \qquad x \geq 1.$$

Notice that $\int_1^{\infty} f(x)dx = \int_1^{\infty} \alpha x^{-\alpha-1}dx = 1$, so $f(x)$ is a valid probability distribution.

Because $r(x) = \frac{\alpha}{x}$ decreases with x, the Pareto distribution has decreasing failure rate (DFR). Thus the older a job is (the more CPU it has used up so far), the greater its probability of using another second of CPU.

Question: For a Pareto with $\alpha \leq 1$, what are the mean and variance of the distribution?

Answer: The calculations are straightforward, by integration over the density function. If $0 < \alpha \leq 1$,

$$\mathbf{E}\left[\text{Lifetime}\right] = \infty$$
$$\mathbf{E}\left[i\text{th moment of Lifetime}\right] = \infty, \quad i = 2, 3, \ldots$$
$$\mathbf{E}\left[\text{Remaining Lifetime} \mid \text{age} = a > 1\right] = \infty.$$

Question: How do these answers change when α is above 1?

Answer: Both the expected lifetime and the expected remaining lifetime are now finite. Higher moments of lifetime are still infinite.

Question: Under the Pareto distribution with $\alpha = 1$, what is the probability that a job of CPU age a lives to CPU age b, where $b > a$?

Answer:

$$\mathbf{P}\left\{\text{Life} > b \mid \text{Life} \geq a > 1\right\} = \frac{1/b}{1/a} = \frac{a}{b}.$$

Using this expression, for the Pareto($\alpha = 1$) distribution, we can interpret the distribution in the following way:

- Of all the jobs currently of age 1 sec, half of those will live to age ≥ 2 sec.
- The probability that a job of age 1 sec uses $> T$ sec of CPU is $\frac{1}{T}$.
- The probability that a job of age T sec lives to be age $\geq 2T$ sec is $\frac{1}{2}$.

20.4 The Bounded Pareto Distribution

When we look for a curve fit to the *measured data*, we observe that the measured data have a minimum job lifetime and a *maximum* job lifetime. Thus the measured data have all *finite* moments. To model the measured data, we therefore want a distribution with a Pareto shape, but truncated on both ends. We refer to such a distribution as a *Bounded Pareto* distribution.

Definition 20.2 The **Bounded Pareto(k, p, α)** distribution has density function

$$f(x) = \alpha x^{-\alpha - 1} \cdot \frac{k^{\alpha}}{1 - \left(\frac{k}{p}\right)^{\alpha}},$$

for $k \leq x \leq p$ and $0 < \alpha < 2$. We often write $BP(k, p, \alpha)$ for short.

The factor $\frac{k^{\alpha}}{1-(k/p)^{\alpha}}$ in Definition 20.2 is a normalization factor needed to make the integral of the density function between k and p come out to 1. For the Bounded Pareto distribution, obviously all of the moments are finite.

For the UNIX job sizes that I measured, the squared coefficient of variation, C^2, was finite, ranging between $C^2 = 25$ and $C^2 = 49$. This may seem like a very high level of variability, but computer workloads today exhibit even higher squared coefficients of variation.

20.5 Heavy Tails

The following are three properties of the Pareto distribution:

1. **Decreasing failure rate (DFR)** — The more CPU you have used so far, the more you will continue to use.
2. **Infinite or near-infinite variance**
3. **Heavy-tail property** — A minuscule fraction of the very largest jobs comprise half of the total system load. For example, when $\alpha = 1.1$, the largest 1% of the jobs comprise about $\frac{1}{2}$ of the load. (Note that this is much more biased than the often quoted 80–20 rule.)

The last property, which we call the "heavy-tail property," comes up in many other settings. For example, in economics, when studying people's wealth, it turns out that the richest 1% of all people have more money between them than all the remaining 99% of us combined. The heavy-tail property is often referred to as "a few big elephants (big jobs) and many, many mice (little jobs)," as illustrated in Figure 20.4. For comparison, in an Exponential distribution with the same mean, the largest 1% of the jobs comprise only about 5% of the total demand.

Figure 20.4. Heavy-tail property: "Elephants and mice."

The parameter α can be interpreted as a measure of the variability of the distribution and the heavy-tailedness: $\alpha \to 0$ yields the most variable and most heavy-tailed distribution, whereas $\alpha \to 2$ yields the least variable and least heavy-tailed distribution. These properties are explored in more depth in the exercises.

These properties largely hold for the Bounded Pareto distribution as well as the Pareto, although clearly the Bounded Pareto cannot have pure DFR, because there is an upper bound on job size.

20.6 The Benefits of Active Process Migration

Now, let's return to the original question of CPU load balancing.

Question: What does the DFR property of the Pareto distribution tell us about whether it pays to migrate older jobs?

Answer: DFR says that older jobs have higher expected remaining lifetimes. This leads us to think that it may pay to migrate *old* jobs. Although an old job may have a high migration cost because it has accumulated a lot of state (memory), if the job is really old then it has a high probability of using a lot more CPU in the future. This means that the cost of migration can then be amortized over a very long lifetime, as the job gets to spend its long remaining lifetime running on a lightly loaded machine.

Question: What does the heavy-tail property of the Pareto distribution tell us?

Answer: By the heavy-tail property, it may only be necessary to migrate the 1% biggest jobs, because they contain most of the work.

However, it is not clear which jobs are "old enough" as a function of their migration cost. The confusion comes from the fact that for a Pareto distribution with $\alpha \leq 1$, *all* jobs (regardless of age) have the same expected remaining lifetime, namely ∞. Does this mean all jobs are "old enough" to make them worth migrating? The difficulty in working with distributions with infinite moments is coming up with a modeling approach that gets around all the infinities.

We need some *criterion* to determine if a job is "old enough." This criterion should take into account the job's age and its migration cost, as well as the difference in load at the source and target host.

Allen Downey (a fellow grad student) and I developed such a criterion, based on the Pareto job size distribution. The trick for getting around the "infinities" was to look at the expected *slowdown* of a job, rather than its expected response time (recall that the slowdown of a job is its response time normalized by its size). In experiments involving networks of workstations, we showed that active process migration, based on our criterion, ends up migrating fewer than 4% of jobs, while vastly reducing mean slowdown when compared with remote execution. We will not spend time discussing the criterion here, but if you are intrigued at this point, we encourage you to read the paper [85].

20.7 Pareto Distributions Are Everywhere

It is not just UNIX jobs that fit a heavy-tailed Pareto distribution. Pareto job size distributions are everywhere! Here are some more practical and interesting stories.

Around 1996–98, Mark Crovella, Azer Bestavros, and Paul Barford at Boston University were measuring the sizes of files at websites. They found that these sizes had a Pareto distribution with $\alpha \approx 1.1$. They also found similar results for the sizes of files requested from websites. Their SURGE web workload generator is based on these findings [14, 47, 48].

Around this same time, the three Faloutsos brothers were observing a similar distribution when looking at the Internet topology. They observed, for example, that most nodes have low out-degree, but a very few nodes have very high out-degree, and the distribution of the degrees follows a Pareto distribution. This and other observations were published in their beautiful 1999 paper that won the Sigcomm Test of Time award [54].

In 1999, Jennifer Rexford, Anees Shaikh, and Kang Shin at AT&T were working on routing IP flows to create better load balancing. They did not want to have to reroute all flows because the overhead would be too high. Ideally, they wanted to have to reroute only 1% of the IP flows. Would that be enough? Fortunately, their measurements showed that the number of packets in IP flows follows a heavy-tailed Pareto distribution. Consequently, the 1% largest IP flows (those with the most packets) contain about 50% of the bytes in all flows. Thus by rerouting only 1% of the flows, they were able to redistribute half the load. Their paper appeared in Sigcomm 99 [166] and generated a large group of follow-up papers dealing with sampling methods for how to detect which flows are large, based on using the DFR property and the knowledge of how many packets the flow has sent so far.

Around this same time, my students and I, in collaboration with Mark Crovella at Boston University, started a project called SYNC (Scheduling Your Network Connections). The goal was to improve the performance of web servers by changing the order in which they scheduled their jobs to favor requests for small files over requests for large files. Clearly favoring requests for small files over large ones would decrease mean response time. However people had not tried this in the past because they were afraid that the requests for large files would "starve" or at least be treated unfairly compared to requests for small files. Using the heavy-tail property of web file sizes, we were able to prove analytically and in implementation that this fear is unfounded for the distribution of web files. The crux of the argument is that, although short requests do go ahead of long requests, all those short requests together make up very little load (more than half the load is in the top 1% of long requests) and hence do not interfere noticeably with the long requests [12, 46, 92]. In 2004, Ernst Biersack, Idris Rai, and Guillaume Urvoy-Keller extended the SYNC results to TCP flow scheduling by exploiting the DFR property of the Pareto distribution to discern which flows have short remaining duration [144, 142].

There are many, many more examples of the Pareto distribution in measured distributions involving jobs created by humans. Wireless session times have been shown to follow a Pareto distribution [22]. Phone call durations have been shown to follow a distribution similar to a Pareto. Human wealth follows a Pareto distribution. Natural phenomena too follow Pareto distributions. For example, John Doyle at Caltech has shown that the damage caused by forest fires follows a Pareto distribution, with most forest fires causing little damage, but the largest few forest fires causing the majority of the damage. The same property holds for earthquakes and other natural disasters.

Given the prevalence of the Pareto distribution, there has been a great deal of research interest in **why** the Pareto distribution comes up everywhere. Ideally, we would like to prove something similar in nature to the Central Limit Theorem, which explains the ubiquity of the Normal distribution, but this time for the Pareto distribution. We do not have room to delve into the many theories proposed for the origin of the Pareto distribution (e.g., the HOT theory [37]). To date, this is still an open research problem of great practical importance.

20.8 Exercises

20.1 Simulation of M/BP/1

In this problem you will simulate a single FCFS server, where jobs arrive according to a Poisson process with rate λ, and job sizes are distributed according to a Bounded Pareto distribution, $BP(k, p, \alpha)$, with mean 3,000. We will experiment with two values of α: $\alpha = 1.5$ (high variability and heavier tail) and $\alpha = 2.9$ (low variability and light tail).[1] Fix $p = 10^{10}$, and set k appropriately so as to keep the mean steady at 3,000 (for example, when $\alpha = 1.5$ you want $k \approx 1,000$, and when $\alpha = 2.9$ you want $k \approx 1,970$). Now set λ appropriately to create a server utilization of $\rho = 0.8$.

Your goal is to measure the mean time in the queue, $\mathbf{E}[T_Q]$. You will do this by averaging independent samples.

Let one "run" of the simulator consist of running the system from empty state for fifty thousand arrivals and then recording the time in queue experienced by arrival number 50,001.

You will perform n (independent) runs, each of which will generate one sample and then you will determine the mean of the n samples.

For each of the two values of α:

(a) Perform $n = 5,000$ runs of the simulator. Let $X_1, X_2, \ldots, X_n$ denote the n samples you obtain for T_Q. Determine the sample mean, S_M:

$$S_M = \frac{X_1 + X_2 + \cdots + X_n}{n}$$

Determine the sample variance, S_V, via the following well-known formula:

$$S_V = \frac{1}{n-1} \sum_{i=1}^{n} (X_i - S_M)^2$$

(b) Compute the "true" $\mathbf{E}[T_Q]$ and $\mathbf{Var}(T_Q)$ using the following formulas (these will be proven in Chapter 23) for the M/G/1 queue, where S denotes the job size, which is in this case two instances of a Bounded Pareto:

$$\mathbf{E}[T_Q] = \frac{\rho}{1-\rho} \cdot \frac{\mathbf{E}[S^2]}{2\mathbf{E}[S]} \tag{20.1}$$

$$\mathbf{Var}(T_Q) = (\mathbf{E}[T_Q])^2 + \frac{\lambda \mathbf{E}[S^3]}{3(1-\rho)} \tag{20.2}$$

Compare your results with the sample mean and sample variance.

(c) For the lower α case, it will likely turn out that your analytically derived values for $\mathbf{E}[T_Q]$ and $\mathbf{Var}(T_Q)$ are much higher than your measured (simulated) values. Why is this?

(d) Why did we ask you to make each run consist of so many arrivals before taking a sample point? For example, why couldn't you just have used 1,000 arrivals in each run?

---

[1] When the α parameter is this high, the distribution is often no longer considered to be Pareto because the tail is so light.

20.2 The Heavy-Taile Property

We explore three distributions for job size:

(1) Exponential distribution with mean 3,000

(2) Bounded Pareto distribution $BP(k = .0009, p = 10^{10}, \alpha = 0.5)$ with mean 3,000

(3) Bounded Pareto distribution $BP(k = 332.067, p = 10^{10}, \alpha = 1.1)$ with mean 3,000

In each case, compute the fraction of load made up by just the top 1% of all jobs. Also report the size cutoff x defining the top 1% of jobs. It is easiest to use a symbolic math package to do this calculation.

20.3 Why It Is So Hard to Simulate the Bounded Pareto

This problem will illustrate why it is so hard to correctly generate instances of the Bounded Pareto. To generate instances of $BP(k, p, \alpha)$, we follow the usual Inverse-Transform procedure, obtaining

$$x = \frac{k}{\left(1 + u\left(\left(\frac{k}{p}\right)^{\alpha} - 1\right)\right)^{\frac{1}{\alpha}}}$$

where x is an instance of $BP(k, p, \alpha)$, and u is an instance of Uniform(0,1). This formula is correct except that u is not really an instance of Uniform$(0, 1)$, because the UNIX random number generator function rand() actually returns integers between 0 and $2^{31} - 1$. Thus u is actually an instance of Uniform$(0, 1 - 2^{-31})$. Close enough, right? We will see . . .

Table 20.1 shows different Bounded Pareto distribution parameters. Fill in the blank entries for this table. In particular, for the column p_{Actual}, fill in the actual maximum value possible, given that u is never higher than $1 - 2^{-31}$. Use p_{Actual} to compute C^2_{Actual} for the Bounded Pareto that is actually generated, as compared with C^2_{Theory}, the value we should have obtained if we had used p_{Theory}.

As p_{Theory} gets higher, what do you notice about C^2_{Actual} as compared with C^2_{Theory}?

Table 20.1. *Theory versus what is actually generated*

k	p_{Theory}	α	$\mathbf{E}\left[X_{\text{Theory}}\right]$	C^2_{Theory}	p_{Actual}	$\mathbf{E}\left[X_{\text{Actual}}\right]$	C^2_{Actual}
0.297	10^3	1.4	1				
0.290	10^4	1.4	1				
0.287	10^5	1.4	1				
0.286	10^6	1.4	1				
0.286	10^7	1.4	1				

CHAPTER 21

Phase-Type Distributions and Matrix-Analytic Methods

We have seen many examples of systems questions that can be answered by modeling the system as a Markov chain. For a system to be well modeled by a Markov chain, it is important that its workloads have the Markovian property. For example, if job sizes and interarrival times are independent and Exponentially distributed, and routing is probabilistic between the queues, then the system can typically be modeled easily using a CTMC. However, if job sizes or interarrival times are distributed according to a distribution that is not memoryless, for example Uniform$(0, 100)$, then it is not at all clear how a Markov chain can be used to model the system.

In this chapter, we introduce a technique called "the method of stages" or "the method of phases." The idea is that almost all distributions can be represented quite accurately by a mixture of Exponential distributions, known as a phase-type distribution (PH). We will see how to represent distributions by PH distributions in Section 21.1. Because PH distributions are made up of Exponential distributions, once all arrival and service processes have been represented by PH distributions, we will be able to model our systems problem as a CTMC, as shown in Section 21.2.

The Markov chains that result via the method of phases are often much more complex than Markov chains we have seen until now. They typically cannot be solved in closed form. Thus, in Section 21.3, we introduce the matrix-analytic method, a very powerful numerical method that allows us to solve many such chains that come up in practice.

21.1 Representing General Distributions by Exponentials

Variance plays a big role in representing general distributions.

Definition 21.1 The *squared coefficient of variation (SCV)*, C_X^2, of r.v. X, is given by

$$C_X^2 = \frac{\mathbf{Var}(X)}{\mathbf{E}[X]^2} = \frac{\mathbf{E}[X^2]}{\mathbf{E}[X]^2} - 1.$$

One can view C^2 as a normalized variance, because the variance is being scaled down by the square of the mean. Recall that if $X \sim \text{Exp}(\mu)$, then $\mathbf{E}[X] = \frac{1}{\mu}$, $\mathbf{Var}(X) = \frac{1}{\mu^2}$, and $C_X^2 = 1$. We will now consider distributions with lower C^2 and higher C^2.

Suppose that we would like to model a service time distribution with $C^2 < 1$ by using Exponential distributions. For example, we might be trying to describe the transmission time of a packet through a wire, which we denote by r.v. T. Although T may exhibit some small variability, the distribution of T is much closer to a Deterministic (constant-valued) distribution, with $C^2 = 0$, than to an Exponential.

Question: How can we mix Exponential distributions to create a Deterministic or near-Deterministic distribution?

Hint: Think about putting Exponential distributions in series.

Answer: We could model T as the time to pass through k stages, each requiring $\text{Exp}(k\mu)$ time, as shown in Figure 21.1. That is, let $T_i \sim \text{Exp}(k\mu)$, where

$$T = T_1 + T_2 + T_3 + \cdots + T_k.$$

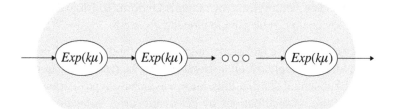

Figure 21.1. The time, T, to pass through all k stages has an Erlang-k distribution.

Definition 21.2 If T is the sum of k i.i.d. Exponential random variables, then T is said to have an **Erlang-k** distribution. A **generalized Erlang** distribution (also called a Hypoexponential distribution) is a sum of Exponential random variables with different rates.

Question: What are $\mathbf{E}[T]$, $\mathbf{Var}(T)$, and C_T^2 for Figure 21.1?

Answer:

$$\mathbf{E}[T] = k \cdot \frac{1}{k\mu} = \frac{1}{\mu}.$$

$$\mathbf{Var}(T) = k \cdot \mathbf{Var}(\text{Single Stage}) = k \cdot \left(\frac{1}{k\mu}\right)^2 = \frac{1}{k} \cdot \frac{1}{\mu^2}.$$

$$C_T^2 = \frac{\mathbf{Var}(T)}{\mathbf{E}[T]^2} = \frac{1}{k}.$$

Question: What happens to T as $k \to \infty$?

Answer: As $k \to \infty$, $C_T^2 \to 0$, and T converges to the Deterministic distribution of value $\frac{1}{\mu}$.

Thus with an infinite number of Exponential phases (or stages), we can approach a Deterministic distribution. The important point is that, given any mean $\mathbf{E}[T] = \frac{1}{\mu}$ and

C_T^2 of the form of $C_T^2 = \frac{1}{k}$, for some integer $k > 1$, one can construct an Erlang-k distribution matching that given $\mathbf{E}[T]$ and that C_T^2.

In the same way that an Erlang-k distribution is useful for approximating distributions with $C^2 < 1$, we can also define a mixture of Exponentials that is useful for approximating distributions with $C^2 > 1$. For example, it is well known that the time to serve web requests has high variability [47]. If T represents the time to serve a web request, we might have $\mathbf{E}[T] = 1$ seconds and $C_T^2 = 25$.

Question: How do we create a distribution with $C^2 > 1$ using Exponential stages?

Answer: Rather than putting the Exponential stages in series, we instead view these "in parallel," as shown in Figure 21.2.

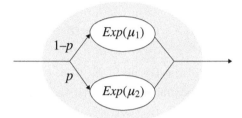

Figure 21.2. Hyperexponential distribution.

Definition 21.3 If T is distributed as $\text{Exp}(\mu_1)$ with probability p and is distributed as $\text{Exp}(\mu_2)$ with probability $1 - p$, then we say that T follows a ***Hyperexponential*** distribution, denoted by H_2.

$$T \sim \begin{cases} \text{Exp}(\mu_1) & \text{with probability } p \\ \text{Exp}(\mu_2) & \text{with probability } 1 - p \end{cases}$$

This is also sometimes referred to as a 2-phase Hyperexponential. If there are $k > 2$ phases, where T is distributed as $\text{Exp}(\mu_i)$ with probability p_i, for $1 \leq i \leq k$, then we say that T follows a ***k-phase Hyperexponential*** distribution, denoted by H_k.

Observe that the Hyperexponential distribution has three parameters: μ_1, μ_2, and p. Thus it seems reasonable that, given a mean and a C^2 value, we should be able to find some setting of the parameters of the Hyperexponential to match them. It turns out that the (2-phase) Hyperexponential distribution suffices to match any mean and C^2, provided $C^2 > 1$; see [152]. It can even be used to match 3 moments of a distribution, provided that the third moment is sufficiently high; see [185]. (One can express each of 3 moments of T as an equation involving the 3 parameters. This system of 3 equations and 3 parameters often has a solution.) However, the Hyperexponential is not useful for the case of $C^2 < 1$.

To gain some intuition for why the Hyperexponential is good at representing high-variability distributions, let us analyze the simple case of a **Degenerate Hyperexponential** distribution, where one of the phases is identically zero:

$$T \sim \begin{cases} \text{Exp}(p\mu) & \text{with probability } p \\ 0 & \text{with probability } 1 - p \end{cases}$$

Question: What is $\mathbf{E}[T]$?

Answer: $\mathbf{E}[T] = p \cdot \frac{1}{p\mu} = \frac{1}{\mu}$.

Question: What is C_T^2?

Answer:

$$\mathbf{E}[T^2] = p \cdot 2 \left(\frac{1}{p\mu}\right)^2 .$$

$$\mathbf{Var}(T) = \mathbf{E}[T^2] - (\mathbf{E}[T])^2 = p \cdot 2 \left(\frac{1}{p\mu}\right)^2 - \left(\frac{1}{\mu}\right)^2 = \frac{2-p}{p} \cdot \left(\frac{1}{\mu}\right)^2 .$$

$$C_T^2 = \frac{2-p}{p} = \frac{2}{p} - 1.$$

Observe that by definition $C_T^2 > 1$. As the value of p decreases, the value of C_T^2 increases.

The important point is that, given *any* mean $\mathbf{E}[T] = \frac{1}{\mu}$ and any $C_T^2 \geq 1$, we can find a Degenerate Hyperexponential to match that mean and C_T^2 (by setting $p = 2/(C_T^2 + 1)$).

Question: Does the (non-degenerate) Hyperexponential distribution have increasing failure rate or decreasing failure rate or neither?

Hint: There is an easy way to argue this intuitively without doing any derivations.

Answer: In Exercise 21.5, we will prove that the failure rate is decreasing, by going back to the original definition of failure rate. Here is a more intuitive argument: Imagine that T is distributed Hyperexponentially with 2 branches, where $\mu_1 > \mu_2$. The longer T has lasted so far, the greater the probability that we are in the μ_2 branch, and thus the greater the probability that T will last even longer.

Thus far we have seen how to model distributions with $C^2 < 1$, with an Erlang distribution, and distributions with $C^2 > 1$, with a Hyperexponential distribution. By combining these ideas of phases in series and phases in parallel, we can represent (almost) any distribution.

A phase-type distribution (PH) denotes the most general mixture of Exponential distributions in series and parallel.

Definition 21.4 *A k-phase PH distribution* with parameters $(\vec{a}, \mathbf{T})$ is the distribution of time until absorption in the following $(k+1)$-state CTMC:

- States 1 through k are transient, and state 0 is absorbing.
- $\vec{a} = (a_0, a_1, \ldots, a_k)$ where a_i denotes the probability that the starting state is i, and $\sum_{i=0}^{k} a_i = 1$.
- $\mathbf{T}$ is a $k \times (k+1)$ rate transition matrix from states $\{1, 2, \ldots, k\}$ to $\{0, 1, \ldots, k\}$, where $T_{ij} = \mu_{ij}$ is the rate of moving from state i to state j, where $i \neq j$.

There is no transition out of state 0, and none from a state back to itself.

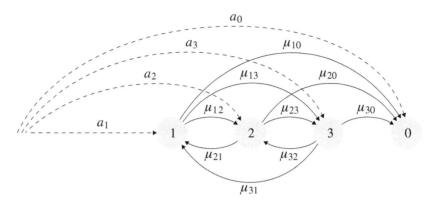

Figure 21.3. A 3-phase PH distribution is the time until absorption in this CTMC, where the initial state is chosen according to probability vector $\vec{a} = (a_0, a_1, a_2, a_3)$.

An illustration of a 3-phase PH distribution is given in Figure 21.3.

The power of PH distributions lies in the fact that they are dense in the class of all non-negative distribution functions. Practically speaking, this means that a PH distribution with a sufficient number of phases can approximate any non-negative distribution arbitrarily closely (see [8], Theorem 4.2).

A k-phase PH distribution has more than k^2 parameters. It is not obvious that one needs so many parameters to be able to well approximate arbitrary distributions. The class of Coxian distributions is still dense in the class of non-negative distribution functions [153, 154], yet Coxian distributions have many fewer parameters (they are a subset of the PH distributions). A k-stage Coxian distribution, depicted in Figure 21.4, looks similar to an Erlang-k, except that there are probabilities of stopping after each stage.

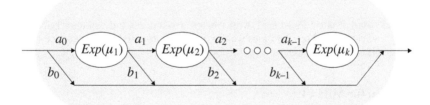

Figure 21.4. A k-stage Coxian distribution. The a_i's and b_i's are probabilities, where $a_i + b_i = 1, \forall i$.

In general, modeling an arbitrary distribution as a Coxian distribution is non-trivial, but doable. It is very common for researchers to match the first 3 moments of a given distribution using a 2-phase Coxian distribution, see Section 21.6. This allows us to represent problems involving general distributions via Markov chains, which we can often solve. We will see this in the next section.

Remark: The fact one can match the several moments of a distribution by a Coxian or PH distribution does not always mean that one has truly "captured" the character of the distribution, particularly its tail behavior, $\mathbf{P}\{X > t\}$. The question of how to best characterize a distribution using Exponential phases is still part of ongoing debate.

21.2 Markov Chain Modeling of PH Workloads

In this section we consider four simple examples of using Markov chains to model PH workloads. We defer discussion of how to solve these Markov chains to Section 21.3.

Markov Chain for M/E$_2$/1

Consider a single FCFS queue, with Poisson arrivals of rate λ, where the service times follow an Erlang-2 distribution. Specifically, the mean job size is $\frac{1}{\mu}$, and a job's service requires first passing through an $\text{Exp}(\mu_1)$ hurdle and then passing through an $\text{Exp}(\mu_2)$ hurdle, where $\mu_1 = \mu_2 = 2\mu$.

Question: What do we need to track in the state space?

Answer: Observe that, because the service order is still FCFS, only the earliest arrival can be serving. Assuming there is at least one job in the system, the job at the head of the queue is in either phase 1 or phase 2. The other jobs are waiting in the queue.

Thus a reasonable choice of state space is (i, j) where i indicates the number of jobs that are queueing (not serving) and j takes on value 1 or 2, depending on whether the job in service is in phase 1 or phase 2. Figure 21.5 shows the resulting Markov chain.

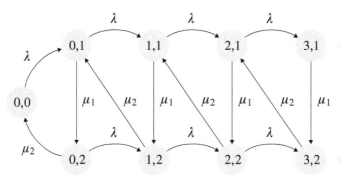

Figure 21.5. Markov chain for M/E$_2$/1, with average arrival rate λ and average service rate μ. State (i, j) indicates that there are i jobs waiting in the queue and the job in service (if there is one) is in phase j. Throughout $\mu_1 = \mu_2 = 2\mu$.

Markov Chain for M/H$_2$/1

Next consider a single-server FCFS queue, with Poisson arrivals of rate λ, where the service times follow a Hyperexponential distribution. Specifically, with probability p, a job will require $\text{Exp}(\mu_1)$ service, and with probability $1 - p$ the job will require $\text{Exp}(\mu_2)$ service.

Question: What should the Markov chain look like?

Hint: It is tempting to assign the job size at the time that the job arrives. What is the problem with doing this?

Answer: If we assign the job size at the time that it arrives, then for every job in the queue we need to track whether it has size $\text{Exp}(\mu_1)$ or $\text{Exp}(\mu_2)$. Thus, it is wiser to hold off determining the job's size until it is about to serve. Only when a job finishes serving is the size of the next job determined.

Question: What then is the state space?

Answer: One reasonable choice is to again use (i, j), where i denotes the number of jobs in the queue (not serving) and j denotes that the job in service (assuming there is one) has size $\text{Exp}(\mu_j)$. The resulting chain is shown in Figure 21.6.

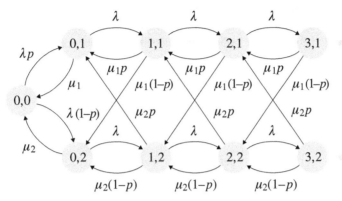

Figure 21.6. Markov chain for M/H$_2$/1, with average arrival rate λ. State (i, j) indicates that there are i jobs waiting in the queue and the job in service (if there is one) has size $\text{Exp}(\mu_j)$.

Markov Chain for E$_2$/M/1

Sometimes it is the arrival process, not the service process, that is non-Markovian. The E$_2$/M/1 queue is a single-server FCFS queue where job sizes are distributed as $\text{Exp}(\mu)$, but the interarrival times between jobs follow an Erlang-2 distribution. The mean interarrival time is $\frac{1}{\lambda}$; hence the rate of each phase of the Erlang-2 is 2λ.

Question: What should the Markov chain look like?

Answer: The key is to realize that the time until the next arrival involves two phases (two hurdles), and a second arrival cannot begin until both those hurdles have completed. That is, two arrivals cannot be "in progress" at the same time.

The resulting state space is therefore (i, j), where now i denotes the number of jobs in the system (including the job in service) and $j \in \{1, 2\}$ denotes the phase of the arrival in progress. The resulting chain is shown in Figure 21.7.

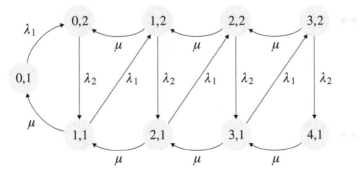

Figure 21.7. Markov chain for E$_2$/M/1 with average arrival rate λ and service rate μ. State (i, j) indicates that there are i jobs in the system, including the job in service, and j denotes the phase of the arrival in progress. The top row indicates that there is an arrival in progress that has just completed phase 1 and is trying to complete phase 2. The bottom row indicates that there is an arrival in progress that is still trying to complete phase 1. Throughout $\lambda_1 = \lambda_2 = 2\lambda$.

Markov Chain for $M_t/M/1$

Another example of a queue with a non-Markovian arrival process is the case of a time-varying arrival rate, where the arrival rate fluctuates between λ^H (some high rate) and λ^L (some low rate), spending $\text{Exp}(\alpha^H)$ time in the high arrival rate regime and $\text{Exp}(\alpha^L)$ time in the low arrival rate regime, as depicted in Figure 21.8. Time-varying load is denoted by M_t. The notation $M_t/M/1$ indicates that the arrival rate changes over time. The notation $M/M_t/1$ indicates that the service rate changes over time.

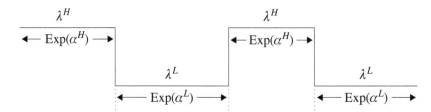

Figure 21.8. The arrival process is called a Markov-modulated Poisson process.

Question: What should the Markov chain look like for the $M_t/M/1$?

Answer: We need to track whether the system as a whole is operating in the high-load phase or the low-load phase. We use the upper (respectively, lower) row of the chain to denote that the system is in the high load (respectively, low load) phase. The resulting Markov chain is shown in Figure 21.9.

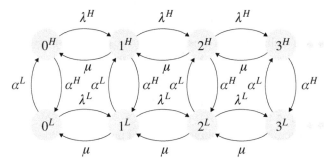

Figure 21.9. Markov chain for $M_t/M/1$, where the arrival rate oscillates between λ^H for $\text{Exp}(\alpha^H)$ duration and λ^L for $\text{Exp}(\alpha^L)$ duration. The state indicates the number of jobs in the system, and the superscript indicates the current regime.

21.3 The Matrix-Analytic Method

Consider the infinite-state Markov chains from Section 21.2. These look like the random walk of the M/M/1; however, rather than having just one row, they have two rows – and possibly more than two rows if more than two phases are used in the PH distribution. If we attempt to write out the balance equations for these chains, we quickly see that they are quite complex, and there is no obvious "guess" for the limiting distribution.

Developed by Marcel Neuts [129, 130], matrix-analytic methods are approximate numerical methods for solving Markov chains where the chains (i) repeat (after some point) and (ii) grow unboundedly in no more than one dimension. In particular, matrix-analytic methods can be used to solve all the chains we have seen in Section 21.2. All these chains grow unboundedly in one dimension (increasing number of jobs), yet they have only a finite number of states (two, in all the examples we have seen) in the other dimension, and they all repeat. By saying that matrix-analytic methods are "numerical methods," we mean that they do not provide a closed-form symbolic solution, in terms of λ's and μ's, but rather we can only solve an instance of the chain (where the rates are all numbers). The solution is obtained by iteration, and there is an error associated with the solution. In practice, the number of iterations is not too large, allowing the solution of chains such as those in Section 21.2 to be obtained within seconds. Also in practice the error is quite small, except for very unusual PH distributions with highly unbalanced rates, created for example by modeling workloads with extremely high C^2 values in the thousands.

The remainder of this chapter serves as a very brief introduction to matrix-analytic methods. For a more comprehensive treatment, we refer the reader to [115].

21.4 Analysis of Time-Varying Load

Our first illustration of matrix-analytic methods is the M_t/M/1 queue, shown earlier in Figure 21.8. This is a particularly nice example, because the repetition starts right from the beginning.

21.4.1 High-Level Ideas

We think of the M_t/M/1 chain as being divided into levels. Level 0 consists of the states 0^H and 0^L. Likewise, level i consists of the states i^H and i^L. In the same way that for the M/M/1 we sought π_i, we now seek $\vec{\pi}_i$, where

$$\vec{\pi}_i = (\pi_{i^H}, \pi_{i^L}).$$

The high-level idea behind matrix-analytic methods is that we recursively express $\vec{\pi}_i$ in terms of $\vec{\pi}_{i-1}$. However, rather than being related by a constant, ρ, as in the M/M/1, they are instead related by a matrix $\mathbf{R}$, such that

$$\vec{\pi}_i = \vec{\pi}_{i-1} \cdot \mathbf{R},$$

which, when expanded, yields

$$\vec{\pi}_i = \vec{\pi}_0 \cdot \mathbf{R}^i.$$

Finding this matrix $\mathbf{R}$ requires solving a matrix equation by iteration. Note that throughout, we still denote the limiting distribution by $\vec{\pi}$, where $\vec{\pi}$ is the vector of all limiting probabilities. In the case of the $M_t/M/1$,

$$\vec{\pi} = \left(\pi_{0^H}, \pi_{0^L}, \pi_{1^H}, \pi_{1^L}, \pi_{2^H}, \pi_{2^L}, \ldots \right).$$

21.4.2 The Generator Matrix, $\mathbf{Q}$

To illustrate the method, it is useful to start by rewriting the balance equations in terms of a "generator matrix," $\mathbf{Q}$. This is a matrix such that

$$\vec{\pi} \cdot \mathbf{Q} = \vec{0} \qquad \text{where } \vec{\pi} \cdot \vec{1} = 1. \tag{21.1}$$

Here $\vec{\pi}$ is the limiting distribution, and $\vec{1}$ is always an appropriately sized vector of 1s.

Question: Try to write down $\mathbf{Q}$ for the case of an $M/M/1$, just to get the feel of it.

Answer: $\mathbf{Q} =$

$$\begin{array}{c c} & \begin{array}{c c c c c} {\scriptstyle 0} & {\scriptstyle 1} & {\scriptstyle 2} & {\scriptstyle 3} & \end{array} \\ \begin{array}{c} {\scriptstyle 0} \\ {\scriptstyle 1} \\ {\scriptstyle 2} \\ {\scriptstyle 3} \\ {\scriptstyle \vdots} \end{array} & \left[\begin{array}{c c c c c} -\lambda & \lambda & & & \\ \mu & -(\lambda+\mu) & \lambda & & \\ & \mu & -(\lambda+\mu) & \lambda & \\ & & \mu & -(\lambda+\mu) & \cdots \\ & & & \mu & \ddots \end{array} \right]. \end{array}$$

Equation (21.1) directly translates to the balance equations:

$$0 = \pi_0 \cdot (-\lambda) + \pi_1 \cdot \mu$$

$$0 = \pi_0 \cdot \lambda + \pi_1 \cdot (-(\lambda+\mu)) + \pi_2 \cdot \mu$$

$$0 = \pi_1 \cdot \lambda + \pi_2 \cdot (-(\lambda+\mu)) + \pi_3 \cdot \mu$$

$$\vdots$$

Observe that the diagonal entries of $\mathbf{Q}$ are all negative and represent the negation of the total rate of leaving the corresponding state.

Question: Let $\mathbf{Q}(*, i)$ denote the ith column of $\mathbf{Q}$. What is the value of the dot product $\vec{\pi} \cdot \mathbf{Q}(*, i)$?

Answer: Each column of $\mathbf{Q}$, when multiplied by $\vec{\pi}$, corresponds to a single balance equation. Thus, by definition, the dot product is 0.

Question: Now try to write $\mathbf{Q}$ for the $M_t/M/1$.

Answer: It helps to recall that $\vec{\pi} = \left(\pi_{0^H}, \pi_{0^L}, \pi_{1^H}, \pi_{1^L}, \pi_{2^H}, \pi_{2^L}, \ldots \right)$.
Now, viewing each column as the coefficients of a balance equation, we have

$$
\mathbf{Q} =
\begin{array}{c}
{}^{0^H} \\ {}^{0^L} \\ {}^{1^H} \\ {}^{1^L} \\ {}^{2^H} \\ {}^{2^L} \\ {}_{\cdots}
\end{array}
\left[
\begin{array}{cc|cc|cc|c}
-\left(\lambda^H + \alpha^H\right) & \alpha^H & \lambda^H & 0 & & & \\
\alpha^L & -\left(\lambda^L + \alpha^L\right) & 0 & \lambda^L & & & \\
\hline
\mu & 0 & -\left(\lambda^H + \alpha^H + \mu\right) & \alpha^H & \lambda^H & 0 & \\
0 & \mu & \alpha^L & -\left(\lambda^L + \alpha^L + \mu\right) & 0 & \lambda^L & \\
\hline
& & \mu & 0 & -\left(\lambda^H + \alpha^H + \mu\right) & \alpha^H & \\
& & 0 & \mu & \alpha^L & -\left(\lambda^L + \alpha^L + \mu\right) & \\
\hline
& & & & & & \ddots
\end{array}
\right].
$$

We can see that this $\mathbf{Q}$ matrix is composed of three 2×2 matrices that repeat, plus one 2×2 matrix that does not repeat:

$$
\mathbf{B} =
\begin{array}{c} {}^{i^H} \\ {}_{i^L} \end{array}
\begin{bmatrix} \mu & 0 \\ 0 & \mu \end{bmatrix}
\quad \text{(``Backwards'')} \quad i > 0
$$

$$
\mathbf{L} =
\begin{array}{c} {}^{i^H} \\ {}_{i^L} \end{array}
\begin{bmatrix} -(\lambda^H + \alpha^H + \mu) & \alpha^H \\ \alpha^L & -(\lambda^L + \alpha^L + \mu) \end{bmatrix}
\quad \text{(``Local'')} \quad i > 0
$$

$$
\mathbf{F} =
\begin{array}{c} {}^{i^H} \\ {}_{i^L} \end{array}
\begin{bmatrix} \lambda^H & 0 \\ 0 & \lambda^L \end{bmatrix}
\quad \text{(``Forwards'')} \quad i \geq 0
$$

$$
\mathbf{L}_0 =
\begin{array}{c} {}^{i^H} \\ {}_{i^L} \end{array}
\begin{bmatrix} -(\lambda^H + \alpha^H) & \alpha^H \\ \alpha^L & -(\lambda^L + \alpha^L) \end{bmatrix}
\quad \text{(``Initial Local'')} \quad i = 0
$$

We can now write $\mathbf{Q}$ more economically as

$$
\mathbf{Q} =
\begin{array}{c} {}_{2|} \\ {}_{2|} \\ {}_{2|} \\ {}_{2|} \end{array}
\begin{bmatrix}
\mathbf{L}_0 & \mathbf{F} & & \\
\mathbf{B} & \mathbf{L} & \mathbf{F} & \\
& \mathbf{B} & \mathbf{L} & \mathbf{F} \\
& & \mathbf{B} & \ddots
\end{bmatrix}.
$$

Using the notation $\vec{\pi}_i = (\pi_{i^H}, \pi_{i^L})$, we now rewrite the balance equations $\vec{\pi} \cdot \mathbf{Q} = \vec{0}$ as **matrix equations**:

$$\vec{0} = \vec{\pi}_0 \cdot \mathbf{L_0} + \vec{\pi}_1 \cdot \mathbf{B}$$
$$\vec{0} = \vec{\pi}_0 \cdot \mathbf{F} + \vec{\pi}_1 \cdot \mathbf{L} + \vec{\pi}_2 \cdot \mathbf{B}$$
$$\vec{0} = \vec{\pi}_1 \cdot \mathbf{F} + \vec{\pi}_2 \cdot \mathbf{L} + \vec{\pi}_3 \cdot \mathbf{B}$$
$$\vec{0} = \vec{\pi}_2 \cdot \mathbf{F} + \vec{\pi}_3 \cdot \mathbf{L} + \vec{\pi}_4 \cdot \mathbf{B}$$
$$\vdots$$

21.4.3 *Solving for* $\mathbf{R}$

We make the educated guess that

$$\vec{\pi}_i = \vec{\pi}_0 \cdot \mathbf{R}^i, \quad \forall i > 0$$

for some matrix $\mathbf{R}$, to be determined, where $\vec{\pi}_0 = (\pi_{0^H}, \pi_{0^L})$ and $\vec{\pi}_i = (\pi_{i^H}, \pi_{i^L})$. Substituting this guess into the matrix equations yields the following:

$$\vec{0} = \vec{\pi}_0 \cdot \mathbf{L_0} + \vec{\pi}_0 \cdot \mathbf{RB} \quad \Rightarrow \quad \vec{\pi}_0 (\mathbf{L_0} + \mathbf{RB}) = \vec{0}$$
$$\vec{0} = \vec{\pi}_0 \cdot \mathbf{F} + \vec{\pi}_0 \cdot \mathbf{RL} + \vec{\pi}_0 \cdot \mathbf{R}^2\mathbf{B} \quad \Rightarrow \quad \vec{\pi}_0 (\mathbf{F} + \mathbf{RL} + \mathbf{R}^2\mathbf{B}) = \vec{0}$$
$$\vec{0} = \vec{\pi}_1 \cdot \mathbf{F} + \vec{\pi}_1 \cdot \mathbf{RL} + \vec{\pi}_1 \cdot \mathbf{R}^2\mathbf{B} \quad \Rightarrow \quad \vec{\pi}_1 (\mathbf{F} + \mathbf{RL} + \mathbf{R}^2\mathbf{B}) = \vec{0}$$
$$\vec{0} = \vec{\pi}_2 \cdot \mathbf{F} + \vec{\pi}_2 \cdot \mathbf{RL} + \vec{\pi}_2 \cdot \mathbf{R}^2\mathbf{B} \quad \Rightarrow \quad \vec{\pi}_2 (\mathbf{F} + \mathbf{RL} + \mathbf{R}^2\mathbf{B}) = \vec{0}$$
$$\vdots$$

Observe the common portion is: $\mathbf{F} + \mathbf{RL} + \mathbf{R}^2\mathbf{B} = \mathbf{0}$. We use this common portion to determine $\mathbf{R}$ as follows:

$$\mathbf{F} + \mathbf{RL} + \mathbf{R}^2\mathbf{B} = \mathbf{0}$$
$$\Rightarrow \mathbf{RL} = -\left(\mathbf{R}^2\mathbf{B} + \mathbf{F}\right)$$
$$\Rightarrow \mathbf{R} = -\left(\mathbf{R}^2\mathbf{B} + \mathbf{F}\right)\mathbf{L}^{-1}$$

We now solve for $\mathbf{R}$ by iterating (here $\mathbf{R}_n$ denotes the nth iteration of $\mathbf{R}$):

1. Let $\mathbf{R}_0 = \mathbf{0}$ (or a better guess, if available).
2. While $||\mathbf{R}_{n+1} - \mathbf{R}_n|| > \epsilon$,
   Set $\mathbf{R}_{n+1} = -\left(\mathbf{R}_n^2\mathbf{B} + \mathbf{F}\right)\mathbf{L}^{-1}$.

This process keeps iterating until it determines that $\mathbf{R}$ has "converged." Sadly there is no known closed-form solution for the above matrix quadratic in general; thus iteration is the approach that is used.[1] Once $\mathbf{R}$ converges, we set $\vec{\pi}_i = \vec{\pi}_0\mathbf{R}^i$. These limiting probabilities satisfy the balance equations.

There are several points related to solving for $\mathbf{R}$ that we have not defined. First, there are several possible definitions of the metric: $||\mathbf{R}_{n+1} - \mathbf{R}_n||$. The typical definition is the maximum of all the elements in the matrix $\mathbf{R}_{n+1} - \mathbf{R}_n$. Thus, while the biggest

---

[1] For some special chains $\mathbf{R}$ can be expressed in closed form; see [115].

difference exceeds ϵ, we continue iterating. Only when all the element-wise differences are smaller than ϵ do we stop iterating. Also, the definition of ϵ is unspecified. We typically start with $\epsilon = 10^{-7}$; however, if convergence is slow, we might try increasing ϵ by a factor of 10. This is tricky because small differences in $\mathbf{R}$ can have a profound effect on the final limiting probabilities.

21.4.4 Finding $\vec{\pi}_0$

The only value remaining is $\vec{\pi}_0 = (\pi_{0^H}, \pi_{0^L})$. We have two equations involving $\vec{\pi}_0$: First, we have the first matrix balance equation listed in Section 21.4.3:

$$\vec{\pi}_0 \left(\mathbf{L_0} + \mathbf{RB} \right) = \vec{0} \tag{21.2}$$

Second we have the normalizing equation:

$$\vec{\pi} \cdot \vec{1} = 1 \tag{21.3}$$

Just as we did in the scalar case, we are going to replace one of the balance equations with the normalization equation. We start by rewriting the normalizing equation (21.3) in terms of $\vec{\pi}_0$:

$$\sum_{i=0}^{\infty} \vec{\pi}_i \cdot \vec{1} = 1, \quad \text{where} \quad \vec{1} = (1, 1)$$

$$\sum_{i=0}^{\infty} \vec{\pi}_0 \mathbf{R}^i \cdot \vec{1} = 1$$

$$\vec{\pi}_0 \left(\sum_{i=0}^{\infty} \mathbf{R}^i \right) \vec{1} = 1$$

$$\vec{\pi}_0 \left(\mathbf{I} - \mathbf{R} \right)^{-1} \vec{1} = 1 \tag{21.4}$$

For notational simplicity, let $\mathbf{\Phi} = \mathbf{L_0} + \mathbf{RB}$ and $\mathbf{\Psi} = (\mathbf{I} - \mathbf{R})^{-1} \vec{1}$. Thus, (21.2) becomes $\vec{\pi}_0 \mathbf{\Phi} = \vec{0}$ and (21.4) becomes $\vec{\pi}_0 \mathbf{\Psi} = 1$.

Expanding out $\vec{\pi}_0 \mathbf{\Phi} = \vec{0}$ to show its components, we have

$$\begin{bmatrix} \pi_{0^H} & \pi_{0^L} \end{bmatrix} \begin{bmatrix} \Phi_{00} & \Phi_{01} \\ \Phi_{10} & \Phi_{11} \end{bmatrix} = \begin{bmatrix} 0 & 0 \end{bmatrix}.$$

After replacing one balance equation (one column) with the normalizing equation, we get:

$$\begin{bmatrix} \pi_{0^H} & \pi_{0^L} \end{bmatrix} \begin{bmatrix} \Psi_0 & \Phi_{01} \\ \Psi_1 & \Phi_{11} \end{bmatrix} = \begin{bmatrix} 1 & 0 \end{bmatrix}.$$

This system of equations has a unique solution, and we solve this system for $\vec{\pi}_0 = (\pi_{0^H}, \pi_{0^L})$. Using $\vec{\pi}_i = \vec{\pi}_0 \mathbf{R}^i$, we now have all the $\vec{\pi}_i$.

21.4.5 *Performance Metrics*

From the limiting probabilities, we now develop a closed-form expression for $\mathbf{E}[N]$ in terms of only $\vec{\pi}_0$ and $\mathbf{R}$:

$$
\begin{aligned}
\mathbf{E}[N] &= \sum_{i=0}^{\infty} i \cdot \vec{\pi}_i \cdot \vec{1} \\
&= \sum_{i=0}^{\infty} i \cdot \vec{\pi}_0 \cdot \mathbf{R}^i \cdot \vec{1} \\
&= \vec{\pi}_0 \cdot \sum_{i=1}^{\infty} i \cdot \mathbf{R}^{i-1} \cdot \mathbf{R} \cdot \vec{1} \\
&= \vec{\pi}_0 \cdot \frac{d}{d\mathbf{R}} \left(\sum_{i=0}^{\infty} \mathbf{R}^i \right) \cdot \mathbf{R} \cdot \vec{1} \quad \text{(matrix calculus)} \\
&= \vec{\pi}_0 \cdot \frac{d}{d\mathbf{R}} (\mathbf{I} - \mathbf{R})^{-1} \cdot \mathbf{R} \cdot \vec{1} \\
&= \vec{\pi}_0 \cdot (\mathbf{I} - \mathbf{R})^{-2} \cdot \mathbf{R} \cdot \vec{1}
\end{aligned}
$$

Similarly, we can define higher moments of N.

To determine $\mathbf{E}[T]$, we first define the average arrival rate λ_{avg}, by

$$
\lambda_{\text{avg}} = \frac{\frac{1}{\alpha^H} \lambda^H + \frac{1}{\alpha^L} \lambda^L}{\frac{1}{\alpha^H} + \frac{1}{\alpha^L}}.
$$

Then, via Little's Law,

$$
\mathbf{E}[T] = \frac{1}{\lambda_{\text{avg}}} \mathbf{E}[N] = \frac{1}{\lambda_{\text{avg}}} \cdot \vec{\pi}_0 \cdot (\mathbf{I} - \mathbf{R})^{-2} \cdot \mathbf{R} \cdot \vec{1}.
$$

The analysis of the $M_t/M/1$ is discussed further in Exercise 21.2.

Question: Suppose that we applied the matrix-analytic method to derive the limiting probabilities for the M/M/1. What would $\mathbf{R}$ look like?

Answer: In this case, $\mathbf{R}$ is just a 1×1 matrix, namely a scalar, and does not require iteration to obtain. You will solve for it in Exercise 21.1.

21.5 More Complex Chains

Sometimes the repeating portion of a chain only starts after level M. In this case, we can still use matrix-analytic methods to solve the chain. However, the initial matrix, $\mathbf{L}_0$, must be larger, so as to encompass the entire non-repeating portion of the chain.

To illustrate how this works, consider the following example, which we refer to as the $M^*/E_2^*/1$. Here the arrival process is Poisson, but the average arrival rate is λ whenever the system is non-empty and is λ' when the system is empty (imagine that the queue is sent additional work from another source when it is empty, as part of a load balancing effort). The job service distribution is a two-phase generalized Erlang, where the first

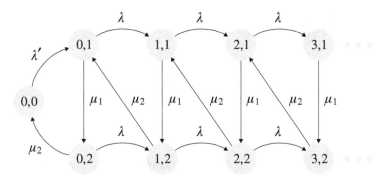

Figure 21.10. Markov chain for $M^*/E_2^*/1$.

phase is distributed as $\mathrm{Exp}(\mu_1)$ and the second is distributed as $\mathrm{Exp}(\mu_2)$. We define the state as (i, s), where i is the number of jobs in queue (not counting any job in service) and s is the phase of the job in service, or 0 if there is no job in service.

Figure 21.10 shows the CTMC for this system.

Question: Defining $a_1 = -(\lambda + \mu_1)$ and $a_2 = -(\lambda + \mu_2)$, express $\mathbf{Q}$ using a_1 and a_2.

Answer:

$$
\mathbf{Q} =
\begin{array}{c}
\begin{array}{c} \\ (0,0) \\ (0,1) \\ (0,2) \\ (1,1) \\ (1,2) \\ (2,1) \\ (2,2) \\ (3,1) \\ (3,2) \\ \end{array}
\begin{array}{c}
\begin{array}{cccccccccc} (0,0) & (0,1) & (0,2) & (1,1) & (1,2) & (2,1) & (2,2) & (3,1) & (3,2) & \cdots \end{array} \\
\left[
\begin{array}{ccc|cc|cc|cc|c}
-\lambda' & \lambda' & 0 & 0 & 0 & & & & & \\
0 & a_1 & \mu_1 & \lambda & 0 & & & & & \\
\mu_2 & 0 & a_2 & 0 & \lambda & & & & & \\
\hline
0 & 0 & 0 & a_1 & \mu_1 & \lambda & 0 & & & \\
0 & \mu_2 & 0 & 0 & a_2 & 0 & \lambda & & & \\
\hline
 & & & 0 & 0 & a_1 & \mu_1 & \lambda & 0 & \\
 & & & \mu_2 & 0 & 0 & a_2 & 0 & \lambda & \\
\hline
 & & & & & 0 & 0 & a_1 & \mu_1 & \\
 & & & & & \mu_2 & 0 & 0 & a_2 & \\
\hline
 & & & & & & & & & \ddots
\end{array}
\right]
\end{array}
\end{array}
$$

More succinctly, this can be written as

$$
\mathbf{Q} = \begin{array}{c} \\ 3| \\ 2| \\ 2| \\ 2| \\ 2| \end{array}
\begin{array}{ccccc} \overset{3}{} & \overset{2}{} & \overset{2}{} & \overset{2}{} & \overset{2}{} \end{array}
\left[\begin{array}{ccccc}
\mathbf{L_0} & \mathbf{F_0} & & & \\
\mathbf{B_0} & \mathbf{L} & \mathbf{F} & & \\
 & \mathbf{B} & \mathbf{L} & \mathbf{F} & \\
 & & \mathbf{B} & \mathbf{L} & \mathbf{F} \\
 & & & \mathbf{B} & \ddots
\end{array} \right].
$$

In this case $\mathbf{L_0}$ is a 3×3 matrix, representing the non-repeating portion of the chain. Also observe that we needed to introduce $\mathbf{F_0}$ and $\mathbf{B_0}$ which are very similar to $\mathbf{F}$ and $\mathbf{B}$, respectively, but have asymmetric dimensions, which are needed to "link" the non-repeating portion of the chain to the repeating portion of the chain.

We define $\vec{\pi}_0 = \left(\pi_{(0,0)}, \pi_{(0,1)}, \pi_{(0,2)} \right)$ and $\vec{\pi}_i = \left(\pi_{(i,1)}, \pi_{(i,2)} \right)$, $\quad \forall i > 0$. Now we rewrite the balance equations $\vec{\pi} \cdot \mathbf{Q} = \vec{0}$ as matrix equations:

$$
\vec{0} = \vec{\pi}_0 \cdot \mathbf{L_0} + \vec{\pi}_1 \cdot \mathbf{B_0}
$$

$$
\vec{0} = \vec{\pi}_0 \cdot \mathbf{F_0} + \vec{\pi}_1 \cdot \mathbf{L} + \vec{\pi}_2 \cdot \mathbf{B}
$$

$$
\vec{0} = \vec{\pi}_1 \cdot \mathbf{F} + \vec{\pi}_2 \cdot \mathbf{L} + \vec{\pi}_3 \cdot \mathbf{B}
$$

$$
\vec{0} = \vec{\pi}_2 \cdot \mathbf{F} + \vec{\pi}_3 \cdot \mathbf{L} + \vec{\pi}_4 \cdot \mathbf{B}
$$

$$
\vec{0} = \vec{\pi}_3 \cdot \mathbf{F} + \vec{\pi}_4 \cdot \mathbf{L} + \vec{\pi}_5 \cdot \mathbf{B}
$$

$$
\vdots
$$

We now guess that

$$
\vec{\pi}_{M+i} = \vec{\pi}_M \cdot \mathbf{R}^i. \tag{21.5}
$$

Question: What is M here?

Answer: In the time-varying load example from Section 21.4, M was 0, but for this chain, $M = 1$.

Substituting the above guess into the balance equations yields the following matrix equations:

$$
\vec{0} = \vec{\pi}_0 \cdot \mathbf{L_0} + \vec{\pi}_1 \cdot \mathbf{B_0}
$$

$$
\vec{0} = \vec{\pi}_0 \cdot \mathbf{F_0} + \vec{\pi}_1 \cdot \mathbf{L} + \vec{\pi}_1 \cdot \mathbf{RB}
$$

$$
\vec{0} = \vec{\pi}_1 \cdot \mathbf{F} + \vec{\pi}_1 \cdot \mathbf{RL} + \vec{\pi}_1 \cdot \mathbf{R^2 B} \quad \Rightarrow \quad \vec{\pi}_1 \left(\mathbf{F} + \mathbf{RL} + \mathbf{R^2 B} \right) = 0
$$

$$
\vec{0} = \vec{\pi}_2 \cdot \mathbf{F} + \vec{\pi}_2 \cdot \mathbf{RL} + \vec{\pi}_2 \cdot \mathbf{R^2 B} \quad \Rightarrow \quad \vec{\pi}_2 \left(\mathbf{F} + \mathbf{RL} + \mathbf{R^2 B} \right) = 0
$$

$$
\vec{0} = \vec{\pi}_3 \cdot \mathbf{F} + \vec{\pi}_3 \cdot \mathbf{RL} + \vec{\pi}_3 \cdot \mathbf{R^2 B} \quad \Rightarrow \quad \vec{\pi}_3 \left(\mathbf{F} + \mathbf{RL} + \mathbf{R^2 B} \right) = 0
$$

$$
\vdots
$$

The common portion is again $\mathbf{F} + \mathbf{RL} + \mathbf{R}^2\mathbf{B} = \mathbf{0}$. Thus

$$\mathbf{RL} = -\left(\mathbf{R}^2\mathbf{B} + \mathbf{F}\right)$$
$$\implies \mathbf{R} = -\left(\mathbf{R}^2\mathbf{B} + \mathbf{F}\right)\mathbf{L}^{-1}.$$

We now solve for $\mathbf{R}$ by iterating:

1. Let $\mathbf{R}_0 = \mathbf{0}$ (or a better guess, if available).
2. While $||\mathbf{R}_{n+1} - \mathbf{R}_n|| > \epsilon$,
   Set $\mathbf{R}_{n+1} = -\left(\mathbf{R}_n^2\mathbf{B} + \mathbf{F}\right)\mathbf{L}^{-1}$.

As before, we iterate until $\mathbf{R}$ has "converged."

All that is left is to determine the initial limiting probabilities. In this case, this means determining both $\vec{\pi}_0 = \left(\pi_{(0,0)}, \pi_{(0,1)}, \pi_{(0,2)}\right)$ and $\vec{\pi}_1 = \left(\pi_{(1,1)}, \pi_{(1,2)}\right)$.

The "local" portion of the balance equations can be written as

$$\begin{bmatrix} \vec{\pi}_0 & \vec{\pi}_1 \end{bmatrix} \begin{bmatrix} \mathbf{L}_0 & \mathbf{F}_0 \\ \mathbf{B}_0 & \mathbf{L} + \mathbf{RB} \end{bmatrix} = \vec{0},$$

or equivalently $\begin{bmatrix} \vec{\pi}_0 & \vec{\pi}_1 \end{bmatrix} \mathbf{\Phi} = \vec{0}$ where

$$\mathbf{\Phi} = \begin{bmatrix} \mathbf{L}_0 & \mathbf{F}_0 \\ \mathbf{B}_0 & \mathbf{L} + \mathbf{RB} \end{bmatrix}. \tag{21.6}$$

Here $\vec{0}$ refers to $[0,0,0,0,0]$.

We also have the normalizing equation $\vec{\pi} \cdot \vec{1} = 1$. We again replace one of the balance equations with the normalization equation. Rewriting the normalization equation in terms of $\vec{\pi}_0$ and $\vec{\pi}_1$,

$$\vec{\pi}_0 \cdot \vec{1} + \sum_{i=1}^{\infty} \vec{\pi}_i \cdot \vec{1} = 1.$$

$$\vec{\pi}_0 \cdot \vec{1} + \sum_{i=0}^{\infty} \vec{\pi}_1 \mathbf{R}^i \cdot \vec{1} = 1.$$

$$\vec{\pi}_0 \cdot \vec{1} + \vec{\pi}_1 \left(\sum_{i=0}^{\infty} \mathbf{R}^i\right) \vec{1} = 1.$$

$$\vec{\pi}_0 \cdot \vec{1} + \vec{\pi}_1 \left(\mathbf{I} - \mathbf{R}\right)^{-1} \vec{1} = 1.$$

Note that the first $\vec{1}$ in each equation above has dimension 3, while the second $\vec{1}$ has dimension 2. We define

$$\mathbf{\Psi} = \begin{bmatrix} \vec{1} \\ \left(\mathbf{I} - \mathbf{R}\right)^{-1} \cdot \vec{1} \end{bmatrix}$$

to be a column vector of size 5.

Then we can write the normalization equation as

$$\begin{bmatrix} \vec{\pi}_0 & \vec{\pi}_1 \end{bmatrix} \boldsymbol{\Psi} = 1.$$

To combine the balance equations with the normalization equation, we return to equation (21.6), repeated here for easy reference:

$$\begin{bmatrix} \vec{\pi}_0 & \vec{\pi}_1 \end{bmatrix} \boldsymbol{\Phi} = [0, 0, 0, 0, 0], \quad \text{where} \quad \boldsymbol{\Phi} = \begin{bmatrix} \mathbf{L}_0 & \mathbf{F}_0 \\ \mathbf{B}_0 & \mathbf{L} + \mathbf{RB} \end{bmatrix}$$

We replace the first column of $\boldsymbol{\Phi}$ with $\boldsymbol{\Psi}$, and the first element of the zero vector with 1. We then solve the resulting system of 5 linear equations for $(\vec{\pi}_0, \vec{\pi}_1)$. From (21.5), we now obtain all the remaining limiting probabilities.

21.6 Readings and Further Remarks

Some additional information on phase-type distributions is provided in [5], pp. 148–59. Representing general distributions by phase-type distributions is a very powerful technique. It is often the only technique known for Markov modeling of problems involving general distributions. To make the Markov chain tractable, it is important that the PH representation of these general distributions does not require too many phases or too many parameters. There is a great deal of research into finding PH representations of general distributions that use few phases and yet accurately represent the given distribution. We recommend [135] and [137] as examples of moment matching and [56] as an example of tail fitting.

Unfortunately there are not many books that explain matrix-analytic methods. Latouche and Ramaswami [115] have an excellent textbook devoted to matrix-analytic methods. The book goes much further than this chapter, explaining the meaning behind the $\mathbf{R}$ matrix. The book also discusses convergence properties of the iteration. Matrix-analytic methods are also covered in Nelson's book [127].

One final remark: There are situations where matrix-analytic methods break down because higher powers of $\mathbf{R}$ become singular. This can happen for a number of reasons, but one condition that induces such behavior is highly variable distributions. Suppose for example that one is studying delay in the $M/H_2/2$ system. If one chooses H_2 with $C^2 < 100$, matrix-analytic methods are excellent for deriving mean delay. However, with $C^2 > 1000$, matrix-analytic methods can sometimes break down.

21.7 Exercises

21.1 Applying Matrix-Analytic Methods to the M/M/1

Consider the M/M/1 with arrival rate λ and service rate μ. Solve for the limiting probabilities using the matrix-analytic method in this chapter. Specifically, derive $\mathbf{Q}$, $\mathbf{B}$, $\mathbf{L}$, $\mathbf{F}$, and $\mathbf{R}$, and then use these to write out the limiting probabilities.

21.2 Time-Varying Load

Consider the M_t/M/1 with a mean job size of 1 and mean load 0.7, where the arrival rate fluctuates between high-load, 1.2, and low-load, 0.2, with $\text{Exp}(\alpha)$ time in each state. Apply the matrix-analytic procedure described in this chapter to determine the mean response time, $\mathbf{E}[T]$, for a range of switching rates, α, ranging from very quick alternation to very slow alternation (use a log scale).

(a) Create a plot of $\mathbf{E}[T]$ versus α.
(b) When alternation is very fast (high α), what does your $\mathbf{E}[T]$ converge to? Why?
(c) When alternation is very slow (very low α), what happens to $\mathbf{E}[T]$? Why?
(d) Suppose that the arrival rate instead fluctuates between 0.9 and 0.5 with $\text{Exp}(\alpha)$ time in each state. Again the mean is 0.7. What should the mean response time look like now in the case when alternation is very slow (very low α)? Why?

Remark: Unfortunately, exact closed-form solutions for the M_t/M/1 require solving a cubic, and thus are not straightforward, nor has much been developed in terms of approximations. See [78] for additional insights.

21.3 Applying Matrix-Analytic Methods to the M/Cox/1

Use the matrix-analytic method to analyze the M/Cox/1 queue. The arrival process is Poisson(λ). The service time distribution is *phase-type* with 2 stages, the first of duration $\text{Exp}(\mu_1)$ and the second of duration $\text{Exp}(\mu_2)$, where the second stage is only invoked with probability p (with probability $1 - p$, service completes immediately after the first stage). Derive $\mathbf{E}[N]$ and $\mathbf{E}[T]$ when $\lambda = 1$, $\mu_1 = 2$, $\mu_2 = 3$, and $p = 0.4$.

Here are some steps:

(a) Define a state space.
(b) Draw out the Markov chain.
(c) Write out the generator matrix $\mathbf{Q}$ (it is infinite, so a portion will do).
(d) Write out the matrices: $\mathbf{F_0}, \mathbf{L_0}, \mathbf{B_0}, \mathbf{F}, \mathbf{L}, \mathbf{B}$. [Check: $\mathbf{L}$ should be a 2×2 matrix.]
(e) Write out the balance equations, and make the appropriate guess for the repeating part of the limiting probabilities.
(f) Solve for the matrix $\mathbf{R}$. [Check: $\mathbf{R}$ should be a 2×2 matrix.]
(g) Use the initial (non-repeating) balance equations together with the normalization constraint to solve for the initial limiting probabilities. Remember that these may be vectors. [Check: Compute the probability of there being zero jobs in the system. This should equal $1 - \rho \approx 0.367$.]
(h) At this point you should have all the limiting probabilities. Use these to compute $\mathbf{E}[N]$ and $\mathbf{E}[T]$.

21.4 Effect of Variability in Service Time

Create a Hyperexponential distribution, H_2, with balanced branches $\left(\frac{p}{\mu_1} = \frac{1-p}{\mu_2}\right)$, fixed mean $\mathbf{E}[S] = 1$, and $C^2 = 10$. Now use matrix-analytic methods to determine mean response time, $\mathbf{E}[T]$, for the M/H_2/1 when the average load is $\rho = 0.8$. Hold ρ and $\mathbf{E}[S]$ fixed but increase C^2. Try $C^2 = 20$,

$C^2 = 30$, $C^2 = 40$, and $C^2 = 50$. What happens to $\mathbf{E}[T]$? Why do you think this occurs?

21.5 Hyperexponential Distribution: DFR

Prove that the H_2 Hyperexponential distribution has decreasing failure rate (DFR). Derive the failure rate function, $r(x) = \frac{f(x)}{\overline{F}(x)}$, and then take its derivative to show that $r(x)$ is decreasing in x. Also explain intuitively why the Hyperexponential has DFR.

21.6 Variance of Number of Jobs

In the same way that we derived a closed-form expression for the mean number of jobs, $\mathbf{E}[N]$, in terms of $\mathbf{R}$, we can also write a closed-form expression for $\mathbf{Var}(N)$ in terms of $\mathbf{R}$, using a little more matrix calculus. Derive this expression.

21.7 Effect of Variability in Service Time in Multi-Server Systems

In this problem we repeat the analysis from Exercise 21.4, except that we deal with a 2-server system. Again create an H_2 with balanced branches $\left(\frac{p}{\mu_1} = \frac{1-p}{\mu_2}\right)$ and fixed mean $\mathbf{E}[S] = 1$ and $C^2 = 10$. This time, use matrix-analytic methods to determine $\mathbf{E}[T]$ for the M/H_2/2 when the system load is $\rho = 0.8$. Hold ρ and $\mathbf{E}[S]$ fixed but increase C^2. Try $C^2 = 20$, $C^2 = 30$, $C^2 = 40$, and $C^2 = 50$. What happens to $\mathbf{E}[T]$? Is the effect of increased variability more or less pronounced than for the case of a single server? Give as much intuition as you can for what is going on.

There is no known closed-form solution for the mean response time in an M/H_2/2. The best known approximation is due to Lee and Longton [118] who state that

$$\mathbf{E}\left[T_Q^{\text{M/G/k}}\right] \approx \left(\frac{C^2 + 1}{2}\right) \mathbf{E}\left[T_Q^{\text{M/M/k}}\right],$$

where G here denotes any general distribution, including the H_2. How do your results compare to the Lee and Longton approximation?

21.8 Understanding Setup Times

The effect of setup times is not well understood in multi-server systems, see [68]. This exercise uses matrix-analytic methods to analyze these systems numerically.

Setup times for the M/M/1 were introduced in Exercise 15.10. We define a setup time for a multi-server system as follows: When a server goes idle, it immediately shuts off. When a job arrives, it needs to set up a server before it can use the server. The setup time is denoted by I. If a server, $s1$, is in setup mode, and another server $s2$ becomes free, then the job waiting for $s1$ is routed to $s2$. At this point server $s1$ is shut off, unless there is a job in the queue, in which case the queued job takes over waiting for $s1$.

(a) Draw a CTMC for an M/M/1 with setup time, I, where $I \sim \text{Exp}(\alpha)$.

(b) Draw a CTMC for an M/M/1 with setup time, I, where $I \sim$ Erlang-2 with mean $\frac{1}{\alpha}$.

(c) Draw a CTMC for an M/M/2 with setup time, I, where $I \sim \text{Exp}(\alpha)$.

(d) Draw a CTMC for an M/M/2 with setup time, I, where $I \sim$ Erlang-2 with mean $\frac{1}{\alpha}$.

(e) For parts (a) and (c), use matrix-analytic methods to analyze response time, assuming $\mu = 1$, $\alpha = 0.1$, and $\rho = 0.5, 0.7, 0.9$. How does setup affect the M/M/2 as compared with the M/M/1?

CHAPTER 22

Networks with Time-Sharing (PS) Servers (BCMP)

In Chapter 21, we saw one application for phase-type (PH) distributions: If we need to analyze a system whose workload involves distributions that are non-Exponential (e.g., high-variability workloads), then we can use a PH distribution to at least match 2 or 3 moments of that workload distribution. This allows us to represent the system via a Markov chain, which we can often solve via matrix-analytic methods.

In this chapter we see another application of PH distributions. Here, we are interested in analyzing networks of Processor-Sharing (time-sharing) servers (a.k.a. PS servers). It will turn out that networks of PS servers exhibit product form solutions, even under general service times. This is in contrast to networks of FCFS servers, which require Exponential service times. Our proof of this PS result will rely on phase-type distributions. This result is part of the famous BCMP theorem [16].

22.1 Review of Product Form Networks

So far we have seen that all of the following networks have product form:

- Open Jackson networks: These assume probabilistic routing, FCFS servers with Exponential service rates, Poisson arrivals, and unbounded queues.
- Open classed Jackson networks: These are Jackson networks, where the outside arrival rates and routing probabilities can depend on the "class" of the job.
- Closed Jackson networks
- Closed classed Jackson networks

We have also seen (see Exercise 19.3) that Jackson networks with load-dependent service rates have product form. Here the service rate can depend on the number of jobs at the server. This is useful for modeling the effects of parallel processing. Note that all of our results thus far have assumed FCFS scheduling at each server.

22.2 BCMP Result

In 1975 Baskett, Chandy, Muntz, and Palacios-Gomez wrote a very famous paper providing a broad classification of networks with product form. We describe here a *subset* of the results in this paper and refer the reader to the original paper [16] for full results.

The results can be subdivided based on the type of service discipline (scheduling policy) at the servers. The first set of results assumes FCFS servers (we are already familiar with these). The second set of results assumes either Processor-Sharing (PS) service discipline or one of a few other service disciplines at the servers.

22.2.1 *Networks with FCFS Servers*

For networks with FCFS servers with unbounded queues, BCMP states that product form solutions exist for open, closed, single-class, and multi-class networks with probabilistic routing with the following restrictions:

Conditions

- The outside arrivals must be Poisson.
- The service times at the servers must be Exponentially distributed.
- The service rate at a server may be load dependent but **cannot** be class dependent.

The BCMP results for the case of networks of FCFS servers are very powerful. They say that, for the purpose of performance evaluation, we can think of the servers as independent M/M/1 queues.

However, the BCMP requirements (for the case of FCFS servers) are also unrealistic in two ways. First, the fact that the service times must be Exponentially distributed is somewhat restrictive.

The second drawback is referred to as **"Kleinrock's independence assumption."** This says that every time a job visits a server, its service time at the server is a new independent random variable. In particular, a job may visit the same server twice and experience different service times during the two visits.

The issue is that the service time is associated with the *server*, not with the *job*. We need this in order to get product form. If we could at least allow the service rate to be associated with the *class* of the job, then we could model the idea of different job sizes (e.g., "small jobs" that have very fast service rates at *every* server and "big jobs" that have slow service rates at *every* server). That is, we could maintain the "size" of a job as it moves between servers, so that subsequent visits of a job to the same server do not result in different service requirements. But alas, in the case of networks of FCFS servers, we cannot analyze the model where the service rate depends on the job class.

Usefulness for Communication Networks

Nevertheless, despite the Exponential service rates and the highly unrealistic Kleinrock's independence assumption, the BCMP results are highly useful for predicting delays in communication networks. In communication networks, the "jobs" are just fixed-size packets (all packets have the same size). Time is only spent when a packet is transmitted on a link. Servers are thus used to model the *links* leaving a router – one server per outgoing link. The service time of a job at a server corresponds to the packet's transmission time (the time to put the packet onto the wire). There is an FCFS queue associated with each server, made up of packets waiting to go onto that corresponding link. Note that a job's "service time" (transmission time for the packet) is really some constant (depending on the link bandwidth). An Exponential service time distribution does a decent enough job of modeling that situation, because the Exponential has somewhat low variability. A Jackson network with Exponential service times actually provides an upper bound (with respect to mean response time) on the same network with constant service times, see [81] for a proof. Furthermore, it is especially convenient that we can make the routing of packets be class dependent to represent the fact that certain packets follow one route while other packets follow other routes.

22.2.2 *Networks with PS Servers*

The main BCMP results deal with networks where the servers use Processor-Sharing service order. In this case the results are much more powerful!

> **Definition 22.1** A server with service rate μ operates under ***Processor-Sharing (PS)*** service order if, whenever there are n jobs at the server, each of the jobs is processed at rate $\frac{\mu}{n}$.

Under PS scheduling, every job in the queue receives service at all times. However, the *share* received by a job depends on how many other jobs are currently present.

Question: Give an example of Processor-Sharing in computer systems.

Answer: A time-sharing CPU rotates in round-robin order between the n jobs in the system, giving the first job one quantum, then the second job one quantum, . . . , then the nth job one quantum, and then returning back to the first job to repeat. If we think of the quantum size as approaching 0, we get PS. Note that under PS there is no cost for switching between jobs, whereas in time-sharing CPUs there is a small overhead for context-switching.

Question: Suppose n jobs arrive at time 0 to a PS server with service rate 1. They each have service requirement 1. At what time do they complete? What is their slowdown?

Answer: All jobs complete at time n and have slowdown n.

Question: The previous question/answer may make it seem that PS is a poor scheduling policy. When is PS scheduling useful?

Answer: PS scheduling is useful when job sizes have high variability. PS prevents short jobs from having to wait behind long jobs, without requiring knowledge of the size of the job a priori. We will learn more about this in Chapter 30.

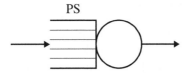

Figure 22.1. PS server

To indicate the fact that in a PS server all jobs are being worked on at once, we will often draw the queue as in Figure 22.1.

BCMP states that for networks where servers use PS service order, product form solutions exist for open, closed, single-class, or multi-class networks with probabilistic routing, with the following conditions:

Conditions

- The outside arrivals must be Poisson.
- The service times at servers can follow **any Coxian distribution**.
- The service rate at a server may be load dependent, and the service time distribution is also allowed to depend on the *class* of the job.

The last two "conditions" are not actually restrictions. Recall from Chapter 21 that Coxian distributions are dense in the class of non-negative distributions. Hence, given enough phases, the service time at the servers can approximate any general non-negative distribution arbitrarily closely.

The Processor-Sharing (PS) result is often ignored by most books. This is probably because most books are concerned with communication networks and thus FCFS servers. However, in analyzing networks of workstations, it is much more common that the workstations are time-sharing machines, scheduling their jobs in PS order. This makes the PS result very important to computer system designers.

Why the PS Result is Important

The standard weakness in queueing networks is that service time is affiliated with the server, not with the job. However, observe that for networks of PS servers, we can circumvent this drawback: We make the service time affiliated with the job by making the service time affiliated with the *class* of the job! The job's class then determines the job's service time at all servers. Observe that service time can even be a (near) *constant* dependent on the class. Thus some jobs always have size 1, and some have size 2, and some have size 3, etc. We can even go so far as to create a realistic workload distribution by using enough different classes. To take this idea even further, we could use the fact that jobs can change classes to model the notion of a job's remaining service time increasing based on its service time so far.

The possible ideas for networks of PS servers are limitless. Much more research needs to be done on exploiting this fantastic result.

Outline of the Rest of the Chapter

We have discussed why the PS result is so powerful. The rest of this chapter is devoted to proving a small piece of the PS result. To keep from losing the intuition, we derive the limiting probabilities for only the cases of 1 PS queue and 2 PS queues in tandem, with only a single class of jobs. The proof for the case of k PS queues is very similar to that for the case of 2 PS queues, and we expect the reader to be able to see how to expand the 2-server proof to k servers. Rather than state the general result upfront, we keep the suspense alive by deriving the results one at a time, because the derivations are as beautiful as the results themselves. We refer the reader to the BCMP paper [16] for a description of the full product form formulas in the case of multi-classed networks and the case of class-dependent service rates.

Remark: The BCMP paper [16] describes many results that we will not be proving. For example, the results for the PS service discipline are extended to the Preemptive-Last-Come-First-Served (PLCFS) service discipline. Under PLCFS a running job is always preempted by the last job to arrive. Surprisingly, PLCFS exhibits product form as well, and the proofs are similar in style to the proofs we present for PS service order. We will not study the PLCFS service order until Chapter 30. The BCMP results also allow for service stations with an infinite number of servers (no delay). The BCMP paper also allows for mixing different types of servers – for example, both PS and FCFS servers – within the same network.

22.3 M/M/1/PS

Before we discuss Coxian service times, it is instructive to start by considering Exponentially distributed service times and see what we can say about the M/M/1/PS queue.

Consider a single M/M/1/PS queue with arrival rate λ and service rate μ. The server services jobs in PS order; namely, when there are n jobs at the server, each is being serviced with rate μ/n.

Question: What is the limiting probability of there being n jobs in the M/M/1/PS queue? How does your answer compare with that of an M/M/1/FCFS server?

Hint: This may seem like a really hard problem. The trick is to model the M/M/1/PS queue via a CTMC.

Answer: Figure 22.2 describes the CTMC for M/M/1/PS. States represent the number of jobs at the server. The arrival rate at each state is λ, so the forward transitions are

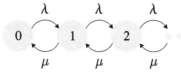

Figure 22.2. CTMC for M/M/1/PS.

clear. To understand the backward transitions, suppose that the chain is in state i. The rate at which an individual job gets serviced in state i is μ/i, because the server is shared among the i jobs. However, because all i jobs are running, the rate at which *some* job completes is $i \cdot (\mu/i) = \mu$ (recall that the minimum of i Exponentially distributed random variables is still Exponentially distributed with rate equal to the sum of their rates). So, given that the CTMC is in state i, the rate of moving to state $i-1$ is μ. Thus this CTMC looks exactly like the regular M/M/1/FCFS. We already know how to solve this chain:

$$\pi_n = \mathbf{P}\{n \text{ jobs at server}\} = \rho^n(1-\rho).$$

22.4 M/Cox/1/PS

Now consider a single M/Cox/1/PS server. A general k-phase Coxian distribution is shown in Figure 22.3, where the p_i's are probabilities. We simplify the computation by just doing the analysis for an abridged 2-phase Coxian service distribution, as shown in Figure 22.4, because the idea is the same as you increase the number of phases.

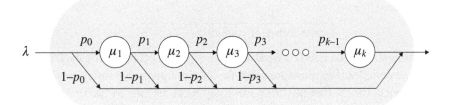

Figure 22.3. Service time is Coxian with k phases.

In the abridged Coxian distribution with 2 phases, each job independently must first complete phase 1 and then, with probability p, must complete phase 2. However, this is a PS server, not a FCFS server. Thus there is no queue, and all jobs are actually serving at once (they are all in the gray region). Specifically, there may be several jobs

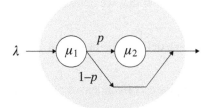

Figure 22.4. Service time is abridged Coxian distribution with 2 phases.

working on completing phase 1, and there may be several others working on completing phase 2.

We define the state of our system to be

$$(n_1, n_2),$$

where n_1 represents the number of jobs currently in phase 1 and n_2 represents the number of jobs currently in phase 2. We define π_{n_1, n_2} to be the probability of the server being in state (n_1, n_2).

The way to picture this is to imagine a professor with n graduate students. Each of her students is in one of two phases of graduate school – the "quals" phase, where the student is preparing for qualifier exams, which takes time $\text{Exp}(\mu_1)$, and the "thesis" phase, where the student is writing a thesis, which takes time $\text{Exp}(\mu_2)$. At any moment of time the professor has n_1 students simultaneously trying to get through the "quals" phase and n_2 students simultaneously trying to get through the "thesis" phase. The egalitarian professor splits her time evenly between all n students.

Question: What is the service rate experienced by a student in phase 1 (the "quals" phase)?

Answer: If there were no other students, a student in phase 1 would be served at rate μ_1. However, because the student has to share the professor with all other students of the professor, the student is actually served at rate

$$\frac{\mu_1}{\text{total number of students}} = \frac{\mu_1}{n_1 + n_2}.$$

To determine π_{n_1, n_2}, we need to write balance equations for the M/Cox/1/PS. These can get quite complex. We therefore solve for the limiting probabilities via the method of local balance, except that this time we apply local balance to each *phase*. That is, we will equate

$$B_i = \frac{\text{Rate leave state } (n_1, n_2)}{\text{due to a departure from phase } i} = \frac{\text{Rate enter state } (n_1, n_2)}{\text{due to an arrival into phase } i} = B_i'.$$

Note about notation: We use B_0 to represent the rate that we leave state (n_1, n_2) due to a departure from phase 0, where phase 0 represents the outside. Thus a departure from phase 0 represents an arrival from outside. Hence B_0 represents the rate that we leave state (n_1, n_2) due to an arrival from outside. Likewise B_0' represents the rate that we enter state (n_1, n_2) due to an arrival into phase 0, where phase 0 represents the outside. Hence B_0' represents the rate that we enter state (n_1, n_2) due to a departure to the outside.

Question: Warmup: How do we define B_1, the rate of leaving state (n_1, n_2) due to a departure from phase 1?

Answer: There are n_1 jobs at phase 1. Each leaves phase 1 with Exponential rate

$$\pi_{n_1, n_2} \cdot \frac{\mu_1}{n_1 + n_2}.$$

Note: We divided by $n_1 + n_2$ because the job is slowed down by all the other jobs in the PS server – not just in its phase. Thus the total rate of leaving state (n_1, n_2) due to a departure from phase 1 is

$$n_1 \cdot \pi_{n_1,n_2} \cdot \frac{\mu_1}{n_1 + n_2}.$$

B_i: Rate leaving state (n_1, n_2) due to a departure from phase i:

$$B_0 = \pi_{n_1,n_2} \lambda$$
$$B_1 = \pi_{n_1,n_2} \frac{\mu_1 n_1}{n_1+n_2}$$
$$B_2 = \pi_{n_1,n_2} \frac{\mu_2 n_2}{n_1+n_2}$$

(Recall that B_0 means "leaving the outside" or, equivalently, arriving from outside into the system.)

B_i': Rate entering state (n_1, n_2) due to an arrival into phase i:

$$B_0' = \pi_{n_1+1,n_2} \frac{\mu_1 (n_1+1)(1-p)}{n_1+n_2+1} + \pi_{n_1,n_2+1} \frac{\mu_2 (n_2+1)}{n_1+n_2+1}$$
$$B_1' = \pi_{n_1-1,n_2} \lambda$$
$$B_2' = \pi_{n_1+1,n_2-1} \frac{\mu_1 (n_1+1)p}{n_1+n_2}$$

(Recall that B_0' means "entering outside" or leaving the system.)

We now need to make a guess for the limiting probability π_{n_1,n_2}.

Question: Look at equating B_1 and B_1'. What guess makes $B_1 = B_1'$?

Hint: Observe that

$$B_1 = B_1' \implies \pi_{n_1,n_2} = \rho_1 \frac{n_1 + n_2}{n_1} \pi_{n_1-1,n_2}, \quad \text{where } \rho_1 = \frac{\lambda}{\mu_1}.$$

Answer: The fact that the limiting probabilities differ by factors involving $n_1 + n_2$ and n_1 suggests a combinatorial choose. A guess for the limiting probabilities is:

$$\pi_{n_1,n_2} = \binom{n_1 + n_2}{n_1} \rho_1^{n_1} \rho_2^{n_2} \pi_{0,0}, \tag{22.1}$$

where $\rho_1 = \frac{\lambda}{\mu_1}$ and $\rho_2 = \frac{\lambda p}{\mu_2}$. Note that ρ_1 and ρ_2 do not mean anything here. This is just a notational convenience.

Let's verify this guess by checking $B_i = B_i'$ for all i.

Check for $i = 1$:

$$B_1' = \pi_{n_1-1,n_2} \lambda$$

$$= \binom{n_1+n_2-1}{n_1-1} \rho_1^{n_1-1} \rho_2^{n_2} \pi_{0,0} \lambda$$

$$= \binom{n_1+n_2}{n_1} \frac{n_1}{n_1+n_2} \rho_1^{n_1} \rho_2^{n_2} \pi_{0,0} \frac{\lambda}{\rho_1}$$

$$= \pi_{n_1,n_2} \frac{n_1}{n_1+n_2} \frac{\lambda}{\rho_1}$$

$$= \pi_{n_1,n_2} \frac{\mu_1 n_1}{n_1+n_2}$$

$$= B_1$$

Check for $i = 2$:

$$B_2' = \pi_{n_1+1,n_2-1} \frac{\mu_1(n_1+1)p}{n_1+n_2}$$

$$= \binom{n_1+n_2}{n_1+1} \rho_1^{n_1+1} \rho_2^{n_2-1} \pi_{0,0} \frac{\mu_1(n_1+1)p}{n_1+n_2}$$

$$= \binom{n_1+n_2}{n_1} \frac{n_2}{n_1+1} \rho_1^{n_1} \rho_2^{n_2} \pi_{0,0} \frac{\mu_1(n_1+1)p}{n_1+n_2} \frac{\rho_1}{\rho_2}$$

$$= \pi_{n_1,n_2} \frac{n_2}{n_1+1} \frac{\mu_1(n_1+1)p}{n_1+n_2} \frac{\rho_1}{\rho_2}$$

$$= \pi_{n_1,n_2} \frac{\mu_2 n_2}{n_1+n_2}$$

$$= B_2$$

Check for $i = 0$:

$$B_0' = \pi_{n_1+1,n_2} \frac{\mu_1(n_1+1)(1-p)}{n_1+n_2+1} + \pi_{n_1,n_2+1} \frac{\mu_2(n_2+1)}{n_1+n_2+1}$$

$$= \binom{n_1+n_2+1}{n_1+1} \rho_1^{n_1+1} \rho_2^{n_2} \pi_{0,0} \frac{\mu_1(n_1+1)(1-p)}{n_1+n_2+1} + \binom{n_1+n_2+1}{n_1} \rho_1^{n_1} \rho_2^{n_2+1} \pi_{0,0} \frac{\mu_2(n_2+1)}{n_1+n_2+1}$$

$$= \pi_{n_1,n_2} \frac{n_1+n_2+1}{n_1+1} \rho_1 \frac{\mu_1(n_1+1)(1-p)}{n_1+n_2+1} + \pi_{n_1,n_2} \frac{n_1+n_2+1}{n_2+1} \rho_2 \frac{\mu_2(n_2+1)}{n_1+n_2+1}$$

$$= \pi_{n_1,n_2} \lambda(1-p) + \pi_{n_1,n_2} \lambda p$$

$$= \pi_{n_1,n_2} \lambda$$

$$= B_0$$

So the guess in (22.1) works. Let's use this guess to express $\mathbf{P}\{n \text{ jobs in system}\}$. Let $n = n_1 + n_2$. Then by (22.1) we have

$$\mathbf{P}\{n \text{ jobs in system}\} = \sum_{n_1=0}^{n} \pi_{n_1,n-n_1} = \sum_{n_1=0}^{n} \binom{n}{n_1} \rho_1^{n_1} \rho_2^{n-n_1} \pi_{0,0}.$$

Note that the last expression on the right is just a binomial expansion:

$$\sum_{n_1=0}^{n} \binom{n}{n_1} {\rho_1}^{n_1} {\rho_2}^{n-n_1} \pi_{0,0} = (\rho_1 + \rho_2)^n \pi_{0,0}.$$

So

$$\mathbf{P}\{n \text{ jobs in system}\} = (\rho_1 + \rho_2)^n \pi_{0,0}. \tag{22.2}$$

Question: What is $\rho_1 + \rho_2$?

Answer:

$$\rho_1 + \rho_2 = \frac{\lambda}{\mu_1} + \frac{\lambda p}{\mu_2}$$

$$= \lambda \cdot \left(\frac{1}{\mu_1} + \frac{p}{\mu_2}\right).$$

Question: Does this term $\left(\frac{1}{\mu_1} + \frac{p}{\mu_2}\right)$ have a meaning?

Answer: Yes! Observe that

$$\left(\frac{1}{\mu_1} + \frac{p}{\mu_2}\right) = \text{Average service requirement of job entering the system} = \mathbf{E}\left[S\right].$$

So

$$\rho_1 + \rho_2 = \lambda \cdot \mathbf{E}\left[S\right]$$
$$= \rho = \text{load for the single-server system.}$$

Thus we have from (22.2),

$$\mathbf{P}\{n \text{ jobs in system}\} = \rho^n \pi_{0,0}.$$

Now, we just need the normalization constant $\pi_{0,0}$, which allows

$$\sum_{n=0}^{\infty} \mathbf{P}\{n \text{ jobs in system}\} = 1.$$

Clearly, because $\pi_{0,0}$ is the fraction of time that the server is idle,

$$\pi_{0,0} = 1 - \rho.$$

Hence,

$$\mathbf{P}\{n \text{ jobs in system}\} = \rho^n (1 - \rho).$$

But this is the same as for an M/M/1.

UNBELIEVABLE!

The fact that the limiting probabilities of the M/G/1/PS are independent of the job size distribution (they depend only on its mean) is called an **insensitivity property**.

Insensitivity properties are rare and always very interesting. It is hard to find intuitive explanations for why certain queueing networks exhibit insensitivity.

Example 1 – Single Server

Consider a time-sharing CPU, shown in Figure 22.5. The jobs arriving to this server have service requirements (sizes) that come from some unknown distribution. The arrival process is Poisson with rate $\lambda = 3$ jobs/sec. The mean job service requirement is $1/5$ sec.

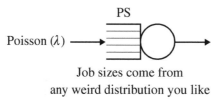

Poisson (λ)

Job sizes come from
any weird distribution you like

Figure 22.5. M/G/1/PS.

Question: What is the mean response time for this system?

Answer: The solution is the same as if we had an M/M/1/FCFS:

$$\mathbf{E}\left[T\right] = \frac{1}{\mu - \lambda} = \frac{1}{5 - 3} = \frac{1}{2} \text{ sec}$$

Example 2 – Server Farm

Suppose you have a distributed server system consisting of two hosts. Each host is a time-sharing host. Host 1 is twice as fast as Host 2.

Jobs arrive to the system according to a Poisson process with rate $\lambda = 1/9$ jobs/sec. The job service requirements come from some general distribution with mean 3 seconds if run on Host 1, but take twice as long on Host 2. When a job enters the system, with probability $p = \frac{3}{4}$ it is sent to Host 1, and with probability $1 - p = \frac{1}{4}$ is sent to Host 2.

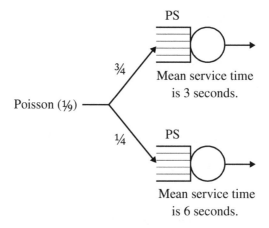

PS

¾

Mean service time
is 3 seconds.

Poisson (⅑)

¼

PS

Mean service time
is 6 seconds.

Figure 22.6. PS server farm.

Question: What is the mean response time for jobs?

Answer: Figure 22.6 shows the server farm.
The mean response time is simply

$$\mathbf{E}\left[T\right] = \frac{3}{4} \cdot (\text{Mean response time at server 1}) + \frac{1}{4} \cdot (\text{Mean response time at server 2})$$

$$= \frac{3}{4} \cdot \frac{1}{\frac{1}{3} - \frac{1}{9} \cdot \frac{3}{4}} + \frac{1}{4} \cdot \frac{1}{\frac{1}{6} - \frac{1}{9} \cdot \frac{1}{4}} = \frac{24}{5} \text{ sec.}$$

22.5 Tandem Network of M/G/1/PS Servers

Figure 22.7 displays two PS servers in tandem, each with two phases. Here, the state is the number of jobs at every phase of every server: (n_1, n_2, m_1, m_2). To determine the limiting probabilities, once again we apply local balance to each *phase*. That is, we equate

$$B_i = \frac{\text{Rate leave state } (n_1, n_2, m_1, m_2)}{\text{due to a departure from phase } i} = \frac{\text{Rate enter state } (n_1, n_2, m_1, m_2)}{\text{due to an arrival into phase } i} = B_i'.$$

Here we have 5 phases: phase 0 corresponds to "outside," and phases 1, 2, 3, and 4 are as shown in Figure 22.7. We now define the rates of leaving/entering a state.

B_i: Rate leaving state (n_1, n_2, m_1, m_2) due to a departure from phase i:

$$B_0 = \pi_{n_1, n_2, m_1, m_2} \lambda$$

$$B_1 = \pi_{n_1, n_2, m_1, m_2} \frac{\mu_1 n_1}{n_1 + n_2}$$

$$B_2 = \pi_{n_1, n_2, m_1, m_2} \frac{\mu_2 n_2}{n_1 + n_2}$$

$$B_3 = \pi_{n_1, n_2, m_1, m_2} \frac{\mu_3 m_1}{m_1 + m_2}$$

$$B_4 = \pi_{n_1, n_2, m_1, m_2} \frac{\mu_4 m_2}{m_1 + m_2}$$

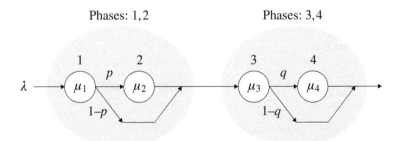

Figure 22.7. Tandem network.

B_i': Rate entering state (n_1, n_2, m_1, m_2) due to an arrival into phase i:

$$B_0' = \pi_{n_1, n_2, m_1+1, m_2} \frac{\mu_3(m_1+1)(1-q)}{m_1+m_2+1} + \pi_{n_1, n_2, m_1, m_2+1} \frac{\mu_4(m_2+1)}{m_1+m_2+1}$$

$$B_1' = \pi_{n_1-1, n_2, m_1, m_2} \lambda$$

$$B_2' = \pi_{n_1+1, n_2-1, m_1, m_2} \frac{\mu_1(n_1+1)p}{n_1+n_2}$$

$$B_3' = \pi_{n_1, n_2+1, m_1-1, m_2} \frac{\mu_2(n_2+1)}{n_1+n_2+1} + \pi_{n_1+1, n_2, m_1-1, m_2} \frac{\mu_1(n_1+1)(1-p)}{n_1+n_2+1}$$

$$B_4' = \pi_{n_1, n_2, m_1+1, m_2-1} \frac{\mu_3(m_1+1)q}{m_1+m_2}.$$

The following is a product form guess for the limiting probabilities:

$$\pi_{n_1, n_2, m_1, m_2} = \binom{n_1+n_2}{n_1} \rho_1^{n_1} \rho_2^{n_2} \binom{m_1+m_2}{m_1} \rho_3^{m_1} \rho_4^{m_2} \pi_0, \qquad (22.3)$$

where $\rho_1 = \lambda/\mu_1$, $\rho_2 = \lambda p/\mu_2$, $\rho_3 = \lambda/\mu_3$, $\rho_4 = \lambda q/\mu_4$, and π_0 is a short form for $\pi_{0,0,0,0}$.

It is easy to see that this guess satisfies the local balance equations ($B_i = B_i'$) for $i = 0, 1, 2, 3, 4$ using very similar algebra to what was used in the case of a single server. The algebra is left to Exercise 22.2.

We now need to find π_0 to determine the limiting probabilities. Let $n = n_1 + n_2$, and $m = m_1 + m_2$. Note that the load on the first server, ρ_a, is $\rho_a = \rho_1 + \rho_2$, and the load on the second server, ρ_b, is $\rho_b = \rho_3 + \rho_4$. So we have

$$\mathbf{P}\{n \text{ jobs at server 1}, m \text{ jobs at server 2}\}$$

$$= \sum_{n_1=0}^{n} \sum_{m_1=0}^{m} \pi_{n_1, n-n_1, m_1, m-m_1}$$

$$= \pi_0 \sum_{n_1=0}^{n} \binom{n}{n_1} \rho_1^{n_1} \rho_2^{n-n_1} \sum_{m_1=0}^{m} \binom{m}{m_1} \rho_3^{m_1} \rho_4^{m-m_1}$$

$$= \pi_0 (\rho_1 + \rho_2)^n (\rho_3 + \rho_4)^m$$

$$= \pi_0 \rho_a^n \rho_b^m.$$

Now, using the fact that

$$\sum_{n=0}^{\infty} \sum_{m=0}^{\infty} \mathbf{P}\{n \text{ jobs at server 1}, m \text{ jobs at server 2}\} = 1,$$

we get

$$\pi_0 = (1 - \rho_a)(1 - \rho_b).$$

Furthermore,

$$\mathbf{P}\{n \text{ jobs at server } 1\} = \sum_{m=0}^{\infty} \pi_0 \rho_a{}^n \rho_b{}^m = \sum_{m=0}^{\infty} (1-\rho_a)(1-\rho_b) \cdot \rho_a{}^n \rho_b{}^m$$
$$= (1-\rho_a)\rho_a{}^n$$

and likewise

$$\mathbf{P}\{m \text{ jobs at server } 2\} = (1-\rho_b)\rho_b{}^m.$$

Thus,

$$\mathbf{P}\{n \text{ jobs at server } 1, m \text{ jobs at server } 2\}$$
$$= \rho_a{}^n(1-\rho_a)\rho_b{}^m(1-\rho_b)$$
$$= \mathbf{P}\{n \text{ jobs at server } 1\} \cdot \mathbf{P}\{m \text{ jobs at server } 2\}.$$

So two M/G/1/PS servers in tandem have a product form solution, where the distribution of the number of jobs at each server again follows an M/M/1.

22.6 Network of PS Servers with Probabilistic Routing

Given a network of PS servers, with Poisson outside arrivals, and general (Coxian) service times, we still have product form and the format of the product form looks exactly like it did for the case of Jackson networks with FCFS servers. Namely,

$$\mathbf{P}\left\{\begin{array}{c} \text{Number of jobs at each queue is} \\ (n_1, n_2, \ldots, n_k) \end{array}\right\} = \prod_{i=1}^{k} \mathbf{P}\{n_i \text{ jobs at server } i\}$$
$$= \prod_{i=1}^{k} \rho_i^{n_i} \cdot (1-\rho_i)$$

where $\rho_i = \lambda_i \mathbf{E}[S_i]$.

The proof follows along the same lines as that in Section 22.5. Again, we say that a network of PS servers exhibits the *insensitivity property*, because only the mean of the job size distribution is relevant.

Question: Why don't these nice product form results come up when we have a network of FCFS servers with Coxian service times? Why doesn't the same analysis go through?

Answer: The state space and job behavior look very different for a network of FCFS servers than for a network of PS servers. In the case of PS servers, all jobs are inside the gray bubble (representing the server) at all times, and all jobs move through the phases independently of each other (with the other jobs only affecting their rate). In the case of FCFS servers, *only one job at a time* can be processing within the gray bubble. The rest of the jobs are queued outside the bubble. The movement of jobs is thus very restricted. Generally, insensitivity arises in situations where there is no strict queueing – jobs receive service right away, as in PS queues or an M/G/∞ system.

22.7 Readings

The purpose of this chapter was to illustrate another application of the method of phases. We saw that we could prove that the M/Cox/1/PS queue behaves like an M/M/1/FCFS queue, and furthermore that a network of PS queues with Coxian service times and probabilistic routing between queues has product form and can be decomposed into M/Cox/1/PS queues. These results and the further extension to classed networks are provided in the original BCMP paper [16]. The BCMP result has also been rederived via other techniques, see for example Harrison's work [95].

The product form results described in this chapter have been extended by Frank Kelly [106] to networks of *quasi-reversible queues*, which allow for more general queueing disciplines than PS or PLCFS. Some good references describing this broader class of product form networks are [127] and [38].

22.8 Exercises

22.1 M/BP/1/PS

Recall Exercise 20.1, which asked you to simulate the M/G/1/FCFS queue, where G was a Bounded Pareto(k, p, α) distribution with mean 3,000. There were two settings of parameters for the Bounded Pareto: (i) $k = 1,000$, $p = 10^{10}$, $\alpha = 1.5$, and (ii) $k = 1,970$, $p = 10^{10}$, $\alpha = 2.9$. The arrival rate, λ, was set to create a server load of $\rho = 0.8$. Suppose now that you are asked to redo the experiment in Exercise 20.1 under PS scheduling. That is, you now need to simulate an M/BP/1/PS queue, first under $\alpha = 1.5$ and then under $\alpha = 2.9$, with the goal of measuring mean response time. What do you expect the mean response time to be in the two cases? Either figure it out analytically, or simulate it and find out.

22.2 Verifying Product Form Solution for Tandem Network of PS Servers

In Section 22.5, we considered a tandem network of PS servers. We made the following "guess" for the limiting probabilities of this network:

$$\pi_{n_1,n_2,m_1,m_2} = \binom{n_1 + n_2}{n_1} \rho_1^{n_1} \rho_2^{n_2} \binom{m_1 + m_2}{m_1} \rho_3^{m_1} \rho_4^{m_2} \pi_0,$$

where $\rho_1 = \lambda/\mu_1$, $\rho_2 = \lambda p/\mu_2$, $\rho_3 = \lambda/\mu_3$, $\rho_4 = \lambda q/\mu_4$, and π_0 is a short form for $\pi_{0,0,0,0}$. This expression represents the probability that there are n_1 jobs in phase 1 at server 1, and n_2 jobs in phase 2 at server 1, and m_1 jobs in phase 3 (this is phase 1 at server 2) and m_2 jobs in phase 4 (this is phase 2 at server 2).

Prove that this guess satisfies the local balance equations: $B_i = B_i'$ for $i = 0, 1, 2, 3, 4$, as defined in Section 22.5.

CHAPTER 23

The M/G/1 Queue and the Inspection Paradox

In Chapter 22 we studied the M/G/1/PS queue and derived simple closed-form solutions for π_n, $\mathbf{E}[N]$, and $\mathbf{E}[T]$ (assuming G is any Coxian distribution).

In this chapter we move on to the M/G/1/FCFS queue. We have already had some exposure to thinking about the M/G/1/FCFS. Using the matrix-analytic techniques of Chapter 21, we saw that we could solve the M/PH/1/FCFS queue numerically, where PH represents an arbitrary phase-type distribution. However, we still do not have a simple closed-form solution for the M/G/1/FCFS that lets us understand the effect of load and the job size variability on mean response time.

This chapter introduces a simple technique, known as the "tagged job" technique, which allows us to obtain a simple expression for mean response time in the M/G/1/FCFS queue. The technique will not allow us to derive the variance of response time, nor will it help us understand the higher moments of the number of jobs in the M/G/1/FCFS – for those, we will need to wait until we get to transform analysis in Chapter 25. Nonetheless, the resulting simple formula for mean response time will lead to many insights about the M/G/1 queue and optimal system design for an M/G/1 system.

23.1 The Inspection Paradox

We motivate this chapter by asking several questions. We will come back to these questions repeatedly throughout the chapter. By the end of the chapter everything will be clear.

Question: Suppose buses arrive at a bus stop every 10 minutes on average, and the time between arrivals at the bus stop is Exponentially distributed. I arrive at the bus stop at a random time. How long can I expect to wait for a bus?

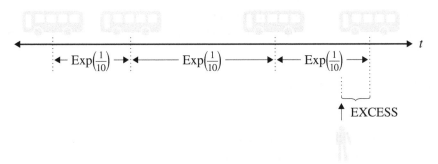

Figure 23.1. The Inspection Paradox.

Question: While you are thinking about the answer to the first question, also ask yourself whether your answer changes if we change the distribution of the time between buses (the mean time between buses is still 10 minutes). What is the range of possible answers across all distributions?

Definition 23.1 is associated with Figure 23.1.

> **Definition 23.1** Let A denote the time between bus arrivals. Let's suppose a person arrives at a random time. Then the time that person has to wait until the next bus is denoted by the random variable A_e and is called the *excess of A*.

23.2 The M/G/1 Queue and Its Analysis

An M/G/1 queue consists of a single server and queue with Poisson job arrivals, where the size (a.k.a. service time) of a job has a *general* distribution (see Figure 23.2). That is, the job service time, denoted by the random variable S, may follow any distribution, where $\mathbf{E}[S] = 1/\mu$. First-Come-First-Served (FCFS) service order is assumed unless otherwise stated.

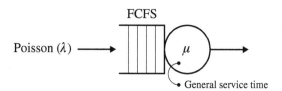

Figure 23.2. An M/G/1 queue.

In this chapter we study the **tagged-job** technique, in which we "tag" an *arbitrary arrival* and reason about the time that the tagged arrival spends in the queue. We will need the following notation:

T_Q : time in queue
N_Q : number in queue
N_Q^A : number in queue as seen by the arrival
S : service time of a job, where $\mathbf{E}[S] = 1/\mu$
S_i : service time of the ith job in the queue
S_e : excess of S – the remaining service time of the job in service, *given* that there is some job in service.

The definition of S_e is elucidated by Figure 23.3.

We now have

$$\mathbf{E}[T_Q] = \mathbf{E}[\text{Unfinished work that an arrival witnesses in the system}]$$
$$= \mathbf{E}[\text{Unfinished work in queue}] + \mathbf{E}[\text{Unfinished work at the server}]$$
$$(\text{Expectations add even if r.v.s are not independent.})$$

$$= \mathbf{E} \left[\sum_{i=1}^{N_Q^A} S_i \right] + \mathbf{E} \left[\text{Unfinished work at server} \right] \tag{23.1}$$

$$= \mathbf{E} \left[N_Q^A \right] \cdot \mathbf{E} \left[S \right] + \mathbf{P} \left\{ \text{Arrival sees job in service} \right\} \cdot \mathbf{E} \left[S_e \right] \tag{23.2}$$

$$= \mathbf{E} \left[N_Q \right] \mathbf{E} \left[S \right] + \left(\text{Time-avg probability server busy} \right) \cdot \mathbf{E} \left[S_e \right] \tag{23.3}$$

$$= \mathbf{E} \left[N_Q \right] \cdot \mathbf{E} \left[S \right] + \rho \cdot \mathbf{E} \left[S_e \right] \tag{23.4}$$

$$= \mathbf{E} \left[T_Q \right] \cdot \lambda \cdot \mathbf{E} \left[S \right] + \rho \cdot \mathbf{E} \left[S_e \right]$$

$$= \mathbf{E} \left[T_Q \right] \cdot \rho + \rho \cdot \mathbf{E} \left[S_e \right]$$

$$= \frac{\rho}{1 - \rho} \cdot \mathbf{E} \left[S_e \right].$$

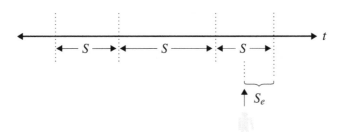

Figure 23.3. Given that there is a job in service (system is busy), a Poisson arrival sees S_e time remaining on the job in service.

We have thus easily obtained a formula for the mean time in queue in an M/G/1 system (a.k.a. mean delay), provided we can compute $\mathbf{E}\left[S_e\right]$ where S_e is the excess of the service time S:

$$\mathbf{E} \left[T_Q \right] = \frac{\rho}{1 - \rho} \cdot \mathbf{E} \left[S_e \right] \tag{23.5}$$

Question: Why were we allowed to break up the expectation in (23.1) into a product of expectations?

Answer: The S_i, $i = 1, 2, \ldots, N_Q^A$, are all independent of N_Q^A, because these jobs have not run yet, and hence their size has not influenced the queueing time seen by the tagged arrival.

Question: Where in the previous derivation have we used the fact that the arrival process is a Poisson process?

Answer: We invoked PASTA twice when moving from (23.2) to (23.3). First, we used the PASTA assumption in stating that

$\mathbf{P} \left\{ \text{Arrival sees a job in service} \right\} = $ Time-average probability the server is busy.

Second, we used PASTA in stating that

$$\mathbf{E}\left[N_Q^A\right] = \mathbf{E}\left[N_Q\right].$$

We will soon derive a general formula for $\mathbf{E}\left[S_e\right]$, but first it is instructive to go through some examples:

Examples

- **M/M/1 Queue:** The service time, S, is Exponentially distributed with mean $1/\mu$. Because the service time distribution is memoryless, $\mathbf{E}\left[S_e\right] = 1/\mu$. Therefore,

$$\mathbf{E}\left[T_Q\right] = \frac{\rho}{1-\rho} \cdot \frac{1}{\mu}.$$

  This agrees with our previous results for the M/M/1 queue.

- **M/D/1 Queue:** The service time is Deterministic (constant) and equal to $1/\mu$. $\mathbf{E}\left[S_e\right] = \frac{1}{2\mu}$, because the remaining service time of a job in service is Uniformly distributed between 0 and $\frac{1}{\mu}$. Therefore,

$$\mathbf{E}\left[T_Q\right] = \frac{\rho}{1-\rho} \cdot \frac{1}{2\mu}.$$

  Note that the expected time in queue is *half* that of the M/M/1 queue.

- **M/E$_k$/1 Queue:** The service time has an Erlang-k distribution (see Definition 21.2). The E_k distribution consists of k stages in series, each with Exponential service time with mean $1/k\mu$. If there is a job in service at the time of an arrival, then it is equally likely that the job is at each of the k stages. On average, the job in service will be at the middle stage, leaving $\left\lceil \frac{k+1}{2} \right\rceil$ stages left to be completed. We therefore should have

$$\mathbf{E}\left[S_e\right] = \left\lceil \frac{k+1}{2} \right\rceil \cdot \frac{1}{k\mu}.$$

  Mean time in queue is then given by

$$\mathbf{E}\left[T_Q\right] = \frac{\rho}{1-\rho} \cdot \left\lceil \frac{k+1}{2} \right\rceil \cdot \frac{1}{k\mu}.$$

  Observe that for $k = 1$ this is equal to the M/M/1 expression and for $k \to \infty$ this is equal to the M/D/1 expression.

- **M/H$_2$/1 Queue:** The service time has a Hyperexponential distribution, H_2, as in Definition 21.3. Here it is not as obvious how to derive $\mathbf{E}\left[S_e\right]$.

To compute $\mathbf{E}\left[S_e\right]$ exactly, for any random variable S, we need to use the **Renewal-Reward theorem**, which we describe in the next section.

23.3 Renewal-Reward Theory

Renewal-Reward theory is a powerful technique that allows us to obtain time averages of many quantities by considering only the average over a single renewal cycle. We can then compute the time-average excess, which, by PASTA, is also the excess seen by a random Poisson arrival.

We start with a reminder of the definition of a renewal process and a reminder of the Renewal theorem. We then build up from there.

> **Definition 23.2 (restated from Definition 9.32)** Any process for which the times between events are i.i.d. r.v.s with a common distribution, F, is called a ***renewal process***.

Figure 23.4 illustrates a renewal process.

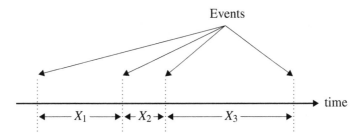

Figure 23.4. A renewal process. The X_i's all have common distribution F.

> **Theorem 23.3 (restated from Theorem 9.33)** *For a renewal process, if $\mathbf{E}[X] > 0$ is the mean time between renewals (events), and $N(t)$ is the number of renewals (events) by time t, then we have, with probability 1,*
> $$\frac{N(t)}{t} \to \frac{1}{\mathbf{E}[X]} \quad \text{as } t \to \infty. \tag{23.6}$$

Now consider a renewal process having i.i.d. interarrival times X_n, $n \geq 1$ with distribution F and mean $\mathbf{E}[X]$, and suppose that each time a renewal occurs we receive a reward. We denote by R_n the reward earned over the course of the nth renewal. We shall assume that the R_n, $n \geq 1$, are i.i.d. with mean $\mathbf{E}[R] \geq 0$. However, we do allow for the possibility that the R_n may (and often will) depend on X_n, the length of the nth renewal interval. If we let $R(t)$ represent the *total* reward earned by time t, then

$$\sum_{n=1}^{N(t)} R_n \leq R(t) \leq \sum_{n=1}^{N(t)+1} R_n.$$

Theorem 23.4 (Renewal-Reward) *If* $0 \leq \mathbf{E}[R] < \infty$ *and* $0 < \mathbf{E}[X] < \infty$, *then with probability 1,*

$$\frac{R(t)}{t} \to \frac{\mathbf{E}[R]}{\mathbf{E}[X]} \text{ as } t \to \infty.$$

Question: Interpret Theorem 23.4.

Answer: The Renewal-Reward theorem says that the average rate at which we earn reward is equal to the expected reward earned during a cycle, divided by the expected cycle length. This should make a lot of sense intuitively, because every cycle is probabilistically identical. The result is non-trivial, however, because normally it is meaningless to just divide two expectations. Therein lies the power of the theorem.

Proof

$$\sum_{n=1}^{N(t)} R_n \leq R(t) \leq \sum_{n=1}^{N(t)} R_n + R_{N(t)+1}$$

$$\frac{\sum_{n=1}^{N(t)} R_n}{t} \leq \frac{R(t)}{t} \leq \frac{\sum_{n=1}^{N(t)} R_n}{t} + \frac{R_{N(t)+1}}{t}. \tag{23.7}$$

We know that

$$\frac{\sum_{n=1}^{N(t)} R_n}{N(t)} \longrightarrow \mathbf{E}[R] \text{ as } t \to \infty, \text{ w.p.1.} \quad \text{(by SLLN)}$$

$$\frac{N(t)}{t} \longrightarrow \frac{1}{\mathbf{E}[X]} \text{ as } t \to \infty, \text{ w.p.1.} \quad \text{(by Theorem 23.3)}$$

Combining these, we have that

$$\lim_{t \to \infty} \frac{\sum_{n=1}^{N(t)} R_n}{t} = \lim_{t \to \infty} \frac{\sum_{n=1}^{N(t)} R_n}{N(t)} \cdot \lim_{t \to \infty} \frac{N(t)}{t} = \frac{\mathbf{E}[R]}{\mathbf{E}[X]}. \tag{23.8}$$

Putting together (23.8) and (23.7), we have that

$$\frac{\mathbf{E}[R]}{\mathbf{E}[X]} \leq \lim_{t \to \infty} \frac{R(t)}{t} \leq \frac{\mathbf{E}[R]}{\mathbf{E}[X]} + \lim_{t \to \infty} \frac{R_{N(t)+1}}{t}.$$

Observing that $\frac{R_{N(t)+1}}{t} \to 0$ as $t \to \infty$, because rewards are finite, we have the desired result. ∎

23.4 Applying Renewal-Reward to Get Expected Excess

We now apply Renewal-Reward theory to derive the expected excess. The definition of excess presumes that the server is busy. We thus consider a renewal process consisting of a sequence of service times, each an instance of the r.v. S, as shown in Figure 23.5:

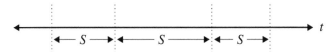

Figure 23.5. Renewal occurs at the end of each service time.

Here the server is assumed to be always busy, with a renewal occurring at the end of each service.

Figure 23.6 illustrates the function $S_e(t)$, the excess at time t.

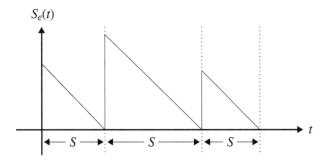

Figure 23.6. The function $S_e(t)$ represents the excess service time at time t.

Question: How do we express $\mathbf{E}[S_e]$ in terms of $S_e(t)$?

Answer:

$$\mathbf{E}[S_e] = \text{Time-average Excess} = \lim_{s \to \infty} \frac{\int_0^s S_e(t)dt}{s}.$$

To compute $\mathbf{E}[S_e]$, we need to express it as a long-run average award. Let $R(s)$ denote the total "reward" earned by time s.

Question: What is $R(s)$ for our problem?

Answer:

$$R(s) = \int_0^s S_e(t)dt.$$

Question: So what is the time-average reward?

Answer:

$$\text{Time-average Reward} = \lim_{s \to \infty} \frac{R(s)}{s} = \lim_{s \to \infty} \frac{\int_0^s S_e(t)dt}{s} = \mathbf{E}[S_e]$$

Now, by Renewal-Reward theory, the time-average reward is equal to the reward earned during one cycle divided by the expected length of one cycle.

Question: What is a "cycle?"

Answer: A cycle is one service time.

Now we can use Renewal-Reward theory to determine the time-average reward, which is the same as the time-average excess:

$$\text{Reward earned during a cycle} = \int_0^S (S - t)dt = S^2 - \frac{S^2}{2} = \frac{S^2}{2}$$

$$\mathbf{E}\left[\text{Reward earned during a cycle}\right] = \frac{\mathbf{E}\left[S^2\right]}{2}$$

$$\mathbf{E}\left[\text{Length of one cycle}\right] = \mathbf{E}\left[S\right]$$

$$\text{Time-avg Reward} = \frac{\mathbf{E}\left[\text{Reward during cycle}\right]}{\mathbf{E}\left[\text{Cycle length}\right]} = \frac{\mathbf{E}\left[S^2\right]}{2\mathbf{E}\left[S\right]}$$

Hence,

$$\mathbf{E}\left[S_e\right] = \frac{\mathbf{E}\left[S^2\right]}{2\mathbf{E}\left[S\right]}.$$

This derivation was a calculus-based argument, which is needed when the reward function is a complex curve. For this particular problem, the following simple geometric argument suffices: Looking at Figure 23.6, the reward earned during one cycle is just the area under a triangle, where the height and base of the triangle have length S. Thus the area is $S^2/2$. Hence the expected reward earned during a cycle is $\mathbf{E}\left[S^2\right]/2$. Now because the expected length of a cycle is $\mathbf{E}\left[S\right]$, we have, by Renewal-Reward, the result that the time-average reward is $\frac{\mathbf{E}\left[S^2\right]}{2\mathbf{E}\left[S\right]}$.

23.5 Back to the Inspection Paradox

We now return to our buses question.

Question: Suppose buses arrive at a bus stop every 10 minutes on average and the time between arrivals at the bus stop is *Exponentially* distributed. I arrive at the bus stop at a random time. How long can I expect to wait for a bus?

Answer: Let r.v. S denote the time between arrivals of buses. Then the average time until the next bus is just the average excess, $\mathbf{E}\left[S_e\right]$; namely

$$\text{Time-average Excess} = \mathbf{E}\left[S_e\right] = \frac{\mathbf{E}\left[S^2\right]}{2\mathbf{E}\left[S\right]}. \tag{23.9}$$

If S has an Exponential distribution, then the above quantity is equal to $\mathbf{E}\left[S\right]$, namely 10 minutes. If S has a Deterministic (constant) distribution, then the above quantity is just $\mathbf{E}\left[S\right]/2$, namely 5 minutes. If S has very high variability, as in the Pareto distribution, then the expected excess will be *much higher* than $\mathbf{E}\left[S\right]$.

Thus far we have been interested in the "time until the next bus arrives." We could also have asked about the time since the last bus arrived. If S denotes the time between buses, then the time since the last bus arrived is called the **age of S**.

Question: What would you guess is the mean age of S?

Answer: The age of S has the same mean and even the same distribution as S_e, the excess of S. To understand why, see Exercises 23.5 and 23.11, which are argued using a Renewal-Reward argument.

Adding the expected age and the expected excess, we see that a random arrival is likely to land in an interval where

$$\text{Expected time between buses as seen by arrival} = \frac{\mathbf{E}\left[S^2\right]}{2\mathbf{E}\left[S\right]} + \frac{\mathbf{E}\left[S^2\right]}{2\mathbf{E}\left[S\right]} = \frac{\mathbf{E}\left[S^2\right]}{\mathbf{E}\left[S\right]}.$$

If S is highly variable, this quantity can be far higher than $\mathbf{E}\left[S\right]$.

Question: Is this just "Murphy's Law," or is there some reason why a random arrival is likely to experience a bigger-than-average time between buses?

Answer: If you think about the renewal process represented by the interarrival times between buses, you will see that some renewals are short and some are long. It is more likely that a random arrival lands in a long interval than in a short interval. This is called the **Inspection Paradox**.

We can also express $\mathbf{E}\left[S_e\right]$ in terms of the squared coefficient of variation of S, C_S^2. Recalling that

$$C_S^2 = \frac{\mathbf{Var}(S)}{\mathbf{E}\left[S\right]^2} = \frac{\mathbf{E}\left[S^2\right]}{\mathbf{E}\left[S\right]^2} - 1,$$

it follows that

$$\mathbf{E}\left[S_e\right] = \frac{\mathbf{E}\left[S^2\right]}{2\mathbf{E}\left[S\right]} = \frac{\mathbf{E}\left[S\right]}{2} \cdot \frac{\mathbf{E}\left[S^2\right]}{\mathbf{E}\left[S\right]^2} = \frac{\mathbf{E}\left[S\right]}{2} \cdot (C_S^2 + 1). \qquad (23.10)$$

This says that higher variability implies higher excess. In fact, observe that when $C_S^2 = 1$, we have that $\mathbf{E}\left[S_e\right] = \mathbf{E}\left[S\right]$, and for $C_S^2 \gg 1$, $\mathbf{E}\left[S_e\right]$ explodes. In practical terms, you arrive at the bus stop and find that the time until the next bus is many times higher than the mean time between buses.

Remark: We refer to S_e as the **excess** of S, but this is also commonly referred to as the **equilibrium distribution** of S.

23.6 Back to the M/G/1 Queue

Recall that when analyzing the M/G/1/FCFS queue we proved equation (23.5), repeated below for reference:

$$\mathbf{E}\left[T_Q\right] = \frac{\rho}{1-\rho}\mathbf{E}\left[S_e\right], \qquad (23.11)$$

where $\mathbf{E}\left[S_e\right]$ was defined as the expected remaining service time on the job in service at the time of an arrival, given that there is a job in service.

From (23.10), we know that

$$\mathbf{E}\left[S_e\right] = \frac{\mathbf{E}\left[S^2\right]}{2\mathbf{E}\left[S\right]} = \frac{\mathbf{E}\left[S\right]}{2} \cdot (C_S^2 + 1). \tag{23.12}$$

Substituting (23.12) into (23.11), we get the **Pollaczek-Khinchin (P-K)** formula [141, 107], written here in several equivalent forms:

$$\mathbf{E}\left[T_Q\right] = \frac{\rho}{1-\rho} \cdot \frac{\mathbf{E}\left[S^2\right]}{2\mathbf{E}\left[S\right]} \tag{23.13}$$

$$\mathbf{E}\left[T_Q\right] = \frac{\rho}{1-\rho} \cdot \frac{\mathbf{E}\left[S\right]}{2} \cdot (C_S^2 + 1) \tag{23.14}$$

$$\mathbf{E}\left[T_Q\right] = \frac{\lambda \mathbf{E}\left[S^2\right]}{2(1-\rho)} \tag{23.15}$$

Question: Looking at (23.14), why does C_S^2 play such a key role in determining delay?

Answer: What causes delays is "bunching up of jobs."

- For the D/D/1 queue, with arrival rate λ and service rate $\mu > \lambda$, there are no delays, because arrivals see no one in service.
- For the M/D/1 queue, delays occur because arrivals sometimes "bunch up."
- For the M/M/1 queue, "bunching up" is also created by occasional long service times. Thus the expected delay in M/M/1 is greater than that in M/D/1.
- For the M/G/1 queue, with highly variable job size, there is even more "bunching up" of jobs.

So what creates delays is the occasional extra-long service time (or extra-large number of arrivals) in some service period. That is, delay is proportional to the *variance* in the *arrival* and *service* processes. Of course once one job is delayed, that affects all jobs in the queue behind it. The P-K formula assumes a Poisson arrival process, and the C_S^2 refers only to variability in the service times.

Very Important Observation: Expected waiting time in an M/G/1 queue can be *huge*, even under very low utilization, ρ, if C_S^2 is huge. For example, if $\rho = 0.5$, $\mathbf{E}\left[S\right] = 1$, but $C_S^2 = 25$ (which is not unusual, as pointed out in Chapter 20), then $\mathbf{E}\left[T_Q\right] = 13$, which is 13 times the mean job size, even though system load is low.

Final Remark: The result below follows from the transform of waiting time, which we will derive in Chapter 26:

$$\mathbf{Var}(T_Q) = (\mathbf{E}\left[T_Q\right])^2 + \frac{\lambda \mathbf{E}\left[S^3\right]}{3(1-\rho)}$$

What is interesting here is that the second moment of delay depends on the third moment of service time, similarly to the way that the first moment of delay depends on the second moment of service time. In general the ith moment of delay is related to the $(i+1)$th moment of service time.

23.7 Exercises

23.1 M/H$_2$/1
For the M/H$_2$/1 queue with arrival rate λ, where the job sizes are specified in Definition 21.2, derive expressions for $\mathbf{E}$ [Excess] and $\mathbf{E}$ $[T_Q]$.

23.2 M/G/1 – Doubling Service Rate and Arrival Rate
Jobs arrive to a CPU according to a Poisson process with rate λ. The CPU requirement of each job is drawn from some general distribution G, with finite moments. The CPU currently has load $\rho = \lambda \cdot \mathbf{E}$ $[S] < 1$, where S denotes the CPU requirement of jobs. The current mean response time is denoted by $\mathbf{E}$ $[T^{\text{current}}]$. Suppose that the arrival rate now increases by a factor of two. To compensate, we buy a CPU that is twice as fast, so each job's service requirement on the new CPU is half what it was on the old CPU. Apply the P-K formula to determine the new mean response time and compare it with the original mean response time.

23.3 M/G/1 with Different Job Types
Consider an M/G/1 queue that serves two types of jobs: red and blue. Red jobs arrive according to a Poisson process with rate $\lambda_R = \frac{1}{4}$ jobs/sec, and blue jobs arrive according to a Poisson process with rate $\lambda_B = \frac{1}{2}$ jobs/sec. Red job sizes have mean 1 and variance 1, whereas blue job sizes have mean 0.5 and variance 1. All jobs arrive to the same FCFS queue, so that, at any time, the server might be serving a red job or a blue one, and there might be jobs of one or both types in the queue. What is the mean response time of red jobs, and what is the mean response time of blue jobs?

23.4 Understanding the Inspection Paradox
Imagine that there are two types of renewals: short renewals of length exactly 1 and long renewals of length exactly 10. Suppose that short renewals occur with probability $\frac{2}{3}$ and long renewals occur with probability $\frac{1}{3}$.
(a) What is the average length of a renewal?
(b) What is the probability that a randomly thrown dart lands in a long renewal?
(c) What is the expected length of a renewal that I see if I arrive at a random time (use part (b))?
(d) How does your answer to (c) compare with your answer to (a)? This difference is the Inspection Paradox.

23.5 Deriving the Expected Age
Let A be a random variable denoting the time between bus arrivals, with mean $\mathbf{E}$ $[A]$ and second moment $\mathbf{E}$ $[A^2]$. The time *since* the last bus arrival is called the **age of A** and is denoted by A_a. Use Renewal-Reward theory to derive $\mathbf{E}$ $[A_a]$, the mean age of A. Follow the approach given in this chapter, showing the diagram of age across time. How does your answer compare with $\mathbf{E}$ $[A_e]$, the mean excess of A?

23.6 Effect of Variability on Waiting Time in M/G/1
Consider a single M/G/1 queue. Let the service time, S, follow a 2-point distribution:

$$S = \begin{cases} 0 & \text{with probability } q \\ \frac{1}{1-q} & \text{with probability } 1-q \end{cases}$$

Observe that as q gets close to 1, most jobs have service time 0.

(a) Determine $\mathbf{E}[S]$, the expected service time. Is this affected by q?

(b) Determine $\mathbf{E}[S_e]$.

(c) Determine C_S^2, the squared coefficient of variation of the service time. What is the range of possible values of C_S^2 as a function of q?

(d) Now determine $\mathbf{E}[T_Q]$, the mean waiting time for this system, as a function of q, assuming load $\rho < 1$. Simplify your expression as much as you can so that it is in terms of q and ρ. What happens in the system as q approaches 1? Give some intuition for what is going on.

23.7 Application of Renewal Reward – M/G/1 Busy Period

Consider an M/G/1 queue with arrival rate λ and mean service time $\mathbf{E}[S]$. A busy period starts when the server becomes busy and ends when it goes idle. Determine the mean length of a busy period. Do *not* solve this problem via transforms or via conditioning on the job size: Use only Renewal-Reward, thinking about busy and idle periods. [Hint: The answer is very short (3 lines) if you see the trick for how to apply Renewal-Reward.]

23.8 Application of Renewal-Reward – M/M/∞ Busy Period

Recall the M/M/∞ system from Section 15.2: Jobs arrive according to a Poisson process with rate λ. Job sizes are Exponentially distributed with mean $\frac{1}{\mu}$. There are an infinite number of servers, so that whenever a job arrives, it is given a new server. A busy period is defined to be the time from when the M/M/∞ first becomes busy (a single job arrives) until the M/M/∞ becomes idle. Derive the mean length of a busy period. [Hint: This is again a 3-line argument. It may help to recall that for the M/M/∞, $\pi_i = e^{-R}\frac{R^i}{i!}$, where $R = \frac{\lambda}{\mu}$.]

23.9 Application of Renewal-Reward – Mean Time between Visits to a State in a CTMC

Consider the expected time between visits to state i in a CTMC. Use a Renewal-Reward type argument to prove that

$$\mathbf{E}[\text{Time between visits to state } i] = \frac{1}{\pi_i} \cdot \frac{1}{\nu_i},$$

where ν_i is the total rate of leaving state i in the CTMC, given that we are in state i. (Note the difference between this result and that for a DTMC.)

23.10 Semi-Markov Process

Consider a stochastic process that moves between states according to some transition probability matrix, $\mathbf{P}$, where P_{ij} represents the probability of next moving to state j given that we are currently in state i. However, when the process is in state i, it stays there for some holding time, H_i, where the H_i's are generally distributed random variables, from possibly different distributions. Such a process is called a semi-Markov process. We will be interested in π_i^{SM}, the stationary probability of being in state i for the semi-Markov process.

To understand π_i^{SM}, it helps to consider π_i^D, the stationary probability for the *embedded DTMC* with the same transition matrix $\mathbf{P}$, where one spends exactly time 1 in each state. The goal of the problem is to prove that

$$\pi_i^{SM} = \frac{\pi_i^D \cdot \mathbf{E}\left[H_i\right]}{\sum_k \pi_k^D \cdot \mathbf{E}\left[H_k\right]}. \tag{23.16}$$

(a) Explain why (23.16) makes intuitive sense.

(b) Consider a long period of time, consisting of n state transitions. Let $N_i(n)$ denote the number of visits to state i during these n transitions. Pick n large enough, so that $N_i(n)$ is large. Let $H_i^{(j)}$ denote the time spent in state i during the jth visit to state i. Let

$$f(n) = \frac{\sum_{j=1}^{N_i(n)} H_i^{(j)}}{\sum_k \sum_{j=1}^{N_k(n)} H_k^{(j)}}.$$

What does $f(n)$ represent?

(c) Use tricks similar to those in the proof of Theorem 23.4 to reformulate $f(n)$ so that it becomes the expression in (23.16) as $n \to \infty$.

23.11 Distribution of Excess

Consider a renewal process where X represents the time between renewals. $F(x)$ and $f(x)$ are the c.d.f. and p.d.f. for X, respectively. We use X_e to denote the excess of X. Use Renewal-Reward to derive $F_e(k) = \mathbf{P}\{X_e < k\}$.

23.12 Server with Failures and Repairs

Consider an M/G/1 queue, where at any time when the server is busy it can fail. The time until the next failure is Exponentially distributed with rate α. Once the server fails, it goes into repair mode. The repair time is a generally distributed random variable denoted by R. After the server is repaired, it continues serving the job that it was serving from the point that it left off (i.e., no work is lost). Assume that the repair times are i.i.d. and are independent of the job sizes. Compute the mean response time of a job arriving to this M/G/1 queue. [Hint: This problem is challenging. Exercise 11.6 and Theorem 3.34 may help.]

CHAPTER 24

Task Assignment Policies for Server Farms

In this chapter we revisit server farms, however this time in the context of high-variability job sizes (indicative of the workloads described in Chapter 20), rather than Exponential job sizes.

The server farm architecture is ubiquitous in computer systems. Rather than using a single, powerful server to handle all incoming requests (assuming such a beast can even be purchased), it is more cost efficient to buy many slow, inexpensive servers and pool them together to harness their combined computational power. The server farm architecture is also popular for its flexibility: It is easy to add servers when load increases and easy to take away servers when the load drops. The term **server farm** is used to connote the fact that the servers tend to be co-located, in the same room or even on one rack.

Thus far, we have primarily studied server farms with a *central queue*, as in the M/M/k system, which we initially examined in Chapter 14 and then revisited from a capacity provisioning perspective in Chapter 15. In the M/M/k, jobs are held in a central queue, and only when a server is free does it take on the job at the head of the queue.

By contrast, in computer systems, most server farms do *immediate dispatching* (also known as *task assignment*), whereby incoming jobs are immediately assigned to servers (also known as *hosts*). There is typically no central queue; instead the queues are at the individual hosts.

Such server farms with immediate dispatching of jobs require an important policy decision, known as the **task assignment policy**. This is the rule that is used by the front-end router (also known as a *dispatcher* or *load balancer*) to assign incoming jobs to servers. For example, incoming jobs may be assigned to servers in round-robin order, or each incoming job might be assigned to the server with the shortest queue. The choice of task assignment policy hugely influences the response time of jobs at the server farm, sometimes by orders of magnitude. Using the right task assignment policy is particularly important when the job size distribution has high variability. A major question in computer systems design is finding a good task assignment policy to minimize mean response time (or some other performance variant).

Figure 24.1 illustrates the server farm model that is the focus of this chapter. The high-speed front-end router deploys the *task assignment policy*, which assigns incoming jobs to hosts. Observe that the *scheduling policy* deployed at an individual host is not fixed, but is typically application dependent. For example, in web server farms, the servers are typically time-sharing servers, and each server "simultaneously" serves all

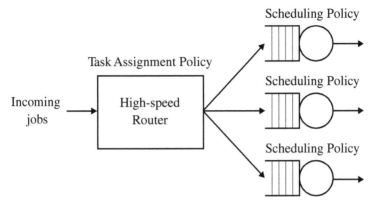

Figure 24.1. Server farm model.

jobs in its queue; that is, each server deploys the PS scheduling policy. By contrast, in manufacturing systems and in many supercomputing settings, jobs are often non-preemptible, and each server serves one job at a time in FCFS order.

The goal of this chapter is to understand the performance of different task assignment policies. The literature is so vast in this area that we can only hope to highlight some important results. Our goal throughout is to provide intuition. The readings noted in Section 24.4 contain greater depth.

In Section 24.1, we consider the case where jobs are non-preemptible and each server serves the jobs in its queue in FCFS order, as shown in Figure 24.2. In Section 24.2, we assume that jobs are preemptible and each server serves the jobs in its queue in PS order, as shown in Figure 24.6. For each of the settings in Sections 24.1 and 24.2, we look for task assignment policies that minimize mean response time. To facilitate analysis in these sections, we assume a Poisson arrival process. In Section 24.3, we ask more broadly how one could design optimal server farms in the case where jobs are preemptible and all design decisions are open (i.e., we can use any task assignment policy and any scheduling policy at the servers). Throughout we assume that job

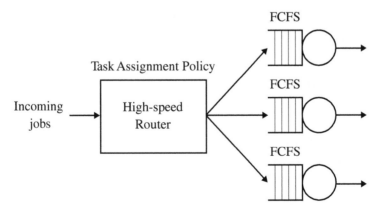

Figure 24.2. Server farm model with FCFS scheduling at hosts.

sizes are drawn from a high-variability distribution, such as the Bounded Pareto from Chapter 20, because such distributions reflect empirically measured job sizes.

24.1 Task Assignment for FCFS Server Farms

In this section, we assume the server farm model as shown in Figure 24.2, with k servers. In particular, we assume that *jobs are not preemptible* and that each server processes jobs in its queue in FCFS order. For simplicity, we assume that servers are *homogeneous*. We assume that job sizes are independently and identically distributed according to some high-variability distribution, G, with mean $\frac{1}{\mu}$. We also assume that jobs arrive according to a Poisson process with average rate λ. As usual, we denote the system utilization, ρ, by

$$\rho = \frac{\lambda}{k\mu}, \qquad 0 \le \rho \le 1$$

and the resource requirement, R, by

$$R = \frac{\lambda}{\mu} = k\rho, \qquad 0 \le R \le k$$

in accordance with Definition 14.4.

This model is common in manufacturing settings where it is often difficult, if not impossible, to preempt a job in progress. It is also common in supercomputing settings, where jobs are typically parallel computations, which makes them very difficult to preempt.

There are many choices for task assignment policies under this model. Many policies are not analytically tractable. However, in some cases their performance can be approximated. In others, even approximations are poor. Our discussion of these policies therefore sometimes relies on empirical results.

We can divide task assignment policies into those that make use of knowing the size (service requirement) of an arrival and those that do not assume any knowledge of the size of an arrival.

Question: What are some examples of task assignment policies for Figure 24.2 that do not assume any knowledge of the size of an arrival?

Answer: We list some common policies:

Under the **RANDOM** policy, each job is assigned to one of the k hosts with equal probability. The aim of the RANDOM policy is to equalize the expected number of jobs at each host.

Under the **ROUND-ROBIN** policy, jobs are assigned to hosts in a cyclical fashion with the ith job being assigned to host number $(i \mod k) + 1$. This policy also aims to equalize the expected number of jobs at each host.

Under the **JSQ (Join-the-Shortest-Queue)** policy, each incoming job is assigned to the host that has the shortest queue (the queue with the fewest *number* of jobs) at the time when the job arrives. If several hosts have the same fewest number of jobs, then JSQ picks one of these hosts at random. This policy tries to equalize the instantaneous number of jobs at each host.

All three policies immediately dispatch jobs to hosts, where there is a queue of jobs at each host. Alternatively, we could instead imagine a single *central* queue (like in the M/M/k), where a host, when free, picks the job at the head of the queue to run. Because we are assuming generally distributed i.i.d. job sizes, this architecture is referred to as the **M/G/k**. Note that, although the M/G/k is not strictly within our model because there are not queues at the hosts, it still obeys the general framework of our model, because jobs are non-preemptible and the (single) queue is serviced in FCFS order, and we do not need to know job sizes. Thus we include M/G/k as one of our policies.

Question: Which of these policies – RANDOM, ROUND-ROBIN, JSQ, or M/G/k – would you guess has the lowest mean response time?

Answer: We will discuss and compare the policies one at a time ... but hold on to your guess.

Question: Which do you think is superior: ROUND-ROBIN or RANDOM? Why?

Answer: It turns out that ROUND-ROBIN slightly outperforms RANDOM. To see why this is so, observe that the arrival process into each queue under RANDOM is a Poisson process, by Poisson splitting. By contrast, the interarrival time into each queue under ROUND-ROBIN is a sum of Exponentials – namely, an Erlang-k distribution – which has less variability than an Exponential. Hence, in RANDOM each queue behaves like an M/G/1, with average arrival rate λ/k, where G is the job size distribution, whereas under ROUND-ROBIN each queue behaves like an E_k/G/1, with average arrival rate λ/k. The lower variability of the E_k, compared to the M (Exponential), results in ROUND-ROBIN having lower mean response time.

Comparing ROUND-ROBIN with JSQ is more difficult, because for JSQ it is not possible to boil down the behavior of each queue to some simple G/G/1 queue. The issue is that the arrival process into a given queue under JSQ depends on the state of the other queues. To precisely analyze JSQ, one would need a k-dimensional Markov chain that tracks the number of jobs in each of the k queues. Unfortunately, no one knows how to analyze such a k-dimensional chain that grows unboundedly in all k dimensions. Even the case of just $k = 2$ dimensions and Exponential service times does not yield a closed form, and, for higher k $(k > 2)$, only approximations exist (see Section 24.4 for details). Based on the approximations that are known, it seems clear that JSQ is far superior to ROUND-ROBIN with respect to mean response time under higher job size variability. In fact, for high-variability job size distributions, JSQ can lower mean response time by an order of magnitude compared to ROUND-ROBIN.

Question: Intuitively, why does it make sense that JSQ should outperform ROUND-ROBIN under higher job size variability?

Answer: JSQ balances the instantaneous number of jobs at each queue, whereas ROUND-ROBIN balances the expected number of jobs. The difference is that JSQ can react quickly. Imagine that all queues have 5 jobs, but there is a lot of variability among job sizes and one of the queues empties suddenly. JSQ can quickly remedy the situation by sending the next 5 arrivals to that queue, whereas ROUND-ROBIN would have to wait for $k/2$ more arrivals on average before even one job could be sent to the empty queue. During that period of waiting for $k/2$ arrivals, the server corresponding to the empty queue is not being utilized, increasing the load on all other servers and increasing overall mean response time. When job size variability is high, queues can empty very suddenly. This is why the dynamic properties of JSQ are so important.

> **Definition 24.1** A *dynamic* policy is one that adapts based on changes in the state of the system (e.g., the number of jobs at each queue), whereas a *static* policy is oblivious to the changes in state.

Thus JSQ is *dynamic*, whereas ROUND-ROBIN is *static*.

Question: How would you guess that JSQ compares with M/G/k under high job size variability? Why?

Answer: Both M/G/k and JSQ are dynamic policies, and both are good at making sure that no host is left idle. However M/G/k has a big additional advantage: It holds off on assigning jobs to hosts as long as possible. Observe that in JSQ it could happen that all queues have 5 jobs, and suddenly one queue empties, creating a situation where one server is unutilized. This underutilization can never happen under M/G/k, because whenever there are $\geq k$ jobs, every host is busy.

Empirical results show that M/G/k can outperform JSQ by an order of magnitude with respect to mean response time when job size variability is high.

Now suppose that we know the *size* of a job when it arrives. Clearly there are many more task assignment policies possible if we know the job size. One obvious example is the LWL policy.

Under the **LWL (Least-Work-Left)** policy, each job goes to the queue where it will achieve the lowest possible response time. This is a *greedy* policy, because each job is acting in its own best interest. Specifically, each incoming job is assigned to the queue that has the least total work at the time when the job arrives. Note that the work a job sees ahead of it is exactly its waiting time. Unlike some of the policies we saw earlier that aim to equalize the *number* of jobs at each host, the LWL policy aims to equalize the total *work* at each host.

The LWL policy is exactly what we do when we go to the supermarket. We look at each line and count not the number of people (jobs) there, but rather we look at the number of items in each person's basket (the job size) for every person in each line. We then join the line with the smallest total number of items (least work remaining).

Recall that under JSQ we only look at the number of jobs in each queue in deciding where to route a job. When job size variability is high, the number of jobs in a queue can be a poor estimate of the total work in that queue. In this sense LWL is far superior to JSQ.

Question: How do LWL and M/G/k compare?

Answer: We will prove in Exercise 24.4 that LWL and M/G/k are actually equivalent, (i.e., LWL = M/G/k). Specifically, if both policies are fed the same arrival sequence of jobs, and ties are resolved in the same way in both systems, then it can be shown that the same job goes to the same host at the same time under both policies. Observe that when a job arrives to the M/G/k system, it may sit in the central queue for a while before being dispatched. However, the host that it will eventually go to is exactly the host that had the least work in front of it under LWL.

Unfortunately the analysis of M/G/k (and hence LWL) is a long-standing open problem in queueing theory. It is hard to imagine why the M/G/k is so hard to analyze, given that the M/M/k is so simple. Many young queueing theorists have devoted several years to beating their heads against the problem of analyzing the M/G/k system. Of course, one can always replace the job size distribution G with some phase-type distribution, PH, and use matrix-analytic methods to solve the M/PH/k system (see Exercise 21.7). Although this yields numerical solutions, it does not provide insight into which properties of the job size distribution matter and how these properties affect the solution. Also, even from a numerical standpoint, matrix-analytic solutions are not a panacea, because they can become very unstable (the matrices become near singular) when the distributions are highly skewed (e.g., when the squared coefficient of variation of the job size distribution, C^2, is very high).

The first closed-form approximation for waiting time in an M/G/k was proposed by Lee and Longton [118] over a half-century ago; it says that the waiting time in an M/G/k is basically the same as that in an M/M/k, but scaled up by a simple factor related to C^2:

$$\mathbf{E}\left[T_Q^{\text{M/G/k}}\right] \approx \left(\frac{C^2 + 1}{2}\right) \mathbf{E}\left[T_Q^{\text{M/M/k}}\right] \tag{24.1}$$

Many other authors have also proposed closed-form approximations for mean delay in the M/G/k, all involving only the first 2 moments of the job size distribution (see Section 24.4). Unfortunately, any approximation of mean delay based on using only the first 2 moments is provably inaccurate for some job size distributions; in addition, the inaccuracy of the approximation can be off by a factor proportional to C^2 [76].

Table 24.1 (borrowed from [76]) illustrates why two moments of the job size distribution are insufficient for predicting $\mathbf{E}[T_Q]$. The first row of the table shows $\mathbf{E}[T_Q]$ for an M/G/10 with mean job size of 1 and $C^2 = 19$ (first column) or $C^2 = 99$ (second column) according to approximation (24.1). The remaining rows show various distributions, all of which have been parameterized to have the same mean job size, $\mathbf{E}[S] = 1$, and appropriate C^2. As shown, the difference in $\mathbf{E}[T_Q]$ across distributions can be very high – $\mathbf{E}[T_Q]$ differs by a factor of close to 2 when $C^2 = 19$ and by a factor of more than 3 when $C^2 = 99$.

Table 24.1. *Simulation results for the 95% confidence intervals in an M/G/k, with $k = 10$, $\rho = 0.9$, and $\mathbf{E}[S] = 1$*

	$\mathbf{E}[T_Q]$ for $C^2 = 19$	$\mathbf{E}[T_Q]$ for $C^2 = 99$
2-Moment Approximation (24.1)	6.6873	33.4366
Weibull	6.0691 ± 0.01	25.9896 ± 0.18
Bounded Pareto ($\alpha = 1.1$)	5.5277 ± 0.02	24.6049 ± 0.28
Lognormal	4.994 ± 0.025	19.543 ± 0.42
Bounded Pareto ($\alpha = 1.3$)	4.879 ± 0.025	18.774 ± 0.36
Bounded Pareto ($\alpha = 1.5$)	3.947 ± 0.032	10.649 ± 0.54

The first line shows $\mathbf{E}\left[T_Q\right]$ for the 2-moment approximation given in (24.1). The remaining lines show various distributions with appropriate C^2.

Table 24.2 summarizes the task assignment policies that we have considered so far. There is one more commonly employed policy shown in the table that also makes use of knowing the size of jobs, namely the SITA policy.

Table 24.2. *Examples of common task assignment policies*

RANDOM	Each job is assigned to one of the k hosts with equal probability.
ROUND-ROBIN	The ith job is assigned to host $(i \mod k) + 1$.
JSQ	Each job is assigned to the host with the fewest number of jobs.
LWL	Each job is assigned to the host with the least total work.
M/G/k	When a server is free, it grabs the job at the head of the central queue.
SITA	Small jobs go to host 1, mediums to host 2, larges to host 3, etc.

Under the **SITA (Size-Interval-Task-Assignment)** policy [83], each host is assigned to a size interval, where the size intervals are non-overlapping and span the full range of possible job sizes. For example, the first host is assigned only "small" jobs (those of size between 0 and s, for some s); the second host is assigned only "medium" jobs (those of size between s and m, for some $m > s$); the third host is assigned only "large" jobs (those of size between m and l, for some $l > m$), etc. Every incoming job is routed to the appropriate host based on its size.

Question: What is the point of the SITA policy? Why does it make sense?

Answer: The SITA policy is similar to the "express lane" in your local supermarket, where one or two queues are reserved for "short" jobs only. When job size variability is high, there can be some very large jobs and some very small ones. By dedicating certain queues to short jobs only, we provide isolation for short jobs, so that they do not get stuck waiting behind long jobs.

Observe that we have not fully specified the SITA policy, because we have not specified the size cutoffs.

Question: Under SITA, what size cutoffs make sense?

Answer: One might think that choosing cutoffs that balance expected load among the queues makes sense. That is, we would choose s, m and l such that

$$\int_0^s tf(t)dt = \int_s^m tf(t)dt = \int_m^l tf(t)dt.$$

However, it turns out that choosing the cutoffs to balance expected load can be very far from optimal. This point is explored in Exercise 24.6.

Finding the optimal cutoff is very counterintuitive and often involves severely unbalancing the load between the servers. For example, for a Bounded Pareto with $\alpha < 1$, one wants to choose cutoffs that unbalance the load, favoring small jobs by underloading the servers of small jobs, whereas for a Bounded Pareto with $\alpha > 1$, one wants to choose cutoffs that unbalance the load, favoring large jobs by underloading the servers of large jobs [93, 82]. In the case of just $k = 2$ servers, the optimal cutoff can be obtained by search; however, the search becomes less feasible with more than 2 servers. As of the date of this book, the problem of finding closed-form cutoffs that minimize mean response time for general job size distributions is still wide open [93].

Question: How can we analyze SITA given that we know the cutoffs?

Answer: Once we are given size cutoffs, the analysis of SITA (under a Poisson arrival process) is very straightforward. Because the size of the incoming job is drawn at random from the size distribution, G, we can view the splitting of jobs into queues as probabilistic Poisson splitting of the arrival process. The ith queue can then be modeled as an M/G_i/1 queue, where G_i represents the job size distribution of jobs arriving at queue i. An example is provided in Exercise 24.1.

Question: How does the performance of SITA and LWL = M/G/k compare?

Answer: This is a surprisingly difficult question. Part of the problem, of course, is that neither SITA (with unknown cutoffs) nor LWL is analytically tractable in closed form. We start with some intuitions about each policy and then move on to what results exist in the literature.

One advantage of the LWL policy over any other policy is that it is ideal at keeping servers utilized. This can be seen by viewing LWL as M/G/k. It is impossible under LWL for one server to have zero jobs while another server has a job queueing.

One advantage of the SITA policy is that it is ideally suited to reducing variability at each queue. Suppose that the original job size distribution, G, has high variability. Under most policies, this same high variability is transferred to all the queues. This is problematic because we know, from the P-K formula (Chapter 23), that queueing delay is directly proportional to the variability of the job size distribution. SITA specifically divides up the job size distribution so that each queue sees only a portion of the domain of the original distribution, greatly decreasing the job size variability at each queue. Another way of putting this is that SITA provides short jobs *protection* from long jobs. Because most jobs in computing-based systems are short jobs, and because long jobs can be very, very long, isolating the many short jobs from long jobs greatly reduces mean response time.

The SITA policy and its variants have been part of the common wisdom for a long time and have been the focus of many papers (see Section 24.4 for references). Because of SITA's benefits in reducing job size variability, for a very long time it was believed that SITA, or some SITA-like variant, was far superior to LWL = M/G/k with respect to mean response time when the job size variability was very high. Many papers specifically compared the performance of SITA to LWL and found that as job size variability is *increased*, SITA becomes far superior to LWL.

Figure 24.3 illustrates SITA's superiority on a server farm with $k = 2$ servers. The job size distribution shown is a Bounded Pareto (k,p,α) with $\alpha = 1.4$. The resource requirement is $R = 0.95$, equivalent to $\rho = 0.95/2$. C^2 is increased while holding $\mathbf{E}[S]$ fixed by increasing the upper limit, p, while decreasing the lower limit, k. The SITA mean response times are computed analytically by first numerically deriving the optimal splitting cutoff. The LWL mean response times are not analytically tractable, so we use a (very loose) upper bound on LWL performance, given in [157]. Figure 24.3 shows the effect on mean response time, $\mathbf{E}[T]$, as C^2 is increased, under LWL and SITA. According to the figure, SITA is far superior to LWL. Although the results for LWL are loose, the trend of SITA's superiority over LWL is in good agreement with simulation results and those in earlier research papers.

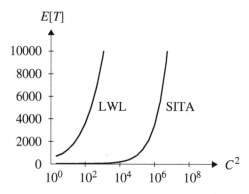

Figure 24.3. Expected response time, $\boldsymbol{E}[T]$, for SITA and LWL versus C^2 in a 2-server system with Bounded Pareto job size distribution with $\alpha = 1.4$ and resource requirement $R = 0.95$.

To more clearly illustrate SITA's superiority, we consider a server farm, again with $k = 2$ servers, where this time $R = 1.8$ and the job size distribution is a Hyperexponential, H_2, with unbalanced means (specifically $Q = 0.7$ fraction of the load is contained in one of the Hyperexponential branches). The advantage of using an H_2 is that we can analytically solve for the (nearly) exact mean response time under LWL via matrix-analytic methods, so that we do not have to use any upper bound. The H_2 also lends itself nicely to increasing C^2 while holding $\mathbf{E}[S]$ constant. Figure 24.4 clearly illustrates SITA's superiority over LWL for this H_2 job size distribution.

Despite comparisons such as those depicted in Figures 24.3 and 24.4 which show that SITA outperforms LWL by orders of magnitude for high job size variability, a *proof* of SITA's superiority over LWL never materialized. SITA itself is difficult to analyze, even for Poisson arrivals, because in general there is no closed-form expression for the optimal size cutoffs and for the resulting response time. Furthermore, LWL (which is equivalent to M/G/k) is in general only approximable. Thus, many of the existing comparisons have used simulation to assert their claims or have compared response time only under heavy-traffic regimes.

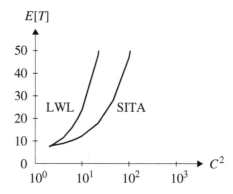

Figure 24.4. Expected response time, $\boldsymbol{E}[T]$, for SITA and LWL versus C^2 in a 2-server system with $R = 1.8$ and job size distribution H_2 with unbalanced branches ($Q = 0.7$).

In 2009, a surprising result was proven, showing that the common wisdom is actually *wrong* [90]: There are cases where SITA is not superior to LWL under high C^2, and in fact, SITA is provably *unboundedly worse* than LWL as $C^2 \rightarrow \infty$ in some regimes. An example of such a regime is provided in Figure 24.5.

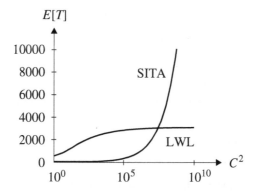

Figure 24.5. Expected response time, $\boldsymbol{E}[T]$, for SITA and LWL versus C^2 in a 2-server system with Bounded Pareto job size distribution with $\alpha = 1.6$ and $R = 0.95$.

Figure 24.5 considers a server farm identical to that of Figure 24.3, except that the Bounded Pareto parameter α has changed from $\alpha = 1.4$ to $\alpha = 1.6$. As in the case of Figure 24.3, the mean response time for SITA is computed analytically, while we use an upper bound from [157] for the mean response time for LWL. This time, however, the comparison between SITA and LWL looks very different. For lower C^2, SITA still improves on LWL; however, there is a crossover point, at sufficiently high C^2, after which SITA's response time diverges, whereas LWL's response time converges. This crossover point is actually at a much lower C^2 than it appears in the graph, because the upper bound for LWL is loose.

This crossover point, after which SITA's response time diverges but LWL's response time converges, was not observed in prior work (which mostly relies on simulation, numerical methods, heavy-traffic approximations or 2-moment M/G/2 approximations), possibly because the earlier literature did not consider the very high C^2 regions, thus (incorrectly) concluding that SITA is always superior to LWL.

Question: But why would SITA be inferior to LWL under high job size variability? Isn't SITA specifically designed to combat high variability?

Answer: Consider a server farm with two hosts, and the Bounded Pareto (k, p, α) job size distribution from Figure 24.5 as $p \to \infty$ and $C^2 \to \infty$. SITA needs to place its size cutoff somewhere. If it places the size cutoff at any finite value, x, then the first host sees a job size distribution with finite variance (because sizes range from k to x); however, the second host sees a job size distribution with infinite variance (because sizes range from x to ∞, as $p \to \infty$). Since mean response time is a weighted sum of the response time at the two hosts, the mean response time under SITA will tend to infinity as $C^2 \to \infty$. Note that we can instead make the cutoff, x, increase with p. This however, means that as $p \to \infty$, the first host experiences infinite variability, which again means that SITA has infinite mean response time.

By contrast, under LWL performance is only bad if two big jobs arrive near to each other, blocking off both servers. But the probability of such a bad event can be very low if the resource requirement is sufficiently light (e.g., $R < 1$ with 2 servers). In this case the second server is not really needed, and is thus available to serve shorter jobs if one server gets blocked with a long job.

In general, for a system with k servers, we define the number of **spare servers** as

$$\text{Number spare servers} = k - \lceil R \rceil.$$

These spare servers can be extremely effective in combating variability. Even if C^2 for the job size distribution approaches infinity, the spare servers can be used to let the smaller jobs have a "freeway" so that they do not get stuck behind large jobs, allowing the response time of LWL to converge.

One might think that SITA could similarly benefit from spare servers, but the strict routing in SITA makes it unable to enjoy this benefit.

Question: But why was there a difference between the Bounded Pareto with $\alpha = 1.4$, shown in Figure 24.3, and the Bounded Pareto with $\alpha = 1.6$, shown in Figure 24.5, given that both cases were run with one spare server?

Answer: The Bounded Pareto with $\alpha = 1.4$ has a fatter tail, implying there are more medium and large jobs. This increases the probability of a "bad event" where two large jobs arrive at near the same time. It turns out that in this case one spare server is insufficient for LWL. The difference is captured more precisely in the $3/2$ moment of the job size distribution. Observe that $\mathbf{E}\left[S^{\frac{3}{2}}\right]$ is infinite for $\alpha = 1.4$, whereas $\mathbf{E}\left[S^{\frac{3}{2}}\right]$ is finite for $\alpha = 1.6$. Theorem 24.2 explains that the $3/2$ moment of S is crucial in understanding the response time of the M/G/2 (LWL).

> **Theorem 24.2** *[155, 156, 157, 158] For (almost) all job size distributions with r.v. S, the mean response time of the M/G/2 is bounded (finite) if and only if $\mathbf{E}\left[S^{\frac{3}{2}}\right]$ is finite and there is at least one spare server.*

Although we do not have space to prove this theorem, in Section 24.4 we elaborate on generalizations of the result to $k > 2$ servers. Note that this stability result is very different from an M/G/1, whose mean response time is finite if and only if $\mathbf{E}\left[S^2\right]$ is finite.

Summary

This section has dealt with finding task assignment policies for server farms in the case where jobs are not preemptible and job size variability is high. Our discussion covers only the highlights of a vast body of literature in the area. The main point is that task assignment is non-obvious and can be counterintuitive. Many common, well-known policies, such as RANDOM, ROUND-ROBIN, and JSQ, are virtually worthless when job size variability is high. Furthermore, it is difficult to *rank* the policies: As we have seen, sometimes SITA can be *far* superior to LWL, and sometimes the reverse is true. Even a seemingly innocuous and obvious goal like "load balancing" is questionable, because SITA can perform far better when the load across servers is purposely unbalanced. Finally, the analysis of task assignment policies is often very difficult and is still in its infancy. We have collected some important references in Section 24.4.

Question: So far we have only considered the case of high job size variability. Suppose that instead the job size variability is very low. How do the policies that we have considered compare in this situation?

Answer: When job sizes are Deterministic (e.g., all jobs have size 1), the ROUND-ROBIN policy is optimal, because the arrivals to a server are maximally spaced out; in fact, if job sizes and interarrival times are both Deterministic, then no job will be delayed under ROUND-ROBIN, assuming that the system is not in overload. The JSQ policy will actually end up doing the same thing as ROUND-ROBIN, because the shortest queue will be that which has not received a new job in the longest time. By the same logic, LWL will end up doing the same thing as ROUND-ROBIN. In contrast, RANDOM will sometimes make the "mistake" of sending two consecutive arrivals to the same queue, incurring some delay. SITA will reduce to RANDOM, because all jobs have the same size. Even with occasional mistakes by RANDOM, we expect mean response time to be very low. To see this, consider the case of RANDOM with Deterministic job sizes and Poisson arrivals. By Poisson splitting, each queue becomes an M/D/1 queue, which we know has only half the delay of an M/M/1.

24.2 Task Assignment for PS Server Farms

We now turn to a very different model of a server farm. Figure 24.6 depicts a queueing model of a web server farm. Here the incoming requests are HTTP requests. These must be immediately dispatched to one of the server hosts, because they are connections that need immediate attention. Requests are fully preemptible in that any request can be stopped and restarted where we left off. Given that this is a network-based application, running on TCP, it is important that the service seem immediate and constant. For this reason, we cannot have requests waiting in a FCFS queue. Instead, each host time-shares among all the requests in its queue, so that each HTTP request receives "constant" service. This scheduling is modeled as Processor-Sharing (PS).

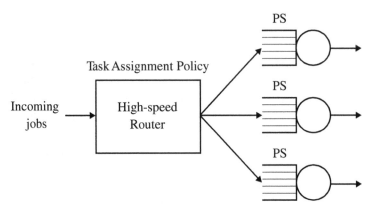

Figure 24.6. Server farm model with PS scheduling at hosts.

There are many common high-speed routers used for dispatching HTTP requests in a web server farm. Some examples are Cisco's LocalDirector [42], IBM's Network Dispatcher [140], and F5's BIG-IP [21]. The job size distribution for websites is known to be highly variable and heavy-tailed [47, 48]. To ease the analysis, we assume that the arrival process is a Poisson process with average rate λ and that job sizes are i.i.d. Assuming a Poisson arrival process is not necessarily unrealistic, particularly if the arrival process is the merge of many disparate users. However, our assumptions that job sizes are independent of each other and independent of the interarrival times are not true in practice, as pointed out in several papers, [70, 47, 169]. As before, we assume k identical servers and use S to denote the job size, where $\mathbf{E}\left[S\right] = \frac{1}{\mu}$. The system load is denoted by $\rho = \frac{\lambda}{k\mu}$ and the resource requirement by $R = \frac{\lambda}{\mu}$.

Given the huge prevalence of web server farms, it is important to consider what task assignment policies are best for the PS server farm model and how they compare. We again consider the policies in Table 24.2; all except for the M/G/k (which by definition uses a FCFS queue) are reasonable options for a PS server farm. Let's see how these compare.

Question: Consider first the RANDOM policy and the SITA policy. Recall that for the FCFS server farm, the SITA policy was far superior to RANDOM when the job size distribution was highly variable. How do these policies compare for the PS server farm, again assuming high job size variability?

Hint: Analyzing SITA of course depends on the size cutoffs. It turns out that, in contrast to FCFS server farms, the optimal size cutoffs for PS server farms are those that *balance* load between the servers (see Exercise 24.2). Thus the load at every server is ρ, just like the overall system load. It is therefore easiest to express the response time of each policy in terms of ρ.

Hint: Both RANDOM and SITA experience Poisson splitting, because the size cutoffs in SITA can be viewed as sending a fraction, p_i, of jobs to server i.

Answer: For RANDOM, we note that an arrival goes to a random queue with load ρ and arrival rate λ/k. By Poisson splitting, this random queue is an M/G/1/PS queue, but the mean response time for M/G/1/PS is the same as that of M/M/1/FCFS (see Chapter 22). Thus, the random arrival goes to a queue with (on average) $\frac{\rho}{1-\rho}$ jobs. By Little's Law, its response time at this queue is then

$$\mathbf{E}\left[T\right]^{\text{RANDOM}} = \frac{1}{\lambda/k} \cdot \frac{\rho}{1-\rho} = \frac{k}{\lambda} \cdot \frac{\rho}{1-\rho}.$$

For SITA, WLOG assume that the job size distribution ranges from 0 to ∞ and that the size cutoffs are $s_1, s_2, \ldots s_{k-1}$, where jobs in the interval $(0, s_1)$ go to host 1, jobs of size (s_{i-1}, s_i) go to host i, and jobs of size (s_{k-1}, ∞) go to host k. The fraction of jobs that go to host i is p_i where $p_i = \int_{s_{i-1}}^{s_i} f(t)dt$, where $f(t)$ is the density of the job size distribution. The load at queue i is ρ (see the first hint). By Poisson splitting, queue i is an M/G/1/PS queue (see second hint). The arrival rate into queue i is λ_i, where $\lambda_i = \lambda p_i$. Putting these facts together we have

$$\mathbf{E}\left[T \mid \text{job goes to host } i\right]^{\text{SITA}} = \frac{1}{\lambda_i} \cdot \frac{\rho}{1-\rho}.$$

$$\mathbf{E}\left[T\right]^{\text{SITA}} = \sum_{i=1}^{k} p_i \cdot \mathbf{E}\left[T \mid \text{job goes to host } i\right]$$

$$= \sum_{i=1}^{k} p_i \cdot \frac{1}{\lambda_i} \cdot \frac{\rho}{1-\rho}$$

$$= \sum_{i=1}^{k} \frac{1}{\lambda} \cdot \frac{\rho}{1-\rho}$$

$$= \frac{k}{\lambda} \cdot \frac{\rho}{1-\rho}.$$

Thus we have that

$$\mathbf{E}\left[T\right]^{\text{RANDOM}} = \mathbf{E}\left[T\right]^{\text{SITA}}. \tag{24.2}$$

The fact that RANDOM and SITA have the same mean response time (for server farms with PS servers) might be surprising, because these policies yield very different performance for FCFS servers. The reason that RANDOM and SITA were so different for server farms with FCFS servers is that RANDOM does nothing to reduce job size variability, whereas SITA does a lot to reduce variability. However, PS scheduling is invariant to job size variability, and hence the benefit of SITA in reducing job size variability is superfluous.

Question: For server farms with PS servers, which is better: JSQ or LWL? Which was better for server farms with FCFS servers?

Answer: Recall that for the case of server farms with FCFS servers, LWL was superior to JSQ. For FCFS servers, LWL represented the *greedy* policy, whereby each job was routed to the host where it would itself experience the lowest response time, namely the host with the least total work.

For the case of PS servers, JSQ represents the *greedy* policy that routes jobs to the host where it will likely experience the lowest response time. Specifically, under JSQ, each job is routed to the host where it will time-share with the fewest jobs. By contrast, knowing the total work at a PS host does not necessarily have any bearing on the job's response time at that host.

Unfortunately, analyzing JSQ is no easier for a PS server farm than for a FCFS server farm, even when the job size distribution is Exponential. Modeling JSQ requires tracking the number of jobs at each queue, so that we can determine to which host an arrival should be routed. But tracking the number of jobs in each queue necessitates a state space that grows unboundedly in k dimensions (one for each queue), making it intractable. The problem is only amplified for LWL where we need to track the total work at each queue.

One idea for analyzing JSQ in a PS server farm is to approximate the dependence between the queues while only tracking what is going on in a single *one* of the k queues, WLOG queue 1 [79]. The dependence is captured by making the arrival rate into queue 1 be dependent on the number of jobs at queue 1. For example, the average arrival rate into queue 1 should be λ/k. However, if queue 1 currently has 0 jobs, then the arrival rate into queue 1 should be greater than λ/k, because it is likely that the other queues have more jobs than queue 1. Likewise, if queue 1 currently has many jobs, then the arrival rate into queue 1 will be less than λ/k, because the other queues likely have fewer jobs. By deriving the correct load-dependent arrival rate into queue 1, one can approximate the influence of the other $k - 1$ queues on queue 1. Finally, since queue 1 was chosen WLOG, the delay experienced by an arrival to queue 1 is the system delay.

A recent finding is that JSQ is surprisingly (nearly) insensitive to job size variability for PS server farms [79]. At first, this may seem to follow from the insensitivity of the M/G/1/PS queue. However, there is more to it than that, because LWL, as we will soon see, is not at all insensitive to job size variability for PS server farms. A proof of the near insensitivity of JSQ has not yet been found, as of the time of writing of this book.

Figure 24.7 shows simulation results for the performance of all the task assignment policies we have considered over a range of job size distributions, described in

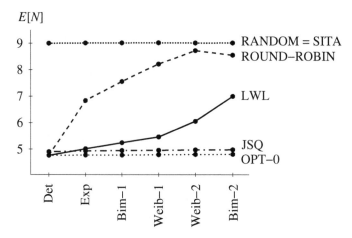

Figure 24.7. Simulation results for a server farm with two PS hosts, under different task assignment policies. The x-axis shows a variety of job size distributions (described in Table 24.3) in order of increasing variability from left to right. The y-axis depicts the mean number of jobs *per host* of the server farm, under each job size distribution. The server farm load is $\rho = 0.9$.

Table 24.3. *Job size distributions, each with mean 2, but increasing variance from top to bottom*

Distribution	Mean	Variance
Deterministic: point mass at 2	2	0
Erlang-2: sum of two Exp(1) random variables	2	2
Exponential: Exp(0.5) random variable	2	4
Bimodal-1: $\begin{cases} 1 & \text{w.p. } 0.9 \\ 11 & \text{w.p. } 0.1 \end{cases}$	2	9
Weibull-1: (shape parameter 0.5, scale parameter 1)	2	20
Weibull-2: (shape parameter $\frac{1}{3}$, scale parameter $\frac{1}{3}$)	2	76
Bimodal-2: $\begin{cases} 1 & \text{w.p. } 0.99 \\ 101 & \text{w.p. } 0.01 \end{cases}$	2	99

Table 24.3.[1] Each distribution has mean 2, but the distributions have increasing variance, ranging from a variance of 0 for the Deterministic distribution to a variance of 99 for the Bimodal-2 distribution. As we consider distributions with higher and higher variance, we see that the performance of ROUND-ROBIN and LWL both deteriorate. By contrast, the performance of SITA, RANDOM, and JSQ appear insensitive to the job size variability (JSQ is not actually insensitive, because there is a 1% variation, not visible by eye). The JSQ policy is clearly the best of the policies we have considered thus far.

To gauge the optimality of JSQ, we also compare policies against the **OPT-0** policy. The OPT-0 policy, introduced in [25], assigns each incoming job so as to minimize the mean response time for all jobs currently in the system, *assuming that there are 0 future arrivals*. Note that we are not being greedy from the perspective of the incoming job, but rather trying to minimize across all the jobs in the system. This policy is followed for each successive incoming arrival. Although the JSQ policy is far simpler than OPT-0, its performance is within about 5% of OPT-0, for all job size distributions in the table. Thus the JSQ policy appears to be near optimal.

Summary

This section has dealt with finding task assignment policies for server farms in the case where jobs are preemptible, the scheduling at the servers is PS, and job size variability is high. Unlike the previous section that dealt with FCFS scheduling at the servers, there is presently very little literature on this topic, see [6], [79], and [101], probably because the operations research community deals far less with PS servers than with FCFS servers.

The main point of this section is that task assignment is very different for server farms composed of PS servers as compared to FCFS servers. Whereas JSQ is a pretty bad policy for server farms of FCFS servers, because of its ineffectiveness in alleviating delays created by high job size variability, JSQ is an excellent policy for server farms of PS servers. Similarly, SITA, a top performer for server farms with FCFS servers, is

---

[1] The Weibull distribution has p.d.f. $f(t) = \frac{\alpha}{\lambda} \left(\frac{t}{\lambda} \right)^{\alpha-1} e^{-\left(\frac{t}{\lambda} \right)^{\alpha}}$, for $t > 0$, where $\alpha > 0$ is called the shape parameter and $\lambda > 0$ is called the scale parameter; see [181]. The parameters that we chose in the table result in heavy-tailed distributions.

among the worst performers for server farms with PS servers. Under server farms of PS servers, job size variability is not a big problem, and some policies, like JSQ, are nearly insensitive to job size variability.

The analysis of server farms with PS servers is a wide open area, full of open problems. For example, we did not even discuss the very interesting problem of task assignment policies for the case of heterogeneous servers.

24.3 Optimal Server Farm Design

We now turn to the more theoretical question of how to optimally design a server farm if one is allowed to choose *both* the task assignment policy and the scheduling policy at the individual hosts; both these decisions are shown in Figure 24.1. This is a theoretical question, because typically the scheduling policy at the individual hosts is dictated by the operating system at the servers and the application. To give ourselves maximum flexibility, we further assume that jobs are fully preemptible and that we know a job's size when it arrives (of course we do not know future jobs). Finally, we allow ourselves the flexibility of having a central queue at the router, if we want one. As usual, we assume a job size distribution with high variability, mean job size $\mathbf{E}\,[S]$, and a Poisson arrival process with average rate λ.

Unfortunately, there exists almost no stochastic analysis in the area of optimal server farm design. All the work in the area of optimal server farm design deals with worst-case analysis and competitive ratios. In **worst-case analysis**, one is no longer looking at the performance of a policy, $\mathcal{P}$, under a Poisson arrival process with i.i.d. job sizes taken from some distribution, as we have been assuming. Instead, one imagines an adversary who can generate any arrival sequence, where the arrival sequence consists of arrival times of jobs and their sizes. The policy $\mathcal{P}$ is now evaluated on each possible arrival sequence and is compared with the optimal policy for that arrival sequence. Specifically, we imagine some algorithm **OPT** that behaves optimally on each arrival sequence. We do not know what OPT looks like, and it does not have to be consistent across arrival sequences (that is, OPT can follow a different algorithm on each arrival sequence); we just use OPT to denote the best possible solution for every arrival sequence. Now consider the whole space of possible arrival sequences. For each arrival sequence, $\mathcal{A}$, consider the following ratio:

$$r_{\mathcal{P}}(\mathcal{A}) = \frac{\mathbf{E}\,[T(\mathcal{A})]^{\mathcal{P}}}{\mathbf{E}\,[T(\mathcal{A})]^{\text{OPT}}},$$

where $\mathbf{E}\,[T(\mathcal{A})]^{\mathcal{P}}$ is the expected response time of policy $\mathcal{P}$ on arrival sequence $\mathcal{A}$. Then the **competitive ratio** of policy $\mathcal{P}$ is defined as

$$\text{Competitive ratio of } \mathcal{P} \;=\; \max_{\mathcal{A}} r_{\mathcal{P}}(\mathcal{A}).$$

In worst-case analysis, the higher the competitive ratio of a policy, the "worse" that policy is. Note that a policy $\mathcal{P}$ can have a high competitive ratio even if it performs poorly on just a single arrival sequence.

Worst-case analysis can yield a very different ranking of policies than that obtained by the stochastic analysis described in most of this book. A policy $\mathcal{P}$ can be viewed as very poor in a worst-case sense, because it performs badly on one particular arrival sequence, but that arrival sequence can be a very low-probability event in a stochastic sense.

Question: Returning to the question of optimal server farm design, what are good routing/scheduling policy choices?

Hint: For the case of a single queue, with fully preemptible jobs, where we know the size of the job, what is the best scheduling policy on every arrival sequence?

Answer: In Exercise 2.3, we proved that the SRPT policy, which always (preemptively) runs that job with the shortest remaining processing time, is optimal with respect to mean response time, for the case of a single queue. This result was originally proved in [159] and holds under any arrival sequence of job sizes and arrival times.

The optimality of SRPT for a single queue inspires the server farm configuration shown in Figure 24.8. It is like an M/G/k, except that the central queue is served in SRPT order. Specifically, the k hosts are always serving those k jobs with the currently shortest remaining processing times. Suppose, WLOG, that server i is working on a job with remaining processing requirement r_i, where $r_i > r_j$, for all active servers j. Then, if a job comes in with shorter remaining time than r_i, that arrival is immediately put into service at the ith server, and the prior job being served at the ith server is put back into the queue. We refer to this as the **Central-Queue-SRPT** policy.

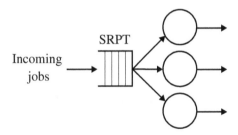

Figure 24.8. Server farm with Central-Queue-SRPT policy.

The Central-Queue-SRPT policy looks very good. Because at every moment of time the k jobs with shortest remaining processing time are those in service, the server farm behaves very much like a single queue with a server that is k times the speed.

Question: Is Central-Queue-SRPT optimal in the worst-case sense? That is, does Central-Queue-SRPT minimize $\mathbf{E}[T]$ on every arrival sequence?

Answer: Sadly, the answer is no. The following is an example of a "bad" arrival sequence, for the case of a 2-server system, where Central-Queue-SRPT does not produce the minimal mean response time. This is adapted from [119]:

- At time 0, 2 jobs of size 2^9 arrive, as well as 1 job of size 2^{10}.
- At time 2^{10}, 2 jobs of size 2^8 arrive, as well as 1 job of size 2^9.
- At time $2^{10} + 2^9$, 2 jobs of size 2^7 arrive, as well as 1 job of size 2^8.
- At time $2^{10} + 2^9 + 2^8$, 2 jobs of size 2^6 arrive, as well as 1 job of size 2^7.
- And so forth . . .

Let's name our two servers, server A and server B. The optimal algorithm, at time 0, will run the 2 jobs of size 2^9 on server A and will simultaneously run the job of size 2^{10} on server B. By time 2^{10}, all work that arrived at time 0 will be complete. At time 2^{10}, the optimal algorithm will run the 2 jobs of size 2^8 on server A and will simultaneously run the job of size 2^9 on server B, and so forth. The point is that the optimal algorithm is always able to pack the jobs in such a way that the servers are both fully utilized at all times.

By contrast, Central-Queue-SRPT makes a mess of this arrival sequence. At time 0, it tries to run one of the jobs of size 2^9 on server A and the other job of size 2^9 on server B, because these are the jobs with smallest remaining time. Only when these complete does Central-Queue-SRPT start to run the job of size 2^{10}, leaving one of the servers idle. Unfortunately, this does not leave enough time to complete the job of size 2^{10}, which must be preempted at time 2^{10} when the next batch of jobs comes in. Central-Queue-SRPT continues its mistakes, by now running one of the jobs of size 2^8 on server A and the other job of size 2^8 on server B. Only when these complete does it start to run the job of size 2^9. Unfortunately, there is not enough time for the job of size 2^9 to complete before the new batch of jobs arrive, etc. Central-Queue-SRPT packs the jobs badly, so that the two servers are not both fully utilized; hence, resources are wasted and jobs do not complete.

Although the Central-Queue-SRPT algorithm performs particularly badly on this arrival sequence, Leonardi and Raz [119] prove that it is still the best possible online algorithm from a worst-case competitive-ratio perspective. It is shown in [119] that the competitive ratio of Central-Queue-SRPT is proportional to $\log\left(\frac{b}{s}\right)$, where b is the biggest job size possible and s is the smallest job size possible, and that no online algorithm can improve on this competitive ratio by more than a constant multiplicative factor.

It is important to note that, although the Central-Queue-SRPT algorithm is not optimal in a worst-case sense, that does not mean that it is not optimal in a *stochastic* sense. For example, it might be the best possible policy given a Poisson arrival process and i.i.d. job sizes from any general distribution. Unfortunately, we do not know the answer to this question, because no one to date has been able to analyze the Central-Queue-SRPT policy from a stochastic perspective, even under a Poisson arrival process and Exponentially distributed job sizes. The closest approximation to this is [89], which analyzes an M/PH/k queue with an arbitrary number of preemptive priority classes, where jobs are prioritized in order of shortest expected remaining time. Unfortunately, the results in [89] are numerical in form; no closed-form analysis exists. Analyzing Central-Queue-SRPT stochastically is an important open problem in queueing.

A related open problem is the question of optimal task assignment under the restriction that jobs need to be **immediately dispatched** to hosts, meaning that they cannot be held in a central queue. This restriction is of practical importance, because, in many applications, like web servers, the request needs to be assigned to a host that can immediately establish a connection with the client. In the case where jobs need to be immediately assigned to hosts, it is optimal to run SRPT scheduling at the individual hosts.[2] Thus we have the architecture shown in Figure 24.9.

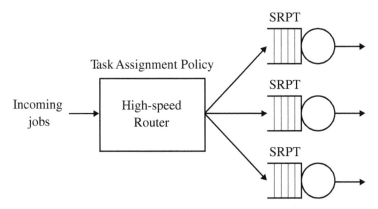

Figure 24.9. Server farm with immediate dispatch and SRPT scheduling at the hosts.

Question: Given SRPT scheduling at the individual hosts as in Figure 24.9, what is a good (immediate dispatch) task assignment policy for minimizing mean response time?

Hint: SRPT is very effective at getting short jobs out.

Answer: Simple RANDOM task assignment is not a bad policy here, because each queue then looks like an M/G/1/SRPT queue with arrival rate λ/k and mean job size $\mathbf{E}[S]$. The idea proposed independently by [9] and by [49] is to go a step further and make sure that the short jobs are spread out over all the SRPT servers, so that the servers can each be working on getting as many short jobs out as possible. Specifically, the **IMD** algorithm in [9] divides jobs into size classes (small, medium, large, etc.) and then assigns each incoming job to the server with the smallest number of jobs in that size class. The point is to make sure that each server has some smalls, some mediums, and some larges, so that their SRPT scheduling can be maximally effective.

Avrahami and Azar [9] prove that when the server farm in Figure 24.9 is run with the IMD task assignment policy, the performance is on the order of that achieved by Central-Queue-SRPT in a worst-case sense, meaning that the two algorithms result in competitive ratios within a constant factor of each other. An exact stochastic analysis of IMD is not known, although an approximation is given in [49].

Summary

This section has looked at server farm configurations using "optimal" task assignment/ scheduling policy pairings. Almost all the available analysis is worst-case analysis.

---

[2] Using proof by contradiction, one can argue that not running SRPT scheduling at the host will only increase mean response time.

Unfortunately, there is almost no stochastic analysis known for any of the models that we considered. This is also a wide-open area. A reader interested in working on such analysis should first read Chapters 32 and 33, which consider SRPT and related variants for a single-server system.

24.4 Readings and Further Follow-up

Below we list additional references on the topic of task assignment for server farms.

More on SITA and Its Variants for Server Farms with FCFS Servers

It is not clear where the idea of size-based task assignment originated, because it has been part of the common wisdom for a long time. Size-based splitting was used in the Cornell Theory Center [99]. The SITA policy was formally introduced by Harchol-Balter, Crovella, and Murta in [83]. In a follow-up paper [82], Harchol-Balter introduced a variant of SITA called TAGS that does not require knowing the size of the job, but nevertheless achieves response times close to those of SITA. The SITA policy and its variants have been the focus of many papers including [99, 83, 82, 177, 50, 134, 41, 172, 65, 32, 11, 59, 36, 161]. Because of SITA's benefits in reducing job size variability, for a very long time it was believed that SITA, or some SITA-like variant, was far superior to LWL = M/G/k with respect to mean response time when the job size variability was very high. Many papers specifically compared the performance of SITA to LWL and found that, as job size variability is *increased*, SITA becomes far superior to LWL [32, 41, 50, 65, 82, 83, 134, 172, 177]. Although the above papers suggest that SITA should be superior to LWL under high job size variability, [90] finds that the opposite can actually be true for certain job size distributions and loads, as explained in this chapter. This work was further extended in [91], where variants of SITA were considered that combine the strengths of SITA and LWL. For example [91] considers an M/G/2 server farm, where the top server only serves small jobs, but the bottom server can serve any job, referred to as **Hybrid**. Surprisingly, [91] proves that even Hybrid can sometimes be inferior to LWL.

More on M/G/k and G/G/k

The mean response time for the M/G/k, and hence also G/G/k, remains a longstanding open problem in the queueing literature [76]. After the Lee and Longton [118] approximation in 1959, many other authors proposed alternative simple closed-form approximations for mean waiting time; see [97, 98, 112, 132, 26, 196]. Unfortunately, all of these closed-form approximations also involve only the first 2 moments of the job size distribution, which is shown to be insufficient in [76].

There are several key analytical papers that are concerned with the G/G/k under high job size variability. Scheller-Wolf and Sigman [156, 155] prove an upper bound on mean delay in a G/G/k system where this upper bound does not depend on any moment of service time higher than the $\frac{k+1}{k}$ moment, and it particularly does not depend on the variance of job size. The [155] result requires that the resource requirement, R, is not too high: $R < \lfloor k/2 \rfloor$ (where $R = k\rho$). However, [156] generalizes the result to allow for higher load, $R < k - 1$. The converse of the [156, 155] results was presented by Scheller-Wolf and Vesilo in [158] for a large class of distributions. It is known that if $R > k - 1$, then the G/G/k diverges as $C^2 \to \infty$ [157], where C^2 is the squared coefficient of variation of the job size.

Whitt [184] and Foss and Korshunov [64] consider a G/G/2 and study the delay tail behavior when job size is heavy-tailed. They find that for low load, the delay tail grows like the tail of the equilibrium distribution, squared, whereas for high load the delay tail grows like the tail of the equilibrium distribution. These results are consistent with [155] and [158].

More on JSQ

For the case of server farms with PS servers, there has been very little analysis of JSQ, see [79]. However, there is a substantive simulation study by Bonomi [25] that examines both JSQ and a few policies that improve slightly over JSQ (5% improvement) by exploiting knowledge of the remaining service times of jobs.

By contrast, there is a lot of work on JSQ for server farms with FCFS scheduling at the servers. For workloads with non-decreasing failure rate, where job sizes are not known a priori, the JSQ policy is provably optimal [180, 194, 52]. As we have pointed out, however, JSQ is far from optimal for FCFS servers with *highly variable* job sizes [83, 82].

Almost all papers analyzing JSQ for server farms with FCFS servers are limited to $k = 2$ servers, an Exponential job size distribution, and the mean response time metric. Even here, the papers are largely approximate and often require truncation of the state space or of some infinite sums [108, 61, 73, 44, 146, 122, 3]. Sometimes the results are exact, but are not computationally efficient and do not generalize to higher values of k [27].

For analyzing JSQ with more than $k = 2$ servers, for the case of server farms with FCFS servers, again with Exponential job sizes, only approximations exist. Nelson and Philips [128] use the following idea: They look at the steady-state probability of the M/M/k queue (with a central queue) as an estimate for the total number of jobs in the JSQ/FCFS system; they then assume that the jobs in the system are divided equally (within 1) among each of the queues. Lin and Raghavendra [120] follow the approach of approximating the number of busy servers by a Binomial distribution and then also assume that the jobs are equally divided among each of the queues (within 1). Both approximations are surprisingly accurate, with reported accuracy in the 2% to 8% error range. There are also some numerical methods papers that do not lead to a closed-form solution, but are accurate and computationally efficient for not-too-large k; see for example [2, 122, 4].

Finally, Bramson, Lu, and Prabhakar [30] consider the limiting regime where the number of queues goes to infinity ($k \to \infty$). In this regime they prove that, for any fixed number of queues, the numbers of jobs at each of the queues become independent. This allows them to derive various performance metrics, including queue lengths.

Cycle Stealing in Server Farms

The performance of server farms can be improved dramatically by allowing servers to share their work. *Cycle stealing* is the idea of allowing an idle server to take on some work from a busy server's queue. Analyzing the performance of a server farm with cycle stealing has the same difficulties as analyzing JSQ, because one needs to track the number of jobs at each server, resulting in a Markov chain that grows unboundedly in k dimensions. Even for $k = 2$ this is only approximable. There are a long list of approximations for different variants of cycle stealing, including approximations based on truncating the state space along one of the dimensions [74, 170, 171]; approximations based on boundary-value methods [55, 113, 43]; heavy-traffic techniques [17, 63]; approximations based on the idea of Dimensionality Reduction of Markov chains [86, 136, 89, 88, 192, 20, 137, 138, 87, 135]; and others [168, 193] .

24.5 Exercises

24.1 Server Farm with Size-Interval-Task-Assignment
We are given a server farm with 2 identical FCFS hosts. Arrivals into the system occur according to a Poisson process with rate λ. Job sizes follow a power-law distribution, denoted by random variable S, where $\mathbf{P}\{S > x\} = x^{-2.5}$, for $1 \le x < \infty$. Small jobs (those of size < 10) are routed to the first server, and large jobs (those of size ≥ 10) are routed to the second server.
(a) Derive the mean response time, $\mathbf{E}[T]$, for this system.
(b) What would $\mathbf{E}[T]$ be if the job size distribution were changed to $\mathbf{P}\{S > x\} = x^{-1.5}$, for $1 \le x < \infty$.

24.2 PS Server Farm
Consider a server farm with 2 identical PS hosts and SITA task assignment. Arrivals into the system occur according to a Poisson process with rate λ. Job sizes follow some (general) distribution. Prove that the SITA cutoff which minimizes mean response time is that which balances load between the two hosts.

24.3 Hybrid Server Farm
We are given a server farm with 2 identical hosts. Arrivals into the system occur according to a Poisson process with rate λ. Job sizes are denoted by the random variable S, with p.d.f. $f_S(t)$, where $0 \le t \le \infty$, and c.d.f. $F_S(t) = \mathbf{P}\{S < t\}$.

Because our job size distribution F_S has high variability, we decide to combat this by using a variant of size-interval scheduling, where small jobs are sent to server 1, where they are scheduled in FCFS order, and large jobs are sent to server 2, where they are scheduled according to PS. Assume that the size cutoff is chosen such that load is balanced between "small" and "large" jobs. Specifically, $\rho = \frac{\lambda \mathbf{E}[S]}{2}$ represents both the load of the server farm and the load at each host. Suppose that this (balanced-load) size cutoff is 10. Thus a job is considered "small" if its size is less than 10, and is called "large" otherwise.

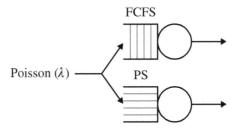

Write an expression for $\mathbf{E}[T]$, the mean response time experienced by an arriving job, as a function of ρ, λ, $f_S(t)$, and $F_S(t)$.

24.4 Equivalence of LWL and M/G/k

Assume that LWL and M/G/k are fed the same arrival sequence of jobs and are both run on k servers. Assume also that ties are resolved the same way in both systems. Prove by induction that each job is served by the same server in both the systems. Furthermore, the job begins and ends service at the same time in both systems.

24.5 One Fast Machine versus Two Slow Ones

Consider the question of whether one fast machine or two slow ones is better for minimizing mean waiting time, $\mathbf{E}[T_Q]$. Each slow machine works at half the rate of the single fast machine. Specifically, a job that requires s seconds of processing time on the fast machine will require $2s$ seconds of processing time on a single slow machine.

(a) Back in Chapter 14, we addressed this question for the M/M/k, where job sizes were drawn from an Exponential distribution. Which architecture (one fast or two slow) was superior there?

(b) Does the answer change when the job size distribution is not Exponential? Specifically, consider the following distribution of job sizes:
   - $\frac{100}{101}$ fraction of the jobs have service requirement (size) 0.01 seconds when run on a slow machine. These are called small jobs.
   - $\frac{1}{101}$ fraction of the jobs have service requirement (size) 1 second when run on a slow machine. These are called large jobs.

   Observe that this job size distribution has the *heavy-tail* property, whereby the 1% largest jobs comprise about half the total load. Assume jobs arrive according to a Poisson process with rate λ, and consider two ways of processing the workload:

   1. Use a single "fast" machine: M/G/1.
   2. Use two slow machines and split the incoming jobs so that small jobs go to machine 1 and large jobs go to machine 2.

   Compute $\mathbf{E}[T_Q]$ as a function of λ in both of these cases. Which case results in a lower $\mathbf{E}[T_Q]$? Explain what is going on. If we had defined the job size distribution to be less heavy-tailed, would the answer change?

24.6 To Balance Load or Not to Balance Load?

The purpose of this problem is to determine whether load balancing between two *identical* FCFS hosts is always a good idea for minimizing $\mathbf{E}[T_Q]$, or whether we might want to purposely *unbalance* load. Assume that jobs arrive from outside according to a Poisson process with rate λ, where S denotes the job size, and the system load is $\rho = \frac{\lambda \mathbf{E}[S]}{2} = 0.5$. Assume a Bounded Pareto $(k = .0009, p = 10^{10}, \alpha = 0.5)$ job size distribution with mean 3,000.

(a) First consider the SITA-E task assignment policy, where the size cutoff, x, is chosen to equalize the load at the two hosts (E stands for "equalize load").

    i. What is the cutoff x under SITA-E?

    ii. What fraction of jobs are sent to each host under SITA-E?

    iii. What is the mean delay, $\mathbf{E}[T_Q]$, under SITA-E?

    iv. What is $\mathbf{E}[T_Q]$ under RANDOM, and how does this compare with $\mathbf{E}[T_Q]$ under SITA-E?

(b) Returning to SITA-E, now purposely unbalance the load by dropping x, the SITA-E cutoff.

    i. Try different values of x and record the corresponding $\mathbf{E}[T_Q]$. Approximately how low should x be to minimize $\mathbf{E}[T_Q]$?

    ii. What is the load at each host under this new cutoff x?

    iii. What fraction of jobs are sent to each host under this new cutoff x?

24.7 A Better SITA-E?

Based on [10]. Consider a server farm with two identical FCFS hosts and SITA-E task assignment (see Exercise 24.6). Eitan proposes a new cutoff heuristic: rather than finding cutoffs which balance load, we instead derive cutoffs which equalize the expected number of queued jobs, $\mathbf{E}[N_Q]$, at each host. Determine whether Eitan's idea is useful by evaluating it on the workload from Exercise 24.6: Assume that jobs arrive from outside according to a Poisson process, with system load $\rho = \frac{\lambda \mathbf{E}[S]}{2} = 0.5$. Assume a $BP(k = .0009, p = 10^{10}, \alpha = 0.5)$ job size distribution with mean 3,000. Which cutoff scheme (balanced load or Eitan's scheme) is better for minimizing overall mean delay, $\mathbf{E}[T_Q]$? How does Eitan's heuristic for finding cutoffs compare with using the optimal cutoff?

24.8 Additional Recommended Problem

Exercise 21.7 on understanding the effect of job size variability in an M/G/2 system is recommended as well.

CHAPTER 25

Transform Analysis

This chapter is a very brief introduction to the wonderful world of transforms. One can think of the transform of a random variable as an onion. This onion is an expression that contains inside it all the moments of the random variable. Getting the moments out of the onion is not an easy task, however, and may involve some tears as the onion is peeled, where the "peeling process" involves differentiating the transform. The first moment is stored in the outermost layer of the onion and thus does not require too much peeling to reach. The second moment is stored a little deeper, the third moment even deeper (more tears), etc. Although getting the moments is painful, it is entirely straightforward how to do it – just keep peeling the layers.

Transforms are a hugely powerful analysis technique. For example, until now we have only learned how to derive the *mean* response time, $\mathbf{E}[T]$, for the M/G/1. However, by the end of the next chapter, we will be able to derive the transform of T, which will allow us to obtain any desired moment of T.

The subject of transforms is very broad. In this chapter we only cover a small subset, namely those theorems that are most applicable in analyzing the performance of queues. We use transforms heavily in analyzing scheduling algorithms in Part VII.

25.1 Definitions of Transforms and Some Examples

Definition 25.1 The *Laplace transform*, $L_f(s)$, of a continuous function, $f(t)$, $t \geq 0$, is defined as

$$L_f(s) = \int_0^\infty e^{-st} f(t) dt.$$

You can think of s as just being some parameter, where the Laplace transform is a function of s. When we speak of the Laplace transform of a continuous random variable (r.v.), X, we are referring to the Laplace transform, $L_f(s)$, of the p.d.f., $f_X(\cdot)$, associated with X. We write $\widetilde{X}(s)$ to denote the Laplace transform of X.

Observe that if X is a continuous r.v. and $f(t)$, $t \geq 0$, is the p.d.f. of X, then

$$\widetilde{X}(s) = L_f(s) = \mathbf{E}\left[e^{-sX}\right].$$

Example: Derive the Laplace transform of $X \sim \text{Exp}(\lambda)$:

$$\widetilde{X}(s) = L_f(s) = \int_0^\infty e^{-st}\lambda e^{-\lambda t}dt = \lambda \int_0^\infty e^{-(\lambda+s)t}dt = \frac{\lambda}{\lambda+s}$$

Example: Derive the Laplace transform of $X = a$, where a is some constant:

$$\widetilde{X}(s) = L_f(s) = e^{-sa}$$

Example: Derive the Laplace transform of $X \sim \text{Uniform}(a,b)$, $a, b \geq 0$:

$$\widetilde{X}(s) = L_f(s) = \int_0^\infty e^{-st}f(t)dt$$

$$= \int_a^b e^{-st}\frac{1}{b-a}dt$$

$$= \left(\frac{-e^{-sb}}{s} + \frac{e^{-sa}}{s}\right)\frac{1}{b-a}$$

$$= \frac{e^{-sa} - e^{-sb}}{s(b-a)}$$

(Observe that here $f(t)$ is defined to be 0 when it is outside the (a,b) range.)

Question: How do we know that the Laplace transform as defined necessarily converges?

Answer: (Partial) It does if $f(t)$ is a p.d.f. of some non-negative random variable and $s \geq 0$. To see this observe that

$$e^{-t} \leq 1,$$

for all non-negative values of t. Thus

$$e^{-st} = \left(e^{-t}\right)^s \leq 1,$$

assuming that s is non-negative. Thus,

$$L_f(s) = \int_0^\infty e^{-st}f(t)dt \leq \int_0^\infty 1 \cdot f(t)dt = 1.$$

Definition 25.2 The *z-transform*, $G_p(z)$, of a discrete function, $p(i)$, for $i = 0, 1, 2, \ldots$ is defined as:

$$G_p(z) = \sum_{i=0}^\infty p(i)z^i.$$

Observe that the z-transform is a polynomial in z. When we speak of the z-transform of a discrete r.v. X, we are referring to the z-transform of the p.m.f., $p_X(\cdot)$, associated with X. We write $\widehat{X}(z)$ to denote the z-transform of X. Observe that if X is a discrete r.v. and $p(i)$, $i = 0, 1, 2, \ldots$, is its p.m.f., then

$$\widehat{X}(z) = G_p(z) = \mathbf{E}\left[z^X\right].$$

Example: Derive the z-transform of $X \sim \text{Binomial}(n, p)$:

$$\widehat{X}(z) = G_p(z) = \sum_{i=0}^{n} \binom{n}{i} p^i (1-p)^{n-i} z^i$$

$$= \sum_{i=0}^{n} \binom{n}{i} (zp)^i (1-p)^{n-i}$$

$$= (zp + (1-p))^n$$

Example: Derive the z-transform of $X \sim \text{Geometric}(p)$:

$$\widehat{X}(z) = G_p(z) = \sum_{i=1}^{\infty} p(1-p)^{i-1} z^i$$

$$= zp \sum_{i=1}^{\infty} (z(1-p))^{i-1}$$

$$= \frac{zp}{1 - z(1-p)}$$

Definition 25.3 The random variable A_t will be used to denote the ***number of arrivals by time t***, where the arrival process is $\text{Poisson}(\lambda)$.

Example: Derive the z-transform of A_t:

$$\widehat{A_t}(z) = G_p(z) = \sum_{i=0}^{\infty} \frac{(\lambda t)^i e^{-\lambda t} z^i}{i!}$$

$$= e^{-\lambda t} \sum_{i=0}^{\infty} \frac{(\lambda t z)^i}{i!}$$

$$= e^{-\lambda t} \cdot e^{\lambda t z}$$

$$= e^{-\lambda t(1-z)}$$

Definition 25.4 The random variable A_S will be used to denote the ***number of arrivals by time S***, where S is a random variable (typically denoting service time), and the arrival process is $\text{Poisson}(\lambda)$.

Example: Derive the z-transform of A_S:

$$
\begin{aligned}
\widehat{A_S}(z) &= \sum_{i=0}^{\infty} \mathbf{P}\{A_S = i\}\, z^i \\
&= \sum_{i=0}^{\infty} \left(\int_0^{\infty} \mathbf{P}\{A_S = i \mid S = t\}\, f_S(t)dt \right) z^i \\
&= \sum_{i=0}^{\infty} \left(\int_0^{\infty} \frac{e^{-\lambda t}(\lambda t)^i}{i!} f_S(t)dt \right) z^i \\
&= \int_0^{\infty} e^{-\lambda t} f_S(t) \sum_{i=0}^{\infty} \frac{(\lambda t z)^i}{i!} dt \\
&= \int_0^{\infty} e^{-\lambda t} f_S(t) e^{\lambda t z}\, dt \\
&= \int_0^{\infty} e^{-\lambda(1-z)t} f_S(t)dt \\
&= L_S(\lambda(1-z)) \\
&= \widetilde{S}(\lambda(1-z))
\end{aligned}
\tag{25.1}
$$

(We will see a quicker way to derive $\widehat{A_S}(z)$ soon.)

25.2 Getting Moments from Transforms: Peeling the Onion

Theorem 25.5 *Let X be a continuous r.v. with p.d.f. $f(t)$, $t \geq 0$. Then*

$$
\mathbf{E}[X^n] = (-1)^n \frac{d^n L_f(s)}{ds}\bigg|_{s=0}.
$$

Even if $f(t)$ is not a p.d.f., it still holds that

$$
\int_{t=0}^{\infty} t^n \cdot f(t)dt = (-1)^n \frac{d^n L_f(s)}{ds}\bigg|_{s=0}.
$$

Note: If the above moments are not defined at $s = 0$, one can instead consider the limit as $s \to 0$, where evaluating the limit may require using L'Hospital's rule.

Proof

$$
e^{-st} = 1 - (st) + \frac{(st)^2}{2!} - \frac{(st)^3}{3!} + \dots
$$

$$
e^{-st}f(t) = f(t) - (st)f(t) + \frac{(st)^2}{2!} f(t) - \frac{(st)^3}{3!} f(t) + \dots
$$

$$L_f(s) = \int_0^\infty e^{-st} f(t)dt$$

$$= \int_0^\infty f(t)dt - \int_0^\infty (st)f(t)dt + \int_0^\infty \frac{(st)^2}{2!} f(t)dt - \int_0^\infty \frac{(st)^3}{3!} f(t)dt + \dots$$

$$= 1 - s\mathbf{E}[X] + \frac{s^2}{2!}\mathbf{E}[X^2] - \frac{s^3}{3!}\mathbf{E}[X^3] + \dots$$

$$\frac{dL_f(s)}{ds} = -\mathbf{E}[X] + s\mathbf{E}[X^2] - 3\frac{s^2}{3!}\mathbf{E}[X^3] + \dots$$

$$\left.\frac{dL_f(s)}{ds}\right|_{s=0} = -\mathbf{E}[X]$$

$$\frac{d^2 L_f(s)}{ds} = \mathbf{E}[X^2] - s\mathbf{E}[X^3] + \dots$$

$$\left.\frac{d^2 L_f(s)}{ds}\right|_{s=0} = \mathbf{E}[X^2]$$

We can see from the original Taylor series expansion that each time we take another derivative, we get a higher moment, with alternating sign. ∎

Example: Compute the kth moment of $X \sim \text{Exp}(\lambda)$:

$$\widetilde{X}(s) = L_f(s) = \frac{\lambda}{\lambda + s}$$

$$\mathbf{E}[X] = -\left.\frac{dL_f(s)}{ds}\right|_{s=0} = -\left.\frac{-\lambda}{(\lambda + s)^2}\right|_{s=0} = \frac{1}{\lambda}$$

$$\mathbf{E}[X^2] = (-1)^2 \left.\frac{d^2 L_f(s)}{ds}\right|_{s=0} = \left.\frac{d}{ds}\left(\frac{-\lambda}{(\lambda + s)^2}\right)\right|_{s=0} = \left.\frac{2\lambda}{(\lambda + s)^3}\right|_{s=0} = \frac{2}{\lambda^2}$$

$$\mathbf{E}[X^k] = (-1)^k \left.\frac{d^k L_f(s)}{ds}\right|_{s=0} = \left.\frac{k!\lambda}{(\lambda + s)^{k+1}}\right|_{s=0} = \frac{k!}{\lambda^k}$$

Theorem 25.6 *For X a discrete r.v. with p.m.f. $p(i)$, $i = 0, 1, 2, \dots$, the sequence*

$$\left\{ \left.G_p^{(n)}(z)\right|_{z=1} : n \geq 1 \right\}$$

provides the moments of X, as follows:

$$G_p'(z)|_{z=1} = \mathbf{E}[X]$$
$$G_p''(z)|_{z=1} = \mathbf{E}[X(X-1)]$$
$$G_p'''(z)|_{z=1} = \mathbf{E}[X(X-1)(X-2)]$$
$$G_p^{(n)}(z)|_{z=1} = \mathbf{E}[X(X-1)(X-2)\cdots(X-n+1)]$$

Note: If the above moments are not defined at $z = 1$, one can instead consider the limit as $z \to 1$, where evaluating the limit may require using L'Hospital's rule.

Proof Here we illustrate how the moments pop out of the sequence. The proof can be obtained formally via induction.

$$G_p(z) = \sum_{i=0}^{\infty} p(i)z^i$$

$$G_p'(z) = \frac{d}{dz}\left(\sum_{i=0}^{\infty} p(i)z^i\right) = \frac{d}{dz}\left(\sum_{i=1}^{\infty} p(i)z^i\right) = \sum_{i=1}^{\infty} ip(i)z^{i-1}$$

$$G_p'(z)\big|_{z=1} = \sum_{i=1}^{\infty} ip(i) = \mathbf{E}[X]$$

$$G_p''(z) = \frac{d}{dz}\left(\sum_{i=1}^{\infty} ip(i)z^{i-1}\right) = \frac{d}{dz}\left(\sum_{i=2}^{\infty} ip(i)z^{i-1}\right) = \sum_{i=2}^{\infty} i(i-1)p(i)z^{i-2}$$

$$G_p''(z)\big|_{z=1} = \sum_{i=2}^{\infty} i(i-1)p(i) = \mathbf{E}[X(X-1)]$$

$$G_p'''(z) = \frac{d}{dz}\left(\sum_{i=2}^{\infty} i(i-1)p(i)z^{i-2}\right) = \frac{d}{dz}\left(\sum_{i=3}^{\infty} i(i-1)p(i)z^{i-2}\right)$$

$$= \sum_{i=3}^{\infty} i(i-1)(i-2)p(i)z^{i-3}$$

$$G_p'''(z)\big|_{z=1} = \sum_{i=3}^{\infty} i(i-1)(i-2)p(i) = \mathbf{E}[X(X-1)(X-2)] \qquad \blacksquare$$

Example: Compute the variance of $X \sim \text{Geometric}(p)$:

$$\widehat{X}(z) = \frac{zp}{1 - z(1-p)}$$

$$\mathbf{E}[X] = \frac{d}{dz}\left(\frac{zp}{1 - z(1-p)}\right)\bigg|_{z=1} = \frac{p}{(1 - z(1-p))^2}\bigg|_{z=1} = \frac{1}{p}$$

$$\mathbf{E}[X^2] = \widehat{X}''(z)\big|_{z=1} + \mathbf{E}[X] = \frac{2p(1-p)}{(1 - z(1-p))^3}\bigg|_{z=1} + \frac{1}{p}$$

$$= \frac{2(1-p)}{p^2} + \frac{1}{p} = \frac{2-p}{p^2}$$

$$\mathbf{Var}(X) = \mathbf{E}[X^2] - (\mathbf{E}[X])^2 = \frac{1-p}{p^2}$$

Example: Use transforms to compute the first moment of A_S, the number of arrivals during a service time, where $S \sim \text{Exp}(\mu)$.

We show here two ways to do this. It is good to know both. The first way is by expanding the transform and then differentiating it:

$$\widehat{A_S}(z) = \widetilde{S}(\lambda(1-z)) = \frac{\mu}{\mu + \lambda(1-z)}$$

$$\widehat{A_S}'(z) = \frac{\mu\lambda}{(\mu + \lambda(1-z))^2}$$

$$\mathbf{E}[A_S] = \widehat{A_S}'(z)\bigg|_{z=1} = \frac{\mu\lambda}{\mu^2} = \frac{\lambda}{\mu}$$

The second way does not expand the transform, so the chain rule needs to be applied.

$$\mathbf{E}[A_S] = \widehat{A_S}'(z)\bigg|_{z=1}$$

$$= \frac{d}{dz}\widetilde{S}(\lambda(1-z))\bigg|_{z=1}$$

$$= \widetilde{S}'(\lambda(1-z))\bigg|_{z=1} \cdot (-\lambda)\bigg|_{z=1}$$

$$= \widetilde{S}'(0) \cdot (-\lambda)$$

$$= -\mathbf{E}[S] \cdot (-\lambda)$$

$$= \frac{\lambda}{\mu}$$

25.3 Linearity of Transforms

Theorem 25.7 *Let X and Y be continuous, independent random variables with p.d.f. $x(t)$, $t \geq 0$, and $y(t)$, $t \geq 0$, respectively. Let $Z = X + Y$ where $z(t)$, $t \geq 0$, is the p.d.f. of Z. Then the Laplace transform of Z is given by*

$$\widetilde{Z}(s) = \widetilde{X}(s) \cdot \widetilde{Y}(s). \tag{25.2}$$

In particular, if $X_1, \ldots, X_n$ are i.i.d. random variables, and $Z = X_1 + \cdots + X_n$, then $\widetilde{Z}(s) = (\widetilde{X}(s))^n$.

Let the convolution of $x(\cdot)$ and $y(\cdot)$ be $g = x \otimes y$, where

$$g(t) = \int_0^t x(t-k)y(k)dk.$$

Then the Laplace transform of $g(t)$, denoted by $L_g(s)$, is given by

$$L_g(s) = L_{x \otimes y}(s) = L_x(s)L_y(s), \tag{25.3}$$

even when X and Y are <u>not</u> independent (although $g(t)$ only equals $z(t)$ when $X \perp Y$).

Proof   Let $X \perp Y$, and $Z = X + Y$. Then

$$\widetilde{Z}(s) = \int_0^\infty e^{-st} z(t) dt$$

$$= \int_0^\infty e^{-st} \int_{k=0}^t z(t \mid Y = k) \cdot y(k) dk \, dt \tag{25.4}$$

$$= \int_0^\infty e^{-st} \int_{k=0}^t x(t - k \mid Y = k) \cdot y(k) dk \, dt \tag{25.5}$$

$$= \int_0^\infty e^{-st} \int_{k=0}^t x(t - k) \cdot y(k) dk \, dt \tag{25.6}$$

$$= \int_{k=0}^\infty y(k) \int_{t=k}^\infty e^{-st} x(t - k) dt \, dk \tag{25.7}$$

$$= \int_{k=0}^\infty y(k) e^{-sk} \int_{t=k}^\infty e^{-s(t-k)} x(t - k) dt \, dk$$

$$= \int_{k=0}^\infty y(k) e^{-sk} \int_{v=0}^\infty e^{-sv} x(v) dv \, dk \quad \text{(letting } v = t - k, dv = dt)$$

$$= L_y(s) \cdot L_x(s)$$

$$= \widetilde{Y}(s) \cdot \widetilde{X}(s) \tag{25.8}$$

∎

Question: In proving (25.2), where was the independence of X and Y used?

Answer: In moving from (25.5) to (25.6).

Question: The proof of (25.3) should *not* require that X and Y are independent. How is this possible?

Answer: The proof of (25.3) starts on line (25.6) above. It therefore does not depend on X and Y being independent.

Here is an alternative proof of (25.2), assuming that X and Y are independent:

Proof $\widetilde{Z}(s) = \mathbf{E}\left[e^{-sZ}\right]$

$$\qquad\qquad = \mathbf{E}\left[e^{-s(X+Y)}\right]$$

$$\qquad\qquad = \mathbf{E}\left[e^{-sX} \cdot e^{-sY}\right]$$

$$\qquad\qquad = \mathbf{E}\left[e^{-sX}\right] \cdot \mathbf{E}\left[e^{-sY}\right] \quad \text{(because } X \perp Y)$$

$$\qquad\qquad = \widetilde{X}(s) \cdot \widetilde{Y}(s) \qquad\qquad\qquad ∎$$

Theorem 25.8 *Let X and Y be discrete independent random variables. Let $Z = X + Y$. Then the z-transform of Z is given by $\widehat{Z}(z) = \widehat{X}(z) \cdot \widehat{Y}(z)$.*

Proof The proof follows exactly the lines of the proof of Theorem 25.7 and can again be done in two ways; see Exercise 25.1. ■

Example: Let $X \sim \text{Binomial}(n, p)$ and $Y \sim \text{Binomial}(m, p)$ be independent random variables. What is the distribution of $X + Y$?

$$\widehat{Z}(z) = \widehat{X}(z) \cdot \widehat{Y}(z)$$
$$= (zp + (1 - p))^n (zp + (1 - p))^m$$
$$= (zp + (1 - p))^{m+n}$$

Observe that $(zp + (1 - p))^{m+n}$ is the z-transform of a Binomial random variable with parameters $m + n$ and p. Thus, the distribution of $X + Y$ is $\text{Binomial}(m + n, p)$.

25.4 Conditioning

Theorem 25.9 *Let X, A, and B be continuous random variables where*

$$X = \begin{cases} A & \text{with probability } p \\ B & \text{with probability } 1 - p \end{cases}.$$

Then

$$\widetilde{X}(s) = p \cdot \widetilde{A}(s) + (1 - p) \cdot \widetilde{B}(s).$$

Proof

$$\widetilde{X}(s) = \mathbf{E}\left[e^{-sX}\right]$$
$$= \mathbf{E}\left[e^{-sX} \,\middle|\, X = A\right] \cdot p + \mathbf{E}\left[e^{-sX} \,\middle|\, X = B\right] \cdot (1 - p)$$
$$= p\mathbf{E}\left[e^{-sA}\right] + (1 - p)\mathbf{E}\left[e^{-sB}\right]$$
$$= p\widetilde{A}(s) + (1 - p)\widetilde{B}(s)$$

■

Theorem 25.10 *Let X, A, and B be discrete random variables where*

$$X = \begin{cases} A & \text{with probability } p \\ B & \text{with probability } 1 - p \end{cases}.$$

Then

$$\widehat{X}(z) = p \cdot \widehat{A}(z) + (1 - p) \cdot \widehat{B}(z).$$

Proof

$$
\begin{aligned}
\widehat{X}(z) &= \mathbf{E}\left[z^X\right] \\
&= \mathbf{E}\left[z^X \mid X = A\right] \cdot p + \mathbf{E}\left[z^X \mid X = B\right] \cdot (1-p) \\
&= \mathbf{E}\left[z^A\right] \cdot p + \mathbf{E}\left[z^B\right] \cdot (1-p) \\
&= p\widehat{A}(z) + (1-p)\widehat{B}(z)
\end{aligned}
$$ ∎

We can generalize Theorems 25.9 and 25.10. Theorem 25.11 is a generalization of Theorem 25.9. The generalization for Theorem 25.10 follows similarly.

Theorem 25.11   *Let Y be a continuous random variable, and let X_Y be a continuous random variable that depends on Y. Then, if $f_Y(y)$ denotes the density function of Y, we have that*

$$
\widetilde{X_Y}(s) = \int_{y=0}^{\infty} \widetilde{X_y}(s) f_Y(y) dy.
$$

Proof

$$
\begin{aligned}
\widetilde{X_Y}(s) = \mathbf{E}\left[e^{-sX_Y}\right] &= \int_{y=0}^{\infty} \mathbf{E}\left[e^{-sX_Y} \mid Y = y\right] \cdot f_Y(y) dy \\
&= \int_{y=0}^{\infty} \mathbf{E}\left[e^{-sX_y}\right] \cdot f_Y(y) dy \\
&= \int_{y=0}^{\infty} \widetilde{X_y}(s) \cdot f_Y(y) dy
\end{aligned}
$$ ∎

Example

Recall the lengthy derivation of $\widehat{A_S}(z)$, resulting in (25.1). We now show a much faster derivation via conditioning. We condition on S as follows:

$$
\begin{aligned}
\widehat{A_S}(z) &= \int_0^{\infty} \widehat{A_S}(z \mid S = t) f_S(t) dt \\
&= \int_0^{\infty} \widehat{A_t}(z) f_S(t) dt \\
&= \int_0^{\infty} e^{-\lambda(1-z)t} f_S(t) dt \\
&= \widetilde{S}(\lambda(1-z))
\end{aligned}
\tag{25.9}
$$

25.5 Distribution of Response Time in an M/M/1

Suppose we want to derive the distribution of the response time T for the M/M/1. We can leverage the fact that we know the distribution of N, the number in system, to get the Laplace transform of T.

Let T_k be the response time, given that the arrival finds k jobs in the system. Then, by Theorem 25.9 and its generalizations, we have

$$\widetilde{T}(s) = \sum_{k=0}^{\infty} \widetilde{T_k}(s) \cdot P(k \text{ in system}).$$

Now observe that

$$T_k = S_1 + S_2 + \cdots + S_k + S_{k+1},$$

where S_i is the size of the ith job in the system, and S_{k+1} is the size of the arrival. Since the S_i's are i.i.d., by Theorem 25.7,

$$\widetilde{T_k}(s) = \left(\widetilde{S}(s)\right)^{k+1} = \left(\frac{\mu}{s + \mu}\right)^{k+1}.$$

Finally,

$$\begin{aligned}
\widetilde{T}(s) &= \sum_{k=0}^{\infty} \left(\frac{\mu}{s + \mu}\right)^{k+1} \cdot \rho^k (1 - \rho) \\
&= \frac{(1 - \rho)\mu}{s + \mu} \cdot \sum_{k=0}^{\infty} \left(\frac{\mu}{s + \mu} \cdot \rho\right)^k \\
&= \frac{(1 - \rho)\mu}{s + \mu} \cdot \frac{1}{1 - \frac{\mu\rho}{s+\mu}} \\
&= \frac{(1 - \rho)\mu}{s + \mu} \cdot \frac{s + \mu}{s + \mu - \mu\rho} \\
&= \frac{\mu - \lambda}{s + (\mu - \lambda)}.
\end{aligned}$$

Question: What does this say about the distribution of T?

Answer:

$$T^{\text{M/M/1}} \sim \text{Exp}(\mu - \lambda).$$

25.6 Combining Laplace and z-Transforms

Theorem 25.12 (Summing a Random Number of i.i.d. Random Variables) *Let*

$$Z = Y_1 + Y_2 + \ldots + Y_X,$$

where the Y_i's are i.i.d. continuous r.v.'s, and where X is a discrete random variable, where $X \perp Y_i, \forall i$. Let $\widehat{X}(z)$ be the z-transform of X, and let $\widetilde{Y}(s)$ be the Laplace transform of Y_i. Then

$$\widetilde{Z}(s) = \widehat{X}\left(\widetilde{Y}(s)\right).$$

Example: Derive the Laplace transform of a Poisson(λ) number of i.i.d. Exp(μ) random variables. Recall that for $X \sim$ Poisson(λ) we have that

$$\widehat{X}(z) = e^{-\lambda(1-z)}.$$

Recall likewise that for $Y \sim$ Exp(μ) we have that

$$\widetilde{Y}(s) = \frac{\mu}{s+\mu}.$$

From this it follows that

$$\widetilde{Z}(s) = \widehat{X}\left(\widetilde{Y}(s)\right) = e^{-\lambda(1-z)}\Big|_{z=\frac{\mu}{s+\mu}} = e^{-\lambda\left(1-\frac{\mu}{s+\mu}\right)} = e^{-\frac{\lambda s}{s+\mu}}.$$

Proof (Theorem 25.12) Let $\widetilde{Z}(s \mid X = n)$ denote the Laplace transform of Z given that $X = n$. Then, by Theorem 25.7, $\widetilde{Z}(s \mid X = n) = \left(\widetilde{Y}(s)\right)^n$. Now, by conditioning,

$$\widetilde{Z}(s) = \sum_{n=0}^{\infty} \mathbf{P}\{X = n\}\, \widetilde{Z}(s \mid X = n)$$

$$= \sum_{n=0}^{\infty} \mathbf{P}\{X = n\} \left(\widetilde{Y}(s)\right)^n$$

$$= \widehat{X}\left(\widetilde{Y}(s)\right). \qquad \blacksquare$$

Question: Can we apply Theorem 25.12 to a sum of a random variable number of *discrete* random variables?

Answer: Yes, the same proof works, and the final result is then $\widehat{Z}(z) = \widehat{X}\left(\widehat{Y}(z)\right)$.

25.7 More Results on Transforms

Normally we look at the Laplace transform of the p.d.f., but we could also ask what is the Laplace transform of any function. Theorem 25.13 considers the Laplace transform of the c.d.f. and relates that to the Laplace transform of the p.d.f.

Theorem 25.13 *Consider a p.d.f., $b(\cdot)$, where $B(\cdot)$ is the cumulative distribution function corresponding to $b(\cdot)$. That is,*

$$B(x) = \int_0^x b(t)dt.$$

Let

$$\widetilde{b}(s) = L_{b(t)}(s) = \int_0^\infty e^{-st} b(t)dt.$$

Let

$$\widetilde{B}(s) = L_{B(x)}(s) = \int_0^\infty e^{-sx} B(x)dx = \int_0^\infty e^{-sx} \int_0^x b(t)dt\,dx.$$

Then

$$\widetilde{B}(s) = \frac{\widetilde{b}(s)}{s}.$$

Proof

$$\begin{aligned}
\widetilde{B}(s) &= \int_{x=0}^\infty e^{-sx} \int_{t=0}^x b(t)dt\, dx \\
&= \int_{x=0}^\infty e^{-st} \cdot e^{-s(x-t)} \int_{t=0}^x b(t)dt\, dx \\
&= \int_{t=0}^\infty b(t)e^{-st}dt \int_{x=t}^\infty e^{-s(x-t)}dx \\
&= \int_{t=0}^\infty b(t)e^{-st}dt \int_{y=0}^\infty e^{-sy}dy \\
&= \widetilde{b}(s) \cdot \frac{1}{s} \qquad\blacksquare
\end{aligned}$$

Here is one last little bit of information that comes in handy when differentiating transforms.

Theorem 25.14 *For all random variables, X,*

$$\widetilde{X}(0) = 1 \quad and \quad \widehat{X}(1) = 1.$$

25.8 Readings

There is a lot more that can be said on transforms. For an entire book on the use of transforms in probability modeling, see [71].

25.9 Exercises

25.1 Sums of Discrete Random Variables
Let X and Y be discrete independent random variables. Let $Z = X + Y$. Prove that the z-transform of Z is given by $\widehat{Z}(z) = \widehat{X}(z) \cdot \widehat{Y}(z)$.

25.2 Sum of Poissons
Let $X_1 \sim \text{Poisson}(\lambda_1)$. Let $X_2 \sim \text{Poisson}(\lambda_2)$. Suppose $X_1 \perp X_2$. Let $Y = X_1 + X_2$. How is Y distributed? Prove it using z-transforms. Note that the parameter for the Poisson denotes its mean.

25.3 Moments of Poisson
Let $X \sim \text{Poisson}(\lambda)$. Derive $\mathbf{E}\left[X(X-1)(X-2)\cdots(X-k+1)\right]$ for $k = 1, 2, 3, \ldots$

25.4 Moments of Binomial
Let $X \sim \text{Binomial}(n,p)$. Derive $\mathbf{E}\left[X(X-1)(X-2)\cdots(X-k+1)\right]$ for $k = 1, 2, 3, \ldots$

25.5 Convergence of z-Transform
Let $p_X(i)$ represent the p.m.f. of a discrete, non-negative r.v. X, and let $\widehat{X}(z) = \sum_{i=0}^{\infty} p_X(i)z^i$ denote the z-transform of X. Prove that if $|z| \le 1$, then $\widehat{X}(z)$ converges. Specifically, show that $\widehat{X}(z)$ is bounded from above and below.

25.6 Sum of Geometric Number of Exponentials
Let $N \sim \text{Geometric}(p)$. Let $X_i \sim \text{Exp}(\mu)$, where the X_i's are independent of each other and of N. Let $S_N = \sum_{i=1}^{N} X_i$. Prove that S_N is Exponentially distributed and derive the rate of S_N.
(a) First do this using δ-step arguments.
(b) Now do this again using transforms via Theorem 25.12.
(c) Suppose we are given a Poisson process, where packets are colored "blue" with probability p. What does the above result tell us about the distribution of the spacing between blue packets?

25.7 Practice with Laplace Transforms: A Useful Identity
Let X be an arbitrary random variable. Let $Y \sim \text{Exp}(\lambda)$, where X and Y are independent. Prove that

$$\mathbf{P}\left\{X < Y\right\} = \widetilde{X}(\lambda).$$

25.8 Review of M/M/1

(a) What do we know about the distribution of N, the number of jobs in an M/M/1? [Hint: It is not quite a Geometric, but it can be expressed as a Geometric plus or minus something.]

(b) Given your previous answer, what are $\mathbf{E}[N]$ and $\mathbf{Var}(N)$?

(c) What do we know about the distribution of T, the M/M/1 response time?

(d) Given your previous answer, what are $\mathbf{E}[T]$ and $\mathbf{Var}(T)$?

(e) Recall the derivation in this chapter for the Laplace transform of T. Follow a similar approach to derive the Laplace transform of T_Q, the waiting time for the M/M/1.

(f) How can you check that your answer for $\widetilde{T_Q}(s)$ is correct, given that you know $\widetilde{T}(s)$?

25.9 Downloading Files

You need to download two files: file 1 and file 2. File 1 is available via source A or source B. File 2 is available only via source C. The time to download file 1 from source A is Exponentially distributed with rate 1. The time to download file 1 from source B is Exponentially distributed with rate 2. The time to download file 2 from source C is Exponentially distributed with rate 3. You decide to download from *all three* sources simultaneously, in the hope that you get both file 1 and file 2 as soon as possible. Let T denote the time until you get *both* files. What is $\widetilde{T}(s)$?

25.10 Two-Sided Laplace Transform

In the case where a distribution can take on negative values, we define the Laplace transform as follows: Let X be a random variable with density function $f(t)$, $-\infty < t < \infty$:

$$\widetilde{X}(s) = L_f(s) = \int_{-\infty}^{\infty} e^{-st} f(t) dt$$

Let $X \sim \text{Normal}(0, 1)$ be the standard Normal. Show that

$$\widetilde{X}(s) = e^{\frac{s^2}{2}}.$$

25.11 Transforms Derivation of Burke's Theorem

In an M/M/1, when the server is busy, jobs depart at rate μ. However, when the M/M/1 is idle, then no jobs depart. Thus, the interdeparture times are either distributed $\text{Exp}(\mu)$ (when the server is busy), or $\text{Exp}(\lambda) + \text{Exp}(\mu)$ (when idle) – this latter term comes from having to wait for an arrival and then for that arrival to depart. It is not at all clear how having interarrival times switch between these modes could form a $\text{Poisson}(\lambda)$ departure process.

Let T denote the time between departures. Prove that $T \sim \text{Exp}(\lambda)$ by deriving its Laplace transform via conditioning.

25.12 M/M/2/3

In the M/M/2/3, jobs arrive according to a Poisson process with rate λ. There are 2 servers, each serving at rate μ, and a single central queue; however, there is only room for 3 jobs total (one waiting job and two serving jobs).

When an arrival finds 3 jobs already in the system, the arrival is dropped; see
Figure 25.1. Let T denote the response time for the M/M/2/3. Derive $\widetilde{T}(s)$.

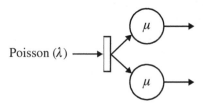

Figure 25.1. The M/M/2/3.

25.13 Busy Period in M/M/1

Derive the duration of a busy period in an M/M/1 queue with arrival rate λ and
service rate μ. A busy period, B, is the time from when a job arrives at an idle
system until the system is first empty again. (Obviously, the number of jobs
may go up and down a lot in between going from state 1 to state 0.)

(a) First derive $\mathbf{E}[B]$. How does $\mathbf{E}[B]$ compare with $\mathbf{E}[T]$ for the M/M/1?

(b) At this point, you may be wondering if the busy period is Exponentially
distributed. Find out by deriving the Laplace transform of the busy period,
$\widetilde{B}(s)$. [Hint: Conditioning helps. Also, at the very end, you may need to
make use of the fact that $\widetilde{B}(0) = 1$].

25.14 Transform of S_e and Moments of Excess[1]

Consider a renewal process where S represents the time between renewals.
$F(x)$ and $f(x)$ are the c.d.f. and p.d.f. for S. We use S_e to denote the excess
of S (a.k.a. the equilibrium distribution of S), and $F_e(x)$ and $f_e(x)$ to denote
its c.d.f. and p.d.f. Your job is to calculate the first 2 moments of excess: $\mathbf{E}[S_e]$
and $\mathbf{E}[S_e^2]$.

(a) Use Renewal-Reward to derive $F_e(k)$, the time-average fraction of time
that $S_e < k$.

(b) Differentiate your result in (a) to derive $f_e(k)$. You should get

$$f_e(k) = \frac{\overline{F}(k)}{\mathbf{E}[S]}. \tag{25.10}$$

(c) Derive $\widetilde{S_e}(s) = L_{f_e}(s)$ and simplify to get

$$\widetilde{S_e}(s) = \frac{1 - \widetilde{S}(s)}{s\mathbf{E}[S]}. \tag{25.11}$$

(d) Differentiate $\widetilde{S_e}(s)$ appropriately to determine the first 2 moments of S_e.

25.15 Heuristic Proof of Central Limit Theorem via Transforms

In this problem, you will derive a heuristic proof of the Central Limit Theorem
(CLT). Let X_1, X_2, ... be a sequence of i.i.d. random variables, each with
mean μ and variance σ^2. CLT says that the distribution of

$$\frac{X_1 + X_2 + \cdots + X_n - n\mu}{\sigma\sqrt{n}} \tag{25.12}$$

---

[1] Warning: the result of this problem will be used repeatedly throughout the rest of the book.

tends to the standard Normal as $n \to \infty$. Specifically,

$$\mathbf{P}\left\{\frac{X_1 + X_2 + \cdots + X_n - n\mu}{\sigma\sqrt{n}} \le a\right\} \to \frac{1}{\sqrt{2\pi}} \int_{-\infty}^{a} e^{-x^2/2} dx, \text{ as } n \to \infty.$$

The high-level idea in our approach is to show that the Laplace transform of (25.12) roughly converges to the Laplace transform of the standard Normal distribution, as given in Exercise 25.10. Showing that the two transforms are the same implies that (25.12) and the standard Normal agree on all moments, thus having the same distribution. Let

$$S = \frac{X_1 + X_2 + \cdots + X_n}{\sqrt{n}}.$$

(a) Start with the case where $\mu = 0$ and $\sigma^2 = 1$.

    i. Show that

$$\widetilde{S}(s) \approx \left(1 - \frac{s\mathbf{E}[X]}{\sqrt{n}} + \frac{s^2\mathbf{E}[X^2]}{2n}\right)^n.$$

    ii. Using what you know about μ and σ^2, show that

$$\widetilde{S}(s) \to \widetilde{N_{(0,1)}}(s), \text{ as } n \to \infty.$$

(b) Now generalize your solution to arbitrary μ and σ.

25.16 M/M/2 Transform

For the M/M/2 with arrival rate λ, where each server serves at rate μ, derive: $\widehat{N}(z)$, $\widehat{N_Q}(z)$, and $\widetilde{T_Q}(s)$. The z-transforms are obtained directly from the limiting probabilities on the number of jobs in the system. The Laplace transform is obtained by conditioning on the number of jobs seen by an arrival. This same approach can be used to derive the M/M/k transform.

CHAPTER 26

M/G/1 Transform Analysis

In this chapter we derive the Laplace transform of the response time for an M/G/1 queue. Among other benefits, the transform allows us to get moments of response time.

We follow the two-step outline shown in Figure 26.1 that involves first computing the z-transform of the number of jobs in the M/G/1, $\widehat{N}(z)$ (see Section 26.1), and then using that to get the Laplace transform of the response time for the M/G/1, $\widetilde{T}(s)$ (see Section 26.2). Note that we cannot simply use Little's Law to make the conversion, because it applies only to means.

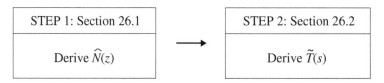

Figure 26.1. Two-step outline.

26.1 The z-Transform of the Number in System

We define

$$\widehat{N}(z) = \sum_{i=0}^{\infty} \pi_i^{\text{M/G/1}} z^i. \tag{26.1}$$

Here $\pi_i^{\text{M/G/1}}$ denotes the long-run fraction of time that there are i jobs in the M/G/1. We sometimes write simply π_i when the context is clear. We could get $\widehat{N}(z)$, if we knew $\pi_i^{\text{M/G/1}}$.

Question: How can we get $\pi_i^{\text{M/G/1}}$? Can we do the same thing we did for the M/M/1?

Answer: (Attempt 1) For the M/M/1, we created a CTMC, where the state was the current number of jobs, and then we solved the CTMC. It is not obvious how to do this for the M/G/1 because the service times are not Exponential. To create a Markov chain, we need to know that the time until we leave a state does not depend on history, such as how much time we have already spent in the state. Yet for an M/G/1, the time until a job departs could certainly depend on how long it has been running so far (think decreasing failure rate, as in Chapter 20).

So we need another idea for getting $\pi_i^{\text{M/G/1}}$. Here is a hint:

Hint: Sometimes it is easier to think about the embedded discrete-time Markov chain (DTMC) that ignores the time spent at each state. How can we use this?

Answer: (Attempt 2) The solution is to consider the M/G/1 *only* at points in time where a departure occurs. The *state* of the chain is defined to be *the number of jobs at the server at the time of the last departure.* We can form a stochastic process $X_1, X_2, X_3, \ldots, X_i, \ldots$, where X_i denotes the number of jobs left behind at the time of the ith departure. This is the **embedded discrete-time Markov chain.** In the embedded DTMC, there is a probability (not a rate) of moving from state to state, which we define shortly.

Let π_i^{embed} denote the limiting probability of being in state i of the embedded DTMC. This is the fraction of M/G/1 departures that leave behind i jobs.

Question: How do π_i^{embed} and $\pi_i^{\text{M/G/1}}$ compare?

Answer: They are the same:

$$\pi_i^{\text{embed}} = \pi_i^{\text{M/G/1}}$$

Recall from Chapter 13 that the probability that a departure leaves behind i jobs (d_i) is equal to the probability that an arrival sees i jobs (a_i), but by PASTA this in turn is equal to the proportion of time that there are i jobs (p_i).

Thus it suffices to derive π_i^{embed} and use that as $\pi_i^{\text{M/G/1}}$ in (26.1). To derive π_i^{embed} we solve the embedded DTMC.

Question: What is P_{ij} for the embedded DTMC process: $X_1, X_2, X_3, \ldots$?

Warning: Be careful. The sequence of states followed by the embedded DTMC is just a subset of those followed by the original M/G/1, because we consider only those states left behind by a departure of the M/G/1.

Answer: If $j < i - 1$, then $P_{ij} = 0$.

For $j \geq i - 1$, where $i \neq 0$, we have

$$P_{ij} = \mathbf{P}\left\{j \text{ jobs at time of next departure} \mid i \text{ jobs at time of current departure}\right\}$$

$$= \mathbf{P}\left\{j - i + 1 \text{ arrivals during a job's service time, } S\right\}$$

$$= \int_x \mathbf{P}\left\{j - i + 1 \text{ arrivals during time } x\right\} \cdot \mathbf{P}\left\{\text{service time of job} = x\right\}$$

$$= \int_x \frac{e^{-\lambda x}(\lambda x)^{j-i+1}}{(j-i+1)!} f_S(x) dx.$$

Observe that $P_{0j} = P_{1j}$ because we have to wait for an arrival before the next departure can occur. When that new arrival departs, there will be a probability, P_{1j}, of transitioning to state j (where state j denotes the state of having j jobs left behind by the last departure).

Now that we have P_{ij} for the embedded DTMC, we can get π_i^{embed} from the stationary equations:

$$\pi_j^{\text{embed}} = \sum_i \pi_i^{\text{embed}} P_{ij}, \qquad \sum_i \pi_i^{\text{embed}} = 1 \qquad (26.2)$$

Unfortunately, given the complexity of the expressions for P_{ij}, trying to solve these simultaneous equations does not seem very appealing. What we really want is a way to determine

$$\widehat{N}(z) = \sum_{i=0}^{\infty} \pi_i^{\text{M/G/1}} \cdot z^i = \sum_{i=0}^{\infty} \pi_i^{\text{embed}} \cdot z^i \qquad (26.3)$$

without having to ever figure out a closed-form formula for π_i^{embed}.

A New Idea!

Here is how to achieve this. We will express

$$\pi_j = \pi_j^{\text{M/G/1}} = \pi_j^{\text{embed}} = \mathbf{P}\left\{\text{M/G/1 departure leaves } j \text{ jobs in system}\right\}$$

in terms of

$$a_j = \mathbf{P}\left\{j \text{ arrivals during } S\right\}.$$

Once we do this, we will be able to express

$$\widehat{N}(z) = \text{ z-transform of number of jobs in system as seen by departure}$$

in terms of

$$\widehat{A}_S(z) = \text{ z-transform of number of jobs which arrive during service } S.$$

This is good because we already know $\widehat{A}_S(z)$ from (25.9), which will allow us to skip over actually deriving the π_j's. We will follow three steps:

Step 1: Express π_j in terms of a_j,

$$P_{0j} = a_j$$
$$P_{ij} = a_{j-i+1}, \ 1 \le i \le j+1$$

where

$$a_j = \int_0^\infty \frac{e^{-\lambda x}(\lambda x)^j}{j!} \cdot f_S(x) dx.$$

Thus we have that

$$\pi_j = \pi_0 a_j + \sum_{i=1}^{j+1} \pi_i a_{j-i+1}. \qquad (26.4)$$

Step 2: Multiply every term of (26.4) by z^j, so that we can express $\widehat{N}(z)$ in terms of $\widehat{A}_S(z)$.

$$\pi_j = \pi_0 a_j + \sum_{i=1}^{j+1} \pi_i a_{j-i+1}$$

$$\sum_{j=0}^{\infty} \pi_j z^j = \pi_0 \sum_{j=0}^{\infty} a_j z^j + \sum_{j=0}^{\infty} \sum_{i=1}^{j+1} \pi_i a_{j-i+1} z^j$$

$$\widehat{N}(z) = \pi_0 \widehat{A}_S(z) + \sum_{i=1}^{\infty} \sum_{j=i-1}^{\infty} \pi_i a_{j-i+1} z^j$$

$$= \pi_0 \widehat{A}_S(z) + \sum_{i=1}^{\infty} \pi_i z^{i-1} \sum_{j=i-1}^{\infty} a_{j-i+1} z^{j-i+1}$$

$$= \pi_0 \widehat{A}_S(z) + \frac{1}{z} \sum_{i=1}^{\infty} \pi_i z^i \sum_{u=0}^{\infty} a_u z^u \quad (\text{where } u = j - (i-1))$$

$$= \pi_0 \widehat{A}_S(z) + \frac{1}{z} \left(\widehat{N}(z) - \pi_0 \right) \cdot \widehat{A}_S(z)$$

$$z\widehat{N}(z) = z\pi_0 \widehat{A}_S(z) + \widehat{N}(z)\widehat{A}_S(z) - \pi_0 \widehat{A}_S(z)$$

$$\widehat{N}(z) = \frac{(z-1)\pi_0 \widehat{A}_S(z)}{z - \widehat{A}_S(z)}$$

All that is left is to determine π_0.

Question: We already know that $\pi_0 = 1 - \rho$, where $\rho = \lambda \mathbf{E}\,[S]$ is the fraction of time that the server is busy. But suppose that you were working on a problem where you did not know π_0. What would you do then?

Answer: You could try to set $z = 1$ in the expression in Step 2 for $\widehat{N}(z)$ and then solve for π_0. Note that it is often the case when you do this that you need to use L'Hospital's rule . . . sometimes repeatedly!

For this example in Step 2, you can immediately see that

$$1 = \lim_{z \to 1} \widehat{N}(z) = \frac{0}{0}$$

$$= \lim_{z \to 1} \frac{(z-1)\pi_0 \widehat{A}'_S(z) + \pi_0 \widehat{A}_S(z)}{1 - \widehat{A}'_S(z)}$$

$$= \frac{\pi_0}{1 - \lambda \mathbf{E}\,[S]}$$

$$\Rightarrow \pi_0 = 1 - \lambda \mathbf{E}\,[S] = 1 - \rho.$$

So we have finally

$$\widehat{N}(z) = \frac{\widehat{A}_S(z)(1-\rho)(z-1)}{z - \widehat{A}_S(z)}. \tag{26.5}$$

Step 3: Substitute in our known formula for $\widehat{A}_S(z)$.

Recall that from (25.9)

$$\widehat{A}_S(z) = \widetilde{S}(\lambda - \lambda z). \tag{26.6}$$

Substituting this into Equation (26.5) we have

$$\widehat{N}(z) = \frac{\widetilde{S}(\lambda - \lambda z)(1-\rho)(1-z)}{\widetilde{S}(\lambda - \lambda z) - z}. \tag{26.7}$$

26.2 The Laplace Transform of Time in System

Our goal is to get $\widetilde{T}(s)$, using the fact that we know $\widehat{N}(z)$. To do this, first consider again the equation we have seen so many times:

$$\widehat{A}_S(z) = \widetilde{S}(\lambda - \lambda z), \tag{26.8}$$

where A_S is the number of Poisson arrivals within service time S. What we want is a result about T.

Question: Equation (26.8) holds for any r.v. S (review the derivation of (25.9)). What random variable would you like to substitute for S?

Answer: Let's substitute T for S in (26.8):

$$\widehat{A}_T(z) = \widetilde{T}(\lambda - \lambda z) \tag{26.9}$$

Equation (26.9) equates the Laplace transform of T (what we want) to the z-transform of A_T.

Question: Is there a nicer name for A_T?

Answer: A_T is the number of arrivals during T, which is equivalently the number of jobs in the system as seen by a departure!

So

$$A_T = N,$$

where N is the number of jobs seen by a departure. Hence,

$$\widetilde{T}(\lambda - \lambda z) = \widehat{A}_T(z) = \widehat{N}(z). \tag{26.10}$$

Substituting in Equation (26.7) for $\widehat{N}(z)$, into (26.10), we get

$$\widetilde{T}(\lambda - \lambda z) = \frac{\widetilde{S}(\lambda - \lambda z)(1-\rho)(1-z)}{\widetilde{S}(\lambda - \lambda z) - z}. \tag{26.11}$$

We now make a simple change of variables. Let

$$s = \lambda - \lambda z.$$
$$z = 1 - \frac{s}{\lambda}.$$

Then (26.11) becomes

$$\widetilde{T}(s) = \frac{\widetilde{S}(s)(1 - \rho)\left(\frac{s}{\lambda}\right)}{\widetilde{S}(s) - 1 + \frac{s}{\lambda}}.$$

Or equivalently,

$$\widetilde{T}(s) = \frac{\widetilde{S}(s)(1 - \rho)s}{\lambda \widetilde{S}(s) - \lambda + s}. \tag{26.12}$$

We are done! Now we can differentiate (26.12) with respect to s to get all moments of T. This is done in Exercise 26.2. You will see that you need to apply L'Hospital's rule twice when differentiating just to get the mean. So it is not so easy, but it is straightforward.

Question: How could we get the Laplace transform of T_Q?

Answer: Observe

$$T = S + T_Q.$$

So

$$\widetilde{T}_Q(s) = \frac{\widetilde{T}(s)}{\widetilde{S}(s)} = \frac{(1 - \rho)s}{\lambda \widetilde{S}(s) - \lambda + s}. \tag{26.13}$$

One thing that may seem surprising is that the above expression for $\widetilde{T}_Q(s)$ does not involve S_e, the excess of S. The excess is in there – it just takes a few more steps to extract.

Recall from (25.11) that the Laplace transform for the excess is

$$\widetilde{S_e}(s) = \frac{1 - \widetilde{S}(s)}{s\mathbf{E}[S]}.$$

We can then express $\widetilde{T}_Q(s)$ in terms of $\widetilde{S_e}(s)$ as follows:

$$\widetilde{T}_Q(s) = \frac{(1 - \rho)s}{\lambda \widetilde{S}(s) - \lambda + s}$$

$$= \frac{1 - \rho}{\lambda \left(\frac{\widetilde{S}(s) - 1}{s}\right) + 1}$$

$$= \frac{1 - \rho}{\rho \left(\frac{\widetilde{S}(s) - 1}{s\mathbf{E}[S]}\right) + 1}$$

$$= \frac{1 - \rho}{1 - \rho \widetilde{S_e}(s)} \tag{26.14}$$

We will discuss some cool properties of (26.14) in Chapter 30, after we have covered some scheduling results, which will provide insight into interpreting (26.14).

26.3 Readings

This material in this chapter borrows from three excellent texts [110, 149, 45].

26.4 Exercises

26.1 M/H$_2$/1 Transform
You are given an M/G/1 queue where the job size, S, has an H_2 distribution:

$$S \sim \begin{cases} \text{Exp}(\mu_1) & \text{with probability } p \\ \text{Exp}(\mu_2) & \text{with probability } 1 - p \end{cases}$$

(a) Derive $\mathbf{E}[T_Q]$.
(b) Derive $\widetilde{T_Q}(s)$.

26.2 Variance of Response Time for the M/G/1
Derive $\mathbf{Var}(T_Q)$ for the M/G/1 by differentiating $\widetilde{T}_Q(s)$.

26.3 z-Transform of N_Q
In this chapter we derived $\widehat{N}(z)$, the z-transform of the number of jobs in system in an M/G/1. Suppose that we instead wanted $\widehat{N_Q}(z)$, the z-transform of the number of jobs queued. Show how to get that from $\widehat{N}(z)$.

26.4 Distributional Little's Law for M/G/1 and M/G/c
Consider an M/G/1 queue with average arrival rate λ, where N denotes the number of jobs in the system and T denotes the response time. The Distributional Little's Law states that, for all integers $k \geq 1$,

$$\mathbf{E}[N(N-1)(N-2)\cdots(N-k+1)] = \lambda^k \mathbf{E}[T^k] \qquad (26.15)$$

(a) Derive (26.15) from (26.10). [Hint: Differentiate.]
(b) Does the law also hold if N is replaced by N_Q and T by T_Q?
(c) Now consider an M/G/c, with arrival rate λ, but look only at the queue portion of this system. What can you say about how the moments of $N_Q^{\text{M/G/c}}$ are related to the moments of $T_Q^{\text{M/G/c}}$?

The Distributional Little's Law is very powerful in settings like the M/H$_2$/c, where we can derive moments of N_Q via matrix-analytic methods, but have no easy way to get moments of T_Q.

26.5 M/M/2 Transform
In this chapter, we saw how to convert $\widehat{N}(z)$ to $\widetilde{T}(s)$ for the M/G/1. In this problem, you will apply this same technique to the M/M/2. First derive $\widehat{N_Q}(z)$ for the M/M/2. Then convert $\widehat{N_Q}(z)$ to $\widetilde{T_Q}(s)$ using the approach in Exercise 26.4. This same approach can be applied to derive the M/M/k waiting time transform.

CHAPTER 27

Power Optimization Application

This chapter combines and applies many analytical techniques we have studied thus far (Renewal-Reward, general transform analysis, and M/G/1 response time analysis) toward analyzing the problem of power management of a single server. The goal is to understand when a server should be turned off to save on power (sometimes called "power napping") and when it should be left on.

In Section 27.1 we provide background on powering a server and state the specific power optimization problem that we address. To solve this problem, we first need to develop two more analysis topics.

The first topic is *busy period analysis* for the M/G/1. We have touched on busy periods in the exercise sections of prior chapters, but in Section 27.2, we go into much more depth in describing busy periods, including different types of busy periods and the Laplace transform of the busy period.

The second topic is the analysis of an M/G/1 with *setup time*, where the first job starting a busy period incurs an extra delay, known as the setup time. Setup times have also been discussed in earlier exercises; however, in Section 27.3 we consider their effect on the M/G/1.

Finally, in Section 27.4, we combine the analyses in Sections 27.2 and 27.3 to solve our power optimization problem.

27.1 The Power Optimization Problem

Consider the operation of a single-server system, specifically an M/G/1/FCFS queue. Thus far, we have only been concerned about the response time of the system. We now discuss the power usage. We distinguish between three states that a server can be in:

ON: The server is on and is busy serving a job. The server burns power at a rate of P_{on}.

IDLE: The server is on and available, but is currently idle. The server burns power at a rate of P_{idle}.

OFF: The server is off.

In the ON state, a server might burn power at a rate of 240 Watts[1] (i.e., $P_{on} = 240$). In the OFF state, a server burns 0 Watts.

---

[1] All the numbers given here involving power measurements and setup costs are based on measurements in our data center lab at Carnegie Mellon University during the year 2011.

Question: At what rate would you guess that power is burned when the server is in the IDLE state?

Answer: Surprisingly, the answer is that P_{idle} is almost as much as P_{on}. An IDLE server typically burns power at a rate of about $P_{\text{idle}} = 180$ Watts. Thus a server running at load ρ burns power at an average rate of

$$\mathbf{E}\left[\text{Power}\right] = \rho \cdot 240 \text{ Watts} + (1 - \rho) \cdot 180 \text{ Watts}.$$

Because this seems very wasteful when ρ is low, the obvious idea is to turn off the server when it is idle.

Question: What is wrong with turning off a server when it is idle?

Answer: There is a huge setup cost to turning a server back on.

The **setup cost** is the cost required to transition a server from the OFF state to the ON state. (*Note:* there is no cost for transitioning from the IDLE state to the ON state). The setup cost consists of *two components:* a time component and a power component. The exact setup time varies depending on the type of application and server. However, a setup time of 200 seconds or so is not at all uncommon for most data center servers, and it can be much higher. The second component is power: During the entire setup time, the server is burning power at a rate of P_{on}.

Given the setup cost, it is no longer obvious that one wants to turn off the server when it becomes idle. From the perspective of solely minimizing response time, one never wants to turn off the server. From a power perspective, if the setup cost is not too high relative to mean job size, one may want to turn off the server when it goes idle.

The power optimization problem aims to resolve this power/response time tradeoff. Specifically, we would like to maximize the Performance-per-Watt (Perf/W):

$$\text{Performance-per-Watt} = \frac{1}{\mathbf{E}\left[\text{Power}\right] \cdot \mathbf{E}\left[\text{Response Time}\right]}$$

That is, we want to minimize both mean response time and mean power.

In this chapter, we do not solve the general power management problem. However, we do analyze and compare two simple policies:

ON/OFF – Under this policy, the server is switched to the OFF state immediately when it goes idle. When a job arrives, the server is then turned on, involving a setup cost.

ON/IDLE – Under this policy, the server is never turned off. Hence it moves between the ON state and the IDLE state.

Our goal is to determine the parameter regime (in terms of ρ and setup cost) under which the ON/OFF policy is superior to the ON/IDLE policy with respect to Perf/W.

27.2 Busy Period Analysis of M/G/1

An important component in overall power usage is understanding how long the server is busy. In the case of a single-server system, the **busy period** is defined to be the time from when the server first becomes busy until the server first goes idle. If one looks at an M/G/1 over time, one can see that the M/G/1 alternates between being in the "busy" state and the "idle" state. We use B to denote the length of a single busy period. Throughout, we assume that the average arrival rate is λ, that job sizes are denoted by the r.v. S, and that load is $\rho = \lambda \mathbf{E}[S]$.

Question: What is the distribution of the length of an idle period?

Answer: The length of an idle period is distributed $\text{Exp}(\lambda)$, because the idle period is just the time until an arrival occurs, see Figure 27.1.

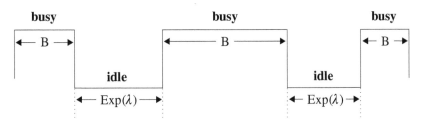

Figure 27.1. Busy and idle periods.

Busy periods are hard to describe because they are *recursive*. Consider a single busy period, started by a job, j, of size S. If no new arrivals come in while j runs, then the length of the busy period is just S. However, any new arrival that occurs while j runs will need to run once j completes and will create the opening for more new arrivals to occur while it runs. Specifically, if a single job j' arrives before j completes, then the length of the busy period is $S + B$, where S is the time for job j and B is the busy period created by job j'. Likewise, if two jobs j' and j'' arrive before j completes, then they each start their own busy period. In this case the length of the busy period is $S + B_1 + B_2$, where $B_1 \perp B_2$ and $B_i \sim B, i = 1, 2$. The job that starts the initial busy period is often referred to as the *parent*, and the jobs that arrive during a busy period are often called the *offspring*. Each offspring can be viewed as starting its own busy period. It may look like a single busy period never ends! But we know that is not true, because the system is idle $1 - \rho$ fraction of the time.

When we talk about the busy period, B, we implicitly assume that all jobs during the busy period come from the same job size distribution. However, in general, one can also talk about a busy period started by a fixed amount of work, x, which is present when the server first turns on, where all future jobs have size S. The duration of such a busy period is denoted by $B(x)$.

Our first goal is to derive $\widetilde{B}(s)$, the Laplace transform of B. It turns out that to fully define B, we need to first look at $B(x)$.

Question: How can we write a general expression for $B(x)$? Feel free to use B within your expression.

Hint: Let A_x denote the number of Poisson arrivals that occur during time x.

Answer:

$$B(x) = x + \sum_{i=1}^{A_x} B_i \qquad (27.1)$$

where the B_i's are independent and are each distributed identically to B. That is, we start with the job of size x and then each arrival during that time x can be thought of as starting its own busy period, where that busy period is a busy period started by an arbitrary job of random size S.

Observe an important property of busy periods:

$$B(x + y) = B(x) + B(y), \qquad (27.2)$$

meaning that a busy period started by $x + y$ work can be viewed as a busy period started by x work, followed by a busy period started by y work.

Equation (27.1) does not look like it is helping us get any closer to getting B, but it is. The next step is to derive the Laplace transform of $B(x)$.

Question: How can we use (27.1) to derive an expression for $\widetilde{B(x)}(s)$?

Hint: Use the fact that we know $\widehat{A_x}(z)$.

Answer: Taking the Laplace transform of (27.1), we have

$$\widetilde{B(x)}(s) = \widetilde{x} \quad \cdot \quad \left(\widetilde{\sum_{i=1}^{A_x} B_i} \right)$$

$$= e^{-sx} \quad \cdot \quad \widehat{A_x}\left(\widetilde{B}(s)\right) \quad \text{(by Theorem 25.12)}.$$

Now we can use our knowledge of $\widehat{A_x}(z)$, from (25.1) to get

$$\widehat{A_x}\left(\widetilde{B}(s)\right) = e^{-\lambda x \left(1 - \widetilde{B}(s)\right)}.$$

And so,

$$\widetilde{B(x)}(s) = e^{-sx} \cdot e^{-\lambda x \left(1 - \widetilde{B}(s)\right)} = e^{-x\left(s + \lambda - \lambda \widetilde{B}(s)\right)}. \qquad (27.3)$$

Equation (27.3) provides an expression for the Laplace transform of $B(x)$. The next step is to *uncondition*, by integrating over all x, to turn (27.3) into an expression for the Laplace transform of B as follows:

$$\widetilde{B}(s) = \int_0^\infty \widetilde{B(x)}(s) f_S(x) dx = \int_0^\infty e^{-x\left(s + \lambda - \lambda \widetilde{B}(s)\right)} f_S(x) dx$$

Question: Is there a nicer way of writing the above expression?

Answer: Yes,

$$\widetilde{B}(s) = \widetilde{S}\left(s + \lambda - \lambda\widetilde{B}(s)\right). \tag{27.4}$$

Equation (27.4) defines the transform of B in terms of itself. Unfortunately, this is the best we can do. Fortunately, this is sufficient to get the moments of B. We do this next.

The first moment, $\mathbf{E}[B]$, is given by

$$\mathbf{E}[B] = -\widetilde{B}'(s)|_{s=0} = -\widetilde{S}'\left(s + \lambda - \lambda\widetilde{B}(s)\right)\Big|_{s=0} \cdot \left(1 - \lambda\widetilde{B}'(s)\right)\Big|_{s=0}$$

$$= -\widetilde{S}'(0 + \lambda - \lambda(1))(1 + \lambda\mathbf{E}[B])$$

$$= -\widetilde{S}'(0)(1 + \lambda\mathbf{E}[B])$$

$$= \mathbf{E}[S](1 + \lambda\mathbf{E}[B]).$$

Solving for $\mathbf{E}[B]$, we get

$$\mathbf{E}[B] = \frac{\mathbf{E}[S]}{1 - \lambda\mathbf{E}[S]} = \frac{\mathbf{E}[S]}{1 - \rho}. \tag{27.5}$$

To get the second moment, we differentiate $\widetilde{B}'(s)$ again and evaluate the result at $s = 0$. This yields

$$\mathbf{E}\left[B^2\right] = \widetilde{B}''(s)|_{s=0} = \frac{d}{ds}\left[\widetilde{S}'\left(s + \lambda - \lambda\widetilde{B}(s)\right)\left(1 - \lambda\widetilde{B}'(s)\right)\right]\Big|_{s=0}$$

$$= \widetilde{S}''(0)\left[1 - \lambda\widetilde{B}'(0)\right]^2 + \widetilde{S}'(0)\left(-\lambda\widetilde{B}''(0)\right)$$

$$= \mathbf{E}\left[S^2\right]\left[1 + \lambda\mathbf{E}[B]\right]^2 + \lambda\mathbf{E}[S]\mathbf{E}\left[B^2\right].$$

Substituting $\mathbf{E}[B] = \frac{\mathbf{E}[S]}{1-\rho}$ and solving for $\mathbf{E}[B^2]$ we get

$$\mathbf{E}\left[B^2\right] = \frac{\mathbf{E}[S^2]}{(1 - \rho)^3}. \tag{27.6}$$

Question: What role does the variability of S play in the mean busy period duration, $\mathbf{E}[B]$, and how does this compare to its role in mean response time, $\mathbf{E}[T]$? Why is there a difference?

Answer: The variability of S plays a key role in $\mathbf{E}[T]$ due to the Inspection Paradox and the effect of $\mathbf{E}[S_e]$ (see Chapter 23). By contrast, $\mathbf{E}[B]$ does not involve an $\mathbf{E}[S_e]$ component, because there are no jobs already in service when the busy period starts; thus there is no "excess" to contend with. The variability of B is naturally affected by the variability of S, because B is a sum of S's, and in general the ith moment of B is dependent on the ith moment of S. By contrast, the ith moment of T is dependent on the $(i + 1)$th moment of S.

Now that we understand standard busy periods, consider how we can modify this analysis to derive different types of busy periods. For example, let B_W denote the length of a busy period started by W work, where W is a random variable and the jobs in the busy period have size S.

Question: What is the transform of B_W?

Answer: Starting with (27.3), we have that

$$\widetilde{B(x)}(s) = e^{-x\left(s+\lambda-\lambda\widetilde{B}(s)\right)}$$

$$\widetilde{B_W}(s) = \int_0^\infty \widetilde{B(x)}(s) f_W(x)dx$$

$$= \int_0^\infty e^{-x\left(s+\lambda-\lambda\widetilde{B}(s)\right)} f_W(x)dx$$

$$= \widetilde{W}\left(s+\lambda-\lambda\widetilde{B}(s)\right).$$

Question: What is the mean length of B_W?

Answer:

$$\mathbf{E}[B_W] = \frac{\mathbf{E}[W]}{1-\rho}. \tag{27.7}$$

This result follows from the following calculation:

$$\mathbf{E}[B_W] = -\widetilde{B_W}'(s)\Big|_{s=0} = -\widetilde{W}'\left(s+\lambda-\lambda\widetilde{B}(s)\right)\Big|_{s=0} \cdot \left(1-\lambda\widetilde{B}'(s)\right)\Big|_{s=0}$$

$$= -\widetilde{W}'(0+\lambda-\lambda(1))(1+\lambda\mathbf{E}[B])$$

$$= -\widetilde{W}'(0)(1+\lambda\mathbf{E}[B])$$

$$= \mathbf{E}[W](1+\lambda\mathbf{E}[B])$$

Substituting $\mathbf{E}[B] = \frac{\mathbf{E}[S]}{1-\rho}$, we get $\mathbf{E}[B_W] = \frac{\mathbf{E}[W]}{1-\rho}$.

Intuitively, (27.7) can be viewed as the size of the job (or work) starting the busy period, $\mathbf{E}[W]$, scaled up by a factor, $\frac{1}{1-\rho}$, related to the load of jobs that make up the busy period. The higher the load, $\rho = \lambda\mathbf{E}[S]$, the more jobs that arrive during W and the longer the busy period.

27.3 M/G/1 with Setup Cost

We now switch gears and consider a different problem: How does setup cost affect response time?

Suppose that the first job to start each busy period experiences an initial setup time, I, before its service is started, where I is a continuous random variable. Here I denotes the time required to "initialize" or power up the server, switching it from being in the OFF state to the ON state. Again we are dealing with an M/G/1 with job sizes denoted by r.v. S.

Our goal is to derive the Laplace transform of T_Q^{setup}, where T_Q^{setup} is the delay experienced by an arrival into an M/G/1 with setup cost I.

A few remarks before diving into the derivation: First, observe that the setup cost, I, affects more than just the job that starts the busy period; many jobs could arrive during the setup time itself, all of which have to wait for the machine to finish powering up.

Question: What is the mean duration of a busy period in an M/G/1 with setup I?

Answer: We can think of the busy period, B^{setup}, as a busy period that is started by total work, $I + S$, where I is the setup time and S is the size of the job starting the busy period. Then by (27.7), we have

$$\mathbf{E}\left[B^{\text{setup}}\right] = \frac{\mathbf{E}\left[I\right] + \mathbf{E}\left[S\right]}{1 - \rho}. \tag{27.8}$$

Equation (27.8) can also be viewed as a sum of two terms, where the first is a busy period started by the setup time and the second is a standard M/G/1 busy period, which starts after the setup busy period is over. Looking at things that way, we have

$$\mathbf{E}\left[B^{\text{setup}}\right] = \frac{\mathbf{E}\left[I\right]}{1 - \rho} + \mathbf{E}\left[B\right].$$

Question: In an M/G/1 with setup I, what fraction of time is the server busy? Here "busy" includes setting up, because that too requires power.

Answer: Clearly, the answer is no longer simply ρ. Let ρ^{setup} denote the fraction of time that the server is busy for the M/G/1 with setup I. To determine ρ^{setup}, we think in terms of renewals. The server is busy for $\frac{\mathbf{E}[I]+\mathbf{E}[S]}{1-\rho}$ time (where $\rho = \lambda\mathbf{E}\left[S\right]$), followed by a period of length $\frac{1}{\lambda}$ of being idle, and then the cycle repeats itself. By the Renewal-Reward theorem (Theorem 23.4), it suffices to look at the fraction of time that the server is busy during one cycle:

$$
\begin{aligned}
\rho^{\text{setup}} &= \frac{\mathbf{E}\left[\text{Busy during cycle}\right]}{\mathbf{E}\left[\text{Cycle time}\right]} = \frac{\frac{\mathbf{E}[I]+\mathbf{E}[S]}{1-\rho}}{\frac{\mathbf{E}[I]+\mathbf{E}[S]}{1-\rho} + \frac{1}{\lambda}} \\
&= \frac{\lambda\mathbf{E}\left[I\right] + \rho}{\lambda\mathbf{E}\left[I\right] + \rho + 1 - \rho} \\
&= \frac{\lambda\mathbf{E}\left[I\right] + \rho}{\lambda\mathbf{E}\left[I\right] + 1}. \tag{27.9}
\end{aligned}
$$

We are now ready to derive $\widetilde{T}_Q^{\text{setup}}(s)$. We follow the same approach used for the M/G/1 without setup, by looking at the embedded DTMC, as in Chapter 26. Again π_i denotes the probability that the last departure left behind i jobs, which by PASTA is equal to the time-average probability that there are i jobs. There is only one difference: The transition probabilities for leaving the 0 state must reflect the initial cost.

Let

$$a_j = \mathbf{P}\left\{j \text{ arrivals in } S \text{ seconds}\right\}$$

and let

$$a'_j = \mathbf{P}\left\{j \text{ arrivals in } S + I \text{ seconds}\right\}.$$

Then

$$P_{ij} = a_{j-i+1}, \text{ for } i > 0 \quad \text{and} \quad P_{0j} = a'_j.$$

Thus we can write

$$\pi_j = \pi_0 a'_j + \sum_{i=1}^{j+1} \pi_i a_{j-i+1}$$

$$\sum_{j=0}^{\infty} \pi_j z^j = \pi_0 \sum_{j=0}^{\infty} a'_j z^j + \sum_{j=0}^{\infty}\sum_{i=1}^{j+1} \pi_i a_{j-i+1} z^j$$

$$\widehat{N}^{\text{setup}}(z) = \pi_0 \widehat{A}_{S+I}(z) + \frac{1}{z}\sum_{i=1}^{\infty} \pi_i z^i \sum_{j=i-1}^{\infty} a_{j-i+1} z^{j-i+1}$$

$$= \pi_0 \widehat{A}_S(z)\widehat{A}_I(z) + \frac{1}{z}\left(\widehat{N}^{\text{setup}}(z) - \pi_0\right)\widehat{A}_S(z)$$

$$\Rightarrow \widehat{N}^{\text{setup}}(z) = \pi_0 \frac{z\widehat{A}_S(z)\widehat{A}_I(z) - \widehat{A}_S(z)}{z - \widehat{A}_S(z)}. \tag{27.10}$$

We now continue to follow the approach in Chapter 26 to convert $\widehat{N}^{\text{setup}}(z)$ to $\widetilde{T}^{\text{setup}}(s)$ by following the usual sequence of observations:

$$\widehat{A}_S(z) = \widetilde{S}(\lambda(1-z)), \quad \text{for any } S$$

$$\Rightarrow \widehat{A}_{T^{\text{setup}}}(z) = \widetilde{T}^{\text{setup}}(\lambda(1-z)), \quad \text{setting } S = T^{\text{setup}}$$

$$\Rightarrow \widehat{N}^{\text{setup}}(z) = \widetilde{T}^{\text{setup}}(\lambda(1-z)), \quad \text{since } A_{T^{\text{setup}}} = N^{\text{setup}}$$

$$\Rightarrow \widetilde{T}^{\text{setup}}(\lambda(1-z)) = \pi_0 \frac{z\widehat{A}_S(z)\widehat{A}_I(z) - \widehat{A}_S(z)}{z - \widehat{A}_S(z)}, \quad \text{by (27.10)}$$

$$\Rightarrow \widetilde{T}^{\text{setup}}(\lambda(1-z)) = \pi_0 \frac{z\widetilde{S}(\lambda(1-z))\widetilde{I}(\lambda(1-z)) - \widetilde{S}(\lambda(1-z))}{z - \widetilde{S}(\lambda(1-z))}$$

$$\Rightarrow \widetilde{T}^{\text{setup}}(s) = \pi_0 \frac{(1-s/\lambda)\widetilde{S}(s)\widetilde{I}(s) - \widetilde{S}(s)}{1 - s/\lambda - \widetilde{S}(s)}, \quad \text{via } s = \lambda(1-z)$$

$$= \pi_0 \frac{(\lambda - s)\widetilde{S}(s)\widetilde{I}(s) - \lambda\widetilde{S}(s)}{\lambda - s - \lambda\widetilde{S}(s)}$$

Hence,

$$\widetilde{T}_Q^{\text{setup}}(s) = \frac{\widetilde{T}^{\text{setup}}(s)}{\widetilde{S}(s)} = \pi_0 \cdot \frac{\lambda - (\lambda - s)\widetilde{I}(s)}{s - \lambda + \lambda\widetilde{S}(s)}. \tag{27.11}$$

Question: What is π_0?

Answer: From (27.9), we have

$$\pi_0 = 1 - \rho^{\text{setup}} = \frac{1 - \lambda \mathbf{E}[S]}{1 + \lambda \mathbf{E}[I]}. \tag{27.12}$$

Substituting π_0 into (27.11) yields

$$\widetilde{T}_Q^{\text{setup}}(s) = \frac{1 - \lambda \mathbf{E}[S]}{1 + \lambda \mathbf{E}[I]} \cdot \frac{\lambda - (\lambda - s)\widetilde{I}(s)}{s - \lambda + \lambda \widetilde{S}(s)}$$

$$= \frac{(1 - \rho)s}{s - \lambda + \lambda \widetilde{S}(s)} \cdot \frac{\lambda - (\lambda - s)\widetilde{I}(s)}{(1 + \lambda \mathbf{E}[I])s}$$

$$= \widetilde{T}_Q^{\text{M/G/1}}(s) \cdot \frac{\lambda - (\lambda - s)\widetilde{I}(s)}{(1 + \lambda \mathbf{E}[I])s}. \tag{27.13}$$

To get the mean, we differentiate (27.13) and also apply L'Hospital's rule to get:

$$\mathbf{E}[T_Q]^{\text{setup}} = \frac{\lambda \mathbf{E}[S^2]}{2(1 - \rho)} + \frac{2\mathbf{E}[I] + \lambda \mathbf{E}[I^2]}{2(1 + \lambda \mathbf{E}[I])}. \tag{27.14}$$

Question: What is the effect of setup when the setup, I, is Exponentially distributed?

Answer: In the case of $I \sim \text{Exp}(\alpha)$, we have $\mathbf{E}[I^2] = 2(\mathbf{E}[I])^2$, which reduces to

$$\mathbf{E}[T_Q]^{\text{setup}} = \mathbf{E}[T_Q] + \mathbf{E}[I]. \tag{27.15}$$

Thus, in the case where $I \sim \text{Exp}(\alpha)$, the setup cost is just an *additive* cost.

The delay for the M/G/1 with setup in (27.13) and (27.14) can be written in terms of two distinct components, the first involving delay for an M/G/1 without setup and the second involving just some setup-related terms. It is really neat (and rare) when results decompose in such a pretty way. Such results are referred to as **decomposition results.**

27.4 Comparing ON/IDLE versus ON/OFF

We are now ready to derive the mean power consumption and mean response time for the ON/OFF and ON/IDLE power management policies.

The analysis of ON/IDLE is simple. The response time is just that of an M/G/1 queue. The power is P_{on} when the server is busy and P_{idle} when it is idle. Hence we have

$$\mathbf{E}[\text{Power}]^{\text{ON/IDLE}} = \rho P_{\text{on}} + (1 - \rho) P_{\text{idle}} \tag{27.16}$$

$$\mathbf{E}[T]^{\text{ON/IDLE}} = \frac{\lambda \mathbf{E}[S^2]}{2(1 - \rho)} + \mathbf{E}[S] \tag{27.17}$$

where $\rho = \lambda \mathbf{E}[S]$.

The analysis of ON/OFF is more involved, but at this point we have all the computations we need. With respect to power, the server might be in one of three states: ON, in SETUP, or OFF. When the server is ON or in SETUP, the power used is P_{on}. Otherwise the power is zero. Fortunately, we already know the fraction of time that the server is busy from (27.9). Hence we have

$$\mathbf{E}\left[\text{Power}\right]^{\text{ON/OFF}} = \rho^{\text{setup}} \cdot P_{\text{on}} = \frac{\lambda \mathbf{E}\left[I\right] + \rho}{\lambda \mathbf{E}\left[I\right] + 1} \cdot P_{\text{on}}, \qquad (27.18)$$

where $\rho = \lambda \mathbf{E}\left[S\right]$ and $\mathbf{E}\left[I\right]$ represents the expected setup time.

The response time under ON/OFF is just the response time for an M/G/1 with setup, which we have from (27.14), namely

$$\mathbf{E}\left[T\right]^{\text{ON/OFF}} = \frac{\lambda \mathbf{E}\left[S^2\right]}{2(1-\rho)} + \frac{2\mathbf{E}\left[I\right] + \lambda \mathbf{E}\left[I^2\right]}{2(1 + \lambda \mathbf{E}\left[I\right])} + \mathbf{E}\left[S\right]. \qquad (27.19)$$

These two formulas allow us to compare the ON/IDLE and ON/OFF policies with respect to the following Perf/W metric:

$$\text{Performance-per-Watt} = \frac{1}{\mathbf{E}\left[\text{Power}\right] \cdot \mathbf{E}\left[\text{Response Time}\right]}.$$

Table 27.1 compares our policies for a range of values of $\rho = 0.1, 0.3, 0.5, 0.7, 0.9$ and $\mathbf{E}\left[I\right] = \frac{1}{8}, \frac{1}{4}, \frac{1}{2}, 1, 2, 4, 8$. Throughout, we assume $\mathbf{E}\left[S\right] = 1$, $\mathbf{E}\left[S^2\right] = 20$, and $\mathbf{E}\left[I^2\right] = 5\mathbf{E}\left[I\right]^2$ (there is no particular reason for choosing these values).

Table 27.1 shows the *ratio* of Perf/W under ON/IDLE versus that under ON/OFF. When the ratio exceeds 1, then the ON/IDLE policy is better (has higher Perf/W), and when the ratio is less than 1, then the ON/OFF policy is better. Looking at the table, we see that, under low load and low setup time, the ON/OFF policy is about 6 times better (ratio is 0.152), whereas under low load and high setup time, the ON/IDLE policy is almost 5 times better. It makes sense that, as the setup time increases, ON/IDLE will become preferable, because turning OFF the server becomes costly.

Table 27.1. *The* $\dfrac{\textit{Performance-per-Watt}^{ON/IDLE}}{\textit{Performance-per-Watt}^{ON/OFF}}$ *ratio*

	$\mathbf{E}\left[I\right] = \frac{1}{8}$	$\mathbf{E}\left[I\right] = \frac{1}{4}$	$\mathbf{E}\left[I\right] = \frac{1}{2}$	$\mathbf{E}\left[I\right] = 1$	$\mathbf{E}\left[I\right] = 2$	$\mathbf{E}\left[I\right] = 4$	$\mathbf{E}\left[I\right] = 8$
$\rho = 0.1$	0.152	0.177	0.231	0.361	0.705	1.708	4.720
$\rho = 0.3$	0.404	0.445	0.528	0.702	1.085	1.964	3.962
$\rho = 0.5$	0.612	0.652	0.726	0.866	1.130	1.645	2.674
$\rho = 0.7$	0.787	0.815	0.865	0.950	1.092	1.340	1.803
$\rho = 0.9$	0.935	0.945	0.963	0.990	1.032	1.099	1.219

When the ratio is < 1, the ON/OFF policy is superior.

What is more surprising is the effect of load. One would expect that increasing the load makes ON/OFF perform worse, relative to ON/IDLE, because under high load it does not pay to turn the server OFF and suffer the setup cost. This intuition is true, provided that the setup cost is not too high. However, when the setup cost is high, the reverse trend seems to happen – namely as the load increases, ON/IDLE's superiority over ON/OFF decreases. This could be due to the fact that the values of $\mathbf{E}\left[T\right]$ and $\mathbf{E}\left[\text{Power}\right]$ are just so high under both policies when both setup costs and load are high that the ratios of the policies become closer to each other.

27.5 Readings

The formulas (27.13) and (27.14) for the M/G/1 with setup time were first obtained in [182]. Setup time is also known as *exceptional first service* in the queueing literature. The material in this chapter, on the M/G/1 with setup times, was applied by a former student, Brian Gold, in the well-known paper, "PowerNap: Eliminating Server Idle Power" [124].

Although this chapter only dealt with a single-server queue, it is natural to ask how policies like ON/OFF might perform in a multi-server system, like the M/M/k system, for example. Surprisingly, analyzing the M/M/k with setup cost is a very difficult problem. The exact analysis is not yet known, but approximations exist in [68].

27.6 Exercises

27.1 Review of Formulas
Throughout, assume that you have an M/G/1 (FCFS) queue, except in part (j), where M/M/1 is stated. The average arrival rate is λ, and S represents job size. Ten quantities are given, labeled (a) through (j). Many of these quantities are equivalent. Your job is to form them into equivalence classes.
(a) $\mathbf{E}\left[A_T\right]$: mean number of arrivals during response time T
(b) $\mathbf{E}\left[A_S\right]$: mean number of arrivals during time S
(c) $\mathbf{E}\left[N\right]$: mean number of jobs in the system
(d) $\mathbf{E}\left[T_Q\right]$: mean queueing time
(e) ρ: load
(f) $\mathbf{E}\left[W\right]$: mean work in system
(g) $\lambda \cdot \mathbf{E}\left[T\right]$: product of arrival rate and mean response time
(h) $\mathbf{E}\left[N\right] - \mathbf{E}\left[N_Q\right]$: mean number of jobs in service
(i) $\mathbf{E}\left[B\right]$: mean duration of busy period
(j) $\mathbf{E}\left[T^{\text{M/M/1}}\right]$: mean response time in M/M/1 queue

27.2 Server Vacations
Imagine you are running a shop with a lazy server. The server serves customers in an M/G/1 queue when there are customers in the shop. However, when the shop is empty, the server walks next door to get coffee. The time to get coffee is denoted by V and is known as a *server vacation*. When the server returns from getting coffee, there may or may not be new customers queued, waiting for the server. If there is no one waiting when the server returns, the server goes to get another cup of coffee, and this continues until the server finds someone in the queue. Assume that "vacation times" are i.i.d. instances of V.

Let $T^{\text{M/G/1/Vac}}$ denote the response time in an M/G/1 with Vacations. Prove the following decomposition result:

$$\widetilde{T}^{\text{M/G/1/Vac}}(s) = \widetilde{T}^{\text{M/G/1}}(s) \cdot \widetilde{V}_e(s)$$

where V_e is the excess of V. [Hint: Follow the derivation of M/G/1/setup in this chapter.]

27.3 Shorts-Only Busy Period

Consider an M/G/1 queue where job sizes have p.d.f. $f(\cdot)$ and c.d.f. $F(\cdot)$. Define a job to be "short" if its size is $< t$ and "long" otherwise. Suppose that short jobs have preemptive priority over long ones. That is, whenever there is a short job in the system, there can never be a long job in service. We define a "short busy period" to be a busy period started by a short job, containing only short jobs. Derive the mean and Laplace transform of a short busy period.

27.4 ON/OFF for M/M/∞

Consider a very large data center, comprising tens of thousands of servers, as is common in companies like Google, Facebook, and Microsoft. Such a data center might be approximated by an M/M/∞ system, where there is no queue and all jobs are immediately served (see Section 15.2). To save power, when a server goes idle, we assume that it is immediately shut off. When a job arrives, it needs to turn on a server, requiring setup time I, where $I \sim \text{Exp}(\alpha)$. If a server, $s1$, is in setup mode and another server, $s2$, becomes free, then the job waiting for $s1$ goes to $s2$. At this point, server $s1$ is shut off.

The effect of setup times for the M/M/∞ was first derived in [68], where the following beautiful decomposition property was observed. Here λ is the outside arrival rate, μ is the service rate at each server, and $R = \frac{\lambda}{\mu}$.

$$\mathbf{P}\{i \text{ servers are busy \& } j \text{ servers are in setup}\}$$
$$= \mathbf{P}\{i \text{ servers are busy}\} \cdot \mathbf{P}\{j \text{ servers are in setup}\} \quad (27.20)$$

where

$$\mathbf{P}\{i \text{ servers are busy}\} = e^{-R} \cdot \frac{R^i}{i!} \quad (27.21)$$

$$\mathbf{P}\{j \text{ servers in setup}\} = C \prod_{\ell=1}^{j} \frac{\lambda}{\lambda + \ell\alpha} \quad (27.22)$$

That is, the number of busy servers follows a Poisson distribution with mean R, just as in an M/M/∞ without setup, and is independent of the number of servers in setup.

In this problem, you will verify the above result:

(a) Draw the CTMC for the M/M/∞ with setup, where the states are (i, j) as defined above.

(b) Write the balance equation for state (i, j) and verify that the above formulas satisfy the balance equation.

(c) Equation (27.21) makes intuitive sense because the long-run number of busy servers should not be affected by the fact that servers first need a setup; hence a Poisson(R) distribution is reasonable. What is the intuition for equation (27.22)? [Hint: Assume that there are always exactly R servers that are busy and draw a birth-death chain representing the number of servers that are in setup, given that assumption.]

27.5 Number of Jobs Served during M/M/1 Busy Period

Let N_B denote the number of jobs served during an M/M/1 busy period.

(a) Derive $\mathbf{E}[N_B]$.

(b) Derive the z-transform: $\widehat{N_B}(z)$. Determine the first and second moments of N_B by carefully differentiating your transform.

27.6 Number of Jobs Served during M/G/1 Busy Period

Let N_B denote the number of jobs served during an M/G/1 busy period. Derive the z-transform: $\widehat{N_B}(z)$. Determine the first and second moments of N_B by carefully differentiating your transform.

27.7 Number of Jobs Served during M/G/1 Busy Period with Setup Time

This problem builds on Exercise 27.6. Consider an M/G/1 system where the server shuts off whenever it goes idle and where there is a generally distributed setup time, denoted by I, needed to turn on a server if an arrival finds the server off. Let N_B^{setup} denote the number of jobs served during a busy period of this M/G/1/setup system. Derive the z-transform: $\widehat{N_B^{\text{setup}}}(z)$. Then derive its mean, $\mathbf{E}\left[N_B^{\text{setup}}\right]$, and provide intuition for this result.

In your derivations, be careful to distinguish between N_B^{setup} and N_B. Both refer to the number of jobs served during a busy period, but the former is a busy period in an M/G/1/setup, whereas the latter is a busy period in an M/G/1.

27.8 A New Power-Saving Policy: DelayedOff

This problem builds on Exercise 27.7. Anshul suggests the following power-saving policy for an M/G/1 system. When the server becomes idle, rather than turning off the server immediately, we set a timer of duration t_{wait}. The server idles until either the timer goes off, in which case the server is shut off, or until there is a new arrival, in which case the server resumes running. The goal of this policy, called *DelayedOff*, is to obviate the setup cost by not turning off the server every time that it goes idle.

Your job is to evaluate the DelayedOff policy, and to determine how much power is saved over policies like ON/OFF and ON/IDLE and what the optimal t_{wait} constant should be. Here are the parameters you should assume: The server consumes power at rate 240 Watts when on, 180 Watts when idle, and 0 Watts when off. Arrivals occur with average rate λ. When an arrival finds the server off, it requires a setup cost to get it on. The setup time is denoted by the general random variable I. Power is consumed at a rate of 240 Watts during the entire period I. In expressing your solution you may use $\rho = \lambda \mathbf{E}[S]$ or $\rho^{\text{setup}} = \frac{\lambda \mathbf{E}[I] + \rho}{\lambda \mathbf{E}[I] + 1}$.

(a) Derive mean response time, $\mathbf{E}[T]$, for the DelayedOff policy.

(b) Derive $\mathbf{E}[\text{Power}]$ for the DelayedOff policy.

(c) Which value of t_{wait} minimizes $\mathbf{E}[T]$?

(d) Which value of t_{wait} minimizes $\mathbf{E}[\text{Power}]$?

(e) Does the DelayedOff policy make sense for the M/G/1 queue?

The DelayedOff policy ends up being very powerful in multi-server systems with the appropriate routing, see [67].

27.9 ON/OFF for M/M/1

[This is a repeat of Exercise 15.10.] The analysis of the ON/OFF policy in this chapter was based on using transforms. For this problem, we revisit the ON/OFF policy, this time for an M/M/1, with average arrival rate λ and service rate μ, where the setup time is distributed as $\text{Exp}(\alpha)$. This time, the approach is to set up a Markov chain for the system and derive the following quantities:

(a) limiting probabilities for all states
(b) limiting probability that the number of jobs in the system exceeds k
(c) mean response time

For each of these quantities, compare with the case of an M/M/1 without setup time.

PART VII

Smart Scheduling
in the M/G/1

Part VII is dedicated to scheduling.

Scheduling is an extremely important topic in designing computer systems, manufacturing systems, hospitals, and call centers. The right scheduling policy can vastly reduce mean response time without requiring the purchase of faster machines. Scheduling can be thought of as *improving performance for free*. Scheduling is also used to optimize performance metrics other than mean response time, such as "fairness" among users, and to provide differentiated levels of service where some class of jobs is guaranteed lower mean delay than other classes.

Stochastic scheduling analysis, even in the case of the M/G/1 queue, is not easy and is omitted from most textbooks. A notable exception is the 1967 Conway, Maxwell, and Miller book, *Theory of Scheduling* [45], which beautifully derives many of the known scheduling analyses.

In this part, we study scheduling in the M/G/1 queue, where G is continuous with finite mean and variance. We are interested in mean response time, the transform of response time, and other metrics like slowdown and fairness. Throughout we are interested in the effects of high variability in job size distribution.

Scheduling policies can be categorized based on whether the policy is preemptive or non-preemptive. A policy is *preemptive* if a job may be stopped partway through its execution and then resumed at a later point in time from the same point where it was stopped (this is also called *preemptive-resume*). A policy is *non-preemptive* if jobs are always run to completion. Scheduling policies can be differentiated further based on whether the policy assumes knowledge of the job sizes.

The chapters are organized as follows. Chapter 28 covers the different performance metrics commonly used in evaluating scheduling policies. Chapter 29 considers non-preemptive scheduling policies that do not make use of job size. Examples are First-Come-First-Served, RANDOM, and Last-Come-First-Served. Chapter 30 considers preemptive scheduling policies that do not make use of job size. Examples include Processor-Sharing, Preemptive-Last-Come-First-Served, and Foreground-Background scheduling (also known as Least-Attained-Service). Chapter 31 considers non-preemptive policies that make use of size. These include Shortest-Job-First and non-preemptive priority queues. Chapters 32 and 33 consider preemptive policies that make use of size. These include Preemptive-Shortest-Job-First and Shortest-Remaining-Processing-Time. Also included are preemptive priority queues.

Performance Metrics

This is a very short chapter that explains some performance metrics that will be used in evaluating the different scheduling policies that we will study in this part. In our discussion below, we will be assuming an *open* system with some arbitrary outside arrival process.

28.1 Traditional Metrics

We have already been using the following traditional performance metrics:

$\mathbf{E}[T]$: mean response time or "mean time in system"

$\mathbf{E}[T_Q] = \mathbf{E}[T] - \mathbf{E}[S]$: mean waiting time or "wasted" time, also known as mean delay or mean queuing time

$\mathbf{E}[N]$: mean number in system

$\mathbf{E}[N_Q]$: mean number in queue

Question: Suppose someone tells you they have a super scheduling algorithm that improves mean waiting time in their system by a factor of 100. Before you buy the algorithm, what question should you ask?

Hint: Just because $\mathbf{E}[T_Q]$ improves by a factor of 100, does $\mathbf{E}[T]$ necessarily improve by a comparable factor?

Answer: In fact, you need to know the mean job size, $\mathbf{E}[S]$, so you can determine the benefit to $\mathbf{E}[T]$.

Suppose

$$\mathbf{E}[S] > \mathbf{E}[T_Q].$$

Then an improvement in $\mathbf{E}[T_Q]$ by a factor of 100,000 still yields less than a factor of 2 improvement in $\mathbf{E}[T]$.

More typically, we have

$$\mathbf{E}[T_Q] \gg \mathbf{E}[S],$$

so improvements in $\mathbf{E}[T_Q]$ translate to comparable improvements in $\mathbf{E}[T]$.

28.2 Commonly Used Metrics for Single Queues

Suppose you have a single queue. Consider these two metrics:

Work in system: remaining work left to do in the system

Utilization of device: fraction of time that the device is busy

Define an *arrival sequence* as a sequence of arrival times and job sizes.

Question: Suppose you are told that two scheduling policies, run on the same arrival sequence, result in the same work in system over all time and the same device utilization. Does that mean that the two policies also have the same mean response time?

> **Definition 28.1** A *work-conserving* scheduling policy is one that always performs work on some job when there is a job in the system. Also, the policy does not create new work (e.g., by re-running parts of jobs).

Observe that "work in system" is the same across all work-conserving scheduling policies, and so is the server utilization. Let's reformulate the question then.

Question: Do all work-conserving scheduling policies have the same mean response time?

Answer: No. Consider two work-conserving policies A and B. Suppose policy A serves the shortest available job first, so that only a few big jobs are left, whereas B serves the longest available job first, so that many more jobs are left. Then $\mathbf{E}[N]$ is much higher for policy B, and by Little's Law, $\mathbf{E}[T]$ is thus higher for B.

28.3 Today's Trendy Metrics

> **Definition 28.2** The *slowdown* of a job is its response time divided by its size:
>
> $$\text{Slowdown} = \frac{T}{S}.$$

Observe that the slowdown of a job is always at least 1.

Question: Why is mean slowdown preferable to mean response time?

Answer: Ideally, one wants the response time of a job to be correlated with the job's size. We would like small jobs to have small response times and big jobs to have big response times. We would like to make sure the slowdown of *every* job is no more than, say, 10.

Question: But why does knowing mean slowdown is low tell us anything about the max slowdown?

Answer: If we know $\mathbf{E}[\text{Slowdown}] = 2$, then we know there cannot be many jobs with slowdown much greater than 3. In particular, fewer than half the jobs can have slowdown greater than or equal to 3 (note that all jobs have slowdown of at least 1). Fewer than $1/4$ of the jobs can have slowdown of at least 5. Fewer than $\frac{1}{n-1}$ fraction of jobs can have slowdown of at least n.

So by making the mean slowdown low, we have also restricted the fraction of jobs with very high slowdowns, which means that few jobs have response time too much greater than their service requirement.

There are many other performance metrics of interest. Variability in response time, $\mathbf{Var}(T)$, and variability in slowdown, $\mathbf{Var}(\text{Slowdown})$, are sometimes even more important to system designers than mean metrics. This is why we often derive the Laplace transform of response time, rather than just the mean.

Another metric of importance is the *tail behavior of response time* (or tail of slowdown). This is defined as the probability that the response time exceeds some level x, namely $\mathbf{P}\{T > x\}$. Understanding the tail behavior is very important in setting Service Level Agreements (SLA's), where a company might be willing to pay to ensure that their response time stays below x with probability 95%. Unfortunately, tail behavior is often not easy to derive. Boxma and Zwart [28] survey recent research in understanding the tail behavior of different scheduling policies.

28.4 Starvation/Fairness Metrics

The increasing popularity of mean slowdown as a performance metric has led some researchers to worry that certain scheduling policies might be achieving low mean slowdown at the expense of *starving* the few big jobs. For example, the Shortest-Remaining-Processing-Time (SRPT) policy results in low mean slowdown because most jobs are small and they get treated well, at the expense of delaying large jobs.

Question: What performance metric will tell us if jobs are being starved?

Answer: We recommend looking at *mean slowdown as a function of job size*. For example, consider asking "What is the expected slowdown of jobs of size x?" or "What is the expected slowdown of the max job size?" or "What is the expected slowdown of jobs in the 99th percentile of the job size distribution?"

We use $\mathbf{E}[\text{Slowdown}(x)]$ to denote the expected slowdown of a job of size x. We might then say that scheduling policy $\mathcal{P}$ is "starving some jobs" or at least "treating some jobs unfairly" if the expected slowdown of a job of size x is higher under policy $\mathcal{P}$ than it is under Processor-Sharing (PS), for some x. We compare with PS because PS provides equal expected slowdown to all jobs (this statement will become more clear when we get to Chapter 30) and hence is considered "fair." We likewise might say that a scheduling policy $\mathcal{P}$ is "fair" even if it does not provide equal expected slowdown to all job sizes, as long as $\mathbf{E}[\text{Slowdown}(x)]$ under policy $\mathcal{P}$ is lower than that under PS, for all x.

Starvation is often a deceptive thing. Consider the following example.

Question: Suppose I tell you that switching from scheduling policy A to scheduling policy B resulted in strictly improving the response time of *almost all* jobs and in *no* job ending up with a *worse* response time under policy B than under A. Is this possible?

Answer: Sure it is. Consider the case of a single server, where n jobs all arrive at time 0 and have size 1. Under Processor-Sharing, they each have response time of n. Now we switch to FCFS. The response time of $n - 1$ of the jobs strictly improves. The response time of one job stays the same. No job has a worse response time.

Section 33.4 proves more counterintuitive results on fairness, such as the "All-Can-Win" theorem for SRPT scheduling.

28.5 Deriving Performance Metrics

In the next few chapters, we consider various scheduling policies for the M/G/1 queue. Typically, for every scheduling policy we derive $\mathbf{E}[T]$ (mean time in system) and $\mathbf{E}[T(x)]$ (mean time in system for a job of size x).

Question: How can we derive $\mathbf{E}[\text{Slowdown}]$, given $\mathbf{E}[T]$ and $\mathbf{E}[T(x)]$?

Hint: It is *not* $\mathbf{E}[T]/\mathbf{E}[S]$.

Answer: First derive the mean slowdown for a job of size x as follows:

$$\mathbf{E}[\text{Slowdown}(x)] = \mathbf{E}\left[\frac{T}{S} \mid \text{job has size } S = x\right] = \mathbf{E}\left[\frac{T(x)}{x}\right] = \frac{1}{x}\mathbf{E}[T(x)].$$

Notice that we were able to pull out the x because it is just a constant. Now we use $\mathbf{E}[\text{Slowdown}(x)]$ to get mean slowdown:

$$\mathbf{E}[\text{Slowdown}] = \int_x \mathbf{E}[\text{Slowdown} \mid \text{job has size } x]\, f_S(x)dx$$

$$= \int_x \mathbf{E}[\text{Slowdown}(x)]\, f_S(x)dx$$

$$= \int_x \frac{1}{x}\mathbf{E}[T(x)]\, f_S(x)dx$$

To derive the transform of response time, we typically first derive the transform of $T(x)$ and then integrate that to get the transform of response time, as follows:

$$\widetilde{T}(s) = \int_x \widetilde{T(x)}(s) f_S(x)dx$$

Similarly, for the transform of slowdown, we first derive the transform of Slowdown(x) and then integrate that.

28.6 Readings

The fairness metric that we use here was introduced in [12]. The slowdown metric has received very little attention in the world of scheduling until recently, see [100] and the references therein.

CHAPTER 29

Scheduling: Non-Preemptive, Non-Size-Based Policies

This chapter and all the remaining chapters focus on scheduling for the case of an M/G/1 queue. We always assume $\rho < 1$ and that G is continuous with finite mean and finite variance. Every scheduling policy we consider is work-conserving (i.e., whenever there is a job to be worked on, some job will receive service).

> **Definition 29.1** A ***non-preemptive service order*** is one that does not preempt a job once it starts service (i.e., each job is run to completion).

This chapter focuses on non-preemptive scheduling policies that do not make use of knowing a job's size.

29.1 FCFS, LCFS, and RANDOM

The following three non-preemptive policies do not assume knowledge of job size:

FCFS: When the server frees up, it always chooses the job at the head of the queue to be served and runs that job to completion.

LCFS (non-preemptive): When the server frees up, it always chooses the last job to arrive and runs that job to completion.

RANDOM: When the server frees up, it chooses a random job to run next.

Question: When would one use LCFS?

Answer: Consider the situation where arriving jobs get pushed on a stack, and therefore it is easiest to access the job that arrived last (e.g., the task at the top of the pile on my desk!).

Question: Which of these three non-preemptive policies do you think has the lowest mean response time?

Answer: It seems like FCFS should have the best mean response time because jobs are serviced most closely to the time they arrive, whereas LCFS may make a job wait a very long time. However, surprisingly, it turns out that all three policies have exactly the *same* mean response time. In fact, an even stronger statement can be made.

> **Theorem 29.2** [45] *All non-preemptive service orders that do not make use of job sizes have the same* distribution *of the number of jobs in the system.*

Corollary 29.3 *All non-preemptive service orders that do not make use of job sizes have the same* $\mathbf{E}[N]$, *and hence the same* $\mathbf{E}[T]$.

Question: Does this mean that all these policies also have the same $\mathbf{E}[\text{Slowdown}]$?

Answer: See Exercise 29.2.

Question: Any ideas for how the proof for Theorem 29.2 might go?

Hint: It will help to recall the embedded DTMC formulation for the M/G/1/FCFS queue. The idea is to look at the M/G/1 queue just at the point of departures.

Answer: For the M/G/1/FCFS queue in Chapter 26, we let the current state be the number of jobs in the M/G/1 system at the time of the last departure. The sequence of states $\{X_i, i \geq 0\}$ forms a DTMC, where, for $i > 0$,

$$P_{ij} = \text{Probability that when leave state } i \text{ we next go to state } j$$

$$= \mathbf{P}\left\{ \begin{array}{l} \text{The next departure will leave behind } j \text{ jobs,} \\ \text{given that the last departure left behind } i \text{ jobs} \end{array} \right\}$$

$$= \mathbf{P}\{j - i + 1 \text{ jobs arrive during the service time } S\}$$

$$= \int_x \mathbf{P}\{j - i + 1 \text{ arrivals during time } x\} f_S(x)dx$$

$$= \int_x \frac{e^{-\lambda x}(\lambda x)^{j-i+1}}{(j - i + 1)!} f_S(x)dx.$$

The limiting probability, π_i, for this DTMC process specifies the fraction of jobs that leave behind i jobs. This in turn, by PASTA (see Chapter 13), equals the limiting probability that there are i jobs in the M/G/1.

Question: So, having recalled this argument for M/G/1/FCFS, what would the argument be like to determine the limiting number of jobs in the system for M/G/1/LCFS?

Answer: The argument does not change at all when the service order is LCFS. In fact it is the same analysis for *any* service order that does not make use of job size.

Question: Why do we require that the scheduling policy not make use of size?

Answer: If you used size in determining which job got to serve next, then that would affect the distribution of the number of jobs that arrive during one service time.

Question: Consider again the set of all non-preemptive scheduling policies that do not make use of size. Is $\mathbf{Var}(T)$ the same for all these policies?

Answer: No. Observe that LCFS can generate some extremely high response times because we have to wait for the system to become empty to take care of that first arrival. It turns out that, in agreement with intuition, we have

$$\mathbf{Var}(T)^{\text{FCFS}} < \mathbf{Var}(T)^{\text{RANDOM}} < \mathbf{Var}(T)^{\text{LCFS}}.$$

We already know how to derive $\mathbf{Var}(T)^{\text{FCFS}}$. We now show how to derive $\mathbf{Var}(T)^{\text{LCFS}}$. We do this by computing the Laplace transform of waiting time, $\widetilde{T}_Q^{\text{LCFS}}(s)$. Before we begin, it helps to recall a few formulas from Chapter 27 and Exercise 25.14.

$$B(x) = \text{length of busy period started by a job of size } x$$

$$= x + \sum_{i=1}^{A_x} B_i, \quad \text{where } A_x = \text{number arrivals by } x$$

$$\widetilde{B(x)}(s) = e^{-x\left(s+\lambda-\lambda\widetilde{B}(s)\right)}$$

$$B = \text{length of busy period made up of jobs of size } S$$

$$\widetilde{B}(s) = \int_{x=0}^{\infty} \widetilde{B(x)}(s) f_S(x) dx = \widetilde{S}\left(s+\lambda-\lambda\widetilde{B}(s)\right)$$

$$B_W = \text{length of busy period made up of jobs of size } S, \text{ started by work } W$$

$$\widetilde{B_W}(s) = \widetilde{W}\left(s+\lambda-\lambda\widetilde{B}(s)\right)$$

$$S_e = \text{excess of } S$$

$$\widetilde{S_e}(s) = L_{f_e}(s) = \frac{1-\widetilde{S}(s)}{s\mathbf{E}[S]}$$

Consider an arrival into the M/G/1/LCFS queue. Conditioning on whether the arrival sees an empty system or a busy system, we can immediately write

$$\widetilde{T}_Q^{\text{LCFS}}(s) = (1-\rho) \cdot \widetilde{T}_Q^{\text{LCFS}}(s \mid \text{idle}) + \rho \cdot \widetilde{T}_Q^{\text{LCFS}}(s \mid \text{busy}). \tag{29.1}$$

Question: What is $\widetilde{T}_Q^{\text{LCFS}}(s \mid \text{idle})$?

Answer: If the arrival sees an empty system, then the waiting time is zero, so

$$\widetilde{T}_Q^{\text{LCFS}}(s \mid \text{idle}) = 1.$$

Question: How long does the arrival wait if it finds the server busy?

Answer: At first one might think that the waiting time is just the excess of a service time, S_e, because the arrival has to wait for the job in service to finish serving. This is, however, not quite correct, because more jobs may arrive during S_e, and those jobs have precedence over our arrival. In fact, the waiting time for our arrival is the length of a busy period started by a job of size S_e.

$$\widetilde{T}_Q^{\text{LCFS}}(s \mid \text{busy}) = \widetilde{S_e}\left(s+\lambda-\lambda\widetilde{B}(s)\right)$$

$$= \frac{1-\widetilde{S}\left(s+\lambda-\lambda\widetilde{B}(s)\right)}{\left(s+\lambda-\lambda\widetilde{B}(s)\right)\mathbf{E}[S]}$$

$$= \frac{1-\widetilde{B}(s)}{\left(s+\lambda-\lambda\widetilde{B}(s)\right)\mathbf{E}[S]}$$

Returning to (29.1) we have

$$\widetilde{T}_Q^{\text{LCFS}}(s) = (1 - \rho) \cdot \widetilde{T}_Q^{\text{LCFS}}(s \mid \text{idle}) + \rho \cdot \widetilde{T}_Q^{\text{LCFS}}(s \mid \text{busy})$$

$$= (1 - \rho) + \rho \cdot \frac{1 - \widetilde{B}(s)}{\left(s + \lambda - \lambda \widetilde{B}(s)\right) \mathbf{E}\,[S]}$$

$$= (1 - \rho) + \frac{\lambda(1 - \widetilde{B}(s))}{\left(s + \lambda - \lambda \widetilde{B}(s)\right)}.$$

From this transform, we can derive the second moment of waiting time, $\mathbf{E}\left[T_Q^2\right]$. We find that

$$\mathbf{E}\left[T_Q^2\right]^{\text{LCFS}} = \frac{\lambda \mathbf{E}\,[S^3]}{3(1 - \rho)^2} + \frac{(\lambda \mathbf{E}\,[S^2])^2}{2(1 - \rho)^3}.$$

In comparison, for FCFS scheduling we saw

$$\mathbf{E}\left[T_Q^2\right]^{\text{FCFS}} = \frac{\lambda \mathbf{E}\,[S^3]}{3(1 - \rho)} + \frac{(\lambda \mathbf{E}\,[S^2])^2}{2(1 - \rho)^2}.$$

So

$$\mathbf{E}\left[T_Q^2\right]^{\text{LCFS}} = \mathbf{E}\left[T_Q^2\right]^{\text{FCFS}} \cdot \frac{1}{1 - \rho}.$$

Thus, although the mean waiting times are the same for FCFS and LCFS, the second moment of waiting time differs by a factor that depends on ρ, but not on the job size distribution. Under high loads, the second moment of waiting time under LCFS becomes very high compared with the second moment of waiting time under FCFS.

29.2 Readings

Theorem 29.2 was taken from [45], Section 8.5. Very few books analyze scheduling policies in a stochastic setting. However, two good ones with lots of insights are [45, 111].

29.3 Exercises

29.1 Reviewing LCFS
Derive the mean queueing time under LCFS, $\mathbf{E}\,[T_Q]^{\text{LCFS}}$. Derive this by conditioning on whether an arrival finds the system busy or idle, but *without* using transforms.

29.2 Non-Preemptive, Non-Size-Based Policies
In this chapter, we saw that the FCFS, LCFS and RANDOM scheduling disciplines all have the same distribution of the number of jobs in the system for an M/G/1 queue. How do they compare with respect to mean slowdown (again, for an M/G/1)? Prove your answer.

CHAPTER 30

Scheduling: Preemptive, Non-Size-Based Policies

This chapter is about preemptive scheduling policies that do not make use of knowing a job's size or its priority class.

> **Definition 30.1** A policy is *preemptive* if a job may be stopped partway through its execution and then resumed at a later point in time from the same point where it was stopped (this is also called *preemptive-resume*).

We define three preemptive scheduling policies during this chapter, none of which make use of job size. The policies are Processor-Sharing (PS) (Section 30.1), Preemptive-Last-Come-First-Served (PLCFS) (Section 30.2), and Generalized Foreground-Background (FB) (Section 30.3).

30.1 Processor-Sharing (PS)

30.1.1 *Motivation behind PS*

In Chapter 29, we saw that all non-preemptive, non-size-based scheduling policies for the M/G/1 result in the

same distribution on $N \Rightarrow$ same $\mathbf{E}[N] \Rightarrow$ same $\mathbf{E}[T] \Rightarrow$ same $\mathbf{E}[T_Q]$.

Thus all non-preemptive, non-size-based service orders for the M/G/1 have $\mathbf{E}[T]$ equal to that for M/G/1/FCFS, namely

$$\mathbf{E}[T] = \frac{\lambda \mathbf{E}[S^2]}{2(1 - \rho)} + \mathbf{E}[S].$$

We also saw that for all these policies,

$$\mathbf{E}[T(x)] = x + \frac{\lambda \mathbf{E}[S^2]}{2(1 - \rho)}.$$

(*Note:* $\mathbf{E}[T_Q(x)] = \mathbf{E}[T_Q]$ for all x.)

The problem is that this mean response time can be very high when $\mathbf{E}[S^2]$ is high (job size variability is high). Intuitively, short jobs queue up behind long jobs, resulting in long delays. In particular, the mean slowdown, $\mathbf{E}[\text{Slowdown}(x)] = \frac{\mathbf{E}[T(x)]}{x}$, is very high for small x.

Processor-Sharing, by contrast, is not negatively affected by high job size variability.

Question: Why are short jobs not affected by long ones under PS?

Answer: When a short job arrives, it immediately time-shares with all the jobs in the system. It does not have to wait for long jobs to finish.

Historically, CPU scheduling has always involved time-sharing, where each job is given a tiny quantum and the CPU takes turns serving jobs in a round-robin fashion. If the quantum size goes to zero, we get the Processor-Sharing abstraction.

There are two reasons, historically, why PS is used in CPU scheduling. The first is that PS allows short jobs (which require just a few quanta of service) to get out quickly. Because PS helps the many short jobs finish quickly, it should in theory also help reduce $\mathbf{E}[T]$ and particularly $\mathbf{E}[\text{Slowdown}]$, as compared to FCFS. The other reason for PS is that time-sharing the CPU might allow an increase of overall system throughput in a multi-resource system. Imagine, for example, a multi-resource system, including a CPU, disk, memory, etc. It is useful to have many jobs running simultaneously (rather than just one job at a time), because jobs requiring different resources can be overlapped to increase throughput.

But PS is not better than FCFS for **every** arrival sequence.

Question: Give an example of an arrival sequence for which PS is worse than FCFS for both $\mathbf{E}[T]$ and $\mathbf{E}[\text{Slowdown}]$?

Answer: Consider two jobs, both arriving at time 0, and both having size 1:

$$\mathbf{E}[T]^{\text{FCFS}} = 1.5 \quad \mathbf{E}[\text{Slowdown}]^{\text{FCFS}} = 1.5$$
$$\mathbf{E}[T]^{\text{PS}} = 2 \quad \mathbf{E}[\text{Slowdown}]^{\text{PS}} = 2$$

Question: We have seen that PS does not outperform FCFS on every arrival sequence. Can we say that M/G/1/PS outperforms M/G/1/FCFS with respect to expected response time in a stochastic setting? If so, what conditions, if any, are needed on G?

Answer: Recall that we proved in Chapter 22 that the distribution of the number of jobs in the M/G/1/PS system is the same as that in an M/M/1/FCFS system (for any Coxian distribution G). Hence the mean number of jobs and mean response time are the same for the M/G/1/PS and the M/M/1/FCFS.

So M/G/1/PS is better in expectation than M/G/1/FCFS exactly when M/M/1/FCFS is better than M/G/1/FCFS, namely when

$$C_G^2 > 1,$$

where C_G^2 is the squared coefficient of variation of G.

In summary, it is the fact that the mean response time for PS is insensitive to job size variability that makes PS so powerful in practice.

30.1.2 *Ages of Jobs in the M/G/1/PS System*

Definition 30.2 The *age* of a job is the total service it has received so far.

By definition, $0 \leq \text{age}(j) \leq \text{size}(j)$, where $\text{age}(j)$ denotes the age of job j and $\text{size}(j)$ denotes the (original) size of job j.

Although the steady-state number of jobs in the M/G/1/PS and M/M/1/FCFS queues is the same,

$$\mathbf{P}\left\{n \text{ in system}\right\} = \rho^n (1 - \rho),$$

the distribution of the *ages* of their jobs is very different. Under FCFS, the jobs in queue all have age 0 and the job in service (if there is one) has age (and excess) distributed according to the equilibrium distribution, where the equilibrium distribution has probability density function, $f_e(\cdot)$, defined by

$$f_e(x) = \frac{\overline{F}(x)}{\mathbf{E}[S]}. \tag{30.1}$$

Hence S denotes job size, $f(\cdot)$ is the job size p.d.f. of arriving jobs, and $\overline{F}(x) = \int_x^\infty f(t)dt$ is the probability that an arriving job has size $\geq x$ (see Exercise 25.14 for the derivation and Chapter 23 for more intuition).

Question: Can you guess at how the ages of the jobs in PS are distributed?

Answer: Under PS, all jobs are worked on simultaneously, and thus an arrival sees every job through an Inspection Paradox. It therefore is unsurprising that an arrival to the M/G/1/PS finds that *all* jobs in the system have i.i.d. ages, distributed according to the equilibrium distribution.

Theorem 30.3 *For the M/G/1/PS queue, given there are n jobs in the system, their ages are independent and have distribution density $f_e(\cdot)$. Furthermore, the departure process is a Poisson process with rate λ.*

Proof The proof of this theorem is sketched in [149]. The proof is very technical and does not provide intuition, so we have not repeated it here. The basic idea is to make a guess about the reverse process, whereby we guess that the excesses of jobs in the reverse process are distributed according to the equilibrium distribution, and then we prove that this guess satisfies the balance equations. ∎

30.1.3 *Response Time as a Function of Job Size*

We now show that in the M/G/1/PS, every job has the same expected slowdown.

Theorem 30.4

$$\mathbf{E}\left[T(x)\right]^{\text{M/G/1/PS}} = \frac{x}{1 - \rho}.$$

Corollary 30.5

$$\mathbf{E}\left[\text{Slowdown}(x)\right]^{\text{PS}} = \frac{1}{1-\rho}$$

$$\mathbf{E}\left[\text{Slowdown}\right]^{\text{PS}} = \frac{1}{1-\rho}$$

The remainder of this section is devoted to proving Theorem 30.4.

Recall Little's Law for red jobs: "The average number of red jobs in the system equals the average arrival rate of red jobs multiplied by the average time a red job spends in the system." To figure out the mean time in system for a job of size x, we thus need to figure out the mean number of jobs in the system with size x. (Note that we are talking here about "original size" x, not "remaining service requirement" x).

Question: Can we express the expected number of jobs in the system with size between x and $x + h$ as $\mathbf{E}[N] f(x) h + o(h)$?

Answer: No. Although original job sizes are drawn from distribution density $f(\cdot)$, the sizes of those jobs in the system have a p.d.f. possibly different from $f(\cdot)$, because PS finishes off small jobs more quickly.

Let

$$f(\cdot) = \text{ job size p.d.f. for arriving jobs.}$$

$$f^{\text{sys}}(\cdot) = \text{ job size p.d.f. for jobs in the system.}$$

Question: Sadly, we do not know anything about the probability that a job in the system has size, say, w. However, we do know the probability that a job in the system has age w. Can we use this?

Answer: Yes! Our approach will be to condition on the job's age:

$$f^{\text{sys}}(w) = \int_{x=0}^{w} f^{\text{sys}}(w \mid \text{ job has age } x) \cdot \mathbf{P}\{\text{job has age } x\}$$

$$= \int_{x=0}^{w} f^{\text{sys}}(w \mid \text{ job has age } x) \cdot f_e(x) dx, \quad \text{by Theorem 30.3}$$

$$= \int_{x=0}^{w} f(w \mid \text{ job has size } \geq x) \cdot f_e(x) dx$$

$$= \int_{x=0}^{w} \frac{f(w)}{\overline{F}(x)} \cdot f_e(x) dx$$

$$= \int_{x=0}^{w} \frac{f(w)}{\mathbf{E}[S]} dx, \quad \text{by (30.1)}$$

$$= w \frac{f(w)}{\mathbf{E}[S]}$$

So

$$f^{\text{sys}}(w) = f(w) \cdot \frac{w}{\mathbf{E}\left[S\right]}. \tag{30.2}$$

Question: Explain the intuition behind (30.2).

Answer: In (30.2), the factor that $f(w)$ gets weighted by is $\frac{w}{\mathbf{E}[S]}$. When w is small compared to $\mathbf{E}\left[S\right]$, this factor is less than 1. When w is large compared to $\mathbf{E}\left[S\right]$, this factor is greater than 1. This indicates that more large jobs are going to be *in the system* than would be true under $f(w)$.

Using (30.2), we have, for small h,

$$\mathbf{E}\left[\text{Number of jobs in system with (original) size} \in (x, x+h)\right]$$

$$= \mathbf{E}\left[N\right] \cdot f^{\text{sys}}(x) \cdot h + o(h)$$

$$= \frac{\rho}{1-\rho} \cdot x \cdot \frac{f(x)}{\mathbf{E}\left[S\right]} \cdot h + o(h)$$

$$= \frac{\lambda}{1-\rho} \cdot x \cdot f(x) \cdot h + o(h).$$

$$\mathbf{E}\left[\text{Rate of arrivals of jobs into system with size} \in (x, x+h)\right]$$

$$= \lambda \cdot f(x)h + o(h).$$

Now applying Little's Law, we have

$$\mathbf{E}\left[\text{Time in system for jobs with (original) size} \in (x, x+h)\right]$$

$$= \frac{\frac{\lambda}{1-\rho} \cdot x \cdot f(x) \cdot h + o(h)}{\lambda \cdot f(x)h + o(h)}$$

$$= \frac{\frac{\lambda}{1-\rho} \cdot x \cdot f(x) + \frac{o(h)}{h}}{\lambda \cdot f(x) + \frac{o(h)}{h}}$$

$$= \frac{\frac{\lambda}{1-\rho} \cdot x \cdot f(x)}{\lambda \cdot f(x)} \quad \text{as } h \to 0$$

$$= \frac{x}{1-\rho}.$$

Hence we have shown that

$$\mathbf{E}\left[T(x)\right]^{\text{M/G/1/PS}} = \frac{x}{1-\rho},$$

completing the proof of Theorem 30.4.

30.1.4 *Intuition for PS Results*

Consider Theorem 30.4 and its corollary. These say that the expected slowdown for a job of size x under the M/G/1/PS is a *constant*, independent of the size x. Remember that for non-preemptive non-size-based scheduling, the mean slowdown for small jobs was greater than the mean slowdown for large jobs. By contrast, under PS, all jobs have same slowdown. For this reason, people always refer to PS as **fair scheduling**.

In Chapter 28, we discussed what would be a good metric for evaluating whether a policy, like SRPT, is starving big jobs. The criterion we advocate using is to determine mean slowdown of big jobs under SRPT and see whether the big jobs have much higher mean slowdown under SRPT than they would have under PS, which produces equal slowdown for all jobs. We will discuss *fairness* in detail in Chapter 33.

Question: What is the intuition behind Theorem 30.4?

Hint: An arrival sees

$$\mathbf{E}[N] = \frac{\rho}{1 - \rho}$$

jobs in the system.

Answer: The arrival is slowed by a *factor* of $\mathbf{E}[N] + 1$, where

$$\mathbf{E}[N] + 1 = \frac{\rho}{1 - \rho} + 1 = \frac{1}{1 - \rho}.$$

Thus, any arrival of size x should take $\mathbf{E}[T(x)] = x \cdot \frac{1}{1-\rho}$ time to leave the system. (This is not a proof, just intuition.)

Question: What else that we have studied recently has the form $\frac{x}{1-\rho}$?

Answer: $\mathbf{E}[B(x)] = \frac{x}{1-\rho}$ is the expected length of a busy period started by a job of size x.

Thus the mean response time for a job of size x for the M/G/1/PS queue is also equal to the mean length of a busy period started by a job of size x. Although this may lead one to think that the response time under M/G/1/PS is really just a busy period duration, higher moment analysis shows this not to be true.

Remark: Although results for $\mathbf{E}[T]^{\text{PS}}$ and $\mathbf{E}[T(x)]^{\text{PS}}$ are really simple and beautiful, this is not true for $\mathbf{Var}(T)^{\text{PS}}$, which cannot even be expressed in a closed form. There are still theses being written today on the M/G/1/PS queue. There are pretty solutions when G is Deterministic, and obviously when it is Exponential, but not for much else (see Section 30.4).

30.1.5 *Implications of PS Results for Understanding FCFS*

Recall the transform equation for waiting time (delay) in the M/G/1/FCFS queue from (26.14):

$$\widetilde{T_Q}^{\text{FCFS}}(s) = \frac{1 - \rho}{1 - \rho \widetilde{S_e}(s)} \tag{30.3}$$

Remember that we needed an entire chapter (all of Chapter 26) to prove this result. We now rederive this result in one page. We start by writing (30.3) as a summation.

Question: How can we express (30.3) as a sum?

Answer:

$$\widetilde{T_Q}^{\text{FCFS}}(s) = (1 - \rho) \sum_{k=0}^{\infty} \left(\rho \widetilde{S_e}(s) \right)^k = \sum_{k=0}^{\infty} (1 - \rho) \rho^k \left(\widetilde{S_e}(s) \right)^k. \qquad (30.4)$$

Question: What does $\left(\widetilde{S_e}(s) \right)^k$ represent?

Answer: $\left(\widetilde{S_e}(s) \right)^k$ is the Laplace transform of $\sum_{i=1}^{k} S_e^{(i)}$ where the $S_e^{(i)}$, for $1 \leq i \leq k$, represent i.i.d. instances of S_e.

Kleinrock, vol. I [110] writes that no one has been able to explain the curious formulation of $\widetilde{T_Q}^{\text{FCFS}}(s)$ given in (30.4). Indeed it seems quite strange to see the term $\rho^k(1 - \rho)$ within an expression for the M/G/1/FCFS queue.

Question: Using what we have learned about PS, explain in four lines why

$$\widetilde{T_Q}^{\text{FCFS}}(s) = \sum_{k=0}^{\infty} (1 - \rho) \rho^k \left(\widetilde{S_e}(s) \right)^k.$$

Answer: Let W^{FCFS} denote the stationary work in an M/G/1/FCFS system. W^{FCFS} is the same as the work in system as witnessed by a Poisson arrival. This in turn equals the delay experienced by a Poisson arrival under FCFS.

Let W^{PS} denote the stationary work in an M/G/1/PS system.

$$
\begin{aligned}
\widetilde{T_Q}^{\text{FCFS}}(s) &= \widetilde{W}^{\text{FCFS}}(s) \\
&= \widetilde{W}^{\text{PS}}(s) \quad \text{(both FCFS and PS are work-conserving)} \\
&= \sum_{k=0}^{\infty} \widetilde{W}^{\text{PS}}(s \mid \text{arrival sees } k \text{ jobs}) \cdot \mathbf{P}\{\text{arrival sees } k \text{ jobs}\} \\
&= \sum_{k=0}^{\infty} \left(\widetilde{S_e}(s) \right)^k \cdot \rho^k (1 - \rho)
\end{aligned}
$$

That completes the derivation of the M/G/1/FCFS delay transform.

30.2 Preemptive-LCFS

Another preemptive non-size-based scheduling policy is **Preemptive-LCFS (PLCFS)**, defined as follows: Whenever a new arrival enters the system, it immediately preempts the job in service. Only when that arrival completes does the preempted job get to resume service.

Question: What do you recall about the performance of the (non-preemptive) LCFS policy?

Answer: It was identical in performance to FCFS – and thus not very good for highly variable job size distributions.

Question: Any guesses as to what the performance of PLCFS will be like?

Answer: We will prove the following theorem:

Theorem 30.6

$$\mathbf{E}\left[T(x)\right]^{\text{PLCFS}} = \frac{x}{1 - \rho}$$

$$\mathbf{E}\left[\text{Slowdown(x)}\right]^{\text{PLCFS}} = \frac{1}{1 - \rho}$$

The remainder of this section is devoted to proving Theorem 30.6. The derivation is actually quite simple and instructive. We derive the mean, $\mathbf{E}\left[T(x)\right]$, here, and in Exercise 30.6 we will derive the full transform, which will yield additional insight.

Consider a particular tagged job of size x.

Key Observation: Once a job is interrupted, it will not get back the processor until all jobs arriving after that point are completed (refer to Figure 30.1).

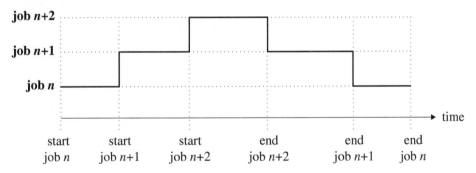

Figure 30.1. Jobs under Preemptive-LCFS.

Question: So how long will it be, on average, from when our tagged job is interrupted until it gets back the processor?

Answer: We can think of the point when our job gets interrupted as marking the beginning of a busy period in an M/G/1 queue, because the job will not resume until the interruption, and all work that arrives during its busy period, completes. So,

$$\mathbf{E}\left[\text{Time until job gets back processor}\right] = \mathbf{E}\left[\text{Length of busy period}\right] = \frac{\mathbf{E}\left[S\right]}{1 - \rho}.$$

Note: The mean length of the busy period is the same regardless of the service order in the M/G/1 so long as the service order is work-conserving.

Question: What is $\mathbf{E}$ [# times our tagged job gets interrupted]?

Answer: Because our job has size x, the expected number of times it will be interrupted is just λx, the expected number of arrivals during time x.

Let Wasted-Time(x) refer to the time the tagged job is in the system but not serving.

$$\mathbf{E}\left[\text{Wasted-Time}(x)\right] = \mathbf{E}\left[\text{# times tagged job is interrupted}\right] \cdot \mathbf{E}\left[\text{length of interruption}\right]$$

$$= \lambda x \cdot \frac{\mathbf{E}\left[S\right]}{1 - \rho}$$

$$= \frac{\rho x}{1 - \rho}$$

$$\mathbf{E}\left[T(x)\right] = x + \mathbf{E}\left[\text{Wasted-Time}(x)\right] = x + \frac{\rho x}{1 - \rho} = \frac{x}{1 - \rho}$$

$$\mathbf{E}\left[\text{Slowdown}(x)\right] = \frac{1}{1 - \rho}$$

Thus although the PLCFS policy looks very different from PS, its mean performance is the same as for PS – even its mean performance on jobs of size x. We have now completed the proof of Theorem 30.6.

Question: Can you see any advantage to using PLCFS over PS?

Answer: PLCFS offers the same expected performance with many fewer preemptions.

Question: Exactly how many preemptions will we have under PLCFS?

Answer: Each job creates two preemptions – one when it arrives and one when it departs. Thus we have only two preemptions per job in PLCFS, whereas in a real-world implementation of PS, with small quantum sizes, the number of preemptions can be much higher. If preemptions actually have a cost, then PLCFS wastes less time doing them, as compared with PS.

30.3 FB Scheduling

So far, all the preemptive non-size-based scheduling policies we have seen produce the same mean slowdown for all job sizes:

$$\mathbf{E}\left[\text{Slowdown}(x)\right] = \frac{1}{1 - \rho}$$

Wouldn't it be nice if we could somehow get lower slowdowns for the smaller jobs, so that we could drop our mean slowdown?

Question: But how can we give preference to the smaller jobs if we do not know job size?

Answer: We *do* know a job's age (the service it has received so far), and age is an indication of the job's remaining CPU demand.

If the job size distribution has DFR (decreasing failure rate), as does the Pareto distribution, then the greater the job's age, the greater its expected remaining demand. So we should give preference to jobs with low age (younger jobs), and this will have the effect of giving preference to jobs that we expect to finish quickly.

UNIX does this using Multi-Level Processor-Sharing (MLPS), also called Foreground-Background scheduling. There are two queues served by the same one server, where queue 1 is high priority and queue 2 is low priority. All jobs start out in queue 1. Jobs in queue 1 are run using PS. When a job hits a certain age a, it is moved to queue 2. Jobs in queue 2 get service only when queue 1 is empty.

We will study this idea in the limit as the number of queues goes to infinity. This limiting algorithm is called **Generalized Foreground-Background (FB) scheduling** and is defined as follows:

- The job with the lowest CPU age gets the CPU to itself.
- If several jobs have same lowest CPU age, they share the CPU using PS.

This algorithm is known in the literature both under the name FB and under the name Least-Attained-Service (LAS).

Question: Consider the following arrival sequence:

- At time 0, a job (customer) of size 3 arrives.
- At time 1, a job (customer) of size 2 arrives.
- At time 2, a job (customer) of size 1 arrives.

When will each of these complete under FB?

Answer: The size 1 job leaves at time 3; the size 2 job leaves at time 5; and the size 3 job leaves at time 6, as shown in Figure 30.2.

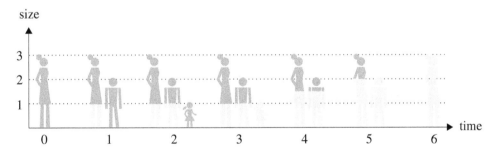

Figure 30.2. State of system at several points in time under FB scheduling. As jobs (customers) are worked on, they start to "disappear." When a job becomes "invisible," it departs.

The performance improvement of FB over PS obviously has to do with how good a predictor age is of remaining size, which depends on the distribution of job sizes. Our goal is to compute $\mathbf{E}\left[T(x)\right]^{\text{FB}}$. Before we start, let's work through a small mathematical exercise that will come in handy later.

Let $f(y)$ be the probability density function (p.d.f.) for our size distribution. Define $f_{\overline{x}}(y)$ to be the p.d.f. for the transformed size distribution, where each job of size $> x$ has been replaced by a job of size x, as shown in Figure 30.3.

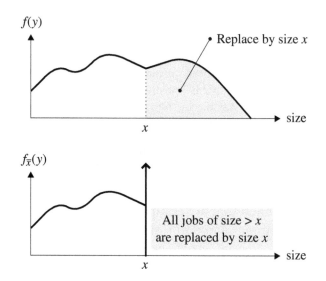

Figure 30.3. Original p.d.f., $f(y)$, and the transformed p.d.f., $f_{\overline{x}}(y)$.

If $S_{\overline{x}}$ denotes the job size under the transformed distribution, then

$$\mathbf{E}\left[S_{\overline{x}}\right] = \int_0^x yf(y)dy + x(1 - F(x)) \overset{\left(\substack{\text{integration} \\ \text{by parts}}\right)}{=} \int_0^x \overline{F}(y)dy.$$

$$\mathbf{E}\left[S_{\overline{x}}^m\right] = \int_0^x y^n f(y)dy + x^n(1 - F(x)) \overset{\left(\substack{\text{integration} \\ \text{by parts}}\right)}{=} \int_0^x y^{n-1}\overline{F}(y)dy.$$

$$\text{Utilization}: \rho_{\overline{x}} = \lambda\mathbf{E}\left[S_{\overline{x}}\right].$$

Now let us return to the problem of deriving $\mathbf{E}\left[T(x)\right]^{\text{FB}}$. Let *job x* denote a job of size x. To derive $\mathbf{E}\left[T(x)\right]^{\text{FB}}$, think about all the units of work that have to get done before job x can leave the system:

(1) x units (this is just the size of job x).

(2) The expected remaining work in the system when job x arrives, *except that* in doing this computation we need to pretend that every job in the system has a service requirement no more than x. That is, every job of size $> x$ is assumed to have size x, for the purpose of computing the remaining work in the system when job x arrives. To understand this, realize that from job x's viewpoint, a job j with size $> x$ looks exactly like it has size x, because once job j reaches age x it will never again affect job x. So in totaling the expected remaining work in

the system that will affect job x, we need to shrink each job's size to x. If a job has already reached age $\geq x$, we just ignore that job, because it will not receive service until after job x completes.

(3) The expected work due to new arrivals while job x is in the system, where again jobs are counted only by how much they can affect job x.

We use $S_{\overline{x}}$ in determining quantities (2) and (3) in $\mathbf{E}\left[T(x)\right]^{\text{FB}}$:

Derivation of (2): Item (2) basically says that when job x arrives into the system, it looks at all jobs through "transformer glasses" (see Figure 30.4), which "decapitate" each job of size $> x$ to form to a job of size x. Then we total the remaining work in the transformed system.

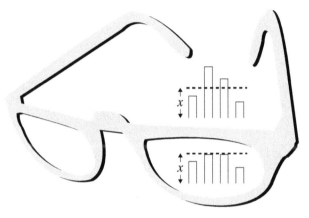

Figure 30.4. Transformer glasses for FB.

Claim 30.7 *If the queue is using FB scheduling, then the remaining work in the suddenly transformed system is the same as if we had simply transformed each job at the instant it arrived to the system.*

Proof Let system A be the original system, no transformations. Let system B be a system where each job is transformed the instant it arrives. Whenever system B is working, system A is also working on a job of age $< x$. The only time system A is working on a job of age $> x$ is when both (i) system B is idle and (ii) all jobs in system A have age $> x$. Thus, if we walked up to system A at any moment and suddenly put on our transformer glasses, system A would look just like system B. ∎

Thus, (2) is asking for the remaining work in a system doing FB scheduling where each job is transformed immediately on arrival. In other words, (2) is asking for the remaining work in an FB system where the job size is $S_{\overline{x}}$.

Question: But what is the remaining work in such a system?

Answer: Remember, the remaining work in any work-conserving system is the same as any other, so we may as well ask what is the expected remaining work in a M/G/1/FCFS where the job size is $S_{\bar{x}}$. But this is simply

$$\mathbf{E}\left[\text{Remaining work in M/G/1/FCFS}\right] = \mathbf{E}\left[T_Q\right]^{\text{M/G/1/FCFS}} = \frac{\lambda \mathbf{E}\left[S_{\bar{x}}^2\right]}{2(1 - \rho_{\bar{x}})}.$$

So

$$(2) = \frac{\lambda \mathbf{E}\left[S_{\bar{x}}^2\right]}{2(1 - \rho_{\bar{x}})}.$$

Derivation of (3): To derive (3), observe that

$$(3) = \mathbf{E}\left[\text{\# arrivals during } T(x)\right] \cdot \mathbf{E}\left[\text{size of arrivals as viewed by job } x\right]$$
$$= \lambda \mathbf{E}\left[T(x)\right]^{\text{FB}} \mathbf{E}\left[S_{\bar{x}}\right].$$

So,

$$\mathbf{E}\left[T(x)\right]^{\text{FB}} = (1) + (2) + (3)$$

$$= x + \frac{\lambda \mathbf{E}\left[S_{\bar{x}}^2\right]}{2(1 - \rho_{\bar{x}})} + \lambda \mathbf{E}\left[T(x)\right]^{\text{FB}} \mathbf{E}\left[S_{\bar{x}}\right]$$

$$= x + \frac{\lambda \mathbf{E}\left[S_{\bar{x}}^2\right]}{2(1 - \rho_{\bar{x}})} + \rho_{\bar{x}} \mathbf{E}\left[T(x)\right]^{\text{FB}}.$$

Now collecting the $\mathbf{E}\left[T(x)\right]^{\text{FB}}$ terms together we have

$$\mathbf{E}\left[T(x)\right]^{\text{FB}} (1 - \rho_{\bar{x}}) = x + \frac{\lambda \mathbf{E}\left[S_{\bar{x}}^2\right]}{2(1 - \rho_{\bar{x}})}.$$

So

$$\mathbf{E}\left[T(x)\right]^{\text{FB}} = \frac{x + \frac{\lambda \mathbf{E}\left[S_{\bar{x}}^2\right]}{2(1 - \rho_{\bar{x}})}}{1 - \rho_{\bar{x}}} \tag{30.5}$$

$$= \frac{x(1 - \rho_{\bar{x}}) + \frac{1}{2}\lambda \mathbf{E}\left[S_{\bar{x}}^2\right]}{(1 - \rho_{\bar{x}})^2}. \tag{30.6}$$

Expression (30.5) gives us another way of thinking about $\mathbf{E}\left[T(x)\right]^{\text{FB}}$ – as the mean length of a busy period. Consider a busy period started by only the job itself (x) plus the "relevant" work that it finds in the system when it arrives $\left(\frac{\lambda \mathbf{E}\left[S_{\bar{x}}^2\right]}{2(1 - \rho_{\bar{x}})}\right)$, where all jobs arriving during the busy period have job sizes $S_{\bar{x}}$. Then (30.5) is the mean length of that busy period (see Section 27.2).

Several interesting results regarding FB will be explored in the exercises:

- If the job size distribution has DFR, then younger jobs have lower remaining service times, so

$$\mathbf{E}\left[T\right]^{\text{FB}} < \mathbf{E}\left[T\right]^{\text{PS}}$$

as expected; see [189] for a formal proof.

- If the job size distribution has increasing failure rate (IFR), then younger jobs have higher remaining service time, so favoring the younger jobs (as FB does) is bad and

$$\mathbf{E}\left[T\right]^{\text{FB}} > \mathbf{E}\left[T\right]^{\text{PS}}$$

as expected.

- If the job size distribution has constant failure rate (Exponentially distributed), then remaining time is independent of age, so we might expect that

$$\mathbf{E}\left[T\right]^{\text{FB}} = \mathbf{E}\left[T\right]^{\text{PS}}.$$

In Exercise 30.3, you will prove this equality for the Exponential distribution.

- Also for an Exponential job size distribution, we will see in Exercise 30.2 that

$$\mathbf{E}\left[\text{Slowdown}\right]^{\text{FB}} < \mathbf{E}\left[\text{Slowdown}\right]^{\text{PS}}.$$

Question: Why would the slowdown under FB, under an Exponential job size distribution, be strictly smaller than under PS, although their mean response times are equal?

Answer: Here is a heuristic argument: Under an Exponential workload, age is independent of remaining time. So, biasing toward jobs with small ages does not favor jobs with small *remaining* service requirement, and remaining service requirement is what affects $\mathbf{E}\left[T\right]$. However, biasing toward jobs with small ages does slightly favor jobs with smaller expected original size. So FB is in essence giving slight preference to short jobs even under the Exponential distribution, and this is what improves $\mathbf{E}\left[\text{Slowdown}\right]$.

30.4 Readings

Athough the M/G/1/PS has simple solutions for $\mathbf{E}\left[T\right]$ and $\mathbf{E}\left[T(x)\right]$, the variance of response time, $\mathbf{Var}(T)$, is far more difficult to analyze and is not known in a simple closed form. For those interested in learning more, a good place to start is the survey paper by Yashkov and Yashkova [197]. There are also many variants of PS in the literature, which allow for time-sharing with different weights, including Discriminatory Processor-Sharing (DPS) and Generalized Processor-Sharing (GPS). A survey of these and other variants is given in [1].

Foreground-Background (FB) scheduling, also known as Least-Attained-Service (LAS), has received a lot of attention, both analytically and from a practical perspective. On the analytical front, we recommend the thesis by Misja Nuijens [133] and [143]. On the implementation front, FB has been used for IP flow scheduling; see [144, 142].

Policies like PS and FB that do not make use of size are sometimes called *blind*; see [60]. Additional references on all these scheduling policies can be found in Adam Wierman's thesis [188].

30.5 Exercises

30.1 Review of Scheduling Formulas

Match each of the following 12 expressions to *one* of the formulas (a) through (g). Read the glossary to make sure you understand all the expressions.

(1) $\mathbf{E}\left[T\right]^{\text{M/G/1/FCFS}}$

(2) $\mathbf{E}\left[T\right]^{\text{M/G/1/PS}}$

(3) $\mathbf{E}\left[T\right]^{\text{M/G/1/LCFS}}$

(4) $\mathbf{E}\left[T\right]^{\text{M/G/1/PLCFS}}$

(5) $\mathbf{E}\left[T\right]^{\text{M/M/1/FCFS}}$

(6) $\mathbf{E}\left[T\right]^{\text{M/M/1/PS}}$

(7) $\mathbf{E}\left[T\right]^{\text{M/M/1/FB}}$

(8) ρ

(9) $\mathbf{E}\left[B\right]^{\text{M/G/1/FCFS}}$

(10) $\mathbf{E}\left[B\right]^{\text{M/M/1/FCFS}}$

(11) $\mathbf{E}\left[S_e\right]$

(12) $\mathbf{E}\left[W\right]^{\text{M/G/1/FCFS}}$

Formulas:

(a) $\lambda\mathbf{E}\left[S\right]$ (b) $\frac{\mathbf{E}\left[S^2\right]}{2\mathbf{E}[S]}$ (c) $\frac{\mathbf{E}[S]}{1-\rho}$ (d) $\frac{\rho}{1-\rho}\mathbf{E}\left[S_e\right]$ (e) $\frac{\rho}{1-\rho}\mathbf{E}\left[S_e\right]+\mathbf{E}\left[S\right]$

(f) $\frac{\mathbf{E}[S_e]}{1-\rho}$ (g) None of the above

Glossary:

ρ = load = fraction of time server is busy

T = response time

B = busy period duration

λ = average arrival rate

S = service requirement for jobs

S_e = excess of S

W = work seen by an arrival into the queue

30.2 Comparison of FB and PS Scheduling Policies

Consider an M/G/1 server with load $\rho = 0.8$. Consider two job size distributions:

(a) Exponential distribution with mean 3,000

(b) Bounded Pareto distribution $BP(k = 332.067, p = 10^{10}, \alpha = 1.1)$ with mean 3,000

For each distribution, compute $\mathbf{E}\left[T\right]$ and $\mathbf{E}\left[\text{Slowdown}\right]$ under both FB and PS scheduling. Use a symbolic math package to do the computations.[1]

30.3 FB versus PS under Exponential Workloads

In Exercise 30.2 you should have found that the mean response time under FB and under PS was the same if the job size distribution was Exponential. In the chapter, we gave intuition for why this might be true. Prove formally that this should be the case. [Hint: There is an ugly long proof and a very beautiful short proof.]

30.4 Starvation under FB

Consider an M/G/1 server with load $\rho = 0.8$. Consider two job size distributions:

---

[1] The following link provides all the functions that you will need already coded for use with Mathematica™: http://www.cs.cmu.edu/~harchol/PerformanceModeling/software.html.

(a) Exponential distribution with mean 3,000.
(b) Bounded Pareto distribution, $BP(k = 332.067, p = 10^{10}, \alpha = 1.1)$, with mean 3,000.

The FB policy favors small jobs (or those that are expected to be small). In this way it improves on the performance of PS. However, there is a fear that this benefit may come at the cost of causing large jobs to suffer unfairly. In this problem, we compare the mean slowdown of large jobs under FB and under PS to study the effect of this unfairness. You will need to use a symbolic math package (use the link in Footnote 1).

(a) Compare the mean slowdown of a job in the 90th percentile under FB and under PS.
(b) Compare the mean slowdown of a job in the 99th percentile under FB and under PS.
(c) What is the first percentile where a job does worse under FB than under PS?
(d) Explain why so few jobs suffer under FB.

30.5 Analysis of Preemptive-LCFS

This question develops a clearer understanding of PLCFS.

(a) Determine the Laplace transform for time in system under PLCFS, $\widetilde{T}(s)^{\text{PLCFS}}$. Follow exactly the approach we used in the chapter where we first consider the response time of a job of size x and then look at how many times that job gets interrupted and what the contribution of each such interruption looks like.
(b) Use this transform to determine the first 2 moments of response time.
(c) You should notice something very simple about your transform. It should look identical to a transform that you derived recently. This will give you a new way of looking at PLCFS. Explain why this alternative, simpler, view of PLCFS is also correct.

30.6 M/G/1/FB Transform

In this chapter we derived the mean response time for FB. Use the same arguments to derive the transform of response time.

30.7 Database Performance

Bianca observes that her database throughput drops when she runs too many transactions concurrently (this is typically due to thrashing). She also observes that if she runs too few transactions concurrently, her database throughput drops as well (this is often due to insufficient parallelism). To capture these effects, Bianca models her time-sharing database system as an M/M/1/PS queue with load-dependent service rate, $\mu(n)$, where n denotes the number of concurrent transactions. The function $\mu(n)$ is shown in Figure 30.5.

(a) Solve for the mean response time under Bianca's M/M/1/PS system. Assume arrival rate $\lambda = 0.9$. [Hint: Use a Markov chain.]
(b) Bianca has a great idea: Rather than allow all transactions into the database as before, she decides to allow at most 4 transactions to run concurrently in the database, where all remaining transactions are held in a FCFS queue. Bianca's new queueing architecture is shown in Figure 30.6. Compute the mean response time for Bianca's new architecture, again assuming

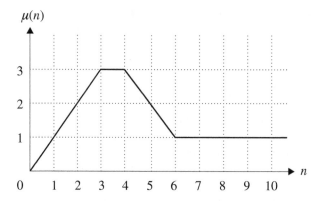

Figure 30.5. Service rate in the database changes depending on number of concurrent transactions, n, staying constant at 1 for $n \geq 6$. Ignore non-integral values of n.

$\lambda = 0.9$, and Exponentially distributed service times with rates from Figure 30.5. What is the intuition behind Bianca's hybrid FCFS/PS architecture?

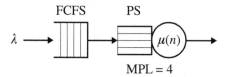

Figure 30.6. Processor-Sharing with limited multiprogramming level, MPL $= 4$.

(c) Varun suggests that if the job size distribution is highly variable (much more variable than an Exponential), it may be better to increase the MPL to more than 4, even though that causes the service rate to drop. What is the intuition behind Varun's suggestion? [Hint: Observe that Bianca's FCFS/PS architecture has some properties of FCFS and some properties of PS.]

If you would like to learn more about analyzing the limited Processor-Sharing system in Figure 30.6, we recommend [77, 198, 199].

Scheduling: Non-Preemptive, Size-Based Policies

Until now, we have only considered scheduling policies that do not have any knowledge of the job sizes. In this chapter and the next two chapters, we will look at size-based scheduling policies, starting with non-preemptive size-based policies (this chapter) and followed by preemptive size-based policies (next two chapters). The size-based policies that we will be studying include the following:

SJF – (non-preemptive) Shortest-Job-First (Chapter 31)

PSJF – Preemptive-Shortest-Job-First (Chapter 32)

SRPT – (preemptive) Shortest-Remaining-Processing-Time (Chapter 33)

It will be convenient to evaluate these size-based policies as special cases of *priority queueing,* so we start by analyzing priority queues, which are important in their own right.

Size-based scheduling is a very important topic, which is why we devote three chapters to it. The proper size-based scheduling policy can greatly improve the performance of a system. It costs nothing to alter your scheduling policy (no money, no new hardware), so the performance gain comes for free. The above size-based policies are implemented in real systems. For web servers serving static content, SRPT scheduling has been implemented in the Linux kernel to schedule HTTP requests [92]. It has also been used to combat transient overload in web servers [162]. Priority queues are likewise prevalent in computer systems. Prioritization of jobs is used in databases to provide differentiated levels of service, whereby high-priority transactions (those that bring in lots of money) are given priority over low-priority transactions (those that are less lucrative). Prioritization can be implemented in different ways in database servers, sometimes internally by scheduling the database lock queues, and sometimes externally by limiting the multiprogramming level in the database to favor high-priority transactions; see [123, 164, 163] and the references therein.

31.1 Priority Queueing

We now describe a model for an M/G/1 priority queue. Arriving jobs are divided into n priority classes, where class 1 is the highest priority and class n is the lowest priority. Class k job arrivals form a Poisson process with rate $\lambda_k = \lambda \cdot p_k$, where $\sum_{k=1}^{n} p_k = 1$. The service time distribution for a job of class k has moments $\mathbf{E}[S_k]$ and $\mathbf{E}[S_k^2]$.

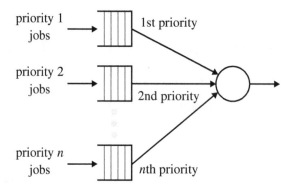

Figure 31.1. When a server frees up, it takes the job at the head of the highest priority, non-empty queue.

We can picture the M/G/1 priority queue as maintaining a separate (imaginary) queue for each class. When the server becomes free, it always chooses the job at the head of the highest priority non-empty queue to work on, as shown in Figure 31.1.

We consider two types of priority queueing:

1. **Non-Preemptive Priority Queueing** – Once a job starts running, it cannot be preempted, even if a higher priority job comes along.
2. **Preemptive Priority Queueing** – The job in service is preempted if a higher priority job arrives, and the higher priority job is then served. No work is lost.

Question: What are some examples where non-preemptive priority queueing is used and where preemptive priority queueing is used?

Answer: Non-preemptive priority queueing is used whenever a job cannot be stopped once it has started running. For example, airline ticket counters want to ticket the first-class customers before the coach customers, but once they start ticketing a coach customer, they cannot stop midway if a first-class customer arrives.

Preemptive priority queueing is often used for job scheduling in computer systems. Interactive jobs get precedence over batch jobs and can preempt a running batch job.

Notation

We always write the priority in parentheses. Class 1 jobs have highest priority; class 2 next highest priority, etc. Class n jobs have lowest priority.

As you can probably guess, priority will eventually become related to size; a job's size will be its priority, where a job of size x has priority over a job of size y if $x < y$, for real-valued x and y.

$$S_k = \text{size of priority } k \text{ job}$$
$$\mathbf{E}\left[N_Q(k)\right] = \text{average number of priority } k \text{ jobs in the queue}$$
$$\mathbf{E}\left[T_Q(k)\right] = \text{average time in queue for priority } k \text{ jobs}$$

$$\mathbf{E}\left[T(k)\right] = \text{average time in system for priority } k \text{ jobs}$$

$$\lambda_k = \lambda \cdot p_k = \text{average arrival rate of jobs of priority } k$$

$$\rho_k = \lambda_k \mathbf{E}\left[S_k\right] = \text{contribution to the load due to jobs of priority } k$$

We will require that the server utilization, ρ, is less than 1:

$$\sum_{i=1}^{n} \rho_i = \sum_{i=1}^{n} \lambda_i \mathbf{E}\left[S_i\right] = \sum_{i=1}^{n} \lambda \cdot p_i \mathbf{E}\left[S_i\right] = \lambda \mathbf{E}\left[S\right] = \rho < 1 .$$

Note that S, as usual, represents an arbitrary job's size. Hence,

$$\mathbf{E}\left[S\right] = \sum_{k=1}^{n} p_k \mathbf{E}\left[S_k\right] \quad ; \quad \mathbf{E}\left[S^2\right] = \sum_{k=1}^{n} p_k \mathbf{E}\left[S_k^2\right] \quad ; \quad \mathbf{E}\left[S_e\right] = \mathbf{E}\left[S^2\right] / \mathbf{E}\left[S\right]^2$$

31.2 Non-Preemptive Priority

We will use a "tagged-job" type of argument to derive the performance of a non-preemptive M/G/1 priority queue. It will help greatly to review the "tagged-job" argument for the M/G/1/FCFS queue from Chapter 23 before reading this section.

Deriving $T_Q(1)$ – Time in Queue for Jobs of Priority 1

Consider a priority 1 arrival. That arrival has to wait for both

  (i) The job currently in service, if there is one.
 (ii) All jobs of priority 1 in queue when the job arrives.

$$\mathbf{E}\left[T_Q(1)\right] = \mathbf{P}\left\{\text{Server busy}\right\} \cdot \mathbf{E}\left[S_e\right] + \mathbf{E}\left[N_Q(1)\right] \cdot \mathbf{E}\left[S_1\right]$$

$$= \rho \cdot \mathbf{E}\left[S_e\right] + \mathbf{E}\left[T_Q(1)\right] \cdot \lambda_1 \cdot \mathbf{E}\left[S_1\right]$$

$$= \rho \cdot \mathbf{E}\left[S_e\right] + \mathbf{E}\left[T_Q(1)\right] \cdot \rho_1$$

$$= \frac{\rho \cdot \mathbf{E}\left[S_e\right]}{1 - \rho_1}$$

Deriving $T_Q(2)$ – Time in Queue for Jobs of Priority 2

Consider a priority 2 arrival. That arrival has to wait for

  (i) The job currently in service, if there is one.
 (ii) All jobs of priority 1 or 2 in queue when the job arrives.
(iii) All jobs of priority 1 that arrive while the new job is waiting (not in service).

$$\mathbf{E}\left[T_Q(2)\right] = \rho \cdot \mathbf{E}\left[S_e\right] + \mathbf{E}\left[N_Q(1)\right] \cdot \mathbf{E}\left[S_1\right] + \mathbf{E}\left[N_Q(2)\right] \cdot \mathbf{E}\left[S_2\right]$$

$$+ \mathbf{E}\left[T_Q(2)\right] \cdot \lambda_1 \mathbf{E}\left[S_1\right]$$

$$= \rho \cdot \mathbf{E}\left[S_e\right] + \mathbf{E}\left[T_Q(1)\right] \cdot \rho_1 + \mathbf{E}\left[T_Q(2)\right] \cdot \rho_2 + \mathbf{E}\left[T_Q(2)\right] \cdot \rho_1$$

$$\mathbf{E}\left[T_Q(2)\right] \cdot (1 - \rho_1 - \rho_2) = \rho \mathbf{E}\left[S_e\right] + \rho_1 \cdot \mathbf{E}\left[T_Q(1)\right]$$

$$\mathbf{E}\left[T_Q(2)\right] \cdot (1 - \rho_1 - \rho_2) = \rho \mathbf{E}\left[S_e\right] + \rho_1 \cdot \frac{\rho \mathbf{E}\left[S_e\right]}{1 - \rho_1} = \frac{\rho \mathbf{E}\left[S_e\right]}{(1 - \rho_1)}$$

$$\mathbf{E}\left[T_Q(2)\right] = \frac{\rho \mathbf{E}\left[S_e\right]}{(1 - \rho_1)(1 - \rho_1 - \rho_2)}$$

Deriving $T_Q(k)$ – Time in Queue for Jobs of Priority k

Consider a priority k arrival. That arrival has to wait for

(i)   The job currently in service, if there is one.
(ii) All jobs of priority $1, 2, \ldots, k$ in queue when the job arrives.
(iii) All jobs of priority $1, 2, \ldots, k - 1$ that arrive while the new job is waiting.

After some algebra, we can show by induction that

$$\mathbf{E}\left[T_Q(k)\right]^{\text{NP-Priority}} = \frac{\rho \mathbf{E}\left[S_e\right]}{\left(1 - \sum_{i=1}^{k} \rho_i\right)\left(1 - \sum_{i=1}^{k-1} \rho_i\right)}.$$

Finally, substituting in the formula for $\mathbf{E}\left[S_e\right]$, from (23.9), we have

$$\mathbf{E}\left[T_Q(k)\right]^{\text{NP-Priority}} = \frac{\rho \frac{\mathbf{E}[S^2]}{2\mathbf{E}[S]}}{\left(1 - \sum_{i=1}^{k} \rho_i\right)\left(1 - \sum_{i=1}^{k-1} \rho_i\right)}. \tag{31.1}$$

Interpreting the Formula for $\mathbf{E}\left[T_Q(k)\right]^{\text{NP-Priority}}$

Question: Explain the difference between the formula for $\mathbf{E}\left[T_Q(k)\right]^{\text{NP-Priority}}$ and the formula for $\mathbf{E}\left[T_Q\right]^{\text{FCFS}}$.

Answer: Recall that for the M/G/1/FCFS queue

$$\mathbf{E}\left[T_Q\right]^{\text{FCFS}} = \frac{\rho \frac{\mathbf{E}[S^2]}{2\mathbf{E}[S]}}{1 - \rho}.$$

Recall in the tagged job analysis for the M/G/1/FCFS queue that the numerator, $\rho \frac{\mathbf{E}[S^2]}{2\mathbf{E}[S]}$, is due to waiting for the job in service. Specifically, this numerator represents the probability that there is a job in service (ρ) multiplied by the expected remaining time on that job given that there is a job in service ($\mathbf{E}\left[S_e\right] = \frac{\mathbf{E}[S^2]}{2\mathbf{E}[S]}$). This is also the case in the numerator for the M/G/1/NP-Priority queue.

Recall next that in the M/G/1/FCFS queue, the denominator, $1 - \rho$, is due to waiting for the jobs already in the queue. In the M/G/1/NP-Priority formula, the denominator has two components. The

$$\left(1 - \sum_{i=1}^{k} \rho_i\right)$$

term can be thought of as the contribution due to waiting for jobs in the queue of higher or equal priority. Observe that a job of class k only needs to wait behind those jobs in the queue of class up to k. The

$$\left(1 - \sum_{i=1}^{k-1} \rho_i\right)$$

term can be thought of as the contribution due to those jobs that arrive after our job, but have strictly higher priority than our tagged job (i.e., jobs of class 1 to $k-1$ arriving after our job). This second part of the denominator obviously does not occur under FCFS.

Question: Now compare what happens to high-priority jobs (low k) under non-preemptive priority queueing versus under FCFS.

Hint:

$$\mathbf{E}\left[T_Q(k)\right]^{\text{NP-Priority}} \approx \frac{1}{(1 - \sum_{i=1}^{k} \rho_i)^2} \cdot \frac{\rho \mathbf{E}\left[S^2\right]}{2\mathbf{E}\left[S\right]}.$$

$$\mathbf{E}\left[T_Q(k)\right]^{\text{FCFS}} = \mathbf{E}\left[T_Q\right]^{\text{FCFS}} = \frac{1}{1 - \rho} \cdot \frac{\rho \mathbf{E}\left[S^2\right]}{2\mathbf{E}\left[S\right]}.$$

Answer: The $\mathbf{E}\left[T_Q(k)\right]^{\text{NP-Priority}}$ formula has the disadvantage of the squared denominator, due to having to wait behind later arrivals. However it has the advantage of only seeing load due to jobs of class k or less. Here is the point: Suppose k is low (i.e., we have a high-priority job). Then,

$$\sum_{i=1}^{k} \rho_i \ll \rho.$$

So

$$\mathbf{E}\left[T_Q(k)\right]^{\text{NP-Priority}} < \mathbf{E}\left[T_Q\right]^{\text{FCFS}}.$$

Now let's suppose that the job's priority is related to its size, where the smaller the job is, the higher its priority. Recall that if the service time distribution has the heavy-tail property, then the largest 1% of the jobs make up most of the load. Thus, even for higher values of k (but not the max k) we have that

$$\sum_{i=1}^{k} \rho_i \ll \rho.$$

So

$$\mathbf{E}\left[T_Q(k)\right]^{\text{NP-Priority}} < \mathbf{E}\left[T_Q\right]^{\text{FCFS}},$$

even for higher values of k. Of course, for a job of class n, NP-Priority is worse than FCFS, because of the squared term in the denominator.

Question: How do we get $\mathbf{E}\left[T_Q\right]^{\text{NP-Priority}}$, given $\mathbf{E}\left[T_Q(k)\right]$?

Answer:

$$\mathbf{E}\left[T_Q\right]^{\text{NP-Priority}} = \sum_{k=1}^{n} \mathbf{E}\left[T_Q(k)\right] \cdot p_k = \sum_{k=1}^{n} \mathbf{E}\left[T_Q(k)\right] \cdot \frac{\lambda_k}{\lambda}.$$

31.3 Shortest-Job-First (SJF)

One way of assigning priorities is as a function of the job size.

Question: If your goal is minimizing mean response time, which do you think should have higher priority: the large jobs or the small ones?

Answer: The small ones. See Exercise 31.1.

Shortest-Job-First (SJF) is a non-preemptive scheduling policy (once a job is running, it is never interrupted). Whenever the server is free, it chooses to work on the job with the *smallest size*.

Question: How can we analyze the performance of SJF given what we have just seen?

Answer: We can use our results for non-preemptive priority queueing. We model SJF by having an infinite number of priority classes, where the smaller the job, the higher its priority.

Analysis of SJF

Consider again the situation of n priority classes. Let's assume that the job sizes range between $x_0 = 0$ and x_n. Define boundary points $x_1, x_2, \ldots x_{n-1}$ such that

$$x_0 < x_1 < x_2 < \cdots < x_{n-1} < x_n.$$

Assign all jobs of size $\in (x_{k-1}, x_k)$ to class k, as shown in Figure 31.2. Then,

$$\mathbf{E}\left[T_Q(k)\right]^{\text{NP-Priority}} = \frac{\rho \mathbf{E}\left[S^2\right]}{2\mathbf{E}\left[S\right]} \cdot \frac{1}{\left(1 - \sum_{i=1}^{k-1} \rho_i\right)\left(1 - \sum_{i=1}^{k} \rho_i\right)}$$

where $\mathbf{E}\left[T_Q\right]^{\text{NP-Priority}} = \sum_{k=1}^{n} p_k \cdot \mathbf{E}\left[T_Q(k)\right].$

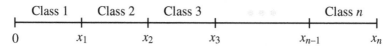

Figure 31.2. Defining classes based on job size.

Observe that p_k, the fraction of jobs in class k, equals $F(x_k) - F(x_{k-1})$, where $F(x_n) = 1$, and $F(x_0) = 0$. So far we have not used anything but the original NP-Priority formulas.

Now consider the situation where $n \to \infty$ and $x_k - x_{k-1} \to 0$. That is, the number of classes, n, is allowed to grow to ∞, in such a way that $(x_k - x_{k-1})$ becomes arbitrarily small $\forall k$.

We are interested in the expected waiting time for a job of size x_k. As $n \to \infty$,

Load of jobs in class 1 to k $\to$ Load of jobs of size $< x_k$

$$\sum_{i=1}^{k} \rho_i = \lambda \sum_{i=1}^{k} p_i \mathbf{E}[S_i] \to \lambda \int_{t=0}^{x_k} tf(t)dt.$$

Load of jobs in class 1 to $k-1$ $\to$ Load of jobs of size $< x_{k-1}$

$$\sum_{i=1}^{k-1} \rho_i = \lambda \sum_{i=1}^{k-1} p_i \mathbf{E}[S_i] \to \lambda \int_{t=0}^{x_{k-1}} tf(t)dt \to \lambda \int_{t=0}^{x_k} tf(t)dt.$$

So,

$$\mathbf{E}[T_Q(x)]^{\text{SJF}} = \frac{\rho \mathbf{E}[S^2]}{2\mathbf{E}[S]} \cdot \frac{1}{(1 - \lambda \int_{t=0}^{x} tf(t)dt)^2}. \tag{31.2}$$

And

$$\mathbf{E}[T_Q]^{\text{SJF}} = \int_{x=0}^{x_n} \mathbf{E}[T_Q(x)] f(x)dx$$

$$= \frac{\rho \mathbf{E}[S^2]}{2\mathbf{E}[S]} \cdot \int_{x=0}^{x_n} \frac{f(x)dx}{(1 - \lambda \int_{t=0}^{x} tf(t)dt)^2}. \tag{31.3}$$

Now, let's compare SJF with FCFS for a job of size x. To do this, we first need to define a term.

Definition 31.1 Let

$$\rho_x = \lambda \int_{t=0}^{x} tf(t)dt. \tag{31.4}$$

The term ρ_x denotes the load composed of jobs of size 0 to x. Note that we can express ρ_x equivalently as

$$\rho_x = \lambda F(x) \int_{t=0}^{x} t \frac{f(t)}{F(x)} dt, \tag{31.5}$$

which shows more explicitly that we are multiplying the arrival rate of jobs of size no more than x, namely $\lambda F(x)$, by the expected size of jobs of size no more than x, namely $\int_{t=0}^{x} t \frac{f(t)}{F(x)} dt$.

Note: ρ_x is different from $\rho_{\bar{x}}$, which we saw in the FB policy analysis.

Rewriting (31.2) using ρ_x, we have

$$\mathbf{E}\left[T_Q\left(x\right)\right]^{\text{SJF}} = \frac{\rho\mathbf{E}\left[S^2\right]}{2\mathbf{E}\left[S\right]} \cdot \frac{1}{\left(1 - \rho_x\right)^2}.$$

By comparison we have, for FCFS:

$$\mathbf{E}\left[T_Q\left(x\right)\right]^{\text{FCFS}} = \frac{\rho\mathbf{E}\left[S^2\right]}{2\mathbf{E}\left[S\right]} \cdot \frac{1}{1 - \rho}.$$

Observe that ρ_x is typically much less than ρ. For small jobs (small x), $\mathbf{E}\left[T_Q\left(x\right)\right]^{\text{SJF}}$ should be lower than $\mathbf{E}\left[T_Q\left(x\right)\right]^{\text{FCFS}}$. For very large jobs, $\mathbf{E}\left[T_Q\left(x\right)\right]^{\text{SJF}}$ is higher than $\mathbf{E}\left[T_Q\left(x\right)\right]^{\text{FCFS}}$ because of the squared factor in the denominator. If the service time distribution is heavy-tailed, then $\mathbf{E}\left[T_Q\left(x\right)\right]^{\text{SJF}}$ is only higher for the *very, very* large jobs. Because most jobs are small,

$$\mathbf{E}\left[T_Q\right]^{\text{SJF}} < \mathbf{E}\left[T_Q\right]^{\text{FCFS}}.$$

31.4 The Problem with Non-Preemptive Policies

Question: Nonetheless, we claim that SJF is still a poor choice of scheduling policies in the case of a heavy-tailed job size distribution, when trying to minimize mean time in queue. Why is this?

Answer: The expression for mean time in queue contains an $\mathbf{E}\left[S^2\right]$ term, and in heavy-tailed job size distributions, the variance is huge! It would be much better to use a scheduling policy whose mean delay does not involve an $\mathbf{E}\left[S^2\right]$ term. For example, we might use the PS, PLCFS, or FB policies that we discussed in the last chapter.

Question: What about the mean time in queue for really small jobs?

Answer: Even for small jobs, performance is still affected by the variance in the job size distribution. True, a system with high load ρ may appear as if it has low load from the perspective of a small job; however, the variance in the job size distribution can dominate everything! So even a small job may not do well under SJF.

Question: Explain intuitively (without using the formula) why it is that even a small job is not expected to do well under SJF.

Answer: A small job can still get stuck behind a big job, if the big job started running before the small job got there.

So what we really need in order to get good performance is the ability to **preempt** jobs. This is the topic of the next chapter.

Question: What can be done if preemption is not available?

Answer: The ability to preempt jobs is, in fact, so important that in cases where preemption is not naturally available, it pays to take up extra time to checkpoint the job, saving its state, so that it can be stopped and restarted again from that point.

Question: But what if checkpointing is not available either? It seems one has no choice then but to run jobs to completion?

Answer: If the job size variability is high enough and one does not know how long a job is going to take, it can actually be better to kill a running job after some time, given that there are other jobs queued up. This may seem foolish, because the killed job will eventually have to be restarted from scratch, and this creates extra work. However, if there are many jobs queued up, they are likely to include many short jobs, and mean response time will improve by letting those short jobs get a chance to run. This is the idea behind the TAGS policy [82].

31.5 Exercise

31.1 Why Small Jobs Should Get Priority

Consider an M/G/1 system with non-preemptive priority scheduling. Suppose there are two customer classes of jobs – S (small) and L (large) – with arrival rates λ_S and λ_L and mean job size $\mathbf{E}[S_S]$ and $\mathbf{E}[S_L]$, where

$$\mathbf{E}[S_S] < \mathbf{E}[S_L].$$

Prove that, to minimize the mean waiting time over all jobs, we should give class S jobs priority over class L jobs. Do this by deriving $\mathbf{E}[T_Q]^{\text{NP-Priority}}$ for the case where S has priority and for the case where L has priority.

CHAPTER 32

Scheduling: Preemptive, Size-Based Policies

In this chapter, we discuss preemptive scheduling policies that make use of knowing the size of the job. As in the last chapter, we start by defining and evaluating preemptive priority queueing, and then we extend that analysis to the Preemptive-Shortest-Job-First (PSJF) scheduling policy.

32.1 Motivation

Recall that we can divide scheduling policies into non-preemptive policies and preemptive policies.

Question: What is discouraging about the mean response time of all the *non-preemptive* scheduling policies that we have looked at?

Answer: They all have an $\mathbf{E}\left[S^2\right]$ factor that comes from waiting for the excess of the job in service. This is a problem under highly variable job size distributions.

We have also looked at *preemptive* policies. These tend to do better with respect to mean response time under highly variable job size distributions. Not all of these have equal performance, however. Preemptive policies like PS and PLCFS that do not make use of size have mean response time equal to that of M/M/1/FCFS; namely, they are insensitive to the job size distribution beyond its mean. This is already *far* better than non-preemptive scheduling policies, when the job size distribution has high variability. However, preemptive policies that make use of size or age can do even better by biasing toward jobs with small size. So far, we have seen this only for the FB scheduling policy that favors jobs with small age. In this chapter and the next, we will examine policies that make use of a job's (original) size and remaining size.

32.2 Preemptive Priority Queueing

We start with preemptive priority queueing. As in the non-preemptive case, we assume the following:

- There are n classes.
- Class 1 has highest priority.
- Class k jobs arrive according to a Poisson process with rate $\lambda_k = \lambda \cdot p_k$.
- Class k jobs have service requirements with moments $\mathbf{E}\left[S_k\right]$ and $\mathbf{E}\left[S_k^2\right]$.
- The load of class k is $\rho_k = \lambda_k \cdot \mathbf{E}\left[S_k\right]$.

At every point in time, the server is working on the highest priority job in the system. Preemptive priority queueing differs from non-preemptive queueing in that whenever a job arrives with a higher priority than the job currently in service, the job in service is preempted and the higher priority job begins service. No work is lost under preemptions.

One application of preemptive priority queueing is a network where a number of different packet streams with different priorities are trying to use the same communication link. Each stream consists of a sequence of packets. Only one stream flows through the communication link at a time. If a higher priority stream starts up, the current stream suspends its service and waits for the higher priority stream to finish.

We will compute $\mathbf{E}\left[T(k)\right]^{\text{P-Priority}}$, the mean time in system for a job of priority k in a system with preemptive priority. To do this, imagine a job of priority k entering the system and consider all the work that must be completed before the job can leave the system. This work is made up of three components:

1. $\mathbf{E}\left[S_k\right]$ – the mean service time for a job of priority class k
2. the expected time required to complete service on all jobs of priority 1 to k already in the system when our arrival walks in
3. the expected total service time required for all jobs of priority 1 to $k-1$ that arrive before our arrival leaves

Observe that component (3) is simply

$$(3) = \sum_{i=1}^{k-1} \mathbf{E}\left[T(k)\right] \cdot \lambda_i \cdot \mathbf{E}\left[S_i\right] = \mathbf{E}\left[T(k)\right] \sum_{i=1}^{k-1} \rho_i.$$

But, how do we compute component (2)?

Question: Can we do what we did in the case of non-preemptive priority, namely, add up the expected number of jobs in each class for classes 1 to k, each weighted by the mean job size for that class?

Answer: No. The jobs in queue may already have been partially worked on (remember, this is a preemptive queue).

To determine (2), we make the following arguments:

$(2) = \left(\begin{array}{l}\text{Expected remaining work in the system due to only jobs of priority}\\ \text{1 through } k.\end{array}\right)$

$= \left(\begin{array}{l}\text{Total expected remaining work in preemptive priority system if the}\\ \text{system only ever had arrivals of priority 1 through } k \text{ (because jobs}\\ \text{of class} > k \text{ do not affect jobs of class 1 through } k).\end{array}\right)$

$= \left(\begin{array}{l}\text{Total expected remaining work in system if the system only ever had}\\ \text{arrivals of class 1 through } k \text{ } and \text{ the scheduling order was any work-}\\ \text{conserving order; for example, FCFS (because all work-conserving}\\ \text{policies have the same remaining work).}\end{array}\right)$

$$= \left(\begin{array}{l} \mathbf{E}\left[T_Q\right] \text{ under FCFS scheduling order, where the system only has} \\ \text{arrivals of class 1 through } k \end{array} \right)$$

$$= \frac{\sum_{i=1}^{k} \rho_i}{1 - \sum_{i=1}^{k} \rho_i} \cdot \frac{\sum_{i=1}^{k} \frac{p_i}{F_k} \mathbf{E}\left[S_i^2\right]}{2 \sum_{i=1}^{k} \frac{p_i}{F_k} \mathbf{E}\left[S_i\right]}, \quad \text{where } F_k = \sum_{i=1}^{k} p_i$$

This can be simplified a bit as follows:

$$(2) = \frac{\lambda \sum_{i=1}^{k} p_i \mathbf{E}\left[S_i\right]}{1 - \sum_{i=1}^{k} \rho_i} \cdot \frac{\sum_{i=1}^{k} p_i \mathbf{E}\left[S_i^2\right]}{2 \sum_{i=1}^{k} p_i \mathbf{E}\left[S_i\right]} = \frac{\lambda \sum_{i=1}^{k} p_i \mathbf{E}\left[S_i^2\right]}{2(1 - \sum_{i=1}^{k} \rho_i)} = \frac{\sum_{i=1}^{k} \rho_i \frac{\mathbf{E}\left[S_i^2\right]}{2\mathbf{E}\left[S_i\right]}}{1 - \sum_{i=1}^{k} \rho_i}.$$

So, finally, adding (1) and (2) and (3), we have

$$\mathbf{E}\left[T(k)\right]^{\text{P-Priority}} = \mathbf{E}\left[S_k\right] + \frac{\sum_{i=1}^{k} \rho_i \frac{\mathbf{E}\left[S_i^2\right]}{2\mathbf{E}\left[S_i\right]}}{1 - \sum_{i=1}^{k} \rho_i} + \mathbf{E}\left[T(k)\right] \sum_{i=1}^{k-1} \rho_i$$

$$\mathbf{E}\left[T(k)\right]\left(1 - \sum_{i=1}^{k-1} \rho_i\right) = \mathbf{E}\left[S_k\right] + \frac{\sum_{i=1}^{k} \rho_i \frac{\mathbf{E}\left[S_i^2\right]}{2\mathbf{E}\left[S_i\right]}}{1 - \sum_{i=1}^{k} \rho_i}$$

$$\mathbf{E}\left[T(k)\right]^{\text{P-Priority}} = \frac{\mathbf{E}\left[S_k\right]}{1 - \sum_{i=1}^{k-1} \rho_i} + \frac{\sum_{i=1}^{k} \rho_i \frac{\mathbf{E}\left[S_i^2\right]}{2\mathbf{E}\left[S_i\right]}}{(1 - \sum_{i=1}^{k-1} \rho_i)(1 - \sum_{i=1}^{k} \rho_i)}. \quad (32.1)$$

Interpretation of $\mathbf{E}\left[T(k)\right]^{\text{P-Priority}}$

We now look for a way to interpret (32.1). For preemptive service disciplines, one can view the time in system of a job as divided into two components:

1. the time until the job first starts serving (also called **waiting time**), denoted by *Wait*
2. the time from when the job first receives some service, until it leaves the system (also called **residence time**), denoted by *Res*

Question: Is residence time the same as service time?

Answer: No. The residence time is a lot longer. It includes all interruptions.

Question: Consider the expression (32.1) for the mean time in system for a job of class k under preemptive priority queueing. What does the first term

$$\frac{\mathbf{E}\left[S_k\right]}{1 - \sum_{i=1}^{k-1} \rho_i} \quad (32.2)$$

represent?

Answer: This represents the mean residence time of the job of class k, $\mathbf{E}\left[Res(k)\right]$. You should recognize this formula as being the expected length of a busy period started by a job of size $\mathbf{E}\left[S_k\right]$, where the only jobs that are allowed in the busy period (after the first job) are those of class 1 through $k - 1$.

Observe that once the job of class k starts to serve, it can only be interrupted by jobs of class 1 through $k - 1$. The time until our job of class k can leave is thus the length of the busy period created by those interruptions of class 1 through $k - 1$.

Question: Now explain the second term in (32.1).

Answer: By definition, the remaining term in (32.1) is

$$\mathbf{E}\left[Wait(k)\right] = \frac{\sum_{i=1}^{k} \rho_i \frac{\mathbf{E}\left[S_i^2\right]}{2\mathbf{E}[S_i]}}{\left(1 - \sum_{i=1}^{k-1} \rho_i\right)\left(1 - \sum_{i=1}^{k} \rho_i\right)},$$

representing the mean time until the job of priority k first receives service. Note that this term is almost identical to $\mathbf{E}\left[T_Q(k)\right]$ for the *non*-preemptive priority queue (31.1), except that the numerator (corresponding to excess of the job in service) now represents only excess due to jobs of class 1 through k.[1] This is clear, because a job in service of class greater than k will just be immediately preempted.

It is sometimes convenient to rewrite (32.1) as

$$\mathbf{E}\left[T(k)\right]^{\text{P-Priority}} = \frac{\mathbf{E}\left[S_k\right]}{1 - \sum_{i=1}^{k-1} \rho_i} + \frac{\frac{\lambda}{2} \sum_{i=1}^{k} p_i \mathbf{E}\left[S_i^2\right]}{(1 - \sum_{i=1}^{k-1} \rho_i)(1 - \sum_{i=1}^{k} \rho_i)}. \tag{32.3}$$

Question: Recall that in the case of non-preemptive priority and SJF, we found that a high priority job (or a "small" job in SJF) does not necessarily obtain good performance because it still has to combat the variability in the job size distribution. Is that the case here as well?

Answer: No. Observe that both terms in $\mathbf{E}\left[T(k)\right]^{\text{P-Priority}}$ depend *only* on the first k priority classes, as we would expect, as compared with the non-preemptive priority system.

This means that a high priority (low k) job in preemptive priority queueing really does win, even in a high-variability job size distribution, because it only sees the variability

---

[1] In the non-preemptive case, we had

$$\mathbf{E}\left[T_Q(k)\right]^{\text{NP-Priority}} = \frac{\rho \frac{\mathbf{E}[S^2]}{2\mathbf{E}[S]}}{\left(1 - \sum_{i=1}^{k} \rho_i\right)\left(1 - \sum_{i=1}^{k-1} \rho_i\right)}.$$

The denominator of this expression is equal to that for the preemptive priority queue. The numerator of this expression can be viewed as

$$\rho \frac{\mathbf{E}[S^2]}{2\mathbf{E}[S]} = \frac{\lambda}{2} \mathbf{E}[S^2] = \frac{\lambda}{2} \sum_{i=1}^{n} p_i \mathbf{E}[S_i^2] = \sum_{i=1}^{n} \lambda_i \cdot \frac{\mathbf{E}[S_i^2]}{2} = \sum_{i=1}^{n} \underbrace{\rho_i}_{\substack{\uparrow \\ \text{Probability there is a job} \\ \text{in service of class } i}} \cdot \overbrace{\frac{\mathbf{E}[S_i^2]}{2\mathbf{E}[S_i]}}^{\substack{\text{Expected excess for job} \\ \text{in service of class } i}}.$$

Thus for the non-preemptive priority queue, all n classes (rather than just k classes) contribute to the excess.

created by the first k classes and not the variability of the entire distribution. Also, it sees only the *load* created by the first k classes and not the entire system load (this latter property is also true for non-preemptive priority and SJF).

32.3 Preemptive-Shortest-Job-First (PSJF)

The PSJF policy is defined similarly to the SJF (Shortest-Job-First) policy, except that the size-based priorities are enforced preemptively. Thus at any moment in time, the job in service is the job with the smallest *original* size. A preemption only occurs when a new job arrives whose size is smaller than the original size of the job in service.

Question: How can we analyze the mean response time of PSJF?

Answer: There are two approaches. We cover both here.

The first approach is to make use of our results for scheduling with preemptive priority classes, where we assume that a job's class is its size, and we take the limit as the number of classes goes to infinity. Starting with the preemptive priority response time for class k, (32.3),

$$\mathbf{E}\left[T(k)\right]^{\text{P-Priority}} = \frac{\mathbf{E}\left[S_k\right]}{1 - \sum_{i=1}^{k-1} \rho_i} + \frac{\frac{\lambda}{2} \sum_{i=1}^{k} \rho_i \mathbf{E}\left[S_i^2\right]}{\left(1 - \sum_{i=1}^{k-1} \rho_i\right)\left(1 - \sum_{i=1}^{k} \rho_i\right)},$$

and performing the same limiting operations as we did in analyzing SJF (where we imagine that jobs of size x form one "class" and that there are an infinite number of classes), we have

$$\mathbf{E}\left[T(x)\right]^{\text{PSJF}} = \frac{x}{1 - \rho_x} + \frac{\frac{\lambda}{2} \int_0^x f(t)t^2\, dt}{(1 - \rho_x)^2}, \qquad (32.4)$$

where $f(t)$ is the p.d.f. of job size, S, and $\rho_x = \lambda \int_0^x t f(t)\, dt$ is defined to be the load made up by jobs of size less than x, see (31.4).

Now let's pretend that we did not have a preemptive priority class formula and look at how we could have derived the mean response time for PSJF from scratch. We start by breaking up response time into waiting time and residence time:

$$\mathbf{E}\left[T(x)\right]^{\text{PSJF}} = \mathbf{E}\left[Wait(x)\right]^{\text{PSJF}} + \mathbf{E}\left[Res(x)\right]^{\text{PSJF}}$$

Here *Wait(x)* represents the time until job x receives its first bit of service, and *Res(x)* represents the time from when job x receives its first bit of service until it is complete.

Question: What is $\mathbf{E}\left[Res(x)\right]^{\text{PSJF}}$?

Answer: *Res(x)* is just the duration of a busy period started by a job of size x, where the only jobs that make up this busy period are jobs of size $\leq x$. Thus

$$\mathbf{E}\left[Res(x)\right]^{\text{PSJF}} = \frac{x}{1 - \rho_x}.$$

Question: Can we also think of $\mathbf{E}\left[Wait(x)\right]^{\text{PSJF}}$ as a busy period duration?

Answer: Yes! When a job of size x walks in, it sees some work. However, not all the work that it sees is relevant to it. The only relevant work is that made up by jobs of (original) size $\leq x$. Let's call that work W_x. Now, *Wait(x)* can be viewed as the length of a busy period started by a phantom job of size W_x, where the only jobs that make up this busy period are jobs of size $\leq x$.

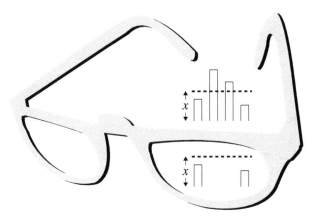

Figure 32.1. Transformer glasses for PSJF. Whereas in FB, the transformer glasses truncate all jobs of size $> x$ to size x, in PSJF, the transformer glasses make jobs of size $> x$ invisible.

Question: What is $\mathbf{E}\left[W_x\right]^{\text{PSJF}}$?

Answer: This is the work in the system as seen when job x puts on transformer glasses that make anyone whose (original) size is greater than x invisible (see Fig. 32.1). But given that the policy is PSJF (so jobs of size $\leq x$ are always worked on before jobs of size $> x$), we see that this is the same as the amount of work under PSJF, where the only jobs allowed into the system are jobs of size $\leq x$. However, because PSJF is work-conserving, this is the same as the amount of work in an FCFS system where the only jobs in the system are jobs of size $\leq x$. But that work is the same as the time-in-queue in an FCFS system where the only jobs in the system are jobs of size $\leq x$.

We will use the random variable S_x to denote the size of a job of size $\leq x$. The density of S_x is $\frac{f(t)}{F(x)}$ where $f(t)$ is the density of S.

So,

$$
\begin{aligned}
\mathbf{E}\left[Wait(x)\right]^{\text{PSJF}} &= \frac{\mathbf{E}\left[W_x\right]}{1-\rho_x} \quad \text{(mean length of busy period)} \\[2mm]
&= \frac{\mathbf{E}\left[T_Q \mid \text{where job sizes are } S_x\right]^{\text{FCFS}}}{1-\rho_x} \\[2mm]
&= \frac{\frac{\lambda F(x)\mathbf{E}\left[S_x^2\right]}{2(1-\rho_x)}}{1-\rho_x}
\end{aligned}
$$

$$= \frac{\lambda F(x) \int_0^x t^2 \frac{f(t)}{F(x)} dt}{2(1 - \rho_x)^2}$$

$$= \frac{\lambda \int_0^x t^2 f(t) dt}{2(1 - \rho_x)^2}. \tag{32.5}$$

Thus

$$\mathbf{E}\left[T(x)\right]^{\text{PSJF}} = \frac{x}{1 - \rho_x} + \frac{\lambda \int_0^x t^2 f(t) dt}{2(1 - \rho_x)^2},$$

just like (32.4).

32.4 Transform Analysis of PSJF

We now derive the Laplace transform of the response time of the M/G/1/PSJF queue. Before reading this, it is helpful to review Section 27.2.

Let

$$T = \text{Response time.}$$

$$T(x) = \text{Response time for a job of size } x.$$

Given the Laplace transform of $T(x)$, we can get the transform for T by conditioning on job size as follows:

$$\widetilde{T}(s) = \int_x \widetilde{T(x)}(s) f(x) dx.$$

Thus we only need to determine $\widetilde{T(x)}(s)$:

$$\widetilde{T(x)}(s) = \widetilde{Wait(x)}(s) \cdot \widetilde{Res(x)}(s), \tag{32.6}$$

where *Wait(x)* denotes the waiting time of a job of size x and *Res(x)* denotes the residence time of a job of size x. Both these quantities will be analyzed in terms of busy periods.

We need the following notation:

$$\lambda_x = \lambda F(x) = \text{arrival rate of jobs of size} \leq x$$

$$S_x = \text{arbitrary size of a job whose size is} \leq x$$

$$\text{Note: } \mathbf{E}\left[S_x\right] = \int_0^x t \frac{f(t)}{F(x)} dt$$

$$\rho_x = \lambda_x \mathbf{E}\left[S_x\right] = \lambda \int_0^x t f(t) dt = \text{load made up of jobs of size} \leq x$$

$$W_x = \text{work in system made up of jobs of size} \leq x$$

$$B_x = \text{duration of busy period of jobs of size} \leq x \text{ only}$$

$$A_y^x = \text{number of arrivals of size} \leq x \text{ during time } y$$

Question: Pop Quiz: What is $\widetilde{B_x}(s)$?

Answer:

$$\widetilde{B_x}(s) = \widetilde{S_x}\left(s + \lambda_x - \lambda_x \widetilde{B_x}(s)\right).$$

We are now ready to describe $\widetilde{Wait(x)}(s)$ and $\widetilde{Res(x)}(s)$.

$Res(x) = $ duration of a busy period started by a job of size x made up by arrivals of size $\leq x$

Question: Is $\widetilde{Res(x)}(s) = \widetilde{B_x}(s)$?

Answer: No. Both B_x and $Res(x)$ are busy periods composed of jobs of size $\leq x$. However, the starting job in B_x is any job of size $\leq x$, whereas $Res(x)$ must start with a job of size exactly x.

$$Res(x) = x + \sum_{i=1}^{A_x^x} B_x^{(i)} \quad (B_x^{(i)} \text{ is the } i\text{th busy period})$$

$$\widetilde{Res(x)}(s) = e^{-sx} \cdot \widetilde{A_x^x}(\widetilde{B_x}(s))$$

$$= e^{-sx} \cdot e^{-(\lambda_x)x\left(1 - \widetilde{B_x}(s)\right)}$$

$$= e^{-x\left(s + \lambda_x - \lambda_x \widetilde{B_x}(s)\right)} \tag{32.7}$$

Now we move on to *Wait(x)*.

$Wait(x) = $ duration of a busy period started by W_x, where the only arrivals are of size $\leq x$

$$\widetilde{Wait(x)}(s) = \widetilde{W_x}\left(s + \lambda_x - \lambda_x \widetilde{B_x}(s)\right) \tag{32.8}$$

Question: What do we know about $\widetilde{W_x}(s)$?

Answer:

$W_x = $ work in PSJF system made up by jobs of size $\leq x$

  $= $ work in PSJF system if there only existed those jobs of size $\leq x$ and no others

  $= $ work in FCFS system if there only existed jobs of size $\leq x$ and no others

  $= $ queueing time in FCFS system where there are only jobs of size $\leq x$

Hence, from (26.13), using S_x, λ_x, and ρ_x, we have

$$\widetilde{W_x}(s) = \frac{(1 - \rho_x)s}{\lambda_x \widetilde{S_x}(s) - \lambda_x + s}. \tag{32.9}$$

Combining equations (32.9), (32.8), (32.7), and (32.6), we have the Laplace transform of response time for jobs of size x under PSJF:

$$\widetilde{T(x)}^{\text{PSJF}}(s) = \widetilde{Wait(x)}(s) \cdot \widetilde{Res(x)}(s)$$

$$= \widetilde{W_x}\left(s + \lambda_x - \lambda_x \widetilde{B_x}(s)\right) \cdot e^{-x\left(s + \lambda_x - \lambda_x \widetilde{B_x}(s)\right)}$$

$$= \frac{(1 - \rho_x)\left(s + \lambda_x - \lambda_x \widetilde{B_x}(s)\right) \cdot e^{-x\left(s + \lambda_x - \lambda_x \widetilde{B_x}(s)\right)}}{\lambda_x \widetilde{S_x}\left(s + \lambda_x - \lambda_x \widetilde{B_x}(s)\right) - \lambda_x + \left(s + \lambda_x - \lambda_x \widetilde{B_x}(s)\right)}$$

32.5 Exercises

32.1 Warmup: Preemptive Priority Queue

Consider an M/M/1 with n preemptive priority classes, where class i jobs arrive with rate λ_i. Assume that all job sizes are Exponentially distributed with mean 1. Use the formulas in this chapter to derive a very simple expression for the mean response time of the kth class.

32.2 The $c\mu$-Rule

(Contributed by Urtzi Ayesta) Suppose you have a single-server queue with n classes of jobs and Exponential service times. Class i jobs arrive with some average rate λ_i and have mean service time $\frac{1}{\mu_i}$. Assume that there is a *holding cost*, c_i, associated with class i, meaning that a class i job incurs a cost of c_i dollars for every second that it spends in the system. Let $\mathbf{E}[N_i^\pi]$ denote the mean number of jobs of class i under some scheduling policy π. Let $\mathbf{E}[W_i^\pi]$ denote the mean total work of all class i jobs in the system under scheduling policy π. Let $Cost(\pi) = \sum_{i=1}^n c_i \mathbf{E}[N_i^\pi]$ denote the mean operational cost under policy π; $\mathbf{E}[N^\pi]$ denote the mean number of jobs in the system under policy π; and $\mathbf{E}[T^\pi]$ denote the mean response time under policy π.

Without loss of generality, assume that

$$c_1 \mu_1 > c_2 \mu_2 > \cdots > c_n \mu_n$$

Let $c\mu$ denote the policy that gives preemptive priority to jobs in order of their class (class 1 has priority over class 2, which has priority over class 3, etc.), i.e., the class with the highest product of $c \cdot \mu$ gets highest priority. Observe that it makes sense to give these jobs priority because they either have a high holding cost, or are small, or both.

The $c\mu$-Rule states that the $c\mu$ policy is optimal for minimizing $Cost(\pi)$, over all policies π, where we limit ourselves to policies that do not know the exact sizes of jobs, only the mean size for that class. This exercise will lead you through a very simple proof of the $c\mu$-Rule. The key idea in the proof is to first show that the $c\mu$ policy minimizes a certain sum of work and then to translate the work result into a result about $Cost(\pi)$.

(a) If we set all the costs to be the same, i.e., $c_i = c, \forall i$, what does the $c\mu$-Rule say about mean response time?

(b) Explain via sample-path arguments why the following work sum inequality holds for all policies π:

$$\sum_{i=1}^{j} \mathbf{E}\left[W_i^{c\mu}\right] \le \sum_{i=1}^{j} \mathbf{E}\left[W_i^{\pi}\right] \quad \forall j \qquad (32.10)$$

(c) Prove the following simple identity, where the a_i's and b_i's are constants and $a_{n+1} = 0$:

$$\sum_{i=1}^{n} a_i b_i = \sum_{i=1}^{n} (a_i - a_{i+1}) \sum_{j=1}^{i} b_j \qquad (32.11)$$

(d) Prove that

$$Cost(c\mu) = \sum_{i=1}^{n} c_i \mathbf{E}\left[N_i^{c\mu}\right] \le \sum_{i=1}^{n} c_i \mathbf{E}\left[N_i^{\pi}\right] = Cost(\pi)$$

for all policies π. To do this, you will need to first translate $\mathbf{E}\left[N_i\right]$ into $\mathbf{E}\left[W_i\right]$, by observing that

$$\mathbf{E}\left[W_i^{\pi}\right] = \mathbf{E}\left[N_i^{\pi}\right] \cdot \frac{1}{\mu} \quad (\text{why??})$$

Then apply both (32.11) and (32.10) to produce the result.

CHAPTER 33

Scheduling: SRPT and Fairness

In this chapter, we introduce Shortest-Remaining-Processing-Time (SRPT) scheduling. SRPT is even superior to the PSJF policy that we saw in the last chapter, because it takes a job's *remaining service requirement* into account, not just the *original job size*. We also compare all the scheduling policies that we have studied so far with respect to mean response time as a function of load and the variability of the job size distribution. Finally, we study the *fairness* of SRPT by comparing it to the (fair) PS policy and proving the All-Can-Win theorem.

33.1 Shortest-Remaining-Processing-Time (SRPT)

Under SRPT, at all times the server is working on that job with the shortest remaining processing time. The SRPT policy is preemptive so that a new arrival will preempt the current job serving if the new arrival has a shorter remaining processing time.

Observe that, under SRPT, once a job, j, starts running, it can only be preempted by a new arrival whose size is shorter than j's remaining time. In particular, any jobs that are in the system with j, while j is running, will never run before j completes.

Remember that in Exercise 2.3 we proved that SRPT achieves the lowest possible mean response time on every arrival sequence. In this section, we analyze the mean response time for SRPT in the M/G/1 setting.

Question: Can we look at SRPT as some type of preemptive priority system with classes?

Answer: *No!* The problem is that in SRPT a job's priority is its "remaining" size, which *changes* as the job ages. The preemptive priority model does not allow jobs to change priorities while in queue.

It turns out that the response time analysis of SRPT is somewhat involved. The proof is outlined in two different ways in the Schrage and Miller paper from 1966 [160]. In this section we give another sketch of the proof of response time for SRPT. This sketch may feel precise, but it is missing a few details. In Section 33.2, we fill in these missing details.

We start by looking at the final result and then try to understand where each term comes from:

$$
\mathbf{E}\left[T(x)\right]^{\text{SRPT}} = \mathbf{E}\begin{bmatrix} \text{Time until job of size} \\ x \text{ first receives service} \\ \text{(waiting time)} \end{bmatrix} + \mathbf{E}\begin{bmatrix} \text{Time from when job first} \\ \text{receives service until it is} \\ \text{done (residence time)} \end{bmatrix}
$$

$$
= \mathbf{E}\left[Wait(x)\right] + \mathbf{E}\left[Res(x)\right]
$$

$$
= \frac{\frac{\lambda}{2}\int_{t=0}^{x} t^2 f(t)dt + \frac{1}{2}x^2\left(1 - F(x)\right)}{(1 - \rho_x)^2} + \int_{t=0}^{x} \frac{dt}{1 - \rho_t} ,
$$

where $\rho_x = \lambda \int_0^x t f(t)dt$ as in (31.4).

Understanding the Residence Time

Recall that the term representing mean residence time for the preemptive priority queue for a job of class k was

$$
\frac{\mathbf{E}\left[S_k\right]}{1 - \sum_{i=1}^{k-1} \rho_i} .
$$

This term represents the job size, slowed down by the load of all jobs of higher priority than itself.

If we just tried to translate this directly to the continuous case we would have the mean residence time for a job of size x under PSJF; namely,

$$
\mathbf{E}\left[Res(x)\right]^{\text{PSJF}} = \frac{x}{1 - \rho_x} ,
$$

which represents a busy period started by a job of size x ("job x") and consisting of only jobs of size $\leq x$.

By contrast, in SRPT, a job of size x has mean residence time

$$
\int_{t=0}^{x} \frac{dt}{1 - \rho_t} .
$$

To understand this expression, first observe that in SRPT, a job's "priority" increases as it ages. Thus the factor by which the job is slowed down, once it has started service, should depend on its remaining service requirement, t, and should be related to the load of all jobs of size less than t. Now think of the job of size x as broken into $\frac{x}{dt}$ pieces of size dt each. The job starts out with remaining time x and slowly receives service. Consider the time required for the job to move from having $t + dt$ remaining service time to t remaining service time. This is a busy period, started by dt work, where only jobs of size $< t$ are included in the busy period, because they are the ones that have priority over our job. The length of such a busy period is exactly $\frac{dt}{1-\rho_t}$.

The first busy period, needed for the job to decrease from remaining size x to remaining size $(x - dt)$, takes a long time, because almost every job counts in the busy period.

However the later busy periods, needed for the job to decrease from say $x/2$ to $(x/2 - dt)$, go a lot faster, because only smaller jobs count.

The residence time of job x is just the sum (integration) of all these busy periods.

Understanding the Waiting Time

Let's now think about the intuition behind the expression for waiting time:

$$\mathbf{E}\left[\textit{Wait(x)}\right] = \frac{\frac{\lambda}{2}\int_{t=0}^{x} t^2 f(t)dt + \frac{\lambda}{2}x^2(1 - F(x))}{(1 - \rho_x)^2}$$

Question: If you ignore the second term in the numerator, what does this expression remind you of?

Answer: Ignoring the second term in the numerator, we have exactly the mean waiting time from the M/G/1/PSJF; see (32.5). Recall that the mean waiting time from the M/G/1/PSJF is the duration of a busy period, started by W_x, the total remaining work in the system from jobs of size $\leq x$, and made up of all new arrivals of size $\leq x$ that occur during W_x. (Recall that $\mathbf{E}\left[W_x\right]^{\text{PSJF}} = \frac{\frac{\lambda}{2}\int_{t=0}^{x} t^2 f(t)dt}{1-\rho_x}$ and that $\mathbf{E}\left[\textit{Wait(x)}\right]^{\text{PSJF}} = \frac{\mathbf{E}[W_x]^{\text{PSJF}}}{1-\rho_x}$.)

The mean waiting time for SRPT also looks like such a busy period; however, the work starting the busy period includes an extra term:

$$\frac{\lambda}{2}x^2\overline{F}(x)$$

Question: What is this extra term? Why does it occur?

Answer: It looks like all jobs of original size $> x$ (the jobs that occur with probability $\overline{F}(x)$) are contributing x^2 to the SRPT expression. To understand this, observe that in PSJF only jobs of size $< x$ can contribute to job x's waiting time. By contrast, in SRPT *all* jobs contribute to job x's waiting time. However, the big jobs only contribute at most x to job x's waiting time, because job x only sees the big jobs once their remaining time is reduced to x.

Question: Does the numerator of $\mathbf{E}\left[\textit{Wait(x)}\right]^{\text{SRPT}}$ remind you of another distribution we have seen?

Answer: Yes, it is like the $S_{\overline{x}}$ job size, which we used for FB scheduling, where jobs of size $> x$ are transformed into jobs of size x; see Section 30.3.

In SRPT, the numerator in the waiting time expression is $\frac{\lambda}{2}\mathbf{E}\left[S_{\overline{x}}^2\right]$, as in FB; see (30.6). However, the denominator of the SRPT expression involves ρ_x as in PSJF, not $\rho_{\overline{x}}$ as in FB, because only jobs of size $\leq x$ are allowed to enter the busy period.

In fact, SRPT is related to both FB and to PSJF. The exact relationship will become clearer in the next section.

33.2 Precise Derivation of SRPT Waiting Time*

Section 33.1 provided a proof sketch for response time of SRPT. The derivation of *Res(x)* was precise. We now make the derivation of *Wait(x)* precise as well.

Let W_x^{SRPT} denote the work that an arrival of size x finds in the system that is "relevant" to itself (i.e., work in the system that will run before the arrival of size x gets to start running). Then *Wait(x)* is simply a busy period started by W_x^{SRPT}, where the only jobs allowed to enter are those of size $\leq x$. Hence,

$$\mathbf{E}\left[Wait(x)\right]^{\text{SRPT}} = \frac{\mathbf{E}\left[W_x^{\text{SRPT}}\right]}{1 - \rho_x}. \tag{33.1}$$

We spend the rest of the section analyzing $\mathbf{E}\left[W_x^{\text{SRPT}}\right]$. W_x^{SRPT} is composed of two types of jobs:

Type a: These are jobs that job x finds in the system of (original) size $\leq x$.

Type b: These are jobs that job x finds in the system of (original) size $> x$ that now have remaining size $\leq x$.

If all we had to worry about was work made up of type a jobs, this would be an easy problem. The work made up of type a jobs is the same as W_x^{PSJF}. Unfortunately, we also have type b jobs.

Question: How many jobs can there be of type b?

Answer: There can be *at most one* job of type b. Furthermore, no more type b's will enter the system until job x has left the system entirely.

The difficulty in analyzing the work made up of type a and b jobs lies in the strangeness of the type b jobs. From the perspective of job x, jobs of type b appear at the server, having size x, according to some non-Poisson process, where there can only be *at most* one type b job in the system at a time. The fact that there can only be one type b job is particularly at odds with respect to all the analysis techniques we have used so far.

To determine the total work in the system made up of type a and type b jobs, we use the following trick: We imagine that our queueing system is broken into two pieces, the *queue part* and the *server part*. Note that by definition there can only be one job of either type in the server at a time. We imagine type b jobs as arriving directly into the server, whereas all other jobs arrive at the queue. We also imagine type b jobs as always having priority over type a jobs, so that they never leave the server once they are in there. That is, they always run to completion. Making type b jobs have priority over type a jobs does not change the amount of work in the system, but it does allow us to ensure that type b's never enter the *queue part*.

---

* *Warning:* This is a difficult section and can be skipped.

Thus we can think of the *queue part* as a system made up of only type a jobs and the *server part* as consisting of jobs from distribution $S_{\overline{x}}$ from the FB analysis (this includes both the type a jobs and the type b jobs). We call this system of a's and b's "system X."

Our goal is to understand the work in system X. This work is the same as the delay experienced (T_Q) by an arrival of type a into system X, if we now pretend that all arrivals of type a are of equal priority with respect to each other and hence are served FCFS.

We now use a tagged-job argument to determine the mean delay for a type a arrival into system X. Note that we cannot simply pretend that system X is a regular FCFS queue, because type b jobs only enter the server. Hence we cannot just apply the P-K formula, and we instead need to do the tagged-job analysis from scratch.

A type a arrival to system X will see some number of jobs in the queue, N_Q. These will all be of type a. Hence their size can be represented by S_x, which denotes the job size for jobs of size $\leq x$ only. The probability that a type a arrival sees a job in service is $\rho_{\overline{x}}$, where $\rho_{\overline{x}} = \lambda \mathbf{E}\left[S_{\overline{x}}\right]$ (as in the FB policy). To understand why this is so, we think about the server as a separate system and look at it from a Renewal-Reward perspective. It is important to note that *every single job* eventually enters the server. However, the jobs of size $> x$ that enter the server enter it as being size x. Thus, the job size distribution of jobs entering the server is $S_{\overline{x}}$, and the fraction of time that the server is busy is $\rho_{\overline{x}}$. Going back to our type a arrival, that (Poisson) arrival sees time-average behavior; namely, with probability $\rho_{\overline{x}}$ it sees a busy server, and the expected remaining service time of the job serving is the expected excess of $S_{\overline{x}}$.

Putting these together we have

$$
\begin{aligned}
\mathbf{E}\left[T_Q\right] &= \mathbf{E}\left[N_Q\right] \cdot \mathbf{E}\left[S_x\right] + \rho_{\overline{x}}\mathbf{E}\left[\text{Excess of } S_{\overline{x}}\right] \\
&= \mathbf{E}\left[T_Q\right]\lambda F(x) \cdot \mathbf{E}\left[S_x\right] + \rho_{\overline{x}} \cdot \mathbf{E}\left[\text{Excess of } S_{\overline{x}}\right] \\
&= \mathbf{E}\left[T_Q\right]\rho_x + \rho_{\overline{x}} \cdot \mathbf{E}\left[\text{Excess of } S_{\overline{x}}\right] \\
&= \frac{\rho_{\overline{x}}\mathbf{E}\left[\text{Excess of } S_{\overline{x}}\right]}{1 - \rho_x} \\
&= \frac{\rho_{\overline{x}}}{1 - \rho_x} \cdot \frac{\mathbf{E}\left[S_{\overline{x}}^2\right]}{2\mathbf{E}\left[S_{\overline{x}}\right]} \\
&= \frac{\lambda \mathbf{E}\left[S_{\overline{x}}\right]}{1 - \rho_x} \cdot \frac{\mathbf{E}\left[S_{\overline{x}}^2\right]}{2\mathbf{E}\left[S_{\overline{x}}\right]} \\
&= \frac{\lambda}{1 - \rho_x} \cdot \frac{\mathbf{E}\left[S_{\overline{x}}^2\right]}{2} \\
&= \frac{\lambda}{2} \cdot \frac{\int_0^x t^2 f(t)dt + \overline{F}(x) \cdot x^2}{1 - \rho_x}.
\end{aligned}
$$

This expression for $\mathbf{E}\left[T_Q\right]$ represents W_x^{SRPT}. Hence, returning to (33.1), we have

$$\mathbf{E}\left[Wait(x)\right]^{\text{SRPT}} = \frac{\mathbf{E}\left[W_x^{\text{SRPT}}\right]}{1 - \rho_x} = \frac{\lambda}{2} \cdot \frac{\int_0^x t^2 f(t)dt + \overline{F}(x) \cdot x^2}{\left(1 - \rho_x\right)^2}$$

as desired.

33.3 Comparisons with Other Policies

Let's return to the formula for SRPT response time:

$$\mathbf{E}\left[T(x)\right]^{\text{SRPT}} = \frac{\frac{\lambda}{2}\int_{t=0}^x t^2 f(t)dt + \frac{\lambda}{2}x^2(1 - F(x))}{(1 - \rho_x)^2} + \int_{t=0}^x \frac{dt}{1 - \rho_t} . \quad (33.2)$$

We can make several immediate observations. First, observe that the response time for a job of size x is not influenced by the variance of the entire job size distribution, but rather just by the variance of the distribution up to size x. $\mathbf{E}\left[T(x)\right]$ is also not influenced by the entire load, but rather just by the load made up of jobs of size $\leq x$. Also, once our job of size x starts receiving service, the only influencing factor is the load made up of jobs of size less than the current remaining service time of our job. This explains why *small* jobs (small size x) do so well under SRPT.

33.3.1 *Comparison with PSJF*

It's clear that the waiting time for SRPT is greater than that for PSJF because of the extra x^2 term in the numerator. In contrast, the residence time for SRPT is clearly better than that for PSJF, because a job only has to wait for those jobs smaller than its current remaining service requirement under SRPT, whereas it has to wait behind all jobs smaller than its original size in PSJF. Compare (32.4) with (33.2) and imagine integrating over all x. It turns out that this benefit in $\mathbf{E}\left[Res(x)\right]$ makes SRPT superior to PSJF with respect to *overall* mean response time, $\mathbf{E}\left[T\right]$, where $\mathbf{E}\left[T\right]$ is the weighted integral of $\mathbf{E}\left[T(x)\right]$ over all x.

33.3.2 *SRPT versus FB*

Without looking at the formulas, it might not seem obvious how SRPT and FB compare. SRPT and FB are in a sense complements. In SRPT, a job gains priority as it receives more service. Its response time can be thought of as a snowball rolling downhill, which at first rolls slowly, but gains momentum and moves faster and faster. In FB, the reverse is true. A job has highest priority when it first enters. As time goes on, it loses priority. One might imagine that the performance of SRPT and FB are somehow related. Lemma 33.1 shows that, on every job size x, SRPT beats FB.

Lemma 33.1 *In an M/G/1, for all x and for all ρ,*

$$\mathbf{E}\left[T(x)\right]^{\text{SRPT}} \leq \mathbf{E}\left[T(x)\right]^{\text{FB}} .$$

Proof   The proof follows from the fact that both the mean residence time and the mean waiting time are lower under SRPT as compared with FB. In the case of mean waiting time, SRPT and FB have the same numerator, but FB has a $(1 - \rho_{\overline{x}})^2$ term in the denominator, as compared to $(1 - \rho_x)^2$ in SRPT, where $\rho_{\overline{x}} > \rho_x$.

$$
\begin{aligned}
\mathbf{E}\left[T(x)\right]^{\mathrm{FB}} &= \frac{x(1 - \rho_{\overline{x}}) + \frac{1}{2}\lambda\mathbf{E}\left[S_{\overline{x}}^2\right]}{(1 - \rho_{\overline{x}})^2} \\[2mm]
&= \frac{x}{1 - \rho_{\overline{x}}} + \frac{\frac{1}{2}\lambda\left(\int_0^x y^2 f(y)dy + x^2\overline{F}(x)\right)}{(1 - \rho_{\overline{x}})^2} \\[2mm]
&\geq \frac{x}{1 - \rho_x} + \frac{\frac{1}{2}\lambda\left(\int_0^x y^2 f(y)dy + x^2\overline{F}(x)\right)}{(1 - \rho_x)^2} \\[2mm]
&\geq \int_{t=0}^{x} \frac{dt}{1 - \rho_t} + \frac{\frac{1}{2}\lambda\int_0^x y^2 f(y)dy + \frac{1}{2}\lambda x^2\overline{F}(x)}{(1 - \rho_x)^2} \\[2mm]
&= \mathbf{E}\left[T(x)\right]^{\mathrm{SRPT}} \quad\blacksquare
\end{aligned}
$$

33.3.3 *Comparison of All Scheduling Policies*

At this point we have derived at least $\mathbf{E}\left[T(x)\right]$ for all scheduling policies. However, it is not obvious just from looking at these formulas how these policies compare with respect to overall mean response time, $\mathbf{E}\left[T\right]$ – most of us are not born doing triple nested integrals in our heads :-).

To facilitate understanding, we have evaluated all the formulas for $\mathbf{E}\left[T\right]$ using Mathematica for the different policies. Mean response time as a function of load is given in Figure 33.1, and mean response time as a function of C^2 is given in Figure 33.2. In both figures, we have used a Weibull job size distribution. The Weibull, defined by

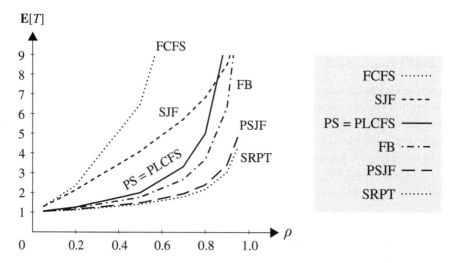

Figure 33.1. Mean response time as a function of load for the M/G/1 with various scheduling policies. The job size distribution is a Weibull with mean 1 and $C^2 = 10$.

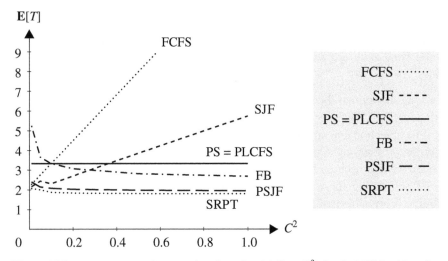

Figure 33.2. Mean response time as a function of variability (C^2) for the M/G/1 with various scheduling policies. Load is fixed at $\rho = 0.7$. The job size distribution is a Weibull with fixed mean 1 and changing C^2.

$\overline{F}(x) = e^{-\left(\frac{x}{\lambda}\right)^{\alpha}}$ with parameters λ and $\alpha > 0$, is convenient because when $\alpha < 1$, it has decreasing failure rate (DFR) and C^2 can be made as high as desired.

Looking at Figure 33.1, we see that the policies are ordered as we would expect. Knowing the size helps. Being able to preempt jobs helps even more.

Question: The SJF policy is not so great for low loads (due to the high C^2). However, it suddenly starts looking a lot better, comparatively, under high loads, even beating PS. Why is this?

Answer: There is a $1 - \rho_x$ term in the denominator of $\mathbf{E}\left[T_Q(x)\right]^{\text{SJF}}$, as compared with a $1 - \rho$ term in the denominator of $\mathbf{E}\left[T(x)\right]^{\text{PS}}$. That helps SJF a lot under high load.

Looking at Figure 33.2, we see that under high C^2, the policies are ranked as expected.

Question: Why is the line for PS = PLCFS flat?

Answer: These policies are invariant to the variability of the job size distribution.

Question: Why do policies like FB look *worse* for low C^2?

Answer: FB needs DFR to perform well, and higher DFR is coupled with higher C^2.

33.4 Fairness of SRPT

Although the SRPT scheduling policy is optimal with respect to mean response time and has a comparatively low second moment as well, it is rarely used for scheduling jobs. Consider for example a typical web server.

Question: Which scheduling policy best represents scheduling in a web server?

Answer: PS. The server time-shares between HTTP requests. Both the CPU and the outgoing bandwidth are scheduled in round-robin order, approximating Processor-Sharing.

This seems suboptimal, because the mean response time for PS is clearly far higher than that for SRPT. One might wonder whether there are other issues in applying SRPT. A possible objection to using SRPT is that the job size is not always known. However, for web servers serving static (GET File) requests, the sizes of these files are known by the server and accurately represent the job service requirement. Implementation of SRPT scheduling for web servers is also easy, it turns out. In [92, 162], SRPT scheduling is implemented for an Apache web server running on Linux by modifying the Linux kernel to schedule outgoing bandwidth so as to favor HTTP requests with small remaining file size.

Question: So what is the problem with using SRPT?

Answer: The problem is that people deeply fear that SRPT will cause long jobs to "starve."

Now clearly, when $\rho < 1$, no job actually starves, because every busy period is finite, so every job will eventually get to run. When people talk about "starvation," they are really talking about jobs doing worse under SRPT than they would under a *fair* policy like PS. By **fair** we mean a policy that affords every job the same expected slowdown, regardless of its size.

Question: Consider the question illustrated in Figure 33.3. An M/G/1 queue is shown, where the job size distribution is a Bounded Pareto ($k = 332$, $p = 10^{10}$, $\alpha = 1.1$).

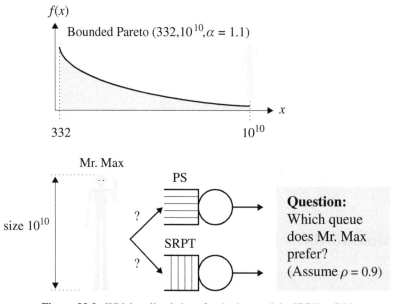

Figure 33.3. Which policy is best for the largest job: SRPT or PS?

The load is $\rho = 0.9$. Consider now the very biggest job in the job size distribution (we call him, Mr. Max). Mr. Max is a job of size $x = 10^{10}$. The question is whether Mr. Max prefers to go to an M/G/1/PS queue, or an M/G/1/SRPT queue. That is, is $\mathbf{E}\left[T(10^{10})\right]$ lower under PS scheduling or under SRPT scheduling?

Discussion: Clearly small jobs should favor SRPT. By contrast, large jobs have the lowest priority under SRPT, but they get treated like equal citizens under PS, where they time-share equally with all other jobs. It therefore seems much better for Mr. Max to go to the PS queue, where he will be treated as an equal citizen. That is, it seems that $\mathbf{E}\left[T(10^{10})\right]^{\text{PS}}$ should be far lower than $\mathbf{E}\left[T(10^{10})\right]^{\text{SRPT}}$.

Answer: This intuition turns out to be wrong!

In fact, for the same M/G/1 setup as in Figure 33.3, we produced Table 33.1 via Mathematica™.

As seen in Table 33.1, not only does the *largest* job prefer SRPT to PS, but almost all jobs (99.9999%) prefer SRPT to PS by more than a factor of 2. In fact 99% of jobs prefer SRPT to PS by more than a factor of 5.

Table 33.1. $\mathbf{E}[\text{Slowdown}(x)]$ *under SRPT and under PS for increasing* x

Percentile of job size distribution	Expected slowdown under SRPT	Expected slowdown under PS
90%-tile	1.28	10
99%-tile	1.62	10
99.99%-tile	2.69	10
99.9999%-tile	4.73	10
99.999999%-tile	8.50	10
99.99999999%-tile	9.53	10
100%-tile (Mr. Max)	9.54	10

But how can this be? Can every job really do better in expectation under SRPT than under PS? The answer is YES, and not just for the Bounded Pareto job size distribution.

Theorem 33.2 (All-Can-Win [12]) *Given an M/G/1, if* $\rho < \frac{1}{2}$, *then,* $\forall x$,

$$\mathbf{E}\left[T(x)\right]^{\text{SRPT}} \leq \mathbf{E}\left[T(x)\right]^{\text{PS}}.$$

The All-Can-Win theorem says that every single job (every x) prefers SRPT to PS in expectation, assuming $\rho < \frac{1}{2}$. Remarkably, the All-Can-Win theorem holds for all job size distributions G. For many G, the restriction on ρ is much looser. In fact, for the Bounded Pareto distribution with $\alpha = 1.1$, shown in Figure 33.3, the All-Can-Win theorem holds whenever $\rho < 0.96$.

Question: Do you have any intuition for *why* the All-Can-Win theorem should hold?

Answer: Here is the intuition. First realize that, although it seems that large jobs are ignored under SRPT, this is only the case until the large job gets some service. Once a large job starts to get some service, it gains priority over other jobs. In the end, even the largest job will have a period where it has highest priority. Now imagine that load is light. Then it seems plausible that the $\mathbf{E}\left[Wait(x)\right]$ component of SRPT is low, because an incoming job often finds the system empty. In this case, the $\mathbf{E}\left[Res(x)\right]$ component could be a major part of a job's response time under SRPT. Now compare with PS. PS has no $Wait(x)$ component, only a $Res(x)$. However, the $Res(x)$ component for PS is clearly way higher than that for SRPT. Thus, it seems plausible that under light load conditions even a job of large size x could do worse under PS than under SRPT.

Here is the formal proof:

Proof *(All-Can-Win)*

$$\mathbf{E}\left[T(x)\right]^{\text{SRPT}} \leq \mathbf{E}\left[T(x)\right]^{\text{PS}}$$

$$\Updownarrow$$

$$\frac{\frac{\lambda}{2}\int_{t=0}^{x} t^2 f(t)dt + \frac{\lambda}{2}x^2(1-F(x))}{(1-\rho_x)^2} + \int_{t=0}^{x} \frac{dt}{1-\rho_t} \leq \frac{x}{1-\rho}$$

$$\Updownarrow$$

$$\frac{\frac{\lambda}{2}\int_{t=0}^{x} t^2 f(t)dt + \frac{\lambda}{2}x^2(1-F(x))}{(1-\rho_x)^2} \leq \frac{x}{1-\rho} - \int_{t=0}^{x} \frac{dt}{1-\rho_t}$$

$$\Updownarrow$$

$$\frac{\frac{\lambda}{2}\int_{t=0}^{x} t^2 f(t)dt + \frac{\lambda}{2}x^2(1-F(x))}{(1-\rho_x)^2} \leq \int_{t=0}^{x} \frac{dt}{1-\rho} - \int_{t=0}^{x} \frac{dt}{1-\rho_t}$$

$$\Updownarrow$$

$$\frac{\frac{\lambda}{2}\int_{t=0}^{x} t^2 f(t)dt + \frac{\lambda}{2}x^2(1-F(x))}{(1-\rho_x)^2} \leq \int_{t=0}^{x} \frac{\rho - \rho_t}{(1-\rho)(1-\rho_t)}dt$$

Now, because

$$\int_{t=0}^{x} \frac{\rho - \rho_t}{(1-\rho)(1-\rho_t)}dt > \int_{t=0}^{x} \frac{\rho - \rho_t}{(1-\rho)}dt,$$

it suffices to show that

$$\frac{\frac{\lambda}{2}\int_{t=0}^{x} t^2 f(t)dt + \frac{\lambda}{2}x^2(1-F(x))}{(1-\rho_x)^2} \leq \int_{t=0}^{x} \frac{\rho - \rho_t}{(1-\rho)}dt.$$

Before showing this, we observe, using integration-by-parts, that

$$\int_{t=0}^{x} \frac{\rho - \rho_t}{(1-\rho)}dt = \frac{1}{1-\rho}\left((\rho - \rho_t)\,t\,\big|_{t=0}^{t=x} + \int_{0}^{x} t\rho_t' dt\right)$$

$$= \frac{(\rho - \rho_x)x}{1-\rho} + \frac{\lambda\int_{0}^{x} t^2 f(t)dt}{1-\rho}.$$

So it suffices to show that

$$\frac{\frac{\lambda}{2}\int_{0}^{x} t^2 f(t)dt + \frac{\lambda}{2}x^2(1-F(x))}{(1-\rho_x)^2} \leq \frac{(\rho - \rho_x)x}{1-\rho} + \frac{\lambda\int_{0}^{x} t^2 f(t)dt}{1-\rho}.$$

We further observe that

$$x(\rho - \rho_x) = \lambda x \int_x^\infty t f(t) dt > \lambda x^2 (1 - F(x)).$$

Thus it suffices to show that

$$\frac{\frac{\lambda}{2} \int_0^x t^2 f(t) dt + \frac{\lambda}{2} x^2 (1 - F(x))}{(1 - \rho_x)^2} \leq \frac{\lambda x^2 (1 - F(x))}{1 - \rho} + \frac{\lambda \int_0^x t^2 f(t) dt}{1 - \rho}.$$

From the above expression, it suffices to show that

$$2(1 - \rho_x)^2 > 1 - \rho.$$

Because $\rho > \rho_x$, it suffices to show that

$$2(1 - \rho_x)^2 > 1 - \rho_x.$$

Dividing both sides by $1 - \rho_x$, we see that this is clearly true when

$$\rho_x < \frac{1}{2},$$

which is true by the theorem assumption that $\rho < \frac{1}{2}$. ∎

We have shown that fairness is counterintuitive. A seemingly "unfair" policy, like SRPT, can outperform a fair policy, like PS, in expectation, on every job size.

33.5 Readings

There is a lot of recent work on fairness of scheduling policies. The proof technique from Section 33.2 is illustrated more generally in [191]. Many references and further results can be found in the thesis of Adam Wierman [188], in [190], and in a wonderful book by Hassin and Haviv [96].

Bibliography

[1] S. Aalto, U. Ayesta, S. Borst, V. Misra, and R. Núñez Queija. Beyond processor sharing. *Performance Evaluation Review*, 34(4):36–43, 2007.

[2] I.J.B.F. Adan, G.J. van Houtum, and J. van der Wal. Upper and lower bounds for the waiting time in the symmetric shortest queue system. *Annals of Operations Research*, 48:197–217, 1994.

[3] I.J.B.F. Adan, J. Wessels, and W.H.M. Zijm. Analysis of the symmetric shortest queue problem. *Stochastic Models*, 6:691–713, 1990.

[4] I.J.B.F. Adan, J. Wessels, and W.H.M. Zijm. Matrix-geometric analysis of the shortest queue problem with threshold jockeying. *Operations Research Letters*, 13:107–112, 1993.

[5] A.O. Allen. *Probability, Statistics, and Queueing Theory with Computer Science Applications*. Academic Press, 2nd edition, 1990.

[6] E. Altman, U. Ayesta, and B. Prabhu. Load balancing in processor sharing systems. *Telecommunication Systems*, 47(1–2):35–48, 2011.

[7] E. Arthurs and J.S. Kaufman. Sizing a message store subject to blocking criteria. In *Proceedings of the Third International Symposium on Modeling and Performance Evaluation of Computer Systems*, pages 547–564, 1979.

[8] S. Asmussen. *Applied Probability and Queues*. Springer-Verlag, 2nd edition, 2003.

[9] N. Avrahami and Y. Azar. Minimizing total flow time and total completion time with immediate dispatching. In *Proceedings of the Annual ACM Symposium on Parallel Algorithms and Architectures (SPAA)*, pages 11–18, 2003.

[10] E. Bachmat and A. Natanzon. Analysis of the large number of hosts asymptotics of SITA queues. In *Workshop on Mathematical Performance Modeling and Analysis (MAMA)*, 2012.

[11] E. Bachmat and H. Sarfati. Analysis of size interval task assignment policies. *Performance Evaluation Review*, 36(2):107–109, 2008.

[12] N. Bansal and M. Harchol-Balter. Analysis of SRPT scheduling: investigating unfairness. In *Proceedings of the 2001 ACM Sigmetrics Conference on Measurement and Modeling of Computer Systems*, pages 279–290. Cambridge, MA, June 2001.

[13] A. Barak, S. Guday, and R.G. Wheeler. *The Mosix Distributed Operating System: Load Balancing for Unix*. Springer Verlag, 1993.

[14] P. Barford and M.E. Crovella. Generating representative web workloads for network and server performance evaluation. In *Proceedings of the 1998 ACM Sigmetrics Conference on Measurement and Modeling of Computer Systems*, pages 151–160, July 1998.

[15] L.A. Barroso and U. Hölzle. The case for energy-proportional computing. *Computer*, 40(12):33–37, 2007.

[16] F. Baskett, K.M. Chandy, R.R. Muntz, and F. Palacios-Gomez. Open, closed and mixed networks of queues with different classes of customers. *Journal of the ACM*, 22:248–260, 1975.

[17] S.L. Bell and R.J. Williams. Dynamic scheduling of a system with two parallel servers in heavy traffic with complete resource pooling: asymptotic optimality of a continuous review threshold policy. *Annals of Applied Probability*, 11(3):608–649, 2001.

[18] D. Bertsekas and R. Gallager. *Data Networks*. Prentice Hall, 1992.

[19] D. Bertsimas and D. Nakazato. The distributional Little's law and its applications. *Operations Research*, 43(2):298–310, 1995.

531

[20] A. Bhandari, A. Scheller-Wolf, and M. Harchol-Balter. An exact and efficient algorithm for the constrained dynamic operator staffing problem for call centers. *Management Science*, 54(2):339–353, 2008.

[21] Big-IP. F5 Products. http://www.f5.com/products/big-ip.

[22] D.P. Blinn, T. Henderson, and D. Kotz. Analysis of a wi-fi hotspot network. In *International Workshop on Wireless Traffic Measurements and Modeling*, pages 1–6, June 2005.

[23] G. Bolch, S. Greiner, H. de Meer, and K.S. Trivedi. *Queueing Networks and Markov Chains*. John Wiley and Sons, 2006.

[24] A. Bondi and W. Whitt. The influence of service-time variability in a closed network of queues. *Performance Evaluation*, 6(3):219–234, 1986.

[25] F. Bonomi. On job assignment for a parallel system of processor sharing queues. *IEEE Transactions on Computers*, 39(7):858–869, 1990.

[26] O. Boxma, J. Cohen and N. Huffels. Approximations in the mean waiting time in an *M/G/s* queueing system. *Operations Research*, 27:1115–1127, 1979.

[27] O.J. Boxma and J.W. Cohen. *Boundary Value Problems in Queueing System Analysis*. North Holland, 1983.

[28] O.J. Boxma and B. Zwart. Tails in scheduling. *Performance Evaluation Review*, 34(4):13–20, 2007.

[29] M. Bramson. *Stability of Queueing Networks*. Springer Verlag, 2008.

[30] M. Bramson, Y. Lu, and B. Prabhakar. Randomized load balancing with general service time distributions. In *Proceedings of the 2010 ACM Sigmetrics Conference on Measurement and Modeling of Computer Systems*. New York, NY, pages 275–286, June 2010.

[31] P. Bratley, B. Fox, and L. Schrage. *A Guide to Simulation*. Springer-Verlag, 2nd edition, 1983.

[32] J. Broberg, Z. Tari, and P. Zeephongsekul. Task assignment with work-conserving migration. *Parallel Computing*, 32:808–830, 2006.

[33] S.L. Brumelle. A generalization of $L = \lambda W$ to moments of queue length and waiting times. *Operations Research*, 20:1127–1136, 1972.

[34] P.J. Burke. The output of a queueing system. *Operations Research*, 4(6):699–704, 1956.

[35] J. P. Buzen. Computational algorithms for closed queueing networks with exponential servers. *Communications of the ACM*, 16(9):527–531, 1973.

[36] V. Cardellini, E. Casalicchio, M. Colajanni, and P.S. Yu. The state of the art in locally distributed web-server systems. *ACM Computing Surveys*, 34(2):1–49, 2002.

[37] J.M. Carlson and J. Doyle. Highly optimized tolerance: a mechanism for power laws in designed systems. *Physical Review E*, 60:1412–1427, 1999.

[38] H. Chen and D.D. Yao. *Fundamentals of Queueing Networks*. Springer, 2001.

[39] H. Chen and M. Frank. State dependent pricing with a queue. *IIE Transactions*, 33(10): 847–860, 2001.

[40] G.L. Choudhury, K.K. Leung, and W. Whitt. Calculating normalization constants of closed queueing networks by numerically inverting their generating functions. *Journal of the ACM*, 42(5):935–970, 1995.

[41] G. Ciardo, A. Riska, and E. Smirni. Equiload: a load balancing policy for clustered web servers. *Performance Evaluation*, 46:101–124, 2001.

[42] Cisco Systems LocalDirector. http://www.cisco.com/warp/public/cc/pd/cxsr/400/index.shtml.

[43] J.W. Cohen and O.J. Boxma. *Boundary Value Problems in Queueing System Analysis*. North-Holland Publishing, 1983.

[44] B.W. Conolly. The autostrada queueing problem. *Journal of Applied Probability*, 21:394–403, 1984.

[45] R.W. Conway, W.L. Maxwell, and L.W. Miller. *Theory of Scheduling*. Addison-Wesley, 1967.

[46] M.E. Crovella, R. Frangioso, and M. Harchol-Balter. Connection scheduling in web servers. In *USENIX Symposium on Internet Technologies and Systems*, pages 243–254, Boulder, CO, October 1999.

[47] M.E. Crovella and A. Bestavros. Self-similarity in World Wide Web traffic: evidence and possible causes. In *Proceedings of the 1996 ACM Sigmetrics International Conference on Measurement and Modeling of Computer Systems*, pages 160–169, May 1996.

[48] M.E. Crovella, M.S. Taqqu, and A. Bestavros. Heavy-tailed probability distributions in the world wide web. In *A Practical Guide To Heavy Tails*, chapter 1, pages 1–23. Chapman & Hall, New York, 1998.

[49] D. Down and R. Wu. Multi-layered round robin scheduling for parallel servers. *Queueing Systems: Theory and Applications*, 53(4):177–188, 2006.

[50] M. El-Taha and B. Maddah. Allocation of service time in a multiserver system. *Management Science*, 52(4):623–637, 2006.

[51] M. El-Taha and S. Stidham. *Sample-Path Analysis of Queueing Systems*. Kluwer Academic Publisher, Boston, 1999.

[52] A. Ephremides, P. Varaiya, and J. Walrand. A simple dynamic routing problem. *IEEE Transactions on Automatic Control*, 25(4):690–693, 1980.

[53] R. Fagin, A. Karlin, J. Kleinberg, P. Raghavan, S. Rajagopalan, R. Rubinfeld, M. Sudan, and A. Tomkins. Random walks with back buttons. *Annals of Applied Probability*, 11(3):810–862, 2001.

[54] M. Faloutsos, P. Faloutsos, and C. Faloutsos. On power-law relationships of the internet topology. In *Proceedings of SIGCOMM*, pages 251–262, 1999.

[55] G. Fayolle and R. Iasnogorodski. Two coupled processors: the reduction to a Riemann-Hilbert problem. *Zeitschrift fur Wahrscheinlichkeitstheorie und vervandte Gebiete*, 47:325–351, 1979.

[56] A. Feldmann and W. Whitt. Fitting mixtures of exponentials to long-tailed distributions to analyze network performance models. *Performance Evaluation*, 31(8):963–976, 1998.

[57] W. Feller. *An Introduction to Probability Theory and Its Applications*, volume I. John Wiley and Sons, 3rd edition, 1968.

[58] W. Feller. *An Introduction to Probability Theory and Its Applications*, volume II. John Wiley and Sons, 2nd edition, 1971.

[59] H. Feng, V. Misra, and D. Rubenstein. Optimal state-free, size-aware dispatching for heterogeneous M/G-type systems. *Performance Evaluation*, 62:475–492, 2005.

[60] H. Feng, V. Misra, and D. Rubenstein. PBS: A unified priority-based scheduler. In *Proceedings of the 2007 ACM Sigmetrics International Conference on Measurement and Modeling of Computer Systems*, pages 203–214, June 2007.

[61] L. Flatto and H.P. McKean. Two queues in parallel. *Communications on Pure and Applied Mathematics*, 30:255–263, 1977.

[62] Flushing away Unfairness. *The Economist*, July 8, 2010.

[63] R.D. Foley and D. McDonald. Exact asymptotics of a queueing network with a cross-trained server. In *Proceedings of INFORMS Annual Meeting*, Applied Probability Cluster, October 2003.

[64] S. Foss and D. Korshunov. Heavy tails in multi-server queue. *Queueing Systems*, 52:31–48, 2006.

[65] B. Fu, J. Broberg, and Z. Tari. Task assignment strategy for overloaded systems. In *Proceedings of the Eighth IEEE International Symposium on Computers and Communications*, pages 1119–1125, 2003.

[66] R. G. Gallager. *Discrete Stochastic Processes*. Kluwer Academic Publishers, 1996.

[67] A. Gandhi, V. Gupta, M. Harchol-Balter, and M. Kozuch. Optimality analysis of energy-peformance trade-off for server farm management. *Performance Evaluation*, 11:1155–1171, 2010.

[68] A. Gandhi, M. Harchol-Balter, and I. Adan. Server farms with setup costs. *Performance Evaluation*, 67(11):1123–1138, 2010.

[69] A. Gandhi, M. Harchol-Balter, R. Das, and C. Lefurgy. Optimal power allocation in server farms. In *ACM Sigmetrics 2009 Conference on Measurement and Modeling of Computer Systems*, pages 157–168, 2009.

[70] S. Ghosh and M. Squillante. Analysis and control of correlated web server queues. *Computer Communications*, 27(18):1771–1785, 2004.

[71] W.C. Giffin. *Transform Techniques in Probability Modeling*. Academic Press, 1975.

[72] J.J. Gordon. The evaluation of normalizing constants in closed queueing networks. *Operations Research*, 38(5):863–869, 1990.

[73] W.K. Grassmann. Transient and steady state results for two parallel queues. *Omega*, 8:105–112, 1980.

[74] L. Green. A queueing system with general use and limited use servers. *Operations Research*, 33(1):168–182, 1985.

[75] D. Gross and C.M. Harris. *Fundamentals of Queueing Theory*. John Wiley and Sons, 3rd edition, 1998.

[76] V. Gupta, J. Dai, M. Harchol-Balter, and B. Zwart. On the inapproximability of M/G/k: why two moments of job size distribution are not enough. *Queueing Systems: Theory and Applications*, 64(1):5–48, 2010.

[77] V. Gupta and M. Harchol-Balter. Self-adaptive admission control policies for resource-sharing systems. In *ACM Sigmetrics 2009 Conference on Measurement and Modeling of Computer Systems*, pages 311–322, 2009.

[78] V. Gupta, M. Harchol-Balter, A. Scheller-Wolf, and U. Yechiali. Fundamental characteristics of queues with fluctuating load. In *Proceedings of the 2006 ACM Sigmetrics Conference on Measurement and Modeling of Computer Systems*, pages 203–215, 2006.

[79] V. Gupta, M. Harchol-Balter, K. Sigman, and W. Whitt. Analysis of join-the-shortest-queue routing for web server farms. *Performance Evaluation* 64(9–12):1062–1081, 2007.

[80] P.R. Halmos. *Measure Theory*. Graduate Texts in Mathematics. Springer, 2000.

[81] M. Harchol-Balter. *Network Analysis without Exponentiality Assumptions*. PhD thesis, University of California, Berkeley, 1996.

[82] M. Harchol-Balter. Task assignment with unknown duration. *Journal of the ACM*, 49(2):260–288, 2002.

[83] M. Harchol-Balter, M.E. Crovella, and C. Murta. On choosing a task assignment policy for a distributed server system. *IEEE Journal of Parallel and Distributed Computing*, 59:204–228, 1999.

[84] M. Harchol-Balter and A. Downey. Exploiting process lifetime distributions for dynamic load balancing. In *Proceedings of the 1996 ACM Sigmetrics Conference on Measurement and Modeling of Computer Systems*, pages 13–24, Philadelphia, May 1996.

[85] M. Harchol-Balter and A. Downey. Exploiting process lifetime distributions for dynamic load balancing. *ACM Transactions on Computer Systems*, 15(3):253–285, 1997.

[86] M. Harchol-Balter, C. Li, T. Osogami, A. Scheller-Wolf, and M. Squillante. Cycle stealing under immediate dispatch task assignment. In *15th ACM Symposium on Parallel Algorithms and Architectures*, pages 274–285, San Diego, June 2003.

[87] M. Harchol-Balter, C. Li, T. Osogami, A. Scheller-Wolf, and M. Squillante. Task assignment with cycle stealing under central queue. In *23rd International Conference on Distributed Computing Systems*, pages 628–637, Providence, RI, May 2003.

[88] M. Harchol-Balter, T. Osogami, and A. Scheller-Wolf. Robustness of threshold policies in a beneficiary-donor model. *Performance Evaluation Review*, 33(2):36–38, 2005.

[89] M. Harchol-Balter, T. Osogami, A. Scheller-Wolf, and A. Wierman. Multi-server queueing systems with multiple priority classes. *Queueing Systems: Theory and Applications*, 51(3–4):331–360, 2005.

[90] M. Harchol-Balter, A. Scheller-Wolf, and A. Young. Surprising results on task assignment in server farms with high-variability workloads. In *ACM Sigmetrics 2009 Conference on Measurement and Modeling of Computer Systems*, pages 287–298, 2009.

[91] M. Harchol-Balter, A. Scheller-Wolf, and A. Young. Why segregating short jobs from long jobs under high variability is not always a win. In *Forty-Seventh Annual Allerton Conference on Communication, Control, and Computing*, University of Illinois, Urbana-Champaign, pages 121–127, October 2009.

[92] M. Harchol-Balter, B. Schroeder, N. Bansal, and M. Agrawal. Size-based scheduling to improve web performance. *ACM Transactions on Computer Systems*, 21(2):207–233, 2003.

[93] M. Harchol-Balter and R. Vesilo. To balance or unbalance load in size-interval task allocation. *Probability in the Engineering and Informational Sciences*, 24(2):219–244, 2010.

[94] P.G. Harrison. On normalizing constants in queueing networks. *Operations Research*, 33:464–468, 1985.

[95] P.G. Harrison. Reversed processes, product forms and a non-product form. *Linear Algebra and Its Applications*, 386:359–381, 2004.

[96] R. Hassin and M. Haviv. *To Queue or not to Queue*. Kluwer Academic Publishers, 2003.

[97] P. Hokstad. Approximations for the *M/G/m* queue. *Operations Research*, 26(3):510–523, 1978.

[98] P. Hokstad. The steady state solution of the $M/K_2/m$ queue. *Advances in Applied Probability*, 12(3):799–823, 1980.

[99] S. Hotovy, D. Schneider, and T. O'Donnell. Analysis of the early workload on the Cornell Theory Center IBM SP2. Technical Report 96TR234, Cornell Theory Center, January 1996.

[100] E. Hyytiä, S. Aalto, and A. Penttinen. Minimizing slowdown in heterogeneous size-aware dispatching systems. In *Proceedings of the 2012 ACM Sigmetrics Conference on Measurement and Modeling of Computer Systems*. London, U.K., pages 29–40, June 2012.

[101] E. Hyytiä, J. Virtamo, S. Aalto, A. Penttinen. M/M/1-PS queue and size-aware task assignment. *Performance Evaluation*, 68:1136–1148, 2011.

[102] J.R. Jackson. Jobshop-like queueing systems. *Management Science*, 10(1):131–142, 1963.

[103] G. Jain. *A Rate Conservation Analysis of Queues and Networks with Work Removal*. PhD thesis, Columbia University, IEOR Department, 1996.

[104] R. Jain. *The Art of Computer Systems Performance Analysis*. John Wiley and Sons, 1991.

[105] S. Karlin and H. M. Taylor. *A First Course in Stochastic Processes*. Academic Press, 2nd edition, 1975.

[106] F. P. Kelly. *Reversibility and Stochastic Networks*. John Wiley and Sons, 1979.

[107] A. Khinchin. Mathematical theory of a stationary queue. *Matematicheskii Sbornik*, 39(4):73–84, 1932.

[108] J.F.C. Kingman. Two similar queues in parallel. *Biometrika*, 48:1316–1323, 1961.

[109] J. Kleinberg. Authoritative sources in a hyperlinked environment. *Journal of the ACM*, 46(5):604–632, 1999.

[110] L. Kleinrock. *Queueing Systems, Volume I: Theory*. Wiley-Interscience Publication, 1975.

[111] L. Kleinrock. *Queueing Systems, Volume II. Computer Applications*. John Wiley & Sons, 1976.

[112] J. Köllerström. Heavy traffic theory for queues with several servers. I. *Journal of Applied Probability*, 11:544–552, 1974.

[113] A. Konheim, I. Meilijson, and A. Melkman. Processor-sharing of two parallel lines. *Journal of Applied Probability*, 18:952–956, 1981.

[114] J.F. Kurose and K.W. Ross. *Computer Networking: A Top-Down Approach Featuring the Internet*. Pearson Education, 2003.

[115] G. Latouche and V. Ramaswami. *Introduction to Matrix Analytic Methods in Stochastic Modeling*. ASA-SIAM, Philadelphia, 1999.

[116] A.M. Law and W.D. Kelton. *Simulation Modeling and Analysis*. McGraw-Hill Companies, 2000.

[117] E. Lazowska, J. Zahorjan, G. Graham, and K. Sevcik. *Quantitative System Performance: Computer System Analysis Using Queueing Network Models*. Prentice Hall, 1984.

[118] A.M. Lee and P.A. Longton. Queueing process associated with airline passenger check-in. *Operations Research Quarterly*, 10:56–71, 1959.

[119] S. Leonardi and D. Raz. Approximating total flow time on parallel machines. In *Proceedings of the Annual ACM Symposium on Theory of Computing (STOC)*, pages 110–119, 1997.

[120] H.C. Lin and C.S. Raghavendra. An analysis of the join the shortest queue (JSQ) policy. In *Proceedings of the 12th International Conference on Distributed Computing Systems*, pages 362–366, 1992.

[121] J.D.C. Little. A proof of the queueing formula $L = \lambda W$. *Operations Research*, 9:383–387, 1961.

[122] J.C.S. Lui, R.R. Muntz, and D.F. Towsley. Bounding the mean response time of the minimum expected delay routing policy: an algorithmic approach. *IEEE Transactions on Computers*, 44(12):1371–1382, 1995.

[123] D. McWherter, B. Schroeder, N. Ailamaki, and M. Harchol-Balter. Improving preemptive prioritization via statistical characterization of OLTP locking. In *Proceedings of the 21st International Conference on Data Engineering*, pages 446–457. San Francisco, April 2005.

[124] D. Meisner, B. Gold, and T. Wenisch. Powernap: Eliminating server idle power. In *Proceedings of ASPLOS*, pages 205–216, 2009.

[125] D.A. Menascé, V.A.F. Almeida, and I.W. Dowdy. *Capacity Planning and Performance Modeling*. Prentice Hall, 1994.

[126] M. Miyazawa. Rate conservation laws: a survey. *Queueing Systems*, 15(1–4):1–58, 1994.

[127] R. Nelson. *Probability, Stochastic Processes, and Queueing Theory*. Springer-Verlag, 1995.

[128] R.D. Nelson and T.K. Philips. An approximation to the response time for shortest queue routing. *Performance Evaluation Review*, 17:181–189, 1989.

[129] M.F. Neuts. Probability distributions of phase type. In *Liber Amicorum Prof. Emeritus H. Florin*. University of Louvain, Belgium, pages 173–206, 1975.

[130] M.F. Neuts. *Matrix-Geometric Solutions in Stochastic Models*. Johns Hopkins University Press, 1981.

[131] Normal Distribution Table for Finite Mathematics. www.zweigmedia.com/RealWorld/normaltable.html.

[132] S.A. Nozaki and S.M. Ross. Approximations in finite-capacity multi-server queues with Poisson arrivals. *Journal of Applied Probability*, 15(4):826–834, 1978.

[133] M. Nuijens. *The Foreground-Background Queue*. PhD thesis, Universiteit van Amsterdam, 2004.

[134] K. Oida and K. Shinjo. Characteristics of deterministic optimal routing for a simple traffic control problem. In *Performance, Computing and Communications Conference, IPCCC*, pages 386–392, February 1999.

[135] T. Osogami and M. Harchol-Balter. Closed form solutions for mapping general distributions to quasi-minimal PH distributions. *Performance Evaluation*, 63(6):524–552, 2006.

[136] T. Osogami, M. Harchol-Balter, and A. Scheller-Wolf. Analysis of cycle stealing with switching times and thresholds. In *Proceedings of the 2003 ACM Sigmetrics Conference on Measurement and Modeling of Computer Systems*, pages 184–195, San Diego, June 2003.

[137] T. Osogami, M. Harchol-Balter, and A. Scheller-Wolf. Analysis of cycle stealing with switching times and thresholds. *Performance Evaluation*, 61(4):374–369, 2005.

[138] T. Osogami, M. Harchol-Balter, A. Scheller-Wolf, and L. Zhang. Exploring threshold-base policies for load sharing. In *Forty-Second Annual Allerton Conference on Communication, Control, and Computing*, pages 1012–1021, University of Illinois, Urbana-Champaign, October 2004.

[139] L. Page, S. Brin, R. Motwani, and T. Winograd. The pagerank citation ranking: bringing order to the web. Technical Report 1999–66, Stanford InfoLab, November 1999.

[140] M. Pistoia and C. Letilley. *IBM WebSphere Performance Pack: Load Balancing with IBM SecureWay Network Dispatcher*, International Technical Support Organization, October 1999.

[141] F. Pollaczek. Über eine aufgabe der wahrscheinlichkeitstheorie. *Mathematische Zeitschrift*, 32:64–100, 1930.

[142] I.A. Rai, E. W. Biersack, and G. Urvoy-Keller. Size-based scheduling to improve the performance of short TCP flows. *IEEE Network*, January 2005.

[143] I.A. Rai, G. Urvoy-Keller, and E.W. Biersack. Analysis of LAS scheduling for job size distributions with high variance. In *Proceedings of the ACM Sigmetrics Conference on Measurement and Modeling of Computer Systems*, pages 218–228, 2003.

[144] I.A. Rai, G. Urvoy-Keller, and E.W. Biersack. LAS scheduling approach to avoid bandwidth hogging in heterogeneous TCP networks. *Lecture Notes in Computer Science*, 3079:179–190, 2004.

[145] S. Raman and S. McCanne. A model, analysis, and protocol framework for soft state-based communication. In *Proceedings of SIGCOMM*, pages 15–25, 1999.

[146] B.M. Rao and M.J.M. Posner. Algorithmic and approximation analyses of the shorter queue model. *Naval Research Logistics*, 34:381–398, 1987.

[147] M. Reiser and S. Lavenberg. Mean-value analysis of closed multichain queueing networks. *Journal of the ACM*, 27(2):313–322, 1980.

[148] S.M. Ross. *Simulation*. Academic Press, 2002.

[149] S.M. Ross. *Stochastic Processes*. John Wiley and Sons, New York, 1983.

[150] S.M. Ross. *Introduction to Probability Models*, 9th edition, Elsevier, New York, 2007.

[151] C.H. Sauer and K.M. Chandy. *Computer Systems Performance Modeling*. Prentice-Hall, 1981.

[152] C.H. Sauer and K.M. Chandy. Approximate analysis of central server models. *IBM Journal of Research and Development*, 19:301–313, 1975.

[153] R.S. Schassberger. On the waiting time in the queueing systems GI/G/1. *Annals of Mathematical Statistics*, 41:182–187, 1970.

[154] R.S. Schassberger. *Warteschlangen*. Springer-Verlag, 1973.

[155] A. Scheller-Wolf and K. Sigman. New bounds for expected delay in FIFO GI/GI/c queues. *Queueing Systems*, 28:169–186, 1997.

[156] A. Scheller-Wolf. Further delay moment results for FIFO multiserver queues. *Queueing Systems*, 34:387–400, 2000.

[157] A. Scheller-Wolf and K. Sigman. Delay moments for FIFO GI/GI/s queues. *Queueing Systems*, 25:77–95, 1997.

[158] A. Scheller-Wolf and R. Vesilo. Structural interpretation and derivation of necessary and sufficient conditions for delay moments in FIFO multiserver queues. *Queueing Systems*, 54:221–232, 2006.

[159] L.E. Schrage. A proof of the optimality of the shortest remaining processing time discipline. *Operations Research*, 16:687–690, 1968.

[160] L.E. Schrage and L. W. Miller. The queue M/G/1 with the shortest remaining processing time discipline. *Operations Research*, 14:670–684, 1966.

[161] B. Schroeder and M. Harchol-Balter. Evaluation of task assignment policies for supercomputing servers: the case for load unbalancing and fairness. *Cluster Computing: The Journal of Networks, Software Tools, and Applications*, 7(2):151–161, 2004.

[162] B. Schroeder and M. Harchol-Balter. Web servers under overload: how scheduling can help. *ACM Transactions on Internet Technologies*, 6(1):20–52, 2006.

[163] B. Schroeder, M. Harchol-Balter, A. Iyengar, and E. Nahum. Achieving class-based QoS for transactional workloads. In *Proceedings of the 22nd International Conference on Data Engineering Poster Paper*, pages 153–155, Atlanta, GA, April 2006.

[164] B. Schroeder, M. Harchol-Balter, A. Iyengar, E. Nahum, and A. Wierman. How to determine a good multi-programming level for external scheduling. In *Proceedings of the 22nd International Conference on Data Engineering*, pages 60–70, Atlanta, GA, April 2006.

[165] B. Schroeder, A. Wierman, and M. Harchol-Balter. Open versus closed: a cautionary tale. In *Proceedings of Networked Systems Design and Implementation (NSDI)*, 2006.

[166] A. Shaikh, J. Rexford, and K.G. Shin. Load-sensitive routing of long-lived IP flows. In *Proceedings of ACM SIGCOMM*, pages 215–226, September 1999.

[167] K. Sigman. Lecture Notes borrowed from Karl Sigman's Stochastic Processes Class, 2005.

[168] M.S. Squillante, C.H. Xia, D.D. Yao, and L. Zhang. Threshold-based priority policies for parallel-server systems with affinity scheduling. In *Proceedings of the IEEE American Control Conference*, pages 2992–2999, June 2001.

[169] M.S. Squillante, D.D. Yao, and L. Zhang. Internet traffic: periodicity, tail behavior and performance implications. E. Gelenbe, editor, *Systems Performance Evaluation: Methodologies and Applications*, pages 23–37, CRC Press, 2000.

[170] D.A. Stanford and W.K. Grassmann. The bilingual server system: a queueing model featuring fully and partially qualified servers. *INFOR*, 31(4):261–277, 1993.

[171] D.A. Stanford and W.K. Grassmann. Bilingual server call centers. D.R. McDonald and S.R.E. Turner, editors, *Analysis of Communication Networks: Call Centers, Traffic and Performance*, pages 31–47, American Mathematical Society, 2000.

[172] Z. Tari, J. Broberg, A. Zomaya, and R. Baldoni. A least flow-time first load sharing approach for a distributed server farm. *Journal of Parallel and Distributed Computing*, 65:832–842, 2005.

[173] Y.C. Tay. *Analytical Performance Modeling for Computer Systems*. Morgan & Claypool Publishers, 2010.

[174] E. Thereska. *Enabling What-If Explorations in Systems*. PhD thesis, Carnegie Mellon University, 2007.

[175] E. Thereska, M. Abd-El-Malek, J.J. Wylie, D. Narayanan, and G.R. Ganger. Informed data distribution selection in a self-predicting storage system. In *Proceedings of the International Conference on Autonomic Computing (ICAC'06)*, pages 187–198, June 2006.

[176] G.B. Thomas and R.L. Finney. *Calculus and Analytic Geometry*. Addison-Wesley, 9th edition, June 1996.

[177] N. Thomas. Comparing job allocation schemes where service demand is unknown. *Journal of Computer and System Sciences*, 74:1067–1081, 2008.

[178] H.C. Tijms. *A First Course in Stochastic Models*. John Wiley and Sons, 2003.

[179] K.S. Trivedi. *Probability and Statistics with Reliability, Queueing and Computer Science Applications*. Prentice-Hall, 1982.

[180] R.W. Weber. On optimal assignment of customers to parallel servers. *Journal of Applied Probability*, 15:406–413, 1978.

[181] Weibull Distribution. Characteristics of the Weibull. http://www.weibull.com/hotwire/issue14/relbasics14.htm.

[182] P.D. Welch. On a generalized M/G/1 queueing process in which the first customer of each busy period receives exceptional service. *Operations Research*, 12:736–752, 1964.

[183] W. Whitt. A review of $L = \lambda W$ and extensions. *Queueing Systems*, 9:235–268, 1991.

[184] W. Whitt. The impact of a heavy-tailed service-time distribution upon the M/GI/s waiting-time distribution. *Queueing Systems*, 36:71–87, 2000.

[185] W. Whitt. Approximating a point process by a renewal process: two basic methods. *Operations Research*, 30:125–147, 1982.

[186] W. Whitt. Open and closed models for networks of queues. *AT&T Bell Laboratories Technical Journal*, 63(9):1911–1979, 1984.

[187] W. Whitt. Blocking when service is required from several facilities simultaneously. *AT&T Bell Laboratories Technical Journal*, 64(8):1807–1856, 1985.

[188] A. Wierman. *Scheduling for Today's Computer Systems: Bridging Theory and Practice*. PhD thesis, Carnegie Mellon University, 2007.

[189] A. Wierman, N. Bansal, and M. Harchol-Balter. A note on comparing response times in M/GI/1/FB and M/GI/1/PS queues. *Operations Research Letters*, 32(1):73–76, 2004.

[190] A. Wierman and M. Harchol-Balter. Classifying scheduling policies with respect to unfairness in an M/GI/1. In *Proceedings of the 2003 ACM Sigmetrics Conference on Measurement and Modeling of Computer Systems*, pages 238–249, San Diego, CA, June 2003.

[191] A. Wierman, M. Harchol-Balter, and T. Osogami. Nearly insensitive bounds on SMART scheduling. In *ACM Sigmetrics 2005 Conference on Measurement and Modeling of Computer Systems*, pages 205–215, 2005.

[192] A. Wierman, T. Osogami, M. Harchol-Balter, and A. Scheller-Wolf. How many servers are best in a dual-priority M/PH/k system? *Performance Evaluation*, 63(12):1253–1272, 2006.

[193] R.J. Williams. On dynamic scheduling of a parallel server system with complete resource pooling. D.R. McDonald and S.R.E. Turner, editors, *Analysis of Communication Networks: Call Centers, Traffic and Performance*. American Mathematical Society, pages 49–72, 2000.

[194] W. Winston. Optimality of the shortest line discipline. *Journal of Applied Probability*, 14:181–189, 1977.

[195] R.W. Wolff. *Stochastic Modeling and the Theory of Queues*. Prentice-Hall, 1989.

[196] D.D. Yao. Refining the diffusion approximation for the *M/G/m* queue. *Operations Research*, 33:1266–1277, 1985.

[197] S.F. Yashkov and A.S. Yashkova. Processor sharing: a survey of the mathematical theory. *Automation and Remote Control*, 68(9):1662–1731, 2007.

[198] J. Zhang. *Limited Processor Sharing Queues and Multi-server Queues*. PhD thesis, Georgia Institute of Technology, 2009.

[199] J. Zhang, J.G. Dai, and B. Zwart. Diffusion limits of limited processor sharing queues. *Annals of Applied Probability*, 21:745–799, 2011.

[200] D. Zwillinger. *CRC Standard Mathematical Tables and Formulae*. Chapman & Hall, 31st edition, 2003.

Index

Lightning Source UK Ltd.
Milton Keynes UK
UKHW052138060123
414915UK00021B/51